L3

Fodor's 90
Austria

D0774202

FODOR'S TRAVEL PUBLICATIONS, INC.,
New York & London

Fodor's Austria

Area Editor: GEORGE W. HAMILTON
Editorial Contributors: NICHOLAS ALLEN, LILLIAN LANSETH-
  CHRISTENSEN, GÜNTHER LEIDOLF, MARK LEWES, KENNETH
  LOVELAND
Editor: RICHARD MOORE
Drawings: KEITH HOWARD
Cartographers: CECIL W. BACON, ALEX MURPHY, SWANSTON
  GRAPHICS, BRYAN WOODFIELD
Cover Photograph: E. NAGELE/FPG INTERNATIONAL

Cover Design: VIGNELLI ASSOCIATES

Special Sales

Fodor's Travel Publications are available at special discounts for bulk purchases (100
copies or more) for sales promotions or premiums. Special editions, including personalized
covers, excerpts of existing guides, and corporate imprints, can be created in large
quantities for special needs. For more information, write to Special Marketing, Fodor's
Travel Publications, 201 East 50th Street, New York, NY 10022. Enquiries from the
United Kingdom should be sent to Fodor's Travel Publications, 30–32 Bedford Square,
London WC1B 3SG.

MANUFACTURED IN THE UNITED STATES OF AMERICA
10 9 8 7 6 5 4 3 2 1

CONTENTS

iii

FOREWORD

Although it is one of Europe's smallest countries, Austria manages to pack within its borders as many mountains, lakes and picturesque cities as countries five times its size. On top of which it can boast a people as friendly and welcoming as any in the world, who insist on real comfort in all aspects of life. Sports rank high and skiing highest, with innumerable ski lifts, cable cars, mountaintop lodges, luxurious resorts and connecting highways. And, as icing on the cake, Austria is the most economical of skiing's European Big Three (Austria, France and Switzerland).

Austria is a country in which it is impossible to avoid hourly contact with the very fabric of history. Once the heart of a vast empire that stretched to the New World, Austria today is an attractive amalgam of the rich vestiges of its proud past and a balanced attitude to the modern world. Vienna, for example, contains both the Hofburg, with its Burgundian treasure, and the new Vienna International Center which houses the International Atomic Energy Agency, as well as the U.N. Industrial Development Organization and other U.N. offices. Austria is poised in the very heart of the continent, sharing its cultural heritage with both northern and southern Europe, and yet having very obvious affinities with the lands beyond. It was Metternich who said that "the Orient begins at the Landstrasse," encapsulating thus the critical role of Vienna as the meeting place of East and West for two thousand years.

But, as with most countries, the capital is only a small part of what Austria has to offer. Indeed, most visitors will see only a part of the rich variety, geographical and cultural, that is available. Whether you are looking for a quiet holiday in the green depths of the countryside, ancient abbeys or fairytale castles, exciting skiing, music and drama festivals, churches, museums and galleries, or the chance to extend your skills in a "hobby holiday," or to improve your health at one of the numerous spas, Austria can supply exactly what you want.

We would like to thank the Director of the Austrian National Tourist Office in Vienna and his staff for their considerable help and interest; Director Werner Fritz of the London office, and his staff for their unfailing courtesy and aid during the work on this edition. We would also like to thank George W. Hamilton for his enthusiasm and expertise in revising this edition.

*

While every care has been taken to assure the accuracy of the information in this guide, the passage of time will always bring change, and consequently the publisher cannot accept responsibility for errors that may occur.

All prices and opening times quoted in this guide are based on information available to us at press time. Hours and admission fees may change, however, and the prudent traveler will avoid inconvenience by calling ahead.

Fodor's wants to hear about your travel experiences, both pleasant and unpleasant. When a hotel or restaurant fails to live up to its billing, let us know and we will investigate the complaint and revise our entries where the facts warrant it.

Send your letters to the editors of Fodor's Travel Publications, 201 E. 50th Street, New York, NY 10022.

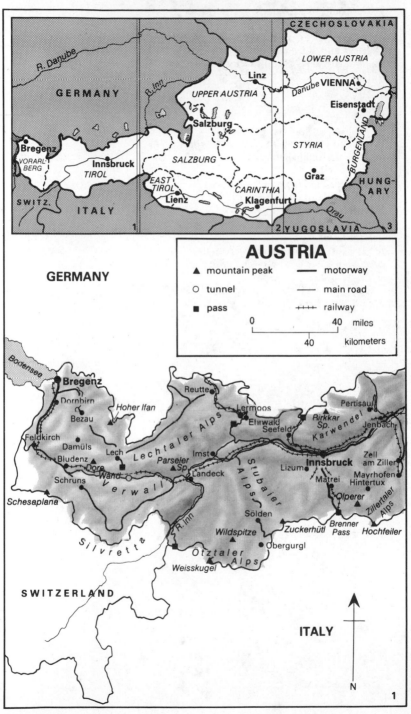

AUSTRIA

- ▲ mountain peak
- ○ tunnel
- ■ pass
- —— motorway
- — main road
- ++++ railway

0   40 miles
40 kilometers

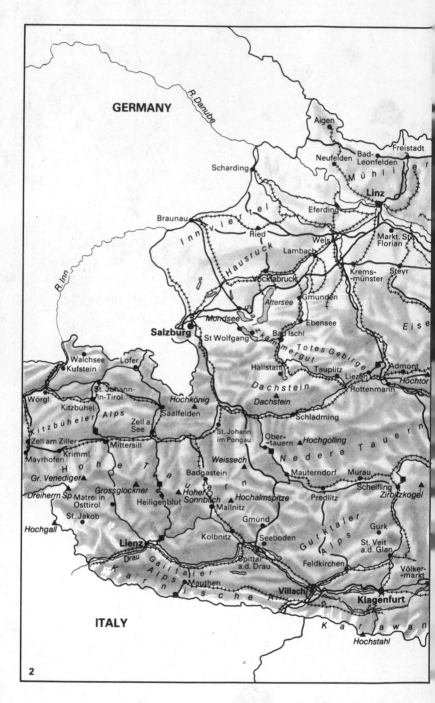

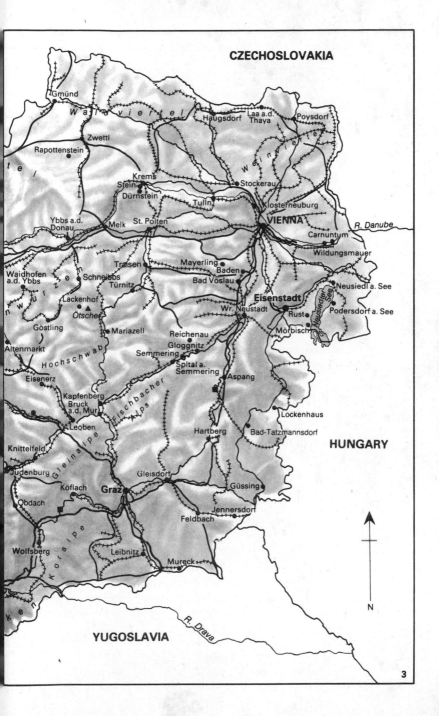

FACTS AT YOUR FINGERTIPS

Planning Your Trip

SOURCES OF INFORMATION. In the U.S. The major source of information for anyone planning a vacation to Austria is the *Austrian National Tourist Office,* 500 Fifth Ave., 20th floor, New York, NY 10110 (212–944–6880); 11601 Wilshire Blvd., Suite 2480, Los Angeles, CA 90025 (213–477–3332); 4800 San Felipe, Suite 500, Houston, TX 77056 (713–850–9999); 500 N. Michigan Ave., Suite 544, Chicago, IL 60611 (312–644–5556). They can supply information on all aspects of travel to and around the country, from which type of vacation is best suited to your needs and purse, to the best and most economical ways of getting around. They will also have a wealth of material on hotels, restaurants, excursions, museums and so on. They produce copious amounts of information, much of it free and all of it useful.

In Canada contact the Tourist Bureaus at 736 Granville St., Suite 1220, Vancouver Block, Vancouver BC V6Z 1J2 (604–683–8695); 2 Bloor St. E., Suite 3330, Toronto, Ontario M4W 1A8 (416–967–3348); 1010 Sherbrooke St. W., Suite 1410, Montreal, Quebec H3A 2R7 (514–849–3709). The office also offers a snow-conditions report during the season (phone 416–967–6870).

In the U.K. the address is—30 St. George St., London W1R OAL (01–629 0461). The office also runs a jazzily-named *Holiday Hotline* for the latest resort and price information—phone 01 629 0461.

PACKAGE TOUR OR INDEPENDENT TRAVEL. Time, convenience, cost and the type of travel that most interests you are the factors to consider when it comes to choosing an all-inclusive, fully-escorted tour, a loose plan-your-own-itinerary package tour, or totally independent travel.

Package tours are the easiest to arrange, and probably the most economical and efficient way for a first-time traveler to Austria to get an overview of the most famous sights. The operator will arrange for all plane, rail, motorcoach and other transportation; transfers wherever needed; tour guides; and generally commodious accommodations. Flight-plus-lodging for many such tours often works out to be less expensive than the flight alone would be if booked as a regular economy fare. Thus, even if you prefer arranging for accommodations at some place other than that offered by the tour operator, and even if you have no intention of participating in any group sightseeing or other package activities, it may still be in your best interest to buy the entire package.

In booking a package tour it is best to go through a travel agent; indeed, except for the likes of American Express, Cook and the airlines, most packagers do not handle their own reservations.

Be sure, when booking a tour, to read the fine print *very carefully.*

Traveling independently allows for greater freedom than does tour travel, but it is usually more expensive (assuming you desire comparable accommodations and services). In contrast, you will almost always get better

1

value for your money (that does not necessarily mean it will be cheaper) when dining on your own. Tour operators have arrangements with particular establishments that can handle busloads of tourists at a time; in order to serve them simultaneously and at a reduced rate, there will usually be a fixed menu offered, or a limited selection from the full menu. The food in such places also tends to play on stereotypes; both your options and the quality of the food you get are likely to be better going it on your own.

If you have not tied yourself to a tour and do require en route assistance in finding accommodations within your budget, go directly to the information kiosk at rail, ship or air terminals in the city or town where you wish to stay. The people manning these kiosks are among the most helpful and reliable sources of information concerning available hotel, hostel, pension, bed-and-breakfast and tourist-home rooms. During peak tourist periods they may suggest some surprisingly viable—and fascinating—alternatives, either one town away, or at a local university, or even a monastery that rents rooms out to the public.

TOUR OPERATORS. Full details of the many operators offering trips to Austria are available from the *Austrian National Tourist Office,* major international airlines and, of course, travel agents. But such is the range of tours available from both North America and the U.K. that a summary of some of the more typical is of interest. (All citations are meant to be representative of typical offerings that are regularly available. Details are as of Spring 1989; check for more current information.)

Not all U.S. travel agents are licensed, as the laws vary from state to state, but membership in the *American Society of Travel Agents* (ASTA) is a safeguard. Similarly, U.K. agents belong to the *Association of British Travel Agents* (ABTA). Members prominently display ASTA or ABTA shields.

From the U.S. there are ski tours, rail tours, self-drive tours, ballooning tours, Vienna-only tours, Danube cruise tours and budget tours, to name a few. Fly-drive tours combining Austria with the Southern part of Germany, and often the Italian and French Alps, are a popular way of seeing more than one country; the *Cortell Group* is one tour operator offering such packages.

Pan Am offers several ski tours in the Austrian countryside during the winter. Prices for a 7-day ski package range from $900–$1,200, depending on the destination city, with some specialist weeks in Innsbruck priced at $700–$750, and include airfare, accommodations and all meals.

Buddy Bombard's Great Balloon Adventure features daily balloon rides in the morning, picnic lunches and afternoon sightseeing in Salzburg, the Alpine foothills and the Lake District. The 5-day trip costs $3,480, land package only, includes air fare and all meals, and is limited to 12 people at a time.

Here are a few firms from among the many specializing in Austrian vacations—

Austrian Airlines, 15 W. 50th St., New York, NY 10020 (212–307–6226).
American Express, 300 Pinnacle Way, Norcross, GA 30071 (800–241–1700).

Bennett Tours, Inc., 270 Madison Ave., New York, NY 10016 (800–221–2420; within New York State, 212–532–5060).

The Bombard Society, 6727 Curran St., McLean VA 22101 (800–862–8537).

Cortell Group, 17310 Red Hill Ave., Suite 360, Irvine, CA 92714 (800–228–2535).

Dial Austria, 342 Madison Ave., New York, NY 10173 (212–661–4660; 800–221–4980).

Extra Value Travel, 683 S. Collier Blvd., Marco Island, FL 33937 (800–255–2847; within Florida, 813–394–3384).

Globus Gateway/Cosmos, 95–25 Queens Blvd., Rego Park NY 11374 (800–221–0090; in New York State, 718–268–7000).

Maupintour, 1515 St. Andrews Dr., Lawrence, KS 66046 (913–843–1211).

Pan Am Holidays, (ski packages only), 810 Belmar Plaza, Belmar, NJ 07719 (800–526–2827; within New Jersey, 800–662–3055 or 201–280–1120).

From the U.K. there are around 75 tour operators handling vacations to Austria—winter and summer. They range from fancy art-tours to excellent budget ski-trips. Among the wide range available are the following (prices quoted are from the 1987 programs)—

Austro Tours have a wide range of skiing vacations. Among them are 7 days in Gastein costing around £479 at peak season; 14 days for around £700–£790. At Filzmoos, a better bet for a family ski vacation, 7 days runs around £270–£310, and 14 days around £410. Austro Tours also run summer packages and city vacations. A *Two Center Tour* (3 nights in Vienna, 4 in Salzburg) begins from around £320, depending on the grade of hotel chosen.

Swan Hellenic, the specialists in art tours, all accompanied by couriers and guest lecturers, who are authorities in their particular fields, do one principal Austrian tour. *Salzburg, the Danube and Vienna* lasts for 15 days and costs about £1,580—visiting many of Austria's most famous sights, abbeys, castles and museums, and includes a cruise on the Danube.

Austria Travel is run by the Anglo-Austrian Society, and it organizes a number of economical packages to city and/or countryside. For example, a 7-day trip to Vienna and the countryside costs from £450 per person, twin sharing, while Vienna combined with one night in Budapest costs about £520 per person. Prices include flights from Gatwick, London, and transfers in Austria.

Here are a few of the firms with Austrian offers—a full list is available from the Austrian National Tourist office.

Austria Travel, 46 Queen Anne's Gate, London SW1H 9AU (tel. 01–222 0366).

Austro Tours Ltd., 5 St. Peter's St., St. Albans, Herts. AL1 3DH (tel. 0727–38191).

Canterbury Travel (London) Ltd., 248 Streatfield Rd., Kenton, Harrow, Middx. HA3 9BY (tel. 01–206 0411).

Ingham Travel, 10–18 Putney Hill, London SW15 6AX (tel. 01–785 7777).

Neilson Ski, Arndale House, Otley Rd., Heatingley, Leeds LS6 2UU (tel. 0532–744422).

Serenissima Travel Ltd., 21 Dorset Sq., London NW1 5PG (tel. 01–730 9841).

Swan Hellenic, 77 New Oxford St., London WC1A 1PP (tel. 01–831 1616).

Thomas Cook, 45 Berkeley St., London W1A 1EB (tel. 01–499 4000).

WHEN TO GO. Austria has two main seasons. The **summer season** starts at Easter and ends about the middle of October. May, June, September and October are the pleasantest for traveling about (except in Vienna), sufficiently warm, and there is less competition for hotel rooms and restaurant tables; also prices tend to be lower.

June through August are the most crowded months, when the main festivals take place. The Vienna Festival is from mid-May to the end of June; the Schubert Festival in Hohenems, Vorarlberg, is in mid-June; the Carinthian Summer Festival is in July and August; and the Salzburg, Bregenz and Mörbisch Festivals are in late July and August. Less international, the Bruckner Festival in Linz and St. Florian is in September; and the Styrian Autumn Festival is from the beginning of October to mid-November.

The **water-sports season** also, obviously, has its peak in July and August when the beaches of the Carinthian lakes, Bodensee (Lake Constance) in Vorarlberg, and Neusiedlersee in Burgenland are positively swarming with swimmers. The waters of the Salzkammergut lakes are cooler, but they have just as much sailing and boating. Water-ski contests are a regular feature on the principal lakes, and on Wörthersee in Carinthia you can see occasionally night water-ski jumping with torches. The summer season in the principal lake resorts is very lively as it is also in the principal spas, such as Bad Hofgastein, Badgastein, Bad Ischl, and Baden near Vienna. In all these places, however, you have to make your reservations well in advance. Even the smallest resort features an openair swimming pool; most better resort hotels have one, many two, indoor and outdoor pools.

The **winter sports season** starts in December and lasts until the end of April. You can ski in Austria as late as the middle of June and on the highest glaciers throughout the year, but if you want to do that you must be prepared to cope with rather high altitudes. Reservations are a must in the main resorts during the peak season. We give more information about Winter Sports possibilities in the *Practical Information* sections at the end of the relevant chapters.

CLIMATE. The traditional four seasons. Generally speaking Austria has a moderate Central European climate. However, as the altitude and general geographical situation vary tremendously from one part of the country to another, it is always wise to check up locally. This is especially true in the winter, when road conditions can be very dangerous due to ice, snow and fog.

Average maximum afternoon temperatures in degrees Fahrenheit and Centigrade:

Vienna	Jan.	Feb.	Mar.	Apr.	May	June	July	Aug.	Sept.	Oct.	Nov.	Dec.
F°	34	38	47	57	66	71	75	73	66	55	44	37
C°	1	3	8	14	19	22	24	23	19	13	7	3

SEASONAL EVENTS. Since Austria is a country that has held firm to its traditions, many of the events that will attract the visitor are traditional, with centuries of history behind them. **New Year** is, of course, one of the highlights of the year, and in some of the fashionable winter resorts, such as Zürs in Vorarlberg and Seefeld in Tirol, its beginning is celebrated with such unusual features as torchlight ski races; Vienna offers *Fledermaus* in both Opera Houses, a choice of superb concerts, and the Kaiserball in the Hofburg—the first of the glittering balls. The Three Magi singing (Sternsingen) is observed almost everywhere in the countryside and special masked processions can be seen around Twelfth Night and in mid-*January* in some localities of Styria where they are known by the name of Glöckerllauf, as well as in the Pongau area of Land Salzburg where they are called Perchtenlauf. January also sees the Mozart week in Salzburg.

Carnival, or Fasching, celebrations get under way immediately afterwards and continue, crescendo, until Ash Wednesday. They include hundreds of balls in Vienna, culminating in the Philharmonic Ball on Jan. 18 and the grand gala Opera Ball on Feb. 22 this year; mummers' parades with old woodcarved masks in several localities in Tirol, masked dances and parties everywhere.

On the first Sunday of Lent, burning discs are sent rolling down some hills of Vorarlberg while on the top of them bonfires are lit. Spring trade fairs open in Vienna in **March** and in Graz in **April.** Easter is celebrated everywhere, with a music festival in Salzburg, and on Good Friday the Vienna Philharmonic gives its traditional Joseph Haydn concert in the Eisenstadt "Bergkirche" Church in Burgenland, where the composer is buried. April also sees the Viennale Film Festival in Vienna.

The first weekend of **May** is most energetically celebrated at Zell am Ziller, in the Ziller valley of Tirol, which is thronged with visitors to the Gauderfest. The many attractions of this festival include Preis-Rangeln (a folk type of wrestling), cockfighting, folk dancing, the serving of a special beer and a tremendous outburst of Gemütlichkeit. Corpus Christi sees colorful processions throughout Austria. Particularly picturesque are those of the Lungau region of Land Salzburg and the water processions with gaily decorated boats and barges on the Traun and Halstätter lakes. The Vienna Festival begins during the second half of May and lasts through mid-June.

On Midsummer's day (**June** 21) great bonfires burn almost everywhere throughout the country, offering a particularly picturesque view in the mountains of Tirol and in Wachau in Lower Austria. In Graz the Styriarte festival of Renaissance music is held, and in Linz the avant-garde "ars electronica." Throughout June is the Lower Austria Danube Arts Festival, with events all over the province. June through July sees the Hohenems Schubertiade music festival.

At the height of the season, in **July** and **August,** the Salzburg Festival, the world's most prestigious, attracts a cosmopolitan audience. In the same months, opera and operettas are performed on water stages at Bregenz on Lake Constance, and at Mörbisch on Neusiedler Lake in Burgenland. Classical plays are presented in the courtyards of the Dominican Convent of Friesach and Porcia Palace, Spittal/Drau, both in Carinthia, where the up-and-coming musical and literary festival of the Carinthian

Summer is shared by Ossiach and Villach. Also shared is the Festival Week of Old Music, Renaissance and Baroque music at the Wilten Stiftskirche and the Silver Chapel of the Hofburg in Innsbruck. Concerts in the Abbey Churches of Garsten, Kremsmünster, St. Florian and Schlierbach in Upper Austria. Bad Ischl has operetta weeks, July to Sept. Music weeks and courses are held in Bad Hofgastein in the second half of July, and there is the renowned summer academy of music in Salzburg at the Mozarteum. The Gmunden Festival takes place during July.

In **August,** Klagenfurt holds its Wood Fair. During the summer, Styria and Tirol hold many brass band and folk festivals.

In **September,** musical interest shifts to Linz, where the Bruckner Festival takes place. There are trade fairs in Vienna and Innsbruck. Many villages have their own harvest or grape festivities throughout this month and **October.** The Graz music and drama festival called Steirischer Herbst (Styrian Autumn) takes place from early October to mid-November.

The 15th of **November** is St. Leopold Day (for Leopold III, one of the early rulers of Austria, later proclaimed a saint), and there is a picturesque folk and religious festival in Klosterneuburg near Vienna where St. Leopold is buried. Similar celebrations in November include the festival honoring St. Martin, patron saint of Burgenland, held throughout this province on November 11 and 13; and parades on horseback in Land Salzburg and Upper Austria on 6 November honoring St. Leonhard, patron saint of cattle and horses. In Vienna, the Musikverein is the scene of the Schubertiade.

St. Nicholas Day, the 6th of **December,** as in many countries of Europe, is the real beginning of the Christmas season, and Christkindl Christmas open-air markets are held in all major towns. If you choose to go to Oberndorf, near Salzburg, for the midnight mass on Christmas Eve, you can hear *Silent Night, Holy Night* sung in the Memorial Chapel where it was first sung.

WHAT TO PACK. There is really only one supreme rule—travel light. This makes more sense than ever now that any journey may suddenly be made more complicated by strikes of baggage handlers at airports. If you realize that what ever you take you may have to carry yourself, then you will be surprised to find how much you can leave at home!

For transatlantic travelers by air the regulations should be noted carefully. Your baggage is subject to a size allowance, not a weight one. First-class passengers may have two pieces of baggage, provided that the total of the height, width and length does not exceed 124 inches (316 cm.). Economy-class passengers may also have two pieces of baggage, but the total sum of their height, length and width must not exceed 106 inches (270 cm.) and neither of the two must exceed a total of 62 inches (155 cm.). All other passengers (i.e. non-transatlantic ones), are still bound by the weight limitations of 66 lb. in First Class and 44 lb. in Economy.

It's a good idea to pack the bulk of your things in one bag and put everything you need for overnight, or for two or three nights, in a carry-on bag, to obviate packing and repacking at brief stops. Motorists will find it advisable to be frugal as well. You should limit your luggage to what can be locked into the trunk or boot of your car when making daytime stops.

Take what you would wear for the same sort of activities you plan to indulge in if you were staying in Britain or the northern United States. Remember, however, that if you are going to investigate any high altitudes (and it's pretty hard in Austria not to), you will find evenings chilly even in midsummer, so a warm sweater or two is a good thing to have. If you are going in for sports, the same sort of sports clothes you wear at home will be appropriate. Do take comfortable walking shoes; women's shoes ought to have broad heels to cope with the diminutive Austrian cobblestones of many city streets.

If you plan to spend much time in cities or the better resorts and go to top-notch places, you will find Austrians more formal, on the whole, than Americans and Britons, and you had better take some evening clothes, or at least fairly sober ones. Even in the summer, gala performances at the festivals tend to be dressy affairs.

COSTS IN AUSTRIA. Austria remains one of Europe's best buys. While not inexpensive, Vienna still offers value for money. Generally, prices directly concerned with tourism (hotels, ski-lifts and restaurants) have, despite high taxes, increased less than in other major tourist countries.

Vienna and Salzburg lead the list of expensive cities in Austria, followed by Innsbruck. Expensive resorts include Kitzbühel, Seefeld, Badgastein, Bad Hofgastein, Velden, Saalbach, Zell am See, Pörtschach.

Farther down the ledger, there are many old and attractive towns and cities (Graz, Linz, Krems, Hallstatt, Feldkirch, Dürnstein, Steyr to mention a few) which offer almost as much history and notable architecture in attractive and comfortable surroundings, but at much lower cost.

Budget Areas. Particularly easy on the pocketbook, and still not overrun with tourists are Burgenland, the area of Waldviertel and Weinviertel in Lower Austria, the smaller lakes, such as Klopeiner See, in Carinthia, the southeastern areas of Land Salzburg (Pongau and Lungau), East Tirol, almost forgotten since history and politics cut it off from the rest of Tirol, and the green mountains and rolling vineyard hills of Styria.

Some Budget Ideas. You can cut your vacation costs considerably by making a European-type, stay-put vacation, selecting one area or place and remaining there for at least a week at a time.

Many hotels, from inexpensive on up to first-class establishments, offer special all-inclusive weekly rates, although not all extend such offers during the high season. Most of these also include *Visitor's Cards,* which entitle the tourist to reductions of 20–30% for all local recreational facilities, including swimming pools, ski lifts, etc. The Visitor's Card scheme is operated by the regional tourist offices, whose addresses you can obtain from the National Tourist Office nearest you.

Even some of the top resorts, such as Kitzbühel and Zell am See, are getting on the all-inclusive bandwagon, and most cities, including Vienna, Salzburg and Innsbruck, offer special weekend rates, often combined with an Austrian Airlines flight.

Another way of cutting down on costs is to take either a bungalow or apartment. In many localities there are vacation apartments and bungalows available and, if your German is up to it, many farmers throughout the country offer room and board in their own Alpine-style farmhouses, which, of course, are the original models of every balconied inn and luxury hotel in Austria. See under *Hotels* later in this section.

Off-season travel is recommended if you are willing to pass up the big events, which necessarily take place in the main season, and are free to take your trip at any time of the year. It is cheaper—air fares and hotel rates are lower out of season. Lower hotel charges off season are very frequent in Austria, especially on full board terms, sometimes amounting to as much as 33 1/3% and even more. Even where prices are the same, you get better accommodations: the choicest rooms in the hotels and the best tables in the restaurants have not been pre-empted and train compartments are not jammed full.

Warning: Other Nasty Taxes. The tax situation becomes more complicated when it comes to beverages: there is, *in addition* to the Value Added Tax, a beverage or refreshment tax, which also applies to ice cream and coffee; then there is an alcohol tax added to beer, wine and liquor; and, finally, champagne gets hit with still another champagne tax. Thus drinking anything but water in Austria (which fortunately is very good) can be an expensive pastime. All these taxes are *included* automatically in the price, so you will not notice them as a separate imposition, but they are there all the same.

Sample costs. It will cost about AS50 to have a shirt laundered; from 120 to dryclean a suit, and from 70 a dress; a shampoo and set for a woman will cost her around 400, a manicure from 60; a man's haircut (without shampoo) from AS100.

Opera tickets cost from AS80–2,000 (Salzburg Festival up to 3,000), more for special performances; theater tickets from 50–600.

TAKING MONEY ABROAD. Traveler's checks are still the standard and best way to safeguard your travel funds; and you will usually get as good a rate of exchange in Austria for traveler's checks as you will for cash. In the U.S., many of the larger banks issue their own traveler's checks—just about as universally recognized as those of American Express, Cook and Barclays—as well as those of one or more of the other firms mentioned. In most instances there is a 1% charge for the checks; there is no fee for Barclays checks. Some banks also issue them free if you are a regular customer. The best-known British checks are Cook's and those of Barclays, Lloyds, Midland and National Westminster banks. It is also always a good idea to have some local currency upon arrival for the airport bus, taxis, tips and so on. Some banks will provide this service; alternatively, contact Deak International Ltd., 630 Fifth Ave., New York, NY 10111 (212–635–0515, call for additional locations). But try to get bills in smaller denominations—it is embarrassing to have local currency which you can't use, although these can be changed at airports and railway stations.

Britons holding a Uniform Eurocheque card and check book—apply for them at your bank—can cash checks for up to £100 a day at banks participating in the scheme *and* write checks for goods and services (hotels, restaurants, shops, etc.) again up to £100.

CREDIT CARDS. Credit Cards are now an integral part of the Western Financial Way of Life and, in theory at least, they are accepted all over Europe. In theory, because Austria is one of the countries where they are less used than elsewhere. There are many thrifty Austrian restaurateurs and hoteliers who are damned if they see why they should turn over any part of their hard-earned money to credit card companies, and stoutly refuse to accept plastic payment. A great many of these are the more atmospheric, regional establishments, most likely the very ones you will want to eat in and, in the countryside, stay in. So keep an eye open for those little signs in the window; you could easily find yourself in an embarrassing situation otherwise.

We have included credit card information wherever possible. There are, however, some surprising omissions of hotels or restaurants that you would think would accept credit cards, but don't. The initials we use for this information are AE, DC, MC and V—which stand for American Express, Diner's Club, MasterCard (alias Access and Eurocard) and Visa (Barclaycard in Britain). Be sure to double check that your particular piece of plastic is accepted before ordering a meal or checking into your hotel.

PASSPORTS. All travelers require a passport for entry into Austria. **In the U.S.,** apply in person at U.S. Passport Agency Offices, local county courthouses or selected Post Offices. If you have a passport not more than eight years old you may apply by mail; otherwise you will need:

1—proof of citizenship, such as a birth certificate;

2—two identical photographs, two inches square, in either black and white or color, on non-glossy paper and taken within the past six months;

3—$35 for the passport itself plus a $7 processing fee if you are applying in person (no processing fee when renewing your passport by mail); for those 18 years and older, or if you are under 18, $20 for the passport plus a $7 processing fee if you are applying in person (again, no extra fee when applying by mail);

4—proof of identity that includes a photo and signature (a driver's license, previous passport or any governmental ID card for example).

Adult passports are valid for 10 years, five years for those 18 and under; they are not renewable. Allow four to six weeks for your application to be processed, but in an emergency, Passport Agency offices can have a passport readied within 24–48 hours, and even the postal authorities can indicate "Rush" when necessary.

If you expect to travel extensively, request a 48- or 96-page passport rather than the usual 24-page one. There is no extra charge. When you receive your passport, write down its number, date and place of issue separately. The loss of a valid passport should be reported immediately to the local police and to the Passport Office, Department of State, Washington DC 20524. If your passport is lost or stolen while abroad, report it immediately to the local authorities and apply for a replacement at the nearest U.S. Embassy or consular office.

Canadian citizens apply in person to regional passport offices, post offices or by mail to Passport Office, Bureau of Passports, External Affairs, Ottawa, Ontario K1A OG3 (613–994–3500) (819–994–3500). A $25 fee, two photographs, a guarantor, and evidence of citizenship are required. Canadian passports are valid for five years and are non-renewable.

U.K. citizens. Apply for passports on special forms obtainable from your travel agency or from the main post office in your town. The application should be sent to the Passport Office in your area (as indicated on the guidance form) or taken personally to your nearest main post office. It is advisable to apply for your passport 4–5 weeks before it is required, although in some cases it will be issued sooner. The regional Passport Offices are located in London, Liverpool, Peterborough, Glasgow and Newport. The application must be countersigned by your bank manager, or by a solicitor, barrister, doctor, clergyman or Justice of the Peace who knows you personally. You will need two photos. The fee is £15. A larger, 94-page passport can be obtained for an extra charge.

British Visitor's Passport. This simplified form of passport has advantages for the once-in-a-while tourist to most European countries (Austria included). Valid for one year and not renewable, it costs £7.50. Application may be made at a local post office (in Northern Ireland at the Passport Office in Belfast); you will need identification plus two passport photographs—no other formalities.

Visas. Citizens of the United States, Great Britain, and Canada do not need visas to visit Austria. Citizens of other nations should get in touch with the nearest Austrian consulate or tourist association representative for the latest developments on this requirement.

Health Certificates. Not required for entry into Austria. Neither the United States, Canada nor Great Britain require a certificate of vaccination prior to re-entry. However, the health regulations can change overnight if there is a scare, so we advise you to check up on the latest status quo, just in case. If you expect to be wandering through the woods in the eastern or southeastern parts of Austria, inoculation against tick bite—these carry encephalitis—is recommended.

INSURANCE. Travel insurance can cover everything from health and accident costs, to lost baggage and trip cancellation. Sometimes they can all be obtained with one blanket policy; other times they overlap with existing coverage you might already have for health and/or home; but there will be times where it is best to buy policies that are tailored to very specific needs. Many travelers unwittingly end up with duplicate coverage, so before purchasing separate travel insurance of any kind, check your regular policies carefully.

Generally, it is best to take care of your insurance needs before embarking on your trip. You'll pay more for less coverage—and have less chance to read the fine print—if you wait until the last minute and make your purchases from, say, an airport vending machine or insurance company counter. If you have a regular insurance agent, that is the person to consult first.

Flight insurance, which is often included in the price of the ticket when the fare is paid via American Express, Visa or certain other major credit cards, is also often included in package policies providing accident coverage as well. These policies are available from most tour operators and insurance companies. While it is a good idea to have health and accident insurance when traveling, be careful not to spend money to duplicate coverage you may already have . . . or to neglect some eventuality which could end up costing a small fortune.

For example, basic Blue Cross–Blue Shield policies do cover health costs incurred while traveling. They will not, however, cover the cost of emergency transportation, which can often add up to several thousand dollars. Emergency transportation *is* covered, in part at least, by many major medical policies such as those underwritten by Prudential and Metropolitan Life. Again, we can't urge you too strongly that in order to be sure you are getting the coverage you need, check any policy carefully before buying. Another important example: Most insurance issued specifically for travel does not cover pre-existing conditions, such as a heart condition.

Travel Assistance International, the American arm of Europ Assistance, offers a comprehensive program providing medical and personal emergency services and offering immediate, on-the-spot medical, personal and financial help. Trip protection ranges from $40 for an individual for up to eight days to $600 for an entire family for a year. Full details from travel agents or insurance brokers, or from Europ Assistance Worldwide Services, Inc., 1133 15th St., N.W., Suite 400, Washington, DC 20005 (800–821–2828). In the U.K., contact Europ Assistance Ltd., 252 High St., Croydon, Surrey (01–680 1234).

Carefree Travel Insurance, c/o ARM Coverage Inc., 120 Mineola Blvd., Box 310, Mineola, NY 11501, underwritten by the Hartford Accident and Indemnity Co., offers a comprehensive benefits package that includes trip cancellation and interruption as well as medical, legal and economic assistance. Trip cancellation and interruption insurance can be purchased separately. Call 800–645–2424 for additional information.

International SOS Assistance Inc., Box 11568, Philadelphia, PA 19116 (800–523–8930), has fees from $25 a person for one to thirteen days, to $195 for a year.

IAMAT (International Association for Medical Assistance to Travelers), 417 Center St. Lewiston, NY 14092 (716–754–4883) in the U.S.; or 40 Regal Rd., Guelph, Ontario N1K 1B5 (519–836–0102) in Canada.

The Association of British Insurers, Aldermary House, 10–15 Queen St., London E.C.4 (01–248 4477), will give comprehensive advice on all aspects of vacation travel insurance from the U.K.

Baggage Loss. It is possible, though often a complicated affair, to insure your luggage against loss through theft or negligence. Insurance companies are reluctant to sell such coverage alone, however, since it is often a losing proposition for them. Instead, it is most often included as part of a package that would also cover accidents or health. Remuneration is often determined by weight, regardless of the value of the specific contents of the luggage. Should you lose your luggage or some other personal possession, be sure to report it to the local police immediately. Without documentation of such a report, your insurance company might be very stingy. Also, before buying baggage insurance, check your homeowners policy. Some such policies offer "off-premises theft" coverage, including the loss of luggage while traveling.

Cancellation Coverage. The last major area of traveler's insurance is trip cancellation coverage. This is especially important to travelers on APEX or charter flights. Should you get sick abroad, or for some other reason be unable to continue your trip, you may be stuck having to buy a new one-way fare home, plus paying for space on the charter you're not using. You can guard against this with "trip cancellation insurance," usually available from travel agents. Most of these policies will also cover last minute cancellations.

STUDENT AND YOUTH TRAVEL. All student travelers should obtain an *International Student Identity Card,* which is in most instances needed to get student discounts, youth rail passes, and Intra-European Student Charter Flights. Apply to *Council on International Educational Exchange,* 205 East 42 St., New York, NY 10017. Cost is $10. Canadian students should apply to the *Association of Student Councils,* 187 College St., Toronto, Ontario M5T 1P7. U.K. students should apply to the *National Union of Student Marketing,* 461 Holloway Rd., London N.7 (01–272 9445).

The following organizations can also be helpful in finding student flights, educational opportunities and other information. Most deal with international student travel generally, but materials for those listed cover Austria.

American Youth Hostels, Box 37613, Washington, DC 20013. Members are eligible for entree to the worldwide network of youth hostels. The organization publishes an extensive directory to same.

Council on International Educational Exchange (CIEE), 205 East 42 St., New York, NY 10017 (and 20 satellite offices around the United States called *Council Travel Services*) provides information on summer study, work/travel programs and travel programs and services for college and high school students. CIEE's *Work, Study, Travel Abroad: The Whole World Handbook* ($8.95 plus $1 postage) is the best listing of both work and study possibilities.

Institute of International Education, 809 United Nations Plaza, New York, NY 10017, is primarily concerned with study opportunities and administers scholarships and fellowships for international study and training. The New York office has a visitor's information center; satellite offices are located in Chicago, Denver, Houston, San Francisco and Washington, DC.

Also worth contacting is *Educational Travel Center,* 438 N. Frances St., Madison, WI 53703. Specific information on rail and other discounts is listed in the appropriate sections hereafter.

Among the leading specialists in the field of youth travel are the following:

Arista Student Travel Assoc., Inc., 11 E. 44th St., New York, NY 10017 (212–687–5121).

Bailey Travel Service Inc., 123 E. Market St., York, PA 17401 (717–854–5511).

Campus Holidays, 242 Bellevue Ave., Upper Montclair, NJ 07043 (201–744–8724).

Harwood Tours & Travel, Inc., 2428 Guadalupe, Austin, TX 78705 (512–478–9343).

Osborne Travel Service, Inc., 3379 Peachtree Rd., N.E., Atlanta, GA 30326 (404–261–1608).

In Canada: *Canadian Federation of Student-Services,* 187 College St., Toronto, Ontario M5T 1P7, is a non-profit student service cooperative owned and operated by over 50 college and university student unions. Its travel bureau, *Travel Cuts,* can arrange transportation, tours, and work programs abroad. Try also *Tourbec,* 535 Ontario East, Montreal, Quebec H2L 1N8.

In Britain: Student travel arrangements may be made through the following:

Australian Student Travel, 117 Euston Rd, London NW1.

CTS (Centro Turistico Studentesco—Italian), 33 Windmill St., London W1.

London Student Travel (including Union of Student International Travel—Irish), 52 Grosvenor Gardens, London SW1.

Worldwide Student Travel, 39 Store St., London WC1.

HANDICAPPED TRAVEL. *Access to the World: A Travel Guide for the Handicapped,* by Louise Weiss, is an outstanding book covering all aspects of travel for anyone with health or medical problems; it features extensive listings and suggestions on everything from availability of special diets to wheelchair accessibility. Available from Facts on File, 460 Park Ave., New York, NY, 10016 (212–683–2244).

Tours specially designed for the handicapped generally parallel those of the non-handicapped traveler, but at a more leisurely pace. For a complete list of tour operators who arrange such travel write to the *Society for the Advancement of Travel for the Handicapped,* (SATH), 26 Court St., Brooklyn, NY 11242. Travel Information Service of *Moss Rehabilitation Hospital,* 12th St. and Tabor Road, Philadelphia, PA 19141, answers inquiries regarding specific cities and countries as well as providing toll-free telephone numbers for airlines with special lines for the hearing impaired and, again, listings of selected tour operators.

International Air Transport Association (IATA) publishes a free pamphlet entitled *Incapacitated Passengers' Air Travel Guide.* Write IATA, 2000 Peel Street, Montreal, Quebec H3A 2R4.

From the U.K.: The *Airline Transport Users Committee,* 129 Kingsway, London W.C.2, publish a very useful booklet, *Care In the Air,* free.

But one of the very best guides is a book published by the *Royal Association for Disability and Rehabilitation,* 25 Mortimer St., London W.1, called *Holidays for Disabled People,* £3 from W.H. Smith or direct from RADAR (no charge for post or packing).

Once in Austria, contact *Öst. Zivilinvalidenverband,* Lange Gasse 60, A-1080 Vienna (0222–48–55–05), for further information. A handicapped guide to Vienna is available from the *Sozialamt der Stadt Wien,* A-1010, Rathaus.

Getting to Austria

FROM THE U.S. By Air. Air fares are in a constant state of flux, and our best advice is to consult a travel agent and let him or her make your reservations for you. New competition on the New York–Vienna route should mean a number of special fares over the coming months. Agents are familiar with the latest changes in fare structures—ever more confusing despite "deregulation" among U.S. carriers who now allegedly base prices on distance traveled—as well as with the rules governing various discount plans. Among those rules: booking (usually) 21 days in advance, minimum stay requirements, maximum stay allowances, the amount that (sometimes) must be paid in advance for land arrangements. Lowest prices overall will, of course, be during the off-season periods.

Generally, on regularly scheduled flights, you have the option, in descending order of cost, of First Class, Club or Business Class, APEX or Stand-by tickets. APEX is by far the most used and the most useful of these categories. Some charter service is still available; again, an agent will be able to recommend which ones are reliable. Sometimes it is also worth investigating package tours even if you do not wish to use the tours' other services (hotels, meals, etc.); because a packager can block book seats, the price of a package can be less than the cost when air fare is booked separately.

If you have the flexibility, you can sometimes benefit from the last-minute sales that tour operators have in order to fill a plane. A number of brokers specializing in such discount sales have also sprung up. All charge an annual membership fee, usually about $35–$50. Among these: *Stand-Buys Ltd.,* 3033 S. Parker Rd., Aurora, CO 80011 (800–255–1488); *Moments Notice,* 40 E. 49th St., New York, NY 10017 (212–486–0503); *Discount Travel Intl.,* 114 Forest Ave., Narberth, PA 19072 (215–668–2182); and *Worldwide Discount Travel Club,* 1674 Meridian Ave., Miami Beach, FL 33139 (305–534–2082).

Try to find out whether the tour operator is reputable and whether you are tied to a precise round trip or whether you will have to wait until the operator has a spare seat in order to return.

Airlines specifically serving Austria from **major U.S. cities** (usually via New York) include:

Austrian Airlines, 15 W. 50th St., New York, NY 10111 (800–843–0002); five or six nonstop flights a week between New York JFK and Vienna.

Pan Am, Pan Am Bldg., New York, NY 10166 (212–687–2600); twice a week from New York JFK to Vienna direct.

Royal Jordanian Airlines, 535 Fifth Ave., New York, NY 10017 (212–949–0050); twice weekly from Los Angeles, Chicago, New York, and Miami.

TWA, 100 S. Bedford Rd., Mt. Kisco, NY 10549 (212–290–2141); connects with Austrian Airlines in Frankfurt and Munich, daily from New York JFK.

From Canada. *Air Canada,* Place Air Canada, Montreal, Quebec H2Z 1X5 (514–393–3333) operates a direct flight to Vienna from Toronto, three times a week. From Montreal, connections to Vienna via London, Zurich and Paris (on other carriers) are available on Air Canada. *Canadian Airlines International,* 1101 St. Catherine's St. W., Montreal, Quebec H3B 1H8 (514–286–1212), flies to Amsterdam where it too connects with Austrian Airlines.

Fares. Typical roundtrip fares as of Spring 1989. New York–Vienna $4,008 first class and $689–$900 APEX (depending on the type of APEX ticket and the season). Charter fares were about the same as (or slightly lower than) APEX.

FROM THE U.K. By Air. There are direct flights from London to both Vienna and Salzburg by *British Airways* and *Austrian Airlines.* Vienna has a minimum of two flights daily from London Heathrow. The flying time is a little over 2 hours. A greater choice of flights is available by flying from either London Heathrow or Gatwick to Frankfurt and then changing.

Salzburg has a direct flight on 5 days a week (Mon., Wed., Fri., Sat., Sun.) in the summer, by Austrian Airlines from London Heathrow. The flying time is again around 2 hours. A more frequent service is available via Zurich.

Other major towns can be reached from London via Frankfurt.

Fares. Discount flights to Austria are becoming easier to find. First, by booking at least one month before flying and paying for the entire round trip at the same time, a substantial saving can be made against the full fares. The British Airways Club Class fare to Vienna works out at around £462 round trip, while the summer APEX fare starts at around £178 round trip. Second, "scheduled charter" flights are becoming more frequently available to Austrian airports. *German Tourist Facilities,* for example, operate several flights every week from Luton to Vienna and also fly several times a week to Salzburg. Flights to Vienna range from around £165 to £200 round trip. They can be booked by anyone. Contact *GTF,* 184–186 Kensington Church St., London W8 4DP (tel. 01–792 0311). Third, the *Anglo-Austrian Society,* 46 Queen Anne's Gate, London S.W.1 offer reduced fare flights for full-time students under 30 to Vienna and Salzburg; reductions are also offered to members.

By Train. Rail services to Austria offer a wide choice of routes. There is a daily through service from Calais to Innsbruck, running via Basel, Zurich and Bludenz. The connecting service departs from London Victoria at 2.30 P.M. and Innsbruck is reached just before noon the next day. For the overnight run from Calais second-class couchettes are available and light refreshments are provided from Basel onwards. Alternatively, there is also the *Ostende Wien* direct link between London and Vienna. Depart London 9.15 A.M., arrive Vienna 9.40 A.M. next day. If changing trains en route doesn't worry you, travel more comfortably via Paris. First of all use the *City Link* Rail–Hovercraft–Rail service from London (Victoria) to Paris (Nord) departing at 10 A.M. and arriving in Paris at 4.30 that afternoon, in good time for an evening out in Paris. In summer, a later service, leaving London at noon, can be used. Then transfer to Paris (Est)—around ½ km away—for the *Arlberg Express* which leaves at 10.40 P.M. and runs via Innsbruck to Vienna. On this train first- and second-class sleepers and second-class couchettes are available as far as Innsbruck.

If time permits the most attractive route to Austria is via Cologne and Munich, with an overnight stop in Cologne en route. Use the rail service from London (Victoria) to Dover, then catch the speedy P & O European Ferries/RTM Jetfoil to Ostend and travel by express train to Cologne. An early morning departure from London will give a late afternoon arrival in Cologne. The following morning board the EuroCity express, the *Johann Strauss,* which leaves Cologne at 5.55 A.M., and runs through to Vienna. This very comfortable train has full restaurant facilities for both breakfast and lunch. Vienna is reached just before 4 A.M.

Fares. Rail fares to Austria are still good value for money, especially if you want to break your journey en route. In Spring 1989, a second class round-trip ticket to Innsbruck worked out at around £179, and to Vienna at around £193. Couchettes and sleepers must be reserved well in advance in high summer, however. A supplement of £7 each way is payable on the Dover–Ostend Jetfoil. Students/young people (under 26) can obtain reduced fare tickets from *Eurotrain* and *Transalpino*—these cut the return fare to Innsbruck to £115 and to Vienna to £129. On these "under-26" tickets a wide choice of routes is available and break of journey is allowed, so work out your route carefully! Details from *Eurotrain,* 52 Grosvenor Gdns., London SW1W OAG (01–730–3402), or *Transalpino,* 71–5 Buckingham Palace Road, London SW1W ORE (01–834–9656).

Young British residents should carefully consider buying an *InterRail* card as this costs around £140 and gives 1 month's unlimited rail travel throughout Europe, including Austria. Remember that the card also entitles you to ½ fare on British Rail and several Channel and North Sea services. Details from any British Rail Travel Centre or Rail Appointed Travel Agent.

Rail Holiday. The German travel service (DER) in conjunction with the German Railways (DB tours) offer a wide range of inclusive holidays in Austria from London and these are well worth investigating. For example, seven nights in Salzburg staying in a small hotel (half board) works out at from £254–£268, upward to £421 in peak season, travel included. The off-peak prices compare very favorably with the rail only fare! Ask for the brochure *Summer Holidays in Germany and Austria.* Details from *DER Travel Service,* 18 Conduit St., London W1R 9TD (01–408–0111) or in the U.S.A. from *German Rail,* 747 Third Avenue, New York, NY 10017.

Planning. For advance planning the *Thomas Cook European Timetable* is invaluable. This can be bought over the counter from any branch of Thomas Cook, or in the U.K. by post from *Thomas Cook Timetable Publishing,* P.O. Box 36, Peterborough PE3 6SB. In the U.S.A. by mail from *Stephen Forsyth Travel Library,* P.O. Box 2975, Shawnee Mission, KS 66201-1375 ($16.95, plus $3 postage). There are major differences between the summer and winter schedules of the European railways so buy the timetable close to your visit.

By Bus. At the time of writing there were no direct bus services to Austria from the U.K. and little prospect of any new services. At present the nearest you can get is Munich. International Express operate a daily service throughout the summer which leaves London (Victoria Coach Station) in mid-evening and arrives in Munich at 7 the following night. Fares work out at around £110 for an adult, round trip, with a reduction for students on production of an International Student Identity Card at time of booking. From Munich there are several bus services to Austrian destinations including Innsbruck. But services are relatively infrequent—a couple of days a week—so it's quicker and easier to go by train.

Details of the International Express services are contained in the International Express brochure, which can be obtained from any National Express coach station, appointed travel agents, or direct from *International Express,* The Coach Travel Center, 13 Lower Regent St., London SW1Y 4LR (tel. 01–439 9368).

By Car. The best way to reach Austria by car from England is to use one of the North Sea/Cross Channel ferries to Ostend or Zeebrugge in Belgium or to Dunkirk in Northern France and then use the toll-free Belgian motorway system (E5) to drive to Aachen, then via Cologne to Frankfurt. From there travel either southwards via Stuttgart towards Innsbruck and the Tirol (A61, A67, A5, E11, A7) or eastwards by way of Nürnberg and Munich to cross into Austria at Walserberg and then on to Salzburg. The most direct way to Vienna is by autobahn via Nürnberg, Regensburg and Passau, entering Austria at Schärding. There is now only a short distance that is not yet autobahn. In summer border delays are much shorter at Schärding than at Salzburg.

Using this route the journey to Innsbruck will occupy 2–3 days depending on the pace you wish to maintain. The ferry crossing takes around 4½ hours which makes an overnight sailing inconvenient. The best method is to take a morning ferry and then stop overnight in Belgium or Germany, continuing refreshed the following morning. By this route it is some 640 miles from Ostend/Zeebrugge to Innsbruck. On the ferry the single fare for a car plus driver and passenger ranges from around £60 in the off-peak period to around £90 in high summer. If using one of the short sea crossings from Dover/Folkestone to Calais/Boulogne the driving distance to Innsbruck is slightly longer, around 655 miles.

Motorail. If the idea of a long drive across Europe doesn't appeal, why not consider one of the Motorail services? There are two alternative routes. Firstly, the service from 's-Hertogenbosch (in central southern Holland about 75 miles from Rotterdam Europort and 90 miles from Vlissingen) which runs to Salzburg and Villach. Secondly, from Schaerbeek (Brussels) to Salzburg and Villach. The service from 's-Hertogenbosch runs once a week, on Thursdays, during the summer, leaving at 7.30 P.M. and arriving in Salzburg at 7.05 and Villach at 10.10 the following morning. The service from Brussels leaves Schaerbeek on Fridays and arrives in Salzburg and Villach on the Saturday at the same time of day as the 's-Hertogenbosch service. The full range of sleeping accommodation from couchettes to first-class single sleepers is available. Details of fares from *DER Travel,* 18 Conduit St., London W1R 9TD (01–408 0111); in the States from *DER Tours* 230 Park Ave., Suite 1515, New York, NY 10169 (212–818–0150).

Staying in Austria

CUSTOMS ON ARRIVAL. The following is the official list of duty-free items you may bring in with you, but there is no necessity to worry about them unduly. Overworked Austrian customs officials are not especially interested in counting to see that you may have 402 cigarettes with you instead of 400.

Travelers over 17 *from European countries* may bring in the following items duty free: 200 cigarettes or 50 cigars or 250 gr. of tobacco; 2 liters of wine and 1 liter of spirits; 1 bottle toilet water (approx. 300 gr), 50 gr. of perfume. All other passengers (e.g., those from the U.S.) can bring in *twice* these amounts.

At the end of your stay you may take out up to $400 worth of goods (for real art objects you need an export permit). For goods of additional value, you can get export forms from the shop of purchase or from the Austrian National Bank in Vienna.

AUSTRIAN MONEY. The unit of Austrian currency is the Schilling, divided into 100 Groschen. In these days of inflation and fluctuating rates of exchange, you would be wise to check regularly on the dollar or sterling rates—both while planning your trip and while on it. A little forethought can save you money. At presstime (Spring '89), the rate of exchange was about AS13 to one US dollar; the pound sterling was around AS22. The recent series of new banknotes has very little differentiation between the AS100 and AS500 notes; be careful, as confusion can be expensive.

Foreign currency and Austrian schillings (AS) may be brought into Austria in unlimited quantities. Any amount of foreign exchange may be taken out, plus AS100,000. Foreign currency may be exchanged at any Austrian bank and exchange offices at the following railway stations: Vienna Westbahnhof, and Süd-Ostbahnhof, Linz, Salzburg, Innsbruck, Kufstein, and Villach. Vienna airport also has a currency exchange office, and the exchange counter at the Reisebüro City on the Stephansplatz is open on Sundays. The 24-hour post offices also have counters where you can change money.

HOTELS. Austrian hotels are officially classified from one to five stars according to strict government standards and inspection. In order to give our readers a clearer picture, in regard to price as well as quality, we have employed our own classification, dividing hotels into four categories. These are geared to peak-season rates (where applicable) and for the more expensive rooms with private bath facilities. By an active program of modernization, the problem of the lack of baths or showers is gradually being overcome, and most rooms in the three higher categories can be taken to possess private facilities unless otherwise stated. Only in the inexpensive category will the number of showers, if any, be mentioned. Most of the better resort hotels insist on half or full board in season; the rest of the year they offer any terms.

Many summer and winter resort and spa hotels are open only seasonally. In summer resorts the peak season is July and August, with pre-season beginning June 1 and the post-season lasting until the middle or end of September. In the skiing centers the peak season is from Dec. 20–Jan. 6, and from Feb. 1–March 15. The peak-season prices at fashionable resorts are 25 to 50 percent higher.

Except in Vienna and Salzburg, there are few *Luxury* hotels, but numerous *Expensive* in all major resorts, usually with swimming pools, often indoor and outdoor, saunas. The *Moderate* in the country areas or smaller cities and towns are on the whole more than adequate; food, service and cleanliness are of high standard. The newer *Inexpensive* have private showers. The sign *Zimmer frei* outside private houses means rooms are available.

Hotel Rates

(in Austrian Schillings)

Category		Vienna, Salzburg, Innsbruck top resorts	State capitals, major resorts	Country, small towns
Luxury (L)	single	1500–2500	1000–1500	—
	double	2000–4000	1500–2500	—
Expensive (E)	single	1000–1500	700–1000	350–450
	double	1500–2200	1000–1500	500–700
Moderate (M)	single	600–1000	350–500	250–300
	double	900–1500	700–1000	400–600
Inexpensive (I)	single	300–500	250–350	150–200
	double	500–900	500–700	250–350

In the countryside and occasionally in the towns, various local terms are common: *Gasthof,* German for a country and small town type of a good-size hotel combined with a fairly large eating and drinking establishment. In bigger cities they are usually old, often colorful but unpretentious; in the resorts, *hof* forms frequently part of the names of even deluxe modern establishments. *Gasthaus,* a country inn (but found also in the cities), smaller in size than Gasthof, but usually with at least a few beds; the emphasis is on the eating and drinking services. *Frühstücks-pension,* a guest house usually offering rooms with breakfast, and occasionally a small evening snack. *Kurhaus*, literally a "cure house" or spa establishment, often offering in addition to baths and other cure facilities such amenities as restaurants, cafés, and entertainment. The ever-more-popular *Kurhotel* offers its guests a wide range of cures under medical supervision, from therapeutic baths to slimming.

The expression *garni* simply means bed and breakfast.

On arrival in any town or village, if you are looking for accommodations, go to the *Verkehrsverein* (tourist office) where you will receive the help you need. They are usually open during shopping hours.

Pensions may charge 10–20% less in their respective categories. Off-season charges are 20–40% less, but many resort hotels keep open only during the slightly cheaper pre- and post-season months.

Service and all taxes included.

All rooms with bath or shower, except in Inexpensive category.

Castle-Hotels. To accommodate travelers in search of something different, Austria has converted many of its famous old castles into hotels. Some historic and atmospheric ones are:

Palais Schwarzenberg in Vienna; Schlosshotels Mönchstein, Sankt Rupert and Fondachhof in the city of Salzburg; Schloss Fuschl nearby on Fuschlsee; Schloss Pichlarn in Irdning in Styria; Schloss Velden, Schloss Seefels and Schloss Leonstain, all on Wörthersee in Carinthia; Schloss Itter near Hopfgarten in Tirol; Schlosshotel Igls near Innsbruck; Schlosshotels Lebenberg and Münichau in Kitzbühel, also in Tirol; and Schloss Drassburg in Burgenland.

For general information on Castle Hotels, contact—*Zentrale Reservierungsstelle der Arbeitsgruppe der Österreichischen Schlosshotels und Herrenhäuser,* Bergstr. 22, A-5024 Salzburg (tel. 0662–88 16 77).

Romantik Hotels and Restaurants. A German organization which now has 16 Austrian members. These are inns of historical interest but with modern comfort and at reasonable prices, they appear in our hotel listings. The addresses to contact for direct information are—in the U.S., Romantik Travel and Tours, Box 1278, Woodinville, WA 98072 (206–486–9394, 800–826–0015); in the U.K., Romantik Hotel, Swynford Paddocks, Six Mile Bottom, Newmarket, Suffolk CB8 0UQ (063–870 234).

Bungalows and Apartments. Self-service vacations are increasingly popular, and, of course, cut down on costs tremendously. There is plenty of scope for this kind of vacation in Austria. Among the larger firms handling villa rental is *Inter Home Ltd.,* which have over 10,000 apartments in 14 countries, including in many parts of Austria. Their address in Britain is 363 Richmond Rd., Twickenham, Middx.; and in Austria, *Inter Home Gesmbh.,* Alpenstr. 54, A-5020 Salzburg. They have a special line in chalets in the Alpine areas, which means that you can combine a relaxed, do-it-yourself holiday with skiing and other winter sports. For more modest accommodations, *Pego Holiday Homes,* Sägeweg 12, A-6700 Bludenz.

The National Tourist Offices can also help with lists of firms doing this kind of business.

Farmhouse Holidays are extremely pleasant, picturesque and economical, especially for families with children. There are about 4,000 farms which take part in the scheme. Most of them provide only bed and breakfast, which leaves you free to enjoy the day as you please. It is the kind of holiday that is better spent with a car, though this is by no means essential.

The Austrian National Tourist Office will provide you with a list and brochures; very often advance booking is not necessary. There are three approximate price categories for bed and breakfast per person: I being from AS 100 up, II 90–100, and III up to 90.

CAMPING. For details contact the *Österreichischer Camping Club,* Johannesgasse 20, A-1010 Vienna (tel. 0222–711 99 0). The club is a subsidiary of the *ÖAMTC Motor Club,* Schubertring 1, A-1010 Vienna (tel. 0222–711 99 0), which offers an informative booklet on camping possibilities.

A list without prices can be obtained from the Austrian Tourist Office, A-1040 Vienna, Margaretenstr. 1 (0222 58–72–000). This leaflet is also available at frontier crossing points. There are about 400 sites in operation at this writing, with new ones in the offing. Most of the campsites in the brochure belong to one or another of the various organizations, although a few are privately owned. Charges per person and per day vary between AS30 and AS40, plus AS30 to AS40 for the car, depending on the quality of the camp. There are about 77 winter camping sites throughout Austria. Some mountain roads are either altogether forbidden, or not recommended for trailers.

YOUTH HOSTELS. Members of the International Youth Hostel Federation are welcome at all Austria's Youth Hostels. Details from *Österr. Jugendherbergsverband,* A-1010 Vienna, Schottenring 28 (533–53–53), *Österr. Jugendherbergswerk,* A-1010 Vienna, Freyung 6/11 (533–18–33) or *Osterr. Jugendferienwerk,* Alpenstr. 108a, A-5020 Salzburg (25 7 58–0). Details are also available from your national Youth Hostelling organization—*American Youth Hostels, Inc.,* Box 37613, Washington, DC 20013-7613, or *Canadian Hostelling Association,* 18 Dyward Market, Vanier City, Ottawa, Ontario K1N 7A1. In England the address is *Youth Hostels Association International Travel Bureau,* 14 Southampton St., London W.C.2. Help for young travelers with problems is now available through "Tramper Treff," A-1010 Vienna, Gonzagagasse 22—open Mon.–Fri., 9–5 (tel. 533 53 53).

RESTAURANTS. Eating in Austria ranges from extremely expensive to good, wholesome food at wholesome prices wherever you are—in Vienna, or smaller towns in the country. The one constant factor is that everywhere there are fine traditional restaurants, bursting with atmosphere and value. In this respect Austria has managed far better than many other parts of Europe which have succumbed to the vice of quick, cheap food in flashy surroundings.

We grade the restaurants in our listings as (E) for Expensive, (M) for Moderate and (I) for Inexpensive. The cost of meals in these gradings is likely to be—(E) AS500 per person without wine—and up, way up; (M), AS300 plus, again for one; (I), AS150–200, but this is a wildly variable category and, if you have the set menu at lunchtime (the Austrians' main meal) you could easily eat (I) in a distinctly (M) spot.

Indeed, it is possible to have excellent meals all over Austria for a modest price, even in Vienna and Salzburg. Among the best places to eat are the wine cellars, which not only provide lowcost meals with delicious wine by the tankard and large helpings, but will also satisfy even the most voracious seeker after atmosphere.

Lunch is served usually between 12 noon and 2 P.M. and dinner between 6 and 9 P.M., except in late-hour restaurants, where it is served much later.

If you can cope with the rather flowery German, buy a copy of Gault-Millau's *Guide Österreich,* which is a mine of information for those wanting to explore the gastronomic territory by themselves. The Falter Press publishes an excellent and exhaustive booklet available at newsstands: *Wien wie es Isst.* Your hotel or pension will have suggestions as well.

Some other liquid costs are—a bottle of wine costs about AS180–300 (more, of course, for special vintages), but the open wines are very good and cost about AS25–45 per ¼ liter carafe. A glass (half liter) of beer varies from AS20–30 depending on the establishment; coffee varies from AS20 to 40; whiskey about 55 to 90; schnapps from 15 to 30; a cocktail in a top bar will cost at least AS90. Mineral water, apple juice, Coca-Cola and similar drinks cost about AS19, all inclusive of taxes.

NIGHTLIFE. Things have livened up over the past two years and there is quite a lot going on into the small hours. For the latest information *Disco Digest* is available from bookstalls, price AS50. It covers all of Austria.

TIPPING. Almost all hotels (among the few exceptions are smaller country inns) now include service charges in their rates. For restaurants this includes 10% service and all the various taxes; it is nevertheless customary to tip about 5% of your bill. You tip the hotel concierge only for special services. Give the hotel porter AS10 per bag. When you take a taxi, no tip is included in the fare; 10% of the fare is the usual. If the driver has been helpful in other ways, give him 15%. The railway station porters charge AS10 a bag. Hat-check girls get AS7–15, depending on the locale. Washroom attendants get about AS5.

MAIL. Postage is about the same as in most European countries. For the first 20 grams (about ¾ ounce) letters cost AS5 for all domestic destinations; 6 for destinations abroad. Regular-size letters (20 grams) and postcards are forwarded within Europe automatically by airmail (with no extra charge); aerograms to U.S. and Canada AS11. Postcards to Austrian destinations 4, abroad 5, airmail postcards to U.S. and Canada 7.50. Have airmail letters weighed at the post office to be sure of correct postage.

Cables, telegrams, and wireless messages are sent from post offices. In addition to being available in post offices, stamps are sold in tobacco shops (Tabak Trafik) and it is often easier to buy them there, as post offices can get very busy.

TELEPHONES. Telephone numbers in Austria consist only of numerals (three to seven digits). Coin-operated street telephone booths in cities are numerous. Direct dialling everywhere within Austria as well as to most countries in the world; otherwise dial 09 for long-distance operator.

Calls within Austria are 33% cheaper between 6 P.M. and 8 A.M. on weekdays and from 1 P.M. on Saturday to 8 A.M. Monday. If you are calling Austria from abroad omit the "O" preceding the area code.

Major developments in the Austrian telephone system mean that numbers will be changing for years to come. We make every effort to keep numbers up to date, but check on the spot should you find it difficult to make your connection. This is particularly the case in Vienna and Innsbruck.

Warning—don't make long-distance calls from your hotel room without checking very carefully what the cost will be. Hotels frequently add several hundred percent to such calls. This is an international practice, not one confined to Austria alone. Go to the main post office or phone center for long-distance calls (in larger towns these are often open late or even round the clock). Alternatively, AT&T have a Teleplan service designed to overcome excessive surcharges. For details, call (in the US) 800–874–4000. If you intend to use phone boxes a lot, buy a "Wertkarte" for AS95 at any post office. Wertkarte call boxes take the card rather than coins registering the time left on your card and give you AS100 worth in calls against the credit card.

CLOSING TIMES. Most stores open at 8.30 or 9 A.M. and close at noon or at 12.30 P.M. for a one- to two-hour lunch interval, and then stay open until 6 P.M.; in most villages opening time is 8 A.M. and lunch hour from 12 to 3 P.M. Some foodstores open at 7 A.M. and close at 6.30 P.M. with a two- to three-hour lunch break. At the Südbahn, Westbahn and Franz Josef stations, as well as in the 3rd District, Landstrasse 3, foodstores remain open till midnight.

Most of the stores in the city centers do not observe the lunch interval and stay open without interruption from 9 A.M. to 6 P.M. On Saturdays shops are open from 9 A.M. to noon. The usual office hours are 8 A.M. to 5 P.M., Sat. closed, except the first Saturday of the month, when most stay open until 5 or 6 P.M. Banking hours at main offices (larger banks) in Vienna are 8–3, branch offices 8–12.30; 1.30–3, Thurs. till 5.30 P.M., closed Sat. Note that banking hours vary from town to town. They are always closed on Saturdays. Most barbers and hairdressers close Monday.

National Holidays 1990. Jan. 1 (New Year's Day); Jan. 6 (Ephiphany); Apr. 15, 16 (Easter); May 1 (May Day); May 24 (Ascension); June 3, 4 (Whitsun); June 14 (Corpus Christi), Aug. 15 (Assumption); Oct. 26 (National Day); Nov. 1 (All Saints); Dec. 8 (Immaculate Conception); Dec. 25, 26 (Christmas).

BALLOONING. This is a growing sport in Austria. Enthusiasts can get information from the Vienna Ballooning Club (tel. 69 29 13, 69 29 16 or 883 03 53).

BICYCLING. Cycle tracks are appearing all over Austria—and one will eventually run the length of the Danube. Hiring facilities are becoming more common, and include 97 railway stations. Bicycles hired at one of these can be returned to any station in Austria. For further details contact the Austrian National Tourist Office or any local tourist office. Details of the now extensive cycle-tracks and trails will be found in the map *Radfahren in Österreich*. Specialist bicycle tours are organized by *Austria Radreisen,* 4780 Schärding (tel. 07712–2409).

FISHING. Well-stocked lakes in Upper Austria are the Traunsee, Attersee, Hallstätter See, and Mondsee; the Danube, Steyr, Traun, Enns, Krems, and Alm rivers also provide good fishing. Tirol is another good fishing region; try the Achensee, Traualpsee, Walchsee, Plansee, and nearby streams, also the Inn and Drau (East Tirol) rivers and the Zillertal streams. Styria provides some of the best trout fishing in Austria, as do the lakes in the Styrian Salzkammergut. Carinthian lakes and Lower Austrian streams and rivers also abound in fish. An excellent guide, *Fishing in Austria,* is obtainable from all Austrian Tourist Offices; it will give you the licenses available and their cost.

GLIDING. From May to September you can glide or learn to glide at one of Austria's schools, located at Zell am See, Niederöblarn (Styria), Graz-Thalerhof (also Styria), Wiener Neustadt, just outside Vienna, and Spitzberg bei Hainburg (Lower Austria). The schools at Zell am See and Wien-Donauwiese also offer passenger flights in 2-seaters.

There are a number of gliding clubs, in addition to those mentioned above, which offer hourly passenger rides, although no instruction. Write to the *Austrian Aero Club,* Prinz Eugenstr. 12, 1040 Vienna (505 10 28), for further details.

GOLF. The golf season starts in Austria in late March. Although all of the more than 80 golf clubs in Austria are private clubs, all of them welcome visitors on a "green-fee" basis as readily as publicly owned courses elsewhere as their membership is rather limited. Over 40 of the courses are 18-hole, and a number are associated with excellent resort hotels. The Austrian National Tourist Office has information, or write Golf Green Austria, Hirtlhof 26, A-4283 Bad Zell (tel. 072 63–361 or 072 63–7153).

HORSE RIDING. Austria is rich in opportunities for the visitor who is interested either in extended tours on horseback, or in just enjoying a happy few hours in some of the best riding country anywhere. Any interest in equitation can be satisfied. Several hotels specialize in equestrian holidays.

Information on accommodations and riding facilities can be obtained from the various provincial tourist offices (*Landesverkehrsamt*). The Austrian National Tourist Office also have a booklet called *Equestrian Sports in Austria.*

MOUNTAIN CLIMBING. *Österreichischer Alpenverein* (Austrian Alpine Club), with headquarters at Wilhelm-Greil-Strasse 15 (tel. 0512–23 171) in Innsbruck, owns and maintains 275 of the 700 mountain refuges, which are sometimes more like mountain inns than huts; one-fourth situated between 2,500 and 3,000 meters. Total capacity 26,000 beds in small rooms and dormitory. ÖAV branches in all major towns for details about climbs, guides, use of huts etc.

Owing to the large numbers of British enthusiasts who have become members of the Austrian Club, there is a U.K. branch of the *Austrian Alpine Club,* 13 Longcroft House, Fretherne Road, Welwyn Garden City, Herts.

The maximum fee charged by mountain guides is AS950 per day for glacier and light-to-medium rock-climbing tours, whereby the guide takes care of his own food. For heavier tours and for longer engagements, a lump-sum rate is usually agreed upon. It is usual to give a good tip at the end of the tour.

Hut charges are on two scales. If you are a member of the Austrian Alpine Club, your hut charges will automatically be 50% less. Membership can be obtained by foreign applicants at any of the Austrian Alpine

Club sections. Various Austrian alpine clubs operate the other two-thirds of the huts.

The mountain climbers' schools, *Alpenschule Glockner-Heiligenblut* in Carinthia, *Hochgebirgsschule Glockner-Kaprun* in Land Salzburg, *Hochgebirgsschule Tyrol* and *Alpinschule Innsbruck,* both in Tirol, and *Bergsteigerzentrum Steiermark* which offers mountain climbing courses in the Dachstein range and in Gesäuse Alps (both in Styria); the base for the school is in Öblarn in Styria. All organize climbing courses and guided tours for beginners and more advanced climbers. In most Alpine areas, specialist guides are available.

HIKING. Austria also provides 50,000 km. of well-maintained and signposted mountain paths through Europe's largest reserve of unpolluted air. A paradise for ecologists and for all lovers of superb landscape.

Apart from the long-distance hiking paths scattered around Austria, there are also three main European ones that lead through the country, for the really fit hiker. These are E5, Pyrenees–Jura–Neusiedler See; E5, Lake Constance–Adriatic; E6, Baltic–Wachau–Adriatic. Bookstores in your resort will have hiking maps of the area. Those to the scales 1:20000 and 1:25000 are the most useful.

If you are planning high-altitude hiking, do remember that cable cars tend to be closed for repairs out of season. Always take protection against rain, an extra layer of clothing, and tell your hotel desk where you are going. It is always worth asking about the weather. Rain in the valleys may give way to sunshine above 1,000 meters.

For information about hiking regions and conditions contact *Alpine Auskunft des Österreichischen Alpenvereins,* Wilhelm-Greil-Str. 15, A-6020 Innsbruck (0512–24 107). Members (US$35) can stay in the countrywide mountain *Hütten* for low rates.

WATER SPORTS. Sailing. Small sailing boats may be hired on all the lakes of the Salzkammergut region and on the large Carinthian lakes in the south. You can rent a rowboat on any of Austria's 100-odd lakes. Information can be obtained from the Austrian National Tourist Offices, and from *Österreichischer Segel-Verband* (Austrian Yachting Association), Grosse Neugasse 8, 1040 Vienna (0222–587 86 88).

Water skiing and sail skiing are popular on the Wörther See, Millstätter See, and Ossiacher See in Carinthia; on Traunsee, Attersee, and Wolfgangsee in Salzkammergut; at Zell am See in Salzburg province; and on Bodensee (Lake Constance) in Vorarlberg.

Kayaking on the Enns River between Schladming and Gesäuse (extremely difficult through Gesäuse) and on most of the Mur, which is very easy below Graz. Boats can be rented at Gröbming and Aich-Assach for the Enns run. Also on Danube, Traun and Steyr.

Windsurfing. This is a fast-growing sport in Austria, especially on Lakes Neusiedl and Attersee.

Swimming. No resort or larger village is without outdoor swimming pools, many of them heated; almost all pools demand the wearing of swimming caps. Swimming facilities exist also on many lake and river beaches.

WINTER SPORTS. Skiers are in luck almost anywhere in Austria. This is a country where skiing is a national sport and the tiniest tot is put on skis almost before it can walk. The season lasts from the end of November to April, depending on snow conditions. But there are enough all-year-round skiing regions on glaciers at altitudes of up to 3,300 m. (11,000 ft.), to satisfy even the keenest snow freak. Among the well-established summer/winter regions are Kitzsteinhorn (Kaprun) in Land Salzburg; in Tirol, Rettenbachferner (Sölden), Stubaier Glacier (Renalt), Wurmkogel (Hochgurgl), Tuxer Ferner (Hintertux), Pitztal, Kaunertal Glacier; and Dachstein (Ramsau) in Styria. A new all-year region was opened in 1984 in Pitztal, St. Leonhard.

In many areas cable cars, chair lifts and T-bars have been built to create "ski-circuses," where skiers can ski all day long (using the same ski pass) without doing one slope twice and yet winding up in the afternoon in exactly the same place as starting out in the morning. Even such a massive dose of the slopes shouldn't detract from the après-ski activities—wining, dining, dancing, horse-sleigh excursions at night.

Nor is the beginner left out, for there are very experienced Austrian instructors at all the centers, some of them with international wins to their credit. Ski-schools take children from the age of 3!

For up-to-date snow data, check with the Austrian National Tourist Office, which provides its branches with twice-weekly reports via telex. You can also get this information from any Lufthansa office.

The *American Skiers Best Friend* network offers special assistance in 23 ski resorts. Contact the Tourist Offices in Badgastein, Bad Hofgastein, Geschurn, Innsbruck, Ischgl, Kaprun, Kirchdorf, Kitzbühel, Lech, Kleinwalsertal, Mayrhofen, Neustift, Obertauern, Saalbach, St. Anton, St. Johann/Pongau, Schladming, Stuben, Seefeld, Soelden, Schruns, Zell am See and Zuers.

Ski Bargains. Good facilities and terrain, at much lower prices, can be found in East Tirol, Styria, Lower Austria, Carinthia, and parts of Salzburg and Upper Austria. Ski areas offer a weekly pass for use on all lifts, cable cars and usually swimming pools, at 20–30% reductions. Consult the local tourist office. In addition, many ski resorts, including several of the more expensive and fashionable ones, offer all-inclusive weekly rates, sometimes also including ski schools and lift facilities. For a complete list, write for the special booklet prepared by the Austrian National Tourist Office.

Skiing holidays for students in some of the finest winter sports areas of Austria, from Dec. to April, are organized by the *Büro für Studentenreisen* (Office for Students' Tours), Schreyvogelgasse 3, A-1010 Vienna (tel. 533 35 89); information also from *ÖKISTA,* Türkenstrasse 4, A–1090 Vienna (tel. 34 75 26), and its partner *OS-Reisen,* Reichstratstrasse 13, A-1010 Vienna (tel. 48 78 21).

Skating and Tobogganing are two winter sports that you can indulge in nearly everywhere in Austria. Skates and shoes are easy to pack but a toboggan you will have to hire—the hotel porter will see to this—or to buy. They are not expensive, an ordinary toboggan will cost about 400 schillings.

A rather more gentle sport is **ice shooting,** a form of curling. The rules are slightly different from those of Scottish curling and you may not use a broom, but the principles are the same. Styria is the stronghold of this sport.

SHOPPING. We deal with specific shopping points in several other places in this book, but here are a few general hints that may be of use.

Wherever possible carry your purchases home with you, especially if they are valuable or fragile.

Find out all about customs regulations. You could be stung for a small fortune and turn a bargain into a very expensive commodity indeed.

If you are shipping goods home, be very sure you have understood the terms, how the shipment will be made, when it should arrive . . . and *get it all in writing*.

If you make expensive purchases you may get a refund on VAT if your purchase was in a tax-free shop and cost more than AS1,000. Ask for details when shopping and make sure the shop itself will handle your refund directly. If not, the central clearing agent is likely to charge a fat fee. Customs clearance is required upon departure, when the tax, which has been paid, is refunded. Finally, don't miss the Advent Christkindl Markets held in all the larger towns.

Getting Around Austria

By Air. There are flights between the major Austrian cities of Vienna and Salzburg, Graz, Linz, Klagenfurt and Innsbruck, but before you think of flying, check the time it would take to go by rail and also the schedules, as they vary considerably from season to season. The success of the Klagenfurt–Vienna route has persuaded Austrian Airlines to launch a daily service, early mornings Klagenfurt to Vienna, evenings in the other direction, six days a week—with Sat. morning, Sun. evening at the weekend.

Most domestic flights are operated by *Austrian Air Services* using 17-passenger metro turboprop equipment. Innsbruck is linked to the outside world by *Tyrolean Airways* which operates regular flights between Innsbruck and Vienna, Zurich, Frankfurt and Graz. They have a Fly and Drive arrangement with *AVIS*. *Rheintalflug* operate two daily flights between Vienna and Altenrhein in Switzerland, over the border from Vorarlberg. This company and air taxis operate to some of the ski resorts in winter. There are helicopter flights from St. Anton to St. Christoph in Tirol over the Arlberg ski terrain that can be combined with ski tours in the higher mountain regions. For private charter flights, contact *Alpenair* (0222–94 52 28); *Jetair* (0222–533 60 33); *Avanti-Air* (0222–7770 2097); or *Polsterer-Jets* (0222–7770 2077).

By Train. Austria and railways go together like chocolate cake and cream. The timetable for the main Inter-City services works on the equal interval basis, so trains are usually hourly and run on the so-many-minutes-past-each-hour principle. Due to the mountainous terrain in many parts of the country speeds are not particularly high. Vienna to Innsbruck, some 580 km. (360 miles), takes around 5½ hours—but who wants to travel quickly through this magnificent scenery? There are many cross-country routes and branch lines which show you the real Austria away from the crowds. Many of the valleys are served by narrow-gauge lines and these are well worth visiting; some, especially in summer, still use steam locomotives.

There are several types of train in Austria, and these are clearly noted in the timetables. A supplement of AS30 is payable on Express (Ex) and Schnell Zug (D) trains, so don't use them for local journeys! For the Eilzug (semi-fast) and Regionalzug (local) trains all tickets are valid. When buying a ticket for one of the fast trains (Ex/D), the supplement is automatically included in the price of the ticket. At busy periods be sure to reserve a seat. This can be done at the station up to a few hours in advance for a small fee.

All four major credit cards are accepted at 127 stations.

Discount Tickets. Several schemes are available which can be useful to the visitor even if staying only for a short period. For AS200, pensioners (women 60 years and up, men 65) can buy a *Seniorenpass* which entitles them to 50% reductions on many journeys. The "seniors" program has many possibilities, so check for those that may apply. Information at most railway stations.

Kilometerbanken—Kilometer Bank. These tickets can be bought for 2,000 km. or 5,000 km. and can be used by up to *six* people at the same time. You enter the starting station and destination on the card and the conductor or booking office clerk deducts the person-kilometers travelled from the "bank." Valid on all trains for trips of 71 km or longer and gives a longer discount of up to 40% of standard fares. The cost is AS1,700. All in 2nd class. For 1st class travel half as many kilometers again will be booked off.

Bundes–Netzkarten. National cards. Unlimited rail travel for 1 month or 1 year. Have a passport photo to hand. These cards also entitle the holder to a 50% reduction on OBB buses and private railway lines. The country-wide card is also valid for the Vienna Suburban rail system, the OBB rack railways and their ships on the Wolfgangsee. Prices are—1st class: AS4,650; 2nd Class: AS3,100 for a month.

Regional Tickets (both 1st and 2nd class) are available for some 18 different areas for any 4 days within a 10-day period. Prices are AS500 1st Class, AS400 2nd Class. Have a passport-size photograph handy.

You can put your car on a train and travel in comfort between Vienna and Salzburg, Innsbruck and Feldkirch, as well as Villach to the South. For information tel. (0222)5650–2989. *Austrian Railways* also offer bicycle hire at many stations for AS80 per day—half price if you arrive by train. You will need a passport or other form of identification.

Eurailpass—for visitors coming from outside Europe. This pass is excellent value for money, being valid for unlimited travel on all the State railways of Western Europe (except G.B.). In Austria it also covers the Puchberg am Schneeberg–Hochschneeberg rack railway (superb!), the steamers on Wolfgangsee and the Danube steamers of the *Erste Donau Dampfschiffartsfahrt Gesellschaft* between Passau and Vienna. The Eurailpass gives *first* class travel for 15 days for $320, 21 days $398, 1 month $498, 2 months $698, 3 months $860, and includes all supplements. For the under-26s there is the *Youthpass*. This is valid for 2nd class travel only and can be bought for one month for $360 or for two months for $470. The Eurailpass must be purchased before leaving for Europe and then validated before use.

In the U.S.A., details from *French National Railroads,* 610 Fifth Avenue, New York, NY 10020 or *German Rail,* 747 Third Avenue, New York, NY 10017; **in Canada** details from *German Rail,* 1290 Bay St., Toronto, Ontario M5R 2C3.

By Steam Train. There are several lines in Austria where delightful little steam engines can be found at work, ambling along valleys or toiling up steep mountain grades. The *Zillertalbahn* meanders up the picturesque

Ziller valley from the mainline station at Jenbach to the village of Mayrhofen (32 km., 20 miles). In the summer there are at least two steam trains each way a day. On Fridays and Saturdays there is also a Hobby train on which, under careful guidance, you can drive the steam locomotive yourself!

Also starting from Jenbach there is the beautifully antiquated *Achenseebahn*. This runs from the main railway station up to the lake steamer landing stage at Achensee. The open carriages are propelled up the rack by superb 0–4–0 locomotives dating from *1899*.

If mountains are more your style it is possible to combine both steam locomotives and splendid mountain scenery. The meter-gauge *Schneebergbahn* runs up the Hochschneeberg from Puchberg. The journey of 9 km. (6 miles) takes an hour and twenty minutes and the service is hauled exclusively by steam power. On Saturdays, Sundays and holidays there is a special mainline train from Vienna and Wiener Neustadt to Puchberg to connect with the mountain rack train. As with most Austrian mountains, there is a good restaurant at the summit. There is also a narrow-gauge line through the Waldviertel running from Gmünd to Gross-Gerungs right along the Czech border.

Also of interest is the *Schafbergbahn* at St. Wolfgang which is not far from Salzburg. This line is only accessible by road and only uses its steam engines in the high summer as it also has some modern diesel locomotives. From the summit of the Schafberg there is an unparalleled view stretching over the Wolfgangsee and the mountains of the Salzkammergut.

In summer steam trains also run between Zell am See and Krimml, and between Murau and Tamsweg. The *Schafkäs* Express plies between Waidhofen/Ybbs and Göstling.

If you are in Vienna the Prater park is a must. Besides the Big Wheel there is a delightful miniature railway which has a circuit in the grounds. During the summer a steam locomotive is used daily. Lovers of "big steam" should not miss the steam museum at Strasshof, north of Vienna.

There are many other lines on which steam trains are run, but not at regular intervals. The only way to find out what's going on is to ask at the local tourist office when you get there, or to buy a copy of the Austrian Railway Timetable, as this contains details of all lines with regular steam operations in the summer. Information is also available in the monthly magazine Schienenverker Aktuell; also from Brenner & Brenner, Schanzstr. 39, A-1140 Vienna (0222–95 34 304) which organizes many steam excursions.

By Car. EEC tourists can bring their cars to Austria without any other documents than their ordinary registration papers and their national driving licenses. Green Card insurance is, however, recommended for them, and is obligatory for others.

Tourists' cars must be equipped with first-aid kit, a set of spare bulbs, and a red warning triangle. In the case of breakdown or accident the triangle must be placed 55 yds behind the car and not more than 1 yd from the edge of the road.

Tourist-owned vehicles must not remain in Austria for more than one year and may not be driven by Austrian residents of whatever nationality. The country's minimum driving age is 18, and children under 12 must ride in the back seat. It is compulsory for front-seat passengers to wear seat belts.

Parking is a problem in all towns and resorts. Parking zones, with various time limits, are clearly indicated and strictly policed. In major towns, parking discs must be fixed to the windshield or a *Kurzparkscheine* properly marked must be placed in view on the dashboard; obtainable at tobacco shops (*Tabak Trafik*) but expensive. Many towns and cities now charge for limited parking. Tickets are obtainable in banks and *Tabak Trafiks*. Streetcars have the right of way at intersections without traffic lights, regardless of the direction from which they are approaching.

Roads. All roads are paved and well-maintained, but most of the secondary country roads are narrow and winding. In winter snow tires are essential, even though salt is used on main roads, in fact obligatory when the signs are out. The Austrian Automobile Club (ÖAMTC) broadcasts taperecorded telephone messages on the current road conditions in all of Austria; dial Vienna (0222) 1590 in case you understand German; if you don't, call Vienna (0222) 711 99, ext. 1215, from 6 A.M.–8 P.M. Eighteen ÖAMTC posts throughout Austria will rent chains up to 60 days to any automobile club member.

The ÖAMTC and ARBÖ road patrol and breakdown services cover most of the main roads all the year round, Sundays and holidays included, from 8 A.M. till dusk. For emergency help, phone ÖAMTC (123) or ARBÖ (123) from anywhere in the country; no area code is necessary.

Speed limits. There is a speed limit of 130 kph. (80 mph.) on all autobahns; on other highways and roads 100 kph. (62 mph.); in built-up areas 50 kph. (31 mph.); for cars with trailers weighing more than 750 kg. (about 1,650 lb.) 80 kph. (49 mph).

Fuel. Gasoline (petrol) prices: AS10.40 per liter for regular and AS11.30 for premium. Motor oils vary between AS50 and 88 per liter. Discount and self-service stations are a bit cheaper. Although the cost fluctuates constantly, it roughly corresponds with the rest of Europe.

Tolls. There are a few toll roads in Austria, mostly over or under mountains. Detailed information on these roads is available from the National Tourist Office, either in the country or abroad, or from the ÖAMTC Motor Club, Schubertring 1–3, A-1010 Vienna. The tolls vary greatly and are liable to change. There are considerable reductions during winter months and for return tickets.

Among the important toll roads, open summer and winter, are—
Villach Alpine Road (Carinthia)
Hochkar Alpine Road (Lower Austria)
Hinterstoder–Höss Road (Upper Austria)
Badgastein–Böckstein Road (Salzburg Province)
Grossglockner High Alpine Road (Salzburg–Carinthia), closed in winter
Gerlos Road (Salzburg–Tirol)
Felbertauern Alpine Road (Salzburg–East Tirol)
Tauplitz Alm Alpine Road (Styria)
Brenner Autobahn (Tirol–Italy)
Arlberg Road Tunnel (Tirol–Vorarlberg)

Tunnel Ferries. The Austrian State Railroads run a car-ferry service through a tunnel from Böckstein near Badgastein in Salzburg to Mallnitz in Carinthia, and vice versa, now mainly of local interest because of the new road over the Tauern range. Count on the tunnel car-ferry service only in the daytime. During the trip you remain in the car together with all other occupants.

Maps. The numerous detailed maps supplied free by the *Austrian National Tourist Office* and regional tourist offices are perfectly adequate. For perfectionists, maps are sold at low cost by the Austrian Automobile Club. Particularly useful is the annually revised map of Austria showing the condition of roads (*Strassenzustandskarte*); also excellent is the more detailed 1:200,000 road map of Austria in 8 sections, printed on 4 maps.

Car Hire. For those who do not wish to bring their own cars to Austria, hire firms, both local and international, will provide self-drive and chauffeur-driven cars for collection at airports, stations or hotels in the larger towns. Approximate charges for a car without chauffeur are from AS550 to AS1,500 per day, depending on type of car, without fuel, plus AS5.50 to AS9.50 per kilometer; insurance extra. On a weekly or monthly basis the charges are considerably lower (about AS5,800 per week). VAT is added at 20% so it can be cheaper to hire your car in Germany or Switzerland and bring it over. Shop around, as rates vary widely; among the cheapest is *Autoverleih Buchbinder,* Schlachthausgasse 38, A-1034 Vienna (tel. 0222–712 26 43), with branches throughout the country.

You can pick up a rental car on arriving in Austria by train at the following stations: Bregenz, Dornbirn, Graz, Innsbruck, Klagenfurt, Leoben, Linz, Salzburg, Vienna (both West and South stations), Villach and Zell am See. Just contact any rail ticket office, travel agency selling rail tickets, or the conductor on an express train up to two hours prior to scheduled arrival of train, to make the arrangements. A car with chauffeur will cost about AS2,400 per day including 100 km.

Automobile Clubs. *Austrian Automobile Club* (Österreichischer Automobil-Motorrad- und Touring-Club), headquarters in Vienna, Schubertring 3, with border offices on the main roads entering Austria, as well as its provincial affiliates, will gladly give any information you may need on motoring. The countrywide emergency number 120 will quickly bring you help.

At Vienna's Schwechat Airport they are open daily until 8 P.M., also for emergency repairs. Provincial automobile clubs: *Carinthia:* Domgasse 5, Klagenfurt; **Salzburg:** Schrannengasse 5, Salzburg; **Styria:** Girardigasse 1, Graz; **Tirol:** Tschamlerstrasse 10, Innsbruck; **Upper Austria:** Gürtelstrasse 20a, Linz; **Vorarlberg:** Bahnhofplatz, Dornbirn.

If you need information on road conditions, traffic situation, breakdown service or border formalities call the Information Service of the club in Vienna (711 99 7, preceded by 02 22 when calling from outside of Vienna but within Austria) between 6 A.M. and 8 P.M. The Austrian Automobile Club also operates a central service for objects lost by motorists; write or call. You can also get motorist assistance from Austria's other automobile club, ARBÖ, by phoning 123 nationwide; no area code is needed.

Motorway Restaurants. Worth noting are the motels and restaurants of the *Rosenberger* chain, spread along Austria's autobahn network. They are reasonably priced and mostly provide good local food, including a salad bar and light snacks, in up-to-date surroundings.

Kilometers Into Miles. This simple chart will help you to convert to both miles and kilometers. If you want to convert from miles into kilometers read from the center column to the right, if from kilometers into miles, from the center column to the left.

Miles		Kilometers	Miles		Kilometers
0.6	1	1.6	37.3	60	96.6
1.2	2	3.2	43.5	70	112.3
1.9	3	4.8	49.7	80	128.7
2.5	4	6.3	55.9	90	144.8
3.1	5	8.0	62.1	100	160.9
3.7	6	9.6	124.3	200	321.9
4.3	7	11.3	186.4	300	482.8
5.0	8	12.9	248.5	400	643.7
5.6	9	14.5	310.7	500	804.7
6.2	10	16.1	372.8	600	965.6
12.4	20	32.2	434.9	700	1,126.5
18.6	30	48.3	497.1	800	1,287.5
24.8	40	64.4	559.2	900	1,448.4
31.0	50	80.5	621.4	1,000	1,609.3

By Bus. Austria has a nation-wide bus and coach system although frequencies are not as great as in some other countries. But their safety record is one of the highest in Europe. The Post Buses (bright orange-yellow for easy recognition) reach to even the remotest areas, especially into mountain valleys which might otherwise be difficult to penetrate. Out of season there is usually no problem in getting a seat, but in peak weeks (winter as well as summer) a reservation is essential. Many of the buses duplicate railway routes but take longer. The main cities also have excellent bus or streetcar networks reaching out into the surrounding country. The buses are kept spotlessly clean and in excellent running order. For central bus information, telephone (0222) 7501.

Europabus tours of Austria, lasting from two to seven days, are frequent and take you through the most scenic areas. *Austrobus* of Vienna runs fast bus services in summer between Vienna and Venice in Italy, Opatija-Zagreb in Yugoslavia, Prague-Karlsbad in Czechoslovakia, and Cracow in Poland; most of these bus lines take you through large portions of Austria. Information from Austrian tourist offices.

By Boat. This is a delightful and leisurely way of traveling "by armchair" to and from Vienna, through some 300 km. of Austria's most beautiful scenery, past romantic castles and ruins, medieval monasteries and abbeys and lush vineyards. One of the high spots, especially in the springtime when the fruit trees are in bloom, is the Wachau near Vienna.

The trip from Passau to Vienna takes two days (including overnight stop in Linz—on board if you wish) and can be made from late June to late September. It leaves Passau at 3 P.M. and arrives in Linz at 8 P.M., from whence it departs at 10 A.M. to arrive in Vienna at 8.15 P.M. The return upstream takes longer and you should check the times.

One-way fare is AS926; cabins for two cost AS400–600 extra for the trip in either direction; meals are extra. There are reductions for groups. The immaculate white-painted Mississippi-type craft each carry about 1,000 passengers on their three decks. As soon as you get on board, hire a deck chair, give the steward a good tip and ask him to place it where you will get the best views. Be sure to book cabins in advance.

A rejuvenated *Danube Steamship Company (DDSG)* has introduced several new services and special trips. The world's largest river cruiser *Mozart* has just gone into service. For details inquire at the company's ticket office at 1021 Vienna, Handelskai 265, tel. 0222–217 50 430 (at the ship landing on the main course of the Danube).

In fact, Vienna is, as it has always been, a gateway to Eastern Europe. From Vienna, river cruise lovers may enjoy a 14-day trip along the Danube to the Black Sea and back, on Austrian, Soviet or Romanian ships. From the Soviet ships you change in the Danube delta to a Soviet Black Sea ship to continue to Yalta. From mid-April to mid-September a Czech hydrofoil runs daily between Vienna and Bratislava, leaving Vienna at 9 A.M. and returning at 5 P.M. Visas obtainable on board; an extra passport photograph necessary. A Hungarian steamer makes the trip to Budapest in 10 hours; a duty-free shop is on board; a hydrofoil makes the Vienna–Budapest round-trip daily. The Austrian old-timer *Schönbrunn* has been restored and now operates nostalgia-trips to Budapest; these are summer only.

Returning Home

CUSTOMS. U.S. Customs. You may bring in $400 worth of foreign merchandise as gifts or for personal use without having to pay duty, provided they have been out of the country more than 48 hours and provided they have not claimed a similar exemption within the previous 30 days. Every member of a family is entitled to the same exemption, regardless of age, and the exemptions can be pooled. For the next $1,000 worth of goods a flat 10% rate is assessed.

Included in the $400 allowance for travelers over the age of 21 are one liter of alcohol, 100 non-Cuban cigars and 200 cigarettes. Only one bottle of perfume trademarked in the U.S. may be brought in. However, there is no duty on antiques or art over 100 years old. You may not bring home meats, fruits, plants, soil or other agricultural products.

Gifts valued at under $50 may be mailed to friends or relatives at home, but not more than one per day of receipt to any one addressee. These gifts must not include perfumes costing more than $5, tobacco or liquor.

If you are traveling with such foreign-made articles as cameras, watches or binoculars that were purchased at home or on a previous trip, either carry the receipt or register them with U.S. Customs, using form 4457, prior to departure.

Canadian Customs. In addition to personal effects, and over and above the regular exemption of $300 per year, the following may be brought into Canada duty-free: a maximum of 50 cigars, 200 cigarettes, 2 pounds of tobacco and 40 ounces of liquor, provided these are declared in writing to customs on arrival. Canadian Customs regulations are strictly enforced; you are recommended to check what your allowances are and to make sure you have kept receipts for whatever you may have bought abroad. Small gifts can be mailed and should be marked "Unsolicited gift, (nature of gift), value under $40 in Canadian funds." For other details, ask for the Canada Customs brochure, *I Declare.*

British Customs. There are two levels of duty free allowance for people entering the U.K.: one, for goods bought outside the EEC or for goods bought in a duty free shop within the EEC; the other, for goods bought in an EEC country but not in a duty free shop.

In the first category you may import duty free: 200 cigarettes or 100 cigarillos or 50 cigars or 250 grammes of tobacco (*Note:* if you live outside Europe, these allowances are doubled); plus one liter of alcoholic drinks over 22% by volume (38.8% proof) or two liters of alcoholic drinks not over 22% by volume or fortified or sparkling wine, or two liters of table wine; plus two liters of table wine; plus 50 grammes of perfume; plus nine fluid ounces of toilet water; plus other goods to the value of £32.

In the second category you may import duty free: 300 cigarettes or 150 cigarillos or 75 cigars or 400 grammes of tobacco; plus 1½ liters of alcoholic drinks over 22% by volume (38.8% proof) or three liters of alcoholic drinks not over 22% by volume or fortified or sparkling wine, or three liters of table wine; plus five liters of table wine; plus 75 grammes of perfume; plus 13 fluid ounces of toilet water; plus other goods to the value of £250 (*Note* though it is not classified as an alcoholic drink by EEC countries for Customs' purposes and is thus considered part of the "other goods" allowance, you may not import more that 50 liters of beer).

In addition, *no animals or pets of any kind* may be brought into the U.K. The penalties for doing so are severe and are strictly enforced; there are *no* exceptions. Similarly, fresh meats, plants and vegetables, controlled drugs and firearms and ammunition may not be brought into the U.K. There are no restrictions on the import or export of British and foreign currencies.

Anyone planning to stay in the U.K. for more than six months should contact H.M. Customs and Excise, Kent House, Upper Ground, London S.E.1 (tel. 01–928 0533) for further information.

DUTY FREE. Duty free is not what it once was. You may not be paying tax on your bottle of whiskey or perfume, but you are certainly contributing to somebody's profits. Duty free shops are big business these days and mark ups are often around 100 to 200%. So don't be seduced by the idea that because it's duty free it's a bargain. Very often prices are not much different from your local discount store and in the case of perfume or jewelry they can be even higher.

As a general rule of thumb, duty free stores on the ground offer better value than buying in the air. Also, if you buy duty free goods on a plane, remember that the range is likely to be limited and that if you are paying in a different currency to that of the airline, their rate of exchange often bears only a passing resemblance to the official one.

The duty free shops at the Austrian airports are run by Austrian Airlines, so prices are similar if not the same as those charged in the air. Vienna airport has a reputation for being among the pricier of the European duty free shops, so look for local goods rather than the international brands. And VAT is charged, unless you point out that you are not a resident, or buy enough to qualify for a refund.

AUSTRIA AND THE
AUSTRIANS

by
LILLIAN LANSETH-CHRISTENSEN

Lillian Lanseth-Christensen is a born New Yorker, who studied design with Josef Hoffman in Vienna, then worked for Joseph Urban in New York, and finally returned to Austria, from where she writes on food, her second love, for Gourmet *magazine.*

Austria is too small and far too full of natural and manmade beauties to fly over or speed through with a clear conscience. It is, partly, a romantic land of castles and fortresses, legends and heroics, mighty mountains and profound lakes. But it is also intimate and friendly, full of intriguing folklore, small villages, wild flowers, and mountain meadows. Austria should be enjoyed at close quarters, seen at eye level, its lilting music should be heard in its natural surroundings, and its food tasted as you go along, accompanied by the wine that grew in the vineyard next to the restaurant's vegetable garden.

The Unpredictable Austrians

You may not be able to fit a walking trip with rucksack and alpenstock into the confines of a short vacation, but you can bicycle, meander by motor, take the railways—wide or narrow gauge—ride a horse, or sail in a Danube steamer. All along the way you will meet the Austrians, basically a friendly, warm, and honest people who embrace and spoil their guests, and open their arms and their doors to them. That is not to say they are above making money, but you are always left with the feeling that they like you, at least in part, for yourself alone.

It seems to me that life in Austria, perhaps more than in any other country, is at the mercy of its national traits—the characteristics of the often misunderstood and unpredictable Austrians. They are capable of the highest elation and the profoundest depression. Always at the mercy of the full moon, or the *Foehn,* a depressing warm wind that originates in North Africa and can be blamed for everything that goes wrong while it is blowing.

The typical Austrian is, first of all, inquisitive, perhaps curious would be a kinder word, a trait he disguises as being interested and caring. He is critical of—and at the same time casual about—situations he knows he could remedy. He will stop on the street to tell you how to drive your car, although he doesn't own or drive one himself, and rarely rides in one. He will tell you exactly how the government should be run, but he will do nothing about it. This wildly misused and abused man has two vacations a year, may draw 14 months' salary, and will scream if the last two months—over and above the normal calendar 12—are taxed.

He is generous, kind to his canary and dachshund, has an indestructible sense of humor, and, while he may yell imprecations at you one minute, he will be your best friend the next. He will peer into an excavation and criticize the building that has not yet been erected, and he will send back his soup because it is too hot or too cold . . . but just you find fault with it and he will defend it with his life. In other words, he is lovable, funny, and at the same time insouciant. He is interested in everything, with an interest that can verge on noseyness.

That is the Austrian—and his wife, too. If they are Viennese, everything is magnified. Sealed envelopes are held up to the light and parcels are shaken. If that doesn't work they resort to direct questions, "Are you two ever going to get married?" or "How much do you weigh?"

The Austrian's wife's curiosity about her neighbor is partly satiated because they share a cleaning woman, a *Putzfrau,* who is a formidable source of intelligence. The wife also goes to market every day, where she limits her purchases to 10 dekagrams of ham and a cucumber, to give her an excuse to shop again next morning—she has a perfectly good refrigerator at home—to see who is buying what. A roast signifies guests, a stewing chicken always means an illness, and cake-makings foretell a birthday.

Flat Feet and Belle Poitrines

The Austrian character developed slowly over the more than 1,000 years since it first emerged as a nation. But, in the last hundred or so of those years, certain archetypes developed to become a characteristic part of the Austrian scene. There was, for example, the restaurant, or café, cashier, a type clearly based on the legendary Frau Anna Sacher, with her cigar and her Belle Poitrine—that pneumatic upthrust of the bust which made ladies of the Belle Epoque look like figureheads on battleships. She had a soft spot for the old Emperor Franz Josef, and a scowl for the poor busboy—called a *piccolo* in Austria, where foreign words were in (now it is American slang, mispronounced).

Next came the Traffic Ladies, who despite their name are nothing to do with autos or even horsedrawn carriages; rather they are the women, clad in mittens and woolen socks, who stood all day in the hole-in-the-wall cubicles called State Tobacco Traffics. There they dispensed cigars, Vienna Woods cigarettes, gossip, Virginias, gossip, newspapers—and gossip. On top of that, they were Notary Publics, and in that capacity they knew what everyone, but everyone, was up to—Austria requires a notarization for every single move.

What with their intimate knowledge of their neighbor's lives, their chilblains, and selling cigarettes by the piece, they were always *grantig,* irritable. Their customers rarely bought newspapers. Why should they bother? After all, their actual source for the news that really mattered was the Traffic Ladies themselves, who knew everything and passed it on with gusto and spice. Full of the cream of the news, the average Austrian then repaired to his coffeehouse, were he could read all the papers, secure on their bamboo frames, for the price of one cup of coffee.

The line of archetypal characters stretches out to include the Kutcher, originally coachmen, now taxi drivers; elderly flower girls; the lavender sellers with their haunting cry; and, above all, the more or less flat-footed Herr Obers, the café head waiters. The Herr Obers are still the factotums, confessors, confidants, analysts, and advisors of Austria's menfolk. They know all about misunderstood husbands, about a little activity called a side-jump, about innocent *fleerts,* and the state of their guests' gall bladders.

But the type for which Austria is perhaps most famous, is Die Schoene Wienerin, strictly speaking "the beautiful Viennese," but who could come from Graz or Innsbruck, or, for that matter, from Kleinkircheim, just so long as she was *mollig*—rounded and buxom, cheerful and a good cook—or the employer of a good cook . . . and, above all, blonde. Although many Austrian women, due to Celtic forebears and confluences of neighboring bloods, are *mollig* and dark, the traditional concept is always blonde. Now, by some miracle of evolution or diet, the once-chubby beauties have become long-legged and svelte.

Tales of the Un-blue Danube

Beside all these favorite human characters—the Traffic Ladies now sell cigarettes by the pack, even by the carton, and are accordingly much more cheerful—Austria is full of well loved natural beauties, foremost among which is the 1,770-mile-long Danube. In Europe, only the Volga is longer, and both of them have memorable theme songs—the Volga's for rowing, the Danube's for dancing. The singularly un-blue Danube is Austria's only link with a salt sea. Its most romantic and dramatic stretch lies between Passau and Vienna or, more precisely, between Krems and Melk, where the stupendous monastery rears its Baroque bulk high on a bluff.

At Durnstein, which overhangs the Wachau's most poetic bend in the river, history, myth, legend, pleasure, and dinner meet. It all began on the night of December 20, 1192, when England's King Richard the Lionheart, on his way home from the Crusades, was recognized and thrown into the dungeons of Hadmar's fortress at Durnstein. Its dramatic ruins stand on a height above the wonderfully luxurious Hotel Schloss Durnstein, with its superb dining terrace and its hypnotizing river views. The tale about the minstrel Blondel's rescue of his king from durance vile is probably a myth, but the very solid ransom that was certainly paid for Richard I's release went toward strengthening and enlarging the fortifications of Vienna, among other places.

The chronicle of the Danube flowed on, gathering myths along the way. In the year 1200 the heroic *Song of the Nibelungen* was chronicled there, centuries before Wagner moved the whole story to the Rhine. The Danube Maidens were definitely *mollig,* the dragon Fafner smoldered in a cave near Melk, while Brunnhilde slept, and the Danube gold was stolen.

In 1301, a small vine was grown in the Ritzling vineyard at Weissenkirchen, to be exported to Germany, then returned to Austria with the name of Riesling. In 1552 a fully grown elephant arrived in Vienna, possibly by barge along the Danube, to show the Austrians how different things could be in the outside world.

In 1683 the event occurred that was to change the Austrian males' way of life for ever. The Turks had been besieging Vienna from the comfortable quarters of their silken tents, under the command of the Grand-Vizier Kara Mustapha. With the help of their allies, the Austrians finally drove them away, and in its haste to depart the Turkish army abandoned cannons, armored camels, a parrot, and mounds of green coffee beans. These were awarded to a spy called Georg Franz Kolschitzky, who was the only one to recognize them for coffee beans and not camel dung. Using them as his stock-in-trade, Kolschitzky opened Austria's first coffeehouse in 1684, placing all subsequent generations of Austrians in his debt.

The Austrian's Home from Home

The Austrian escapes from his home to his coffeehouse, to the airless male world of smoke, naps, billiards, and coffee. It is commonly believed that men are happiest away from home, but not the Austrian. Tucked away in his coffeehouse, he hides behind his newspaper, picking his teeth or dozing. There are discussions and heated arguments, but little hilarity. The great composer Brahms went to his favorite coffeehouse religiously for an hour's nap every afternoon. My professor, Josef Hoffman, walked out of *his* coffeehouse, dragging his entourage behind him like the Pied Piper, never to return, and all because the proprietor had acquired—and refused to get rid of—an artificial palm.

In Paris or Rome the café habitué sits facing outward, watching the world go by. In Austria, he resolutely faces inward—except for a few narrow window seats, often occupied by tourists—and lingers over a single cup of coffee and a glass of water for half a day. In Vienna that vital glass of water is the best that any city can offer. It comes from Semmering, and there have been enthusiasts—Americans among them—who have shipped home a barrel of Vienna water just so that they, too, could make a cup of Wiener Mokka and accompany it with a glass of intoxicatingly pure Wiener Wasser.

It is not as though coffee was simple coffee in Austria: There are many refinements as to quantity, color, what is added to it, and the cups it is served in. There are big cups of coffee and little ones, brown and white ones, gold and *Turkisch* ones. Each kind of coffee fits a time of day or humor, an occasion, or a need. Rum and brandy can be added, but most cups seem to be crowned by the ubiquitous whipped cream.

The Bad Cure Makes Good

Rich and fattening adventures deep into the satisfying world of *Schlag* (whipped cream) are only possible because the Austrians take an annual, or even a semi-annual, cure in a *Bad* (the word for a spa, and nothing to do with the state of their health). Everyone has a favorite Bad, large or small, where the resident spa doctor prescribes his pet cure—salty hot water, mud baths, or starvation, all accompanied by long walks. There was one famous Austrian spa doctor called "Hunger" Meyer, who started off every cure by putting his patient to bed for three days in a darkened room without food. If the patient had not passed on, he started his proper treatment with such an encouraging weight loss that half the battle was already won.

Bads have the advantage of communal suffering. Even the scales used to be placed in a circle so that everyone could comment on his neighbor's progress—if any. After going through all this torture for the sake of *Shlag*, commonsense rears its head and the *Nachkur*, the "after cure," comes into play, to undo half the good that the cure itself accomplished. But you would have to be in one of the less rigid resorts to enjoy its pleasurably corrective effects.

Austria is a lovely—if small—country, and Austrians enjoy and appreciate their homeland to the full. In order not to miss the advantages of a Bad, if one does not happen to be nearby, they are ingenious in turning a favorite inn into a *Luftkurort*, an "air cure place." I remember that we were taken to one when we were children. We were gotten up early and walked to the top of a hill, where Father said, sternly, BREATHE, just as though we had not been doing so all the time. After experiencing a Luft Kur, it is hard to shift back from conscious to unconscious breathing.

Putting First Things First

Once cured at his favorite Bad, the Austrian goes back to his old ways. There is no question but that Austria is a great country for eating and drinking. When two Austrians meet they don't ask "How are you?", or "How's the family?", but "What did you eat this morning?", or "What are you having for dinner?", or "Did you enjoy the *Zwetschkenknodel?*" Zwetschkenknodel are plum dumplings cowering under mountains of buttery breadcrumbs and powdered sugar. There are even organized Plum Dumpling Contests—the architect Adolf Loos used to take part in them— with champions eating over thirty of the gorgeously gooey things.

Austria's cuisine is said to be varied due to its central position in Europe, taking elements from many of its neighbors. But the food is not so much varied as it is frequent! As a rule, the day starts with hot tea, preferably in bed, which is followed by *Frühstück,* the "Early Piece,"—by which you can guess that there are many more "Pieces" to come! This is breakfast, lately defined as either *American*—dry cereal, bacon and eggs—or *Continental*—tea, coffee, or hot chocolate, a roll, butter and jam, and a knife to spread them with. The knife differentiates this kind of breakfast from the more serious one, the *Gabelfrühstück,* Fork Breakfast, which should include something (I always hope it's a dab of gooseliver pâté) that has to be eaten with a fork. The beverage may be coffee, but a glass of sherry or cold *Sekt* (champagne) is always welcome.

After these little stopgaps, the Austrian lightly turns to thoughts of dinner, eaten in the middle of the day. It always starts with a soup with a dumpling or noodles floating in it. The soup is followed by an unbelievable revolving monotony of boiled beef, pork roast, Wiener Schnitzel, and Gulyas (goulash). The routine can be varied by excellent game, fish, or poultry, but the pendulum always swings back to boiled beef with mushroom, horseradish, or Paradise (tomato) sauce. The meal is completed with a *Mehlspeise*, a dish made of flour, such as a strudel or a dumpling. Then comes a coffee, a little nap, a few more hours work—and *Jause.*

The *Jause* is a sit-down meal at the dining room table, with tea, open sandwiches, cakes, callers, and gossip. For theatergoers there is supper after the performance, for stay-at-homes, the *Jause* drifts into a light supper, followed by a *Betthupferl,* a "bed hopper," a little something to insure a good night's rest.

Things have changed a bit in recent years. Husbands rarely come home for lunch, which they eat in a restaurant with their colleagues. There's no question of a contemptible sandwich and a container of coffee at their desks. Also, the American cocktail hour has been added in the early evening, rather than substituted for an already existing excuse for a little nourishment.

The traveler in Austria who stops at country Gasthäuser and inns, is startled to be asked for his drink order before he has decided on his meal. He learns to order the beer or wine of his choice irrespective of what he will eat.

The place where all Austrians, men and women, assemble is the *Konditorei,* the pastryshop. The summit of the confectioner's art was reached at Demel, on the Kohlmarkt in Vienna, and it is still there, not under the same ownership, but with the same delicious recipes.

I remember sitting in Demel's one day, watching a young couple, obviously in love, who interrupted their looking deeply into each other's eyes and their murmured endearments to tear off to the counter for another slab of Malakoff Torte and a second wedge of Spanische Windtorte mit Schlag and raspberries. When their hands were again locked and he seemed on the verge of some momentous declaration, she suddenly remembered seeing the Hasselnuss-Creme-Schnitte and ran off to secure a helping.

Austrians, beside their other charms, have the sweetest teeth, and have treasured generations of the most talented pastry chefs and confectioners who have ministered to their cravings. Not that long ago, two of the leading practitioners took each other to the highest court in the land to settle the vital question of which one of them had invented the Sacher Torte—a, to me, rather dry chocolate/almond cake that needs a liberal whoosh of whipped cream to help it down. After the legal proceedings, which are still the talk of pastryshops across the land, Sacher now stamps his with a handsome seal, "The Original Sacher Torte," and Demel leaves off the word "original." Both ship it all over the world in hoardable wooden boxes and it arrives just as fresh in Japan, say, where it is especially popular, as it left Vienna.

Mad Dogs and Austrians

Vienna lies roughly on the same longitude as Newfoundland—a fact we never considered when we came to live here—and all Austrians, who enjoy heavenly cool, but short, summers are sun hungry. The first little beam in spring brings them out into the parks, or even just to stand at the base of a monument, to soak up the palest sunlight. They fight for the best exposure on the park bench, their dogs growl at each other for their own place in the sun, while the old ladies feed the birds. Sleeves are rolled up, chests bared, and the heat seekers stay out until sunset. They have just the right kind of skin to tan beautifully, and by summer they look like Floridians. If that is the way that they greet the approach of summer, they have just as positive a reaction to the first snowflake. Now calling themselves *Sportlers,* they are immediately off to the ski slopes.

Capital Gains

Austria has fewer cities per capita than most European countries, but the ones that it does have are bursting at the seams with atmosphere.

Salzburg is Baroque, be-domed, and bedecked with putti and arabesques; a city made for festivals, for comfort, and for top food at the Goldener Hirsch. It is a city that sparkles with its own well-being and good fortune—even in the rain. It is essentially a walking city, and has a feature that makes it possible to explore—even in the rain. The Mozart House, on Getreidegasse, and all the buildings around it, are "through houses" or "passage houses," which means that their entrances lead into attractive courtyards, or go straight through into the next street. They have long since become rainy-day, treasure-hunt areas that offer shelter, tiny shops, equally tiny cafés, and small-scale surprises. You can eat, and drink, and shop, and dart back and forward to your heart's content all day.

Innsbruck, the capital of the Tirol, has snow-capped mountains at the ends of its streets, a beautiful castle, arcades, and some historic bronze figures in the Hofkirche. Both Styria and its capital, Graz, are always defined as "green." Graz is the green city that has at its heart a magical square built in the 17th and 18th centuries, untouched by the passing years. Hidden in the surrounding mountains is Piber, where the graceful white Lipizzaner stallions, whose performance at the Spanish Riding School in Vienna takes one's breath away, graze and cavort in the high green meadows.

The capital of all these capitals is Vienna, a beautiful old city in the process of rejuvenation, a city with an endearing personality, relaxed, sometimes a little pompous, but always filled with interest and—there's that word again—curiosity. History may have left it lopsidedly off-center from its former focal position in the Austro-Hungarian Empire, so that it is now just 35 miles from the Hungarian border, but it remains above all a German-speaking city in a German-speaking country that has always faced toward the west.

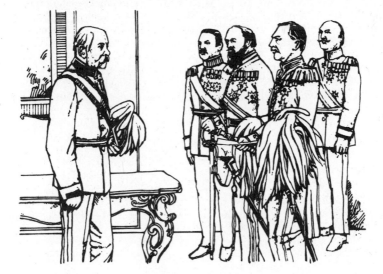

AUSTRIA'S HISTORY

From Empire to Republic

Not only Austria's history, but the very character of its inhabitants has been determined by its geography, by its situation astride natural European highways. Along them came the peoples of many races, marching, fighting, trading and settling, each leaving behind some trace of their passage.

Of all these highways the greatest, of course, was the mighty River Danube. The Celts, whom the Roman legionaries found in possession when they slowly pushed northward through Alpine passes and along the Danube valley about 100 B.C., had probably been supreme in the area for about seven centuries. As the legions advanced, they consolidated their new territories by the construction of successive Roman forts and built those imperishable roads which carried the new civilization from the south. The fortified settlements were defended against the increasing waves of migrating North and East European peoples. The vine was transplanted to the banks of the Danube; baths and arenas were built, above all the Romans established stable laws. Some local inhabitants became Romanized and a number of them received Roman citizenship, and some Celto-Roman towns flourished in the newly established Roman provinces which replaced the old Celtic state formations. But in the countryside, where the Germanic tribes has already begun mixing with the Celts, the Romans were able to rule only by the law of the sword.

Carnuntum, near Petronell, about 46 km. (29 miles) east of Vienna, became the Romans' capital city for the region. By the 2nd century A.D., it was big enough to have an amphitheater that could accommodate 13,000

41

people. Where Vienna's Innere Stadt (Inner City) stands today the Romans built the fortified settlement of Vindobona, in which Marcus Aurelius, the philosopher emperor, died in A.D. 180.

From then on the far-flung Roman Empire was steadily weakened by the attacks of the Germanic tribes, themselves driven westward by the even more formidable Huns. Their great primitive force and systematic restlessness gradually overcame the resistance of the highly civilized but increasingly vitiated Romans, who were preoccupied more with wars at home than with the defense of the frontiers. Before A.D. 400 the invading waves of barbarians were battering down the walls the Romans had built, and in another 80 years the Romans themselves had vanished from Austria.

Charlemagne and the Babenburgs

From the northeast came the West-Goths, the Vandals and Attila, "Scourge of God," with his terrible Huns. Waves of Teutons and Slavs, Franks, Burgundians and Avars flowed over the plains of the Danube, intermingling and leaving their imprint on following generations. These Dark Ages are the period that is imperishably enshrined in the great Nibelung saga. Though the climax of the heroine, Kriemhild's, revenge is supposed to have taken place in West Hungary, much of the Nibelung story happened in the Austrian section of the Danube valley.

A Christian bishop was established in Salzburg early in the 8th century, and the town became the center of missionary activity among the pagan tribes to the east and southeast. Then, between the years 791 and 799, the formidable Frankish ruler, Charlemagne, conquered the lands of present-day Austria. At Christmas in 800, he was crowned Emperor of the West by the pope in Rome, thus reviving a title that had not been used for over 300 years. Charlemagne's mighty empire, which stretched from the Pyrenees to the primeval German forests, lasted only as long as his life. Following his death in 814 it was divided among his descendents, the eastern part becoming the Holy Roman Empire of the German Nation.

Owing to constant rivalries and shaken by the Avar invasion, this empire was only revived under a new dynasty in 962, when Otto the Great was crowned as the first Holy Roman Emperor by the pope in Rome. The rivalries continued—particularly between emperors and popes—but the empire, basically a kind of confederation of German princes, remained a historically continuous unit until 1806, being ruled for most of the period by the Habsburgs of Vienna. The simple imperial diadem, probably first used to crown Otto the Great, is still one of the most valued possessions in the Imperial Treasury in Vienna's Hofburg, where it lies alongside other priceless insignia.

In 976 Emperor Otto II conferred upon the Margrave Leopold of Babenberg the newly created eastern province of the Reich—and Oesterreich (Austria) came into being as a separate country.

Under the Babenbergs, who ruled for 270 years, Austrian peasants and merchants alike prospered and the church accumulated vast wealth. It was also a period of considerable cultural attainment, the writing of the legend of the Nibelungs and the poetry of Walter von der Vogelweide being but two aspects. The Babenbergs were an interesting dynasty. Leopold III "the Holy" (1095–1136) founded several of the oldest monasteries in Austria. Leopold V (1177–94) was called "the Virtuous"—which, in the cynical way of the period, clearly suggests that he was nothing of the sort!—quarreled over a question of honor with Richard the Lionheart during a crusade, and imprisoned him in Dürnstein Castle when the English king attempted to travel through Austria in disguise. As he had harmed a crusader, Leopold—in accordance with the church laws of the time—was excommunicated by the pope and died of an injury received in an accident before he was able to make his peace with the church. Recent studies have revealed that sections of central Vienna, together with the town walls of Wiener Neustadt, Hartberg, and Enns were built with the ransom money.

Under the greatest Babenberg, Heinrich II Jasomirgott (so called from his favorite oath, *Ja, so mir Gott helfe*—So help me God!) the growth of trade and barter made Austria prosperous and in 1156 the country acquired the rank of a Duchy. Heinrich also created Vienna as his capital, building his palace in Am Hof. The last Babenberg, Friedrich II "the Quarrelsome," was killed in battle in 1246 and his tomb can be seen in the cloister at Heilgenkreutz. After a troubled interregnum of 32 years, Austria was awarded to the House of Habsburg, who ruled it until the dissolution of their realm in 1918.

The Habsburgs

And so, in 1278, the 640-year rule of the House of Austria, of the Habsburgs, began; a period which saw the advent of 20 emperors and kings. The name was derived from Habichtsburg, or Hawks' Castle, the original fortress of the family, located in the Aargau region of Switzerland, and still called Habsburg today. But the Habsburgs acquired their vast territorial possessions and power only gradually, and largely by advantageous marriages. The wedding of Maximilian I to Maria of Burgundy, heiress to Burgundy and the Netherlands, in 1477 (though Maximilian did not ascend the throne until 1493) represented the opening move in the famous Habsburg game—"Let others wage war, you, happy Austria, grow by marriages." In 1496 Maximilian's son, Philip, married Joan of Castille and Aragon, thus bringing the Habsburgs Spain and into international politics on a large scale. After Maximilian's death, his grandson, Charles (son of Philip and Joan), inherited the vast Habsburg possessions, becoming Charles I of Spain as well as Charles V of the Holy Roman Empire.

Charles V left the deepest impress on Europe of all the emperors—naturally, for his domains were vast and he hoped to make them vaster still. Becoming king of Spain in 1516, in that country's Golden Century, he controlled also Spain's huge territories overseas, the Netherlands and Burgundy (he himself had been born in Ghent, now in Belgium, in 1500). In 1519 he was elected Holy Roman Emperor, the first ruler to claim, though a little hyperbolically, that the sun never set on his dominions. To the unceasing conflict with France was soon added the struggle with the German Protestant princes and with the Turks. Charles V personally led a successful expedition against Tunis in 1535, but failed against Algiers in 1541. The bitter obligation to recognize the right of German princes to dictate the religion of their subjects led to his abdication in 1556, and he retired to a Spanish monastery where he died two years later.

Right at the beginning of his reign, in 1521, Charles V had divided his territories with his brother Ferdinand, who had married Anna of Hungary and Bohemia in 1515. This division founded the two lines of the Habsburg family—the Austrian line and the Spanish line. When, in 1526, Louis II

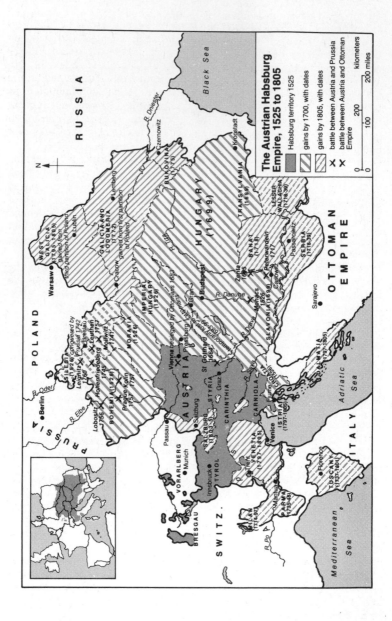

The Austrian Habsburg
Empire, 1525 to 1805

Habsburg territory 1525

gains by 1700, with dates

gains by 1805, with dates

✗ battle between Austria and Prussia

✗ battle between Austria and Ottoman
   Empire

kilometers
0 · · · 100 · · · 200
0 · · · · · · 200 miles

RUSSIA

Black Sea

N

R. Dniester

Czernowitz

POLAND

BUKOVINA
(1775)

Kronstadt

Warsaw

WEST
GALICIA
(1795-1805)
(gained from
the partition of Poland)

Lublin

GALICIA AND
LODOMERIA
(1772)
(gained from the 1st partition
of Poland)

HUNGARY
(1699)

TRANSYLVANIA
(1699)

Berlin

R. Oder

PRUSSIA

SILESIA (conquered by
(1526) Prussia)
Leignitz ✗ 1742
1760 Breslau
✗ Sorhin
Torgau 1745 ✗ 1757
✗ Mollwitz
Liegnitz 1741

Cracow

R. Tisza

Zenta
1695

LESSER
WALLACHIA
(1718-39)

Prague Kolin
✗ 1757 1757

BOHEMIA (1526)

Lobositz
1756

MORAVIA
(1526)

IMPERIAL
HUNGARY
(1526)

BANAT
(1718)

Peterwardein
1717

SERBIA
(1718-39)

Passarowitz

R. Danube

Grätz

Pressburg (Vienna)

Vienna ✗ besieged by Ottomans 1683
1805 R.
St. Gotthard 1664
✗ Győr

Buda 1686

Budapest

Zrinyi
(1526)

Mohács
✗ Mohács 1526

SLAVONIA

Drau

Sarajevo

OTTOMAN
EMPIRE

AUSTRIA

Passau

Salzburg

SALZBURG
(1803-5)

STYRIA

Graz

CARINTHIA

CARNIOLA

R. Sava

Fiume (1797-1805)

DALMATIA
(1797-1805)

VORARLBERG

Munich

Innsbruck

TYROL

VENETIA
(1797-1805)

ISTRIA
(1797-1805)

Venice

Adriatic
Sea

BRESGAU

SWITZ.

R. Po

MILAN
(1714-97)

Florence

PARMA
(1735-48)

Mantua

TUSCANY
(1737-80)

ITALY

Mediterranean
Sea

of Hungary and Bohemia (brother of Anna) fell in battle against the Turks, Ferdinand inherited those two crowns in accordance with previously-made treaties. He also was the first Habsburg to live in the Hofburg in Vienna.

The Turks were an everpresent threat during the 16th and 17th centuries, a threat, moreover, to the whole of Europe, though Austria lay on the main line of their advance. Twice the Turks besieged Vienna, in 1529 and 1683, and on the second attempt were totally defeated. While the 200-year-long struggle with the infidel Turks rumbled on, Austria had to face some of the worst excesses of the Catholic-Protestant confrontation to its north and west. The religious antagonism of the Reformation and its back-lash the Counter-Reformation, crystalized into widespread violence in 1618 with the beginning of the Thirty Years War. Luckily the Turks kept quiet while the war was raging across central Europe.

The Thirty Years' War ended in 1648 with the Peace of Westphalia, not notably in Austria's favor. The empire was, however, firmly back under the control of the crown, and the arts of peace were beginning to flourish once again. The empire covered at different times part or all of what are today Poland, Czechoslovakia, Hungary, the Ukraine, Rumania, Yugoslavia and Italy as well, of course, as Austria. Surprisingly, domination over so vast a territory and such a heterogeneous mixture of races brought few open revolts in its wake.

As a foretaste of the terrors to come, Vienna was struck in 1679 by the plague which claimed around 100,000 victims—commemorated by the Plague Pillar on the Graben, recently refurbished and glowing with gold. No sooner had the plague receded than the Turks arrived.

The Turks and Maria Theresa

The Turks, who had been more or less quiescent for decades, now saw in the torn and exhausted continent of Europe the chance for victory. Backed up by allies who thought that Turkish rule might be preferable to Austrian, a huge army of mixed troops, somewhere in the region of 300,000 strong, rolled towards the gates of Vienna. In 1683 the city gathered itself together for the attack. The defending forces were led by the emperor, Leopold I, the giant and fearless king of Poland, Jan Sobieski, and the Duke of Lorraine. The Turks drew up their besieging lines to the south, east and north of the city while the Austrian forces encamped to the west. For two months the garrison slowly succumbed to hunger and artillery attacks. Eventually the allied forces caught the Turkish army in a pincer movement between themselves and the troops who sallied out of the city. The Turks were routed—one of the most successful elements in their defeat being the magnificent armored Polish cavalry—and fled in total confusion.

There were two spoils of war famous above the rest of the rich loot. A great gold crescent was carried from the plundered Turkish camp and placed on the spire of St. Stephen's Cathedral, and—so the legend goes—a sack of strange seeds yielded the first coffee to be drunk in Europe. It was that year that Vienna's coffee houses opened for business.

This was a period for colorful characters and great military genius. As well as Jan Sobieski, the Siege of Vienna also brought to the fore Prince Eugene of Savoy. His services had at one time been refused by Louis XIV of France, to whom he was related, because the prince did not conform to the Sun King's idea of how an officer should look, one of Louis' more notable misjudgments. True, Prince Eugene was slight and weedy, but his heart was in soldiering and, rejected by France, he joined the army of the Austrian Emperor. Louis XIV, incidentally, supported the Turks, so great was his hatred of the House of Habsburg.

After helping to rout the Turks from Vienna, Prince Eugene joined the Duke of Marlborough and together they defeated the French armies in the War of the Spanish Succession. In his long career he played a decisive military and political role in the reigns of three emperors and left a considerable cultural legacy to Austria. The Belvedere Palace, among others, was built for him and a part of his great library can be still seen in a central position in Vienna's Prunksaal.

It was the misfortune of the Habsburgs that their rich domains were a tempting prize. Any pretext was good enough for foreign monarchs to help themselves to some of it whenever they could. The extinction of the Spanish line in 1700 provided one such occasion; the death of the last male Austrian Habsburg, Charles VI, and the accession of his daughter Maria Theresa as ruler of Austria in 1740 provided a second. These led to the War of the Austrian Succession, soon followed by the Seven Years' War.

Maria Theresa was one of the great queens of history, easily the equal of Catherine the Great and well outranking Victoria. During her 40-year reign she instituted a program of major reforms at home, transforming a gaggle of feudal states into a single, centrally-administered nation. Trade, education, the church, all found themselves being swept by the maternal broom. And a mother she undoubtedly was, not just of her nation, but of her family which numbered sixteen children, guaranteeing the continuity of the Habsburg-Lothringen line. This was a time of cultural expansion, the period of high Baroque in art and architecture, the age of the great composers Gluck, Haydn and Mozart—a truly golden era.

Maria Theresa's reforms were well founded, but her son and successor, Joseph II, who had been co-regent with his mother since 1765 when his father died, went too far too fast. Joseph reigned alone for ten years, 1780–90, and in that time almost created a "Welfare State" long before its time. Unfortunately, he over-reached himself. One of his schemes to tip over into particularly spectacular disaster was the reform of the Church. This entailed the closing down of over 700 monasteries and the seizure of their rich possessions. The news of this draconian measure brought the pope, Pius VI, hotfoot from Rome in 1782 to try to mitigate the severity of the plan. Joseph wrote his own epitaph—"Here lies a Prince whose intentions were honest, but who had the ill-luck to see all his undertakings founder."

Napoleon and Metternich

Then came Napoleon. After his crushing conquest of the Austrians and Russians at Austerlitz in 1805, he stripped Austria of her Italian possessions, the Tirol and Vorarlberg, and in 1806 forced the Emperor Franz to give up the crown of the Holy Roman Empire that had been a Habsburg title virtually continuously since 1438. Thus the great tradition that was not Holy, nor Roman, nor an Empire, faded into history. In 1810 the daughter of the Emperor, Marie Louise, was married to Napoleon and bore him a son, an ill-fated boy known as the Eaglet, L'Aiglon, the Duke of Reichstadt, whose short life (1811–32) was spent as a virtual prisoner in the palace of Schönbrunn.

After his cataclysmic Russian campaign in 1812, Napoleon's enemies took heart and began the effort that was finally to defeat him. At the Battle of Leipzig in 1813, the allied armies were led by an Austrian general, Prince Karl Schwarzenberg. Defeated, Napoleon was banished to the island of Elba, and the victorious allies converged on Vienna for a great Congress. Russia, England, Prussia and Austria chose the Austrian Prince Metternich as President, who in turn brought the brilliant French turncoat, Talleyrand, into the discussions as representative for his country. It was a period of the most magnificently devious diplomacy. Vienna became the glowing center for European hopes, glittering and dancing at incredible cost to the Austrian crown, who had to pay for the whole splendid affair. But Austria was getting her money's worth, and also a well-earned reward for her long humiliations at Napoleon's hands. In the haggling over territory that went on, Austria gained large areas in Italy, and recovered Salzburg, Tirol and the Vorarlberg.

But, just as the Congress seemed resolved and the treaties were agreed, news of Napoleon's escape from Elba and his advance on Paris burst on the unsuspecting delegates. All was to do again. The Allies had to reform, the final chapter in Napoleon's downfall had to be written, Waterloo fought and the Corsican Ogre dispatched to the remotest end of the earth, St. Helena, there to decline into ill-health and die, a process that took six years.

Austria had now regained a dominating position in European affairs. This revival of Austrian power was presided over by Prince Metternich, organizer of the so-called Holy Alliance among the principal victorious European nations, an alliance that was intended to guarantee peace in Europe. The fallacy of "Peace in our time" was to resound at regular intervals for a century and a half, and still echoes hollowly today.

Klemens Lothar Metternich was a brilliant diplomat, but a man of the most rigidly conservative beliefs. Anything that had the slightest taint of liberalism or progressiveness in it was anathema to him, and there were plenty of liberal ideas abroad in the wide territories that Austria now commanded, territories that were riddled with groups who deeply resented the Imperial domination. Slavs, Italians, Hungarians all had to be forced to conform with his concept of a prosperous Austria. Metternich's rule saw out the long reign of the Emperor Franz, who died in 1835, and the "Aimiable" Ferdinand I, who held the throne from the death of Franz until 1848, when he abdicated. That year saw the collapse of all that Metternich had worked for—over 30 years of manipulating the structure of the state, aided by all the trappings of dictatorship, not least censorship and a secret police. It was a year of upheaval throughout Europe, when people in many parts of the Continent, but particularly in the capitals, sought to liberate themselves from oppressive regimes. There were revolutions in Rome, Berlin, Venice, Milan, Naples, Prague, Budapest—and Vienna. In the face of the failure of his authority, Metternich resigned, was smuggled out of Vienna in a laundry cart and fled to London. He did not return to Vienna until 1851 and, though he faded into a kind of *eminence grise,* manipulating affairs away from the public eye, he was never again in complete aristocratic charge. He died in 1859 at the age of 86.

Enter Bismarck and Franz Josef

The 1848 revolutions, motivated partly by nationalism and partly by anti-authoritarian struggles, were accompanied by the emergence of two important figures for the history of Austria: the Prussian Bismarck, later the Iron Chancellor, and a delicately handsome youth of 18, who acceded to the Austrian throne in that fateful year, and who was to occupy it until just before its final collapse in 1918—Franz Josef. His 68-year reign was to be marked by successive disasters at home and abroad, mostly due to the persistent efforts of half-a-dozen nationalities striving for autonomous status. In spite of these constant irritants, in economic and cultural fields Austria had never been richer and happier; thus, to most Austrians the Franz-Josef era has remained a golden one, the warmly-remembered twilight of the House of Habsburg.

Simply stated, Bismarck's aim was to unify Germany under the domination of Prussia. When the proposal to bring the many German states into a single nation was made at Frankfurt in 1848, Bismarck opposed it because it would have been achieved under liberal, non-Prussian, auspices, and also because a union in which Austria was included would almost inevitably accept the leadership of this greatest of German states. Catholic Austria, Catholic Bavaria, the Catholic Rhineland—these would form a mighty bloc against which a Lutheran Prussia would be impotent. It was not Bismarck's aim to submerge Prussia in a German Empire; he wanted to submerge Germany in a Prussian Empire. He had to knock Austria out of the German lineup before he could achieve this. There followed a couple of decades of wars, diplomatic manipulations and complicated maneuvering that culminated with Bismarck triumphant. By means of the successful Franco-Prussian War (1870–71) during which Prussia was able to rally all the German states to its banner, Bismarck acheived his aim. As a result of the French defeat the German Empire was constituted and William I, King of Prussia, was proclaimed emperor in the Hall of Mirrors at Versailles in 1871, after the occupation of Paris by German armies.

Austria remained outside this new German empire. But if she could not be tolerated as a rival within Germany, she was still desirable as an ally, and therefore Franz Josef was readmitted to the good graces of Germany with the signature of the Triple Alliance in 1882.

The Fall of the Empire

Four years after his accession Franz Josef launched himself on an autocratic course, determined to rule alone—which he did for the rest of his long reign with mixed results. He had many of the abilities to make a fine head of state. He was enormously thorough, a stickler for routine and detail but at the same time completely unable to delegate authority. The combination was not a happy one in an autocrat as it led to a pyramid structure of government, the buck always passing upward in the system to land finally on the emperor's desk. Only his enormous courage and dedication carried him through so many years, and postponed the inevitable collapse of the empire for so long.

In 1854 he married Elisabeth, an extremely beautiful Bavarian princess, with whom he was deeply in love all his life. Their heir, Rudolf, was born in 1858. She was not well-equipped for the demanding life of Empress, a fact that began to appear early in their marriage. Endless disputes with her domineering mother-in-law drove Elisabeth first into a brief sally into politics, espousing the cause of the freedom-hungry Hungarians, then, after a breakdown and two rest cures on Madeira, into a restless, wandering life, almost never at home with her husband and children, always traveling in a seemingly desperate effort to escape from her failure as a wife and empress.

The clash with the Prussians under Bismarck, the restlessness of the Hungarians, the struggles with Italy, all created turbulent years for Franz Josef, during which he revealed himself as ill-able to handle the fate of Austria on the European scene. In 1867 a resolution of the Hungarian situation was achieved and the Dual Monarchy of Austria-Hungary was born, with Franz Josef wearing both crowns. The figure of the emperor represented about the only real link between the two halves of the equation, for each was governed by a parliament of its own. But though the *Ausgleich,* or compromise agreement, temporarily eased the strains between Austria and Hungary, it was a settlement riddled with hostilities, especially on the Hungarian side.

The years 1856–90 saw the conversion of Vienna from a near-medieval city into today's elegant one. The rings of fortifications were demolished and in their place great sweeping boulevards came into being, lined with massive public buildings. The Danube was tamed and the whole creation formed a superb backdrop to the golden age of Vienna.

Franz Josef's life was not only continually harassed by national and international problems, but his personal life, too, was a series of fatal disasters. In 1867 his younger brother, Maximilian, who had been manipulated onto the throne of Mexico by Napoleon III of France, was shot by a revolutionary firing squad. His wife, Charlotte, who had been canvassing everyone she could—including the pope—to try and save him, went mad.

In 1889 Rudolf, the heir to the throne, died in mysterious circumstances, together with his girl friend, Maria Vetsera, who was only 21. The hunting lodge at Mayerling, not far from Vienna, where the double tragedy occurred, was pulled down on his father's orders, and the whole tragic affair was so completely hushed up that even today the details are not entirely clear; where facts are few, fiction has a field day. A Carmelite convent was built on the site of the hunting lodge.

In 1898 Elisabeth—who had spent virtually the whole of her married life wandering about Europe, often on horseback until rheumatism intervened—was stabbed to death by an Italian anarchist, just as she was about to board a lake-steamer in Geneva. It appears to have been a random act of violence, without any political intent.

The final blow was a disastrous one, not only for Franz Josef but for the whole of Europe. After the death of Rudolf, the heir to the throne had been the emperor's nephew, the Archduke Franz Ferdinand, a man of wider interests and views than his uncle although he had no chance to put his political ideas into practice. In 1914 he was visiting Sarajevo, the capital of Austria's Bosnian province, when a Serbian terrorist belonging to the "Black Hand" organization shot both him and his wife as they were driving through the town in an open carriage. It was June 28. By the beginning of August the whole of Europe was at war.

World War I and After

Franz Josef died in the night of November 20, 1916. With him passed away nearly six-and-a-half centuries of history. At the end of World War I, in 1918, his successor Karl I, who had ruled for only two years, renounced his throne. A day later the Republic of Austria came into being.

It was a shrunken state. Only the German-speaking part was left to Austria, and not even all of that. The little Austrian Republic of 7 million people was only the rump of the Austria-Hungary which was left after all the prime joints had been cut away. Magyars, Czechs, Slovaks, Poles, Croats and other unwilling subjects of the Habsburgs were no longer part of the Austrian hegemony.

Economically, the break-up was a debacle. The succession states possessed railroads which ran nowhere in particular; they had been built for the days when the flow from what had become Yugoslavia, Poland, Czechoslovakia, Hungary, had been to and from Vienna. Produce was cut off from its markets, ports from their hinterlands. Austria had been bereft of her assets and left with her liabilities. Her problems seemed insoluble; and indeed, her early years were bitter—financial chaos, hyper-inflation of a type never previously known, but which has since been experienced by many peoples, and economic collapse.

Hardly had the League of Nations' loans set Austria somewhat on her feet again than she was rent by internal conflict. After the Social-Democrats left the coalition government in 1920, the Catholic Party dominated the federal and state governments, with the exception of Vienna. Under Chancellor Dollfuss, who took office in 1932, this one-party rule was transformed in 1934 into a full dictatorship, following a five-day civil war conducted by the private military units of both parties. Dollfuss also feared the Nazis, who had already proclaimed their plans to incorporate Austria into Nazi Germany. The Nazis attempted to start a civil war in 1934. Although the conspiracy was unsuccessful, they managed to murder Dollfuss. Schusnigg, his successor, was unable to resist the increasing pressure from Hitler for long. In March 1938 German troops occupied Austria without meeting resistance and without any country lifting a finger in Austria's defense. The country was incorporated into the Third Reich and within 18 months the world was once more plunged into war, this time on a truly global scale. Austria's identity was wiped from the face of Europe—for the moment.

Occupation

Austria was occupied at first by Soviet and then also by the U.S., French and British forces in May 1945. Subsequently, a provisional (all-party) government was established in Vienna under Russian supervision by a Socialist, Dr. Karl Renner, who later became the first President of the Republic. Eventually free and democratic elections were held in November 1945. The resulting parliament consisted of 85 representatives of the Volkspartei (Conservatives), 76 Socialists and 4 Communists.

Britain, the United States and Russia had earlier promised (in the Moscow Declaration of 1943) to restore a free, independent and democratic Austria. A Four-Power Declaration of July 4, 1945 declared that Austria (with its eight states and the city of Vienna) had been restored to its 1937 frontiers. The same declaration divided the country into four zones. France, The United States and Britain were allotted the western regions, Russia the eastern. Thus the approaches to Austria from the Western democracies were controllable by the Western Powers alone, those from the European communist dictatorships only by the Russians.

Vienna was anomalously situated within the Russian Zone but under a special Four Power occupation statute. Although it was divided into four sectors of occupation, there were, in contrast to Berlin, no barriers between sectors and no restriction of movement from one to another for Austrians or foreigners. Which was just as well, considering that the city is honey-combed with a vast network of cellars anyway.

Vienna was the seat of the Allied High Commission for Austria, a genuinely quadripartite body. Vienna's "Inner City"—the first district—was called the International Sector. It fell under the jurisdiction of the Allied Commission's "chairman of the month," British, French, American, or Russian. When the chairmanship passed from one nationality to another, a colorful ceremony complete with band music, marching, flag ceremonies was held, all in marked contrast to the terrible deprivation which gripped the country as a whole.

For almost ten years the Western powers sought a peace treaty for Austria, but it was not until April, 1955, when the Soviets suddenly reversed their position, that the Austrian State Treaty became a reality. The treaty was signed in the Belvedere Palace in Vienna, on May 15, 1955, the ratification was completed by June 27, and the official end of the occupation came on October 25, although most of the troops and equipment were withdrawn considerably earlier.

Austria Today

Present-day Austria is a democratic, federal republic, called the "Second Republic" with a bicameral legislative body similar to those of the Western democracies. Its Nationalrat is the Lower House, its Bundesrat the Upper House. This body is freely elected by the whole nation. The Upper House has only veto rights. Head of State is a President chosen by the electorate for six years; the head of the government, called the Federal Chancellor, is appointed from the majority party by the President of the Republic.

The roots of the present organization of the Austrian federal system go deep into history. The country is divided into nine federal states, or Bundesländer: Burgenland, Carinthia, Lower Austria, Upper Austria, Salzburg, Styria, Tirol, Vienna and Vorarlberg. Each state has its own government, with the governor elected by the state parliament. State dealings with the federal government are through the governor, while "local" affairs such as building, the affairs of young people, conservation, etc., are the business of the state parliament. There are similarities with the political organization of the United States in the way the system works.

Today, despite occasional scandals such as that surrounding the alleged Nazi past of President Kurt Waldheim, Austria still holds a quietly respected place in the family of nations and she contributes largely to international affairs, lending active support to the work of the U.N., sending medical teams and even troops to assist the cause of world peace. Vienna's huge U.N.O. city also bids for international attention, though it has some traits of a white elephant and is not notably popular with the citizens of the capital.

The country has also handled with skill its rather difficult position of outpost of the West in Europe. In June, 1979, to illustrate the focal nature of Austria's situation, the signing of SALT 2 was held in Vienna, and almost every month brings news of the help that Austria has provided to refugees from the East, often from territories which were once part of her own great heritage.

Recent events have shaken but not destroyed Austria's international image; they have also, however, had the effect of raising the level of national awareness and responsibility for past, present and future.

MUSIC IN AUSTRIA

The Year-Round Festival

by
KENNETH LOVELAND

One of Britain's senior music critics and a well-known travel writer, Kenneth Loveland has spent more than half-a-century in journalism, being at one time national President of the Guild of British Newspaper Editors. He now devotes himself to writing and broadcasting entirely about music. His love affair with Austria goes back many years—including nearly 30 consecutive Salzburg Festivals.

For the musical tourist who is excited at the prospect of treading in the footprints of the mighty, seeing where masterpieces were committed to paper, or standing where a long-loved work was either praised or damned at its first appearance, Austria is tops. The land is saturated with musical history.

The fact that a composer was born in a certain house does not of itself make that house interesting, though the contents, if it has become a museum, will attract. Indeed, most composers moved from their birthplace before reaching their creative years. Far more stimulating to see where they worked, to see the suroundings in which a symphony came to life, to see where the music itself was born. Austria has more of this to the square kilometer than anywhere else in the world. And Vienna is the heart of it all.

There is a tram starting from the center of Vienna which runs past the house where Mozart wrote his last three symphonies. Look left, and you will see the end of the street in which Beethoven died, and from which his funeral cortege set out. A young man named Schubert, so tragically soon to go on the same journey, was among the torch-bearers. A little further on, and you will pass the house where he was born. A little further, a house where Beethoven worked, and the journey ends on the edge of the Vienna woods, hymned by Johann Strauss the younger.

Leave the tram, and it is a short walk to the house from which Beethoven set out on that hike which produced the *Pastoral Symphony*. Progress, that relentless mauler of illusions, has dipped its itchy fingers into some of the countryside. But you can still follow that same walk, still find the brook which inspired the slow movement, and on a spring morning, the air will be filled with bird song just as Beethoven found it. And on a fine Sunday afternoon, scores of faithful Viennese will be seen following the trail. It matters. It is inheritance.

The end of that tram ride is haunted by Beethoven. Have a glass of wine in the garden of a tavern where he lodged, then walk the short distance to the house where he wrote that heart-broken testament when he discovered that his deafness was incurable.

Only a hard-boiled cynic can fail to be moved. And back in Vienna itself, only the flint-hearted can stand in the Währingerstrasse and look at the windows behind which Mozart wrote those last three symphonies in the incredible short time of six weeks in the summer of 1788 and not be touched. For this was the time when the Mozart fortunes had slumped to their lowest, the begging letters to their most pathetic. Next year, Mozart was to write to a friend "If you, my best of friends, forsake me, I am unhappily and innocently lost with my poor sick wife and my child." But then Vienna is neither for the hard-boiled nor the flint-hearted. It is for the musical romantic, happy to be where names and events come to life. And so is all of Austria, over which the Vienna tradition cast its influence, and still does.

Strangers in Town

Mozart, Schubert, Beethoven, Haydn, Richard Strauss, Mahler, Bruckner, Lehár, Johann Strauss II, Brahms—what a list they make. Yet hardly any of those who built the Vienna tradition were Viennese themselves, some not even Austrian.

Mozart came there on a visit from Salzburg with his employer, the Archbishop Hieronymus von Colloredo. The Archbishop sacked him, and got his unenviable place in history as the man who fired the most versatile composer who ever lived (he must have been, mustn't he? Those operas, symphonies, piano concertos, all that chamber music, crammed into a life that ended when he was only 35). And Mozart stayed in Vienna.

Beethoven came from the Rhineland, Haydn from Lower Austria, Brahms from Germany, Mahler from Bohemia, Bruckner from Upper Austria, Lehár from Hungary, Richard Strauss from Bavaria. Only Schubert and Johann Strauss II were Viennese-born.

So what were they doing there?

Vienna was the capital of the Habsburg empire, and it was an empire in which music ran strong. The aristocracy not only patronized it, giving employment and commissions to composers. Many of them were skilful musicians themselves. We owe much to those overlords. Let us be grateful for Beethoven's encouragement from the Archduke Rudolph, to Prince Lobkowitz for his patient support of Beethoven, to Prince Lichnowsky (in whose palace Beethoven astutely found lodgings when he arrived in Vienna), to Count Waldstein, to Count Rasoumovsky of the quartets, and those other noblemen who stand behind so much that has come down to us.

Stroll round Vienna, and it is fascinating to think of Beethoven walking there, hands thrust behind him, chin jutting out.

The stories of his deafness range from the comic to the sad. When conducting, he would crouch low in a quiet passage, then suddenly leap in the air for the *crescendo* he could not hear. At the end of the first performance of the *Ninth Symphony,* the ovation was tremendous. Then the mezzo soloist, Karolina Unger, realizing that he knew nothing of it, turned Beethoven round gently, and led him to the front of the platform so that he could see the audience on their feet, cheering and waving hats.

Never embarrass a Viennese policeman by asking where Beethoven lived. The list is too long. He moved all the time. But many of the places associated with him are easily tracked down. The Pasqualati House up on the Molkerbastei, where he wrote much of *Fidelio,* the fourth, fifth and sixth symphonies, has survived the march of time, and so have several others. The Kärntnertortheatre, where the *Ninth Symphony* was first heard, stood on the site now occupied by Sacher's of the delicious cakes, but the palace of Prince Lobkowitz, where the *Eroica Symphony* was first rehearsed, is much as it was in Beethoven's time.

Schubert haunts yield themselves less easily, but are there for the seeking. Many of his songs were written for those parties of artistic friends gathered around him, some for the baritone Johann Michael Vogl, sung perhaps just once or twice, then placed on one side. Yet they included many of the finest ever written. Some have never been recovered. How many gems as precious as *An die Musik, Erlkönig,* or *An Silvia* were among the manuscripts we are told were used to light a fire after his death? Some which had been discarded surfaced years later to become eternally popular. No other great composer can owe his fame today to so much music that came to light posthumously.

He never heard his *Symphony No. 9,* the great C major, today an essential in the repertory of any important orchestra. In rehearsal, the musicians of Vienna found it too difficult and it was withdrawn. Ten years after his death, Schubert's brother Ferdinand sent it to Schumann, who passed it on for Mendelssohn to give it in Leipzig in 1839. For years conductors were deterred by its length. When it was introduced to London, August Manns played for safety by spreading it over two evenings. And Vienna? They played it there at last in 1839, but only the first two movements were given, and they were separated by a Donizetti aria. The imagination wilts.

But strange things happened at concerts in Vienna in the first half of the 19th century. Nothing stranger than that which occurred at the first performance of Beethoven's *Violin Concerto* at the Theater an der Wien on December 23, 1806. Beethoven had been late finishing it, and Franz Clement played it from manuscript. It seems not to have upset him. For good measure, he threw in between the first two movements a sonata of his own played on one string with the violin held upside down.

They had prodigious appetites, too. What about the concert that was given in the same theater on December 22, 1808? It contained what today would be called the world premieres of Beethoven's *Symphony No. 5,* his *Pastoral Symphony,* and his *Piano Concerto No. 4.* Has any single concert ever bequeathed so much music destined to be universally loved?

For the discovery of Schubert's *Unfinished Symphony* we move to Graz in Styria. In 1865, the Viennese conductor Johann Herbeck went there to inquire if Anselm Hüttenbrunner, once a friend of Schubert's, had any of Schubert's manuscripts. The tired old man rummaged in a chest, and produced a mass of papers. Herbeck saw among them a symphony in B minor. "Take it" said Anselm. "There's no hurry to return it." And that is how what is one of the best-known of all symphonies came to light 37 years after its composer's death.

Of all the composers who died young, Schubert is most to be mourned. He was only 31, and his last works show a face turned resolutely forward. As it was, the mantle of succession to Beethoven fell on Brahms. A realist in all things, he accepted the fact, but was cautious about admitting it. "I shall never compose a symphony" he wrote to a friend. "You have no conception of how the likes of us feel when we hear the tramp of a giant like Beethoven behind us." But his first symphony proclaimed that the tradition would go on.

Musical Establishments

I never sit in Vienna's Musikverein without stealing a glance at the balcony and visualizing the scene that day, March 7, 1897, when the Vienna Philharmonic played Brahms's *Symphony No. 4.* Death was already waiting for him, and the Brahms who limped to the front of the artist's box was shrunken and haggard, the hair hanging lank. He bowed slowly to the cheering audience, and walked slowly away. Within a month he was dead, but he had carried away the adoration of an audience who knew they would never see him again.

But the Viennese have not always been kind. They were slow to recognize the genius of Bruckner, and have often given a rough time to composers or musicians on whom they at first lavished acclamation. Mahler, who arrived as conductor of the Court Opera (now the Vienna State) in 1897, brought about numerous reforms, built a brilliant ensemble, and gave Vienna a golden decade which is still discussed. But he made enemies, and worn out by intrigues, eventually left for America.

Neither have the Viennese always been shrewd judges of imported music. Musical history is littered with examples of works which flopped with a resounding thud then bounced back to popularity to the embarrassment of the original critics. The first performance of the Tchaikovsky *Violin Concerto* took place in Vienna at a Philharmonic concert on December 4, 1881, with Adolf Brodsky as soloist. There was much hissing, and Eduard Hanslick, the leading Viennese critic of the time, stalked from the hall to describe the concerto as "stinking in the ear." Wrote Hanslick "We see wild and vulgar faces, we hear curses, we smell bad brandy." But there are not many surer crowd-pullers today.

We have begun to mention the famous Viennese musical institutions, and it is time to consider them in more detail.

The Vienna State Opera is more than just a theater. It is a visual symbol of Vienna's pride in its own status and achievements. They say that when it burned after the bombing of March 13, 1945, hundreds of people who had never ventured inside wept in the streets. To them, it *was* Vienna.

The theater had a chequered early career. It owed its existence to the foresight of the Emperor Franz Josef and his ministers who demolished the walls surrounding the inner city to make way for a wide boulevard fringed by splendid buildings. One of these was to be a new opera house. A competition for the design was won by Eduard van der Null and August Siccard von Siccardsburg. But things were going badly for Austria at this time, and both the expense of the new opera house and its design were useful targets for attack. Eduard van der Null hung himself, and Siccardsburg died of a stroke soon after.

But the theater was soon famous. First Richter, then Mahler brought standards to the height of perfection. And despite the ruin of World War I, the Vienna State Opera (as the former Vienna Court Opera now became), enjoyed another golden era in the 1920s with singers like Slezak, Mayr, Lehmann, Schumann and Tauber. The political events of the 1930s, then World War II, took their toll, and in 1944, with the Allies fighting in Normandy, it was decided that the theater should not re-open for the next season. The following year, it lay in ruins. The last opera performed there, prophetically, had been *Götterdämerung*. Yet when it was re-built, a new generation of great singers ushered in another golden era. Mahler had once declared that tradition was slovenliness, but on a night when everything is going well at the Vienna State, one is conscious of the best that tradition implies, something handed down.

The Volksoper is to operetta what the Staatsoper is to opera. And this is the point at which to emphasise that operetta is not just a junior branch of opera. Thank heavens, this truth, which the Austrians have always understood, is now generally accepted in civilized musical circles throughout the world. As works of art, as examples of musical-theater craftsmanship, operettas like *The Merry Widow, Die Fledermaus* and *The Gipsy Baron* stand infinitely higher than some of the operas through which, as a critic, I am often condemned to sit. And it cannot be a coincidence that the finest singers of Viennese operetta have always been the greatest Mozart singers, the greatest Schubert *lieder* singers. The genuine operetta sound, stylish and cultured, descends in the same line. One thinks of Schumann and Tauber in the past, Schwarzkopf in our own time.

But somehow, I feel always that where the ghosts of the Vienna tradition walk most surely is the Theater an der Wien. Schikaneder, that remarkable showman who was Papageno in the first production of *The Magic Flute* in 1791, built it soon after and it was under his management when *Fidelio* was first performed there. Beethoven lived in it for a while, and as we have seen, much of his music was first heard there.

Its succeeding history is colorful. Barbaia, the former waiter who once managed Naples's San Carlo Theatre where a share of the profits of the royal gaming tables was written into his contract, was one manager. Another was Count Palffy, who hit on a shrewd money-making scheme. He decided to raffle the theater, with the proviso that if the winner did not want it, he could have 300,000 gulden instead. A countryman won, and decided to take the cash, which meant that the Count had made a handsome financial profit and still kept the theatre. But the winner had, if not an outright last laugh, at least a farewell chuckle. He insisted on being paid in 20 gulden pieces. The last we hear of him is setting off for home with the coins loaded on a wagon, and accompanied by an escort of police for safety.

Operetta gave the Theater an der Wien a splendid epoch much later in the 19th century. Offenbach brought his French operettas to Vienna in 1863, triumphed, and the Viennese just had to find an answer. They found it in the enchanting works of Zeller, Millöcker, Suppé, and in particular Johann Strauss II, already famous throughout the world as the Waltz King. Many of the most famous Viennese operettas were first given at the Theater an der Wien, among them *Die Fledermaus* (1874), *The Gipsy Baron* (1885) and *Waldmeister* (1895) all by Johann. As the century died, it seemed that operetta in Vienna would die with it, as first one then another of its composers passed away, Suppé in 1895, Zeller in 1898, Johann Strauss in 1899. Millöcker just failed to make the new century, dying on December 31, 1899.

Then in 1905, Lehár's *The Merry Widow* opened at the Theater an der Wien. Lehár was not the first choice, and picked up the libretto only after others had turned it down. Neither did it succeed at first. But its eventual popularity led to an operetta revival, and paved the way for a new generation of composers, among whom Kalman, with *The Gipsy Princess* (1915) and *Countess Maritza* (1924) and Oscar Strauss with *A Waltz Dream* (1907) were important. Today, Viennese operetta is enjoying success with a new audience, who are finding its eloquent tunes and insinuating rhythms a delightful experience.

The Theater an der Wien has been beautifully restored to look as it did in Beethoven's time. It plays a major role in the annual Vienna Festival. One of the most memorable nights of my life was spent listening to *Fidelio* on the stage where it was first played, on the very night of the 200th anniversary of the composer's birth.

The Vienna Philharmonic, that other radiant jewel in the Austrian musical crown, has a double function, spending part of its time playing for the Vienna State Opera, and giving its regular symphony concerts in the Musikverein on Sunday mornings. Its identifying characteristic (every great orchestra has one) is the beauty of its string tone. It was formed by Nicolai (of *The Merry Wives of Windsor*) in 1842.

Music in the Blood

In Austria, music is for delight as well as inspiration. The statue of Johann Strauss II in the Stadtpark tells all. To see him, violin tucked under the chin, is to imagine those infectious waltzes, *Wine, Women and Song, Voices of Spring,* and best of them all, the *Emperor.* But quite possibly you will not need to imagine them. Somewhere in the distance, an orchestra will be playing them, somewhere heads will be swaying, feet will be tapping. Johann wrote a waltz called *Wiener Blut,* but he might just as well have called it Austrian Blood, for music is in the blood of all the people, whether it echoes from *Don Giovanni* at the State Opera or the Viennese waltzes it gave to the world.

Johann was a fine musician (though he thought his brother Josef was a better one) and worked some adventurous things into his programs. On the night he lay dying, his orchestra was giving an openair concert, and someone tip-toed up to the stand to whisper to the leader. The orchestra stopped, then started to play, very quietly, *The Blue Danube.* And Vienna knew the waltz king had died.

The Vienna Festival takes place in May and June. They call it the festival of 1,000 performances. Into this shop window, Vienna puts the best that Austria can offer as well as playing host to orchestras, opera companies, ballets and famous musicians from all over the world.

Then there is that other Viennese specialty. On a fine evening, seek out the taverns of Grinzing or Heiligenstadt. As the shadows deepen and the lights appear under the trees, a quartet will start to play *Schrammelmusik,* those sentimental, nostalgic songs peculiar to Vienna. Sip the new wine, enjoy the cold meats served with it, and do what the Viennese do. Relax and just let it happen.

But this is starting to look as though music in Austria is mostly a Viennese experience. It is not, but the point is that all the thriving musical life you will find in the provinces somehow flows from the Viennese source. Neither should it be assumed that music in Austria lives entirely in the past. After all, Vienna is where Schönberg, Berg and Webern started the atonal revolution from which few seriously creative composers have been able to escape uninfluenced since.

The Salzburg Festival represents everything that is splendid in its preservation of the operas of Mozart in the city of his birth, and holds a mirror every year to Austria's orchestral heritage. But even Salzburg finds room for experiment. This is where Henze's *The Bassarids* first appeared in 1966, and where Friedrich Cerha's *Baal* had its world premiere in 1981. Cerha's great contribution, of course, has been to complete Berg's unfinished *Lulu.* In 1971, the Vienna Festival brought out Gottfried von Einem's *The Visit of the Old Lady,* one of the more successful new operas of recent years.

But the crowds who throng Salzburg at festival time are mostly there to honor tradition. Mozart's music must be one of the biggest revenue earners the Austrians have. There are nights when one watches the crowds pouring over the bridge across the Salzach on their way, perhaps, to *Cosi Fan Tutte* or *The Marriage of Figaro;* nights when one sees the coaches lined up outside the best hotels to take visitors to the festival theaters, or notes tickets changing hands at black market prices, sees the shops stocked with Mozart souvenirs, and then the cruel irony strikes home. The reason for it, the reason this lovely city is packed with visitors, went to a pauper's grave.

Salzburg and Vienna, they lead the world's festivals. But Austria teems with festivals. Many with contrasted themes. Graz, in October, is about the future. The names I see on the program in front of me are Kagel, Ligeti, Cerha.

The Austrians are skilled at calling up nature to help with the staging. The Bregenz Festival, tucked into that corner of the Vorarlberg where the borders of Austria, Germany and Switzerland tumble over each other, uses a floating stage on Lake Constance, whose shores house the openair audience. The sky darkens, the moon rises, the lights of Lindau on the German shore twinkle, a steamer glides in the distance, and it is all romance—aquatic opera under the stars. Linz, in the early autumn, naturally exploits its proud association with Bruckner, who was at one time organist in the city's cathedral.

Somehow, in Austria, everything seems to come back to music. Who can visit the Burgenland without recalling Haydn and his almost 30 years' service for Prince Nicholas Esterhazy, surely one of the happiest patron-composer relationships in all music? The mountains of the Tirol somehow suggest the proud peaks of a Bruckner symphony, a leisured moment in a Viennese coffee house the nonchalant near-sentimentality of a Schubert impromptu, a picnic by a Carinthian lake the prospect of Brahms sketching a symphony during one of those working holidays he so enjoyed there, a stroll through the park at Bad Ischl, beloved of Lehar, prompts in the mind a tune that really belongs to Hanna Glawari.

It was in a tavern in the Burgenland that I congratulated the waitress, cheerful, fresh in her local costume, on the quality of a meal. She thought. "Austrian cooking" she said "is a symphony in a frying pan." Now, I wonder where she read that. But the remark told a story. In Austria, search for a metaphor and you are bound to come up with something musical.

EATING THE AUSTRIAN WAY

Schlagobers Supreme

In the course of centuries, Slavs, Turks, Italians, Magyars and, of course, Germans, all flourished within the immediate homeland of the Habsburgs. It might be reasonable to suppose that Austria, the inheritor of the remnants of the Empire, would have a cuisine composed of all these varied and exotic elements, fused into one great big cosmopolitan gastronomic United Nations. But it doesn't work out like that. It is true that you will encounter Hungarian restaurants, Balkan restaurants, Italian restaurants, even Russian restaurants in Vienna and other important cities of Austria, but during their long residence in Austria, the various exotic schools of cooking have become Austrianized. Asperities have been smoothed away, exaggerations toned down, and the gamut of tastes brought into harmony. But the chief contribution of the people who created the Viennese waltz and the operetta naturally comes with the dessert course, in the appropriate form of rich and luscious pastries, and in the beloved and universal *Schlagobers* or whipped cream.

This means that the visitor to Austria, while he will be able to enjoy a wide range of international dishes, need not fear that his palate or his stomach will be attacked by fiery or pungent concoctions. He will be able to order without fear anything he discovers on the menu. He will certainly find it advisable to watch his weight, however, because Austrian food is filling, rich, and copious. The portions may strike visitors from countries of less hearty eaters as enormous. But if the new arrival, eating his first meal, is under the impression that he is being so well served because he has stumbled on the one substantial repast of the day, with perhaps a little minor help on a couple of other occasions, he will be quite wrong. Austrians not only eat a lot at one time, they eat a good many times during the day.

Pastry Shops

In case of a feeling of faintness between meals (and in case any time is being wasted between meals), one can always dart into one of the *Konditorei* or pastry shops so numerous in Austria, or the milk and *espresso* bars, now fairly widespread, for a life-preserving snack. The pastry shop *is* thoroughly Austrian. Other countries have pastry shops, but they aren't the same and they don't play so important a role in the daily life of the citizen. A visit to a famous pastry shop, like Demel's on the Kohlmarkt in Vienna, or Zauner's in Bad Ischl, is a must. Both of these shops achieved their fame as imperial court caterers and so far have succeeded in preserving their quality in spite of contemporary difficulties in finding the staff to carry on the pastrycook's delicate art. Many pastry shops do not confine their temptations to pastries alone. They also offer sandwiches, vegetable soufflés, mushrooms stuffed with a herb and cheese mixture, in fact all manner of heavenly tidbits.

All-Purpose Coffeehouses

To savor the atmosphere of the coffeehouses you must take your time. In Vienna you have a wide choice of these establishments; set aside an afternoon, a morning, or at least a couple of hours, and settle down in one of your choice. You can read (many coffeehouses carry not only Austrian papers and magazines but a few English or American ones) or you can catch up on letter writing. There is no need to worry about outstaying one's welcome, even over a single small cup of Mokka.

The decline of the coffeehouse has fortunately been halted, and even reversed. They represent a way of life that is once more sought-after: many coffeehouses are being refurbished and new ones are opening.

The Austrian coffeehouse has a lengthy history. When the Turkish invaders were driven out of Vienna in 1683 they left behind some mysterious brown beans. A former Austrian spy in the Turkish camp learned how to use them. Thus coffee was introduced to Austria, and the first coffeehouse established. This was a momentous moment, for a substantial part of Austrian social life revolves around the coffeehouses. They are scattered all over the nation. They are the club, pub and bistro all rolled into one. They are the places where one meets business associates, relaxes over the paper and generally finds a home from home.

Coffee is not just coffee in Austria. It comes in many forms and under many names. Morning coffee is generally *Melange* (half coffee and half milk), or with little milk, a *Brauner*. The usual afterdinner drink is *Mokka*, very black, and most Austrians like it heavily sweetened. But that is just the beginning. Some restaurants, notably those specializing in Balkan cookery, serve Turkish coffee (*Türkischer*), a strong, thick brew. There is usually considerable sediment in the bottom of the cup, which should not be stirred, and the coffee is often served with a square of Turkish Delight.

More delightful to Western eyes are the coffee-and-whipped-cream combinations (*Kaffee mit Schlag*), but these are tastes that are easily acquired and a menace to all but the very thin. The coffee may be either hot or cold. A customer who wants more whipped cream than coffee asks for a *Doppelschlag*. Hot black coffee in a glass with one knob of whipped cream is an *Einspänner* (one-horse coach). Then you can go to town on a *Mazagran*, black coffee with ice and a tot of rum, or *Eiskaffee*, cold coffee with ice cream, whipped cream and biscuits. Or you can simply order a *Portion Kaffee* and have an honest pot of coffee and jug of hot milk. As you can see, coffee-drinking is a life's work.

The Restaurant Scene

As in any large cosmopolitan community, you can dine in Vienna in an atmosphere of luxury with perfect service and delicious food, including not only the best of Austrian cooking but beautifully prepared foods from other lands. In Vienna, you can also find a tasty meal for a comparatively modest sum. In the larger cities, such as Graz and Innsbruck, there is a similar selection of eating places, although on a smaller scale and with lower prices generally. Out in the country—except in the fashionable tourist resorts—you may enjoy good, modest meals at still lower prices.

The one thing that is common to restaurants throughout the country, whether they are pricey Viennese ones or simple country inns, is that they have a great deal of character, friendliness and atmosphere. This is partly due to the fact that the Austrians have preserved a lot of ceremony and the niceties of social etiquette in their lives, with the result that the rate of change has been much slower in Austria than in many other parts of Europe. But something of a revolution has been taking place in Vienna and to a lesser extent outside. Many new restaurants are opening and new ways of presenting old dishes have been developed with varying success. Emphasis has been placed on local dishes. The Austrian National Tourist Office encouraged restaurants to offer traditional meals, characteristic of their region, and they responded enthusiastically. But, to repeat a point made elsewhere, these local dishes were originally cooked on farms for hard-working hands who needed both sustenance and bulk in their diet— so they tend to be both hearty and rich. You might want to have a schnapps afterwards to help the digestion!

Consult the restaurant guides (first and foremost *Gault Millau Österreich*, if you can cope with German) and restaurant columns in the daily papers.

Don't leave paying the bill till the last minute; Austrian headwaiters are never in a hurry to collect your money. It is customary to add a tip of up to 10% to the final total.

Austrian Specialties

One of the best food buys in Austria is soup, which is consistently good—and inexpensive. Austrian soups range all the way from the highly seasoned *Gulyassuppe*, full of paprika and onions, to mild consommé with a poached egg. Particularly popular with Austrians and visitors is the *Leberknödlsuppe*, a meat broth containing liver dumplings. It contains less calories for the weight-conscious than the many other delicious noodle soups.

Having no seacoast, Austria is naturally not fish country, except for the freshwater varieties. Carp, Fogosch, pike and, best of all, succulent crawfish (when in season, which is rather short) and various trout from the native lakes and rivers are the best bet. Carp is an insipid-tasting fish to those used to the lively savor of the deep sea. Pike and Fogosch come from the Danube and the lakes on the Hungarian border and are often excellent when grilled or fried, much like pike and bass. The crawfish (called Krebs) look like tiny lobsters and make a delicious thick soup in many restaurants. Or they are served cold to be laboriously picked from their shells and dipped in mayonnaise.

Austrian brook trout and rainbow trout are delicious. The most popular way of serving them is "blue," the whole fish boiled in a *court bouillon* and accompanied by drawn butter. Or try it *Müllerin*—sautéed in butter to a crisp brown. In summer try cold smoked trout for a delicate entrée.

If you happen to be in Austria on Ash Wednesday, don't miss a *Hering-schmaus*. On this the strictest fast-day in the church calendar, the Austrians adhere to it by eating no meat. Instead, just about every restaurant holds the above-named feast—a buffet packed with every fish and salad specialty imaginable.

Schnitzels and Other Meat Dishes

Veal and beef dominate the Austrian kitchen, though the various types of schnitzel can also be pork. *Wiener Schnitzel* is usually veal steak, well beaten, dipped in flour, egg and crumbs and fried, usually in deep fat, to golden brown crunchiness. *Natur Schnitzel* is fried as it is, without egg or crumbs. *Holstein Schnitzel* is the same, plus a fried egg on the meat and crossed anchovy strips on the egg. *Pariser Schnitzel* is dipped in flour and egg and fried. There are many other types of schnitzel and related veal specialties. One of the best is *Cordon Bleu:* cheese and ham are rolled in a piece of veal, the whole is dipped as above and fried. *Paprikaschnitzel* is also good.

Pork is highly popular and also less expensive than veal. There's plain roast pork with potatoes or *Knödeln* (dumplings like doughy cannonballs); special cuts like *Schweinscarré,* or a long tender strip from beside the backbone called *Schweinsjungfrau* ("pig's virgin," if you must be literal), and such specialties as pig's shank, kidneys, and a great variety of smoked pork dishes.

Austrians don't care much for lamb, but it is now more widely available than a few years ago. However, venison (*Rehrücken*) and numerous other game dishes (wild boar, hare, pheasant, quail, partridge) are popular and usually served with cranberries. Some of these game dishes are of considerable antiquity, even medieval, and have vanished from the tables of most Western countries.

Steaks are usually good in Austria. Note that the odd word *Lungenbra-ten* may be used to denote what is also called *Filet.* Ask for your steak *durch* (well done), *medium* (medium rare) or *Englisch* (rare).

Austrian *Tafelspitz* (boiled beef) is famous, and deservedly so. It is prepared by being put into boiling water and simmered for about two hours, until it is well cooked. With it come various sauces, a bland sauce, like a thin hollandaise, flavored with chives; and more tangy sauces of grated horseradish, or horseradish and apple which are combined raw and allowed to fuse into a delicious form of dynamite. *Röstkartoffeln* (roasted sliced potatoes) are usually served with the beef, and sometimes a number of other vegetables.

At the other end of the taste gamut is *Gulyas* (goulash), of Hungarian origin, made with beef—or best of all, venison. Highly seasoned, it is usually served with potatoes. Reminiscent of the New England boiled dinner is *Bauernschmaus,* a tasty meat dish of the folksy type. It varies from restaurant to restaurant but usually includes ham, a piece of salt pork, sausage, sauerkraut, and a large dumpling.

Sausage and Chicken

Austrian sausages are excellent. If you want to try a sampling of a number of different varieties, you can order a sausage platter, and you will be given a generous selection of cold sliced sausages. Frankfurters, named after a Viennese butcher, are excellent and are called *Wieners* almost everywhere—*except* in Vienna.

Austrian cuisine offers two superb chicken dishes: *Backhuhn* or *Backhendl,* young, medium-sized chicken breaded and fried in deep fat until it is golden brown; and *Steirisches Brathuhn,* roast chicken, usually turned on a spit. Vienna is believed to be the home territory of the Backhendl, while Styria, where the best chickens in Austria are raised, is the home of the Brathuhn, also called *Poulard.*

The Knödl is an Austrian institution. It leads both rice and potatoes in popularity, but not by much. There is an infinite variety of this dough dish. One group includes the homely hearty unsweetened type, the dumpling, which appears with meat or goes into soup. Then there are the smaller, more delicate sweet ones, eaten as dessert, flavored with jam, poppy seed, cottage cheese, and other unusual ingredients.

There are also fine cheeses, the best of which is the Vorarlberg Farmhouse *Bergkäse* from the villages of the Bregenzerwald.

Vegetables and Bread

Although Austria is not famous for vegetable cookery, it has several delightful specialties. Puréed spinach (*Spinat*) is cooked spinach, chopped and flavored with butter, salt, garlic, perhaps a bit of flour, and a little cream. *Rotkraut* (red cabbage), made sweet-sour and flavored with caraway seed is also good. Mushrooms, fried to a delicious crispness in the manner of Wiener Schnitzel, are not uncommon in better restaurants. Stuffed green peppers and stuffed cabbage in tomato sauce are contributions of Hungarian and Balkan cooking to the Austrian menu.

A fairly good green salad, generally lettuce with a vinegar and oil dressing, usually somewhat sweetened, is served almost anywhere. If you don't like sugar in your salad dressing, say so when you order. A popular alternative, which may or may not please English and American palates, is a *Gemischter Salat,* a dab of several cooked and raw vegetables—not mixed greens as in the States and England; these dabs are neatly arranged in a ring on a plate—a bit of kraut, chopped beets, shredded lettuce, etc. *Slaw,* or cabbage salad, is popular, with a vinegar dressing.

Bread is crisp and excellent, perhaps the best in the world. It will pay any visitor making a long stay to go to a *Bäckerei* (bakery), sample some of the fine breads, and see which ones suit their particular taste. Incidentally, bread and sweet cakes or pastries are not generally made in the same bakery, as they are in the States or in England. You buy fine *Torten,* which are extremely rich cakes, only in pastry shops, never in bakeries. Also, let no unwary visitor look at his pocket dictionary and order *Kuchen,* expecting to receive a beautiful piece of iced, many-layered cake. What he will probably get is a sort of coffee cake or sweet roll, which often turns up as dessert in Austria.

Semmels and salt sticks and the like are commonly served with meals, along with dark rye bread of various types. Wholemeal bread is to be found in every bakery.

Cheese

After years in the doldrums, the Austrian cheese industry has accepted the challenge posed by massive imports, and a wide variety of all sorts of cheeses, carefully made in small quantities, is beginning to come onto the market. Most famous is the Vorarlberg mountain cheese made from raw milk fresh from the Alm. It's a must for cheese lovers.

All About Desserts

And now the desserts—those fabulous desserts! It is impossible to choose the best, for there are so many wonderful sweets, but perhaps the best known is *Strudel.* There are many kinds of strudel, most of them made with fruit, a few with cheese. There are apple strudel, cottage cheese strudel, cherry strudel, strudel made with fruit and nuts, strudel made with fruit and nuts and raisins—and a most delicious Pannonian variety with apples, raisins and poppy seeds, available only in Burgenland.

Palatschinken, thin dessert pancakes, are a distant relative of the French crêpes. They are rolled around a stuffing of fruit, jam, nuts, or other delicious tidbits. *Salzburger Nockerl* is one of the most famous Austrian desserts. It is a delicious soufflé of eggs, sugar, butter, and a bit of flour. Pick your restaurant carefully for this tasty item and don't hurry the chef. It's worth waiting for.

Kaiserschmarren, meaning imperial fluff, is a thicker pancake than the Palatschinken at the beginning of its preparation, but as it is shredded during the cooking process before it becomes quite firm, and is dusted with sugar and served with stewed fruit (mainly plums called *Zwetschkenröster*), it doesn't look anything like a pancake.

Torte is an Austrian specialty and may be very good or very poor. The most famous is the *Sachertorte,* created at the Sacher Hotel in Vienna nearly a hundred years ago. It is a very rich chocolate cake iced with more chocolate. Compare *Sachertorte* from the Sacher Hotel, with apricot jam in the middle, with *Sacher Torte* from Demel's; they put the apricot jam just below the icing! The use of this renowned name was the subject of a much-publicized trial, which came to a decision worthy of Solomon, that the original article should be spelled as one word, those others using the similar recipe must use two words.

Other names in the Torte world are *Dobosch,* hazelnut, *Linzer, Malakoff.* If these rich desserts are too much for the visitor, he may want to try *Guglhupf,* a fine-textured sponge cake, good with coffee. A popular specialty is the *Krapfen,* which used to turn up during Fasching (the Carnival season) and is now available all year. It is a relative of the jam-filled doughnut of Britain, but better, because it is fluffier and crisper.

Characteristic Viennese confections are *Marillenknödel* and *Zwetschkenknödel* made from apricots and plums from which the stones are re-

moved and replaced by lumps of sugar, after which the fruit is wrapped
in a light potato-flour dough and boiled before being rolled in buttered
breadcrumbs. Then there are the yeast dumplings filled with plum jam
(*Powidl*) rolled in poppy seeds and sugar—order just one, the size may
surprise you. And *Powidltatschkerl* (more difficult to pronounce than to
eat), thin potato dough triangles enclosing again plum jam, this time rolled
in breadcrumbs with hot butter and sugar.

A Small Glossary of Specifically Austrian Food Terms:

Ananas	can mean strawberries as well as pineapple
Erdäpfel	potatoes
Faschiertes	minced meat
Fisolen	green beans
Karfiol	cauliflower
Kohlsprossen	brussels sprouts
Marille	apricot
Paradeiser	tomatoes
Schlagobers	whipped cream
Stelze	leg of pork

AUSTRIA'S WINES

Treading the Wine Road

by
NICHOLAS ALLEN

Nicholas Allen is an Englishman, resident in Vienna for more than 20 years, who heads a scheme that takes English-language plays (Thornton Wilder's among them) to schools throughout the country. He knows the highways and byways—especially the byways—of Austria as only someone who spends every winter struggling with avalanches and village inns can.

The cultivation of grapes and the making of wine can be traced in Austria back to Celtic times, even before the Romans arrived. Despite many setbacks over the long centuries winemaking has continued to be a major industry right up to the present day with 250,000 people at work in some 50,000 wineries to produce an average of 3 million hectoliters of wine a year.

Vines have the tendency to thrive in beautiful surroundings and, as attractive buildings and towns often develop close to vineyards, a journey through any wine region can be an alluring prospect. Luckily, Austria has been largely neglected by the "experts," and its deliciously fresh wines will form an ideal treasure-trove to reward those who enjoy drinking wine and dislike the all-too-frequent nonsense that goes with it. One of the things that can impede the easy enjoyment of wine and its creation is the aura of mystique which so often surrounds it, the do's and don't's which have more to do with snobbery than with a love of wine.

This chapter describes a journey that loops through Austria's wine country, one that will give you plenty of chance to sample the changing landscape as well as the varieties of wine. Many of the towns you will pass through are mentioned in other chapters, so the concentration here is on the wine itself. But before starting out, it is worth relaying some basic information about Austrian wine, to provide a background.

Starting with the Romans

Not long after the Roman emperor Domitian had banned the making of wine outside Italy (around 90 A.D.)—an edict that proved hard to enforce—another emperor, Probus, took the more sensible line of encouraging winemaking throughout the empire. He did so particularly in Austria, where the Danube vineyards date back to his time.

Another emperor—Charlemagne—of what had, by then, become the Holy Roman Empire, ordered the bishoprics and monasteries in his lands to oversee the making of wine, thus ensuring continuity through difficult times. To this day there are many monasteries involved in the making of wine in Austria.

Winemaking wasn't easy in those early days. In 1456 the vintage was so sour that the emperor of the time ordered it to be poured into the rivers. In Vienna, however, he decreed that the undrinkable crop be used to mix the mortar for the tower of St. Stephen's Cathedral. It is a miracle that the finished result is not like the Tower of Pisa.

Governments have always been in need of money and they quickly realized that wine was a good source of tax income. During the 16th century the Bavarians evaded these taxes by making—and drinking—more and more beer instead of wine. The Austrians, however, remained faithful to wine and have done so to the present day.

The 19th century spelled disaster everywhere. Phylloxera killed the vines throughout Europe and it took well into the 20th century before new, resistant vines were established and bearing in their place. Then came World War I which left Austria an amputated shadow of its former self. Half its vineyards disappeared behind new boundaries and were lost to other countries forever.

During the 1920s the economic stability of Austria's wine industry was ensured by the development of the *Hochkultur*. Professor Lenz Moser from Krems had the idea of training vines on stakes and letting them leaf and flower at a height of 3–4 feet; this made cultivation, protection, and harvesting much easier and also increased the yield.

During Hitler's Third Reich Austrian wine was submerged into the German wine industry, so it was not until 1955—with the signing of the State Treaty—that the Austrian wine industry was ready to begin the upward course which has continued to the present day.

The "anti-freeze" scandals of 1985 were a big setback for the Austrian wine industry. However, the nation has risen to the occasion, introducing some of the strictest legislation in the world to ensure that such things won't happen again. It is worth pointing out that not one winery on our journey, and not one wine mentioned in this chapter, has been even remotely involved, and that even at the height of the scandal at least 95% of Austrian wines were blameless. By 1988 the beneficial effects of these measures had become apparent. Austrian wines are better than ever before and represent good value for high quality and great variety. Rebuilding its international image will be a long process, but an impressive start has been made by the Austrian wine industry.

A Red and White Dossier

Austrian wines are fresh and usually drunk young. Economics and local preference have led people to underestimate these wines' ability to age and mature. Austrian winemakers tend to let their wines ferment through until there is little residual sugar left; this makes them very different from their sweeter German cousins.

Until recently only the white wines have been of any interest, but in the last ten years there has been a major development leading to some red wines of quality. Winemakers in Austria face the opposite problem to that of their Californian colleagues: in California the steady hot climate leads to magnificent red wines and whites that can easily be too full and heavy, while in Austria the raw climate leads to crisp, clean white wines but to reds that often lack body and roundness. Over recent years there has been a marked trend towards maturing red wines in small oak barrels (*barriques*), thus producing wines with a higher tannin content and more body. These wines take longer to mature but the results are already proving to be wines that are far more complex and interesting.

Here is a list of the seven "types" of wine you may encounter on the wine-road trip:

Tafel- or *Land-wein*—table wine, of Austrian grapes, usually served open and good to "quaff."

Qualitätswein—wine of a specific region and grape conforming to certain standards. Quality wine must be "harmonious" and "typical."

Kabinett—quality wine with no sugar added during fermentation.

Spätlese—late-gathered grapes give rise to a rich, powerful wine which, unlike its German equivalent, need not be sweet.

Auslese—a wine made from late-gathered grapes that have been individually sorted for quality before being crushed.

Beerenauslese—grapes that have been left on the vine to become raisin-like. Attacked by *noble-rot* these grapes are then made into magnificent dessert wines equal to the great Sauternes.

Eiswein—grapes picked when frozen by December frosts. This specialty, found in the Burgenland, is savored drop by drop.

These are the principal grapes found in Austrian wine:

White: *Grüner Veltliner*—a sturdy wine which accounts for 30% of vines in Austria. Particularly at home in lower Austria it can, if cultivated for quality rather than quantity produce great white wines. They are dry, with touch of fruit, fresh to the taste often with a "peppery" aftertaste. This grape is unique to Austria.

Müller Thurgau—a Riesling Sylvaner cross that produces mild rather uninteresting wines.

Welschriesling—found in Burgenland and Styria this grape gives wines of great elegance when allowed to be really dry.

Pinot blanc—the French White Burgundy grape is being planted extensively with good results. When not too heavy the wines have exceptional aroma. Several growers are experimenting with the Chardonnay grape, noble cousin to pinot blanc.

Neuburger—legend has it that in 1860 two growers found this vine floating down the Danube as driftwood. They planted it near Dürnstein and ever since it has produced beautiful wines of a nutty quality; some are dry, some less so.

Rheinriesling—as in Germany, this noblest of all white wine grapes produces superb, dry white wines that mature for many years. At its best in the Wachau.

Muscat Ottonel—a difficult vine that produces delightful muscat-flavoured wines. They range from dry in the Wachau to sweet in the Burgenland.

Zierfandler and Rotgipfler—the two grapes at the heart of the world-famous Gumpoldskirchner wines. Rich, heady and lasting.

Red: *Blauer Portugieser*—when not used for mass wines these can be distinguished. At its best round Retz.

Blaufränkisch—introduced from Franconia at the time of Charlemagne, this is the grape of the Burgenland where many of Austria's finest red wines are produced. At their best these are full, dry and with enough tang to make them interesting.

Blauburgunder—the Pinot Noir from Burgundy also produces good wines but the climate makes it impossible for them ever to come close to the French cousins.

Zweigelt and St. Laurent—two specifically Austrian cross-breeds that can occasionally produce surprising results.

Blauer Wildbacher—a grape unique for hundreds of years to a small corner of West Styria. It produces the wine called *Schilcher*.

These two lists form the basis of the great variety which is Austrian wine; it is hardly known outside the country because both wineries and their output are usually too small to make export and wide marketing viable propositions. This makes it all the more exciting to set off on a journey of discovery.

The journey I am going to suggest is a personal one; it leaves many gaps along the way for the traveler to discover for himself. After all, what is more fun than that wine you—and only you—have unearthed from a small grower in a tiny village—. But before launching on the journey, here are a couple of points to bear in mind.

Always ask on the spot about the vintage: in a climate as varied and as unstable as Austria's there can be great regional differences from year to year. Wine lists in restaurants are now much more informative and extensive, and wine waiters will usually be eager to help you.

Stop wherever you feel interested: no matter whether it is a vineyard or a cellar, a private house or a co-operative, a gasthaus or the smartest restaurant. Those involved, be they in the Seewinkel or in Dürnstein will be pleased to show you around, talk to you, let you taste their wines and maybe at the end of it all even sell you the odd bottle that will surprise your friends back home.

The Wine Trail Begins

The journey starts in Spitz an oder Donau. You could take the West-autobahn from Vienna as far as Melk and, after looking at the famous

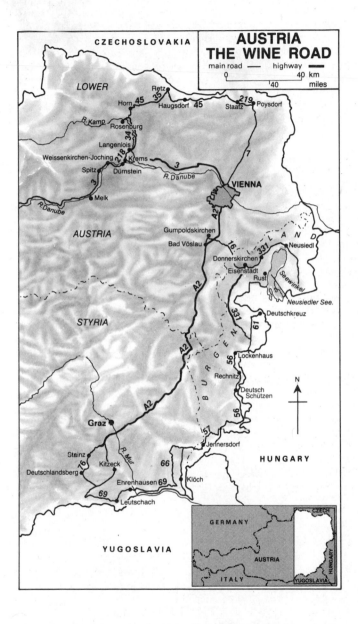

AUSTRIA
THE WINE ROAD
main road —— highway ▬▬
0   40 km
40   miles

CZECHOSLOVAKIA

LOWER

Retz
Horn 45   35
R. Kamp Haugsdorf 45   219 Poysdorf
Rosenburg   Staatz
Langenlois 218 34
Weissenkirchen-Joching Krems 3   7
Spitz Dürnstein
Melk R. Danube
3
R. Danube VIENNA

AUSTRIA

A21

Gumpoldskirchen L A N D
Bad Vöslau 16 331 Neusiedl
Donnerskirchen
Eisenstadt Seewinkel
Rust Neusiedler See.
A2
Deutschkreuz
STYRIA 331
61
B U R G E N
A21 56 Lockenhaus
Rechnitz
56 Deutsch
N Schützen
A2 56
57

Graz

Stainz R. Mur Jennersdorf HUNGARY
76 Kitzeck
Deutschlandsberg 66 Klöch
Ehrenhausen 69
69 Leutschach

GERMANY CZECH
AUSTRIA
YUGOSLAVIA ITALY YUGOSLAVIA HUNGARY

monastery, cross the Danube by the magnificent new bridge. On the other side you join Route 3 and drive 16 km. (10 miles) downstream to Spitz. Villages with ancient churches nestle against the slopes and where there aren't vines there are apricot trees. A drive along this road at blossom-time (usually late April) is unforgettable. Come back in August and eat your fill of golden apricots bought at the roadside.

The vineyards begin at Spitz. Here the Danube valley is high and narrow, reminiscent of the Rhine. The wise Roman Emperor Probus ordered his soldiers to construct the terraces on which the vines thrive to this day; facing south, they are protected from harsh winds. This section of the Wachau from Spitz down to Dürnstein (about 10 km., 6 miles) is the most beautiful and is devoted entirely to wine. Here Austria's noblest white wines grow: look out for Veltliners, Rheinrieslings and above all in Spitz for Neuburgers: they will all be aromatic but dry and light.

Visit the Hirtzberger Winery (02713–209). Try the "Steinfeder" (a new term for Wachau wines guaranteeing no added sugar and a maximum 10.7% alcohol content) *Grüner Veltliner Donaugarten 1984* and the superb *Riesling Spatlese Ried Hochrain 1983*. (When buying wine in the Wachau look for the insignia "Vinea Wachau Nobilis Districtus" on the label. Reputable growers in the area carry out their own strict quality control and this sign means the wine has passed more stringent tests than those set by the State. For instance, a "Federspiel" wine is equal to the Kabinett and must not exceed 11.9% alcohol.)

Time your journey so as to reach the tiny village of Weissenkirchen/Joching shortly before lunch. Don't miss the Franz Prager winery in Weissenkirchen (02 7 15–22 48) and compare two of his Veltliners from two different vineyards: *Hinter der Burg* and *Kaiserberg* in order to see how two wines of the same grape, grown within a few hundred yards of each other, can nevertheless be quite individual. Retain in your mind the taste of his Muscat Ottonel, dry and vigorous, to compare with one of its sweeter cousins in Burgenland. This vineyard is undoubtedly one of the finest in Austria. Having looked at the romantic village with its weathered Gothic church poised on a rock, you will only have to go one kilometer back to Joching where you can find lunch; and where better than at a wine "chateau," that of the Josef Jamek Winery (02 7 15–22 35, closed Sun. and Mon.)? Frau Jamek will cook a superbly light meal, using local ingredients and recipes. If you are lucky Herr Jamek will be on hand to guide you through his palette of wines: a young Veltliner might give way to a noble Rheinriesling which in turn could lead to his remarkable Pinot Blanc Spätlese, *Ried Hochrain:* fruity, yet absolutely dry. As you sip your coffee, round off your meal with his *Apricot Schnapps* before moving on.

It is only a few kilometers to Dürnstein where Richard the Lionheart was imprisoned. But this time, the aim is to seek out the Kellerschlössl, a Baroque palace designed by the great architect Jakob Prandtauer and home of the Dürnstein wine co-operative. While large co-operatives often exist to produce bulk wines, the one at Dürnstein has aimed at producing wines of the highest quality using the modern methods that only a co-operative can afford (02 7 11–22 17). The co-operative has a cellar capacity of 11 million liters at its disposal and you can taste the wines in the Vinothek wineshop in the little town (Tues. and Thurs. from 2.30 P.M. to 5). Compare a dry Neuburger *Ried Burgberg* with its fuller—some would say more characteristic—Neuburger *Ried Gut am Steg*. Don't miss their rich

Veltliner *Ried Lichtgartl* and a Rheinriesling Spätlese from the *Ried Kellerberg:* rich but never cloying.

A few kilometers on to Krems and the narrow valley has broadened and become gentler. Krems, one of the best preserved Baroque towns in Europe is also the home of the Lenz Moser family who did so much for the development of Austrian Wine after both World Wars. In town you can visit the Vinothek of the enormous wine co-operative, but perhaps you should seek out the Fritz Salomon Winery Undhof. Krems is right next door to a town called Stein and these used to be joined by a tiny community called *Und* (and). Hence the name Krems UND Stein. Und has long since been swallowed up, but the Undhof remains as proof. This vineyard is equal to that of Herr Prager in Weissenkirchen (02 7 32–32 26). Unforgettable is his Veltliner *Ried Wieden,* often considered Austria's finest. Try too his Rhein Riesling Spätlese *Ried Kremser Kögl.* Unusually for Austria, Herr Salomon has also experimented with the Pinot Gris grape; lovers of spicy wines will not want to miss his *Ried Wachtberg* Traminers.

The Wachau Tourist Office in Krems also arranges wine tours of the area, and at the beginning of June each year the Krems Wine Fair provides a unique opportunity to encounter many rare wines from the region. Worth noting, too, is the 1656 monastery of Und, now the first Austrian Wine Market. Restored last year, this has become the center of the Austrian Wine Market. For an entrance fee of AS120, you can taste wines from all over the country, take part in cultural events, and dine in a pleasant restaurant (tel. 02732–73074).

It might be wise to stay the night in Krems, across the river in Mautern at the Hotel Bacher. The restaurant is one of Austria's finest and the rooms are delightful. Liesl Wagner, here, was voted "cook of the year" in 1983 and she will cook you a delicate dinner worthy of the honor while her husband helps you choose from his fine Krems wines.

Next morning, take Route 218 out of Krems up to Langenlois. Beethoven liked to come and drink the white wine here and a visit to the Bründlmayer winery (02 7 34–21 72) quickly explains why. Here the wines are richer and fruitier, although not at all sweet; the soil and the flatter valley are the reason. Besides Veltliners and Rheinrieslings, the Bründlmayers have successfully experimented with red wines. Try their Blauburgunder (Pinot Noir) *Ried Dechant* as well as a Rheinriesling *Ried Zöbinger Heiligenstein.*

Leaving Langenlois, turn north up Route 34, following the River Kamp valley. At the end of this beautiful ride it is certainly worth visiting Rosenburg Castle, shortly before the town of Horn (35 km., 22 miles). In Horn take Route 45 to Pulkau and then Route 35 up to Retz, a distance of 29 km. (18 miles). Retz is the principal town of the *Weinviertel* or winedistrict. This ancient town, still surrounded by its medieval walls, with superb patrician houses on the main square, is best visited at harvest-time. About then the barrels are emptied of old wine to prepare for the new and the fountain in the main square runs with wine! Beneath the town are 28 km. (17 miles) of cellar; you can visit these and refresh yourself at the end at an underground wine-bar. Retz is famous for good, rather heavier Veltliners but above all for its red wines: in Act II of the opera *Der Rosenkavalier* the wounded Baron Ochs is offered *Ein Retzer Wein* to make him feel better. He is delighted, and the ensuing waltz is proof of the wine's efficacy.

If there is time, visit the Weinbauschule (Viticultural College, 02 9 42–22 02) and compare a Blauer Portugieser *Ried Züngel Altenburg* with a Blauburger, also from the *Ried Züngel:* both are finely balanced and dry, the latter perhaps the fruitier and more velvety.

Leave Retz on a small road and drive through open, undulating country southeast to Haugsdorf. Notice in many of the villages the rows of cellars built into the sloping ground at the roadside. These cellar-streets, which are a feature of the area, called Kellergassen, are beautiful to look at and provide perfect storage conditions for the wines. In Haugsdorf you won't regret testing the red wines of the Josef Lust Winery (02 9 44–2 87). Compare his *Roter Fasan* Blauer Portugieser with his Pinot Noir. The former grape is so often used to make mass-market wines that a taste of Herr Lust's Blauer Portugiesers comes as a revelation.

Inns to stay in in this area are simple, but all will provide clean, comfortable accommodation and good local food at amazingly low prices. From Haugsdorf travel east along Route 45 to Laa an der Thaya, and join Route 46; this road brings you to the amazing castle of Staatz, perched high on its volcanic rock. A walk up to the ruins will prepare you for the next round of tastings! From Staatz, Route 219 brings you to Poysdorf, about 50 km. (31 miles) altogether from Haugsdorf.

In Poysdorf, centre of the Falkenstein wine district, call at the Gunter Haimer Winery (02 5 52–25 59). In an area often given to mass production he has placed his cards on quality: beautiful Kabinett Veltliners lead one on to his exceptional *Ried Taubenschuss,* a dry Veltliner Spätlese. This wine is proof of what the Veltliner grape is capable of. Also in Poysdorf you can, if you give advance notice, enjoy a gourmet tasting at the Franz Rieder Winery in Kleinhadersdorf-Poysdorf, Untere Ortsstrasse 44 (02552–2241). AS250 per person for ten or more.

Traveling straight down towards Vienna you have the amazing sight of vines growing round endless oil-wells. Here are Austria's largest oil-fields: the two life-bloods exist, happily, side by side—a truly Austrian solution of life's problems.

The Wine Trail Continues

Now, leave Vienna to the west and travel on south to Gumpoldskirchen. This tiny village on the eastern slopes of the last Alpine rocks has lived for wine for two thousand years. It produces the richest, most magnificent white wines in Austria and their fame is widespread. At one stage, there was more Gumpoldskirchner on the world markets than the village could ever have produced—a situation reminiscent of the medieval glut of pieces of the True Cross; in self defense the growers introduced strict measures of control. Always look for the words *Original Gumpoldskirchner* on the bottle. The further word *Königswein* (Wine of Kings) means that the bottle in question is a particularly special wine. But do go easy on the intake—Gumpoldskirchner wines are heavier and go straight to the head.

Stroll down the main street on a warm evening and call in at any of the houses displaying a bunch of fir twigs at the door. Such a house is open for wine and cold food; the courtyard behind the house, usually protected by a huge old tree, will make you linger.

It is here that the Zierpfandler and the Rotgipfler grapes come into their own. Just outside Gumpoldskirchen is the Thallern Winery, belonging to the Heiligenkreuz monastery in the southern Vienna Woods. Try a Zierpfandler *Ried Wiege,* Auslese and Beerenauslese or a golden *Rotgipfler Trockenbeerenauslese.* The winery has a tiny Gothic chapel housing a *Christ on the Vine* by Heiligenkreuz sculptor Giuliani.

By now you will probably need to spend the night in Baden to the south before going on to Bad Vöslau. Here look for the Robert Schlumberger Winery (02 2 52–72 90). This Alsatian family came from the Champagne to Austria in 1845 and were instrumental in starting the production of sparkling wines in Austria. Although no longer made by him, the *Ultra Brut* (sparkling wine) that bears his name is undoubtedly Austria's finest brand of Sekt.

The Schlumbergers are famous for their red wines; indeed one of these was served to Queen Victoria at the Great Exhibition of 1862. She liked it so much that the wine was put on her Kensington Palace wine-list. Remarkable is the Schlumberger *Privatkeller* Cabernet-Merlot; here Herr Schlumberger has used the two great Bordeaux grapes, almost unique in Austria.

From Vöslau take Route 305 east across to Ebreichsdorf where you join Route 16 from Vienna down to Eisenstadt. This jewel of a town, made famous by the Esterhazys and Josef Haydn, is the capital of the Burgenland. You could do worse than stay at the new Hotel Burgenland since from here you can make trips out to Lake Neusiedl. Around this steppe lake, unique in Europe, you can travel north towards Neusiedl and around into the Seewinkel, a huge nature reserve and bird sanctuary. The wine here is good and plentiful. Call in at any house with the *Flaschenwein* sign and ask to taste.

All the Burgenland wines bear the mark of an area that was part of Hungary until after World War I. The wines, as is inevitable in a warm climate, have in the past tended to be heavy and sweet, but enterprising young growers are now producing dry wines of real depth. The Anton Kollwentz Winery, 7051 Grosshöflein (02 6 82/51 58) produces some magnificent *barrique*-matured reds. Don't miss Donnerskirchen, 14 km. (8½ miles) northeast of Eisenstadt on Route 304. A good lunch at the Restaurant Engel will prepare you for a tasting at the St. Martinus co-operative in the village. This co-operative has aimed at a lighter style, reflected in their dry Welschrieslings. It also holds informative wine seminars. Try also Spätlese and Trockenbeerenauslese from the Welschriesling and the Muscat-Ottonel grapes and think back to Herr Prager's Muscat Ottonel many tastings ago in Weissenkirchen. Here too you might finally have the chance to try an Eiswein.

Another outing will take you to the free town of Rust. Unspoilt, this town offers shelter to several families of storks who arrive from Egypt every spring and spend the summer there. A cold lunch in the Rathauskeller can be combined with an on-the-spot tasting of countless local wines.

After a good night's sleep, Route 331 will take you south from Eisenstadt for about 30 km. (18½ miles) to Weppersdorf and there turn east on Route 62 to go about 20 km. (12½ miles) to Deutschkreuz. Make straight for the Hans Igler Winery (02 6 13–365), for Herr Igler has invested his time, his love and his money in creating red wines of international distinction. His Blaufränkisch Kabinett from various barrels emerge the winners at every tasting, year after year.

Returning to Route 61, go for another 26 km. (16 miles) south until you turn off on Route 55 west to Lockenhaus. Here, after a pause to enjoy the scenery, go south on Route 56 and follow the Hungarian border through Rechnitz about 40 km. (25 miles) down to Eisenberg. At this point the lovely wooded steppes open out eastwards to reveal a small, steep area of sloping vineyards facing southeast. These look down past the border watchtowers onto the Hungarian plains. At the foot of the Eisenberg is the village of Deutsch Schützen. Call ahead to the Körper Winery (03365–2203) just outside the village. Herr Körper has an amazing selection of white wines which he will happily open for you to taste. It is his reds, however, from the Eisenberg that are unforgettable. Compare his Blaufränkisch with his Zweigelt, the former being the rounder without in any way being heavy or cloying. His Merlot grape experiments have had remarkable results and 1989 should see his first Cabernet vintage.

Before leaving the Burgenland, spend a night at the Hotel Raffel in Jennersdorf, 30 km. (18½ miles) southwest on Route 57. A comfortable room will await you after a Pannonian dinner of gargantuan proportions, served stylishly in a dining-room of elegance. Herr Kampel, the owner, will enjoy advising you in making a choice from his extensive cellar.

Around 20 km. (12½ miles) south of Jennersdorf you are already well into Styria by the time you get to Klöch, where a visit to the Ducal Stürgkh Winery (03 4 75–223) is a must. Here, on a tiny area, grow Gewürztraminers equal to those of Alsace. Start with the Kabinetts and move on to the *Kellerbraut* Spätlese, in hand-numbered bottles. You will find it justifies its fame as one of the finest in Europe.

Follow the little road south till you come to Route 69, then travel along the River Mur and the Yugoslav border for 30 km. (18½ miles), crossing the main north–south road at Strass. When you reach Ehrenhausen, turn south onto the South Styrian Wine Road. Soon you are on the border with Yugoslavia, literally *on*, half the road is in Yugoslavia and half in Austria! On either side endless vineyards fall away steeply. These are some of the steepest vineyards in the world and have to be worked by hand. Look out for a *Klapotetz*, a large wind-operated moving scarecrow designed to keep the birds off the grapes. To work, they say, these must be made of cherry-wood: you may be lucky and hear one in action.

Output here is not great, but the wines have finesse and richness. Drive slowly, for the road is narrow and twisty, but also to enjoy the unique scenery as beautiful as any wine country in the world. Stop at one of the many *Buschenschanks* and order a Brettljause (a board with cold meats, bread and pickles); try a Welschriesling with it, or a Morillon or a Traminer. Then sit and forget the world outside, which you can do here, for people even forget there is a border; just drink in the view, the wine and the peace. One warning: don't go at the weekend, for most of the citizens of Graz have the same idea.

Rejoin Route 69 at Leutschach, turn right at Arnfels and follow the valley up to Route 74 (about 10 km., 6 miles). Here a small road leads up to the village of Kitzeck, the highest wine-village in Europe, whose sloping vineyards will make you dizzy if you look down. There is a tiny wine-museum, a local labour of love, that is well worth a visit.

From Kitzeck, travel 30 km. (18½ miles) westwards to Deutschlandsberg and join Route 76 leading up to Stainz. Between these towns on the slopes to our left, grows a grape found nowhere else in the world: the Blauer Wildbacher. From this is made a wine called *Schilcher*. This rosé wine, always drunk chilled, is anything from onion-skin colored round Stainz, to a fuller red-pink nearer Deutschlandsberg; the wine is tangy, heady and sometimes almost sour. For many it is an acquired, or not acquired taste, but it is certainly one not to miss. A Schilcher Wine Road has been created and maps are available from the village tourist office (03462-2377). Various *Gasthauses* and *Buschenschanks* have joined to offer the finest wines and traditional local dishes. A particularly fine Schilcher is produced by E. & M. Müller at vineyards belonging to the Liechtenstein family. Their winery is at Gross St. Florian (03 4 64–234) and their *Ried Burgegg* Schilcher has the true onion-skin colour. Indeed, for a cross section of what Styria has to offer, this winery is ideal for a visit.

End of the Trail

And so you have traveled through most of Austria's wine country and finally return to Vienna. What other capital city has vineyards within its bounds? The *Heuriger* (this year's wine) Taverns of Grinzing, Sievering and Nussdorf are lodestones for wine lovers. It is a memorable experience to sit at the edge of a vineyard on the Kahlenberg with a tankard of young white wine, and listen to the *Schrammel* quartet playing sentimental Viennese songs. How far-sighted of the Emperor Joseph to decree in 1784 that winegrowers could sell their wines together with cold food direct to customers whenever they liked. At the same time, the Viennese discovered that it was cheaper to go out to the wine than to bring it inside the city walls where taxes were levied. Mutual interest has thus made an institution of these *Heurigen*.

There are so many of these taverns, that it would be frivolous to single any out: everyone in Vienna has his favorite which is also of course the best. Beethoven, however, knew a good thing when he lived at a house on the Pfarrplatz in Heiligenstadt for some time. Now belonging to the Mayer family, it houses a Heuriger which really serves its own wines (37 12 87, open daily from 4 P.M.) and has long been a favourite of many famous Viennese.. If you go there in the fall, try a glass of *Sturm,* a cloudy drink halfway between grape-juice and wine, with a delicious yeasty fizz. Ing. Mayer also owns vineyards within Vienna that produce some wines of exceptional quality: try his *Alsegger* Rheinriesling, steely and dry and compare this with another Rheinriesling, *Schwarze Katz* from the Nussberg. This second is mellower and they make an interesting contrast, coming as they do from different districts of Vienna.

On your last evening, call a taxi and ask him to take you to Heuriger Sirbu (37 13 19, closed Sun.) on the Kahlenbergerstrasse at the *Eiserner Hand.* Here on a slope high above the Danube, with a tankard of exceptionally good *Heuriger* and a plateful of cold food in front of you, you can sit beneath a trellis of vines and glimpse the stars above. Away to your left are the upper reaches of the Kahlenberg, once occupied by the Turks, and below you Vienna and the Danube, lights sparkling as the dusk turns to night. Way across the other side, just visible, are the lights of Bisamberg, another wine village we haven't even begun to talk about . . .

A Wine Vocabulary

In order to help you find your way through the maze of bottles, *viertels* and barrels of this long liquid adventure, here are a few of the simpler words that are used in the delicious world of Austrian wine.

Abgang	aftertaste
blumig	with a fine bouquet
dünn	watery, thin
feurig	heady
fruchtig	fruity
herb	dry
Körper	body
körperreich	full-bodied
leicht	light
moussierend	sparkling
rassig	aromatic, fragrant
resch	crisp, lively, dry
sauer	sour, sharp, rough
schwer	full-bodied, heady
spritzig	slightly sparkling because young
Ein Spritzer	wine mixed with mineral water
süffig	pleasant to drink
süss	sweet
trocken	dry
Ein Viertel	¼ of a liter, served open
Weinstein	Residual acid crystals in dry white wine. A sure sign of high quality

EXPLORING
AUSTRIA

VIENNA

Splendors of the Past

by
RICHARD MOORE

Used as we are in the cities of the West to a life of instant shocks, endless crime, wall-to-wall noise and the rat-race rush all day long, Vienna comes as a relief. It is a city of civilized behavior, peaceful parks, elegant streets—a place where there is room to breathe. And yet, over the past five years, something of a rejuvenation has taken place. Bars, traffic-free zones, the UN, restoration of countless buildings, a lively avant-garde scene—all have played their part.

It is also a city that is more self-contained than most. According to the Tourist Board—in a fine moment of indiscreet candor—the population is "grumpy and cranky, arrogant and melancholy." But to the casual eye the Viennese are friendly, if reserved, welcoming and, above all, proud of their beloved old dowager of a town. In fact a high proportion of the Viennese themselves are middle-aged or elderly, which gives a sense of stability to the place. Crime is not the problem it is in many metropolitan centers, the streets are kept spotless and you can walk them safely at night. Mark you, the streets are mostly empty at night, although the city center is now lively with plenty on offer for all tastes until the small hours. Apart from the solid joys of the opera, operetta and concerts, among the finest in the world, Vienna has most to offer in the daytime, when you can absorb the remaining echoes of a long and compelling history, enjoy some of the world's greatest art, experience an ambience where music has been a way of life for centuries, and come a little closer to the city where Beethoven and Freud, Maria Theresa and Hitler, Mozart and Klimt all lived. You will sense something of what Europe was like before the pulse of this century quickened to a beat that our grandfathers would never have understood.

The city in which this ambience exists is out of proportion to its modern function. As we have said elsewhere, Austria is today merely the shrunken remnant of a once mighty empire and Vienna was, above all, an imperial city, built as a massive bureaucratic center housing all the offices and functionaries that ordered the affairs of peoples throughout the emperor's vast possessions. It was also the ceremonial center, with a network of palaces that provided aristocratic shelter for the nobility who danced attendance on the emperor when he was resident at either the Hofburg or Schönbrunn. While these magnificent buildings have mostly managed to find a place in the modern state of things—frequently creating a bizarre juxtaposition of Baroque glories and present stridency, as with the Museum of Modern Art at the Palais Liechtenstein—the sheer number of them has meant that the streets of Vienna are lined with magnificent monumental doorways and the cliff-like march of stately facades. The city has been stranded by its time-warp, left high and dry in the Europe of the 1980s, and the miraculous thing is that the Viennese have succeeded in making a virtue out of a necessity.

In fact, one of the most enjoyable aspects of a visit to Vienna is to see just how the Viennese have managed to create a new, and completely valid, way of life out of the shattered world of their past. This will manifest itself to the visitor in a variety of ways, depending largely on personal interest. The best possible equipment for getting the most out of the city is to have a taste for history, a curiosity for the quirks in human nature, and a thirst for art and music. A thirst for good wine comes in handy, too. In fact, sitting in a 13th-century cellar, deep below the streets of Vienna, drinking a goblet of crisp white wine, watching your fellow-drinkers and listening to a quartet playing Mozart, would be difficult to beat as a typical Viennese delight.

The Man That Hath not Music In His Soul . . .

Wherever you turn, you will find how deeply music is engrained in the Viennese, indeed in all Austrians. Vienna has the most enormous variety of musical events to offer, and events of an amazingly high standard. Performances by the Vienna Boys' Choir in the Hofburg Chapel on Sunday mornings are events to remember. You will have an inkling of the world of art that gave birth to Haydn and Schubert (both of whom were connected with the choir in their day) when you hear the purity and immediacy of the boys' singing in its proper setting.

You will gain another insight into the way that music is looked upon if you attend a performance at the Opera. Be careful to dress as formally as you can while traveling, for opera is treated solemnly there, the intermissions becoming a kind of solemn processional rite. In the simple elegance of its reconstructed auditorium, with its ranked boxes, you will find just as much intensity of attention as at the Metropolitan or Covent Garden, but somehow of a different quality, as if the audience were more ritually aware of participation in a theatrical tradition. For music in Vienna is a vital part of the great heritage of the city.

For yet another look at the importance of music in Vienna it is worth visiting the museum of musical instruments in the Hofburg complex. This is a collection of interest to the specialist as well as to the amateur. The pianos that were played by the great composers who graced Vienna's musical life, Beethoven, Brahms, Schumann and Schubert, are there. Pianos painted and carved, embellished with sphinxes and lyres, pianos that look like castles and pianos that look like cathedrals, even pianos that look like pianos.

Nor is the interest in keyboard instruments confined to pianos. That king of instruments, the organ, is well enthroned in Vienna. One of the finest organs in Vienna, and one that has been superbly rebuilt in recent years, is that of the Augustinerkirche. Every Friday in summer at 8 P.M. there is a concert given by international organists. It lasts an hour or so and is completely informal with a minimal charge on the door. The choral music here on Sundays and important church festivals is magnificent too.

The Importance of Serendipity

We mention elsewhere some of the dishes that will give you a taste of Vienna, but we cannot pass by the importance of dropping in to a coffeehouse at some point in your wanderings to sample the relaxed life of the city that goes on there. It is an ideal way of drinking coffee and atmosphere at the same time. The coffeehouse is the club, meeting place, gossip center and home-from-home for many Viennese. Coffee has a long and honorable history in the city. The Turks never managed to conquer Vienna, though, heaven knows, they tried hard enough. But they did leave one legacy, for the first beans to be used are believed to have been captured from the Turkish camp after the second siege was lifted. You will encounter innumerable coffeehouses as you wander round the streets of Vienna. At one time threatened, they have enjoyed a renaissance in recent years. Don't be shy of walking in, ordering a mokka and sitting quietly to enjoy the coming and going of the regulars.

Serendipity is very much a force in Vienna. One of the most unexpected and delightful sights is that to be seen on a bright day in late winter, when the touch of frost is still in the air, but the sun holds a promise of warmth. Then it is in, say, the grounds of the Belvedere, that you will see elderly Viennese, men and women, standing in the shelter of the palace wall, dressed in their sober clothes, with their faces to the sun, enjoying the respite from the winter's chill. Another is to see the troops of schoolchildren, brought from other parts of Austria to learn more of their nation's great heritage, weaving their way in orderly but excited lines through subways, museums and squares. It is a kind of microcosm of the way their mothers and fathers behave, for, though the Austrians are a formal, tidy, orderly people, they manage still to get a great deal of fun out of life.

An Eagle's-Eye View

Before exploring Vienna, it is a good idea to see it whole. No one can pretend that it is easy to climb the 345 steps of the south steeple of St. Stephen's Cathedral, but it is worth it as it affords a magnificent view right in the heart of town. For the less intrepid, there is an elevator to the top of the much lower north tower. The Big Wheel in the Prater affords one of the best and most readily accessible panorama views of Vienna, but the most romantic view is from the last projecting spur of the nearby mountains of the Vienna Woods.

Immediately below flows the Danube—not, unless you are phenomenally lucky, even remotely blue and too well-regulated to be romantic. Over a hundred years ago, a first artificial bed was cut to improve water transport and contain the spring floods which, however, still caused heavy damage when the snows melted abruptly. So a second channel through the broad inundation flats was completed in 1981, and the excavation soil was heaped into a 14-mile-long, 200-yard-wide island, used as a wild-life sanctuary and recreation area. This second bed, though mainly intended for water sports, also raised the groundwater level needed for Vienna's water supply in the extensive meadows round the Alte Donau (Old Danube). The latter is a cut-off branch of the River Danube forming a shallow (about 2-meters deep) lake some seven kilometers long and 300 to 500 yards wide. It is one of the favorite relaxation spots of the Viennese. The area is now a national park, its recreation area comprising the popular bathing beach of Gänsehäufel. The Winterhafen has been enlarged to deal with the increased water transport when the Rhine-Main-Danube canal has been completed.

The great city spreads across an extensive plain which continues over the Marchfeld toward the frontier of Czechoslovakia, marked by the rivers Thaya and March, less than 50 miles away. Upstream, to the left, lies the beautiful monastery of Klosterneuburg with its green-patina cupolas, on an eminence above the Danube.

A little higher up, on the opposite bank, is Korneuburg, with Kreuzenstein Castle atop a low hill. Behind Klosterneuburg rise the tree-clad heights of the Vienna Forest, coming to an end in the Lainzer Tiergarten, a natural wildlife preserve round the Empress Elisabeth's Hermes Villa, open to the public during the summer months. Below the wooded Tiergarten stands Maria Theresa's Baroque palace of Schönbrunn, with its formally laid-out gardens and the ornamental structure of the Gloriette behind. Through the flat country farther to the right the Danube flows on to Bratislava (Pressburg to the Austrians). From that city a spur of the Lower Carpathians runs off to the northeast.

Where the Danube flows through the gap between the Alps and the Carpathians across a broad basin, there Vienna grew up, astride the natural highway from the North Sea to the Adriatic. No political changes have been able to rob her of the importance she derives from this geographical position. Just south of Bratislava, some 65 km. (40 miles) from Vienna, begins the Hungarian Great Plain. Thus from these Viennese observation posts you are actually looking into two countries behind the Iron Curtain, both of which, of course, formed part of the Austro-Hungarian monarchy before World War I.

Legacy of Imperial Prosperity

Vienna does not really lie on the Danube; only the northern outskirts of the city touch it. The heart of Vienna, the Innere Stadt (Inner City) or First District—in medieval times, the entire city of Vienna—is bounded by the Ringstrasse (Ring) which forms almost a circle, with a narrow arc cut off by the Danube canal—dug in 1598—diverted from the main river just above Vienna and flowing through the city to rejoin the parent stream just below it. The Ring follows the lines of what, until an imperial decree ordered their leveling in 1857, were the defenses of the city—ramparts, moats and *glacis*. About 2 km. (just over a mile) beyond the Ring runs the roughly parallel line of the Gürtel, which until 1890 formed the outer fortifications, or Linienwall.

In the 1870's Vienna reached the zenith of its imperial prosperity. This was marked by such gigantic undertakings as the cutting of a new channel (with the overflow meadows) for the Danube, the building of the Great Exhibition of 1873, and the construction of the 90-km. water conduit from the natural underground reservoir in the Styrian mountains to the south of the city, which provides it with the most delicious ice-cold water to be found in any European capital.

This same prosperity found its expression in the series of magnificent buildings erected around the Ringstrasse when the fortifications were leveled—the Opera House, National Art Gallery, and National Museum of Natural History, the "New Wing" of the Hofburg, Parliament, the Rathaus, the University, and the Votivkirche. By the time the Gürtel took the place of the outer fortifications, there was not quite so much money available and, although many open spaces were laid out as parks, it has no noteworthy buildings.

Most of the older buildings are, naturally, to be found in the small area of the Inner City, including many Baroque palaces of the nobility. It was only after the invading Turkish hordes had been repulsed in 1683 that the area immediately beyond the Ring—the so-called "Inner Suburbs"—now numbered Bezirke (Districts) II to IX—began to develop, and the nobility to build summer residences here.

Of recent years many tall, functional, buildings have come to dominate the older, architecturally superior, districts. Notable among these is the United Nations City, situated in the Donau Park, overlooking the Danube. These high buildings, few in number by the standards of most modern cities, give an air of almost irrelevant modernity to a city whose heart beats with the pulse of history—meretricious costume jewelry around the neck of a dignified dowager.

A Crossroads Capital

Vienna is a triple capital. It is the capital of the Federal Republic of Austria and at the same time the capital city of two of the nine federal states that go to make up the country, Lower Austria and Vienna itself. Once the heart of an empire that reached across most of the known world, Vienna is now the chief city of a comparatively small nation and has a population of 1,580,600.

A glance at the map will show you that, though Vienna was once placed centrally in the heart of the Austro-Hungarian territories, since the modern partition of Eastern Europe it is now positioned in the extreme eastern tip of present day Austria. In fact it is less than 50 miles from the Iron Curtain and is actually further east than Prague. Vienna's geographical position and rich history both greatly influence, however subconsciously, what the visitor to the city sees and feels.

Vienna came into being at the point where two main routes of trade and tribal migration crossed. One of these highways was the Danube, a certain means of passage through an uncertain landscape, the other was the route from the Baltic down to the Adriatic. Its position sets it as a meeting ground, a place of parley between the lands to the west and the more oriental lands to the east. In fact the East can almost be said to begin at Vienna.

Where people had lived since the Stone Age there grew up a Celtic settlement, called Vindomina which, in turn, gave way to a Roman garrison, Vindobona. The Romans settled on this site in about 100 B.C., and it was intended to act as part of the fortifications to defend their eastern borders from attacks from the north. It was a big encampment—you can see just how big if you run your finger on the map following Rotgasse up from the Danube Canal, then Kramergasse, Graben into Naglergasse, turn down Tiefer Graben and back along Salzgries. These streets form almost the exact boundaries of Vindobona, and immediately you can see how Vienna's history is still written very clearly in the layout of her streets. To be able to trace a Roman fort 2,000 years later in the plan of a modern city is a delight for the history buff, and Vienna is hiding a lot of such delights. Of course, the early settlements were long before the days of the tamed Danube, and this small plateau rose above the turbulent waters of a frequently-flooding side branch of the great river. Nor was the establishing of this great camp the only act of the Romans which has survived. In these early centuries of the Christian era, the Romans planted vines along the nearby foothills, creating a tradition for wine-growing that has lasted. Not far from Vienna, at what is now Petronell, they built the capital of their province of Pannonia, Carnuntum, with two amphitheaters and all the solidity of a Roman provincial town.

After the Romans had pulled back to defend their heartland, a move completed by 488 A.D., the region became the prey of various Germanic tribes. It was in Vindobona that the *Nibelungenlied* sets the Whitsuntide wedding of Etzel (Attila) and Kriemhild, festivities that lasted for seventeen days with a crowd of guests so great that they could not all be lodged in the city. Which was hardly surprising, for in those days, only a century or so after the Romans had left, the place must have been just a ruined shell of its former self.

Babenbergs and Habsburgs

Tradition has it that Charlemagne visited the city at the end of the 8th century, a fairly safe bet, since he seems to have popped up all over Europe. The history of this period is a trifle unfocused and possibly includes the reign of a character called Samo, a mysterious Frankish merchant with twelve wives and forty-seven children. But the picture clears with the arrival of the Babenbergs. Margrave Leopold III became lord of Vienna in 1135, and the town was designated for the first time in documents as *civitas,* a city, in 1137. However, it was only under the first Duke, Heinrich Jasomirgott, that Vienna became the Austrian capital.

The Babenbergs were, by and large, a civilized clan, especially Leopold VI (1194–1230), under whom the Babenberg court in Vienna became a culturally brilliant center. The city expanded and, with Leopold the Glorious at the helm, defensive walls were finally fixed at the point where they would stay until they were demolished by Franz Josef in 1857.

If the Babenbergs began the expansion of Vienna, it was left to their successors, the Habsburgs, who took formal possession in 1278, to transform it over the next six and a half centuries into one of the great cities of the world. The history of the Habsburg dynasty and the history of Vienna became inextricably intertwined, and, as we explore the city, evidence of this interdependence will constantly appear. Not that, in the earlier days of the Habsburg dynasty, Vienna was the only city to have eminence; others, Graz, Linz and Innsbruck for example, even Prague, came to the fore from time to time, but in the end it was Vienna that won out.

To symbolize briefly the next few centuries—Vienna was afflicted with two great scourges, the Turks and the Plague. They were both deadly and both, also, were the cause of some of Vienna's greatest monuments, built in redemption of vows made in the direst moment of danger.

With the final defeat of the Turks in September 1683, Vienna could come out from behind her protecting, encircling walls, and was able to expand. After centuries of confinement within medieval boundaries, never knowing when the Turks would mount yet another siege, she was able to build once more in spreading safety.

This was the supreme period of Baroque Vienna, the years when the major buildings of the Hofburg, the Karlskirche (plague-inspired), the palaces of Schönbrunn and the Belvedere all appeared, along with many hardly lesser gems. With that strange promptness that often marks important periods in human affairs, native artists and architects, equipped to realize contemporary needs, were suddenly to hand. As if out of thin air Fischer von Erlach and Hildebrandt, Rottmayr, Troger and Daniel Gran materialized to embody the imperial spirit of an upsurging age in that singularly ebullient style, the Baroque. What forces were behind the sudden arrival of a totally indigenous, artistic powerhouse, capable not only of conceiving such huge works of art, but of successfully carrying them out, is one of those puzzles that will remain unanswered. But it is very clear that the challenge to recreate on Austrian soil imperial concepts as grandiose as Versailles and to provide settings fit for the triumphal Habsburgs, fuelled the inspiration of those artists chosen for the task.

The Baroque mold into which Vienna was cast, superseding the Gothic, is still very obvious as you walk around the Inner City, but subsequent ages also left their impression, especially the middle 1800s. It was in 1857 that the young Emperor Franz Josef commanded that the old circle of fortifications which had for so long acted as corset to the city—in fact, one of them was actually called Gürtel, Girdle—should be torn down; an act that gave the signal for the great surge of construction along the Ring. It was a really remarkable experiment in town planning, in many ways even more remarkable than the efforts of Baron Haussmann at exactly the same time in Paris. In a flurry of archeological enthusiasm and technical skill, buildings modeled on ancient Greece, Renaissance Italy and Gothic France began to rise along the new wide boulevards.

At the end of the 19th century another artistic wave broke over Vienna. Otto Wagner's buildings marked the city with the spirit of a new age. The Postsparkasse (Post Office Savings Bank, of all prosaic names for a great building this one has to win a prize) on Georg-Coch-Platz, is one of his finest, while the Secession building (Friedrichstrasse 12), designed by Joseph Olbrich with doors by Klimt, carried modernity a stage further with those touches of fantasy that characterize Jugendstil, the Austrian version of *art nouveau.*

Exploring Vienna

Before setting off around the city, a few general points. It is a good idea to plan your route for the day. Opening times of the major museums and other buildings you may wish to see are very variable, some open for a very short time only. The Prunksaal, for example, the main hall of the National Library, which is one of the glories of Vienna and indeed of the world, is open only from 11 to 12 in the morning from October to May, though during the rest of the year it is open from 10 to 4. Arriving at a museum you particularly wanted to see and finding that it shut half an hour before is intensely irritating, so it is wise to check up in advance. Among their many helpful pamphlets the Vienna Tourist Board have one giving the latest times when "Kultur" can be imbibed. We give some of the opening times in this book, but it is always as well to make sure they haven't changed.

Another extremely useful Tourist Board publication is called *Vienna from A to Z,* which currently costs 30 schillings. To explain. All the major buildings in the city have been equipped with small metal shields on their facades, shields which are decorated with flags in summer and which give basic information in German about the building. *Vienna from A to Z* is a catalog of these shields, in English, keyed to the number in a circle which is on all the shields. This excellent system has, in fact, turned the whole of the city into a wonderfully captioned art gallery.

Don't forget during your explorations that there are hundreds of cafes around the city which are ideal for rest, recuperation and the comfortable study of your guidebook. A half-hour spent over an icecream or a coffee will set you up for further forays and give you a breath of genuine Viennese life at the same time.

One last tip. Carry a lot of 10 schilling pieces with you. In most of the important churches and in many other buildings around town there are coin-operated tape machines that give you a commentary on the main points of interest in English and several other languages; all you have to do is press the right button.

The Opera

As good a place as any to start exploring the city is at the Opern-Passage, a large subterranean crossing under the Ring just by the Opera, that leads to the vast subway station extending as far as the Karlsplatz. While there is a tourist information office here where you can stock up on the various pamphlets and information with which to plan your trip, the main tourist office is now "upstairs," at Kärntnerstrasse 38, at the back of the Opera House, open 9–7 daily.

Above ground you will find the Opera House itself. It is a focus for Viennese life, and one of the chief symbols of resurgence after the cataclysm of World War II. The building was originally constructed in the middle of the 19th century, its first season being launched in 1869 with a performance of Mozart's *Don Giovanni.* In April 1945 it was almost totally destroyed, but the Viennese made it one of their first priorities when the hostilities ceased to rebuild their beloved Opera, restoring the auditorium, but incorporating many up-to-the-minute technical improvements in the stage region. The theater was reopened in November, 1955 and this time the chosen work was that great "resurrection" opera by another of Vienna's musical pantheon, Beethoven's *Fidelio.*

From September through June there are guided tours of the building every afternoon; five times daily in July and August. The auditorium is plain when compared with the red and gold eruptions of London's Covent Garden or some of the Italian opera houses, but it has an elegant individuality which shows to best advantage when the stage and auditorium together are turned into a ballroom for the great Opera Ball. The performances are sumptuous, with a lavish buffet in the intermissions and stately patrols through the fine long halls. If you secure a ticket you would be well advised to go sober-suited, otherwise you will feel rather out of place among the serious Viennese operagoers.

The affairs of the Opera House are of vital interest to the citizens of Vienna. Even those who never darken the Opera's doors read about the doings of the administration—artistic and financial—with avidity, as a long line of directors have had good cause to know. The problem is one that seems extremely odd to the outside world, for the position of Director is virtually the top job in Austria, almost as important as that of President, and one that comes in for even more public attention. Every man-on-the-street thinks he could do it just as well and, since the huge salary comes out of the taxes, he feels that he has every right to criticize, often and loudly. Vienna is a city where opera is taken very, very seriously.

Grouped around the Opera are several famous haunts, the Hotel Bristol, the Café Mozart and, most renowned, Sacher's. Sacher's is firmly ensconced in Viennese legend and, of course, the home of the celebrated chocolate cake, the Sachertorte, about which there raged a famous law suit over who precisely could lay claim to being the makers of the cake. Sachertorte, as opposed to Sacher Torte, is now only made by Sacher's!

When you cross the road behind the Opera to reach the pedestrian zone of the Kärntnerstrasse, you will be introduced to one of the basic facts of Viennese life. One does not jaywalk. You will see throngs of people patiently waiting at pedestrian crossings for the lights to change, even when the street is totally and completely clear of traffic, with apparently nothing in sight as far as the Wienerwald.

Kärntnerstrasse

Stretching ahead from the back righthand corner of the Opera is Kärntnerstrasse and the beginning of a pedestrian precinct that runs through the heart of Vienna's Inner City shopping area. It has openair cafés down the middle in summer and is generally attractive to wander through and to window shop. The Viennese hotly dispute if the introduction of this pedestrian mall has changed one of Europe's smartest shopping streets for the better.

On your left at number 38 is the *Vienna Information* office. A little further down on the right, tucked between shops, is the restored facade of the Malteserkirche, Church of the Knights of Malta, one of the few Orders remaining from the days of the Crusades. The interior is Gothic and some 600 years old, its plain walls decorated with plaques bearing the arms of the Grand Masters of the Order. The present Order is recognized diplomatically in about 40 countries, it numbers some 3,000 members around

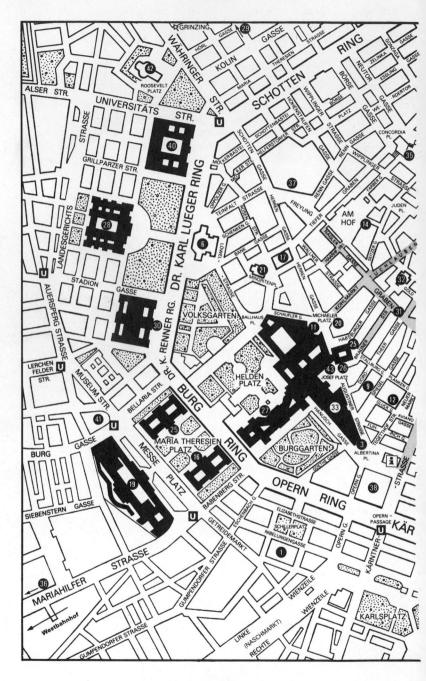

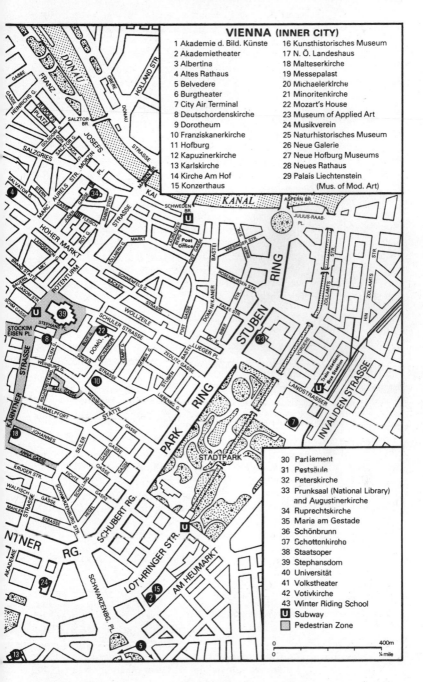

VIENNA (INNER CITY)

1 Akademie d. Bild. Künste
2 Akademietheater
3 Albertina
4 Altes Rathaus
5 Belvedere
6 Burgtheater
7 City Air Terminal
8 Deutschordenskirche
9 Dorotheum
10 Franziskanerkirche
11 Hofburg
12 Kapuzinerkirche
13 Karlskirche
14 Kirche Am Hof
15 Konzerthaus

16 Kunsthistorisches Museum
17 N. Ö. Landeshaus
18 Malteserkirche
19 Messepalast
20 Michaelerkirche
21 Minoritenkirche
22 Mozart's House
23 Museum of Applied Art
24 Musikverein
25 Naturhistorisches Museum
26 Neue Galerie
27 Neue Hofburg Museums
28 Neues Rathaus
29 Palais Liechtenstein
        (Mus. of Mod. Art)

30 Parliament
31 Pestsäule
32 Peterskirche
33 Prunksaal (National Library) and Augustinerkirche
34 Ruprechtskirche
35 Maria am Gestade
36 Schönbrunn
37 Schottenkirche
38 Staatsoper
39 Stephansdom
40 Universität
41 Volkstheater
42 Votivkirche
43 Winter Riding School
U Subway
▨ Pedestrian Zone

the world and the present Grand Master is, technically at least, a Head
of State. It is, in fact, one of the biggest and one of the least known charitable organizations in the world today.

One of the delights of wandering around Vienna is to be able to compare
the architecture and atmosphere of the city's many churches. Around a
dozen will appear in the following pages and that in no way exhausts the
possibilities. It is interesting to trace the changing styles over the centuries
from the simple, almost severe interiors of churches such as this one, to
the enormously elaborate Baroque decorations of those built (or at least
ornamented) in the early 18th century.

The narrow sidestreets to the right of Kärntnerstrasse contain a wealth
of Baroque palaces and houses including (back, before the Malteserkirche)
the 17th-century Annakirche decorated by Daniel Gran; the Kremsmünster Court in Annagasse; the Baroque wing of the Hofkammerarchiv (Imperial Household Records Office) which backs on to the simpler 19th-
century wing in the Johannesgasse, next to the 17th-century Ursulinenkir-
che. The Ministry of Finance's offices are housed in a masterpiece of the
Baroque, Prince Eugene of Savoy's Winterpalace, designed by Fischer von
Erlach—the staircase, with sculptures by Giovanni Guiliani, is breathtaking—and extended by Lukas von Hildebrandt, who likewise inspired the
former Monastery Zur Himmelpforte (At the Gate of Heaven) after which
the street is named.

The Imperial Vault

Back on Kärntnerstrasse, a few yards past the Malteserkirche but on
the left, is a short turning that leads directly into the Neuer Markt. On
the left of this square, opposite, is the Kapuzinerkirche (Church of the
Capuchins), again at least 600 years old. The plain facade has been restored to its original 17th-century design, while the simple white interior
sets off the warm browns of the marquetry work behind the high and side
altars.

Below this church lie the bodies of the imperial house of Austria in the
Kaisergruft, the Imperial Vault. Perhaps this is the wrong way to approach the Habsburgs in Vienna for the first time, starting with their
tombs, but it does give you a chance to get their names in sequence as
they lie in their serried ranks, their coffers ranging from the simplest
through positive explosions of funerary conceit with decorations of skulls
and other morbid symbols to the lovely and distinguished tomb of Maria
Theresa and her husband, designed while the couple still lived. To pass
by these long lines of imperial dead is to take a short journey through history and art, and impresses one with a sense of exactly how the Habsburg
centuries unfolded.

The Capuchin monks guide the groups of visitors among the tombs of
138 Habsburgs, from Ferdinand II in 1633 to Franz Josef in 1916. The
Countess Fuchs was the only non-royal to be buried here—a well-deserved
honor for this dearly-loved surrogate mother to the children of Maria Theresa. The Countess was the Empress's own governess to begin with, and
without her Maria Theresa would never have been able to conduct affairs
of state *and* raise a family. Only one coffin was ever taken away. In 1940,
after Germany defeated France, the remains of the Duke of Reichstadt,
the son of Napoleon and Marie Louise, were transferred to Les Invalides
in Paris upon the personal order of Adolf Hitler, who was hoping to ap-

pease the French with the gesture. Zita, widow of Austria's last Kaiser, Carl, was buried here in 1989, doubtless the last of the Habsburgs to find a final resting place here.

In the center of the Neuer Markt is the Baroque Donner Brunnen, the Providence Fountain, the work of Georg Raphael Donner, one of the leading 18th-century artists of Vienna. The original lead figures are in the Baroque Museum in the Lower Belvedere—and, one has to admit, look better there than the copies do here. Providence stands in the middle and the four figures at the corners represent four Austrian rivers, the Traun, Enns, Ybbs and March. These four figures are among Donner's most attractive works; the poise of the young man with the trident, leaning over the basin, is particularly lifelike, although his accessible pose leaves him open to easy indignities.

Further along Kärntnerstrasse a turning on the right, Weihburggasse, leads past the hotel Kaiserin Elisabeth, where many famous people have stayed over the decades, Wagner and Liszt among them. On the other side of the street is a famous restaurant, the Drei Husaren (Three Hussars) which, although one of Vienna's fanciest and most expensive, you might want to return to one evening. Further along in the next block is the excellent British Bookshop where you can stock up on reading material (and don't be put off by the closed door, it's almost certainly open for business).

Franziskanerplatz is a charming, small square, with a fountain topped off by an exceptionally urbane Moses in the middle. To one side is the former residence of Countess Fuchs, governess of Maria Theresa. It has been restored to its extremely elegant former looks. On the facade of the Gothic-Renaissance Franziskanerkirche (Franciscan Church) is a statue of St. Jerome, lion in attendance and golden cardinal's hat on his head. The interior of this church is a cheerful one, with a most dramatically conceived backing to the altar, containing a painting of *The Immaculate Conception* by Rottmayr.

Kärntnerstrasse opens into Stephansplatz at Stock-im-Eisen (Trunk-in-Iron), a treetrunk into which every 16th-century apprentice blacksmith drove a nail before leaving Vienna. You can still see this odd relic preserved in a glass case up on the wall on a left-hand corner. Hans Hollein's new "Haas Haus" on the corner of Graben and Stock-im-Eisen Platz should be finished by 1990 and promises to provide a controversial talking point, as did the Loos House on Michaelerplatz at the turn of the century (see p. 105).

St. Stephen's Cathedral

Stephansdom (St. Stephen's Cathedral) is another focus for the pride of the Viennese in their city. It shared with the Opera and some other major buildings the fate of having been very heavily damaged in World War II, and of having risen from the fires of destruction like a phoenix. And like the phoenix, it is a symbol of regeneration.

Now that the work on the subway is finished—in this part of the city at least—it is possible to prowl around the cathedral to your heart's content, without being sent flying by raucous traffic. It sits in the middle of a wide piazza, the space round it seeming larger than it actually is. To one side of the great building, close to where Kärntnerstrasse meets the square, you will see the outlines of two buildings superimposed on each other in colored stone on the paving. Two chapels used to stand here, one dedicated to Mary Magdalene and the other to St. Virgilius. The deep delving for the subway, which went right up to the foundations of the cathedral, revealed not only some Roman remains and lots of bones, for the area had once been a graveyard, but also the Virgilkappelle almost complete, as it had been when encased in the crypt of the Maria Magdalena Kappelle. It is now cocooned in the subway ticket hall below Stephansplatz and can be visited. It is a severe vaulted chamber which seems like part of the catacombs. As you go in there is a small collection of pottery from different periods found around the city during various excavations. If the chapel is closed, you can look down into it through a large window in the ticket hall.

A first St. Stephen's was built by Duke Heinrich Jasomirgott in 1147 and, following a fire, replaced by a Romanesque basilica during the reign of King Ottocar of Bohemia. The Great West Front thus dates from the late 13th century, with the soaring Riesentor (Giant Doorway) flanked by two small towers (Heidentürme) on either side. There are a lot of attractive details in the carving here, Samson wrenching open the lion's jaws, a griffin, and all sorts of mythical beasts.

Continuing round to the left, you will pass by the unfinished north tower—unfinished, that is, when compared with its brother on the south side. It was decided not to rival the sky-piercing south spire and to leave the north tower a mere stump, called the Adlerturm. Inside is one of Vienna's traditional treasures, Die Pummerin, the Boomer; a huge bell weighing around 22 tons and measuring 10 feet across. The original Boomer was cast in 1711 from cannon captured from the Turks. In the south tower until 1945, it crashed down into the nave during a fire and was replaced in 1952, in the north tower. The new Boomer was carried in solemn procession from St. Florian in Upper Austria, where it had been cast as part of Upper Austria's contribution to the rebuilding and refurnishing of St. Stephen's. You can visit the bell by an elevator.

The northwest door is another masterpiece of medieval work. As it used to be the women's entrance to the cathedral (the southwest door was for men only) it features mainly female saints and incidents from the life of the Virgin.

Next on the circumambulation comes the openair pulpit named after the monk Capistranus who, in 1450, preached from it to rouse the people of the city to a crusade against the Turks. The elaborate group above the simple pulpit was added in 1737 and shows the saint (he was canonized in 1690) spearing a symbolic Turk to a flourish of flags and cherubs. Close by this spot the body of Mozart rested briefly in 1791 on the way to his burial. He died not far away in a house on Rauhensteingasse (Number 8, although the original house is no longer there).

Further round the east side of the cathedral is the torso of the Man of Sorrows which is irreverently known as *Our Lord of the Toothache*, because of its agonized expression. Nearby are more carvings, especially a 1502 scene of the events on the Mount of Olives.

You are now at the base of Alte Steffl, Old Steve, the dominating feature of the Vienna skyline. It is 450 feet high and was built between 1359 and 1433. If you feel fit enough, you can climb the 345 steps to take advantage of the stupendous view from the top of the tower section, not of the spire itself, of course. From that vantage point you can see out over the city to the rising slopes of the Wienerwald.

St.Stephen's Cathedral

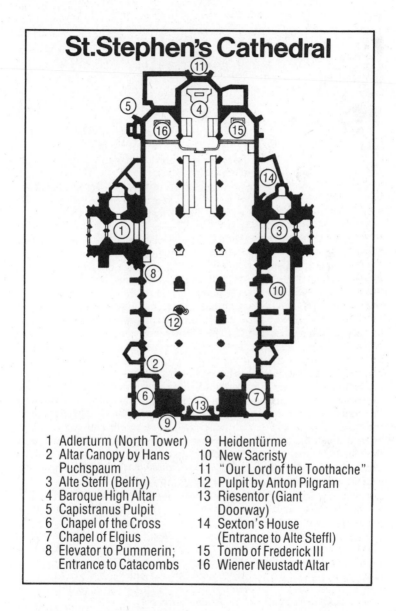

1 Adlerturm (North Tower)
2 Altar Canopy by Hans Puchspaum
3 Alte Steffl (Belfry)
4 Baroque High Altar
5 Capistranus Pulpit
6 Chapel of the Cross
7 Chapel of Elgius
8 Elevator to Pummerin; Entrance to Catacombs
9 Heidentürme
10 New Sacristy
11 "Our Lord of the Toothache"
12 Pulpit by Anton Pilgram
13 Riesentor (Giant Doorway)
14 Sexton's House (Entrance to Alte Steffl)
15 Tomb of Frederick III
16 Wiener Neustadt Altar

To the right of the southwest door stands the statue of Duke Rudolf IV, who ordered the Gothic enlargement of the cathedral, holding a model of the building in his right hand. Both he and his wife, Katharine, who balances him on the other side of the door, are attended by heralds carrying their coats of arms. The arch continues upwards with statues of saints, while four scenes from the life of St. Paul fill in the tympanum.

Inside the cathedral there are many easily identifiable things to see and a great deal of atmosphere to absorb. The fabric was extensively rebuilt after the terrible damage of 1945 when the cathedral was caught in the crossfire of the two locked armies, and suffered not only gunfire but blockbusters and incendiary bombs into the bargain. It is difficult now, sitting quietly, drinking in the shadowed peace, to tell what was original and what parts of the walls and valuting were reconstructed. One of the things that has helped towards this merging of the new with the old is that many of the treasures of medieval carving were rescued. Among these is the pulpit sculptured by Anton Pilgram between 1510 and 1515, with the vivid heads of the early Fathers of the Church, Augustine, Gregory, Jerome and Ambrose, and with Pilgram's own carved face peering out from behind a shutter under the stairs. All the way up the intricate balustrade are delightful animals symbolizing sins.

There is another self-portrait bust of Pilgram under the organ support, like a huge bracket, on the wall of the north side. This one dates from the same time as the pulpit (1513) and is a masterpiece of early portraiture, closely akin to the work of Dürer, who was a contemporary.

The Apostelchor (Apostles' Choir), the south choir, contains the tomb of Frederick III, another masterpiece, this time the work of Nikolaus of Leyden who took 45 years to complete it, from 1467 to 1513. With carvings representing Good and Evil (protective spirits and animals) all round, the monumental marble block on top depicts the emperor in his coronation robes.

The Marienchor (Virgin's Choir) contains the tomb of Rudolph IV, the founder of both the cathedral and of Vienna University whose small statue was on the southwest door. Apart from some lovely medieval figures on the wall here, the thing that draws the eye is the Wiener Neustadt altar which dates from 1447. A riot of wood carving, gilt and color, it was brought to St. Stephen's from the Cistercian Monastery of Wiener Neudstadt in 1884. It represents the three figures of the Virgin and the saints Barbara and Catherine, with the Coronation of the Virgin above and scenes from her life in the wings. Resting on the top of this reredos are the remains of an altarpiece dedicated to St. Andrew (c. 1420).

The central, early Baroque, high altar (1647) is a turmoil of black marble with a picture of the cathedral's patron saint being stoned to death.

There is much else to see; the Catacombs, where the internal organs of the Habsburgs rest, all except their hearts (one has the impression that the Day of Resurrection is going to be an extremely busy one among the various crypts of Vienna while the Habsburgs pull themselves together); in the Catacombs can be seen the vestiges of the original basilica which was burned down in 1258, thus opening the way for the construction of the present building; the Eligius Chapel, to the right of the main entrace, with some exquisite sculpture, especially the statue of St. Ludmilla with her palm leaf, and a Virgin and child; and the Kreuzkappelle (Chapel of the Cross), on the other side of the west door, and a Baroque wrought-iron grille and the tomb of Prince Eugene of Savoy.

On one of the pillars of the nave is a stone plaque telling of the various contributions of other parts of the country to the reconstruction. Each province took responsibility for a particular section of the work. There may be other church interiors which have more striking architectural features, but there are very few that represent the investment of more civic pride than does St. Stephen's. The interior has now finally been cleaned and repainted.

Teutonic Knights and Mozart

Under the very shadow of the cathedral is the Deutschordenskirche (Church of the Teutonic Knights), at Singerstrasse 7. The church is small and deceptively simple, dating back to the middle of the 14th century. It is a perfectly maintained, white interior with the arms of the past Masters on the walls.

The Baltic area was the realm of the Order in the Middle Ages—and realm is not too strong a word, for although the High Master of the Order was not actually a king, he was an unchallenged monarch. At the height of their power in the 14th century, the Teutonic Knights tried to build a Kingdom of God on earth in the lands bordering the Baltic—Danzig, East Prussia, Livonia and Estonia. With military dictatorship, theocracy and colonialism all working in a strange unison, the Knights forged a history that is too little known. A relic from the Order's days in the Baltic is the 16th-century winged altarpiece, painted in the Netherlands and once housed in St. Mary's Church in Danzig. It was moved to its present position in 1808. Sadly, it is not easy to see this lovely work without help, as it is set back on the altar.

On the second floor above the church is the Treasury of the Order. Usually under the guardianship of a brother of the Order is a multifarious collection of items from the Order's long history. Coins and documents, especially a charter of Henry IV of England, with a fine seal; silver and gold table decorations of fine craftsmanship—a salt cellar decorated with "adders tongues", actually fossilized teeth which were supposed to detect poison in food; a stag with antlers and earrings of coral; a complicated astronomical clock, with jewels and filigree work; weapons and ceremonial dress; medieval paintings. From the window of the last room, the one that contains the paintings, there is a fine view down into the beautifully-kept courtyard of the building, dominated by the soaring presence of the cathedral.

Continue a little way down Singerstrasse, turn into Blutgasse and then right into Domgasse. Here, at Number 5, Mozart lived from 1784–87 and composed *The Marriage of Figaro*. It is now a commemorative museum. In the block formed by Domgasse, Blutgasse, Singerstrasse and Grünangergasse there is a grouping of old houses, called Fähnrichshof, that has been restored.

Much restoration of facades has taken place in Vienna. Many buildings have been washed and countless houses have had their frontages repainted. The face of old Vienna is much brighter than for many long years.

A Basilisk and the Old University

The Viennese are essentially apartment dwellers, but apartment dwellers with a difference. Their apartments are inward looking. The whole of the old city consists of high buildings, some with very thick ancient walls, built round central courtyards. These "castles" close up tight in the evening as the citizens pull up their metaphorical drawbridges and prepare for the night's siege. In the daytime one can peek into some of these inner courtyards to see the great variety of architecture they represent, but remember that they are integral parts of private houses, so peek politely.

Across Stephansplatz from the North Tower of the cathedral is the 17th-century Archiepiscopal Palace which houses the very interesting Diocesan Museum. A small lane runs through the buildings here down to Wollzeile, named after the wool merchants and weavers who once lived and worked in the neighborhood.

The next street parallel to Wollzeile, Bäckerstrasse (starting at the small square, Am Lugeck, where there is a statue of the inventor of printing, Gutenberg) has many historic houses, Number 14 being especially interesting with a Renaissance courtyard, dating from the end of the 16th century. Keep your eye roving over the facades as you walk along; you will surprise all sorts of carving and other decorations.

Sonnenfelsgasse, the next down on the left, also has many lovely houses, especially Number 15, with a fine gateway. This is now the area of the Old University. The square, Dr. Ignaz-Seipel-Platz (also known as Universitätsplatz) is named after one of the first Chancellors of the Austrian Republic, who lived from 1876–1932 and was not only a politician but also a Catholic priest and expert on international law, an unusual combination. He was enormously influential in forming modern Austria and steered his country through the chaos of the 1920s, maintaining a simplicity of life that unnerved some of his staff. He would travel to international meetings by third-class railway carriage.

The 1627 facade of the University Church of the Assumption (Jesuitenkirche) takes up one side of the narrow square. It was originally built in the early 17th century, but was given its present sumptuously ornate interior by the architect Andrea Pozzo between 1703 and 1705. An abbé, Pozzo was also a great fresco painter and he brought his talent to the ethereal ceilings here, as well as to the twisting columns and the dramatic altar with its high-flying crown.

Down one of the other sides of the square is the great Ceremonial Hall of the Old University (now called the Akademie der Wissenschaften— Academy of the Sciences) built in the 1750s by a French architect, Jean-Nicolas Jadot de Ville-Issey, a court architect to Maria Theresa. It is very much a neo-classical building and clearly the work of an artist working in the disciplines of French symmetry. The opposite side of the square is taken up by the Alte Universität, where the original University was housed, ruled by the Jesuits. This building is from 1623–27. Careful cleaning is restoring to this small square a large measure of its original elegance and color; indeed the whole complex is to be renovated over the next five years.

Curving round behind the University Church is Schönlaterngasse (Street of the Beautiful Lantern), once part of Vienna's medieval *Quartier Latin* and rapidly becoming so again. Attractive bars, literary cafes, galleries and boutiques are creating a lively atmosphere, very much to the students' taste and intriguing to visitors.

Number 7 is the Basiliskenhaus, one of the earliest houses in the area, parts of it dating from as early as 1212. In those days the house was a bakery and a basilisk, a small fire-breathing and very deadly type of dragon, was living in the well, poisoning the water and turning anyone who came near to stone. A young baker's apprentice, clearly well versed in the classical myths, managed to kill the unpleasant lodger by showing it a mirror and so turning it to stone, in its turn.

Just along from the Basilisk House is Alte Schmiede (The Old Smithy), a commercially run place containing a reconstruction of a medieval blacksmith's workshop, with a restaurant and art gallery.

On the other side of the Basilisk House is an arched gateway leading into the quiet close of the Heiligenkreuzerhof. This was once the city residence of the Cistercian monks from Heiligenkreuz (Holy Cross), which lies not so many miles from Vienna, close to Mayerling. Many of the great monastic foundations of the Middle Ages had their urban headquarters, in much the same way as the great families maintained a city palace so as to be near the corridors of power, and this was one such. The small square, really a large courtyard, contains a lovely Baroque chapel of St. Bernard; unfortunately, rarely open.

Schönlaterngasse leads to the main Post Office next to the church of the Dominicans, after whom a remaining bastion of the old fortifications is named. The regular postal counters and all-night post office facilities are in the building to the left, in the Fleischmarkt.

Adjoining Rotenturmstrasse is Fleischmarkt, since at least 1285 the center of the meat trade, the butcher's quarter, but also meeting place of the Greek merchants, a fact still commemorated in the names Griechengasse and Griechenbeisl (Greek Tavern), the latter an atmospheric old restaurant. The Greek church, next to the Griechenbeisl on the Fleischmarkt, has been cleaned and restored and is now a magnificent fantasia of brick and gold leaf. Part of the ancient city defenses can be seen here at Number 9 (a 13th-century tower, best viewed from the courtyard of Number 7). Number 9 Fleischmarkt has an attractive 16th-century sculpture of the Virgin on its facade.

St. Rupert and the Romans

Just above the point where Fleischmarkt intersects Rotenturmstrasse, lies Hohe Markt. This square is notable as the place where you can see part of the Roman foundations that have been unearthed, for this was roughly the middle of the Roman encampment. In the basement of No. 3 there is a small museum, with sections of two Roman houses which were revealed during drainage work in 1948. Further excavations have made this quite an interesting place to visit, with the Roman central heating (hypocaust) and other remains, as well as excellent maps of the area.

The square as a whole has had a lot of restoration. In the middle is a lovely fountain, now renovated and almost rivaling the Plague Column for interest. It is called the Vermählungsbrunnen (the Fountain of the Virgin's Wedding) and it dates from 1732. High on an arch in one corner of the square is the Anker Clock, a delightful 1911 confection, with many Viennese figures marking the time—among them Marcus Aurelius, and Haydn. Midday is the time to see the full procession in all its splendor. There is a plaque on the wall to the left of the clock which carries details of the figures.

Rotenturmstrasse slopes down from the cathedral to the Danube Canal at Franz Josefs Kai. "Kai" is the same word as "quay," and this was the stretch of the bank where, in the old days, the fishing boats and the merchants' vessels tied up. Turn left, and two blocks along you will come to the Church of St. Rupert (Ruprechtskirche) standing high above the embankment. On street level is the site of the hotel which, during World War II, was the Gestapo headquarters, demolished in postwar disgust. There is a prominent commemoration stone in its place.

St. Rupert's is an old church, parts being from the 11th century, but it was almost certainly built on the site of a gateway of Vindobona, and no doubt some of the Roman masonry was used in the first foundations, laid, so legend says, around 740. St. Rupert was the patron saint of the Danubian salt merchants, and you will notice the carved bucket that accompanies his statue outside the church. The building is often locked, indeed you may only get in by going to a service on Sunday. The nave and tower are pure, simple Romanesque, and the remainder Gothic. There are some attractive modern decorations, including some very contemporary windows in yellow and blue, which harmonize surprisingly well with the ancient stones.

This, then, is the heart of the Roman settlement. A little beyond St. Rupert's is another memory of those early days in the name of the street that runs up from Franz Josefs Kai—Marc Aurelstrasse, called after the Roman philosopher-emperor. Walk up this sloping street (it has no particular points of interest) and along its continuation, Tuchlauben, and then turn right down Bognerstrasse, you will reach . . .

Am Hof

Am Hof is yet another impressive square. In the center stands the Mariensäule (Virgin's Column), erected originally in 1646 after the delivery of the city from the Swedes during the Thirty Years' War. That column was removed and the present one put up in 1667. Around the base are the figures of War, Hunger, Plague and Heresy, all very real dangers during so many of Vienna's long centuries.

Am Hof is so called from the fact that the Babenbergs had their palace (castle might be a better word) here, before the center of power was moved under the Habsburgs to the Hofburg. The site of this court was to one side of the square, where Number 7 now stands. It was, naturally, the scene of intriguing events in medieval times. Vienna was on the route to the Holy Land, and many crusaders, among them Barbarossa, stayed here. Walter von der Vogelweide, the famous Minnesinger who features in Wagner's *Tannhäuser*, was a figure of the Babenberg court in the 1190s when it was a center for art and poetry.

On the opposite side of Am Hof is the Church of the Nine Choirs of Angels, the Kirche Am Hof. The facade is a wonderful example of the early Baroque style, designed by Carlo Carlone in 1662. From the deep central balcony Pope Pius VI blessed the city in 1782 and, on August 6th, 1806 heralds proclaimed the end of the Holy Roman Empire of the German Nation. This facade, with its windows, statues and recessed wings, is more like the varied front of a palace than of a church. The interior seems simpler than it is, with its octagonal pillars, grey and white coloring and very high ceiling. The generally subdued effect provides a muted background for the paintings, and of these the finest is probably the ceiling fresco by Maulpertsch, in one of the side chapels to the left.

Back in the square, notice the attractive house, Number 38, painted in tones of ocher, a simple yet very pleasing facade. Number 83 has an interesting sculpture of the Virgin. In the corner of the square is a facade that is anything but simple, it is an ornate building which looks as if it started life as a triumphal arch and carried on from there. You will be surprised to find that it is the headquarters of the Fire Brigade but, to be fair, it was once the City Armory, was "Baroqued" in the early 1730s and is surely the most unlikely fire house to be found anywhere.

In the tiny streets behind the church, Schulhof and Seitzergasse, you can see the Gothic walls of the choir. You will find a fine old restaurant, the Gösser Bierklinik (Steindlgasse 4) nearby. We enjoy the way they cook game in season so much that we have never dared find out just what a "Beer Clinic" might be. Around the corner, at Schulhof 2, is the Uhrenmuseum (Clock Museum), containing over 3,000 timepieces of every description, from the 1440s to today's electronic marvels. The prize exhibit is an astronomical clock of 1769 by Rutschmann.

Take Parisergasse into Judenplatz where there is a rather clumsy statue of the German dramatist Lessing. This was the medieval ghetto of Vienna and must have witnessed many scenes of human misery. The plight of the Jews in the days before the Enlightenment was not a happy one. In 1421 two hundred and ten were burned alive, and for the next two centuries Jews were constantly humiliated. It is a part of Viennese history that should be remembered today with pain.

There are interesting houses here, in and around the Judenplatz. Number 4 is another Mozart House; at the corner of the square, on Number 12 Kurrentgasse, two pillars support a flying lion and a fish; Number 2 has an attractive Gothic bas relief; and Number 11, which continues through to become Wipplingerstrasse 7, is the former Bohemian Court Chancery, built by Johann Bernhard Fischer von Erlach from 1708 to 1714, though changed later. Walk around this building into Wipplingerstrasse and there you will see two really superb frontages facing each other across the street. The front of the Bohemian Chancellery is the original Fischer von Erlach one, with sculptures by Mattielli, and what sculptures they are! Across the road, its statues protected from the pigeons by netting, is the Alte Rathaus, the Old Town Hall. It had been the Guildhall for centuries before it received its lovely facade in 1699.

Go through one of the short, arched passages into the Alte Rathaus' central courtyard. Against one wall is the Andromeda Fountain, by Georg Raphael Donner. This is a gentle work of bas relief, with Andromeda (whom legend says was an Ethiope, though she certainly isn't in this version) and the dragon in the foreground, and with Perseus about to swoop down for the kill. The work is normally dated 1741, but since Donner died in the February of that year, it must almost certainly be placed a little earlier.

From another corner of the courtyard an archway leads to Salvatorgasse. Turn left and walk a short way along to the Church of Maria am Gestade.

St. Mary on the Banks (Maria am Gestade) is one of the finest Gothic churches in Vienna. It used to stand on the edge of the river, as its name shows, but it is now quite a bit inland from the water. It was built on Roman foundations and also on a 12th-century church, which accounts for the rather strangely angled nature of the floor plan of the present building. The inside has just been restored to reveal much previously unsuspected beauty. The church as it now stands is late 14th century though restored after the damage caused during the Turkish sieges. The tower is seven-sided and culminates in a lacey crown. Inside, the feeling of the nave is pure unadulterated Gothic (it is worth comparing this church with the mock-Gothic of the Votivkirche). In a small chapel to the right, halfway up the nave, are two superb parts of a triptych by the Master of Maria Stiegen (1460); they show the *Annunciation* and the *Coronation of the Virgin* and are of a quality rarely seen in public outside the most prestigious galleries. Also worth remarking are the figures high up around the nave and some of the stained glass.

St. Peter's Church

Leading out of Stephansplatz is the Graben, another attractive shopping street and part of the widespread central pedestrian mall. The Pestsäule (Plague Column) shoots up from the middle of the Graben like a geyser of whipped cream. It was erected between 1682 and 1693 to commemorate the deliverance of Vienna from the Black Death which had raged in the city in 1679. A huge number died and the Emperor Leopold I vowed this memorial while the plague still held sway. Among the sculptors who worked on the column was Johann Bernhard Fischer von Erlach whom, with his son, we will meet constantly around Vienna. It is worth surmounting the overall effect of swirling upward movement to look more closely at many of the excellently sculpted details. This is one of the most exuberant Baroque monuments anywhere (especially in its cleaned and regilded state) and as such deserves close inspection.

Just past the column, on the right, is a short turning leading to Peterskirche (St. Peter's Church). Mind the traffic; frustrated by not getting into the Graben it's fairly fierce. St. Peter's was built at the very beginning of the 18th century, but the site had held several churches before that. There is a panel on the outside showing the first Christian temple in Vienna being founded by Charlemagne, a quite possible legend. True or not, the site was long hallowed by the time the present structure was begun. It was finished by the middle 1730s and so is exactly contemporary with the more imperial Karlskirche.

The main architect was Johann Lukas von Hildebrandt and the interior is probaby the best example of church Baroque in Vienna, certainly the most theatrical. The fresco on the dome is by Rottmayr but is a bit difficult to see clearly unless the light is coming from the right angle. It shows the *Coronation of the Virgin,* a favorite subject for ceilings as it calls for an imitation sky with lots of clouds and flying angels. The pulpit is an especially fine one with a highly ornate canopy and opposite the pulpit is what can only be described as a religious tableau. Its subject is the martyrdom of St. John Nepomuk, who was thrown into the River Moldau, and here, like a scene on stage are the gold figures of the saint and his brutal attackers and the silver waters of the river, frozen as it pours under the bridge. This is a theme which you will recognize in other Austrian churches, as it was a favorite religious story.

The decoration of the high altar with its double grove of soaring pillars and the *trompe l'oeil* above is especially remarkable. As you leave the church, notice the florid ornamentation of the organ and its gallery.

A turning on the left at the end of the Graben, Kohlmarkt, will lead you directly to Michaelerplatz and the Hofburg.

The Hofburg

The Michaelerplatz, the starting point for visiting the Hofburg is worth exploring on its own account. The Michaelerkirche (St. Michael's Church) takes up one side of the strangely shaped square. It is an amalgam of periods, from Romanesque and Gothic through Baroque and Neo-classical, but the chief effect is Gothic. The interior has some very old frescos and fine carvings. The floor of the nave is indented with tombstones and the high altar seems almost a Baroque afterthought. Near the altar is the tomb of the great 18th-century poet, Pietro Metastasio, who lived in a house on the Michaelerplatz for about 40 years, dying there in 1782. He was court poet in the city during the reign of Maria Theresa, and turned out many opera libretti, at least one of which, *La Clemenza di Tito,* survived changing musical tastes to be set by Mozart.

To the right side of the church, in the Michaeler Passage (go through the arch marked No. 6), is a 16th-century carving of the *Agony in the Garden,* with the Betrayal and Crucifixion shown simultaneously in the medieval manner.

Facing St. Michael's across the square is the flat green facade of the Looshaus (The Loos House). The Griensteidl Café, a famous literary haunt, used to stand here, much frequented by such writers as Schnitzler and the young Hofmannsthal. It was pulled down in 1910 to make way for the present building, the work of Adolf Loos (1870–1933) and the cause of a storm of protest. The windows of Franz Josef's private apartments looked straight out on the new building and, staunch conservative as he was in his tastes, he actually went to law to try and get the "monstrosity" demolished; he called it "the house with no eyebrows". He lost the case. The building was a landmark in undecorated architecture.

Easily eclipsing the Loos House is the great entrance gateway to the Hofburg, the Michaelertor, and the facade on either side, now freshly painted. It is flanked by two well-muscled fountains symbolizing imperial sea and land power. Passing through the triple arch is a main roadway with side walks on each side. Here, under the oval dome, are the entrances into the Imperial Apartments (on the left). These rooms are interesting to visit for the glimpses that they give into the lives and characters of the last Habsburgs, especially of Franz Josef and his wife. Her exercising equipment and other personal effects bear mute witness to the attractive woman who was stabbed by an assassin in Switzerland, after having spent most of her married life wandering the face of Europe in an attempt to avoid the rigid duties that awaited her in Austria.

The Hofburg is like a nest of boxes, courtyards opening off courtyards and wings (trakts) spreading far and wide. A large part of it still houses the offices and conference rooms of the Austrian Government and cannot be visited by the public. This great complex was built at several periods and when each expansion was planned, rather than demolish existing buildings, they were partly adapted and swallowed by the new buildings.

Once through the first, covered courtyard, you are in the In der Burg, with its statue of Franz II. In the left wall is the gateway to the Schweizerhof, the original nucleus of the Hofburg. This gateway is a splendid one, built in 1552, as the inscription at the top says, at the direction of Ferdinand I. It is painted a reddish-brown, black and gold, and gives a fine Renaissance flourish to the facade. The disused moat runs on either hand. Through the Schweizertor lies the Schweizerhof's courtyard with the Hofburgkapelle in one corner. In this Court Chapel, from September to June, high mass is celebrated on Sundays and holidays by the Hofmusikkappelle, made up of the Vienna Boys' Choir, opera singers and musicians from the Vienna Philharmonic Orchestra. Needless to say, it is a musical experience of the first order, so it is essential to buy tickets in advance. They can be obtained on the preceding Friday from 5 P.M. in the Schweizerhof.

The Imperial Treasury

After two years' closure for total renovation, the Imperial Treasury reopened in 1987. Exhibition facilities have been thoroughly modernized to provide a fitting setting for this unique collection.

Among the items of historic significance are a wealth of heraldic objects—tabards, those short tunics that heralds used to wear emblazoned with their masters' coats of arms; staves of office, borne by chamberlains and other officers of the court; huge keys, fit for the castle of a sleeping princess; hoods for falcons; in fact all the panoply of a vast and anciently organized court. The time span covered by the multitude of items, both sacred and secular, is impressive, too. From the Imperial Crown, encrusted with roughly shaped gems and thought to date from about 962, through to objects less than a century old, the collection includes treasures covering some thousand years.

The heart of the Treasury's riches is the Burgundian Treasure, and especially those parts of it connected with the Order of the Golden Fleece. This most romantic of medieval orders of chivalry (which is still in existence) passed into the hands of the Habsburgs when, by marriage, they became Dukes of Burgundy. The Burgundian Treasure encompasses robes, vestments, paintings and jewels and spans several centuries, but of all its evocative pieces the most striking are the church vestments. These form a full set for the celebration of mass; copes, altar cloths, dalmatics and so forth. They are covered with the most delicate and brilliant "needle paintings" of angels, scenes from the bible and saints. These embroideries date from the years before 1477 and rank with such works as the *Très Riches Heures* of the Duc de Berri as masterpieces of medieval creativity.

Here and there in the collection are various objects made of "unicorn" horn—actually narwhal horn. They are touching reminders of that mixture of faith and fantasy that characterized the Middle Ages, for not only was the horn considered a symbol of Christ, but the legend that a unicorn could only be captured by a virgin added to its rarity. One extremely long *ainkhürn*, nearly 8 feet, suggests that the virgin officiating at that particular hunt must have been of quite staggering purity.

Part of the collection's historical relics tells the sad story of the son of Napoleon anad Marie Louise, the King of Rome. Among the more poignant items is the cradle presented by the City of Paris in 1811, no everyday cradle, but more of a cradle-throne from which the baby-king could hold court. It is a happy, elaborate piece of furniture, and not unlike a car from a very aristocratic carousel.

Do not miss the large number of reliquaries, each one containing its fragment of bone, tooth, wood, hair, clothing or other relic of saint or martyr. These reliquaries are often of extremely rich workmanship, encasing their freight of holy detritus in objects of earthly beauty.

And while on the subject of relics, one of the most fascinating is the Holy Lance, supposedly the lance which pierced Jesus' side, into which has been embedded a Holy Nail, wrenched from the Cross. Of great historical interest, too, is a saber, perhaps presented by one legendary hero, Haroun al Raschid, to another, Charlemagne; and a mantle from around 1133, embroidered with two heraldic lions, preying on a couple of prostrate camels, a superb relic of the Norman kings of Sicily.

The Neue Hofburg Museums

Return to In der Burg and turn left, go through the vaulted corridor and out into the openair again. This is the Heldenplatz, the Square of the Heroes. There was a plan, when the Hofburg was being extended in the 1880s, to build two huge sweeping wings, facing each other. Only the wing on the left was actually constructed, the Neue Hofburg. In the center of this great sweep stands the statue of Prince Eugene of Savoy on his rearing steed, while over to your right is the Archduke Karl. The opposite side of the Heldenplatz from where you entered is bounded by the Burgtor, a kind of triumphal arch, dedicated now as a war memorial.

The flight of steps up to the center of the Neue Hofburg will lead you to three museums, the Collection of Weapons, the Ephesus Museum and the Collection of Musical Instruments.

The Ephesos (Ephesus) Museum is the newest of the three, and employs the most modern techniques for display. By a clever use of metal scaffolding poles the large sections of masonry rescued during the archeological digs at Ephesus have been placed in exact relation to each other, to give a sense of the scale and form of the original buildings. One of the main features of the exhibition is the remains of a large frieze (dating from the middle of the 2nd century A.D.) from the mausoleum of Lucius Verus, rather in the fashion of latterday Elgin Marbles. It tells of the conquest of the Parthians, confused in movement and without the elegance of its Greek original, but full of vivid details. Also on display are large relief maps, expertly made of wood, which with other models, help the understanding of the terrain that yielded up these fine if fragmented sculptures.

Above the Ephesus Museum is the Collection of Musical Instruments, mentioned at the beginning of this chapter. It is worth visiting, especially if you are interested in early keyboard instruments. On our last visit we had the delight of hearing Beethoven's piano being tuned, and its clear bell-like notes followed us round the galleries like Papageno's magic chimes. The instruments come in all shapes and sizes, a harp in the form of a harpooned fish, a table clavier with drawers and inkwells, one with a curved keyboard, another with the black and white notes reversed. But it is the associations that haunt many of the pianos which make them so interesting. Mahler's piano, one belonging to Brahms, to Clara and Robert Schumann, Haydn's . . . the list is endless. When Mozart called Vienna "Piano Land" he wasn't exaggerating.

The Collection of Weapons (Waffensammlung) is one of the best in the world. The ranks of suits of armor, contained in a maze of rooms, are accompanied by all manner of weapons—swords, crossbows, early guns and pistols, and all backed with fine Flemish tapestry. Many of the pieces are from the most renowned craftsmen of Spain, Italy and Germany. From the Middle Ages up to the 17th century, the possession of the latest fashion in arms and armor was comparable to owning the latest motor car today,

HOFBURG

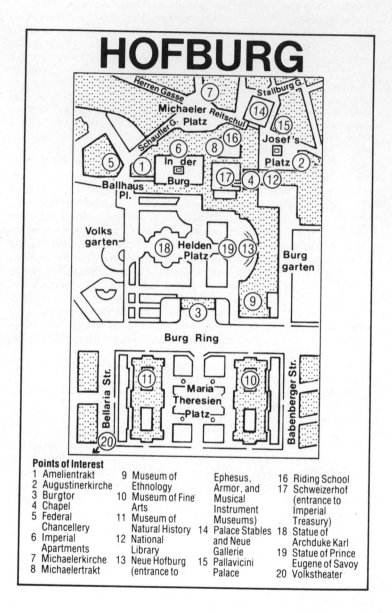

Points of Interest

1 Amelientrakt
2 Augustinerkirche
3 Burgtor
4 Chapel
5 Federal Chancellery
6 Imperial Apartments
7 Michaelerkirche
8 Michaelertrakt

9 Museum of Ethnology
10 Museum of Fine Arts
11 Museum of Natural History
12 National Library
13 Neue Hofburg (entrance to

Ephesus, Armor, and Musical Instrument Museums)
14 Palace Stables and Neue Gallerie
15 Pallavicini Palace

16 Riding School
17 Schweizerhof (entrance to Imperial Treasury)
18 Statue of Archduke Karl
19 Statue of Prince Eugene of Savoy
20 Volkstheater

with a similar balance between the utilitarian and the artistic. Here, too, are exotic items captured from the Turks. Not infrequently, as you walk through the rooms, you will see a suit of armor that seems to embody a sense of menace, to have a brooding, threatening life. One can easily understand what a place of terror a medieval battlefield must have been.

There is a fourth museum in the Neue Hofburg, the Museum für Völkerkunde (Ethnographical Museum). The entrance to this one is at the other end of the Neue Hofburg, by the Ring. It is a very rich collection of pieces from all over the world, illuminating societies and cultures not only thousands of miles, but centuries apart. Among the treasures are the robes and head-dress of Montezuma, miracles of feather work. It gives yet another sidelight on the Habsburgs to realize into what remote corners of the world their empire reached.

The Riding School and the New Gallery

If you return to the Michaelerplatz, you can begin to explore the range of buildings that runs to the right, along Augustinerstrasse. The first one, tucked in to the right, is the Winter (or Spanish) Riding School. This is one part of Vienna known throughout the world, for the elegant white Lippizaner horses have become a kind of trademark for the city. For the last 300 years they have been perfecting their *haute école* riding demonstrations, to the sound of Baroque music. The Winter Riding School was built between 1729 and 1735, and once again the architect was Fischer von Erlach.

The breed was started in 1580 and proved themselves in battle as well as in the complicated "dances" for which they are famous today. While it is easy to see them rehearsing, obtaining a ticket for full performances needs planning well in advance.

Across the road from the Riding School (entrance under the colonnade) is the Neue Galerie (New Gallery) in the Stallburg (Palace Stables), which is where the Lippizaners live. You will have to climb two long flights to reach the pictures as there is no elevator. The New Gallery collection is of paintings from the mid-1800s to just after World War I. The rooms are utterly plain, painted white, with the paintings displayed on simple colored screens. The general effect is to show the pictures to the very best advantage. The artists represented range from Millet and Corot, through Delacroix and Courbet (some fine landscapes) to Monet (a luminous garden), Renoir and van Gogh, and end with two fine canvasses by Munch. Along the way there are several German and Austrian contemporaries of these better-known artists, notably Böcklin (with a remarkably pneumatic *Sea Idyll*) and a group by Lovis Corinth, showing his strikingly bold style. There are rarely more than one or two pictures by any single painter, so that the total effect is of an easily assimilable collection of thoroughly representative works. A delight to wander through and highly recommended.

The National Library and the Augustine Church

Return to the colonnade which opens into Josefsplatz, probably Vienna's loveliest square, with a statue of Josef II in the center. The entrance to the National Library, or rather to that part of the National Library that the public most frequently visits, is at the far left corner of the square. As we mentioned before, the Prunksaal (Grand Hall) of the Library is open for only an hour a day in winter (11–12) though from 10–4 in summer, so plan ahead.

This is one of the grandest Baroque libraries in the world, in every sense a cathedral of books. It was created by Fischer von Erlach the younger from the designs of his father, while the frescos in the dome are the work of Daniel Gran and are superb examples of the difficult art of *trompe l'oeil.* The books around the central space under the dome were bought in 1738 from the library of Prince Eugene of Savoy, which contained thousands of priceless items. They are mainly in uniform red bindings. Behind the high ranks of shelves there are hidden bays onto which sections of the shelves open like doors, increasing the shelf capacity tremendously, giving space for scholars to work and preserving the design of the interior. This Library has a higher proportion of manuscripts of textual or artistic importance than any comparable library outside the Vatican.

Opposite the National Library, across Josefsplatz, are the Pallavicini and Palffy Palaces, both built by great families who needed to be near the court. A little further along, at the corner of Augustinerstrasse and Lobkowitz Square, is the Baroque Lobkowitz Palace, built at two periods, with the top floor being by Fischer von Erlach, senior, in 1709. It was here that Beethoven's *Eroica* was first performed. The building has now been lovingly restored and renovated, and houses the Theater Museum.

Turning right out of Josefsplatz you will come to the Augustinerkirche (the Augustine Church) which nestles into the side of the Hofburg as befits a court parish church. It was built soon after 1330 and has a fairly severe interior following heavy restoration in the 1780s. The severity is relieved by two main features, the lovely organ case, painted in gold and white, and the tomb of the Archduchess Maria Christina, the favorite daughter of Maria Theresa. This eye-catching monument is the first thing you see, straight ahead, on entering the church. It is in the form of a white pyramid with mourning figures walking towards an engulfing black doorway. It was by the great Italian sculptor Canova, who first arrived in Vienna in 1797.

In the little crypt of the Chapel of St. George (1337) are the hearts of the Habsburgs in their urns. This is the third place of burial for the scattered remains of the imperial family. But the Augustine Church is not only a place of death, for it was the scene of some famous marriages over the centuries (Napoleon—by proxy—to Marie Louise, and Maria Theresa to Franz of Lothringen), and it is also the place to hear some of the most beautifully performed church music in Vienna. In addition to the magnificent main Rieger organ in the loft, a beautiful Silbermann Bach organ newly built in Holland was installed during 1985 and is also used for concerts.

The Albertina and the Burggarten

The farthest point of this triangular section of the Hofburg contains the Albertina (continue along Augustinerstrasse to the right), called after its founder, Duke Albert of Saxe-Teschen, husband of Maria Christina (she of the Canova tomb). At the risk of sounding over-lyrical, it must be said that the Albertina is one of the greatest collections of graphic art in the world. It contains well over a million items dating back to the 14th century. Not only does it house the founder's own collection, but a multitude of works collected by Prince Eugene together with many later additions.

The fragility of many of the works makes them difficult to display and some are on view in exact replicas. Also, with 50,000 original drawings and 1,200,000 prints, it is impossible to show the whole collection at once, but the Albertina frequently mounts exhibitions of originals which are always worth visiting, and as money permits, conditions are being improved. The most popular part of the collection are the works of Dürer, and especially his *Praying Hands.*

Across the street in the triangular square is the Hrdlicka memorial to victims of World War II, so named for the sculptor who created it and who, in typical Viennese fashion, insisted that if the pieces weren't placed in this spot, he would resign his commission, triggering a dispute which has by no means ended.

Up the steps by the entrance to the Albertina and round the corner of the ramp lies the Burggarten, an attractive small park which contains the only openair statue of the Emperor Franz Josef in Vienna. It stands in a small Japanese-style thicket. There are two other monuments in the Burggarten, one to Mozart, an 1896 conception of the composer, with too many cherubs and an overromanticized statue; the other, large and impressive, to Goethe.

The Academy of Fine Arts and St. Charles's Church

Facing Goethe, across the Opernring, is Schiller. His statue stands in the center of the Schillerplatz, and behind him you will find the Akademie der Bildenden Künste (Academy of Painting and Fine Arts). This art school, founded in 1692, is the oldest art academy in the German-speaking countries. It was declared the "Arts Authority for the Nation" in 1812, and was the responsibility of Metternich from 1818 to 1848. Hitler's antisemitism may have been partly due to his inability to pass the entrance exams, a failure he attributed to the Jewish professors.

While there are many interesting works to see, a *Conversation Piece* by de Hooch, a serene portrait by Rembrandt, eight views of Venice by Francesco Guardi, a Memling *Crucifixion*—the one masterpiece that dwarfs all the others is the *Last Judgement* by Hieronymus Bosch, one of his best works. It is a triptych which tells the story of the Fall of Man, from the beginning in the Garden of Eden on the left-hand panel, to the tortures of Hell on the right-hand one. The Judgement itself and the sins of mankind fill the central section.

From the Academy, Nibelungenstrasse and Friedrichstrasse lead to Karlsplatz, a huge square above the main subway interchange where, outside Josef Olbrich's Sezession, Marc Anthony is seated in a bronze quadriga drawn by four lions. The Sezession, famous but for many years so drab it escaped notice, has just been restored. The "Golden Cabbage" has been regilded, the facade restored to its pristine white, gold and green. Inside, the rooms have been perfectly restored, and in the newly created cellar you can see the restored *Beethoven Frieze* by Gustav Klimt. The attractive cafe will provide a welcome coffee break in stylish surroundings.

Dominating the Karlsplatz is one of Vienna's greatest buildings, the Karlskirche (St. Charles's Church), dedicated to St. Charles Borromeo. It was begun in 1716 by Johann Bernhard Fischer von Erlach and completed after his death by his son, Joseph Emmanuel. The church was, from the first, a slightly disturbing mixture of styles and now with a large reflecting pool in front of it—in which sits a very fine but totally inappropriate statue by Henry Moore—the effect is of even more artistic confusion, bordering on the bizarre.

The church was another outcome of the plague of 1713, being vowed by Karl VI, whose name, Charles, was thus linked with Charles Borromeo. The front of the church is flanked by two great columns, inspired by Trajan's column in Rome. They are out of keeping with the building as a whole, but were conceived with at least two functions; one was to carry scenes from the life of the patron saint, carved in imitation of Trajan's triumphs, and thus help to emphasize the Imperial nature of the building; and the other was to symbolize the Pillars of Hercules, suggesting the right of the Habsburgs to their Spanish dominions which the Emperor had been forced to renounce.

The interior of the church is based on a central oval shape, faced with chill marble. One is overwhelmingly conscious of a symmetrical and almost musical balance in the way the whole design interacts, leading the eye always upwards to the great dome, where Rottmayr's superb frescos open a new heaven. The high altar is illuminated by stiff shafts of gilt sunlight and cloaked with a penumbra of plaster clouds; not surprisingly it bears a close affinity to the Plague Column on the Graben. The altar pieces are by Prokop, Ricci and Gran.

Next to the church is the City Museum, with exhibits showing the history of Vienna. The displays are arranged chronologically and can give the visitor a very valuable basis of understanding of the way the city developed. Among the items on display are smaller carvings and pieces of stained glass from the cathedral; flags, banners, portraits and documents, all imaginatively exhibited. There is also a fair selection of paintings, Klimt's among them, which have a relevance to the city's history.

Further round the park-like square and above the subway are the two restored entrances to the city railways by Otto Wagner, once derided, but now considered attractive examples of Jungendstil.

Beyond the Otto Wagner pavilions is the Musikverein, home of the Vienna Philharmonic. In the glittering Golden Hall and the two smaller auditoria, some of the best concerts in Vienna are held. Among many other valuable manuscripts, its library contains original scores by such composers as Beethoven, Brahms, Mozart and Schubert. The Archives may have some of these treasures on display in the exhibition room upstairs.

Herrengasse and the Scottish Church

From Michaelerplatz, in the opposite direction to Augustinerstrasse, Herrengasse is lined with interesting buildings, mainly government offices in former palaces. Number 5 is the early 18th-century Wilczek Palace, adjoining the Ministry of the Interior which is housed in a 16th-century palace restored in 1811. Number 9, the 17th-century Mollard-Clary Palace, contains the Museum of Lower Austria, which gives a good idea of the history of the province as well as of the province's natural history. The neo-Classical Landhaus, Number 13, seat of the Provincial Government and Diet of Lower Austria incorporates an early 16th-century chapel by Anton Pilgram, the sculptor of St. Stephen's.

A left turn (Landhausgasse) leads to the Minoritenplatz, Vienna's quietest and most aristocratic square. The 14th-century Minoritenkirche (Church of the Minor Friars, now Mary of the Snow), damaged during both Turkish sieges, was restored in the Gothic manner in the late 18th century. The eight pillars inside divide the nearly square interior into three naves with a floor of plain tiles. There are frescos of heraldic devices on the walls. There is also a large and not entirely successful mosaic copy of Leonardo's *Last Supper* to one side, and a fragment of a fresco of St. Francis.

Among the surrounding palaces, number 1 is the Haus-, Hof- und Staats-archiv (Household, Court and States Archives), whose collection of documents (much of which has now moved to a new building on the outskirts of Vienna), is second only to the Vatican's. Some of this embarrassment of riches is displayed in the fireproof wing of the Bundeskanzleramt (Federal Chancellery), which now also houses the Ministry of Foreign Affairs. It was from this former Court Privy Chancellery, built by Lukas von Hildebrandt on the Ballhausplatz, that the great imperial chancellors determined the fate of Europe. Minoritenplatz 3 is the 17th-century Dietrichstein Palace. Number 5, in the Starhemberg Palace, is the Ministry of Education. It was here that the defender of Vienna against the Turks in 1683 died. Most magnificent is the Liechtenstein Town Palace, which goes through to Bankgasse. This is another palace-lined street and is located between the Burgtheater and the Herrengasse. The Batthyany Palace, the Renaissance Portia Palace and Lukas von Hildebrandt's Kinsky Palace follow one another down it to Freyung, where the Schottenkirche, founded by Duke Jasomirgott in 1155, stands.

The Duke had the Babenberg drive to embellish his court and obviously thought that solid scholarship would help. The monks who gave the foundation its name were actually Irish, not Scottish in the modern use of the word for, in medieval Latin, Ireland was called *Scotia maior*. The church was frequently rebuilt and took its present shape only in the late 1880s. On one side of the various courtyards of the vast Schottenhof, last remodelled in the 1830s, is the Abbey whose Benedictine monks still teach in Austria's oldest High School.

The square beside the church is called Freyung because it commemorates the church's right to grant sanctuary for three days. Opposite the church is the 17th-century Harrach Palace, and, beyond the Austria Fountain whose figures represent the Empire's main rivers, is the vast, imposing Batthyány-Schönborn Palace, a joint enterprise by Fischer von Erlach and Lukas von Hildebrandt (now the Mexican Embassy). Higher up on the Schottengasse—tucked away at the back of a small courtyard on the left— is the Melkstiftkeller, an atmospheric wine cellar.

Between Freyung and Herrengasse is a huge building known as the Palais Ferstl. A beautiful shopping arcade links the two streets and inside they have restored the Cafe Central, once favorite haunt of Lenin, T. Herzl, Karl Kraus and assorted Viennese literary figures, with a lovely staircase. This complex is worth a visit, and if you are lucky, you may even get to see the Grosser Börsesaal, beautifully restored and now a public ballroom and congress hall.

Coming out of the Alte Börse, the second lane on the right is the Naglergasse, leading back to the Graben. What used to be a rather decrepit back street has been newly paved and turned into a chic boutique precinct. A row of five or six medieval houses with early-Baroque frontages have been painstakingly restored to excellent effect.

The Museum of Fine Arts

Across the Burgring from the Heldenplatz and Burgtor is the Maria-Theresien Platz, a formal garden where the focus is a statue of the Empress. It dates from 1880, assembling in one large group below the seated empress, her husband, eldest son, ministers, generals and others who made her reign glorious—Haydn and Mozart among them.

To the left is the Kunsthistorisches Museum (Museum of Fine Arts) and to the right the Naturhistorisches Museum (Museum of Natural History). If natural history interests you, you will be happy to wander in the seemingly endless rooms of stuffed animals on the first floor—but you should be warned that once you get in you may not find it so easy to escape from all those glassy eyes.

The ground floor has prehistoric relics, including many finds from the early Hallstatt civilization. Here, too, is the tiny bulbous *Venus of Willendorf,* some 20,000 years old, carved from limestone and thought to be one of the oldest pieces of sculpture in existence. We warn you, though, you'll have to search for it among much else on display. The Natural History Museum also has collections of meteorites and fossils.

Cross the geometrical gardens to reach the Museum of Fine Arts.

Downstairs are the collections of Egyptian, Greek and Roman art. They are well worth visiting as are the many medieval and Renaissance treasures—including Cellini's glorious gold salt cellar—but space forces us to examine just the painting collection on the first floor.

It is, perhaps, invidious to try to select from the incredible wealth of pictures in the Museum of Fine Arts any for special attention, but, on the other hand, a brief selection might help you to steer around the maze of galleries. The rooms are numbered in two sequences and round two courtyards running clockwise from I–VII (Roman numerals) and 1–13 ordinary numbers; anti-clockwise from IX–XV and 14–24. Room VIII links the two sequences. The rooms with the Roman numerals are the large ones; the smaller, outside rooms, have normal numbering. As you might expect, the large rooms have all the big-scale paintings—some of them striking, some merely pompous; the smaller rooms contain most of the jewel-like pictures, also many of the best portraits. If you suffer from museumitis or are short on time, do the sequences of smaller rooms first. If you have enough time to—take two bites at visiting the Kunsthistorisches Museum, we would heartily advise it. Descriptive information throughout the museum is now in English (and Italian and Japanese) in addition to German.

The museum is undergoing major reconstruction of the upper floors, including the floor that houses its world-famous paintings. Ask for a copy of the free guide leaflet in English at the entry desk; this "floor plan" is a current index to which artists are hung in which rooms. The postcards and reproductions at the sales desk give a clue as to the works the museum (if not the world!) considers the best or most famous in the collection, and if you compare the cards with the artists' names and room numbers on the floor plan, you should be able to find the museum's treasures. The staff is helpful with directions. But this collection is constantly being reshuffled and won't settle down until some future date, when better lighting and air-conditioning installations are completed.

In general, however, the rooms to your right at the top of the stairs will continue to house the works of the Italian, Spanish, and French schools.

Look for the room full of Titians; these give a fine cross-section of portraits and larger compositions. The Tintorettos include his grave signors. The room with the Caravaggios holds his dramatic *David with the Head of Goliath*. The Velazquez portraits of the Habsburgs give a reminder as to how this great collection was indeed formed.

If you move from the Italian, Spanish, and French painters into Room VIII, you begin the transition into the block of rooms at the left of the stairs that house the Dutch and German schools. Here are the hearty Brueghels, which you will instantly recognize, along with Van Dyck, Rubens in both religious and mythical moods, and the great Dúrer portraits of Kleberger and Maximilian I, merciless in their psychological revelation. The peculiar fantasies of Arcimboldo are often out on loan, but the museum seems to have an inexhaustible supply of Rembrandts and Hals to keep the walls covered despite loans to special shows.

The Ring

There are three ways of exploring the Ring. You can ride around it on streetcar 1 or 2; you can walk along it all the way from where it begins by the Danube Canal, at Julius-Raab-Platz, to where it returns to the Canal after its curving flight. Or, and this is the way we recommend, to explore it whenever you happen to cross it on other missions. While it is a pleasant sequence of boulevards, the succession of rather pompous buildings can be a bit overpowering.

There are three points on the Ring we would suggest seeing by themselves. Firstly the Stadtpark, which can be added to your visit to the Karlskirche. It is a romantic park, once dedicated to health cures and now chiefly delightful for visiting an openair café or restaurant, listening to an orchestra playing Viennese music in summer, or looking at the statues of composers, dotted around. The most famous of these is, of course, Johann Strauss himself, fiddling away under the trees and ignoring the symphonic clicking of cameras. Monuments to Bruckner, Franz Lehar, and Robert Stolz are also tucked away here, with Schubert at the other end.

The second stretch of the Ring is that which runs from Maria-Theresien Platz and the great museums along to Rooseveltplatz. This is the part of the Ring that was built up in the secure days of the 1870s and 1880s, where the Parliament Building, the City Hall (Rathaus), the Burgtheater and University all stand, mixtures of Greek revival, Roman and Gothic styles, with a fair measure of Renaissance to hold them together. It makes a pleasant walk, with the Rathauskeller or one of the openair cafés to refresh you *en route*.

At the end of the walk is the Votivkirche, built in 1856–79 to commemorate the escape of the young Franz Josef from the knife of a Hungarian assassin. The Emperor's brother, Maximilian, who died tragically in Mexico, pledged the Votivkirche in thanks. As is often the case with imitative architecture, its mock-Gothic looks tawdry and isn't helped by some truly dreadful modern stained glass and appalling lighting by night.

On this side of town, at Fürstengasse 2, you can find the Palais Liechtenstein (this is the second one, the other is mentioned on page 120), which houses the Museum of Modern Art. The palace was built at the end of the 17th century and is a very large, attractive place, with well-kept grounds and some superb frescos based on the story of Hercules. The collections of modern works assembled in the network of rooms is in strong, sometimes violent, contrast to their faded elegance. As so often with museums of modern art, where time has not yet had a chance to winnow the wheat from the chaff, there is a lot of very forgettable stuff on display, but there are also many pieces that are magnificent. It is well worth while taking time to explore the maze of rooms, as some of the very best works are the most deftly hidden. Among the modern masters represented are Derain, Ernst, Leger, Magritte, Picasso, Lichtenstein, Warhol and many others.

Across the Danube Canal

On the other side of the Canal from the Inner City you will find two parks, the Augarten, once Imperial private gardens but opened to the public first in 1775. A part of the main Augarten Palace, built for the widow of Leopold I, is used by the famous Augarten Porcelain Factory (started in 1717), and another part as the home of the Vienna Boys' Choir, an integral part of the Hofmusikkapelle.

The other park is the Prater, the leisure grounds of Vienna, with the wheel (famous from *The Third Man*), a Planetarium, side-shows, some of the Vienna Fair grounds, a racetrack, golf course and so on. There are parts, such as Krieau, which are not recommended for idle strolling unless you happen to be an expert in judo, though these are some way off. A Prater Pass is available to visitors, giving reduced admission to many attractions.

On the far bank of the Danube, beyond the Prater, is the Donauturm, the 826-foot tower, with rotating restaurant at 541 feet, and observation platform at 492 feet. Next to the Donaupark is the Vienna International Center, a vast complex of highrises round the International Congress Center seating 1,600 in nine halls. Three UN organizations moved in 1979—the International Atomic Energy Commission, the United Nations Industrial Development Organization and a Palestine refugee section—and their advent has turned Vienna into the third most important center for the United Nations. The building costs of 8.5 billion Schilling seem somewhat disproportionate in comparison with the token rent of 1 Schilling a year, and it does not have very much to offer to the sightseer. But for those interested, tours are conducted daily, starting at 11 A.M. and 2 P.M., taking about an hour, from Checkpoint 1. Cost AS40 per person. You will need your passport or other identification to get into the complex (tel. 2631–4193).

The Belvedere

Where Kärntner and Schubert Ring meet, Schwarzenbergplatz leads to the Hochstrahlbrunnen, a fountain spurting a jet of water high in the air, illuminated at night, and the huge Russian War Memorial, whose proletarian realism has been guaranteed by the peace treaty with Russia—however dearly the Viennese would like to remove it, as it blocks out the lovely Schwarzenberg Palace, designed by Hildebrandt (outside) and both Fischer von Erlachs (inside). One wing of the palace is still occupied by the Schwarzenberg family, the other is a luxury hotel. On the left is the Rennweg. Number 6 is the entrance to the Lower Belvedere, the country palace built for Prince Eugene, which consists of two main buildings, one here at the foot of the hill and the other at the top—the Lower and Upper Belvedere—with wide formal gardens in between. The whole complex was masterminded by Hildebrandt and is considered to be one of the most splendid pieces of Baroque architecture anywhere.

The Lower Belvedere contains the Museum of Austrian Baroque, and what better building to house it! This was the home of the prince and the long sequence of lovely rooms now forms the perfect background for the works of art, many of which were created at the time the Belvedere was being built; paintings and sculptures by Daniel Gran, Maulpertsch, Kremser Schmidt, Troger and Georg Raphael Donner. Donner's original lead figures for the Providence Fountain are here. The State Treaty was signed in the Belvedere in 1955 and there is a huge painting of those who took part—it makes an amusing study.

The climb up through the gardens is rewarded by a fine view over Vienna from the terrace, guarded by elegant sphinxes, at the top. The Upper Belvedere was used by the Prince for balls and banquets, and is still used by the Government for such functions. But its main interest lies in the collection of paintings by 19th and 20th century Austrian artists, especially those of Hans Makart, Egon Schiele, Boeckl, Gustav Klimt and Kokoschka. For those who have seen Klimt's work only in reproduction a surprise is in store, for the originals have a richness and incised patterning that gives them an almost three-dimensional quality. These more modern works are on the ground and top floors (with the Klimts and Schieles at the top), while the middle floor contains a lot of mid-19th-century paintings that will, to a non-specialist, seem rather drab. The best scheme is to go right up to the top floor and then work your way down.

The University Botanical Gardens run parallel to the gardens of the Belvedere, while across the Gürtel can be found the Army Historical Museum and the Museum of 20th Century Art. While in the 3rd district, have a cab take you to the corner of Löwengasse and Kegelgasse. There you will see the new apartment house built by the city of Vienna and designed by famous painter Friedensreich Hundertwasser. Not a corner is straight, not a line is horizontal and the facade is filled with trees, golden domes, colored ceramics and countless other details and quotations from other buildings. Hundreds applied for apartments here.

Schönbrunn

Schönbrunn is only a few minutes by subway (U4) from Karlsplatz. You can get off at either the Schönbrunn stop (then walk ahead, or enter the complex from Grünbergstr.) or the Hietzing/Kennedybrücke stop (then walk back). The trip takes a little longer by tram (line 58, from Babenberger Str. and Burgring) up Mariahilferstrasse, main artery leading west, flanked by department stores. You could see the palace and its grounds in a morning, or spend a whole day wandering through the many delights it offers.

It was the favorite residence of the Habsburgs from the time that it was built (1695–1749). Maria Theresa made it her main home, her daughter Marie Antoinette grew up here and carried her memories of Schönbrunn with her to France and to Versailles. Franz Josef was born and died here and preferred to live here above anywhere else. It was also the residence of the last Habsburg Emperor, Karl I, till 1918 and it was here that he abdicated.

The main gates lead into a wide courtyard, the Ehrenhof (Parade Court), bordered by the palace and its wings. To the right is the Coach

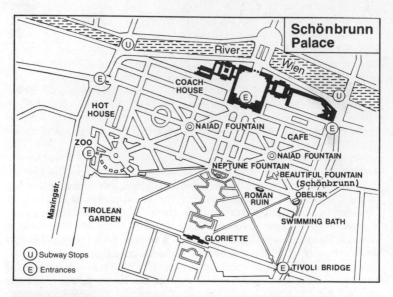

House, Wagenburg, where there is an outstanding collection of ceremonial state coaches, sleighs, hearses, fast private coaches, with the most splendid of all being the Imperial Coronation Coach.

Beside the Coach House is the Rococo Schlosstheater (Palace Theater) now home of a drama school and where performances are given in summer. The theater is beautifully restored, although you will still find a note to the effect that Napoleon witnessed a theatrical performance here.

Of the over 1,440 rooms in the palace, only about 45 can be visited, but those are of great richness and variety.

The tour starts with some of the rooms that Franz Josef and his wife (when she was around) lived in. It is interesting to combine these fairly simple apartments with those in the Hofburg and come up with a fairly clear picture of the kind of life that the old autocrat lived. You will see here the simple iron bedstead on which he died on November 21, 1916. Memories of Maria Theresa and Marie Antoinette come next and are followed by the prettiest sequence of rooms, starting with the Blue Chinese Drawingroom, rich with "Indian" wallpaper and eastern furnishings. The Vieux-Laque Room was a favorite with Maria Theresa, interesting for its Viennese Rococo and black lacquer panels and Chinoiserie decorations, the colored wood flooring is especially noteworthy. Then come the Napoleonic echoes, his own bedroom followed by more Maria Theresa chambers—the Porcelain Room, with around 210 blue ink drawings; the "Millions" Rooms, paneled in a special rosewood, framing in gilt 260 Indian miniatures done on vellum; the Tapestry Room, with its view of Crown Prince Rudolf's private garden. In the Duke of Reichstadt Room the Napoleonic echoes come back in full force, for this is where his son died at the age of 21 of tuberculosis.

The procession of smaller rooms is interrupted halfway round by the great state rooms—especially the Great Gallery, which has featured in many films and is the central glory of Schönbrunn's interior. The ceilings are magnificently frescoed, and one of the sections—that on the east end of incidents in the Seven Years' War—is a modern version, replacing the 18th-century one destroyed in a 1945 air raid.

The Chapel, which you can visit on the way out of the State Apartments, is fairly restrained, when compared with the riot of decorative excess upstairs, but it still houses one or two quiet masterpieces. It dates from 1700, and was slightly altered in Maria Theresa's reign.

Behind the palace lies the large formal park, divided by 40-foot hedges whose geometrically exact tops seem to have been clipped by a pair of celestial shears. The park contains several lovely fountains—two of which are especially attractive; the Schöner Brunnen (Beautiful Fountain), which gave the palace its name, and the Neptune Fountain, dating from 1780 with its triumphant statuary (it only plays in summer). Near to the Schöner Brunn you will find the Roman Ruins, a fake collection of ancient elements, grouped around a reedy pond. It is often besieged by art students, trying to out-draw Piranesi. Another point to head for is the Obelisk, with its fountain, pool and grotto. This 1777 theatrical fantasy terminates a striking view. Also in the gardens is one of the oldest zoos in Europe (founded in 1752) and probably the only Baroque-style zoo anywhere.

On the rising ground at the other side of the park is the colonnaded hall, the Gloriette, surmounted by an Imperial Eagle. It was originally hoped to build the palace on this eminence, but it proved to be impractical. From here, by climbing the winding staircase at one end, there is an extraordinary view across Schönbrunn and its grounds to the city and the Vienna Woods beyond.

Close to the Meidling Gate there is a pleasant outdoor cafe tucked under the trees. It makes an ideal spot for lunch on a summer visit.

PRACTICAL INFORMATION FOR VIENNA

ARRIVING IN VIENNA. By Plane. You can change your money and reserve your hotel room at the airport, if you need to. The airport bus takes you downtown to the City Air Terminal behind the Stadtpark, beside the Hilton Hotel, in about 30 minutes; the buses leave every 20 minutes. Fare—75 sch. Be sure you get the right bus; buses also go to the Westbahnhof via the Südbahnhof. There is now direct fast-train (S-Bahn) service from the airport (underground) to the Terminal at the Hilton. Trains run roughly every hour. A taxi into town from the airport costs about AS350.

By Train. You will end up at either *Westbahnhof* (West Station) if coming from Germany, Switzerland or western parts of Austria, or at *Südbahnhof* (South Station) if coming from southern parts of Austria or Italy. In each there is a Room Information Office *(Information-Zimmernachweis).* Both will make room reservations as well as provide other information.

By Boat. Praterlände/Reichsbrücke, on the main course of the Danube, is only a short taxi ride from the U Bahn station on the Vorgartenstrasse; slightly longer to the city center (taxis wait at the arrival of the ship). During summer information can be obtained from Vienna Tourist Association hostesses on incoming ships and at the landing stage.

TOURIST INFORMATION. For general holiday information on all of Austria inquire at the offices of the *Fremdenverkehrswerbung,* the Austrian National Tourist Office, Margaretenstr. 1, 1040 (587 20 00). Current events (theater performances, concerts, etc.) are given in German and English by telephone (dial 15 15) on a 24-hour basis.

City Tourist Information. *Fremdenverkehrsstelle der Stadt Wien,* Vienna City Tourist Office, with office in the Kärntner Strasse 38, tel. 513 88 92, open daily 9–7 for information on the city of Vienna but not room reservation.

For room reservation you may apply to the following offices:

Information-Zimmernachweis at Westbahnhof, West Station (83 51 85), open daily from 6.15 A.M. to 11 P.M.

Information-Zimmernachweis at Südbahnhof, South Station (65 21 68), open daily from 6.15 A.M. to 10 P.M.

Vienna Booking Service, Opernpassage (586 23 46), open Mon.–Sat. 9–6, Sun. 9–2.

Tourist information and room reservation office at the airport, open from 9 A.M. to 10.30 P.M. (7770–2617).

Tourist Information at Novotel on Westautobahn all year; Rasthaus Föhrenberg on Südautobahn, from April to end of Oct.; 9 A.M. to 7 P.M. both; *Information-Zimmernachweis* at the end of the Westautobahn (97 12 71); *Information-Zimmernachweis* at the end of the Südautobahn, Triesterstr. 149 (67 41 51). Information point at DDSG docking station on the Danube, Handelskai. (218 01 14).

Guides. Inquire in writing to *Verein der Geprüften Fremdenführer,* A-1130 Vienna, Montecuccolipl. 1–3. Vienna Guide Service member Charlotte Speiser, A-1220 Vienna, Rennbahnweg 27 (51 45 00) can help; or contact *Sektion Fremdenverkehr* (Tourist Section) (tel. 514 50 0) at the Chamber of Commerce. Also *Fremdenführerzentrale,* A-1090, Boltzmanngasse 19 (31 42 43). A half day on foot or by car will cost AS800. Also check the Vienna Guide Service branch at tel. 74 52 02. A 1½-hour guided group tour will cost about AS95 per person.

Embassies and Consulates. *British Embassy and Counsulate,* A-1030, Jauresgasse 10 (755 61 17); *Canadian Embassy,* A-1010, Dr. Karl Luegerring 10 (533 36 91). *U.S. Consulate,* A-1010 Gartenbaupromenade 2 (51451).

Motoring Information. *Österreichischer Automobil-, Motorrad- und Touring Club* (ÖAMTC), Schubertring 1–3 (711 99 70) and on the main road in from the airport at Schwechat (777277), open daily (including holidays) until 8 P.M., for emergency repairs also (95 40). Nationwide emergency repair (120). Traffic and road information (1590).

Lost and Found. Fundamt (Police), 1090 Vienna, Wasagasse 22 (31 66 110); Fundamt (Railways), Westbahnhof (56 50–29 96).

Escort Service and Baby Sitters. For these services, as well as for interpreters, translators or help in driving, contact the Meeting Center of the *Österreichischer Akademischer Gästedienst* (Austrian Student Society Service), Mühlgasse 20, 1040 (587 35 25). They have 2,400 students (male and female) on their rolls who are willing to help you.

Emergencies. If you need a doctor and don't speak any German, try *American Medical Society of Vienna,* Lazarettgasse 13 (42 45 68), or call your embassy. In case of an accident, call 133 for Police Accident Squad, and 144 for ambulance service.

Youth Hostels. *Verein der Wiener Jugendherbergen,* 1200, Friedrich-Engels-Platz 24 (35 07 51).

English Language Radio. "Blue Danube Radio" FM102.5, news, music and information in English from 7–9 A.M., 12–2 P.M. and 6–8 P.M. in Vienna area only. The 12–2 programming block is also carried nationwide on the sound channel of the second television program (FS2).

VIENNA DISTRICTS. Vienna is divided into 23 districts, and, if you are to get to know the city, it is as well to have some idea of how the system works and where the districts fall. The districts are numbered by a postal code which is based on the figure of 1000; the center two digits are changed—thus the 1st District (Inner City) is 1010, and the other end of the scale, the 23rd District, is 1230.

Area Code. The area code for phoning Vienna from outside is 0222.

HOTELS. Unless you are motorized—and particularly if you have only a short time to spend in Vienna—you will want to stay in the Inner City (1010), within walking distances of the most important sights, restaurants and shops. Besides, the best way to see Vienna is by strolling around, and this is done more easily if your base is not too far away.

The Inner City has all kinds of hotels, but mostly in the upper grades. There is a fair grouping of moderate and inexpensive ones in the Mariahilferstrasse-Westbahnhof (West Station) area, also within easy reach of most of the Inner City. The hotels a little further out can easily be reached by a short streetcar ride, or even on the subway if you are lucky.

If you are ready to take public transport, it can be a good idea to stay in the green districts, in some small hotel in the Schönbrunn area or outside of the Gürtel (Beltway).

From Easter through October it is advisable to make reservations in advance, as the tourist season is extended at each end by large international conventions. During the Vienna Fair in September, you might have to move further afield to nearby towns such as Tulln (try *Zur Rossmühle*) or Deutsch Wagram *(Marchfelderhof)* with hourly commuter trains to Vienna.

Following is our selection from several hundred hotels available. Within each grade all listings are alphabetical and represent no particular order of preference. All rooms with baths or showers unless otherwise stated; color television usually in the two top categories.

The City Tourist Office has several bureaux to help with accommodations if you are in any difficulty, see *Tourist Information* above.

Luxury

Ambassador, 1010, Neuer Markt 5 (51 4 66). On the square with the famous Donner Fountain, flanked on the other side by Kärntnerstrasse, the world-famous, elegant shopping street in the heart of Vienna. A favorite of diplomats, it has a long tradition of catering to important personalities, including Theodore Roosevelt and Mark Twain. The red brocade walls in the suites and the public rooms, including the restaurants, glitter from chandeliers. 106 airconditioned rooms at the lower price range in this category. AE, DC, MC, V.

Bristol, 1010, Kärntnerring 1 (51516–536). Along from the Opera, one of the venerable Vienna hotels. Founded in 1894, it has preserved its inimitable personality—a fine blend of tradition, elegance and Viennese *savoir-*

faire. 152 rooms, several plush suites; excellent *Korso* restaurant and pleasantly comfortable bar. Special executive club floor. AE, DC, MC, V.

De France, 1010, Schottenring 3 (34 35 40). Near Votivkirche. 230 rooms (those on the courtside are quieter). Restaurant and bar. AE, DC, MC, V.

Hilton, 1030, Am Stadtpark (75 26 52). Above the City Air Terminal, just beyond the Ring. 620 airconditioned rooms and 8 penthouse suites; one of the more attractive of this chain. Fine food in *Prinz Eugen* restaurant, one of the best in the city and much frequented by the Viennese themselves. *Vindobona* wine cellar; bar, cafe, health club with sauna, garage. Executive facilities. AE, DC, MC, V.

Imperial, 1010, Kärntnerring 16 (50 1 10–0). Near the Opera. This almost 100-year-old palace of imperial fame and elegant appearance is the top hotel in the city. Old traditions and modern comfort are reflected in antique furnishings and up-to-date facilities. A large painting of the old Emperor Franz Josef presides over the palatial stairway. Visiting heads of state and other leading dignitaries stay here. All 160 rooms are spacious and have baths with heated floors. Distinguished restaurant *Zur Majestat,* and cafe with Viennese music; cozy and intimate bar. AE, DC, MC, V.

Marriott, 1010, Parkring (51 5 18). Across from the Stadtpark, and an easy stroll to the city center. 304 luxury rooms, sauna, fitness room, indoor pool, good restaurants, particularly for Sunday brunch. 400-car garage. AE, DC, MC, V.

Palais Schwarzenberg, 1030, Schwarzenbergplatz 9 (78 45 15). A small and exclusive hotel in a wing of the Baroque palace still owned by Prince Schwarzenberg; 42 beds, all rooms with authentic period furnishings, most overlooking the garden. Uniquely quiet location off the very center of the city. Large parking area in the palace courtyard. Excellent restaurant and bar, with glorious terrace in garden. AE, DC, MC, V.

Plaza, 1010, Am Schottenring 1 (31390). Vienna's newest luxury hotel, associated with the Hilton chain. 252 rooms, all imaginable facilities, including sauna, fitness room, garage, restaurants. AE, DC, MC, V.

Sacher, 1010, Philharmonikerstr. 4 (51 4 56). Behind the Opera; legendary; original oil paintings, sculptures and *objets d'art* decorate the halls and rooms. Other treasures of the old days include a tablecloth embroidered with signatures of most of the famous crowned and "decrowned" heads of state of seven decades. A portrait of the redoubtable Frau Sacher looks over the bar; her husband Eduard Sacher, a famous chef, left as his legacy the recipe for *Sachertorte,* the world famous chocolate cake. See also *Restaurants.* AE, DC, MC.

SAS Palais, 1010, Parkring (51 5 17–0). Old Ringstrasse Palais rebuilt to house luxury hotel. 165 rooms, bar, restaurant. Ideal for businessmen who like to be housed in style. AE, DC, MC, V.

Vienna Intercontinental, 1030, Johannesgasse 28 (71122). Overlooking the City Park. 500 rooms, streamlined modern comfort; extensive convention facilities. Excellent *Four Seasons* gourmet restaurant; pleasant Brasserie. 250-car underground garage. AE, DC, MC, V.

Expensive

Amadeus, 1010, Wildpretmarkt 5 (63 87 38). Near St. Stephen's. 30 rooms, with mini-bar. Breakfast only. AE, DC.

Am Parkring, 1010, Parkring 12 (512 65 24). 65 airconditioned rooms on 11th and 13th floors, overlooking the City Park, garage. AE, DC, MC, V.

Alba Palace, 1050, Margaretenstr. 92 (55 46 86). 117 comfortable rooms, restaurant, garage. AE, MC, DC, V.

Ananas, 1050, Rechte Wienzeile 101 (55 56 21). Famous *art nouveau* printing works turned into a top-rate hotel. 536 rooms in different categories. 3 restaurants, bars, cafes. AE, DC, MC, V.

Astoria, 1010, Kärntnerstr. 32 (51 57 70). Entrance from Führichgasse. Old and traditional; 108 modernized rooms and good restaurant. AE, DC, MC, V.

Biedermeier, 1030, Landstrasse Hauptstr. 28 (75 55 75). 204 rooms with every comfort in a beautifully renovated 1820s house. Cafe, heuriger, restaurant. A genuine touch of old Vienna. AE, DC, MC, V.

Europa, 1010, Neuer Markt 3 (51 5 94). In the heart of the city. The best of its 102 airconditioned rooms are in the corners of the building. Evening musical entertainment in the restaurant, and a really dry martini in the little bar upstairs; large cafe on the ground floor. AE, DC, MC, V.

Graben, 1010, Dorotheergasse 3 (512 15 31). Just off Graben. 46 rooms, most with bath, rest with shower. Restaurant with diet specialties. AE, DC, MC, V.

Josefshof, 1080, Josefsgasse 4 (43 89 01–0). 38 rooms in Biedermeier style. A hotel to live in. Spacious rooms most with kitchen area. Sauna, buffet breakfast; quiet with garage. AE, DC, MC, V.

K & K Palais Hotel, 1010, Rudolfsplatz 11 (533 13 530). 66 rooms with every comfort. Modern and airy. AE, DC, MC, V.

Kaiserin Elisabeth, 1010, Weihburggasse (51 5 26–0). Near St. Stephen's; old, with 73 rooms, most with bath, some with shower. Homey atmosphere, good value. Once housed Wagner and Liszt. AE, DC, MC, V.

König von Ungarn, 1010, Schulerstr. 10 (515 84). Just behind St. Stephen's. 32 rooms, newly-restored but maintaining old traditions with a fine sense of style. Attractive indoor courtyard bar. Restaurant is in the next door house where Mozart once lived. AE, DC, MC, V.

Kummer, 1060, Maria Hilferstr. 71a (58895). 110 rooms, all with bath or shower. DC, MC, V.

Mailbergerhof, 1010, Annagasse 7 (512 06 41–0). In the center. 40 rooms. Breakfast only. An old house with lovely arcaded courtyard. AE, DC, V.

Mercure, 1010, Fleischmarkt 1a (53460). New hotel in good location. 105 rooms with every comfort. Seminar facilities. Restaurant. AE, DC, MC, V.

Opernring, 1010, Opernring 11 (587 55 18–0). Across from the Opera; 35 rooms, breakfast only. Inside rooms are quieter but lack the magnificent view of the Ring and Opera House. Unusually pleasant, personal touch. AE, DC, MC, V.

Prinz Eugen, 1040, Wiedner Gürtel 14 (505 71 41). Opposite South Station and near Belvedere Palace. 106 rooms, some with terrace and fine views, but noisy on the street side. Restaurant. AE, DC, MC, V.

Rathauspark, 1010, Rathausstr, 17 (42 36 61). Old building completely modernized. 117 rooms, comfortable and convenient. AE, DC, MC, V.

Römischer Kaiser, 1010, Annagasse 16 (512 77 51). Romantik Hotel. Central; 27 rooms in a Baroque palace; bar, breakfast only. AE, DC, MC, V.

Royal, 1010, Singerstr. 3 (512 46 31). Near Graben and St. Stephen's. 81 spacious rooms, on the top floor with terrace; some elegant suites. Bar and Italian restaurant, *Firenze.* AE, DC, MC, V.

Scandic Crown, 1020, Handelskai 269 (217 77). Impressive former warehouse directly on the Danube now turned into vast, luxurious hotel. 367 rooms. Restaurants, tennis courts and countless other facilities. 30 mins to city center via streetcar and subway. AE, DC, V.

Tourotel, 1100, Kurbadstr. 8 (68 16 31). 256 rooms; indoor pool, solarium, fitness room and sauna; garage, bar and restaurant. 45 mins from city center by direct streetcar line 67. AE, DC, MC, V.

Moderate

Albatros, 1090, Liechtensteinstr. 89 (34 35 08). Near U.S. Embassy. 70 airconditioned rooms; sauna, indoor pool, solarium; garage; bar and restaurant. AE, DC, MC, V.

Am Stephansplatz, 1010, Stephansplatz 9 (534 050). Across from St. Stephen's Cathedral. 66 rooms, most with bath or shower; those at the front offer magnificent views of the cathedral. Cafe. AE, DC, V.

Austria, 1010, Wolfengasse 3 (51 5 23). Near the main Post Office. 51 rooms, most with bath or shower. In quiet side street. AE, DC, MC, V.

Erzherzog Rainer, 1040, Wiedner Haupstr. 27–29 (501 110). Near Karlsplatz. 85 rooms, most with bath; those on streetside can be noisy. Fine restaurant. AE, DC, MC, V.

Fürstenhof, 1070, Neubaugürtel 4 (93 32 67). Close to Westbahnhof. Excellent value, spacious, old-fashioned comfort. Cool in summer. All rooms with shower. AE, DC, MD, V.

Ibis, 1060, Mariahilfergürtel 22–4 (56 56 26). 350 rooms, modern, convenient for Westbahnhof; efficient. Surprisingly good restaurant.

Kärntnerhof, 1010, Grashofgasse 4 (512 19 23). Near main Post Office. 45 rooms, all with bath or shower. Good breakfast, friendly. AE, DC, MC, V.

Savoy, 1070, Lindengasse 12 (93 46 46). Modern. 43 rooms; garage. AE, DC, MC, V.

Stefanie, 1020, Taborstr. 12 (21 15 0). Across the Danube canal. 130 rooms, all with bath. Garage, bar, and restaurant. AE, DC, MC, V.

Westbahn, 1150, Pelzgasse 1 (92 14 80). 63 rooms, some with bath or shower. Bar, garage. AE, DC, MC, V.

Westminster, 1090, Harmoniegasse 5 (34 66 04). Near U.S. Embassy. 75 rooms, most with bath. Garage, bar. AE, DC, MC, V.

Wilhelminenberg, 1160. Savoyenstr. 2 (78 66 26). Neo-empire Schloss on the edge of the Vienna Woods overlooking city, built for Archduke Rainer and now converted into a hotel. 96 rooms with shower. About an hour by streetcar and bus from city center. Very comfortable and excellent value. Terrace cafe.

Wimberger, 1070, Neubaugürtel 34 (93 76 36). 97 rooms, some with bath or shower. Well known restaurant and café. MC, V.

Inexpensive

Carlton-Opera, 1040, Schikanedergasse 4 (56 42 15). In quiet side street. 53 rooms, some with shower. Bar and restaurant. AE, DC, MC, V.

Europhaus Wien, 1140, Linzer Str. 429 (97 25 36). Rosenhotel. 22 rooms with bath. Garden. 45 mins from city center by bus and subway or streetcar.

Gabriel, 1030, Landstrasser Hauptstr. 165 (72 67 54). 29 rooms, most with bath or shower, parking. AE, MC.

Gloriette, 1140, Linzer Str. 105 (92 35 33). Not far from Schönbrunn; ask for a quiet room. 60 rooms, 12 with shower. Parking, restaurant.

Goldenes Einhorn, 1050, Am Hundsturm 5 (55 47 55). 17 rooms, some with bath or shower. Old type of family-run *Gasthaus.*

Goldene Spinne, 1030, Linke Bahngasse la (72 44 86). Near City Air Terminal. 43 rooms, some with bath or shower. Bar and restaurant.

Kugel, 1070, Siebensterngasse 43 (93 33 55). Near the Messepalast. 37 rooms, 3 baths, 24 showers.

Mariahilf, 1060, Mariahilferstr, 121B (597 36 05). 75 rooms, some with bath or shower. AE, DC, MC, V.

Post, 1010, Fleischmarkt 24 (51 58 30). Opposite the main Post Office. 106 rooms, some with bath or shower. AE, DC, MC, V.

Rathaus, 1080, Langegasse 13 (43 43 02). 37 rooms with shower.

Rosenhotel International, 1080, Buchfeldg. 8 (43 52 91). 54 rooms with shower. Garage, bar. AE, MC, V.

Schweizerhof, 1010, Bauernmarkt 22 (533 19 31). Central. 55 rooms, 48 showers, 7 baths. Restaurant. AE.

Strudlhof, 1090, Pasteurgasse 1 (31 25 22). Near U.S. Embassy. 48 rooms, all with bath. Garage, bar, and restaurant. AE, DC, MC, V.

Wandl, 1010 Petersplatz 9 (53 45 50). near Graben. 137 rooms, some with bath or shower. Facing the Barquoe St. Peter's Church. Bar.

Zur Wiener Staatsoper, 1010, Krugerstr. 11 (513 12 74). 22 rooms, conveniently situated. AE.

Pensions

There are quite a few pensions in Vienna but their rates are only slightly lower than the corresponding hotel categories. Those classified as top category are sometimes overpriced for the type of accommodations offered. The service personnel may be of lower quality, too. Simply getting into pensions can be a problem—they are often located on the top floors of large buildings, the lifts can be out of order, stairway lights switch off automatically—usually when you are catching your breath between floors—and, to round it off, the building doorman may well be out so you have to remember to carry a key. It sounds like home from home!

The pensions in outlying districts, however, are usually located in separate buildings of their own and are more like normal hotels than the old-fashioned Inner City brand of pension.

Expensive

Arenberg, 1010, Stubenring 2 (512 19 11). 25 rooms, all with bath or shower. In Inner City. Parking. AE, MC, V.

Barich, 1030, Barichgasse 3 (712 12 73). 17 rooms, all but one with bath or shower. Bar, garage.

Domizil, 1010, Schulerstr. 14 (513 30 93). 44 beds, newly opened, every comfort, although at the highest price of any pension. Buffet breakfast. Central; ask for second floor rooms at back. AE, DC, MC, V.

Rothensteiner Appartements, 1070, Neustiftgasse 66 (93 96 43). 19 rooms, all with bath. Parking. Atmospheric cellar-restaurant with good wine and Austro-Greek specialties. Open late.

Sacher Appartements, 1010, Rotenturmstr. 1 (533 32 38). No relation of the hotel of same name. Next to St. Stephen's cathedral. Tops in this category; spacious and friendly.

Wiener, 1010, Seilergasse 16 (512 48 16). 11 rooms, all with bath. Bar. At the top of this category.

Moderate

Some of the best of this category are in the suburban districts.

Christina, 1010, Hafnersteig 7 (533 29 61). 33 rooms, all with bath or shower. In the Inner City. Bar. MC.

City, 1010, Bauernmarkt 10 (63 95 21). 12 rooms, all with bath or shower. In the Inner City; restaurant. AE, DC.

Geissler, 1010, Postgasse 14 (533 28 03). 22 rooms, 3 with bath, 13 with shower. Garage and restaurant. Inner City. AE, DC, MC, V.

Kurpension Oberlaa, 1100, Kurbadstr. 6 (68 36 11). 40 rooms, all with shower. Sauna, indoor pool, solarium, fitness room and cure facilities; restaurant and parking. 45 mins by direct streetcar to city center. AE, DC.

Museum, 1070, Museumstr. 3 (93 44 26). 15 rooms, all with bath or shower. Garage, restaurant. AE, MC.

Neuer Markt, 1010, Seilergasse 9 (512 23 16). Inner City. 37 rooms, most with bath or shower. Restaurant for guests only. AE, DC, MC, V.

Nossek, 1010, Graben 17 (533 70 41). 26 rooms, some with bath or shower. Restaurant. Inner City. Reader recommended.

Inexpensive

Astra, 1090, Alser Str. 32 (42 43 54). 24 rooms, most with shower. AE.

Auer, 1090, Lazarettgasse 3 (43 21 21). Near the General Hospital. 14 rooms, only 2 with shower. DC, MC, V.

Austria, 1090, Garnisongasse 7 (42 21 36). Near Votivkirche. 13 rooms, some with bath or shower.

Felicitas, 1080, Josefsgasse 7 (42 72 12). Clean and friendly. Some rooms with shower.

Milanohof, 1170, Neuwaldegger Str. 44 (46 14 97). 11 rooms, all with showers. Restaurant, diet specialties.

Zipser, 1080, Langegasse 49 (42 02 28). Good value. All rooms with shower. V.

Seasonal Hotels

An excellent bargain are the student homes which operate as seasonal hotels between July and September. Single or double rooms, all with baths or showers. All Rosenhotels can be booked by calling 59 70 68–0.

Moderate

Academia, 1080, Pfeilgasse 3a (43 16 61). 368 rooms; the most luxurious, TV, bar and restaurant. AE, MC, V.

Avis, 1080, Pfeilgasse 4–6 (42 63 74–0). 72 rooms; bar and restaurant. AE, MC, V.

Panorama, 1200, Brigittenauer Lände 224–228 (35 15 41). A little far out, thus the cheapest for the usual fitness rooms, sauna, TV. 356 rooms, bar and restaurant. Parking.

Rosen-hotel Burgenland 1, 1090, Wilhelm-Exner-Gasse 4 (43 91 22). 71 rooms; suana, pool and fitness room; bar and restaurant. AE, MC, V.

Rosen-hotel Burgenland 2, 1060, Mittelgasse 18 (596 12 47–0). 150 rooms; sauna, fitness room; garage, bar and restaurant. AE, MC, V.

Rosen-hotel Burgenland 3, 1060, Burgerspitalg 17 (597 94 75–0).

Rosen-hotel Niederosterreich, 1020, Untere Augartenstr. 31 (35 35 26). 100 rooms; sauna, fitness room; garage, bar and restaurant. AE, MC, V.

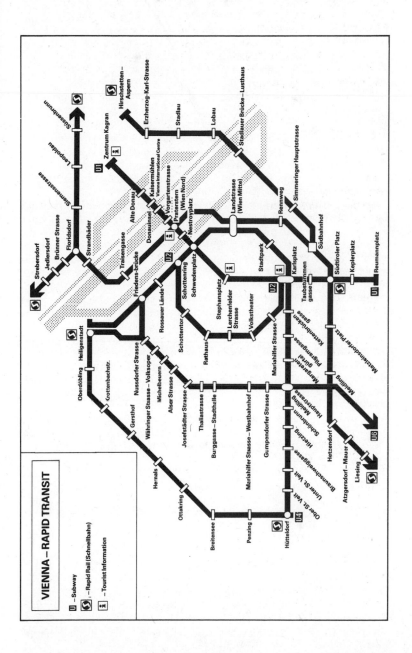

VIENNA – RAPID TRANSIT

U – Subway
S – Rapid Rail (Schnellbahn)
i – Tourist Information

Inexpensive

Alsergrund, 1080, Alser Str. 33 (43 32 31). 58 rooms, TV and restaurant.
Auersperg, 1080, Alser Str. 9 (43 25 49). 80 rooms. MC.
Haus Döbling, 1190, Gymnasiumstr. 85 (34 76 31). 550 rooms. Restaurant with diet cooking. Parking.
Haus Dr. Schärf, 1200, Lorenz-Müller-Gasse 1 (33 81 71). 130 rooms, TV, bar, restaurant and parking.
Josefstadt, 1080, Buchfeldgasse 16 (43 52 11). 40 rooms. TV and restaurant. MC, V.

GETTING AROUND VIENNA. By Subway. Travelers with one eye on the budget would find it advisable to get acquainted with Vienna's public transport system. There are streetcars (trams), buses, a subway, and there is also a *Schnellbahn* (fast railway) serving primarily the northeast, northwest, and southeast suburbs, including the airport.

Of the *U-Bahn* (subway), the U1 runs from Reumannplatz in the 10th District via Stephansplatz, Praterstern, to the Vienna International Center and Zentrum Kagran on the other side of the Danube. The U2 rings the Inner City from Schottenring to Karlsplatz. And the U4 covers Heiligenstadt (Vienna 19), Schwedenplatz (Danube Canal), Karlsplatz, Schönnbrunn and Hütteldorf. You will find the U-Bahn easy to use, with clear colored plans to facilitate travel. The U6 line links Heiligenstadt or Friedensbrücke (be sure to check the destination signs!) and runs along the Gürtel, including a stop at the Westbahnhof, before heading south to Meidling and on to Siebenhirten.

By Streetcar and Bus. In most busy areas, such as would be frequented by a tourist, the streetcars tread on one another's heels. They start at an incredibly early hour of the morning and continue, usually to between 11 and 12 at night. At each streetcar stop there is a sign which tells what cars stop there, where these cars are going and at what hours the first and last trips of the day are made.

Special city buses operate in the Inner City weekdays 7 A.M.–8 P.M. and Sat. until 2 P.M. Numbers 1A, 2A, 3A. At weekends night buses marked "N" operate at half-hourly intervals in all directions from Schwedenplatz. Cost AS25.

If you can't figure out the system yourself, your hotel porter or desk clerk can steer you to the right stop and tell you how to proceed.

There are public transport information booths in the Karlsplatz underpass (587 31 86), open Mon.–Fri. 7–6, Sat. and Sun. 8.30–4, and in the Stephansplatz underpass (52 42 27), open Mon.–Fri. 8–6, Sat. and Sun. and holidays 8.30–4.

Tickets for buses, streetcars and Stadtbahn cost AS20 if bought singly; AS14 if bought in advance in strips of 4 at a *Tabak Trafik* (tobacco store). With a single ticket, cars and means of transport can be changed if continuing in same direction without breaking the journey. Most streetcars have automatic ticket machines in the first car (marked by a yellow sign). They swallow 5 and 10 schilling coins, so have them handy. A 3-day network ticket costs AS102. An 8-day ticket is available for AS 220. This can be used on 8 separate days or by up to 8 people on one day.

Taxis in Vienna charge according to the meter, and they are comparatively cheap; luggage costs AS 10 per case. A tip of 10% is the usual. Taxis can be taken at the stands, which are numerous in the Inner City, or ask a hotel doorman to help. For radio-directed taxis dial 31 30, 601 60, or 43 69.

Horse Cabs. You can still get a *Fiaker,* the Vienna horsecab, on Heldenplatz, Stephansplatz and in front of Albertina, or even order one for a longer ride or a special occasion. Enjoyable but expensive. For longer trips check the price in advance.

By Car. The speed limit within the city limits is 50 km. (about 31 miles) per hour. Honking is forbidden unless absolutely necessary. Priority at intersections not otherwise marked is always to the car on the right. Streetcars (trams) have the right-of-way even when approaching from the left.

Parking. During the daytime it is quite difficult to find parking space in the inner city. In many streets in the center permitted parking time is limited to 1½ hours. In some of these areas special parking tickets are required, available at a Tabak Trafik (tobacco shop) or bank—they come in 3 colors: red for ½ hour, blue for 1 hour, green for 1½ hours, and cost AS 5 per 30 minutes. Parking is forbidden from December–May on all streets with streetcar tracks. There are several large underground parking garages, including Am Hof square near Graben, Karlsplatz, on Kärntnerstr., beside the Opera (there is an underground connection between the garage and the Opera), behind the Cathedral, Franz Josefs Kai near the Rotenturmstr., and on the Ring in front of the Rathaus. The last two tend to be less full. Many shops give a free hour's parking in one of these for every AS 300 spent.

Road Information. Call up 15 90 for recorded and information messages provided by the Austrian Automobile Club.

Car Hire. A variety of self-drive cars can be rented from *Budget Rentacar,* Hotel Hilton, (75 65 65), and at airport (7770–2711); *Carop,* Mollardgasse 15 (597 16 75), and at airport (7770–2699); *Denzel,* 1010, Kärntnerring 14 (65 44 81) and at airport (7770–3316); *Hertz,* Kärntnerring 17 (512 86 77); *Avis,* Opernring 1 (587 35 95); and at airport (7770–2700); *Inter-Rent Austria,* Schubertring 7 (75 67 17), and at airport (7770–2990), mostly VWs, will deliver the car to your hotel. A number of firms provide you with chauffeur-driven cars ranging from Cadillac to Volkswagen bus and with drivers who speak several languages; among them: *Goth,* 1030, Johannesg. 28 (in Hotel Intercont.) (713 71 96); *Franz Mazur,* Hasengasse 18 (604 22 33); *Kalal,* 1030, Rennweg 73 (715 59 25); also in Graz, Linz, Salzburg. *Buchbinder,* 1034, Schlachthausgasse 38 (712 26 43) rents cars at particularly favorable rates.

SEASONAL EVENTS. A monthly guide of events is available at all information centers without charge. The outstanding event of the winter season is Fasching, carnival season, which lasts from New Year's Eve until Mardi Gras. Hundreds of balls are given from Jan. to Feb., often 40 of them a night during its height. The first is the Kaiserball in the Hofburg on New Year's Eve, but the greatest and the most glittering is the Opernball in the Opera; white tie and grand gala evening gown are the requirements here.

Other top balls are Philharmonikerball in the Wiener Musikverein building, Campagnereiterball (Riding Club) in Pallavicini Palace, and Jägerball (Hunter's Ball) all of them very exclusive: invitations, and, of course, formal attire are needed; at the Jägerball you can only wear a festive dirndl and a salon-type of Styrian hunting suit.

There is a wide variety of other balls from those organized by various university departments, intellectual clubs, and artists to the informal dances of plumbers and chimney-sweeps. Vienna Fasching season is much more formal than its Munich and Cologne counterparts. You might also find yourself at a *Gschnas*—a fancy-dress ball. Many coffee-houses are open from the small hours to serve beer and gulasch-soup to weary party-goers on their way home.

February is usually the month for skiing in Vienna's outskirts and, together with Jan., the month of ice skating competitions.

March brings the Spring Trade Fair and the Viennale, a film festival of growing importance.

Art exhibits are often concentrated in **April,** which also marks the start of a long series of conventions. The first of the outdoor restaurants open.

Heurigers begin mushrooming with the warmer **May** weather.

The most prominent summer event is the Festival of Vienna, which takes place annually during May–June. There is a series of performances in all Vienna theaters, and a series of concerts given by famous local and foreign orchestras, choirs, and soloists in the various halls of Musikverein and Konzerthaus, as well as in several other palaces and gardens.

Palace and park concerts (including those in the Rathaus and Schön-brunn Palace), and operetta performances at the Staatsoper and Volksoper continue through **July** and **August,** which are the best months for Danube trips. Check for concert or opera performances by the Haydn Sinfonietta in the Redoutensaal of the Hofburg.

The Autumn Trade Fair is the feature of **Sept.** when the principal theaters re-open their doors. Others stay open all the year.

Grape harvests and wine tasting **Oct.;** this is also the month to get that pheasant—at least garnished with dumplings and cranberries.

Opera runs from **Sept.** 1 to June 30, with various high points, but closing only on Good Friday, Christmas Eve, and one night before and the night of the Opera Ball.

Some of the best church music can be heard in **Dec.,** at the end of which Vienna, with the Strauss introduction played by the Philharmoniker at their traditional Dec. 31 and **Jan.** 1 concerts, plunges with music in her heart into the New Year. Now equally traditional, the Vienna Symphony performs Beethoven's Ninth Symphony on both dates in the Konzerthaus.

SIGHTSEEING TOURS. Apart from the museums and galleries, the parks and gardens, all of which can be visited at your own speed, there are plenty of organized tours to introduce you to the city and its surroundings.

Wiener Rundfahrten (Vienna Sightseeing Tours), Stelzhammergasse 4, offer twice daily (in summer three times a day) sightseeing tours of the city, Kahlenberg and Klosterneuburg, and Heiligenkreuz, Mayerling and Baden; one-hour tours, 10 and 11.30 A.M., departure from the Opera.

Vienna by Night tours are operated by the same firm, as well as by a number of travel agencies offering sightseeing tours: *Cosmos,* Kärntnerring 15; *Cityrama Sightseeing,* Scholzgasse 10.

Vienna Walks, lasting up to 90 minutes, are guided walks that give you the chance to explore unknown Vienna. A monthly leaflet of planned walks is available from the Tourist Office. For details, tel. 74 52 02, 220 66 20 or 93 90 88.

On selected days at 2 P.M., a party leaves the Café Landtmann by the Burgtheater on a guided walk through the 1st. district, lasting about 2½ hours. German, English and Spanish commentary (32 46 774).

On summer Saturdays at 2.30, Sundays and holidays at 10 A.M., there is a special trip around the Ring, to Belvedere, Prater and Schönbrunn with an old-timer (1909) trolley. Departures from Karlsplatz. Get tickets in advance from the Stadtwerke Information office underneath, Mon.–Fri. 7 A.M.–6 P.M., Sat., Sun. and holidays 8.30 A.M.–4 P.M., AS150 for the two-hour trip, children AS50. Book early, as the trip is frequently sold out in advance. Any remaining tickets either at the office or on the tram. Information tel. 587 51 89, 587 31 86.

If you long to visit the sewers made famous by the *Third Man,* visits for parties of 20 people can be arranged on certain days. Tel. 42800–2950 for information.

Buses to nearby areas in Lower Austria leave from *Österreichisches Verkehrsbüro* (Austrian tourist agency), Friedrichstr 7, and from *Austrobus,* Opernpassage, for Mayerling and the Vienna Woods.

From April to Oct. the *Danube Steamship Company* (DDSG) provides sightseeing boat trips along the Danube Canal and the main Danube stream within the city limits. The starting point is at Schwedenbrücke on the Canal.

The caves at Hinterbrühl near Vienna, which were used during the war for the production of the Heinkel jet fighters, can now be visited; here also is the largest (6,200 square meters) underground lake in Europe.

VIENNA FROM A TO Z. All buildings of historic interest are marked by explanatory shields (in summer festooned with red-white banners); a guide in English called *Vienna from A to Z* to these shields can be bought for AS30 in the Vienna Information Office, Kärntnerstr. 38, or in most bookstores.

In most churches of importance there are coin-operated (AS 10) tape machines which will give you an excellent commentary on the history and architecture of the building in English.

SPANISH RIDING SCHOOL. A unique attraction of Vienna are the performances of the Spanish Riding School in Hofburg's Baroque and chandeliered manège. Courbettes, levades, and caprioles are performed to the sounds of Mozart's music. The white stallions, called Lippizaner (until 1918 the stud farm was in Lippiza near Trieste, at that time within the borders of Austria; now it is at Piber in Styria) are trained according to the classical method.

Most performances take place on Sunday mornings (10.45) and Wednesday evenings (7) from March to June and September to November. From mid-April through June, in September and October there are extra shortened half-hour performances on Saturdays at 9 in the morning. Performances are now also held in July and August. During summer occasional performances are held in the gardens of Schönbrunn in the evening; ask about details.

Tickets *must* be booked in advance, and reservations should be made as early as possible. Tickets for Sunday performances may be obtained from the *Spanische Reitschule,* Hofburg, 1010 Vienna. Reservations for Wednesday and shortened Saturday performances handled by ticket offices and travel agents *only.*

The training sessions can be visited from February to June, September till November, every day except Sunday and Monday, 10–12. Visits to the stables are possible, although days and times are not fixed. Check at the stable entrance.

MUSEUMS AND GALLERIES. At present there are over 50 museums and galleries in Vienna. Entrance charges are minimal; for extensive museum visiting, a "Museum Pass" can be bought for AS150—it is very good value as you can use it to gain admission to 39 museums, at any time of day. On the first Sunday of the month admission is usually free; small charge for guided tours. Always study the posters for current special exhibitions.

Important Note. Visiting hours differ from museum to museum and also in some cases between the winter period (Oct. 1 to April 30) and the summer period (May 1 to Sept. 30). Alas, these hours are anything but fixed and can change literally from day to day. With this in mind check carefully before setting out on a museum crawl. There are few things worse than being faced by a closed door with no chance to return when it's open. For information about times call 43 16 08 from 9 A.M. to 7 P.M.

Akademie der Bildenden Künste (Gallery of the Academy of Fine Arts), 1010, Schillerplatz 3 (58 8 16–0). Upstairs from the main entrance to the Academy. About 150 paintings, among them Hieronymus Bosch, Titian, Cranach, Rubens, Rembrandt, Van Dyck. Tues., Thurs. and Fri. 10–2; Wed. 10–1 and 3–6; Sat., Sun. and holidays 9–1.

Albertina, 1010, Augustinerstr. 1 (53 4 83–0). Magnificent collection of graphic arts. Mon., Tues., Thurs. 10–4; Wed. 10–6; Fri. 10–2; Sat., Sun. 10–1. Closed on holidays and Sun. in July/August. Jan.–Feb., special show featuring noted architect Adolf Loos.

Arsenal (Army Museum), 1030, Arsenalstr. (78 23 03). Mon. to Thurs. 10–4; Sat., Sun. 10–4.

Beethoven Museums. Beethoven-Haus, 1190, Probusgasse 6. **Beethoven Apartment,** 1060, Laimgrubengasse 22, where Beethoven lived from 1822–23. **Eroica House,** 1190, Döblinger Hauptstr. 92. Where he composed his 3rd Symphony. **Pasqualati House,** 1010, Mölker Bastei 8. Memorial rooms. All are open May to Sept., Tues. to Sun. 10–12.15 and 1–4.30.

Belvedere (Unteres), Lower Belvedere, The Baroque Musuem, 1030, Rennweg 6 (78 41 58–0). Tues. to Sun. 10–4.

Belvedere (Oberes), Upper Belvedere, 1030, Prinz Eugen Str. 27. Austrian Gallery; works by Klimt, Schiele, Kokoschka, Romanko and Biedermeier painters. Tues. to Sun. 10–4.

Bestattungsmuseum (Funeral Museum), 1040, Goldeggasse 19 (501 95/227). Collection of material connected with funerals. Open Mon. to Fri. 12–3 on request.

Bundessammlung alter Stilmöbel, 1070, Mariahilfstr. 88 (93 42 40–99). Collection of period furniture. Guided tours. Tues. to Fri. 9–4; Sat. 9–12.

Dom- und Diözesanmuseum, Erzbishöfliches Palais, 1010, Stephansplatz 6 (51 5 52–0). Cathedral and religious material, plus the 1365 portrait of Rudolf IV of Habsburg, a very early work. Wed. to Sat. 10–4; Sun. 10–1.

Ephesos Museum, 1010, Heldenplatz in the Neue Burg (93 45 41). Material from the excavations at Ephesus. Mon./Wed./Fri. 10–4, Sat. 9–4.

Fiaker Museum, 1170, Veronikagasse 12 (43 88 52). History of the Viennese horse cab. 1st Wed. of the month, 10–1.

Freud Haus, 1090, Berggasse 19 (31 15 96). Where Sigmund Freud lived and worked, 1891–1938. Mon. to Fri. 9–1; Sat., Sun. 9–3.

Glockenmuseum, 1100, Troststr. 38 (604 34 60). Private collection of bells. Open Wed. 2–5.

Haydn Museum, 1060, Haydngasse 19 (596 13 07). Haydn's apartment; one room commemorates Brahms. Tues. to Sun. 10–12.15 and 1–4.30.

Historisches Museum der Stadt Wien, 1040, Karlsplatz 30 (505 87 47). Excellent survey of Vienna's history, imaginatively displayed. Tues. to Sun. 9–4.30. Special shows this year feature the architect Adolf Loos, *Art in Prague ca. 1400,* Egon Schiele, and *Living in Vienna.*

Hermes Villa, 1130, Lainzer Tiergarten, access Hermesstr (84 13 24). Small palace built for the Empress Elizabeth; used for temporary exhibitions. (See also under *Parks and Gardens,* Lainzer Tiergarten.) Wed. to Sun. 9–4.30. This year's exhibits offer *Rudolf, a Life in the Shadow of Mayerling* (through Feb.) and *Discover—Cover Up, the Art of Seduction* (from Apr.).

Herzgruft, in the Augustinerkirche, Augustinerstr. 3. The "Heart Crypt" where the Habsburg hearts lie in silver caskets. Open on request (533 09 47).

Hoftafel- und Silberkammer, 1010, Hofburg, Michaelertrakt, (93 42 40–99), entrance just inside the Michaelertor, under the dome. Court silverware and porcelain. Tues. to Fri. and Sun. 9–1.

Josefinum (History of Medicine Museum), 1090, Währingerstr. 25 (43 21 54). Display of wax anatomy figures; development of the Vienna School of Medicine. Mon. to Fri. 11–3.

Kaisergruft, 1010, Neuer Markt (512 68 53). Burial place of the Habsburgs. Oct. to April, daily 9.30–12; May to Sept., daily 9.30–4.

Kunsthistorisches Museum, (Museum of Art History), 1010, Burgring 5 (93 45 41). One of the world's greatest artistic treasurehouses. Tues. to Fri. 10–6 (in summer Tues. and Fri. 10–9); Sat. and Sun. 9–6. Closed Mon.

Kunstlerhaus, 1010, Karlsplatz 5 (587 96 63). Daily 9–5, but hours may vary. May–June, *Vienna School of Fantastic Realism;* Dec.–summer 1991, *Mozart and His Era.*

Mozart Erinnerungsräume, 1010, Domgasse 5 (Figarohaus) (513 62 94). Mozart's apartment, where he is said to have spent his happiest years. Tues. to Sun. 10–12.15 and 1–4.30.

Museum des 20. Jahrhunderts (Museum of the 20th Century), 1030, Schweizer Garten (78 25 50–0). Close to the Südbahnhof. Modern art special exhibitions. Daily 10–6, except Wed.

Museum für Angewandte Kunst (Museum of Applied Arts), 1010, Stubenring 5 (711 36 0). A slightly disappointing collection of applied arts. Thurs. to Mon. 11–6.

Museum Moderner Kunst (Museum of Modern Art), 1090, Fürstengasse 1, in former Palais Liechtenstein (34 12 59). Incongruous mixture of magnificent rooms and the latest trends in art; some superb works, but patchy. Daily 10–6; closed Tues. Handy cafe.

Museum für Völkerkunde (Ethnological Museum), 1010, Heldenplatz (93 45 41). Huge collection of material from all over the world and many ages. Tues. to Fri. 9–4.

Museum für Volkskunde (Folklore Museum), 1080, Laudongasse 15–19 (43 89 05–0). Peasant art, furniture and crafts. Tues. to Fri. 9–3; Sat. 9–12; Sun. 9–1.

Nationalbibliothek (National Library), 1010, Josefsplatz 1 (534 10/245). The great Baroque central hall of the library, a cathedral of books—the Prunksaal. May to Oct., Mon. to Sat. 10–4 and Nov. to Apr., Mon. to Sat. 11–12. Special exhibits this year feature Italian Gothic and Renaissance book illustration (mid-May to mid-Oct.), and *Mozart and Salieri* (from Dec.).

Naturhistorisches Museum (Natural History Museum), 1010, Burgring 7 (93 45 41). All you could ever want to know about the animal kingdom (stuffed), rocks, early artifacts (including the Willendorf Venus), etc. Open daily 9–6. Closed Tues.

Niederösterreichisches Landesmuseum (Museum of Lower Austria), 1010, Herrengasse 9 (531 10 0). The landscape and culture of the area around Vienna. Tues. to Fri. 9–5; Sat. 9–2; Sun. 9–12.

Neue Galerie, i.d. Stallburg. 1010, Reitschulg 2. (533 60 45). Wed. to Mon., 10–4.

Planetarium, 1020, PraterHauptallee (near the Giant Wheel) (24 94 32). Sat., Sun. 3 and 5. Special performances for groups. In the same building, a museum of relics from the old Prater.

Schatzkammer (The Hofburg Treasury), 1010, Hofburg, Schweizerhof (93 45 41, weekends 93 44 48). A uniquely magnificent collection of the Habsburg crown jewels. Opening hours Mon., Wed. to Fri. 10–6; Sat. to Sun. 9–6.

Schatzkammer des Deutschen Ordens (Treasury of the Teutonic Knights), 1010, Singerstr. 7, (512 10 65). Daily 10–12; Tues., Wed., Fri. and Sat. 3–5.

Schloss Schönbrunn (Palace of Schönbrunn), 1130, Schönbrunner Schlosstr. (83 36 46). Guided tours only. **Wagenburg** (Carriage museum, closed Mon.) attached. Oct. to April daily 9–12, 1–4; May to Sept. daily 9–12, 1–5. **Gloriette,** daily 8–6. **Zoo,** daily 9–6.

Schubert Museums. Schuberts Geburtshaus, 1090, Nussdorferstr. 54 (34 59 924). Schubert's birthplace, a nice old Biedermeier building. Tues. to Sun. 10–12.15 and 1–4.30. **Schuberts Sterbehaus,** 1040, Kettenbrückengasse 6 (57 39 072). The house where Schubert died. Tues. to Fri. 10–4; Sat. 2–6; Sun. 9–1.

Johann Strauss Apartment, 1020, Praterstr. 54 (24 01 21). Birthplace of the *Blue Danube.* Tues. to Fri. 10–4; Sat. 2–6; Sun. 9–1.

Tabak Museum (Tobacco Museum), in Messepalast, Mariahilferstr. entrance (96 17 16). Tues. 10–5, Wed. to Fri., 10–3, Sat. and Sun., 9–1.

Technisches Museum (Technical Museum), 1150, Mariahilferstr. 212 (83 36 18). Tues. to Fri. 9–4; Sat. 9–1; Sun. 9–4. The first typewriter, among other treasures.

Theater Museum, 1010, Lobkowitzpl., in Palais Lobkowitz (512 24 27). In magnificent new quarters, with excellent rotating exhibitions from the (unseen) vast collection of theater memorabilia. Tues. to Sat., 10–5, Sun., 9–1.

Tramway Museum, 1030, Erdbergstr. 109 (712 12 01). Museum of old Viennese streetcars. May to Sept. Sat., Sun., holidays 9–4.

Uhrenmuseum (Clock Museum), 1010, Schulhof 2 (533 22 65). 3,000 clocks from many periods. Tues. to Sun. 9–12.15, 1–4.30.

Otto Wagner Apartment, 1070, Doblerg. 4. (93 22 33). The architect responsible for Vienna's "Jugendstil" (art nouveau) movement. Open Mon. to Fri. 9–12.

Wine Museum Döbling, 1190, Döblinger Hauptstr. 96 (36 10 042). Sat. 3.30–6; Sun. 10–12.

Zirkus und Clownmuseum, 1020, Karmelitergasse 9 (34 68 15). Museum tracing the development and history of the circus in Vienna. Wed. 5.30–7; Sat. 2.30–5; Sun. 9–12.

PARKS AND GARDENS. The average Viennese loves to do most of his warm-weather walking in the **Wienerwald** (Vienna Woods), romantic locale of Johann Strauss' famous waltz and of many a song and poem. The Wienerwald is not a park, but a range of low, wooded hills, crisscrossed by pathways and roads and framing Vienna on the western side. Among Vienna parks proper the visitor has a wide selection through which to stroll. Bus lines 10A, 39A and 38A will land you on the edge of the woods, as will 49B and 52B.

Belvedere Park. The main part between Lower and Upper Belvedere and a smaller part with an artificial lake between Upper Belvedere and Südbahnhof. Formally laid out in Italian terrace style. Many garden sculptures, wrought-iron gateway by Arnhold and Konrad Küffner made in 1728. Two main entrances, Rennweg 6 or Prinz Eugenstr. 27—both within easy reach of the center. Take the streetcar D marked Südbahnhof up the Prinz Eugen Str. to the Upper Belvedere.

Botanischer Garten, Rennweg 14, also next to Belvedere (the other side), is part of Museum of the Botanical Institute of the University; admission to the garden April 15–Oct. 1, 9 A.M. till dusk. Many rare plants. Permission from superintendent to visit interesting hot-houses.

Burggarten. A small, lovely park next to Neue Hofburg. Mozart Monument, statue of Emperor Franz Josef. On the Burgring.

Donauinsel. Has its own stop on the U1, on the Reichsbrücke. A natural leisure park on a 14-mile island between the two banks of the Danube. All facilities, beaches, walkways, and sunbathing, nude in designated areas.

Donaupark, Arbeiterstrandbadgasse, take the U1 as far as Alte Donau. Danube Park, laid out between the Danube and the so-called Old Danube for the International Garden Show of 1964. One of its most outstanding features is the 826-foot observation tower (Donauturm) with a rotating café-restaurant offering a magnificent view. There are several other cafés and restaurants.

Lainzer Tiergarten. Take streetcar 62 (Lainz) from diagonally opposite the Opera, change to bus 60B (Lainzer Tor), or take the U4 from Karlsplatz to Hütteldorf. A natural game park, formerly imperial game preserve, with deer, boar, and even mouflon, similar to the Rocky Mountain bighorn. The park is very large and it takes several hours to walk across it. In the middle is the Hermes Villa, built originally in the 19th century for the Empress Elisabeth and used today for exhibitions. There is a delightful restaurant at the Villa, indoor and outdoor eating, with good food at reasonable prices. Cars and other vehicles are not allowed and one must walk only along marked paths. There are several entrances. Open 8 A.M. until 1 hour before dusk, April 1 to Oct. 31. Closed Mon. and Tues.

Prater. Subway U1 from Karlsplatz to Praterstern. Very large natural park area (over 10 square km. altogether), once hunting grounds and pleasure park of the emperor, opened to public as early as second half of 18th century. At present includes various sports establishments (stadium, swimming pool, golf course, race track, etc.), Trade Fair exhibition area, and so-called Volksprater. Latter is actually an elaborate amusement park with the famous giant Ferris Wheel as an outstanding feature and several taverns, cafés, dancehalls inside and nearby. Particularly crowded on Sun. afternoons. It has been considerably restored and rejuvenated over the last two years.

Schönbrunn Park. Take subway U4 to Schönbrunn station and walk forward, or one more stop to Hietzing and walk back. A formally laid-out park in Baroque style belonging to Schönbrunn Palace. The Neptun Brunnen and Schöne Brunnen fountains, which gave the palace its name; Gloriette, a colonnade from the top of which there is a beautiful view of the entire Schönbrunn area and beyond; Zoo, Botanical Garden, Palm House, Tiroler Garten, carriage museum and magnificent Baroque theater.

Stadtpark. Along the Park Ring, with small artificial lake, various statues—among them one of Franz Schubert and the famous one of Johann Strauss. Bandstandmusic late afternoons and evenings in summer.

Türkenschanzpark. Next to School of Agriculture, bus 40A from the corner of Schottenring and Liechtensteinstr. The largest rambling wooded variety of park in the city, located on site where Turks built their fortification during siege of Vienna, hence the name.

Volksgarten. Next to Burgtheater, on site of old city wall fortifications. Several monuments, including an attractive one to the Empress Elisabeth and another to the author/playwright Grillparzer. Theseus Temple, occasionally used for exhibitions, and Tilgner Fountain with bronze fauns and nymphs. Refresh yourself in the company of the Austrian government at the delightful Cafe Meierei close to the Ballhausplatz entrance. Reasonable prices and good food and drink.

ENTERTAINMENT. Vienna is one of the main performing arts centers of the German-speaking world . . . indeed, where music is concerned of the world *tout simple*. Which is lucky for most visitors who may have trouble coming to grips with the latest and avant-garde production of a play by an unknown Serbo-Croat intellectual. Indeed, even Shakespeare in an "updated" version may appear in virtually unrecognizable shape, and classics closer to home have been known to suffer similar self-indulgent productions. But with music, and opera especially, the Viennese do not take excessive liberties.

Opera. The main opera house (51 4 44–0) and one of the world's greatest, is the **Staatsoper.** With a pre-season beginning in Sept. and the Festival in June, opera performances go on continuously from Sept. 1 to end June. There is also a new policy of operetta performances here during July and Aug. given by the Volksoper company. The yearly program represents a happy selection from different periods and composers, unlike some world opera houses which tailor their programs to the nationality of their singers. Evening dress and black tie are not compulsory, but they are recommended for first performances and for better seats. Jeans—even designer ones— are frowned upon, even in standing room. In Vienna, opera is a dressy event.

Operas of a lighter type and operettas are presented at the **Volksoper,** a bit out, on the corner of Gürtel and Währingerstr (take streetcar 41, 42 or 43 from "downstairs" at Schottentor on the Ring), but which is significantly cheaper than the Opera. Thus the tradition of Johann Strauss and Franz Lehar is continuing in the city that gave them their great successes.

Operettas and musical shows are also performed at **Theater an der Wien,** Linke Wienzeile 6 and at the newly renovated **Raimundtheater,** 1060, Wallgasse 18, and at the **Ronacher,** 1010, Seilerstätte/ Himmelpfortgasse.

In summer, some chamber opera performances are given in the **Schlosstheater** of Schönbrunn. Chamber opera is also planned for the **Redoutensaal** of the Hofburg.

Drama. Large posters all over town give up-to-the-minute information concerning all theaters. Visitors with sufficient command of the German language should take advantage of the unique attraction offered by Vienna in the field of dramatic arts at the **Burgtheater.** Vienna is one of the leading centers in the cultivation of German theatrical arts and for a German-language actor to play at the Burg means supreme achievement. Closed in summer.

Thanks to this tradition, it is logical that there are many other drama theaters in the city. Among the most important are—**Akademietheater,** Lisztstr. 1 (next to the Konzerthaus), this is the small house of the Burgtheater, classical and modern plays; **Theater in der Josefstadt,** Josefstädterstr. 26, the old theater of Max Reinhardt, classical and modern plays; **Volkstheater,** Neustiftgasse 1, dramas, comedies, folk plays; **Kammerspiele,** Rotenturmstr. 20, modern plays.

There are also a number of small theaters, such as the new **Künstlerhaus, Atelier Theater am Naschmarkt, Theater der Courage,** and **Tribüne.**

Simpl, Wollzeile 36, has a long tradition of poking fun at Austrian and world politics and life in general, but this type of entertainment calls for knowledge of local affairs and dialect.

The **Vienna English Theater,** Josefsgasse 12, 1080 (42 12 60) offers mainly standard pieces in English, featuring the occasional star to supplement the local company. Equally good is the **International Theater,** 1090, Porzellangasse 8 (31 62 72), also performing in English.

Music. The two great orchestras of the capital are the **Vienna Philharmonic** and the **Vienna Symphony.** In addition to their performances, there is an abundance of concerts by soloists, choruses, and chamber music groups.

The most important concert halls in Vienna are in the building of the **Gesellschaft der Musikfreunde** (popularly called *Musikverein*), Dumbastr. 3, the home of the Vienna Philharmonic, and in the **Wiener Konzerthaus,** Lothringerstr. 20. Both of these contain several auditoriums for concerts of different types, and your ticket may be marked with the name of the particular hall in which the concert is being given. Don't hunt vainly for a building with that name. If your ticket is for the **Grosser Musikvereinssaal,** the **Brahmssaal** or the **Kammersaal,** go to the **Musikfreunde** building. If it is for the **Grosser Konzerthaussaal,** the **Mozartsaal** or the **Schubertsaal,** you will find it in the **Konzerthaus.**

Concerts are also given in the small **Figarosaal** of the Palffy Palace, the concert studio of the broadcasting station in **Argentinierstrasse** and the **Bösendorfersaal** of the famous piano manufacturer.

In addition to the Vienna Festival, held late-May and June, there are special summer concerts in the Arkadenhof (Arcade Court) of the Rathaus, in Belvedere garden and Volksgarten, and in many palaces, the most notable being held in Palais Schwarzenberg, Schloss Schönbrunn; but of particular interest are the Mozart concerts given in 18th-century costumes and powdered wigs in the Konzerthaus and the Sofiensäle.

Schubert fans can enjoy occasional piano concerts in the house of his birth, Nussdorferstr. 54.

Church music of high artistic value can be heard during Sunday morning Mass in the following churches in the downtown area—in the Cathedral of St. Stephen, in the Franciscan Church and, above all, in the Augustinerkirche.

Perhaps the most famous of these locales is the Hofburgkapelle where the famous **Wiener Sängerknaben** (Vienna Choirboys) sing at 9.15 A.M. from mid-Sept. to late June. Written ticket reservations for seats (standing room is free) should be made at least eight weeks in advance to: *Hofmusikkapelle Hofburg,* A-1010 Vienna. You will then get a reservation card, which you present to the box office of the Burgkapelle when you pick up and pay for your tickets. A separate contingent of tickets is sold at the box office of the Burgkapelle every Friday from 5 P.M. onwards. It is advisable to queue early (from about 4.30)! A maximum of two tickets per person may be purchased from the box office (tickets also available in ticket and travel agencies, but with a service charge added). Programs published on first of month on church door and in the Saturday papers. There are Wednesday evening organ concerts in St. Stephen's from early May to end Nov.

Try to hear brass band music on various squares and in different parks.

You can hear excellent live jazz at the following: **Jazzland,** 1010, Franz Josefskai 29 (63 25 75), Tues. to Sat. 9 P.M. to 2 A.M.; **Jazzspelunke,** 1060, Dürergasse 3 (587 01 26); **Miles Smiles,** 1080, Lange Gasse 51 (42 84 814); **Opus One,** 1010 Mahlerstr. 11 (513 20 75) to 4 A.M.; **Papa's Tapas,** 1040, Schwarzenbergplatz 10 (65 03 11) from 10 P.M. daily; and **Rotor Engel,** 1010, Rabensteig 5 (535 41 05).

Enquire at your hotel about coffeehouses presenting live music. There is an increasing number.

Getting Tickets. Operas are almost always, and better concerts usually, sold out in Vienna, so it is advisable to buy your tickets several days in advance.

For State theaters (Oper, Volksoper, Akadamietheater, and Burgtheater) you can get tickets in the city ticket office located in a courtyard near the Opera, with entrances from Goethegasse 1 and Hanuschgasse 3, as well as at the individual theaters.

The sale of tickets begins one week in advance for the State theaters, but the tickets may be sold out a couple of hours after the sale is open (people begin waiting in line several hours earlier). Tickets, if any remain, can also be purchased within one hour before the beginning of the performance at the evening ticket office of the theater concerned. You can order tickets by phone, charging them to a credit card (AE, DC, MC, V), up to six days before the performance, by calling (0222) 513 15 13. Credit cards also accepted at the ticket office. Tickets for theaters other than the four mentioned can be purchased during the daily business hours 8 to 10 days ahead or within one hour before the performance at the respective theater ticket office. Sale of tickets for special events starts earlier; for the New Year's Concert it starts on Dec. 17.

For opera and operetta performances write about 2 or 3 months in advance to the nearest Austrian National Tourist Office in the U.S., Canada or the U.K. to get a list of the coming performances and special blank order forms. Then send an order form duly filled in—but no money—to the ticket office Bundestheaterverband, Goethegasse 1, 1010 Vienna. When you get to Vienna, take the reservation card you will receive to that address and pick up and pay for your tickets.

You can buy tickets also at the various ticket agencies and, even more important, particularly for the opera, you can order tickets from them in advance and they will see to it that you get them. The fee charged by the agencies is generally 20% of the ticket price (hotel porters usually charge more) but most of these organizations have a tendency to ignore the existence of cheap seats. Budget tourists would do well to go to the city ticket office themselves.

MOVIES. After a period of neglect, cinemas have come back into fashion in Vienna and many have been converted into multi-auditoria cinecenters. Both the variety and quality of presentation—to say nothing of the comfort—have improved enormously. As most movie houses show films dubbed into German, these two should interest the visitor—the **Burgkino**, at Opernring 19, which shows films of artistic merit in the original language (mostly English); and the **de France kino** on the Schottenring which presents new releases in English only. The **Top Kino** on the Gumpendorferstrasse also presents new releases in English, and the **Filmmuseum** in the Albertina shows older films in the original language, the majority of which are in English.

NIGHTLIFE. Although there are a fair number of night spots in Vienna, the city cannot boast a real nightclub tradition. The average Viennese prefers to go to the opera, theater, and concerts for serious entertainment, and for a relaxed evening, out to dinner or to a wine tavern or Heuriger. The Viennese love to dance, but the dancing is done mostly at the numerous balls during the season, in a few cafes with weekend music, and in dance-bars.

Nightclubs with floor shows are to be avoided in Vienna: they are generally expensive and bad. Having warned you, the following places are the best in town: **Casanova,** Dorotheerg. 6 (512 98 45), open till 4 A.M. DC, MC, V; **Moulin-Rouge,** Walfischg 11 (512 21 30), open 10 P.M.–6A.M.; closed Sun. DC, MC, V.

The leading night spots for dancing are: **Eden-Bar,** Liliengasse 2, near St. Stephen's, (512 74 50), open 10 P.M.–4A.M. AE, DC, MC, V; **Splendid Bar,** Jasomirgottstr. 3 (533 15 15), open till 4 A.M. AE, DC, MC, V; **Fledermaus,** Spiegelgasse 2 (512 84 38). A mixture of literary cabaret and soul singing or whatever else is available; closed Sun. and Mon. DC.

What Vienna does have is innumerable, delightful and quite sophisticated bars. Here are just four suggestions, for a walk along the Rotenturmstr, Räbensteig/Judengasse ("Bermuda Triangle"), Bäckerstr, Schönlaternstr. area will present you with numerous choices: **Chamäleon,** Blutgasse 3 (513 17 03); **Galerie Bar,** 1010, Singerstr. 7 (512 49 29), AE, MC.

Portas, Schulerstr. 6; **Reiss-Bar,** 1010, Marco d'Avianogasse 1, open till 2 A.M.

Other dance bars and discos include—**Atrium,** Schwarzenbergplatz 10
(65 35 94). Popular with students, and boasting 50 types of beer; a disco.
Closed Sun. and Mon.
Casino Cercle Wien, Kärntnerstrasse 41 (512 48 36), for blackjack, rou-
lette and gambling in a former palace.
Chatanooga, Graben 29 (533 50 00), with the accent on youth and jazz;
live music.
Lords Club, Karlsplatz 1 (505 83 08). Occasional live shows.
Magic, in the Volksgarten (63 05 18).
Queen Anne, Johannesgasse 12 (512 02 03).*The* hottest disco in town.
Schwimmende Pyramide, Seilerstätte 5.
Scotch, Parkring 10, chic (512 94 17).
Take Five, Annagasse 3A, open 10 A.M.–4 A.M.
Tenne, Annagasse 3 (512 57 08). Occasional live shows.
Wake Up Disco Club, Seilerstätte 5.

SHOPPING. The finest shops in Vienna line Kärntnerstrasse from the
Opera to St. Stephen's Cathedral, then run left through the Graben and
again left, following Kohlmark to the Imperial Palace. Almost all the
small side streets within and adjoining this roughly outlined square form
part of one of the best shopping districts in Europe. Part of this area is
now a pedestrian precinct, with cafés in the open air in summer.
See *Planning Your Trip* for details of how to recover Value Added Tax.
Vienna's Flea Market, with everything from junk to fine antiques, is
next to the market area at Kettenbrückengasse, 1050, every Sat., 8–6, not
on public holidays. A "quality" flea market operates Sat. and Sun. 2–8
in summer alongside the Danube Canal below Schwedenbrücke.
The following list is of shops dealing with typically Austrian merchan-
dise.
Austrian Jade. *Burgenland,* Opernpassage 4, and Wildpretmarkt 6, AE.
Books. *British Bookshop,* Weihburggasse 8; *Heidrich's,* Plankengasse 7;
Pickwick's, Marc-Aurel-Str. 10–12; *Shakespeare & Co,* Sterngasse 2.
Candles. *Metzger.* Stephansplatz 7; *Jos. Altmann,* Heidenschuss 1 and
Mariahilferstr. 51, 1060. AE. *Marius Retti,* Kohlmarkt 8–10. AE.
Ceramics. *Krolop* (Gmunden ceramics), Kärntnerdurchgang; a few
shops around the corner from Kärntnerstr. 10, AE. *Pawlata,* Kärntnerstr.
14. AE.
Crystal. *Bakalowits,* Spiegelgasse 3; *Lobmeyr,* Kärntnerstr. 26. Best
crystal, tableware and gift articles—they made the crystal glass chande-
liers for New York's Metropolitan Opera. AE, DC.
Dirndls and Trachten for Women. *Lanz,* Kärntnerstr. 10, AE, DC, MC;
Tostmann, Schottengasse 3A, AE, DC, MC, V; *Loden-Plankl,* Michaelerplatz
6, AE; *Modell-Dirndl,* Tegetthofstr. 6, AE, DC; *Resi Hammerer,* Kärntnerstr.
29–31, AE, DC, MC, V.
Glass. *Table-Top,* in exclusive Freyung Arcade in Palais Ferstel. Specialist in exquisite hand-blown Riedel glass. DC.
Handicrafts, Gifts and Souvenirs. *Österreichische Werkstätten,* Kärntnerstr. 6, AE, MC; *Souvenir in der Hofburg,* Hofburg Arcade, AE, MC; *Boutique Gretl,* Bognergasse 7, especially for enamel clocks, AE; *Niederösterreichisches Heimatwerk,* Herrengasse 6–8, AE, DC, MC, V; *Tiroler Werkkunst,*
Mariahilferstr. 89, 1060, AE.
Hats. *Collins Hüte,* Opernpassage; *P & C Habig,* 1040, Wiedner Hauptstr. 15 (65 81 04) AE, DC, V. Note the superb facade.

Jewelry. *A. Haban,* Kärntnerstr. 2, *the* Viennese spot for jewelry, on the corner of St. Stephen's Square, AE, DC, MC, V; *Heldwein,* Graben 13, AE, MC, V; *A. E. Köchert,* Neuer Markt 15, AE, DC, MC, V; *Paltscho,* Graben 14, AE, MC; *Jul. Hügler,* Freisingerstr. 4 and Kärntnerstr. 53, AE, DC; *Juwel,* Kohlmarkt 1, AE, DC, V; *Carius & Binder,* Kärntnerstr. 17, AE, DC, MC, V; *Horwath,* Kärntnerstr. 29–31, AE, DC, MC, V; *Kunz,* Neuer Markt 13, AE, DC, MC, V.

Ladies' Fashions. *Adlmüller,* Palais Esterhazy, Kärntnerstr. Couturier fashions at appropriate prices (also first-rate menswear). AE, DC, MC, V.

Men's Trachten. *Loden-Plankl,* Michaelerplatz 6, AE, DC, MC; *Collins Hüte,* Operngasse 12, for Alpine-style hats. MC, V.

Petit Point. *Berta Smejkal,* Opernpassage 13, Kohlmarkt 9, AE, V; *Stransky,* Hofburg-Passage 2.

Porcelain. *Augarten,* Schloss Augarten, 1060, Stock-im-Eisenplatz 3–4 and Mariahilferstr. 99, AE; *Ernst Wahliss,* Kärntnerstr. 17, AE, DC, MC; *Rasper & Söhne,* Graben 15, AE, DC, MC.

Wrought-iron and Weinhebers. *Horst Zach,* Habsburgergasse 5 and Bräunerstr. 8; *Hamerle,* Annagasse 7; *Reckzügel,* on the Stephansplatz.

RESTAURANTS. First class restaurants in Vienna can be quite expensive—for a full dinner, accompanied by a good bottle of wine, you will pay as much as in most other West European capitals. But in simpler restaurants, particularly in the suburbs, you can still find good food at refreshingly low prices. If you have your main meal at noon (as the Viennese do) you can take advantage of the luncheon specials.

There are still many traditional restaurants, but there has been a tremendous shake-up during the last five years, with many exciting new and high quality restaurants making their mark. Whatever you choose, you will have a relaxed evening, an experience that is difficult to come by in trendier towns.

Most restaurants serve meals only between 12 and 2.30, and between 6 and 10 or 11. An increasing number of restaurants stay open late serving after-theater dinners, but do reserve. Most are closed one day a week and holidays, and many take an annual vacation during July and August.

New bars and small restaurants are opening all the time and closing almost as fast. Many of them are very good, but it is not possible for us to keep track of them all. Check *Wien Wie es Isst,* an excellent comprehensive booklet available at any newsstand.

Expensive

Arche Noah, 1010, Seitenstettengasse 2 (533 13 74). High-class Kosher cooking near 18th-century Synagogue in the Old City. AE, DC, MC, V.

Astoria, 1010, Führichg. 1 (51 57 70). See *Hotels.* Paneled Jugendstil dining room. Excellent cooking, special after-theater set dinners. The best pianist in town. AE, DC, MC, V. Open late.

Balkan Grill, 1160, Brunnengasse 13 (92 14 94). Near West Station. Spicy Balkan specialties. Particular attraction is *Genghis Khan's Flaming Sword,* shashlik served flaming on a sword, with a musical flourish of Viennese and gypsy melodies. In summer an attractive garden. AE, DC, MC, V. Open late, closed Sun.

Csardasfürstin, 1010, Schwarzenbergstr. 2 (512 92 46). An old favorite, now in new hands. Gypsy music, Viennese concept of Hungarian food.

Da Conte, 1010, Kurrentgasse 12 (533 64 46). Small and romantic. Italian cuisine of a standard rare outside Italy. DC, MC, V. Closed Sun.

D'Rauchkuchl, 1150, Schweglerstr. 37 (92 13 81). Revitalized and back on top-form. Popular with celebrities. Closed Sun. evening. AE, DC, MC, V.

Drei Husaren, 1010, Weihburggasse 4 (512 10 92). Just off Kärntnerstr., near St. Stephen's. Candlelight, antique-style furnishings, soft piano music. Magnificent *hors d'oeuvres,* but watch prices! Very good selection of wines and first-class bar. Dinners only. Closes for 4 weeks July to Aug., and Sun. AE, DC, MC, V. Open late.

Four Seasons, Hotel Intercontinental (71122). New furnishings and a new cook have transformed this hotel restaurant into something special. AE, DC, MC, V.

Gottfried, 1030, Marxerg. 3 (73 82 56). Closed Sun., open late. AE, DC, MC, V.

Haas & Haas, 1010, Stephansplatz 4 (513–1916). Elegant snacks and dishes. Good wine. Beautiful shaded courtyard. Closed Sun.

Hauswirth, 1060, Otto Bauergasse 20 (587 12 61). In the 6th District, just off Mariahilferstr., with several large rooms and pleasant courtyard garden in summer. Go to the back room for piano music in the evening. Imaginative modern cooking. Closed Sun. AE, DC, MC, V.

Imperial, 1010, Kärntner Ring 16 (50 1 10–0). Good food and snacks available all day in café with coffee-house atmosphere. Gourmet dining of high quality in restaurant *Zur Majestät.* (501 10 356). Good drinks and music in the intimately arranged bar. Open late. AE, DC, MC, V.

Johanneshof, 1180, Gersthoferstr. 65, (47 83 24). Closed Sun. A Jugendstil jewel.

Kervansaray, 1010, Mahlerstr. 9 (512 88 43). Near the Opera. Turkish specialties, from *Kapama* to *Dönerkebab;* fresh fish from the Bosphorus, including lobsters flown in every day. Turkish décor, no music. Upstairs is a fish restaurant, *Hummer Bar,* which is very expensive—but worth it. Closed Sun. AE, DC, MC, V. Open late.

König von Ungarn, 1010, Schulerstr. 10 (512 53 19). Romantic, intimate setting. Attentive service. Some of the best boiled beef in town. Closed Sat. and August. AE, DC, MC, V.

Korso, Hotel Bristol, 1010, Kärntner Ring 1 (51 5 16–536). Beautifully-designed top gourmet restaurant. Exceptional wine list. AE, DC, MC, V.

Niky's Kuchlmasterei, 1030, Obere Weissgerberstr. 6 (72 44 18). Very good Viennese and French cooking in a pleasant, candlelit, rustic atmosphere. Open Mon. to Sat. 10 A.M. to midnight; closed Sun. and holidays. AE.

Palais Schwarzenberg, 1030, Schwarzenbergpl. 9 (78 45 15). See *Hotels.* In the small, but elegant dining room, there is much to revive belief in old Vienna. Excellent cuisine, wines and service. Stunning terrace overlooking private park. AE, DC, MC, V.

Prinz Eugen, 1030, Am Stadtpark (75 26 52). In the Hilton (see *Hotels*). Opulent surroundings provide a luxurious setting for excellent food. AE, DC, MC, V.

Sacher, 1010, Philharmonikerstr. 4 (512 33 67). See *Hotels.* The main restaurant sparkles as it did in the red-plush era of the Habsburgs, as do the alcoved dining rooms on the upper floor. One of the plusher spots to eat *Tafelspitz* (garnished boiled beef) and its own creation, *Sachertorte.* Open late. AE, DC, MC.

Sailer, 1180, Gersthoferstr. 14 (47 21 21). Near Türkenschanzpark. Modern Austrian specialties, marvelous wines. Paneled dining room, cellar and atmospheric garden in summer. Closed Sun., holidays. AE, DC, MC, V.

Schubert-Stüberl, 1010, Schreyvogelgasse 4 (63 71 87). Near Burgtheater; pleasant, with quiet summer garden; grill and game specialties. Closed Sun. AE, DC, MC, V. Open late.

Steinerne Eule, 1070, Halbgasse 30 (93 22 50). Gourmet restaurant with cozy little rooms. Closed Sun. and Mon. AE, DC, MC, V.

Steirereck, 1030, Rasumovskygasse 2 (73 31 68). On the Danube canal. Ranked among Vienna's best restaurants; lightly cooked Austrian dishes, with the emphasis on freshness. Superb wine list. Closed Sat. and Sun. and holidays. AE.

Moderate

Almhütte, 1090, Schlickgasse (31 67 50). Indigenous haunt of operetta stars. Simple well-cooked food. Excellent pianist Thurs., Fri. and Sat. Closed Sun. evening and all day Mon. MC, V.

Altes Haus, 1190, Himmelstr. 35 (32 23 21). In the wine-growing suburb of Grinzing, where every house is a wine tavern and this one is actually more a wine tavern with food than a restaurant in the proper sense. Try chicken, grilled and skewered meats, and *Topfenstrudl* (*strudl* made with cream cheese). Open evenings only, musical entertainment. Closed Sun. AE, DC, MC, V.

Basteibeisl, 1010, Stubenbastei 10 (512 43 19). Good Viennese cooking, old fashioned specialties. Friendly. Open Mon. to Sat. 9–12 P.M. AE, DC, MC, V.

Donauturm, 1022, Donauturmstr. 4 (23 53 68). On the second floor, at the top of the Danube Tower in Donaupark. Expensive international cuisine in the rotating tower; moderate cafe-restaurant on the lower floor (at 170 m. and 160 m.); rustic **Park Tavern** at foot of tower. AE, DC, V.

Dubrovnik, 1030, Am Heumarkt 5 (713 27 55). Excellent Balkan cooking and atmosphere. Open late. AE, DC, MC, V.

Eckel, 1190, Sieveringstr. 46 (32 32 18). Small house with wood paneled *stuben* and garden. Great cooking such as sweetwater crayfish (in season), trout, game, *Backhendl.* Fluffy, hot soufflé-type desserts such as *Pfannkuchen MarieLouise,* covered with chocolate sauce, ground nuts and whipped cream. A family-run establishment; closed Sun. and Mon. AE, DC, V.

Figlmüller, 1010, Wollzeile 5 (512 61 77). In historic courtyard. Folksy atmosphere. Giant schnitzels and excellent fruity wines from the Südbahn region. Closed Sat./Sun. and August. MC.

Gigerl, 1010, Rauhensteing. 3 (513 44 31). Good food and wine in newly restored house at the heart of Vienna's Old City. Open daily from 4 P.M. DC.

Glacisbeisl, 1070, Messepalast (96 16 58). Between the two museums on the Ring: hard to find, so ask the way. Sit out on what is left of medieval bastions. Excellent local cooking, friendly service. Closed Sun.

Gösser Bierklinik, 1010, Steindlgasse 4 (533 33 36). In a narrow street near Am Hof. One of the oldest inns in the city (1566) with numerous atmospheric rooms.

Himmelpforte, Himmelpfortg. 24 (513 19 66). "Schlemmerkeller" and bar. Excellent cooking and atmosphere. Reasonable. Open late Mon. to Sat. AE, DC, MC, V.

Ilona, 1010, Bräunerstr. 2 (512 61 91). Tiny, serving huge portions of Hungarian specialities. Closed Sun. DC, MC, V.

Johann Strauss, 1010 Schwedenplatz (533 61 33). Large old paddle-steamer beautifully restored and turned into restaurant, bar, café and dance floor. A treat in every way. Live jazz on Sunday mornings. Closed Sun. evening. AE, V.

Lucky Chinese, 1, Kärntnerstr. 24 (512 34 28). Good Chinese food. Open daily. AE, DC, MC, V.

Lugeck, 1010, Lugeck 7 (512 79 79). On the way from St. Stephen's to the Danube canal. Quick bite in the simpler ground-floor premises, more elaborate restaurant fare a few stairs below. AE, DC, MC, V.

Martinkovitz, 1190, Bellvuestr. 4 (32 15 46). Heuriger restaurant famous for its Backhendl. Good home grown wines. Closed Mon. and Tues.

Oswald & Kalb, 1010, Bäckerstr. 14 (512 13 71). Evenings only. Very popular with the young. Open daily and late.

Pastaron, 1010, Jasomirgottstr. 3 (535 55 44). Elegant, modern pasta restaurant of high standard. Good wines. Closed Sun., last orders 11.45.

Rathauskeller, 1010, Rathausplatz 1 (42 12 19). A vast establishment in the basement of the Rathaus (City Hall), with a series of vaulted dining rooms. Evenings, Viennese music in the large *Grinzingerkeller,* where a huge, carved, wooden barrel presides over long tables of tourists. Closed Sun. AE.

Rossini, Schönlaterngasse (52 62 14). Good Italian food. Closed Mon.

Siddartha, 1010, Fleischmarkt 16 (513 11 97). Sophisticated vegetarian spot. Dine healthily by candle-light, with organically grown wines. Delicious food—even for non-vegetarians. Reserve. Closed Sun.

S'Müllerbeisl, 1010, Seilerstätte 15 (512 42 65). Excellent cooking, pleasant surroundings. Open late.

Stadbeisl, 1010, Naglergasse 21 (533 33 23). Small, cozy and usually crowded at noon.

Smutny, 1010, Elisabethstr. 8 (587 13 56). A touch of old Vienna and the Third Man here. Excellent Budweiser beer, good food. Surroundings and waiters untouched by time and fashion. Open daily.

Tabakspfeife, 1010, Goldschmidg. 4 (63 72 86). Regular eating place for many Viennese. Wholesome good value. Closed Sat./Sun.

Tüv-Tam, 1020, Hollandstr. 3 (33 35 65). Strict orthodox Kosher cooking.

Weisse Rauchfangkehrer, 1010, Weihburgasse 4 (512 84 37). "The White Chimneysweep"—a series of rooms in Alpine *Stuben* style with hunting decor, strong on atmosphere. Austrian dishes and wines, with piano music after 8. Check the bill carefully before paying.

Zu Ebener Erd, 1070, Burggasse 13 (93 62 54). Lovely old Viennese house serving delicious local cuisine. DC, V. Closed Sun.

Zum Laterndl, 1010, Landesgerichtsstr. 12 (43 43 58). Near U.S. Library and University. Frequented by students. Good food. Closed Sat. and Sun.

Zur Lotte, 1190, Heiligenstädterstr. 179 (37 41 25). Excellent local cuisine, friendly atmosphere. Good wines and beers. Open daily.

Zur 10-er Marie, 1160, Ottakringerstr. 224 (46 31 16). Heuriger restaurant in an unexpected place. Genuine Schrammelmusik. Very romantic. Garden. Erstwhile haunt of Crown Prince Rudolph. Closed Sun., Mon.

Inexpensive
(see also *Wine Taverns* below)

Bierhof, 1010, Naglergasse 13 (533 44 28). Unusual beers and snacks. Open evenings till late, closed Mon.

Butterfass, 1020, Prater Hauptallee 122 (24 41 05). Near enough to be convenient, far enough from the Prater to afford peace. Simple Viennese food as the Viennese like it. Garden. Closed Mon. AE, DC, MC, V.

Reinthaler, 1010, Glückgasse 5 (512 33 66). Authentic gasthaus, neighborhood public included. Closed Fri. evening, Sat. and Sun.

Stadtkeller, 1010, Singerstr. 6 (512 12 69). Self service at bargain prices. Open daily from 10 A.M.

Schweizerhaus. In Prater (24 23 17) not far from the Big Wheel (from there, ask the way). Where the Viennese go to sit out and listen to the sounds of the funfair while consuming huge *Stelzen* (roast legs of pork), washed down with the best Budweiser in town.

Toni, 1010, Salzgries 6 (66 44 13). Specialty is grilled meats in Turkish and Yugoslav style. Open daily 8 A.M.–11 P.M.

Trzesniewski Buffet, 1010, Dorotheergasse 1 (512 32 91). Hidden away, just off Graben, with spicy canapés to eat on the spot or take away.

Zu den drei Hacken, 1010, Singerstr. (512 58 95). True Viennese *beisl* with simple, freshly-cooked food; large choice, excellent wines, lots of atmosphere, garden. Closed Sat. evenings and Sun.

Zum Braunen Hirschen, 1010, Rudolfsplatz 4 (533 64 62). Genuine Gasthaus, excellent value, friendly. Closed on weekends.

Excursion Dining

Fischerhaus (E), 1190, Hohenstr. (44 13 20). Reached only by car. Good view of the Wienerwald and parts of the city from outdoor terrace. Rustic furnishings. Expensive for what it is, but standards are high. Closed Mon. and 5 Nov. to 25 Feb. AE, DC, MC, V.

Tulbingerkogel Berghotel (E), A-3001, Tulbingerkogel (0 22 73 73 91). On the Tulbingerkogel hill in the Vienna Woods (30 minutes by car). Exceptional Viennese cuisine, Wachau white wines and Vöslau reds. There are also rooms, with bath. AE, DC, MC, V.

La Tour (E), Perchtoldsdorf, Hochstr. 17 (86 47 63). South of the city limits. One of the top luxury dining spots; beautiful setting, excellent food, glorious selection of cheeses and wines. Very expensive, but worth it. Closed Mon. AE, DC, MC, V.

Landhaus Winter (E), 1110, Simmeringerlände (76 23 17). On Danube Canal with summer terrace. Elegant; superb fish and other specialties. Delicious desserts. Children welcome. Closed Mon. AE, DC, MC, V.

Lusthaus (E), 1020, in Prater at end of the Hauptallee (74 17 87). First built in 1560 as the summer pavilion of Emperor Maximilian II. Rebuilt 1770 by Joseph II. Attractive cafe and restaurant. Open Thurs. to Tues. 9 A.M. to midnight.

Höldrichsmühle (M), A-2371, Hinterbrühl bei Mödling (02236–26274). Near Mödling, on the edge of Wienerwald, south of Vienna. Very fine fare from trout to *Milchrahmstrudel* (*strudel* with sour cream) at reasonable prices. Rooms.

Marchfelderhof (M), A-2232, Deutsch Wagram (02247–2243). 8 miles beyond the U.N. City, on the site of Napoleonic battle. Easily reached by *Schnellbahn* in half-an-hour from Wien Mitte station. 5 minutes' walk at the other end. The menu is immense and so are the portions, but prices are reasonable. Claustrophobia guaranteed. Reservations necessary, English spoken. Closed Mon. Rooms. AE, DC, MC, V.

Postschänke (M), 2392 Sulz/Wienerwald (02238/335). Very Biedermeier, typical Viennese excursion restaurant. You expect to see Franz Schubert at the next table. In the heart of the Vienna Woods; beautiful garden. Delicious, wholesome food.

WINE TAVERNS. These are mostly evening institutions intended primarily for drinking, but you can always get at least a bite and often a full dinner. They vary in class from simple to more ornate, and in originality from genuine to pseudo. One of their prominent features is the *Weinheber* (wine siphon), placed in front of you on the table. This should remind you that the wine was drawn straight out of the barrel. Nowadays, however, this is a strictly symbolic gesture since the wine is usually poured into the Weinheber straight from the bottle.

What will undoubtedly strike you as you enter your first wine cellar is the depth. Some of them are two or three floors down in the bowels of the earth and many of them consist of a network of cellars—merely a small part of the vast underground system that honeycombs its way below the streets of Vienna.

Some call themselves city Heurigers which, of course, is only for advertising purposes, since no authentic Heurigers can exist in the city. The Viennese call the more pretentious of these *Nobel-Heuriger,* defining them rather directly as being pretentious, probably overpriced, and less than genuine, although wines served are usually quite good.

Wine taverns in Vienna are many and even an old habitué can always discover a new one. Here are some of the better known ones.

Antiquitäten-Keller, 1060, Magdalenenstr. 32 (566 95 33). Open evenings 7–1; classical music. Closed Aug.

Augustinerkeller, 1010, Augustiner Str. 1 (533 10 26). Tucked in under the building which houses the great Albertina collection, and so handy for lunch (this one *is* open lunchtime) after sightseeing in the Hofburg. Simple and busy, but excellent value for money.

Esterhazykeller, 1010, Haarhof 1 (533 34 82). One of the most extensive—the deep cellars seem like an endless maze. Allow plenty of time on a busy night. Closes 9 P.M.

Melker Stiftskeller, 1010, Schottengasse 3 (533 55 30). Hidden at the back of a small courtyard, the entrance leads down and down, into one of the friendliest and most typical of all wine cellars. Excellent food and wine plus a hard-working clientele. Connected with Melk for a long way back. Evenings only. Closed Sun. and Aug.

Piaristenkeller, 1080, Piaristengasse 45 (42 91 52). Colorful, with restaurant service and zither music. Open late. Closed Mon. DC, MC.

Zwölf-Apostelkeller, 1010, Sonnenfelsgasse 3 (512 67 77). Not far from St. Stephen's. Frequented by students and deep below street level.

HEURIGERS. The *Heuriger* is a seasonal, very simply arranged wine tavern, attached to the premises of a vintner. There are around 700 families in Vienna growing wine, mostly in vineyards on the slopes of Kahlenburg and Bisamberg. Look for the certificate of authenticity on the door. It is here that you will find the best-known areas for wine—Nussdorf, Heiligenstadt, Grinzing, Sievering and Neustift. Other wine-growing regions are on the left bank of the Danube at Stammersdorf, Strebersdorf and Jedlersdorf, while the remoter Mauer and Oberlaa are to the south of the city. Heurigers in these latter districts are much less expensive and more authentic. The wine is sharp but pure and the food simple but good. Quiet courtyards to sit in more than make up for the effort in finding them.

Stammersdorf is especially recommended (Tram 31). Try **Robert Helm,** Stammersdorfer Str. 121 (39 12 44). The wine here will still be a *g'mischter Satz,* as it was in Schubert's day. This type of wine is produced from a variety of grapes, all grown in one vineyard and harvested and vinified together.

When the vintner has drawn off his new wine, he hangs a bough of pine over his door, inviting passers-by in to try his brew. The sale of wine in Vienna is strictly controlled and only the establishments that grow their vines entirely in Vienna or the surrounding rural districts can call themselves *heurigers.*

These delightful places sell food as well, usually local dishes, fairly basic and extremely tasty. You are served with wine by the waitresses—bumper glass mugs, *viertels* (each holding a ¼ liter)—but you have to collect the food yourself, buffet-style.

Naturally, summer and fall are the best time for visiting these outlying areas and spending a convivial evening. Almost all offer some form of mild entertainment, varying from an aged zither player to teams of folk singers extolling the glories of Vienna and its wine in a dialect so thick that not even visitors with fluent German can catch much of it. It's an institution of considerable charm and homely joy, the favorite Saturday afternoon or Sunday evening goal of thousands of Viennese. Here the entire family may go of an evening, bearing its own food or buying a plate of cold cuts and cheese at the wine house. It is all folksy and friendly, and in summer it is especially delightful, for then you sit in the patio or garden. Sadly, nowadays you might feel out of place taking your own food, so always inquire first.

A word of warning: Heurige wine tastes as mild as lemonade, but it is surprisingly potent and leaves a headache in its wake if it is of inferior quality. Austrians accustomed to the heurige eat almost constantly while drinking it, and many dilute it freely with soda water (*Gespritzt*). All good heurigers will furnish proof of the authenticity and purity of their wines on request.

A visit to these areas is possible in winter, too, though then it is the so-called *Noble-Heurigers* that come into their own. These are permanent wine taverns, with classic interiors, often warmed by attractive tiled stoves—like survivals from rich peasant houses.

The easiest to get to (if you don't have a car), are located in Grinzing, Sievering and Nussdorf, which can be reached with streetcar 38, bus 39A and streetcar D respectively. The Vienna Tourist Board puts out an excellent little booklet which will tell you all you want to know about *heuriger* as well as listing many of the best ones; it is called, naturally enough, *Heuriger in Wien* and gives addresses, opening dates and directions on how to reach that district. Our favorite is Stammersdorf, but almost equally high on the list are **Martin Sepp,** Coblenzlgasse 34 in Grinzing (32 32 33); **Haslinger,** 1190, Agnesgasse 3 in Sievering (44 13 47); **Schübl-Auer,** 1190, Kahlenbergerstr. 22 in Nussdorf (37 22 22); and **Stift Schotten,** 1190, Hackhofergasse 17, also in Nussdorf (37 15 75).

CAFES. The old-fashioned Viennese type of cafe, with its marble tables, newspapers, sidewalk terraces in warm weather, is an institution of long tradition that has strengthened its position here and there by adding buffets or partial restaurant service and espresso machines. All of the Viennese cafes offer pastries.

Here we can mention only a few of Vienna's 15,000-odd cafes, ranging from small espresso bars to venerable club-like institutions on and inside the Ring.

Except for those belonging to the famous hotels, mentioned previously, some of the most typical old-fashioned cafes in Vienna are—**Alte Backstube**, 1080, Lange Gasse 34, beautiful Baroque house, lovingly furnished, excellent pastries, open late; **Raimund**, where men of letters meet, at Volksgartenstr. 5, across from the Volkstheater; **Bräunerhof**, 1010, Stallburgg. 2, with music at weekends; **Mozart**, with very pleasant summer lunches on the street terrace, at Albertinaplatz 2, near the Opera; **Prückel** with restaurant service, Stubenring 24, across the street from the Stadtpark; **Tirolerhof**, Fuhrichgasse 8, across the square from Albertina, sometimes afternoon music; **Cafe Central**, 1010, Freyung/Herrengasse in Ferstelpalais complex, a piece of history brought back to life, where Stalin and Trotsky used to play chess; beautiful. Closed in winter; the 100-years-old **Schwarzenberg** on the Ring corner at Schwarzenberg Square; **Frauenhuber**, Himmelpfortgasse 6, all with restaurant service; **Ritter**, Mariahilferstr. 73; **Haag**, at Schottengasse 2, with a garden; **Museum**, corner of Friedrichstr.–Operngasse; **Sperl**, 1060, Gumpendorferstr. 11, a landmark, one of the most famous of all, newly restored.

Cafe Laudon, 1080, Laudongasse 24, a cafe-restaurant with tradition, popular with the chess set. AE.

Among the better modern cafes is **Cafe Europa**, on the ground floor of the hotel of the same name, with large windows facing the Kärntnerstrasse.

The most important downtown coffeehouses are **Cafe Hawelka**, 1010, Dorotheergasse, just off Graben, a meeting place for artists, always crowded. Open 7 A.M. to 2 A.M. except Tues., Sun. 4 P.M. to 2 A.M.; **Cafe Sacher**, behind the Opera House, famous for its cake and its elegance; and **Cafe Landtman**, 1010, on Schottenring, AE, which is a distinguished meeting place for civil servants through its location near the Rathaus, Parliament and headquarters of leading political parties.

Cafes with music—**Kursalon** (also restaurant) in the City Park (Stadtpark), large and popular outdoor cafe during the warmer months with a band playing Austrian light music in the late afternoon and evening. AE. **Volksgarten**, afternoon and evening, with dancing.

PASTRY SHOPS. Demel, the famous pastry shop at 1010, Kohlmarkt 14 (533 55 16), offers at lunch time also magnificent snacks of delicate meats, fish and vegetables. Try stuffed mushrooms or vegetable-cheese combinations. Gorgeous coffee and hot chocolate. Filling your stomach will mean emptying your pocketbook. Open daily 10–6. AE, MC.

Other top pastry shops include: **Gerstner**, Kärntnerstr. 15 (512 49 63); **Heiner**, Kärntnerstr. 21 (512 68 63), with a nice upstairs room, and at Wollzeile 9 (512 48 38); **Lehmann**, Graben 12 (512 18 15). The ubiquitous but less scrumptious **Aida** chain is in the Inner City at Opern Ring 7, Stock-im-Eisenplatz 2, near St. Stephen's and at Wollzeile 28—excellent coffee and pastries at low prices.

Another favorite is **Sluka**, 1010, Rathausplatz 8 (43 88 96). Pretty shop with some of the best pastries and cakes in Vienna. Highly recommended.

The **Kurkonditorei** in Kurhaus Oberlaa, 1100 (68 16 11), is superb and worth a visit. Afterwards there is a park with a naturally-heated swimming pool in which you can work off the calories. You could then call in at the

Reumannplatz and have one of the best ice creams in the world at **Salon Tichy.** There is another swimming pool on the Reumannplatz. The Amalienbad is an indoor complex built in 1926 and now restored to its Art Decor splendor. If you haven't time to travel so far, visit the "Stadthaus" of the Kurkonditorei on the Neuer Markt 16 (513 29 36), and then swing over to Hoher Markt 4 for a breathtaking ice cream at Eissalon Garda.

SPORTS. It is perhaps a surprise to discover that Vienna, a center of arts and sciences of long tradition, is also extremely active in sports. The probable explanation is the average Austrian's love for nature and outdoors. Vienna possesses over 100 sports fields and about 400 recreation grounds, not even counting the two main establishments which are the large **Stadium** in Prater (about 90,000 spectators) and the unique **Stadthalle** (city convention and recreation hall) on Vogelweidplatz near Westbahnhof (17,000 spectators).

BICYCLING. All over Austria tracks are being set up. Bikes can be hired from: 1020, Vivariumstr. 8 (26 66 44); 1020, Praterstern Station (26 85 57); 1100, Waldg. (64 10 113); 1190, Heiligenstädterstr. 180 at DDSG landing, Nussdorf. (37 45 98); or most conveniently, Franz Josefs-Kai, by the Salztorbrücke, on the Danube canal.

GOLF. For golf, you also have to head out to Prater. *Golf-Club Wien* is located at Freudenaustrasse 65a (74 17 86), at the end of the Prater Hauptallee. The course is open from April to Dec.; 18 holes, total length (out and home) 5,810 meters, which is about 6,020 yards. The clubhouse has a restaurant, closed Mon. Guests are welcome. Fees on weekends and holidays are a little higher. The other club is at Wiener Neustadt, the *Föhrenwald-Wiener Neustadt,* (02622/52 171), also with 18 holes, open April–Dec.

HIKING AND CLIMBING. The Austrian national summer sports are hiking and mountain climbing and the Viennese love doing both. Wienerwald—which can be reached by several streetcars and buses—offers any number of walks, light and hard, as short as half an hour and as long as the 220-km. (137-mile) path to Mödling. Pathways are well marked.

The nearest place for rock climbing is Hohe Wand (primarily for training) but the Styrian Alps are only a few hours' drive from the city. Consult the *Österreichischer Alpenverein* which has several branches in Vienna, including Rotenturmstr. 14 (513 10 03) and Walfischgasse 12 (512 69 33).

HORSERACING AND RIDING. For turf fans, there are spring, summer, and fall events at the two racetracks in Prater; flat-racing at Freudenau (74 16 09) and trotting at Krieau (57 72 58).

Horses for riding are available at various riding schools such as *Wiener Reitclub,* Barmherzigengasse 17, 3rd District, *Reitverein St. Stephan,* Weingartenalle, 22nd District, and *Reitschule Kottas,* in Freudenau.

TENNIS. There are many openair tennis courts. Larger ones are in Prater, in the Eislaufverein in Heumarkt (in summer), in Pötzleinsdorf and Hietzing. There are several tennis schools, among them those at Döblinger Hauptstr. 48, 19th District, at Bergmüllergasse 8, 14th District, and in the suburb of Mauer, Kaserngasse 3, which also has indoor courts. Any problem finding somewhere to play, just ask your hotel concierge.

WATER SPORTS. Rowing. The Danube offers many possibilities for rowing. There are about 20 sets of boathouses and numerous rowing clubs. Boats can be rented near the Wagramerstrasse bridge on the left bank of the Old Danube. For further information inquire at the *Österreichischer Ruderverband,* Austrian Rowing Association, 1040, Prinz Eugen-Str. 12 (505 73 07).

Sailing. Sailing boats can be rented on the Old Danube, where there is also a sailing school. *Union-Yacht Club* and *Wiener Yacht-Club* have their boathouses here. The *Vienna Festival Regatta* takes place each June during the Vienna Festival and the Vienna Championship in the fall. Sailing information from *Haus des Sports,* 1040, Prinz Eugen-Str. 12 (505 37 42).

Swimming. There are many openair swimming pools and several bathing establishments on the Danube. One of the best in the open is the *Stadium* pool in Prater, and the most popular among the Danube bathing establishments is Gänsehäufel Island near Kaisermühlen on the Old Danube (cross Reichsbrücke and turn right).

Donau Insel (the Danube Island) is a large recreation area on an artificial island. Its beach, several miles long, runs from Florisdorf well into the Lobau region. You can get there by car (to Florisdorfer Brücke, Reichsbrücke or Praterbrücke, or by U1 as far as Donau Insel).

But perhaps the prettiest is the Krapfenwald pool in Grinzing, near the Cobenzl and overlooking the city. Take the 38 streetcar to Grinzing, then bus 38S.

The best among the indoor establishments are the Stadthallenbad next to Stadthalle and the Dianabad complex just across the canal, which replaces the old turn-of-the-century Dianabad, which in turn replaced the site where *The Blue Danube* was first performed.

WINTER SPORTS. The Austrian national winter sport is **skiing,** but in Vienna the snow usually does not stay long at a time. With sufficient snow, there is very good skiing in various sections of Wienerwald, especially on the Hohe Wand Wiese slope, which is within the city limits (in the 14th District), and which even boasts a 400-meter-long ski lift; in case there is not enough snow, the ten so-called "snow guns" present here produce it artificially. There is also "grass-skiing" here in summer.

On Donau Insel (Danube Island) there is a new cross-country skiing trail accessible from Florisdorfer Brücke.

Otherwise the Vienna skiing grounds are on Semmering, Schneeberg, Hochkar, Türnitz, Annaberg, Josephsberg, and Raxalpe, about 2 slow driving or riding hours from the city, and in Mariazell which is a little farther.

Ice skating is also very popular in Vienna. There are more than 50 ice skating rinks, among them some artificial ones. The artificial openair skating rink of **Eislaufverein** (Ice Skating Union) is at Heumarkt 2 between the Konzerthaus and the Intercontinental Hotel. You can rent skates for a small fee.

LOWER AUSTRIA

Castles, Abbeys and Vineyards

Lower Austria (Niederösterreich) is the largest of the nine federal states. It borders on Upper Austria to the west and Styria to the south. Tiny Burgenland, another federal state, is sandwiched in on the southeast along the Hungarian border. To the north and east is the frontier of Czechoslovakia. The Blue Danube (actually rather a muddy brown most of the year) flows through the heart of Lower Austria from west to east, its banks and surroundings studded with medieval castles, Baroque abbeys and steep vineyards, especially in the beautiful Wachau section. South of the Danube is the area of slowly rising Alpine foothills, deeply cut by mountain streams and reaching their highest points in the Schneeberg, Raxalpe, Göller, Ötscher and Hochkar mountains, all near and on the border with Styria. Northwest of the Danube, the woody slopes of the Waldviertel stretch towards the Bohemian hills, while the northeastern section is rich agricultural land.

There are about 550 castles and fortresses in Lower Austria, some preserved, some reconstructed and others in ruins, since this area, particularly in the Danube valley, was the corridor between east and west Europe and was thus fortified as the defense line of the Germanic Holy Roman Empire. The history of abbeys and other monasteries in this area parallels that of the castles; for the purpose of defense, they were often built as fortresses and they are all steeped in the romance of those lost centuries.

Lower Austria derives its name from the fact that for many centuries it was the "lower" (in the sense of the Danube's course) part of the Archduchy of Austria. The Archduchy of Austria eventually imposed both its

149

name and its capital, Vienna, on the entire territory of today's Austria, but at the same time Vienna also remained the official capital of Lower Austria and the Lower Austrian state government has its offices there. In 1986 St. Pölten was proclaimed Provincial Capital, although, curiously, it will be 20 years before the change over from Vienna to St. Pölten is completed.

Exploring Lower Austria—The Vienna Woods and Baden

Wienerwald, the Vienna Woods, is not a natural park or forest, as you would think from listening to Strauss or the tourist blurbs, but a large range of rolling, densely wooded hills, extending from Vienna's doorstep to the outposts of the Alps in the south. Wienerwald is criss-crossed by country roads and hiking paths, dotted with forest lodges and inns, solidifying every now and then into quaint little villages and market towns. Throughout the year it is the weekend playground of the Viennese and, particularly in summer, thousands of them swarm on foot and by car through its forests and meadows.

Wienerwald reaches its northernmost point at Burg Greifenstein, a medieval castle soaring on a steep rock above the Danube and the tiny village of Greifenstein. A few miles down the Danube is Klosterneuburg, an old market town characterized by its remarkable 12th-century Augustine Abbey: its originally Romanesque church has a beautifully hand-carved wooden choir and oratory; in the Leopold Chapel is the famous *Verduner Altar* (1181) by Nikolaus von Verdun (Werden) decorated with 51 biblical scenes in medieval enamel, medieval stained-glass windows and a 12th-century candelabrum; in the great marble hall there are ceiling frescos by Daniel Gran; in addition, there is a rich library, a museum and treasury. Klosterneuburg is actually located just outside the northwestern boundaries of Vienna.

The panoramic Höhenstrasse (High Road), disclosing beautiful vistas of Vienna and the north section of the Vienna Woods, winds and climbs from Klosterneuburg over the Leopoldsberg, Kahlenberg and Cobenzl elevations to the western suburbs of the city.

The eastern edges of the Vienna Woods are skirted by vineyards beginning at Klosterneuburg, which is also an important wine center, with the Abbey being the biggest and the best wine producer. The vineyards then follow southwards through the wine villages of Nussdorf, Grinzing and Sievering, all of them within the city limits of Vienna, and all of them popular *Heuriger* centers. South of the city, the wine belt resumes at Perchtoldsdorf, a picturesque market town with many wine taverns, the 13th-century Gothic parish church and an imposing defense tower completed in 1511. Perchtoldsdorf, called locally "Petersdorf," is a favorite wine drinking excursion spot of the Viennese. In the nearby town of Mödling, founded in the 10th century, there are even more buildings of historical interest, including the Gothic parish church, a Romanesque 12th-century charnel house and the Town Hall with a Renaissance loggia. Near Mödling is the Romanesque Liechtenstein castle, which received its name from the Styrian minnesinger, Ulrich von Liechtenstein (1199–1275).

A few kilometers east of Mödling, already in the plain, and about 16 km. (10 miles) south of Vienna, is Schloss Laxenburg, a complex consisting of a large Baroque Neues Schloss (New Castle), a small 14th-century Altes Schloss (Old Castle), and an early 19th-century neo-Gothic castle—

now a good restaurant—in the sizeable lake. The large park is populated by many birds as well as small game, such as roe deer and hare. According to the taste of the period, the park is also decorated with statues, cascades, imitation temples and other follies. The Altes Schloss was built in 1381 by Duke Albrecht III as his summer residence, and several Habsburg emperors lived in the Neues Schloss, which now, of all unlikely institutions, houses the International Institute of Applied Systems' Analysis. Opposite is the large Baroque Convent of the Charitable Sisters.

Back in Mödling we follow the Weinstrasse (Wine Road) through the lush grape-growing country to Gumpoldskirchen, one of Austria's most famous wine-producing villages and the home of one of Europe's pleasantest white wines. Vintner houses line the main street, many of them with large wooden gates, typical of this area, leading into the vine-covered courtyard-gardens where the Heuriger (wine of the latest vintage) is served by the owner and his family at simple, wooden tables (sometimes to the tunes of an accordion player). Gumpoldskirchen also has an arcaded Renaissance Town Hall, the market fountain made out of a Roman sarcophagus, and the castle of the Teutonic Knights who still own some of the best vineyard sites in the area.

We can follow the same Wine Road to the famous spa of Baden, which can also be reached more quickly from Vienna via the autobahn, by the local Vienna–Baden streetcar-type of train, or bus, both of which leave from the Opera, or by the main railroad.

Since antiquity, Baden's sulphuric thermal baths have attracted the ailing and fashionable from all over the world. The Roman Aquae Pannonae revived under the Babenbergs in the 10th century; but only with the visit of the Russian Tsar, Peter the Great, in 1698, did Baden's golden age begin, highlighted by the visits of Emperor Franz II, who spent the twelve summers before his death in 1835 in the spa. And in Baden, Mozart composed his *Ave Verum;* Beethoven passed 15 summers and composed large sections of the *Ninth Symphony* and *Missa Solemnis;* Franz Grillparzer wrote his historical dramas and Josef Lanner, Johann Strauss, Karl Michael Ziehrer and Karl Millöcker directed and composed their waltzes, marches and operettas.

The loveliest spot in Baden is the huge and beautiful Kurpark, where one can listen to one of the many public concerts, attend operetta performances in the outdoor Summer Arena (in winter, theater performances are given in the Stadttheater), just sit peacefully under the old trees, or walk through the upper sections of the Kurpark for a view of the town from above. The old Kurhaus, enlarged, renovated, and with a new Kongresshaus (Convention Hall) with all the latest equipment for simultaneous translation and other gadgetry accompanying convention centers, is now known as the Kur-Kongress-Haus.

The baths themselves are built right over the 15 springs which pour forth the sulphuric thermal water to the tune of 8 million liters (1,760,000 gallons) a day. The water is about body temperature and is reported to be particularly good for rheumatic diseases. In addition to the six bath establishments proper, there are also two outdoor thermal-water swimming establishments, the larger one with five pools and a water temperature of 32 degrees C. (89.6 degrees F.).

West of Baden, the quiet and soft Helenental Valley (Route 305) takes you to Mayerling, scene of the tragic death in 1889 of Archduke Rudolf, Emperor Franz Josef's only son, and his young mistress. The mystery surrounding the Mayerling tragedy—largely caused by the instant slamming of a lid of secrecy on the affair by the Emperor and his court—is still a juicy subject for speculation, and is always surfacing in books, films and generally obsessive gossip. The site of the hunting-lodge where the double death took place is marked by a Carmelite convent, built by the bereaved Emperor.

Nearby in the heart of the southern section of the Vienna Woods is Heiligenkreuz, a magnificent Cistercian Abbey with a famous Romanesque and Gothic church, founded by Leopold III, the "Holy", in 1135. The church itself is lofty and serene, with beautifully carved choir stalls, surmounted by busts of Cistercian saints. The cloisters are full of interest, especially a Chapel of the Dead, where the brothers lie in state guarded by four gesticulating skeletons holding candelabra. The Chapterhouse contains the tombs of Babenburg rulers.

The vineyards immediately south of Baden produce some of the best red wine in Austria. Here is the small green spa of Bad Vöslau, resting on a hillside, with a lovely openair thermal swimming establishment at the foot of the hill, and a large and unique forest of pine trees, smelling healthily of tar, beginning in the Kurpark above and extending to the top of the Harzberg hill. The latter can be reached in a half-hour walk; from here there is a fine view of the Vienna Woods, Schneeberg and Wechsel mountains.

From Wiener Neustadt to Semmering

South and southwest of the Vienna Woods lie the highest mountains in Lower Austria, the Semmering, the Schneeberg, Rax and Wechsel groups. In winter the high plateaus of Schneeberg and Rax and the undulating ridges of Semmering and Wechsel are covered with a thick mantle of snow and provide ideal skiing conditions.

To reach these winter-sports and mountain-air resorts, you follow the South Autobahn or the main railroad to Wiener Neustadt, originally built in the 12th century as a fortress town for protection against invasions from the east. The remains of the 12th- and 13th-century town walls can still be seen near the large, pleasant city park; the most prominent among them is a Gothic tower, called Reckturm, which is said to have been built with part of the ransom money exacted for Richard the Lionhearted. As there are several other sites in Austria which claim the same backing, it would seem that the vast sum wrung from the people of England was put to good use.

Wiener Neustadt is usually thought of as an industrial city, but it still has a number of historic artistic treasures, in spite of the heavy destruction through air raids in 1943, when 52,000 bombs (about 1½ bombs for every inhabitant) demolished 3,982 of about 4,000 buildings existing at that time. The city has been rebuilt, naturally, along more functional lines than before. Some of the damaged historic buildings could be repaired, such as the fine 13th-century late Romanesque and Gothic parish church, with later interior Baroque and Rococo additions (tomb of Cardinal Khlesel by Bernini; Rococo choir, twelve apostles and unique Annunciation group by the late Gothic sculptor Lorenz Luchsperger). In addition to several other interesting churches, there is also a beautiful 14th-century sculpture by Master Michael (who also designed St. Stephen's tower in Vienna) located in a small park on Wienerstrasse. Wiener Neustadt is the seat of the Austrian Military Academy, installed by Empress Maria Theresa in the 13th-century castle (open to visitors). It was completely burned out in 1945 and rebuilt between 1949 and 1952. In the west wing of the Military Academy is the 15th-century Georgskapelle, a Gothic church with the grave of Emperor Maximilian I, called the "Last Knight," under the high altar.

For the Wechsel Mountains, continue south on the autobahn (A2) or by train to the market town of Aspang, a summer resort in the Pitten Valley, whose heights are guarded by a line of castles, particularly the notable 11th-century Seebenstein castle-fortress (later rebuilt in Renaissance style). From Aspang, Route 54 winds up to Mönichkirchen (980 m., 3,215 ft.), the summer and winter resort center in this area.

Schneeberg and Raxalpe

Schneeberg and Raxalpe lie west of Wiener Neustadt. The village of Puchberg, a mountain resort in summer and winter, is the departure point for Schneeberg. A small, cog-wheel railway crawls up the crest of the mountain to a point 1,795 m. (5,889 ft.) above sea level. Often steam-pulled, these trains are very popular with only limited seats available, so get there early. Puchberg has a modern Kurmittelhaus, where water cures and other medical treatments are administered. If you want to lose weight or improve your blood circulation, this is the place to try it.

Immediately southwest beyond Schneeberg lies the Raxalpe. Reichenau, a pleasant summer resort in the valley of the river Schwarza, and next-door Hirschwang, which is the valley station of the Rax cable car, are the best departure points for the plateau of Rax. Both can easily be reached by bus from nearby Payerbach, another summer resort and a station on the main railroad line south of Vienna, which in this section makes a steep climb from Gloggnitz, an old town in a deeply cut, scenic valley, up to the Semmering mountain pass.

The Semmering resort center lies around the pass, mostly on the steep slopes on the Lower Austrian side, the other side of the pass being in Styria. Semmering contains rest homes belonging to health insurance and other large firms; but a lot of investment has been made of recent years in reviving hotels and pensions, perched romantically high on the mountainside, to bring back to Semmering some of the luxurious quality of its past. Not least among these rejuvenations is the completely restored Hotel Panhans. In summer there are facilities for swimming, sunbathing, tennis and, of course, easy walks through the refreshing woods as well as harder mountain excursions. Skiing, ski competitions, ice skating, and tobogganing represent the main activities of the winter season. Semmering is also a Höhenluftkurort (a place for high climatic cures) for respiratory and allied ailments.

Höllental, northwest of Semmering, is the wild mountain valley of the River Schwarza that once cut the high mountain plateau into two parts, which today are called Raxalpe and Schneeberg. The road through Höllental leads over the Ochsensattel Pass to St. Aegyd in the Göller mountain area, an unpretentious winter and summer resort, which, however, can be reached much more comfortably through the Traisen Valley from St. Pölten.

The Marchfeld

Marchfeld is the fertile plain to the east of Vienna between the Danube and the river March, which marks the border between Lower Austria and Slovakia. Marchfeld is the granary of Austria, the wide grain fields being interspersed by woods and lush meadows. Pheasant, partridge and quail, as well as other small game, prefer such terrain and for centuries this region has been a hunter's paradise.

Marchauen Nature Preserve is a haven for wildlife, including Austria's only cormorant colony; the Safari Park Gänserndorf, open for cars, contains 340 species of large animals, among them 40 lions. Numerous Baroque castles and sumptuous hunting lodges, now house museums. To the east is Schloss Obersiebenbrunn, given by Charles VI to Prince Eugene, who entrusted Hildebrandt with the construction of a pretty garden pavilion. To the south on Route 49 are Schlosshof, once owned by Empress Maria Theresa, and Niederweiden, which was the hunting castle of Prince Eugen. The Schlosshof has been totally renovated and is the setting for annual exhibitions. Schloss Orth, on the Danube, once a fortress dating from the 12th century, now houses a fishing, honey-making and bee museum, with a 30-million-year-old bee fossilized in a piece of amber. Eckartsau, an 18th-century hunting castle with an imposing stairway and ceiling frescos by Daniel Gran, was given by Archduke Franz Ferdinand, assassinated in 1914 by the Serbs, to his nephew Emperor Charles who abdicated here in 1918, although, interestingly, he never signed the document presented to him by Karl Renner.

Across the Danube from Marchfeld, on the southern bank, lies the Roman town and military camp of Carnuntum, presently partially excavated; in addition to the remainders of the old Roman houses, the sites to visit are the amphitheater and the Heidentor (Heathen Gate), standing alone far out amidst the fields. The objects found during the excavations can be seen in the Museum Carnuntinum in Bad Deutsch-Altenburg, a nearby spa. The town also has a 13th-century Romanesque basilica and an African Museum in the Schloss Ludwigsdorf. In the summer Roman plays are performed in another amphitheater on the road to Petronell, where there is a Danube Museum in a Baroque castle whose one-time owners are buried in a remarkable 12th-century Romanesque circular chapel.

Another few miles to the east is Hainburg with interesting medieval walls and gates, a castle-fortress on an elevation in the town, the ruins of the Rothenstein castle on a hill outside the town, the Baroque parish church and many Gothic, Renaissance and Baroque houses. The population was twice wiped out by the Turks and the town resettled by Swabians from southwest Germany, hence the name Schwab, which is particularly common in Vienna. 8 km. (5 miles) south of Carnuntum is the Castle Rohrau, home of the Counts of Harrach and Austria's only private art museum. It has more than 200 paintings, mostly Italian and Spanish, but is open to the public only in summer, as is Haydn's birthplace, a modest, thatched building in the village, restored and extended for the composer's bicentenary in 1982.

The Weinviertel

North of Vienna, between the Danube and the border of Czechoslovakia, lies the Weinviertel, the Wine District. Though other regions of Lower

Austria are even more noted for their wines, the local dry whites here are pleasing. A string of medieval castles, often in ruins, and many colorful market towns can also be found in this area.

Across the Danube, beside the short North Autobahn (E84, S3), Korneuburg is a small town with a picturesque main square dominated by the Gothic Town Hall tower; the Augustine Church is a remarkable example of Rococo style. On a hill a bit beyond Korneuburg is Kreuzenstein, a 12th-century castle-fortress, destroyed by the Swedes in the Thirty Years' War, restored in the 19th century, and presently a museum and showpiece for old Austrian castle atmosphere. 32 km. (20 miles) to the north at Ernstbrunn, 13th-century St. Martin's contains an altar piece by Kremser Schmidt, while the huge 17th-century castle, in a beautiful park, houses an Empire museum. To the west (on 40) is Hollabrunn, one of the main towns in this area, surrounded by wooded hills. Farther west (on 303) lies the charming little town of Eggenburg, with medieval walls, Gothic churches, Renaissance and Baroque houses, and the Krahuletz Museum, with important prehistoric finds from the area.

On the way to Eggenburg you pass Kleinwetzdorf and "Heldenberg" (Heroes' Mountain). The latter is a formal garden and the incredible burial place of Field Marshal Radetzky. There are innumerable statues and busts, including all the Habsburgs and Babenbergs and countless generals; Radetzky is buried in a crypt along with the baron who paid for the honor of occupying the same tomb as the Field Marshal. The whole complex is a slightly overwhelming military phantasmagoria—but historically fascinating. The Schlosstaverne, open on weekends and holidays, is quite good; the Schloss itself includes a small Radetzky museum.

North of here, near the Czech border, is the wine town of Retz, with its remarkable, vast and colorful central square, renowned also for its Gothic Dominican church, several Renaissance and Baroque buildings, among them a castle with fine interiors, and a windmill. Among the important wine-producing villages here are Röschitz, with the Ludwig Weber Cellar (wall reliefs made of loess); and Haugsdorf, with "cellar streets" lined by wine press houses, (typical for this area).

East on the Thaya River (take Route 45) is the small 13th-century town of Laa, with partially preserved walls and an old fortress. Beer brewing here dates to 1454, accounting in part for the Beer Museum. Southeast of Laa, the fortress ruins of Falkenstein and Staatz still are powerful enough to dominate the countryside around them. Massive 15th-century Schloss Asparn on the Zaya houses the Museum of Lower Austria's Prehistory; in the park are models of dwellings from the Ice Age to the Celts.

Southeast again is Dürnkrut, where in 1278 the famous battle was fought which established the supremacy of the Habsburgs in Austria for the next six and a half centuries. There you are within a stone's throw of the Czech border again.

Along the Danube through the Wachau

If you have time, you should see this part of Austria from the deck of a Danube paddleboat steamer. When the weather is fine and warm, the trip downstream is highly rewarding. The slower trip upstream against the swift-flowing current is even better, allowing more time to take in the magnificent scenery, the charming wine-growing villages, and the fairyland castles perched precariously on the rocky crags on the river bends.

If you cannot spare the time for this leisurely inspection, and go by car, be sure to cross over to the north bank of the Danube and follow the river along the scenic road through the Wachau and Nibelungengau.

Traveling by boat upstream (that is going west) from Vienna, you leave the Klosterneuburg Abbey and Greifenstein castle at your left and enter the area of the fertile Tullner Feld (Tullner Plain), on the south bank, named after the town of Tulln, which is known primarily for its flower cultivation. It was here that Kriemhild met Etzel (Attila) in the *Nibelungen Saga.* The Danube spreads out here in several natural canals among thick river woods, abounding with game. At the end of Tullner Feld, the river Traisen flows into the Danube (south bank), rushing from the high mountains on the Styrian border.

If you are driving and so can leave the Danube, higher up the Traisen are Herzogenburg, with an Augustine Abbey, founded in the 12th century, but whose architecture is partially by the great Baroque masters Fischer von Erlach and Jakob Prandtauer; it has a valuable library and a rich museum of Gothic altars, as well as a wine tavern serving its own wines; and Pottenbrunn, a moated castle with a tin-soldier museum, open in summer only. Still further is St. Pölten, the Provincial Capital and the key railroad and road junction in this district.

The old center of St. Pölten shows a distinct Baroque face and contains many artistic treasures. The originally Romanesque cathedral has a rich Baroque interior and more than a dozen paintings and frescos by Daniel Gran. The Rococo Franciscan church has four altar paintings by Kremser Schmidt. The so-called "Institute of English Maidens" in Linzerstrasse is one of the finest Baroque buildings in the city; the ceiling frescos in its church are by Altomonte and there is also a painting by Lukas Cranach from 1516.

Farther up the Traisen Valley is Lilienfeld, the seat of a medieval Cistercian abbey, founded in 1202 and built in Romanesque style with later Baroque additions; a small gallery of paintings, and a valuable library (1704) are also part of the abbey treasures. Still farther upstream is the small industrial town of Freiland, where the river Türnitz, coming from the winter sports resort of the same name, flows into the Traisen.

Krems and the Wachau

Back on the Danube we continue upstream to Krems, one of the most important cities in Lower Austria and the Austrian wine trade center; the steep vineyards above and near the city produce some of the best Austrian wines. Krems also marks the beginning (when traveling upstream) of the Wachau section of the Danube. It is a delightful old town, founded in 955 or earlier, with partially preserved city walls, a 15th–16th century Rathaus with a Renaissance oriel, a parish church that is one of the oldest Baroque buildings in Lower Austria, a city museum located in the former Dominican Romanesque and Gothic church, a very interesting wine museum in the adjoining former monastery, the Gothic–Renaissance Palais Gozzo on Hoher Markt, where openair plays are staged during the summer, the former Minorite Church in the Stein section of the city (converted into a museum of the work of Kremser Schmidt, the famous Austrian Baroque painter), the former Imperial Toll House, also in Stein (Steiner Landstrasse 84), with splendid Renaissance facade and frescos, and many other Renaissance, Baroque and Rococo buildings, some of them hidden away in the narrow streets on both sides of Obere and Untere Landstrasse, which you enter through the majestic 15th-century Steiner Tor, and others located in the western suburb of Stein, once a town in its own right.

Across the Danube from Krems, in a commanding position on a hill, stands Göttweig, another great abbey, this time Benedictine, founded in the 11th century, but the present Baroque buildings are from the 18th century, built to the plans made by Lukas von Hildebrandt; it has a nice tavern with its own wines, and a beautiful view of Krems and the Danube valley from the terrace. Down in the valley, Klein-Wien and Mautern offer two of Austria's finest and least pretentious restaurants: *Gashaus Schlick* and *Bacher*, respectively. Returning to Krems, visit the chapel in the monastery's town building, the Göttweiger Hof Kapelle: beautiful 14th-century frescos have recently been discovered here and put on show.

Our next stop in the Wachau is Dürnstein, famous for its wines, for its quaint old houses and streets, and for its Baroque reddish church tower. Dürnstein is also known for its castle, now mostly in ruins, where Richard the Lionheart was imprisoned for 13 months; according to the story, it was beneath its battlements that the faithful Blondel played. He had wandered all over the area, trying to find the castle where his king was imprisoned and finally was rewarded by hearing his master's voice. Given the number of castles hereabouts, he certainly had his work cut out.

Farther upstream on the same bank is Weissenkirchen, with a Gothic walled church and the beautiful Teisenhofer patrician house, with a 16th-century arcaded courtyard, presently housing the Wachau Museum. On the other bank, the Aggstein fortress, partially in ruins, is perched upon the top of a 1,000-foot cliff, in a commanding position over the Wachau.

Farther up on the right bank comes Schönbühel Castle. Beyond it on the same bank is the town of Melk, dominated by its mighty Baroque abbey. Originally a 10th-century fortress, and the seat of the Babenberg family who preceded the Habsburgs, it was given to the Benedictines in the early 12th century, but its present Baroque buildings were planned by Jakob Prandtauer in the 18th century. Its library is one of the finest, with some 80,000 volumes and 1,850 old manuscripts dating from the 9th century. This huge and richly endowed complex, though full of art treasures, is also important as an integral part of Austrian history, which can be sensed on every hand. Unfortunately, Melk is in a bad way, physically, with all sorts of decay attacking the fabric of the massive buildings. It may be that you will not be able to visit parts of the complex that have been closed off for repairs. Restoration of the West Front and the interior has been completed. The result is magnificent.

Beyond Wachau the Danube Valley is called Nibelungengau because the Nibelungs are supposed to have settled here, at least for a while; their romantic arrival by ship is enacted every year at the June solstice in a pageant performed at the medieval river town of Pöchlarn; then, both banks of the Danube in this section are ablaze with bonfires and fireworks. This is the area which is supposed to have witnessed some of the events of the *Epic of the Nibelungen*, the great saga that has inspired many versions, mainly that of Wagner's *Ring*. The original story was concerned with the mythical hero Siegfried, his faithful and brave Nibelungs, his marriage to the Burgundian royal daughter Kriemhild and his assassination by Kriemhild's relatives; in revenge Kriemhild then married the King of the Huns and brought about the conflict between the Burgundians and the Huns.

Kriemhild and her brothers, kings of Burgundy, stayed in Bechelaren (Pöchlarn) when they travelled to Attila's court in West Hungary.

Crowning a hill on the left bank is the two-towered Maria Taferl pilgrimage church, in the summer resort village of the same name. 5 km. (3 miles) northeast of Maria Taferl is the castle of Artstetten, burial place of Franz-Ferdinand and his morganatic wife Sophie, both of whom were assassinated in Sarajevo in 1914 (which was one of the triggers of World War I). Nibelungengau ends at the 17th-century Persenbeug Castle, the birthplace of Karl I, the last Austrian Emperor. Across the river and connected by a dam bridge is Ybbs, with remains of medieval walls and towers and a pretty Renaissance fountain on the main square. The natural beauty of the Danube Valley is marred here by a large hydro-electric power station on the river.

The Erlauf and Ybbs Valleys

At Pöchlarn, the small Erlauf River, coming from the Ötscher mountains in the south, joins the Danube. Not far up the Erlauf Valley are the towns of Wieselburg and Purgstall, both with interesting churches and castles. Wieselburg is also known for its beer and for its country fair taking place in late June. Nearby (Route 25) is Scheibbs, another small old town with partially preserved walls, a tower gate and a cluster of Renaissance houses around the Gothic parish church, standing on the main square next to the 16th-century castle, which has a beautiful arcaded courtyard.

In its upper course, skirting the mountain of Gemeinde Alpe and Ötscher, the Erlauf flows through two Erlauf lakes, one natural and one artificial. In this area there are several small summer and winter resorts saddled on wooded and meadowed mountain backs, such as Puchenstuben, Gösing, Annaberg, Josefsberg and Mitterbach, the latter actually on the Styrian border and only three miles from Mariazell, the well-known Styrian resort with the famous pilgrimage church. All these places can also be reached by the main road from St. Pölten.

From Erlauf Lake, a side road takes you to the upper Ybbs Valley to Lunz and Lunzer Lake, nestled among fir-treed slopes. This unpretentious summer resort, whose meadows are covered with white narcissi in late spring, can be reached more easily either by road or train from Gaming and the lower Erlauf Valley. A few miles down the Ybbs River is Göstling, from where a mountain road takes you up to the Hochkar Plateau and a chair lift close to the peak of Hochkar (1,808 m., 5,932 ft.).

The most picturesque town in the lower Ybbs Valley is Waidhofen, with rows of 15th- and 16th-century gabled houses with bay windows and arcaded courtyards; the parish church with winged main altarpiece and several other interesting churches; the high and impressive castle tower; and the massive "city tower", built in 1542 in memory of the city's victorious repulsion of the Turks, with the clock dial still showing the hour of the Turkish defeat—11.45 A.M. A landmark seen miles around is the majestic Baroque pilgrimage church of Sonntagberg (Wahllfahrtskirche), crowning a hill not far from Waidhofen. A few kilometers to the northwest is the historic Benedictine Abbey of Seitenstetten, founded in 1112, with frescos by Kremser Schmidt and a priceless collection of paintings and engravings; to the northeast is the small town of Neuhofen, which likes to call itself the "cradle of Austria", since the oldest known spelling of Österreich (Austria)—Ostarrichi—was found here in an old document dated 996. In its further lower course, the Ybbs passes by Amstetten, and flows into the Danube near the town of Ybbs.

Waldviertel

Waldviertel is the hilly and forested region north of Wachau and Nibelungengau marked by two main rivers: the Kamp, curving through its heart, and the Thaya, winding up and down its northern section. Many a romantic castle is hidden away off the beaten path on wooded hills above the bends of the Kamp and the Thaya. The best departure point for exploring Waldviertel is Krems.

Heading towards the Kamp River, which flows into the Danube some miles below Krems, we reach its vineyard-terraced lower valley near the sunny wine town of Langenlois, with rows of Renaissance and Baroque houses painted blue, pink and yellow. Farther upstream the vineyards disappear and the Kamp rushes through soft and tranquil green hills and through several dams and artificial lakes providing the local hydro-electric power station with energy and the summer vacationers with water sports.

Traveling up the river, some of the most interesting spots on its bank and nearby include: the quiet resort town of Gars with an 11th-century fortress; the imposing Rosenburg castle-fortress with a large tournament courtyard, Gothic chapel and a collection of weapons and furniture; the romantic town of Horn, with five medieval wall towers, several churches of note and a cluster of Renaissance houses; the Benedictine monastery of Altenburg, with a cupola fresco by Paul Troger and a crypt with grotesque paintings representing the *Dance of Death;* the Renaissance castle of Greillenstein, again with works of Troger; the quiet dammed lake of Dobra, framed by woods, with the still powerful medieval Dobra fortress ruins; Ottenstein castle, above the largest of the artificial lakes, with the 12th-century massive chief tower; and Rastenberg castle-fortress, in a side valley nearby.

Zwettl, on the upper course of the Kamp, is a small market town with partially preserved walls, including six towers, located in the center of Waldviertel. Close to town is a beautiful Cistercian monastery with a Romanesque canonical house, one of the oldest of its kind in existence. The Baroque organ, built in 1731, is the largest of its kind in Austria. Occasional concerts are held during the summer. A score of country roads spread out of Zwettl like a spider's web over the surrounding rolling dales and hills. Close by is Schloss Rosenau, which houses a fascinating Freemason's museum in what were once secret Masonic rooms, well worth a visit.

To the southwest, above the upper Kamp River (Route 38, then 124) is Rappottenstein, an excellent example of a medieval castle-fortress. To the west are the towns of Weitra, with medieval walls and Sgraffiti-decorated buildings dating to the 14th century; and Gmünd, right on the border of Czechoslovakia, with a Renaissance face and an interesting glass museum showing the development of glassmaking from the Middle Ages through the 19th century.

Northeast of Gmünd is Heidenreichstein, where you can tour one of the most remarkable "water" castles in Austria. "Water"—or moated—castles were surrounded by a body of water (natural or artificial) for defense purposes whereas the "hill" castles used steep, often rocky and inaccessible, slopes for protection. The most interesting places to the northeast along the Thaya River are the Baroque town of Waidhofen (not to be confused with Waidhofen on the Ybbs River described earlier); Drosendorf, with well-preserved medieval walls; the dreamy castles of Karlstein and Raabs; Fischer von Erlach's Riegersburg, which provides a suitable setting for a Baroque Museum; and 12th-century Hardegg, all on small hills above the river.

PRACTICAL INFORMATION FOR
LOWER AUSTRIA

TOURIST INFORMATION. Lower Austria is, of course, dominated by Vienna, and a great deal of it is visitable on a days-out basis from the capital. However, the province has so much to offer the visitor that to dismiss it as simply an adjunct to Vienna would be a serious mistake. The following list is of the Tourist Offices in the main towns that you are likely to visit, or stay in, while exploring Lower Austria, with their postal codes and phone numbers.

Baden A-2500 (0 22 52/86800–310); Bad Vöslau A-2540 (0 22 52–77 43); Dürnstein A-3601 (0 21 11–219); Gaming-Lackenhof A-3295 (0 74 80–286); Gars am Kamp A-3571 (02985–26 80); Göstling an der Ybbs A-3345 (0 74 84–22 04); Gumpoldskirchen A-2352 (02252–62421); Hainburg an der Donau A-2410 (0 21 65–21 11); Klosterneuburg A-3400 (0 22 43–20 38); Krems A-3500 (0 27 32–26 76).

Langenlois A-3550 (0 27 34–21 01); Maria Taferl A-3672 (0 74 13–302); Melk A-3390 (0 27 52–23 07); Mistelbach an der Zaya A-2130 (0 25 72–25 15); Mönichkirchen A-2872 (0 26 49–225); Neuhofen an der Ybbs A-3364 (0 74 75–27 00); Perchtoldsdorf A-2380 (0 222–86 76 34 34); Pöchlarn A-3380 (0 27 57–310); Puchberg am Schneeberg A-2734 (0 26 36–22 01).

Raabs an der Thaya A-3820 (0 28 46–365); Reichenau an der Rax A-2651 (0 26 66–28 65); Retz A-2070 (0 29 42–27 00); St. Aegyd am Neuwalde A-3193 (0 27 68–290); St. Pölten A-3100 (0 27 42–33 54); Semmering A-2680 (0 26 64–539); Tulln A-3430 (0 22 72–42 85); Weissenkirchen in der Wachau A-3610 (0 27 15–22 32); Wiener Neustadt A-2700 (0 26 22–35 31); Ybbs an der Donau A-3370 (0 74 12–26 12); Zwettl A-3910 (0 28 22–22 33).

Lower Austrian Tourist Information: 1010 Vienna, Heidenschuss 2 (533 31 14).

AREA CODES—MAIL AND PHONE. You will find the postal code (preceded by an "A") and the telephone code (in brackets) after the name of each town in the following Hotel and Restaurant list.

HOTELS AND RESTAURANTS. Hotel facilities in Lower Austria are geared primarily to the needs of budget-minded Viennese vacationists. Although some hotels have few rooms with bath, they are very clean, generally comfortable and range from the Moderate category to the Inexpensive countryside-Gasthaus type. Exceptions are the large, Expensive hotels in resort centers such as Semmering and Baden.

Prices throughout the province are about 25% lower than those of similar hotel categories in Vienna and in the large tourist centers of the Tirol and Salzburg. In the smaller places you will usually eat where you are staying, although any roadside Gasthaus will provide you with a good, if limited, menu.

Aggsbach A-3641 (0 27 12). *Post* (M), (344). 36 rooms, some with shower. Outdoor pool, sauna, tennis; excellent restaurant. Camping site (214).

Alland A-2534 (0 22 58). *Marienhof* (E), (379). 25 simple but clean rooms; lovely building in beautiful setting, near Mayerling, the site of the hunting lodge where Crown Prince Rudolf killed himself; excellent restaurant "Kronprinz" in hotel. Closed Mon. and Tues. AE, DC, MC, V.

Bad Deutsch Altenburg A-2405 (0 21 65). *Kaiserbad* (E), Badg. 4 (2335). 115 rooms; cure facilities; good restaurant. AE, DC, MC.

Baden A-2500 (0 22 52). *Sauerhof zu Rauhenstein* (L), Weilburgstrasse 11–13 (41 2 51). Fine castle in Schönbrunn Yellow; lobby and rooms in period decor or rustic Austrian style, indoor pool, tennis and sauna. Good rotisserie. AE, DC, MC, V.
Caruso (E). Trostgasse 23 (88 66 20). Old villa refurbished as stylish hotel with 74 comfortable rooms. Excellent restaurant. AE, DC, MC.
Clubhotel Baden (E), Schlossgasse 9–11 (48301). 186 beds, all with bath; cure facilities, pool, sauna, tennis; good restaurant. AE, DC, MC, V.
Krainerhütte (E), Helenental (44 5 11). 60 rooms, all with bath and balcony; elegantly furnished. Indoor pool, tennis, fishing. *Parkhotel* (E), Kaiser Franz Ring 5 (44 3 86). 90 rooms, all with bath, most with balcony overlooking the Kurpark. Indoor pool, sauna, cure facilities, conference rooms. DC, MC, V. *Schlosshotel Oth* (E), Schlossgasse 23 (4 44 36). 42 rooms, all with bath; garden, café and wine tavern.
Casino in Kongresshaus. Terrace cafe.

Bad Vöslau A-2540 (0 22 52). *Kurhotel Neydharting* (M), (73 49). Modern, up hill at the edge of the Kurpark; small and quiet. AE.

Deutsch Wagram A-2232 (0 22 47). *Marchfelderhof* (M), Bockflieserstrasse 31 (22 43). 33 beds, most with bath or shower; cozy. Excellent restaurant, original cuisine and famous clientele. (See also Vienna, *Excursion Dining.*) AE, DC, MC, V. Closed Mon.

Dürnstein A-3601 (0 27 11). *Schlosshotel Dürnstein* (L), (212). Baroque castle on rocky terrace overlooking the Danube; heated pool, sauna; famous restaurant. Open March to Nov. AE, DC, MC, V.
Richard Löwenherz (E), (222). 46 rooms. Romantik Hotel. In former convent with atmospheric period decor and historic vaulted dining room; garden terrace overlooking Danube. Restaurant with game and fish specialties; excellent local wines. Open March to Dec. AE, DC, V.
Hotel Sänger Blondel (M), (253). 20 rooms, most with bath or shower; excellent restaurant. Open Feb. to Dec.

Falkenstein A-2112 (0 25 54). *Vinothek* in cellar museum (7703). Wine presentations on 1st and 3rd Sunday in month at 4 P.M.

Feuersbrunn 3483 (0 27 38). On road from Vienna to Krems. *Zur Traube* (E), (2298). Ambitious young son has turned family Gasthaus into an exciting new gourmet restaurant. Closed Wed.

Gars Am Kamp A-3571 (0 29 85). *Bio-Training-Hotel* (E), (26 66). 80 rooms, pleasant garden. Emphasis on health; training rooms, sauna, solarium, indoor pool, specialty restaurant. V.

Gösing A-3221 (0 27 28). On the rail line from St. Pölten to Mariazell. *Alpenhotel Gösing* (E), (217). In striking, isolated position at 915 m. (3,000 ft.), facing the Ötscher range. Mountain lodge style with balconies and terraces; indoor and outdoor pools, sauna, hunting and fishing; good restaurant.

Grafenegg 3485 Haitzendorf (0 27 35). *Schlosstaverne* (M), (616). 18 beds. Next to magnificent Victorian castle, now restored and used for major exhibitions and concerts. Close to Krems/Langenlois. Good food. AE, DC, MC, V.

Gross-Enzersdorf A-2301 (0 22 49). *Seminarhotel am Sachsengang* (E), (2901–0). Conference hotel. Small rooms, but with bath and good furniture; indoor pool, sauna, tennis; restaurant. AE, DC, MC, V.

Gumpoldskirchen A-2352 (0 22 52). *Weingut Aigner* (E), Benediktinerhof, Kirchengasse 3 (62 1 85). 20 rooms, all with bath; indoor pool; wine tavern.
Restaurants. *Rathauskeller* (M), Wienerstrasse 2 (62 4 04). Traditional Austrian fare. AE, DC, V. Closed Tues. *Weinstadl* (M), Jubilaumstr. 42 (62 2 18–0). Rustic wooden interior; grills. AE, DC, MC. *Haus an der Weinstrasse* (M) (02236–4541). On the highest part of the Wine Road, halfway between Gumpoldskirchen and Mödling, at Eichkogel, with outdoor terrace and good view. AE. Closed Sun.

Haag A-3350 (0 74 34). *Schafelner* (E), (24 11). Just off the autobahn between Amstetten and Linz, this country inn serves superb regional cuisine. Wonderful wine list. Closed Mon. AE, DC, MC, V.

Klosterneuburg A-3400 (0 22 43). *Martinschloss* (E), Martinstr. 34–36 (74 26). 50 rooms, most with bath. Baroque castle on the edge of town; big garden, heated pool, hunting facilities. Open Mar. to Nov. DC, MC, V.
Restaurants. *Stiftskeller* (M), (2070). Historic part of the Abbey, interesting cellar section. Open daily. *Cafe Veit,* Niedermarkstr. 13 (20 72). Good food and cakes. Closed Wed.
There are also many good *Heurigers* in the area.

Krems A-3500 (0 27 32). *Bacher.* (E), (29 37). 22 beds in charming rooms. Across the bridge in Mautern. Frau Wagner (the owner) cooks in one of the finest restaurants in Austria. Her husband is responsible for the superb wine cellar and runs his own Vinothek. Reservations essential. Closed Mon. in summer; Mon. and Tues. in winter. DC.
Alte Post (M), Obere Landstr. 32 (22 76). 16th-century house with arcaded Renaissance courtyard, used in warm weather as restaurant garden;

period-style restaurant rooms with good local food and wine. AE. *Rosenhotel Krems* (I), Arbeiterg. 5 (51 06). 90 beds with shower, open July/Aug. Campsite on the bank of the Danube (26 76). **Restaurants.** In the Wachau, *Nikolaihof* (E), (0 27 32–29 01). First class food and wines in relaxed, heuriger atmosphere. South of Danube. Closed Mon., Tues. *Jamek* (E), (0 27 15–22 35). In Weissenkirchen, just beyond Durnstein. Reservations essential. Closed Sun. and Mon., Jan. and Feb. *Schickh* (E), (0 27 36–218). South of Danube in Klein-Wien. First-class food and superb wines. Reservations essential. Closed Wed., Thurs., in winter Mon. and Tues. *Gasthof Jell* (M), Hoher Markt 9 (0 27 32–23 45). Family atmosphere; local dishes imaginatively prepared, plus own wines, superb homemade Schnapps, and delicious *Torte*. Closed Tues. DC. *Prandtauerhof* (M), (0 27 15–23 10). DC. Magnificent local food and wines in Baroque surroundings. Closed Tues., Wed. *Geymüller Gasthof am Tabor* (M), (0 27 39–22 87). South of Danube. High up. A chance to taste the superb Geymüller wines.

Lackenhof A-3295 (0 74 80). *Jagdhof* (E), (300). 20 rooms with bath or shower. Sauna, solarium and gym; skiing resort. Open Dec. to Oct. DC. Youth Hostel (251).

Langenlebarn A-3425 (0 22 72). *Zum Roten Wolf* (M), (25 67). Simple rooms and startlingly good traditional, local food. Near Tulln. Closed Tues. AE, DC, MC, V.

Langenlois A-3550 (0 27 34). *Bründlmayer* (28 83). Heuriger attached to one of Austria's best wineries. Closed Tues., Jan.

Maria Taferl A-3672 (0 74 13). *Kaiserhof* (E), (6357). 50 rooms, most with bath. Indoor pool, sauna. AE, DC, MC, V. *Krone* (E), (63 55). 20 rooms with bath or shower. Indoor pool, sauna; garden terrace with view of the Danube. AE, DC, MC, V.

Markhof A hotel (02285–6106) near Schönfeld-Lassee (A-2294 Marchegg) on an estate about 32 km. (20 miles) east of Vienna, devoted to horsemanship. Only accessible by car. Guest rooms and a *gemütlich* tavern, swimming pool. No restaurant. Bridle paths through open fields and pine forests; indoor ring. Added attraction—four Lippizaners; English owned and run. Inquiries from Reitzentrum Markhof bei Schönfeld-Lassee, A-2294 Marchegg or call Vienna (0222) 47 13 10.

Mayerling: see Alland.

Melk A-3390 (0 27 52). There are several atmospheric hotels in the romantic old town section. Among them *Stadt Melk* (E), Hauptplatz 1 (24 75). 15 rooms with bath or shower. V. *Goldener Ochs* (M), Linzerstr. 18 (23 67). MC, V.
Campsite, large site by the Danube (26 81).
Restaurant. The Abbey's *Stiftskeller* (M), (25 55), serves its own delicious wines. Open daily April–Oct.

Mistelbach A-2130 (0 25 72). *Goldene Krone* (I), (2729). 50 beds. 200 years old; small with modern facilities. Restaurant serving good food. Closed Wed. MC, V.

Mitterndorf A-3452 (02275). *Gasthaus Hütt* (M), (254). Modern style country cooking, try the kid. Own herb garden. Good wines from the Wachau. Closed Wed. and Sat. evenings. DC.

Mödling A-2340 (0 22 36). *Rosenhotel* (M), Guntransdorferstr. 10a (85 1 23). 100 beds with shower, open all year.

Mönichkirchen A-2872 (0 26 49). Summer and winter resort. *Ferienhotel Lang* (E), (257). Indoor pool, tennis, bar with dancing; good restaurant. AE. *Reidinger* (M), (242). Open Dec. to Oct. DC, MC, V in restaurant only.

Neuhofen A-3364 (0 74 75). *Kothmühle* (M), (21 12). 40 rooms, with bath or shower, sauna, solarium and bar. *Ostarrichi* (I), (27 37). 35 rooms, some with shower; heated swimming pool.
Restaurant. Moser (M), (4221). Delightful building. Imaginative cooking using local produce. Good wines.

Neunkirchen A-2620 (0 26 35). *Zum Goldenen Löwen* (M), Triesterstr. 10 (24 26). 20 rooms, some with bath and balcony. Restaurant of some distinction. Closed Fri. and Sat. AE, MC, V.

Puchberg A-2734 (0 26 36). *Kneipp-Kurhotel* (E), (23 10). 40 rooms, most with bath or shower; indoor pool, sauna, solarium, fitness rooms, ski lift; bar. AE. *Puchbergerhof* (M), (22 78). 20 rooms, all with bath or shower. Rustic style; good restaurant with attentive service.
Forellenhof (I), Losenheim 132 (22 05 11). 25 rooms, most with bath or shower; indoor pool, sauna. Open Dec. to Oct. AE. *Hotel Hochschneeberg-Berghaus* (I), (22 57). At the top end of cog-wheel railway at 2000 m (5900 ft.). Open April–Oct.

Raxalpe A-2652 (0 26 66). Northwest of Semmering; railway stop at Payerbach; road to Hirschwang or Prein. *Berghotel Raxalpe* (I), Hirschwang (24 50). 80 beds; at upper station of aerial cable car from Hirschwang. *Ottohaus* (I), (2402). About 2 km. (1¼ miles) from cable car station, reached only by walking in winter.

Reichenau A-2651 (0 26 66), *Knappenhof* (E), Edlach (36 33). 46 beds, all with shower; pool, sauna and thermal baths. Quiet setting on south slope of the Raxalpe. Good restaurant. DC, MC, V.

Rosenau A-3924 (0 28 22). *Schlosshotel* (M), (82 21). Small castle in charming setting. 20 rooms with bath; golf course, riding, tennis; museum of Free Masonry. Good regional cuisine. Closed Feb. DC, MC, V.

Semmering A-2680 (0 26 64). On main road and railway south of Vienna. *Panhans* (L), Hochstrasse 32b (81 81). Reopened in 1983 after restoration that has left former grandeur intact. Great location; indoor pool and notable restaurant—*Kaiser Karl.* AE, DC. *Belvedere* (E), Hochstrasse 60 (270). 22 rooms, 14 with bath; indoor pool, sauna, fitness room. Open Dec. to Oct. AE, DC, MC, V. Good restaurant. *Gartenhotel Alpenheim* (E), (322). 22 rooms, most with bath; pool. Open Dec. to Oct.

Steinakirchen Am Forst A-3261 (0 74 88). *Schloss Ernegg* (M), (214). 16th-century castle with 22 rooms; car service from Amstetten on Vienna–Linz railway. Fine park with hunting, riding, fishing, pool; own stables; 9-hole golf course nearby. Reserve. Good for excursions to Wachau and Mariazell. Open May to Oct. AE, DC, MC, V.

Tulbingerkogel A-3001 (0 22 73). *Silencehotel Berghotel Tulbingerkogel* (E), (73 91). 50 rooms, with bath; lovely setting and famous restaurant. AE, DC, MC, V.

Tulln A-3430 (0 22 72). *Zur Rossmühle* (E), (24 11). Pleasant rooms, excellent restaurant. Fast trains to Vienna. Closed Jan. AE, DC, MC.

Waidhofen/Thaya A-3830 (0 28 42). *Gasthof Haberl* (I), Bahnhofstrasse 2 (25 44). Family-run with spacious and well-appointed rooms. Excellent value, good local food and wines. AE.
Camping Site (23 31).

Waidhofen/Ybbs A-3340 (0 74 42). *Gasthof Schönhuber zum Goldenen Hirschen* (I), (21 32). Pleasant rooms with showers (ask for those on top floor). Family run. Good, simple food.
Restaurant. *Türkenpfeiferl* (E), (35 07). Beautifully-cooked food using local ingredients and recipes. Cozy. Closed Tues. (Wed. in winter). DC, MC.

Wiener Neustadt A-2700 (0 26 22). *Corvinus* (E), Bahngasse 29–33 (2 41 34). By the city wall, modern. Conference facilities. Bar and notable restaurant. AE, DC, MC, V.
Cafe. *Witetschka,* Allerheiligenplatz 1 (2 31 09). On historic square; famous for pastries and ice cream. Closed Sun.

Wolfsgraben A-3012 (02233). *Florianistub'n* (E), (7204). Family gourmet restaurant combined with comfortable Gasthaus. Closed Tues. and Wed. DC.

Ybbs A-3370 (0 74 12). *Weisses Rössl* (M), Kirchengasse 12 (22 92). On the banks of the Danube with restaurant terrace overlooking the river. AE, DC, MC, V.
Restaurant. *Villa Nowotni* (E), Trewaldstrasse 3 (26 20). Tastefully furnished; excellent cuisine. Superb; really worth a visit. Reservations recommended. Closed Mon. AE, DC, MC, V.

GETTING AROUND LOWER AUSTRIA. By Train. Information for Lower Austria available from Niederösterreich Tourist Office, Heidenschuss 2, 1010 Vienna (533 31 14). Railways and roadways follow almost identical routes, but fast train service is provided only on the main railroad lines: Vienna–St. Pölten–Melk–Amstetten–Upper Austria, Vienna–Wiener Neustadt–Semmering, Vienna–Eggenburg–Gmund in Waldviertel. The latter, however, provides only a couple of fast trains daily in each direction. The other two are main international lines to the west and the south and provide many fast trains daily.
Secondary railway lines reach most of the places of interest, but service is slow and trains must be changed often; they are not recommended to

AUSTRIA

anyone wanting to cover more than a few dozen kilometers daily. One exception is the street-car type of train from Vienna (near the Opera) to Baden, which operates almost every half hour between 6 A.M. and 10 P.M.

By Bus. Bus travel is both more interesting and, indeed, sometimes faster than rail travel. Lower Austria has an excellent network of buses. In Vienna inquire at the Niederösterreichisches Landesreiseburo, Heidenschuss 2 (533 31 14 34) in the Inner City, or at any tourist office, and at the post office in smaller towns. Most of the buses in the countryside are run by the postal administration. Bus information from Wien Mitte Bus Station (behind Wien Mitte railway station), A-1030, Landstrasse Hauptstrasse, opposite the Hilton, (75 01). Excursions leave from Austrobus office, Opernpassage (5 34 11–0).

Daily sightseeing tours in summer (in winter two or three a week) to Heiligenkreuz–Mayerling–Baden, Klosterneuburg, Wachau, and Semmering are available from Vienna.

By Boat. For information on traveling by boat in this region—one of the best ways of seeing the many facets of the Danube—see the *Practical Information for Vienna* section.

By Car. From Vienna the best way to visit Lower Austria is by car. If you can manage the German text, an excellent booklet, *Ein Ausflug wie ein Urlaub,* is available from the Niederösterreich Tourist Office and gives details and routes of 29 excursions in various parts of the district. You can make daily trips leaving in the morning and returning in the evening and, in a week or so, can superficially cover the most important points. Routes 7, 2 and 4 (the last two forking after the embryonic North Autobahn past Stockerau) take you north to the Czech border and, with the use of side roads, will enable you to cover the Thaya valley area.

Route 3 will take you to Krems; combined with 34, 38, and 37, it will enable you to cover Kamp valley. From Krems you can continue on a very scenic road along the left bank of the Danube through the Wachau and Nibelungengau to Persenbeug, where you can cross the bridge to Ybbs and return to Vienna on the West Autobahn, A1; if you want to drive along both banks in the Wachau, follow the left bank road as far as Emmersdorf, cross by ferry and bridge to Melk, and return along the right bank on an older but also good road to Mautern; there you can either cross the bridge back to Krems, take 32 to St. Pölten and the autobahn, or drive back to Vienna via Tulln and Klosterneuburg.

Route 1 and the West Autobahn are the main roads west from Vienna and will take you to St. Pölten, Melk, Pöchlarn (off the road), Ybbs (off the road), Amstetten to Upper Austria. From St. Pölten take 20 to Annaberg, Mitterbach and Erlauf Lake, from the vicinity of Ybbs 25 to Lunzer Lake, and from Amstetten 121 to Waidhofen and other localities in the upper Ybbs valley. Semmering is reached by 17, proceeding south of Vienna, and Raxalpe and Schneeberg by side roads branching off 17.

The South Autobahn A2 leads from Vienna to Grimmenstein, whence 54 continues to Mönichkirchen and the Wechsel mountains.

PLACES OF INTEREST. Lower Austria is a land of castles and abbeys. Many of Austria's most magnificent buildings were constructed in this rich area—Melk, Heiligenkreuz, Klosterneuburg, and Schallaburg among the finest. Given the passage of so many violent centuries, to say nothing of the ravages of winter and woodworm, it is not surprising that some of the structures are in a bad way, even in ruins. But sufficient of them still survive intact to give a very clear idea just how impressive they all must have been.

Please check opening time locally, before starting out on your visits. Both times and days of opening are liable to sudden change and are difficult to predict. Where we give routes, they are from Vienna.

Aggstein. A1 to St. Pölten, then local road through Weyersdorf. **Castle,** mostly in ruins, on hill on right bank of Danube. First built in 12th century, last rebuilt in 1606, beautiful view of the Wachau; those interiors still standing are open to public April 1 to Oct. 15.

Altenburg. Route 4 from Stockerau north of Vienna to Horn, then 38. **Benedictine abbey** in town of same name. Founded in 12th century, rebuilt in Baroque style in 18th century; under the library a unique crypt with grotesque paintings representing the *Dance of Death;* cupola fresco in the church is important work of Baroque painter Paul Troger. Guided tours April to Oct., morning and afternoon. Apply in winter.

Baden. South of Vienna, B17 or A2. Operettas in the open-air arena in summer.

Breiteneich. Route 303 from Horn to Göpfritz, then local road to Almosen. One of Lower Austria's oldest Renaissance **castles.** Summer courses in woodwind instruments, with chamber orchestra concerts.

Dürnstein. Near Krems on Left bank of Danube (Route 3). A climb up to the ruined medieval **castle** (prison of Richard the Lionheart); Baroque **abbey,** now being restored; picturesque little town set in vineyards.

Eckartsau. 40 km. (26 miles) from Vienna. 301 via Orth to Pframa. Present Baroque **castle–mansion** mainly built in 18th century as hunting castle; 2 wings from the end of the last century; grand ceiling fresco in Great Hall.

Falkenstein. Route 7 to Poysdorf, about 5 km. (3 miles) after Poysdorf turn left on small local road. Notable **church** and **castle** in imposing location above village of same name near Czech border. Probably built in 11th century, largely in ruins, but marks of past magnificence still visible. Beautifully-preserved *Kellergasse* (wine-cellar lane), with marked walk and cellar museum.

Göttweig. On right bank of Danube, opposite Krems (Route 303). Benedictine **abbey** founded in 11th century, present Baroque buildings from 18th century, constructed according to the plans of Lukas von Hildebrandt; tavern with wines of own production, beautiful view of Krems and Danube valley from the terrace.

Grafenegg. East of Krems near Langenlois. Fine restored Victorian **castle.** Major exhibitions and candlelight concerts.

Greillenstein. Near Horn. Route 38 to Altenburg and Fulgau, then small turning on right for Greillenstein. Renaissance **castle** originating from the 13th century, except for the gate tower and a rare medieval judg-

ment chamber completely reconstructed during 17th century. Very interesting Baroque interiors and ceiling frescos by Paul Troger in the family
crypt.

Hardegg. Route E84 north to Guntersdorf, then 30. **Castle** on Thaya
River in town of same name right on Czech border. Built around 1200,
partially rebuilt at the end of the last century.

Heidenreichstein. Route 303 to Göpfritz, then 5 via Waidhofen. **Castle** in town of same name in northern Waldviertel. First built in 12th century, rebuilt in 15th and 16th centuries, one of the most remarkable Austria
water castles.

Heiligenkreuz. A21 autobahn from Vienna (west). Austria's oldest
Cistercian **abbey** founded in 1135; Romanesque church, built in 12th and
13th centuries, with late Gothic and Baroque additions; stained glass windows from 1300; altar paintings by Rottmayr and Altomonte; cloister
from 1220, with 300 small, red-marble columns; gallery of German and
Austrian Baroque paintings; Baroque library. Guided tours available.

Herzogenburg. From Krems, follow S33 south past Traismauer, local
road to Herzogenburg branches off to the right. Augustine **abbey** founded
in 12th century; present architecture partially by great Baroque masters
Fischer von Erlach and Jakob Prandtauer, frescos and paintings particularly by Altomonte. Baroque library and museum with rich collection of
Gothic winged altars. Wine tavern with wines of own production.

Kirchschlag. Every five years a Passion play is performed in this tiny
town nestling in the eastern foothills of the Alps in the *Bucklige Welt*
(Bumpy World). On the Sunday in question a bus leaves at 1 P.M. from
Wien Mitte station.

Kirchstetten. A1 to exit St. Christophen (32 km.), or regional train
from Westbahnhof to St. Pölten. The home for many years of W. H.
Auden. His simple tomb can be visited in the churchyard. Walk up the
Audenstrasse until you reach his house. It is privately owned and occupied, but a knock on the door will gain you a short look around.

Klosterneuburg. On the edge of Vienna, via the Klosterneuburg autobahn. Augustine **abbey** in town. Founded in 12th century, since then various parts rebuilt several times; church originally Romanesque, beautifully
handcarved wooden choir and oratory, large organ from 17th century; Leopold Chapel with world-famous enameled *Verduner Altar* by Nikolas von
Verdun (Werden) in 1181, stained glass windows from 14th and 15th centuries, and Romanesque candelabrum of 12th century; great marble hall
with Gran's ceiling fresco; library, abbey museum and treasury.

Kreuzenstein. A22 autobahn from Vienna to Korneuburg, then 5 km
(3 miles) on local road. **Castle** first built in 12th century, destroyed by
Swedes during Thirty Years' War in 17th century, reconstructed and re-
furnished in the corresponding style by Count Johann Wilczek at the end
of the last century.

Liechtenstein. Near Mödling just south of Vienna. A2 to Brunn am Gebirge. Castle built in Romanesque style during 12th century, partially destroyed during Turkish wars and rebuilt in same style. Romanesque chapel constructed in 1165 still exists in original form.

Melk. A1 all the way due west. Benedictine **abbey,** largest in Lower Austria, on right bank of Danube. Originally a Roman watchtower, it was turned into a fortress by the Babenbergs about 976. Given to the Benedictines in the 11th century, it was developed by them into a monastery-fortress during the 14th century. The present unique Baroque buildings date from 18th century by Jakob Prandtauer; one of the most beautiful existing Baroque churches; library with huge collection, starting with 9th-century manuscripts. Every summer there are good theater performances and concerts in the pavilion of the monastery.

Orth. 301 due east of Vienna, just before Eckartsau. **Water-castle** originally built in 12th century; today it houses a fishing museum and an apiary museum, with a 30-million-year-old bee in amber.

Persenbeug. A1 to Ybbs. **Castle,** in town of same name on left bank of Danube. Present Baroque building from 17th century, the original castle was probably from the 9th century.

Pöchlarn. Opposite Persenbeug on south bank of Danube. Center of Nibelungen section of the Danube. Birthplace of painter Oskar Kokoschka. Exhibition in the house where he was born, Regensburgerstr. 29. Wed.–Sun., 10–12, 2–5, July to Sept. Gothic parish **Church** of note.

Pottenbrunn. A1 to St. Pölten, then Route 1 north to Pottenbrunn. Moated **castle** noted for its ponds, parks and stairway; also offers a unique tin soldier museum, the figures illustrating actual historical battles.

Raabs. Route 30 due east of Hardegg, on River Thaya. **Castle** first built in 11th century, later rebuilt, present style mainly from 16th century. Renaissance library, Baroque chapel. Concerts held in the castle May to Sept.

Rappottenstein. Route 3 to Krems, 37 and 38 to Zwettl, 38 and 124 to Rappottenstein. First built in 12th century, additions and renovations through 16th century. Fine medieval **castle** fortress, with Austria's best-preserved torture chamber.

Retz. Fine square, 1772 windmill still operating. Sgraffito House 1576. Immense network of cellars; their motto "alles mit der zeit," means all in good time.

Riegersburg. Route 30 from Retz, in the Waldviertel, near the Czech border. Can be combined with a visit to Hardegg. Baroque **castle,** many rooms with original furnishings. Tours in English.

Rohrau. Route 9 due east to Carnuntum, the 211 (off to the right) to Rohrau. The birthplace of Haydn; the house is open to the public. The **castle** houses the Count Harrach collection, Austria's only private art museum, with over 200 paintings, mostly Italian and Spanish Baroque. Open spring to fall.

Rosenau. 8 km. (5 miles) west of Zwettl (37, 38 from Krems). Baroque **palace** housing Freemasonry museum.

Rosenburg. 34 from Stockerau (northwest of Vienna) to Gars, then continue a few km. north again. **Castle,** probably first built in 12th century, rebuilt in 17th century, destroyed by fire in 19th century and rebuilt according to the previous model; 13 towers, large tournament courtyard, Gothic chapel, collection of weapons and furniture.

Schallaburg. A1 to Melk, then a few km. southeast. One of Austria's loveliest Renaissance **castles;** terracotta sculptures line the arcaded courtyard.

Schöngraben. On Highway 2, 5 km. past Hollabrunn. Romanesque **church,** c. 1230. Recently restored and divested of its Baroque trappings. Superb apse and plain interior with remains of frescos. Original stone altar and flooring in apse.

Seebenstein. 16 km. (10 miles) south of Wiener Neustadt on A2. 11th-century **castle,** rebuilt in Renaissance style around 1600.

Seitenstetten. A1 to Amstetten, then 122 to Seitenstetten. Benedictine **abbey** founded in 1112, early Gothic and late-Romanesque church from 13th century with Baroque 17th-century additions; present monastery building of 18th century. Frescos by Kremser Schmidt, Altomonte; large library; picture gallery includes Brueghel, Altomonte, Gran, Kremser Schmidt; collection of engravings.

Staatz. Just southwest of Falkenstein (q.v.). **Castle** ruins in magnificent position. Built in 12th century or earlier, destroyed by Swedes in 17th century during Thirty Years' War. You can walk up from main road.

Waidhofen Ybbs. Steam trains "Schafkäs Express" from June to Sept. Information A-3340, Hohenstr. 49 (0 74 42–26 6 14).

Zwettl. Route 37 from Krems, northwest. Cistercian **abbey.** Church first built betweeen 12th and 14th centuries; mainly Gothic, acquired Baroque additions in 18th century, including most of the altars with notable exceptions of a late Gothic wing altar and some Gothic window glass paintings from 15th century; 13th-century monastery; Romanesque canonical house, one of the oldest of its kind in existence; Baroque library. Stift Zwettl has been restored and looks magnificent.

CASINOS. No self-respecting spa can be without a casino, and Baden is certainly no exception. It is open daily—Sundays and holidays included—from 4 P.M. for roulette, baccara and black jack.

WINTER SPORTS. Lower Austria's main skiing area is in the southern part of the province, particularly in the range of mountains bordering Styr-

ia. Skiing facilities exist also in some places in the Waldviertel region north
of the Danube.

Technical installations have improved greatly during the last decade or
so and this is becoming an increasingly popular—but still relatively inexpensive—winter sports area, with an emphasis on cross-country skiing.
In general, good snow conditions can be expected between December and
March, but in the highest spots you can usually ski until the end of April.

Ötscher Region. This region has a secure place in skiing history. It
was at Lilienfeld that the first slalom took place in 1905. Things have vastly improved since then and all the skiing areas in this group are well-
equipped. The best snow conditions can be found in Lackenhof.

Resorts: Annaberg (973 m., 3,192 ft.); Gaming (430 m., 1,411 ft.); Göstling an der Ybbs (532 m., 1,745 ft.); Hollenstein (487 m., 1,598 ft.); Lackenhof (800 m., 2,625 ft.); Lilienfeld (385 m., 1,263 ft.); Lunz am See (601
m., 1,971 ft.); Mitterbach am Erlaufsee (791 m., 2,592 ft.); Puchenstuben
(850 m., 2,787 ft.); St. Aegyd am Neuwald (582 m., 1,909 ft.); Türnitz
(461 m., 1,513 ft.); Waidhofen an der Ybbs (358 m., 1,175 ft.); Ybbsitz
(404 m., 1,326 ft.).

Facilities. The area has 10 indoor swimming pools, 10 chair lifts, 84
T-bars and 120 km. (75 miles) of popular cross-country trails. There are
superb views from the mountains in the region.

Schneeberg, Rax and Semmering. This is an area that can easily
act as an alternative ski-vacationland for anyone spending time in Vienna.
It is only an hour-and-a-half from the capital by train or car. It is, as one
would expect, popular with the Viennese.

Resorts: Grünbach am Schneeberg (549 m., 1,801 ft.); Gutenstein (482
m., 1,581 ft.); Hirschwang (494 m., 1,648 ft.); Maria Schutz (759 m., 2,490
ft.); Puchberg am Schneeberg (578 m., 1,896 ft.); Reichenau an der Rax
(485 m., 1,591 ft.); Semmering (1,000 m., 3,821 ft.).

Facilities: the area has 10 indoor swimming pools, 2 cable cars, 4 chair
lifts, 16 T-bars and 27 km. (17 miles) of cross-country trails.

Other Areas. Among the other parts of this region which are not really
equipped for full winter-sports status are Waldviertel–Weinviertel,
Wachau–Nibelungengau, the Vienna Woods and the environs of Vienna.
These areas may have some mild ski slopes, but generally they are noted—
and ideal—for long winter walks, skating on the chains of tranquil lakes
and generally having a wonderful time in beautiful wintery surroundings.

BURGENLAND

Puszta and Papa Haydn's Skull

Burgenland, the land of castles and fortresses, corn and wine, is a narrow, fertile belt of vineyards and rich agricultural land running along Austria's eastern frontier with Hungary, touching north on Czechoslovakia and south on Yugoslavia, broken up by the foothills and mountains of the Leitha and Rosalien ranges. Shaped rather like a kidney bean, the state is 65 km. (40 miles) broad at the widest point, and narrows in the center to a "waist" barely three kilometers across. Only 35 km. (22 miles) from Vienna, it is easily reached by frequent bus and train services, and even the most remote parts are accessible in two or three hours.

It is no mere coincidence that the many castles, fortified churches, battlemented villages, and isolated farmsteads have been built on high, strategic ground. Beginning with the Celts in the 4th century B.C. the area has been fought over by Romans, Huns, Goths, Lombards and Slavs. Then came the Bavarians, Hungarians, Austrians and, in the 16th and 17th centuries, the Turks to continue the game of battledore and shuttlecock. In 1648 the area now known as Burgenland finally fell to Hungary, and remained a Hungarian province until the end of World War I. In 1921 it became one of the nine present-day Austrian federal states, except for its capital of Ödenburg (Sopron) and the surrounding area which voted in a plebiscite to remain in Hungary; this accounts for the "wasp waist" in the center of the province.

Although small in size, its scenery is interesting because much of it is quite in contrast to that in the rest of Austria. The face of Burgenland is strongly marked by the large and strange Neusiedler See—a very shallow salt-water lake, the remainder of a prehistoric sea which at one time covered all of the Pannonian Plain. There are myriads of birds in its reeds and on its shores, the most noted among them the famous Rust storks, faithfully returning to their chimney nests every year. On the eastern side of the lake, the landscape turns into the real Hungarian type of *puszta* (steppe), with typical water wells made of tree trunks and the red *"puszta sun"* sinking into the plain in the evening.

Burgenland is the vegetable garden of Vienna and the source of copiously-produced wine, some of it of considerable quality. In many places you will see bunches of drying corn cobs adorning the colorful farm houses, for corn, next to wine, is the main agricultural produce of this state, although other kinds of grain are also grown in large quantity.

Its hard-working, industrious population of small farmers, foresters, vintners and craftsmen is descended from German (88 percent), Croatian (10 percent) and Magyar (2 percent) ancestors, and Burgenland itself looks back on a history as hectic and unsettled as that of any other corner of Europe.

Exploring Burgenland

In 1924 the small town of Eisenstadt at the foot of the Leitha mountains, 40 km. (25 miles) southeast from Vienna, was made the provincial capital. With less than 11,000 inhabitants, it is best known as the place where Josef Haydn lived and worked for 30 years of his life in the service of the Esterhazys. The town is also the center of a region full of vineyards, peach, and almond orchards—made possible by the gentle climate.

The composer's home has now been turned into a museum, and is full of interesting memories of this much-loved and tremendously productive musician. The body of Josef Haydn lies in an elaborate tomb of white marble, built by his grateful master, Prince Esterhazy, in the crypt of Eisenstadt church (Bergkirche). Until the summer of 1954, it was a headless body that lay in this tomb. Haydn's skull could be seen—and handled, if you felt so inclined—in the Musikverein Museum in Vienna. How it came to be there is a long and complicated story.

Ten days after the composer's death in Vienna, a group of young phrenologists persuaded the prince's secretary and an accomplice, a prison warder, to steal the head from the temporary grave in Vienna, and "lend" it to them for a few weeks. In the dead of night the two ghouls, after bribing the cemetery guards, accomplished their mission. It was not until some time later, when the remains were transferred to the final resting place at Eisenstadt, that the theft was discovered.

On his deathbed the secretary confessed to his crime, but refused to part with his treasure—the phrenologists had returned the head to him—unless Prince Esterhazy paid his "heavy expenses," which included a "costly black casket". This the prince refused to do, and the secretary bequeathed the skull to the Musikverein. But the skull had disappeared again. This time it was the doctor attending the accomplice who was the culprit. Finally, it was sold to a famous Austrian professor, and on his death his widow loaned it to the Vienna Pathological Museum.

The Musikverein now claimed the skull, and after a lengthy and costly lawsuit finally managed to secure its "legacy." Since 1895, therefore, the skull had been sitting in a glass case on top of a grand piano in the Musikverein Museum. But the Musikverein finally yielded to the entreaties of those who felt that Haydn's head should be restored to his body. During the Vienna Music Festival in June 1954, the skull was taken in triumphal procession, by way of Haydn's birthplace at Rohrau, to Eisenstadt and placed at last in his coffin with the body from which it had been separated for 145 years.

On the other side of the church where Haydn is entombed, there is a unique structure called the Kalvarienberg, an artificially made "indoor" Calvary Hill, representing the Way of the Cross with life-like, life-size figures placed in cave-like rooms and chapels along an elaborate path. At its highest point, the path reaches the platform of the belfry, offering a beautiful view over the town and this section of Burgenland. The magnificent wooden figures were carved and painted by Franciscan monks, with the aid of simple peasants, more than 250 years ago. Another main point of interest is Eisenstadt in the gracious, sweeping Esterhazy Palace, the home of the famous Hungarian aristocratic family. The palace was originally a medieval castle, but between 1663 and 1672 it was rebuilt to Baroque taste. The Haydn Saal (Haydn Room) is a large frescoed hall, still used for concerts and that can be visited with a guided tour.

East of the palace is the old part of Eisenstadt with three parallel streets—Hauptstrasse, Pfarrgasse and Haydngasse, the latter with the composer's home and the Franziskaner church which houses the Esterhazy tombs. In Esterhazygasse is the Burgenlandisches Landesmuseum (the Burgenland Provincial Museum), with exhibitions of the history, folklore, flora and fauna of the province. Don't miss the small Jewish museum housed in what used to be the ghetto.

Eisenstadt is also the center of one of Austria's best wine-growing areas. The visitor shouldn't miss the chance to taste the deliciously refreshing wine sold in the innumerable inns and taverns.

A few kilometers to the east of Eisenstadt you come to the picturesque towns of Rust, Oggau, and Mörbisch, strung along the western shores of the great, shallow Neusiedler Lake. On nearly every cottage roof you will see the nests of young storks, and occasionally the parent birds standing majestically and motionless beside the chimney stacks. Medieval Rust, once an imperial free town, is known in particular as the "stork capital." Worth visiting is the Gothic Fischerkirche, with interesting frescos and stained-glass windows. Here organ concerts by candlelight are given on occasion. The three parishes are famous, and justly so, for the fine, strong wines made from the small, exceptionally sweet grapes, which have been grown in the district for over 1,000 years.

Near St. Margarethen, on the road between Eisenstadt and Rust, you pass by a giant quarry, already used by the Romans and the source of stone for many 19th-century buildings in Vienna, including the Opera. Today it is a unique outdoor sculptors' workshop—sculptors from all over the world come here during the summer to work in stone cut in the quarry; their finished works remain in this huge atelier until they are sold, thus making the quarry a vast, naturally set, exhibition hall open-to-the-sky.

Mysterious Lake Neusiedl

The 32 km.-long (20-mile) Neusiedler See—one quarter of its huge expanse in Hungary—is nowhere deeper than seven feet, while the size of the lake varies erratically. When the wind blows steadily in one direction for several days, the shallow waters are swept up to one end of the lake, leaving the other end high and dry. Until the last century the lake was almost twice as deep. Land prices led farmers to channel through to the River Raab and drain the lake of half its water. This led to the vast reed banks on the shores and heightened the salt content to 1.8 per cent.

On the farther side of the lake lie vast salt marshes and the ancient villages of St. Andrä and Frauenkirchen, famous for basket weaving.

North of Frauenkirchen, also known for its pilgrimage church, is Halbturn with a Baroque castle-palace, built by Lukas von Hilderbrandt and used by the Empress Maria Theresa as a summer residence; there is a ceiling painting by Maulpertsch in the middle hall and a lovely park. Now restored, it houses a fine gallery of paintings. West of Frauenkirchen is Podersdorf, good for swimming and windsurfing. South is the area known as Seewinkel, with Illmitz and Apetlon and the vast natural wildlife sanctuary with its forests of reeds, hundreds of different types of birds, small steppe animals, and millions of flowers. These lonely, rather desolate marshes hold a collection of flora and fauna unsurpassed anywhere in Europe, and the area is now an international sanctuary, with a Biological Station partially supported by the World Wildlife Fund. Here also begins the real *puszta* (Hungarian type of steppe), with a few windmills and the typical Hungarian-type of well, with long wooden poles for drawing water.

East of Illmitz and St. Andrä, right near the Hungarian border, is the small village of Andau, the famous crossing point during the Hungarian anti-Communist revolution of 1956. Although Hungary is dismantling its border fortifications, here and in a few other places you can still see remnants of the Iron Curtain, with its grim barbed-wire fences and now-empty watchtowers.

Above the lake, in the northeast corner of Burgenland, lies Kittsee, with a Baroque castle and noted ethnographical collection. At the end of the village, a little before reaching Bratislava (Pressburg), the capital of Slovakia, you come to a small cluster of houses, the most easterly settlement west of the Iron Curtain—Chicago.

About 1900, many Burgenlanders emigrated to the United States and regularly sent back their savings to the old country for investment in land and houses. At one time the inhabitants even worked out everything in American dollars rather than in Austrian schillings, so great was the flow of dollars to Burgenland. One émigré, returning to his native land, was astonished at the rapid building progress, and, so the story goes, exclaimed: "Why, you work nearly as fast as back in Chicago!" This particular settlement was promptly called Chicago, and Chicago it is to this day.

Traveling south again to Eisenstadt, you cross the Leitha range, where you can still see, on the Zeilerberg above Winden, where cavemen and great bears lived, according to experts, cheek by jowl as next door neighbors in the Stone Age, 7,000 years ago. All through this area, strip-farming makes many-colored ribbons of the hillsides in summer, and the forested areas are lush and green. Northwest of Eisenstadt is the famous Baroque pilgrimage church of Loretto, visited each summer by up to 100,000 pilgrims. Bronze Age graves, as well as the burial places of Celts and Illyrians were discovered nearby a few years ago. A settlement dating from Roman times is presently in the process of excavation; finds include an old Roman wine press, proving the great age of the surrounding vineyards.

Southwest of Eisenstadt, just before the "waist" you reach the little market town of Mattersburg. Nearby is the village of Neustift an der Rosalia and the mighty, fairyland Castle of Forchtenstein, formerly the stronghold of the highly independent Mattersburg barons. First built in the 13th century and then rebuilt in the 17th century, it is definitely not to be missed. The small spa of Sauerbrunn is also near Mattersburg.

Bernstein is German for "amber," but this charming little hilltop village is not now connected with the warm yellow stone. In Roman times, however, the association was much closer. The "Amber Road" from the Prussian quarries to Rome ran straight down the province, through the Roman settlement at Parndorf in the north, where recent excavations have revealed mosaic floors, skirting Neusiedler Lake and passing quite close to the village of Bernstein. Bernstein, however, has its own specialty: "Bernstein Jade," more correctly called "Serpentine Stone." Much darker than the Chinese gem, almost a jet green, the Bernstein Jade is found in Europe in substantial quantities only in Burgenland. There is a small local industry making ornaments.

The north–south line of mineral springs also runs through this area, and less than 16 km. (10 miles) south of Bernstein is Bad Tatzmannsdorf, the most important spa in Burgenland. On the edge of the Kurpark is an openair museum where old barns, farmhouses and stables have been restored. Near Bad Tatzmannsdorf is the medieval town of Stadtschlaining, with the castle-fortress Burg Schlaining, and farther east is the 13th-century castle-fortress Burg Lockenhaus, with Romanesque frescos in the chapel and a Gothic arcaded Knights Hall.

The whole of the southern part of Burgenland is divided into small-holdings of a few acres each, tilled by industrious small farmers, with the castles of the nobility of the Middle Ages dotted picturesquely all over the countryside. In one way, at least, these ancient strongholds are unique. All of them are built on top of extinct volcanoes. The huge system of fortifications of the castle-fortress of the once proud and mighty Counts of Güssing, in the extreme south, is a good example.

PRACTICAL INFORMATION FOR BURGENLAND

TOURIST INFORMATION. While the main center of information is in Eisenstadt, A-7000 (0 26 82–33 84), many of the smaller towns and villages have Tourist Offices, too. The following are a few of the more important ones with their area codes and telephone numbers. Most of them will be able to help you with accommodation problems, if you have them.

Apetlon A-7143 (0 21 75–22 20); Bad Tatzmannsdorf A-7431 (0 33 53–8284); Bernstein A-7434 (0 33 54–202); Donnerskirchen A-7082 (0 26 83–85 41); Forchtenstein A-7212 (0 26 26–31 25); Güssing A-7540 (0 33 22–23 11).

Illmitz A-7142 (0 21 75–23 83); Jennersdorf A-8380 (0 31 54–200); Lockenhaus A-7442 (0 26 16–22 02); Mattersburg A-7210 (0 26 26–23 33); Mörbisch am See A-7072 (0 26 85–84 30); Neusiedl am See A-7100 (0 21 67–2229); Podersdorf am See A-7141 (0 21 77–2227); Rust A7071 (0 26 85–502); St. Andrä/Zicksee A-7161 (0 21 76–23 00).

AREA CODES—MAIL AND PHONE. You will find the postal code (preceded by an "A") and the telephone code (in brackets) after the name of each town in the following Hotel and Restaurant list.

HOTELS AND RESTAURANTS. Most hotels in Burgenland are on the small side and range from the modest provincial type to simple village Gasthofs. A few exceptions, particularly some spa and castle hotels, belong to higher categories. Prices on the whole are considerably lower than in the regions more frequented by foreign tourists. The current situation is changing slowly as new hotels are being built. There are quite a few private rooms available. If you have any problem with accommodations contact the local—rather than the regional—tourist office, which will be able to help.

Bad Tatzmannsdorf A-7431 (0 33 53). *Kurhotel Bad Tatzmannsdorf* (E), (8581). 50 rooms, with bath or shower; cure facilities, fitness room, solarium; open throughout the year. MC. *Parkhotel* (E), (8287). 35 rooms, with bath or shower and balconies; solarium, fitness room. Open Feb. to Nov. AE, V. *Kurhotel Kastell* (M), (428). 30 rooms, with bath or shower; open all year. AE, DC, MC.

Bernstein A-7434 (0 33 54). *Burg Bernstein* (E), (220). 10 rooms in feudal castle. AE, DC, V.

Deutsch-Schützen A-7474 (0 33 65). *Gasthof Schützenhof* (M), (22 03). Well cooked, plain country fare in simple surroundings. Superb wines (see *Austria's Wines*).

Donnerskirchen A-7082 (0 26 83). *Gasthof Engel* (M), (8502). 4 rooms, 1 with bath; restaurant renowned for good food and wine. Closed Mon., Christmas and March. DC, MC.
Camping site (86 70).

Eisenstadt A-7000 (0 26 82). *Burgenland* (E), Schubertplatz 1 (55 21). Every possible appointment and amenity; underground garage, conference rooms, indoor pool and sauna. Excellent restaurant. AE, DC, MC, V.
Goldener Adler (M), Hauptstrasse 25 (26 45). 42 beds, some with bath or shower. In old part of town, run by same family since 1772. Closed Feb. AE, DC, MC, V. *Parkhotel Mikschi* (M), Haydngasse 38 (43 61). 56 rooms, with bath or shower; garage and garden. DC, MC, V.
Restaurants. *G'würzstöckl* (E), in Hotel Burgenland (55 21). Rustic furniture, good service and very good food. AE, DC, MC, V. *Schlosstaverne* (M), Esterhazyplatz 5 (31 02). In former stable, vaults, candlelight and gypsy music. Selected wines of Count Esterhazy's vineyards. Closed Sun. and Mon. in winter. AE. *Ohr* (M), Rusterstrasse 51 (24 60). Pleasant *Stüberln* and cellar of wines from own vineyard. Closed Mon. and Feb. AE, MC.
There are many other colorful wine restaurants, taverns and gardens around town, particularly near St. Georgen.

Forchtenstein A-7212 (0 26 26). *Gasthof Sauerzapf* (I), (82 17). 14 rooms, some with shower; garden and garage. Closed Wed.
Camping site (31 78). Open May–Sept.
Restaurant. *Reisner* (M), (31 39). People travel from far afield to savor the traditional dishes delicately cooked at this family restaurant. Closed Wed. AE, DC, MC.

Gols A-7122 (0 21 73). *Birkenhof* (M), (2346). Comfortable family hotel with good restaurant. DC, MC, V.

Heiligenkreuz A-7561 (0 33 25). *Gibiser* (M), (2 16). 12 rooms, all with bath or shower. 18th-century log cabins in garden, all with modern amenities. Very good restaurant, serving Hungarian and international food. Closed Mon. in winter. AE, DC, MC.

Illmitz-Apetlon A-7142 (0 21 75). *Traubenmühle* (M), (2304). 10 rooms, all with shower; garden. Open May–Oct. There are several other inexpensive *Gasthöfe* and pensions in town.
Youth hostel in Naturschutzhaus (2500).

Jennersdorf A-8380 (0 31 54). *Raffel* (M), Hauptplatz 6 (328). 33 rooms, with bath or shower. Famous restaurant serving memorable Pannonian cuisine, both rich and plentiful. Exceptional wine cellar. AE, DC, MC.
Campsite (416).

Lockenhaus A-7442 (0 26 16). *Burghotel Lockenhaus* (E), (23 94). In the castle. Baronial meals cooked on open fire are a specialty. Resident ghost among the attractions. MC.

Mörbisch Am See A-7072 (0 26 85). *Steiner* (E), (8444). 50 rooms with bath or shower; sauna, indoor pool and garden. Restaurant. Open April to Nov.

Neusiedl Am See A-7100 (0 21 67). *Wende* (E), Seestrasse 40 (81 11). Restaurant; charming rustic heuriger, Weingwölb, in house next door. 100 rooms, all with bath; indoor pool, sauna, beauty therapy. AE, DC, MC, V.
Mauth (M), Eisenstädterstrasse 205 (570). 15 rooms; garden. Restaurant *Windholz* (in hotel) fast gaining repute. DC, MC.
Restaurant. *Barth Stuben* (M), Franz Listgasse 37 (625). Good use of local produce and traditions. Interesting wines. Closed Mon.
Youth Hostel. *Burgenländisches Jugendherbergswerk* (8830). 80 beds; open throughout the year.

Pamhagen A-7152 (0 21 75). *Pannonia* (E), Storchengasse 1 (21 80). 60 rooms, all with bath or shower, mainly in bungalows; indoor and outdoor tennis, riding, windsurfing. Closed 31 Oct. to 1 April. AE, DC, MC, V.

Podersdorf A-7141 (0 21 77). *Haus Attila* (M), Strandplatz (2415). 20 rooms, some with shower. AE. Under the same management is *Seewirt* (M), Strandplatz 1 (2415). 15 rooms, all with shower or running water. Closed Mon. and Tues. in winter. AE, MC. *Strandhotel Tauber* (M), (2204). 32 beds, most with shower. Restaurant. DC, MC, V.
Campsite (2227 or 2279).
Restaurant. *Zur goldenenen Traube* (M), (2388). Interesting local specialties. DC.

Purbach A-7083 (0 26 83). *Türkenhain* (E), (51 53). 90 apartments for 2 to 4 people; completely furnished, sports facilities, riding, tennis and boating. AE, DC. *Am Spitz* (M), (55 19). 34 beds, all with shower. Attractive building at the end of picturesque *Kellergasse* (street with wine cellars). Good food and wine—apple brandy a specialty. Closed Mon.

Restaurant. *Nikolauszeche* (E), (55 14). 16th-century building. Excellent food in romantic setting. Closed in winter. AE, DC.
Youth Hostel (5538). 110 beds; open 1 April to 31 Oct.
Campsite (5538). Tennis courts, sauna and fishing.

Rust A-7071 (0 26 85). *Seehotel* (E), (381). 90 rooms, with bath; garden, indoor pool, sauna. Beautifully situated. Luxurious. Good restaurant. AE, DC, MC, V. *Sifkovits* (E), (276). Also with acceptable restaurant. Closed Thurs. in winter.
Arkadenhof (M), (246). With good restaurant serving local specialties and wine. *Feriendorf Romantika* (M), (47 70). Bungalows beside the lake. Open April–Oct.
Youth Hostel. *Freistadt Rust* (245). 92 beds, meals. Open April to Oct.
Campsite (595). Open April–Oct.
Restaurants. *Alte Schmiede* (M), Seezeile 24 (467). Fish specialties, gipsy music. Open April to Oct. AE, DC. *Zum Alten Stadttor* (M) (594). Hungarian cuisine. Open April to Oct. *Rathauskeller* (I), Rathauspl. 1 (261). Heurigen specialties and the finest wines of the area (see *Austria's Wines*). Closed Dec./Jan. and Wed.
At nearby **Oslip** A-7000 (0 26 84), *Storchenmühle* (M), (2127). Picturesque old building, good food, gipsy music. AE, MC.
At nearby **Schützen im Gebirge** A-7081 (0 26 54). *Taubenkobel* (M), (22 97). Good food and local wines. Closed Mon. AE, DC, MC, V.

St. Andrä Am Zicksee A-7161 (0 21 76). *Ferienparadies Seewinkel* (M), (21 01). 22 apartments for 2 to 6 people; completely furnished, indoor pool, riding facilities. AE, MC.
Campsite (23 00 or 21 44). Open 1 May to 30 Sept.
Restaurant. *Gasthaus Luntzer* (M), Hauptstrasse 31 (23 04). Fish specialties.

Weiden Am See A-7121 (0 21 67). *Haus Carinthia* (M), (7296). 20 rooms, with shower or running water; garden and garage. *Seepark Weiden* (7322). 84 apartments for 4 to 6 people by the week.

GETTING AROUND BURGENLAND. By Train. The best point of departure by train for the northern part of Burgenland is Vienna; for the southern part, Graz. Except for the Vienna–Budapest (from Westbahnhof) mainline, with only a few stops in Burgenland, train communications are only of the local and slow type. At Parndorf the sections for Eisenstadt and for the area east of Neusiedler See branch off (sometimes necessary to change as only a few trains are direct).
From Wiener Neustadt there is a local line to Sauerbrunn and Mattersburg. Both this line and the line from Eisenstadt traverse Hungarian territory at Sopron to southern Burgenland (these are the so-called "corridor" trains with locked cars through Hungary).
At Friedberg, on the Styrian–Lower Austrian border and on the secondary railroad line between Graz and Vienna, there is a local line for Oberwart.
By Bus. Various bus companies (inquire at travel offices) cover almost the entire province from Vienna and its southern part from Graz. In addition there are bus services between Neusiedl and Eisenstadt and the eastern Neusiedler See area; between Wiener Neustadt and Eisenstadt and

Lockenhaus; between Eisenstadt–Mattersburg–Lutzmannsburg; between Oberwart–Schlaining–Reichnitz–Güssing and some others. Information, Blaguss. A-1040, Wiedner Hauptsstr. 15 (65 16 810).

By Boat. In summer there are motorboat roundtrips on Neusiedler See between Neusiedl, Podersdorf and Rust and between Mörbisch and Ill-mitz.

By Car. If you go by car from Vienna, you can obtain a bird's-eye view of northern Burgenland in a day or day and a half; the same time will be used for the main sights of southern Burgenland from Graz.

From Vienna take Route 10 to Parndorf and the Hungarian border; branching off at Parndorf, use a combination of 304, 51 and 52 to make the Austrian part of the circle of Neusiedler Lake and to reach Eisenstadt. From Eisenstadt continue on the Autobahn, otherwise 331, to Matters-burg; from there it is a short distance to the Castle of Forchtenstein and to Sauerbrunn. To return to Vienna, proceed either to Wiener Neustadt or return in the direction of Eisenstadt and take Route 16.

From Graz take Routes 65 and 307 to Heiligenkreuz on the Hungarian border; from there north on 57 to Güssing, Oberwart (side road to Schlain-ing), Bad Tatzmannsdorf, Bernstein, Oberpullendorf (side road to Raid-ing), and on to northern Burgenland or back along the Hungarian border on 56.

PLACES OF INTEREST. Burgenland does not have the same freight of great abbeys as other parts of Austria, although it has quite a few attrac-tive castles. The places in the following list are all given with the routes from Vienna, as they are mostly within easy reach of the capital and can be seen on a days-out basis. We suggest that you check on opening times before setting out, as they are liable to change at short notice and are diffi-cult to predict.

Bad Tatzmannsdorf. By rail from Vienna (Eastern Sta-tion/Ostbahnhof, in same building as Südbahnhof); or, by road, A2 to Wiener Neustadt, 53 to Mattersburg, then 331 and 50 to Bad Tatzmanns-dorf. **Südburgenländisches Freilichtmuseum** (Openair Museum of Bur-genland farm buildings). Visits year round.

Bernstein. A few kilometers before Bad Tatzmannsdorf on Route 50. **Castle** on medieval site; historical collections, weapons, torture chamber. Open during the summer.The town is also famous for the locally mined Jade-serpentine. It is worked into jewelry and objets d'art, which can be purchased in the village. The **Felsenmuseum** is devoted to the jade indus-try.

Eisenstadt. Bergkirche, with the tomb of Joseph Haydn. Open May 1 to Oct. 31. You can see the Kalvarienberg only with a guide, who is on hand from 8–5, but it is wiser not to arrive after 3.

Burgenlandisches Landesmuseum (Burgenland Provincial Museum), Museumgasse 1–5. The art, history and culture of the province; of only moderate interest.

Esterhazy Palace. Partly used as offices, but open to the public. The Haydn-Saal (Haydn Room) is the great hall of the castle, still used for concerts. Guided tours daily.

Haydn-Haus (Haydn Museum), Josef-Haydn-Gasse 21. Interesting little house with mementos of the composer. Summer only.

Jewish Museum, Unterbergerstr. 6. Synagogue and exhibitions of Jewish history, especially of World War II. Open 10–5 May to Oct; closed Mon.

Forchtenstein. A2 to Wiener Neustadt, 304 to Sauerbrunn, local road via Wiesen to Forchtenstein. Magnificently sited medieval **castle,** part of the defenses against the Turks. Fine armory, the fourth-largest collection in Austria.

Frauenkirchen. Route 10 southeast to Parndorf, then 51 via Neusiedl. Baroque pilgrimage **church.** Beside the church is a remarkable **"Calvary"** laid out on an artificial hill. Jewish cemetery.

Güssing. A2 to Wiener Neustadt, 53 to Mattersburg, 331 to Oberwart, then 57 to Güssing. A classic medieval **castle,** perched high on a solitary volcanic outcrop. **Nature park.**

Halbturn. Route 10 to Parndorf, 304 to Neusiedl, 51 to Mönchhof, local road to Halbturn. Right by the Hungarian border. **Castle** designed by Lucas von Hildebrandt, built in 1701. Only open for summer exhibitions May–Sept. Retail shop for the excellent Schloss wines.

Kittsee. Route 9 due east to Hainburg then Wolfsthal-Berg, then 304 to Kittsee. Horseshoe-shaped **castle** (17th century), with Ethnographical Museum.

Lockenhaus. A2 to Wiener Neustadt, 53 to Mattersburg, then 331. Alternatively (not so scenic) straight south on A2 to Editz turnoff, then on down 55. 13th-century **castle.** Medieval frescos in chapel; unusual vaulting in main hall; cellar treasury. Beautiful music festival in first half July (0 26 26–22 24).

Loretto. Route 16 south to Wampersdorf, local road to Loretto. Baroque **Pilgrimage Church.**

Neusiedl. Route 10 to Parndorf, then 304. Lake **museum** in the town.

Raiding. Route 61 to Weppersdorf, then 62 east to Lackendorf. 3km. south to Raiding, birthplace of Franz Liszt. **Museum** in his birthhouse.

Rust. Much of the town lies within the reed belt of Lake Neusiedl. Boat trips for bird-watchers; **Roman cemetery.** The center of this "Free Town" is strikingly unspoilt. Medieval **Fishermen's Church.**

St. Margarethen. Route 16 to Grosshöflein, then west towards Rust. **Openair workshop** for sculptors in a quarry. Visit as part of a Neusiedler See tour.

BIRD SANCTUARIES. Burgenland's lakes and marshes provide perfect areas for birds to breed and live in safety. Neusiedler See is the central lake for this natural habitat, fringed as it is with thick reeds and secondary lakes and marshes which make up hundreds of acres to the east, an area with the delightful name of Seewinkel. The whole region extends right up to the frontier with Hungary and can sometimes contain up to 250 species, heron and stork, endless varieties of wild duck and such exotic rarities as the golden oriole and the sea eagle. The tourist office in Eisenstadt, as well as those in the heart of Seewinkel—Neusiedl am See, St. Andrä and Podersdorf—can give you details.

SALZBURG

A Lot of Night Music

Salzburg first appeared in history about 500 B.C. as a gathering place for Alpine Celts, whose settlement was called Juvavum or Petena, while the general area was named Noricum. The Romans, arriving about 40 A.D. built roads (their routes are still being followed) to Wels, Augsburg, Regensburg, and to the lakes to the east. In the fourth century St. Maximus arrived to Christianize the people, and incidentally dug the catacombs under the Mönchsberg that are still high on the list of tourist attractions.

In the eighth century, St. Rupert built St. Peter's Monastery in front of the catacombs, as well as the cloisters on the nearby Nonnberg, and started Salzburg on the way to greatness. In 798, 21 years after the founding of the monastery, the city became, as an awe-struck German account puts it, the *Residenz der mächtigen Fürsterzbischöfe von Salzburg*—the see of the powerful bishop-princes of Salzburg. They were indeed powerful. They dominated all the other bishops of the German-speaking world and Salzburg was referred to as the German Rome—the *German* Rome, not the Austrian Rome. The proper adjective is important, for Salzburg, which even today is only barely within Austria's frontier, was not to become a part of that country for another thousand years.

The setting of Salzburg is perfect. It lies on both banks of the Salzach River, at the point where it is pinched between two mountains, the Kapuzinerberg on one shore, the Mönchsberg on the other. All about are enchanting mountain vistas.

Salzburg's many fine buildings complement their surroundings and form a harmonious whole. Salzburg is architecturally a city of a single style, the Baroque. Perhaps nowhere else in the world is there so unanimous a flowering of this school. Salzburg is a riot of Baroque, which is quite proper, for Baroque is itself riotous.

It was in 1077 that the great fortress, now the chief landmark of the whole of Land Salzburg (the State of Salzburg as distinguished from the city), was started by Archbishop Gebhard. This huge pile, sitting high above the city, on the end of the Mönchsberg, became not only the seat of the archbishops who were both spiritual and temporal leaders of western Austria, but also a siege-proof haven during the countless wars that swept the area. Frequently enlarged, the fortress is one of the most impressive sights, both from inside and outside, in Europe. A cog railway up the face of the Castle Hill will take you there the easy way, but the hardy will find the zigzag climb far more exciting.

It was natural that when the Protestant Reformation occurred, the reaction of the mighty Catholic Bishops of Salzburg should be strong. It was so strong, and so successful, that large numbers of Protestants were forced to leave this region—and thus linked the history of Salzburg with that of America. Some of the Pennsylvania Dutch (who, in reality, were not Dutch but Germans) came from Salzburg. Other emigrants from this area helped to found the city of Savannah, Georgia.

In 1816, after the Napoleonic Wars, and as one of the conclusions of the Congress of Vienna, the present territory of Salzburg (city and State) became a part of the Austrian Empire and has remained with Austria ever since. Thanks to the common sense of the opposing German and American generals in 1945, the city was spared the fate of so many European towns. Both men became freemen of the city.

The Mozart Festival

To most people, Salzburg today means the city of Mozart. It is at the time of the Mozart Festival, held annually in July and August, that it receives most visitors.

Wolfgang Amadeus Mozart was born in the city of Salzburg in 1756, and into the 35 short years of his life he crammed a prodigious number of compositions—the mere cataloging of them is the subject of a ponderous work, impressively entitled *Chronologisch-thematisches Verzeichnis sämtlicher Tonwerke Wolfgang Amadeus Mozarts,* the work of one Ludwig von Köchel. His great labor is amply recognized by the fact that his name is perpetuated in the numbering system of Mozart's works, for the "K" which precedes each number stands for "Köchel." It is true that Mozart began early. He started to play the piano at three (to become the outstanding pianist of his time, despite small hands that seemed quite incapable of playing the chords he wrote himself); he was writing compositions at six which already prefigured the musical style he was to develop later and in the same year played before Empress Maria Theresa in Vienna; and he began giving public concerts at the age of seven. It is on record that at the age of eight, George III of England heard him play and "tried him with hard questions." One wonders who prepared the hard questions for George III to ask.

Although Mozart was the wonder child of Europe, his native city did him no particular honor in his lifetime. It is making up for it now. Ever since 1925, on the initiative, among others, of the theatrical director Max Reinhardt, the poet Hugo von Hofmannsthal and the stage designer Alfred Roller, the last week in July and most of August have been given up to Salzburg's internationally famous Festival, which, though it is not devoted exclusively to Mozart, is nevertheless dominated by veneration for this native of the city who stands at the very top in the hierarchy of music. Internationally-celebrated musicians, conductors, singers and instrumentalists come here yearly to take part in the Festival performances.

The heart of the Festival is the Festspielhaus, where most of the operatic performances and the big orchestral concerts are given, described later in the chapter. Other performances take place in the Landestheater. Some concerts and sacred music, such as masses, are presented in the cathedral, where there is a fine locally-designed 4,000-pipe organ, or in the Abbey of St. Peter's, but the finest church music is at the Franziskanerkirche, where masses are performed on Sundays with orchestra and choir. Chamber music concerts are usually given in the hall of the Mozarteum, where a summer music school is conducted, attended by students from all over the world. The Residenz is the scene of serenade concerts held by candlelight, attended by audiences of which the great majority have bought standing-room tickets—somewhat of a misnomer, since the initiated listener prefers to sit somewhere on the wide expanse of marble floor or even to lie full length, head pillowed on a coat, eyes closed, listening in blissful repose to the strains of the music.

Finally, one of the great features of the Festival, and one which has nothing to do with Mozart, is the performance in the square before the cathedral of the morality play *Everyman,* written by Hugo von Hofmannsthal. The cathedral provides a perfect backdrop for the spectacle, with the appearance of Death never failing to make his shattering effect.

Often during the Festival the visitor has half a dozen different performances to choose from in a single day—all of them of a quality that no one would want to miss. But if you find a spare moment, you can complete your homage to Mozart by visiting the house where he was born, at Getreidegasse 9, only a block back from the river on the west bank. It has now been converted into a museum.

Although Salzburg has a seemingly high number of hotels, inns and pensions, they are not always sufficient for the Festival crowds. It is unwise to come to Salzburg without a reservation expecting to be able to find accommodation on the spot. If you haven't time to write individual hotels and wait for replies, try the Stadtverkehrsbüro, Auerspergstr. 7. This office is also a clearing house for placing visitors in rooms in private houses, if you are willing to accept this sort of accommodation. Students who want to take a summer course at the Mozarteum music school and attend the Festival incidentally, can find living quarters through the school if they register early.

If you can't find a place to stay in Salzburg, you can do what many do—find a place in the vicinity. If you have a car, it's fairly simple. Lake resorts nearby are Fuschlsee, Wolfgangsee and Mondsee, served by buses from Salzburg.

The same thing is true for Festival performance tickets—don't arrive without any and expect to be able to pick them up when you reach Salzburg. The demand is always greater than the supply, and tickets are dealt out parsimoniously each year to representatives in different countries. Get them through your travel agent or at the official Austrian tourist agency office in your home country, and be sure to order them well in advance of your trip. *Otherwise, the only tickets you will get will be those sold by hotel concierges at considerably increased prices* and, heaven knows, the prices are high enough to start with!

You can get standing room in Salzburg for the serenade concerts, and sometimes for sacred music or special performances where there is more or less unlimited space, like outdoor concerts, but that's all you can count on without advance booking.

And now, what to wear. If you come at Festival time, bring evening clothes. For the important first night performances evening dress is *de rigueur,* and you will notice that the Austrians particularly dress up. At other times, dress is more informal, and during the skiing season, of course, sportswear is general. Remember that Salzburg is in the mountains and the evenings are apt to be cool even in summer.

Exploring Salzburg

The Number One sight of Salzburg is certainly the Festung Hohensalzburg, the 12th-century fortress that dominates the town (especially at night during the Festival, when it is floodlighted) from one end of the Mönchsberg on the left or west bank of the Salzach. Since at least from a distance the castle hill appears to be standing alone, one usually forgets that it still is, although at the very end, a part of Mönchsberg ridge. You reach it by a cable railway which starts behind St. Peter's cemetery. Its prize exhibit is a later addition, St. George's Chapel, which missed being 15th century by only two years. One year later, in 1502, the fortress acquired the 200-pipe barrel organ, which plays daily during the summer at 7, 11 and 6. During the castle tour, which should not be missed, you are taken through the prince-bishops' marvelous late-Gothic rooms, with their unique stoves and paneling. In adjacent rooms there are the Rainer and Burg museums, with old documents, weapons and armorial decorations. Concerts are held at 8.30 in the summer in the Prince's Chamber. From the Festung there is a marvelous view. You can also enjoy the view from one of the terraces of the Cafe Winkler, especially recommended at night when it is an excellent place from which to view the floodlighting.

Not far from the fortress is the Nonnberg Convent, which was founded by St. Rupert in about the year 700. The church is from the late 1400s and contains, among other riches, a lovely ornate gilded altarpiece. Each evening during May at 6.45 the nuns sing a 15-minute service called "Maiandacht." Their beautiful singing helps create an atmosphere of calm that one hadn't thought possible in Salzburg.

The other end of the Mönchsberg can also be scaled mechanically, this time by a lift from the Gstättengasse. On this side the only attraction is the view, which is marvelous indeed.

You can cover the lower-level sights of the left bank fairly readily in a single walk, starting from the Ferdinand-Hanusch-Platz on the river, between the Museum and Staats bridges. Go up the Hagenauerplatz, which brings you into the Getreidegasse just opposite Mozart's birthplace. As you stroll along Getreidegasse, don't fail to look into doorways en route; more often than not they turn out to be the entrances to passageways leading to idyllic courtyards with attractive shops, coffeehouses and beer gardens. Follow the street westward until you come to an open place, in which stands the Bürgerspital Church (which you can pass up if you don't feel in the mood for minor attractions), and the above-mentioned Mönchsberg lift. Doubling around to the left, you are in Sigmundsplatz, which contains

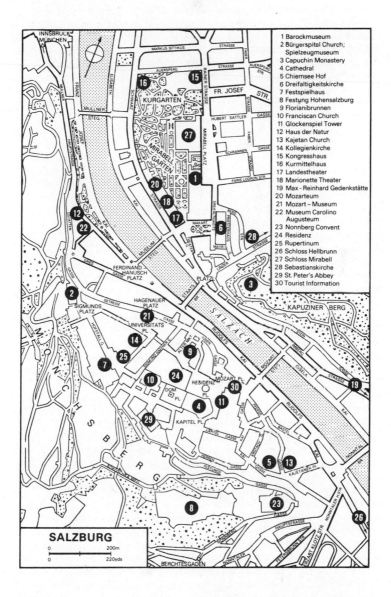

1 Barockmuseum
2 Bürgerspital Church;
  Spielzeugmuseum
3 Capuchin Monastery
4 Cathedral
5 Chiemsee Hof
6 Dreifaltigkeitskirche
7 Festspielhaus
8 Festung Hohensalzburg
9 Florianibrunnen
10 Franciscan Church
11 Glockenspiel Tower
12 Haus der Natur
13 Kajetan Church
14 Kollegienkirche
15 Kongresshaus
16 Kurmittelhaus
17 Landestheater
18 Marionette Theater
19 Max - Reinhard Gedenkstätte
20 Mozarteum
21 Mozart – Museum
22 Museum Carolino
   Augusteum
23 Nonnberg Convent
24 Residenz
25 Rupertinum
26 Schloss Hellbrunn
27 Schloss Mirabell
28 Sebastianskirche
29 St. Peter's Abbey
30 Tourist Information

SALZBURG

0   200m
0   220yds

a somewhat bewildering tribute to the equine race, the Pferdeschwemme, a series of frescos of prancing horses spread out behind a statue dedicated to the same animal. This watering trough was designed especially for the archbishop's horses, which shows they were almost as well treated as Caligula's. Salzburg's love for the horse does not end with this display, nor with the stable ceiling paintings by the same master who performed a similar service for the bishop-princes in their Residenz. When you come to the Kapitelplatz, you will find a Little Pferdeschwemme there (this one was intended for the horses of the church dignitaries to drink at), while in a nearby fountain yet more horses spout jets of water from their flaring nostrils.

Another half-turn left and you pass through Sigmundsplatz and then Hofstallgasse, by the old university building. Though the university was re-opened in 1964, only a few lecture rooms remain here—most of the teaching is done in new buildings out in the district of Nonntal. The old building still contains a large library, with valuable manuscripts. Continue into Universitätsplatz, for the Kollegienkirche. This is an outstanding example of Baroque, not only for Salzburg, but for all Austria—or all Europe, for that matter. This one you should enter, as the interior is as attractive as the outside. It was built by Fischer von Erlach for the University, which is to the right.

On emerging, swing around the corner to the right. Straight ahead, crossing the Hofstallgasse brings you to the Festspielhaus, a large performing-arts complex. The New Festspielhaus is a grandiose, modern construction, decorated with works of art by the leading Austrian artists, among them the painters Oskar Kokoschka, Wolfgang Hutter, Karl Plattner and the sculptor Rudolf Hoflehner, and designed by the architect Clemens Holzmeister. It has space for 2,300 spectators and an especially large stage. The New Festspielhaus is built into the solid rock of the Mönchsberg, with parking space hidden in the hill, so that the audience can get to their seats in the dry. Still in use for the performances is the section of the previous Festspielhaus, now also a part of the complex, which was originally built in 1607 as a court riding school and stable. Called the Winter Riding School, it provides performances with a greater degree of atmosphere than the technically better-equipped, more modern, house.

Along from the Festspielhaus, following the line of the hill, is the Abbey of St. Peter, one of the oldest Benedictine abbeys in German-speaking countries, founded in 696, again by St. Rupert, and its oldest parts date from 847. It is in Romanesque style, with a Gothic cloister, and of its many art treasures, a 1420 Virgin is most highly prized. A favorite visit here is to the catacombs, starting in the interesting old cemetery where St. Virgilius is buried (a resounding name behind which hides this bishop's real name, O'Farrell—he somehow reached Salzburg from Ireland in the eighth century—and helped to make his contemporaries forget that he was crazy, a fact which was evident from his belief that the earth was round).

From St. Peter's (unless you propose to take the inclined cable railway up to the Festung Hohensalzburg from here), cross the Kapitelplatz, with its Neptune Fountain, to what used to be the Prince Bishop's Palace. Across the way is the 17th-century cathedral, which you see from the rear. Circle around it into the Dom Platz. The Cathedral Square is a complete concept. It is not difficult to see why Max Reinhardt chose it as the setting for *Everyman*. In the center rises the Virgin's Column, and at one side is what is considered to be the first early Baroque building north of the

Alps and one of the finest. Its facade is of marble, its towers reach 250 feet into the air, and it holds 10,000 persons. It is not all that usual to find fine modern art allied to superb old buildings, but the Cathedral of Salzburg is an exception. Pay special attention to the three great doors, cast in bronze. The one on the right symbolizes Hope, the one on the left Faith, and the center one by Giacomo Manzù is, of course, Charity. Manzù whose strange episcopal figures, wrapped in their copes, seem to conjure up a world of religious myth and mystery, was a natural choice to bridge the gap between Baroque and modern. The dates on the doors— 774, 1628, 1959—are those of the reconsecrations of the building. Amongst other tribulations, it was badly damaged in World War II. There is an interesting cathedral museum.

Across from the Cathedral, the Franciscan Church, which is now open after extensive restoration and cleaning, is a handbook of architectural history: originally built in the eighth century, it was destroyed by fire in the 12th; Romanesque style from the 13th, Gothic additions in the 15th, followed by Renaissance and Baroque. Its finest possession is a carved Madonna (1495) by Michael Pacher, enshrined on the high altar by Fischer von Erlach (1709).

On the other side of the cathedral from the Kapitelplatz is the Residenzplatz facing the Renaissance Residenz Palace (so called because it was the town residence of the Prince Bishops), with its state rooms, ceiling frescos by Rottmayr and fine furnishings. The rooms of the Residenz are loaded with art treasures, including works by Rembrandt, Rubens, Titian, Brueghel and many others. The 40-foot-high Residenz Fountain in the square before the Palace is lighted at night, and sometimes in fine weather, the serenade concerts otherwise held inside the Residenz are given about the fountain in the openair. Across the square from the palace rises the Glockenspiel Tower, containing a carillon of 35 bells, which performs at 7 A.M., 11 A.M, and 6 P.M. The tunes are taken from the works of Weber, Haydn, and you know who.

Pass from the Residenzplatz into the Alter Markt, the old marketplace, where there are some fine Baroque buildings and the 16th-century Florianibrunnen, St. Florian's Fountain, surrounded by lovely flower stands, where you can buy flowers made of silk and straw, as well as the Salzburg specialty Gewürzsträusserl, bunches of spices—cloves, cinnamon, nutmeg—arranged like flowers. They are a perfect souvenir, attractive and keeping their fragrance for a long time.

East of the Alter Markt is another picturesque part of old Salzburg with small winding streets of ancient houses and interesting shops. If you follow Judengasse you will cross Waagplatz and reach Mozartplatz, with his monument and a Tourist Information office. Across Mozartplatz is Pfeifergasse with the Chiemsee Hof at the end of it. Built originally in 1305, its present form dates from 1700. Up to 1814 it was the residence of the Prince-Bishops and today is the seat of the provincial government. Opposite is the Baroque Kajetan church (1730) with a lovely dome. Close by on Kaigasse no. 8 there is a plaque commemorating Paracelsus (see below). He made his last will in the Wirtshaus that used to stand here, three days before his death in 1541.

The Right Bank

The right bank of the Salzach is rather less crowded with places not to be missed than the left, which contains more of the oldest buildings of Salzburg. You can start to explore it very conveniently just opposite the point where the west bank walk began, in the Platzl, to which the Staatsbrücke (State Bridge) leads. The famous physician and philosopher, Paracelsus von Hohenheim (1494–1541), the scion of a well-known Swabian-German family of that period, who was the first to introduce the use of chemical drugs in medicine, lived here; his neighbors considered him a sorcerer and you can still see the house that they used to look at with superstitious awe—No. 3.

Take Schwarzstrasse out of the Platzl and only after two or three short blocks you will find yourself passing the Landestheater and the Mozarteum, in the garden of which is a little summerhouse in which Mozart finished composing *The Magic Flute*. It is called Zauberflötenhäuschen, a mouthful meaning "the little Magic Flute house."

Between the Landestheater and the Mozarteum, at Schwarzstrasse 24, is the Marionette Theater, where the famous Salzburg marionettes, known round the world, have their home. They have done a great deal of touring, including trips to the United States, and films have been made of them, but this is where you see, during the summer, the puppets of Professor Hermann Aicher at their best. His family has been making and exhibiting marionettes for 200 years.

You are now opposite a large park, originally the private garden of the Schloss Mirabell, which is in a way the Taj Mahal of Salzburg, since it was built in 1606 for his love, Salome Alt, by Wolf Dietrich, who did not abstain from passion simply because he was a bishop—perhaps because he was also a Medici. You may cut across the park to inspect its interior, not neglecting, on the way, the Dwarf's Garden, with its statues of the bishop's favorite midgets, or the delicate wrought-iron gate. Of the splendors inside, the most admired is Rafael Donner's marble stairway, known as the Angel Staircase, though the figures on it are not angels but cupids. As Mirabell houses the Registrar's Office, it is a delightful custom for young newly-weds to have their wedding photo taken close to one of the cupids on the staircase.

While the south portion of the park about Schloss Mirabell is still called the Mirabell Garten, the north part is now called the Kurgarten, since it encloses the very modern Kurhaus, where all kinds of cures can be taken, as well as the Kongresshaus, Salzburg's convention hall. With its Baroque flower beds, statues and the Festung in the background, the gardens make an ideal spot for taking photographs.

Returning along the Mirabellplatz on the other side of the castle, you see the Baroque Holy Trinity Church (Dreifaltigkeitskirche), the first one built in Salzburg by Fischer von Erlach in the 1690s. Mozart's father is buried here, as is his wife and the mother of the later composer, Carl Maria von Weber. Here you are back at your starting point, with a view of the east bank (lower level)—unless, of course, you care to walk back from the river a few blocks up the Linzergasse to visit the Sebastianskirche and its 16th-century graveyard, where Paracelsus and Wolf Dietrich are buried (the latter in a magnificent tiled, but distinctly odd, mausoleum which has just been restored). Directly over Wolf Dietrich's grave you can now see his face in the ceiling. This is a fitting resting place for the spiritual creator of the Salzburg we know.

The upper level on this side of the river is provided by the Kapuzinerberg, which you can climb for the view and the walks in the woods on top, since it is not, like the Mönchsberg opposite, provided with a castle to visit. There are two ways up the Kapuzinerberg, either the climb from Linzergasse or by the stairway from Steingasse. You do, however, begin your climb by passing the Stations of the Cross which lead to the Capuchin monastery that gives the hill its name. If you don't feel up to climbing, from the same point at which you would otherwise start upwards, you can stroll southwards along the Steingasse, at the foot of the slope, and enjoy its lovely old houses. There is, however, a delightful gasthaus built in the courtyard of the old building at the top. You can reward yourself here with delicious and reasonable local specialties if you make the effort to reach the top (closed Tues.).

Excursions from Salzburg

The favorite trip on the outskirts of Salzburg is to what is described as Lustschloss Hellbrunn (the Hellbrunn Pleasure Castle), built in the early 17th century for Bishop Marcus Sitticus, who was Wolf Dietrich's nephew. He allied himself to Duke Maximilian of Bavaria and ensured that his uncle spent the last six years of his life imprisoned in Salzburg castle. The castle is the playground of a mad fountain designer. Some of the fountains operate mechanical figures, others balance balls on water jets and others merely spout water. Wear your old clothes, as one of the games the practical jokers (heavily disguised as fountain builders) played is to drench you suddenly from concealed spouts as you are sitting quietly at a table minding your own business. This Wasserspiele can only be visited in a guided tour. Hellbrunn has a number of other attractions, including the Stone Theater, a natural formation, where the first operatic performance on German-speaking territory was staged in 1617. The interior of the castle, which can be visited with a guided tour, has some fascinating rooms; especially the music room. The *trompe l'oeil* decorations in the banquet hall are especially effective. Also housed at Hellbrunn is the Salzburg Folklore Museum. Special evenings comprising a tour of the castle, the Wasserspiele, a concert and wine tasting can be arranged in advance by calling the Schlossverwaltung 5034 Salzburg, Schloss Hellbrunn (84 16 96). Bus 55, leaving from the main rail station with stops in town as well, stops at Hellbrunn.

A pleasant drive if you have a car is to the north, via Maria Plain (an attractive village with a 1670s pilgrimage church) and Bergheim to Oberndorf (you can get there also by a local railway), much visited because of its one claim to fame—here *Silent Night, Holy Night* was composed by Franz Gruber to verses written by Father Mohr, the village priest. Its birthplace, the old St. Nikolas Church, was destroyed by flood in 1899; on the site is a memorial chapel, and here, and in the new St. Nikolas Church, there are special Christmas midnight masses.

Schloss Leopoldskron is a magnificent 18th-century Rococo palace on the outskirts of town, built by Archbishop Leopold Anton Firmian, later owned by Ludwig I of Bavaria, and still later by Max Reinhardt. Now strictly private property, it can be viewed from across the lake.

Other points are the Gaisberg, served by regular sightseeing buses from Salzburg, and the Untersberg, a mountain whose approaches can be reached by bus and whose top can be reached by a daringly constructed aerial cable car. The spa and casino of Bad Reichenhall, Berchtesgaden, and Königsee, all in Germany, also make a pleasant half-day excursion. Another excursion is to take the newly restored "Oldtimer" tram, built in 1908, from Salzburg Station to Lamprechthausen. Details at the Station information kiosk.

PRACTICAL INFORMATION FOR SALZBURG

TOURIST INFORMATION. Tourist Offices. Stadtverkehrsbüro, the official city tourist office, has its headquarters at Auerspergstr. 7, (80 72–0), and an attractive information center, in traditional Salzburg style, at Mozartplatz 5 (84 75 68). In addition it maintains an information office at the main railway station (7 17 12 and 7 36 38), also open all year, and 4 additional summer offices; Informationsdienst Salzburg-Mitte (3 22 28), open year round at AGIP service station in Münchener Bundesstr., and Informationsdienst Salzburg-West-Airport (85 24 51), April to Oct., at BP service station in Innsbrucker Bundesstr., Informationsdienst Salzburg-Ost, Sterneckstr., and Informationsdienst Salzburg-Süd, Alpenstr. 67 (2 09 66). All year round.

Landesverkehrsamt, the official Salzburg Tourist Department, has its offices at Mozartplatz 1 (80 42–22 32), and shares the above-mentioned information center at Mozartplatz 5 with the city tourist office.

American Express, Mozartpl. 5 (84 25 01); Wagons Lits-Cook, Münzgasse 1 (84 27 55). American Language and Cultural Center, Sportplatzstr. 12 (52754). Open weekdays 2–5.

Consulate. U.S. Consulate, Giselakai 51 (2 86 01), Mon. to Fri., 9–11, 2–4. British Consulate, Alter Markt 4 (84 81 33), Mon. to Fri. 9–12.

Money. Banks are open Mon. to Fri. 8–12, 2–4.30, closed Sat. and Sun. Money can be changed at the rail station from 7 A.M. to 10 P.M., and at the airport 9–4. There is also an exchange at the Griesgasse 11, open Mon. to Fri. 8.30–5.30; Sat. 8.30–5; Sun. 9–4.

Mail. The main post office at Residenzplatz 9 is open weekdays 7–7, Saturdays 8–10 A.M. except during the Festival time, when it is open 7 A.M. to noon. The post office at the Markartplatz is open on weekdays from 7.30 A.M. to 7 P.M. except during the Festival when it is open also Sun. and holidays from 8 A.M. to noon. The post office at the railway station never closes.

AREA CODES—MAIL AND PHONE. The area codes for Salzburg are—mail A-5020; telephone 0 6 62.

HOTELS. It is difficult for a Salzburg hotel not to have a good location, but if you really want a room with a view, you will find some of the better ones on the slopes of the Kapuzinerberg or the Gaisberg, behind it; but at the very top is the Mönchsberg, across the river. The city offers numerous hotels of all price categories, with the accent on the upper categories. Salzburg is as expensive as Vienna. Rates during the summer season (1 June to 30 Sept.) and especially during the Festival, may be as much as 50% higher than during the rest of the year. Many hotels also offer pension terms, but Salzburg has many good restaurants.

Deluxe

Bristol, Markartplatz 4 (7 35 57). 85 rooms with bath or shower; antique furniture. Halfboard only in high season. Two restaurants. Open April to Dec. AE, DC, MC, V.

Fondachhof, Gaisbergstr. 46 (2 09 06). 26 rooms in beautifully furnished rooms of former manor. Elegant lobby, lovely terrace, large park. Restaurant reader-recommended. Open April to Oct. AE, DC, MC, V.

Goldener Hirsch, Getreidegasse 37 (84 85 11). 75 rooms, all with bath. In the main shopping street, 800 year old house which has been an inn since 1564; arched corridors and vaulted stairs, antique and rustic furniture, modern appliances ingeniously hidden. Outstanding food and service. AE, DC, MC, V.

Kobenzl, Gaisberg (21 77 60). 11 km. (7 miles) out and 2,500 ft. up Gaisberg (there is a bus!). Crisp mountain air and fine view over Salzburg. 36 rooms, all with bath; pool, garage and large parking lot, sauna and riding facilities. Excellent restaurant. Family-run. Closed Nov. to March. AE, DC, MC, V.

Osterreichischer Hof, Schwarzstr. 5–7 (7 25 41). Beautiful location near Landestheater and Mozarteum. Now run by the Hotel Sacher, Vienna. 120 rooms, most with bath; panoramic apartments on 4th floor—rooms overlooking the Salzach river also offer a fine view of the fortress and the old city. AE, DC, MC, V.

Schloss Mönchstein, Mönchsberg 26 (84 85 55). On the Mönchsberg in magnificent location above Salzburg. An exclusive castle-hotel of 17 elegant suites; superior service. Superb restaurant. Tennis court. Own wedding chapel. Closed Feb. AE, DC, MC, V.

Sheraton, Auerspergstr. 4 (79 32 10). 143 rooms, 21 elegant apartments. Two restaurants, piano bar. Beautifully situated beside the Mirabell gardens. Very fine restaurant. AE, DC, MC, V.

Expensive

Bayerischer Hof, Kaiserschützenstr. 1 (5 41 70). 60 rooms, all with bath. Newly done up and newly furnished. Two new restaurants. AE, DC, MC, V.

Cottage, Joseph-Messner-Str. 12 (2 45 71). 110 rooms, all with bath. Indoor pool, sauna. AE, DC, MC, V.

Elefant, Sigmund-Haffnergasse 4 (84 33 97). 34 rooms, all with bath. Excellent value within category. Very good restaurant, friendly. AE, DC, MC, V.

Europa, Rainerstr. 31 (7 33 91). 104 rooms, all with bath or shower, in a 15-storey box which sticks uncomfortably out above the rooftops of Salzburg. The roof cafe and restaurant offer a fine view of the city and the Alps. AE, DC, MC, V.

Gablerbräu, Linzergasse 9 (7 34 41). Near main bridge. 50 rooms, some with bath. AE, DC, MC, V.

Kasererhof, Alpenstr. 6 (2 12 65). In Nonntal, near the river. 58 rooms; quiet location with garden and restaurant. AE, DC, MC, V.

Maria-Theresien Schlössl, Morzger Str. 87 (84 12 44). 20 rooms, most with bath, TV. 4 km. (2½ miles) from the center of town. Completely renovated; friendly and personal service. Closed Jan.–March. AE, DC, MC, V.

Pitter, Rainerstr. 6–8 (7 85 71). 200 rooms, all with bath or shower. Near railway station, with restaurant and cafe, beer cellar, musical entertainment; garden in summer. AE, DC, MC, V.

Schlosshotel St. Rupert, Morzgerstr. 31 (84 32 31). 30 rooms, most with bath. Located in lovely area outside the city in the direction of Hellbrunn Castle. Restaurant serves very good food. Open April to Oct. AE, DC, MC, V.

Tannhof, Gaisbergstr. 14a (2 13 50). 12 rooms all with bath or shower. Open March to Oct. AE.

Weisse Taube, Kaig. 9 (84 24 04). 31 rooms, breakfast only, charming. AE, DC, MC, V.

Winkler, Franz Josefstr. 7 (7 35 13). 103 rooms, all with bath and TV. Good restaurant. AE, DC, MC, V.

Wolf Dietrich, Wolf Dietrich Str. 7 (7 12 75). 30 rooms. Pool. AE, DC, MC, V.

Moderate

Auersperg, Auerspergstr. 61 (7 17 21). Most of the 60 rooms with bath; between main station and the Kapuzinerberg. AE, DC, MC.

Drei Kreuz, Vogelweiderstr. 7a (7 27 90). 20 rooms. AE, DC, MC, V.

Johann Strauss, Makart Kai 37 (3 46 19). 30 rooms, 22 rooms with bath. DC.

Kasererbräu, Kaigasse 33 (84 24 45). 37 rooms with bath. Not far from Mozartplatz; small and furnished in old Salzburg style. AE, DC, MC, V.

Koch, Gaisbergstr. 37 (2 04 02). 13 rooms.

Markus Sittikus, Markus Sittikus Str. 20 (7 11 21). 41 rooms, most with bath; near main station. AE, DC, MC, V.

Mozart, Franz Josef Kai 27 (7 22 74). 33 rooms; functional. AE, DC, MC, V.

Pelz, Gaisbergerstr. 40 (2 17 41). 30 rooms; bed and breakfast only. Open April to Oct. AE, DC, MC, V.

Stieglbräu, Rainerstr. 14 (7 76 92). 50 rooms. Large restaurant divided into several sections; garden in summer; parking. AE, DC, MC, V.

Inexpensive

Blaue Gans, Getreidegasse 43 (84 13 17). 40 rooms, half with shower. AE, DC, MC, V.

Emminger, Reisenbergstr. 16 (7 84 61). 25 rooms, all with bath. AE, DC, MC, V.

Gasthof Überfuhr, Ignaz Riederkai 43 (23 0 10). 21 rooms, good food.

Rosenhotel Salzburg, Struberg. 1 (39 6 39). 94 rooms, all with bath. Open July to Oct. AE, DC, MC, V.

Trumerstüberl, Bergstr. 6 (7 47 76). 22 rooms. Friendly, family-run gasthof. Rooms with shower. Reader-recommended.

Vienna, Gaisbergstr. 12 (2 08 70). 16 rooms with shower. AE, MC, V.

Wolf, Kaigasse 7 (84 34 53). 12 rooms, all with bath or shower and TV. AE.

Many more hotels and Gasthöfe (I) are available in Salzburg and suburbs. In the vast majority you'll get a clean room and an honest price.

Pensions

As a major tourist destination, Salzburg has a better selection of pension accommodations than any other city in Austria. They are in all categories and are usually well appointed. For further details, check with the Salzburg Tourist office (see *Tourist Information* above).

Camping

There are 9 campsites in and around Salzburg, the largest ones at Bayerhamerstrasse 14A, in the city; on the Gersbergalm, in the Maxglan section near the airport; and at Schloss Aigen. The Gersbergalm site and Kasern in the city are equipped for winter camping. General information call 74 6 20 or 80 72.

Youth Hostels

Central Information: *Salzburger Jugendherbergswerk,* Kapitelgasse 6, (84 25 91).

There are two year-round hostels in Salzburg and five seasonal ones. The year-round hostels are—

Jugendgästehaus Nonntal, Josef-Preis-Allee 18 (84 26 70, 84 68 57).

Jugendherberge Aigen, Aigner Str., 34 (23 2 48).

The ones only open for a part of the year are—

Jugendherberge Glockengasse 8 (76 2 41); April to mid-Oct.

Jugendherberge Eduard-Heinrich-Haus, Eduard-Heinrich-Str., 2 (25 9 76); July to mid-Aug.

Jugendherberge Haunspergstrasse, Haunspergstr. 27 (75 0 30); July to mid-Aug.

Jugendherberge Walserfeld, 5071 Wals bei Salzburg, Schulstr. 18 (85 13 77); July to mid-Aug.

GETTING AROUND SALZBURG. By Bus. Salzburg is well served by a large number of bus lines, both trolley and motor. There is also a quick City-Bus service through the center of town from the Nonntal carpark to Sigmundsplatz, the city center carpark. A 24-hour network ticket costs AS19.

By Taxi. Taxis are expensive and hard to get, especially just before curtain time during festivals (reserve in advance with hotel porters). For Radio taxis (Salzburg Funktaxi-Vereinigung), Rainerstr. 27 (7 61 11), or to order in advance, 7 44 00. Taxi/Minibus services: *Eiser* (53 7 33); *Erhart* (20 4 00).

Horse Cabs. Salzburg is also an open-carriage city. If you like leisurely promenades behind a horse, this is the place for it. Horse cabs can be hired on Residenzplatz; an hour's ride costs about AS500, half-an-hour AS260.

By Car. Driving in the city is a problem, so park your car on the edge of the city center and proceed by bus or on foot; a city bus runs between the center and the Nonntal parking lot. In Mönchsberg there is a huge garage with a long passage leading directly to the lobby of the Festspielhaus.

If you want to rent a car you may try Hertz or Avis, both at Porschestr. 7 (766 74 for Hertz, 7 72 78–0 for Avis) and the airport; Europcar, Bayernstr. 1(84 37 01); Inter Rent, opposite the main station (5 05 81/338).

By Bicycle. You can hire bikes all year round from Schmidler, Ignaz-Harrer-Str. 88 (3 22 63); from May to Sept. from Zweirad-Center Frey, Alpenstr. 85 (2 35 81) and also from the main railway station.

High Rise. There is an express lift up Mönchsberg and a cable railway to take you swiftly up to the fortress (Festungsbahn). Roughly speaking the first runs from 7 in the morning to about 3 the next morning; the Festungsbahn's timetable is more complex—starting for most of the year at 7.30 and running through till late afternoon or mid-evening.

Sightseeing. Sightseeing flights: carried out with Cessnas by ÖFAG-Flugdienst (85 12 12–0) at the airport. For bus sightseeing tours: Autoreisebüro Salzkraft, Mirabellplatz 2 (7 26 56), Albus, Markartplatz 9 (7 34 45) and Albus Kiosk, Mirabellpl. (7 17 73). Salzburg Panorama Tours, Mirabellplatz (7 40 29) organize minibus trips, chauffeur driven, for up to 8 people. In summer, a Mozart walking tour departs from the Mozarteum, Mon. to Fri. at 11.15 A.M. Cost AS25.

Sightseeing trips in the city and surrounding areas start from the Mirabellplatz. The most scenic are to the Grossglockner and the Dachstein ice caves.

An aerial cable railway, over 2 km. long, takes you to the Untersberg mountain, to an elevation of 5,825 ft. Its valley station is at St. Leonhard, on the road to Berchtesgaden. Each of the two cabins can transport 50 people, and 700 people can be taken to the top in one hour. Take Bus 55 from the city to the base station.

MUSEUMS AND GALLERIES. Opening times are liable to change, so please check locally before planning your day's sightseeing. Several of the museums make special arrangements for Festival time.

Dom Museum (Cathedral Museum) at the Cathedral, Domplatz (84 41 89). Open daily 10–5; Sundays and holidays 11–5. Open May–Oct.

Festspielhaus (Festival Theater) (84 25 41). Guided tours—May, June, Sept., Mon. to Fri. 11 and 3; April and Oct. 3 only. Sat. 11 (subject to variation).

Galerie Welz, Sigmund-Haffnerg. 16 (84 17 71–0).

Glockenspiel the Carillon on the Residenzplatz (80 42–26 81) plays daily 7 and 11 A.M., 6 P.M. Tours daily at 10.45 and 5.45; Nov. to March weekdays only.

Haus der Natur, Museumplatz (84 26 53). A huge natural history exhibition. Open daily 9–5; 1½-hour guided tours available.

Hellbrunn. Castle 5 km. (3 miles) south of the center of Salzburg (84 16 96). Take Bus 55 from downtown. Delightful Baroque park and other attractions (see text). Guided tours April to Oct., daily 9–6; Alpine Zoo (84 11 69). Open Oct. to May 9–4, April to Sept. 9–6.

Hohensalzburg (The Fortress) (80 42–21 23). The Burgmuseum can only be seen as part of a guided tour, May to Sept. 9.30–4.30. Great views. Cog-wheel railway operating daily (see *Getting Around*).

Max-Reinhard-Forschungs- und Gedenkstätte, Schloss Arenberg, Arenbergstr. 10 (75 0 63). Museum and study center dedicated to the great theater director Max Reinhard, who founded the Festival. Open Mon.–Fri. 9–12 (daily during Festival). Closed July and first half of Sept.

Mozarteum, Schwarzstr. 26 (73 1 54). Music academy with two auditoria, the Bibliotheca Mozartiana (huge collection of works by and about Mozart); **Zauberflötenhauschen,** the tiny house in which he composed the *Magic Flute.* Open daily; conducted tours only in July and Aug., weekdays at 11. Walking tours, AS50 per person, leave here at 11.15 Mon. to Fri. during the summer and include Mozart's residence on Markartplatz.

Mozart House, Markartplatz 8 (7 17 76). Open Mon. to Sat. 10–4.

Mozart-Museum, Getreidegasse 9 (84 43 13). Mozart's birthplace. His clavichord, first violin, family pictures and other related material. Open all year, daily 9–6.

Museum Carolino Augusteum, Museumplatz 1 (84 31 45). The city museum outlining the history of Salzburg. Open daily 9–5 except Mon.

Pater-Peter Singer Museum, Hofstallgasse 5. Music collection in a room of the Franciscan monastery.

Residenz, Residenzplatz 1 (80 42–26 90). The city palace of the Salzburg archbishops. Conducted tours through the ornate state rooms daily from 10. **Galerie,** (80 42–22 70). Special Residenz exhibitions. Tues. to Sat. 10–5.

Salzburg Barockmuseum, the Baroque Museum, entrance—appropriately—from the Mirabellgarten (77 4 32). Open daily 9–12, 2–5, mornings only on Sun. Closed Mon.

Spielzeugmuseum (Toy Museum), Bürgerspitalgasse 2 (84 75 60). Open Tues. to Sun. 9–5. Closed Mon.

Rupertinum, Wiener Philharmonikerstr. 9 (80 42–25 41). Provincial art gallery, mainly modern works. Open daily 10–5 except Wed., 10–9 P.M.

St. Peter's Catacombs, (84 45 78). Open May to Sept. 10–5; Oct. to Apr. 11–12, 1.30–3.30.

Trachtenmuseum (Folk Costumes), Griesg. 23/1 (84 31 19). Mon. to Sat. 10–12, 2–5.

SHOPPING. Salzburg stores are open from 9 A.M. to 6 P.M., some of them closing for an hour or two at lunchtime. All of them are shut Sat. afternoons, except the first Sat. of the month, when most shops stay open until 5. The best shopping streets are in the heart of the old city particularly Getreidegasse, Judengasse, Griesgasse, Schwarzstrasse and Linzergasse and the several historic squares such as Waagplatz and Residenzplatz.

Salzburg specialties include dirndls, Lederhosen, petit point, leather goods, jewelry, candles, and sports equipment and clothing.

Candles. *Johann Nagy,* Linzergasse 32. *Hans Nagy,* Getreidegasse 48.

Dirndls and Trachten for Women. *Lanz,* Schwarzstr. 4 and Imbergstr. 5. *Wenger,* Münzgasse 2. *Trachten Forstenlechner,* Mozartplatz 4. *Wally Dirndl* beside Mönschberg lift.

Glass. *Fritz Kreis,* Sigmund-Haffnerg. 14 (841 03 15). Superb hand-engraved glass—also to order.

Handicrafts, Gifts and Souvenirs. *Salzburger Heimatwerk,* Residenzplatz 9. *Hans Schmidjell,* Münzgasse 2.

Petit Point. *Slezak,* Markartplatz 8. *Fritsch,* Getreidegasse 42–44. *J. Ennsmann & Co.,* Getreidegasse 31 and 21, Neutorgasse 32.

Porcelain. *Augarten,* Schwarzstr. 18 (74 6 33).

Silk flowers and Gewürzsträusschen (bunches of flowers made of spices). *Constanze,* Altermarkt and Rainerstr. 25. *Schatzkästlein,* Sigmund-Haffnerg 18.

Toys. *Neumüller,* Rathausplatz 3. *Spielwarenhaus Böhlein,* Markartplatz 4.

Wood Carvings. *Johann Lackner,* Badergässchen 2.

Wrought Iron and Weinhebers. *Hans Schmidjell,* Münzgasse 2. *Gebrüder Roittner,* Getreidegasse 7–8. *Siegfried Kopfberger,* Judengasse 14.

SPORTS. Winter Sports. Gaisberg mountain in the outskirts of Salzburg (the top is only 16 km., 10 miles, from the center of the city by a good mountain road) offers excellent skiing terrain. There are 4 ski lifts and a chair lift on various slopes of the mountain and a ski jump at Zistelsalm. There is a ski school on Gaisberg, and skiing equipment, including boots, can be rented from the Hintner sports store. Ice skating rinks are located in Volksgarten and in Rupertgasse 11. There is also tobogganing on Gaisberg.

Swimming. Among the various pools are—the indoor pool in Kurhaus (Paracelsusbad); AYA-Bad on Alpenstr.; Waldbad Anif on the busline to Hallein; Kreuzbrückl in the suburb of Maxglan; and the pools in Volksgarten (Franz-Josefs-Park) on the way to Aigen; in the park of Klessheim Castle near the golf course; and in the grounds of Leopoldskron Castle. The nearest Salzkammergut lakes (Wallersee, Trumersee) are only 21 km. away, but very cold.

Tennis and Golf. Many tennis courts are available in the city, the best being those of the Salzburger Tennisklub in Volksgarten. Tennis courts are also available in the park of Klessheim Castle, where a 9-hole golf course is open from April to Oct. The Salzburg area boasts over half a dozen golf courses, and new ones are being planned. Details from the tourist office, Mozartplatz 5.

Gliding is another feature of the Salzburg area; starting and landing sites on Gaisberg, at Koppl and at the airport of Maxglan; for further information inquire at Aero-Club-Landesverband, Mozartplatz 8, Salzburg.

Horseback Riding. For horse-riding facilities, contact either Reiterhof Moos, Moosstr. 135 (84 27 91), or Reitstall Doktorbauer, Eberlinggasse 5 (84 57 85).

THE SALZBURG FESTIVAL. The great annual event is, of course, the Festival, from the last week in July to the end of Aug. Details can be obtained from the *Salzburger Festspiele,* Postfach 140, 5010 Salzburg (06222–84 25 41).

As we say earlier in the text of this chapter, don't arrive without tickets and expect to be able to pick them up on the spot. There is always a huge demand for places and, despite the huge cost of seats, they are spread around to the various agencies very sparingly. Almost certainly the only tickets available in Salzburg itself will be from hotel concierges at vastly inflated rates—and the official one's top price is already AS3000—around $225 U.S.

There is standing room available for serenade concerts and some of the less ritzy performances, especially the outdoor ones, but that's all you are likely to be able to come by honestly after arrival.

NIGHTLIFE. The mortality of nightclubs is greater in Salzburg than in Vienna; better inquire from the city tourist office or from the hotel porter (however, bear in mind that he is likely to be getting a commission, which will be added to your bill).

Stieglkeller, Festungsrestaurant and *Sternbräu* have folklore shows on some days of the week during summer.

A number of wine taverns have local atmosphere and musical entertainment, among them: *Bacchus Stuben,* Rudolfskai 16; *Paracelsus Weinstube,* established 1541, Kaigasse 8; *Höllbräu Kerzenstübl,* Judengasse 15; *Steirische Weinstuben,* St.-Julienstr. 9.

Bars. Check the bars in the Lederergasse and Steingasse. *Büro American Bar,* Rich. Mayrstr. 1 (7 72 97); *Casanova,* Linzergasse 23 (7 50 31); *Casino Alm Disco,* Bayerhamerstr. 14 (7 11 69); *Disco Tyrol,* Wolf Dietrichstr. 4 (7 62 79); *Paracelsus Stub'n,* Kaigasse 8 (84 32 77); *Old Grenadier,* Ursulinenpl. 2 (84 37 18); *Saitensprung,* Steing 11, (71 06 82). Wines and cocktails; *Western Saloon,* Linzer Bundesstr. 94 (6617 24).

CASINO. Located at the Café Winkler on Mönchsberg (84 56 65). Roulette, baccara and black-jack are played according to the international rules, daily after 5 P.M. Passport required, knowledge of German advisable and you must be over 21.

RESTAURANTS. Salzburg is well supplied with good restaurants, but they are in great demand and it is wise to make reservations at the more frequented places. The hotel restaurants are all up to standard, and some of them are decidedly atmospheric (especially in the Inexpensive range).

Expensive

Alt Salzburg, Sigmundsplatz 2 (84 14 76). Small elegant dining rooms in red and gold. Excellent cuisine including Tafelspitz, lamb, very good salads. Reserve. Closed Sun. and Feb. AE, DC, MC. Open late.

Bayrischer Hof, Elisabethstr. 12 (54 17 00). Close to railway station. Good Austrian fare, popular among Salzburgers. Reserve. Closed Sat. AE, DC, MC, V.

Café Winkler, Am Mönchsberg 32 (84 12 15). Unsurpassed view of Salzburg from the terrace. Casino in house. Fish and game specialties; good salads. Reserve. Closed Mon. AE, DC, MC, V. Open late.

Goldener Hirsch, Getreidegasse 37 (84 15 11). Famous haunt of famous people. Fine dining in chic atmosphere, but can be very crowded. Reserve. AE, DC, MC, V. Open late.

Kobenzl, Gaisberg (2 76 17). Superb location, high above Salzburg. Excellent Austrian and international cuisine. Reserve. Closed Nov. to March. AE, DC, MC, V.

Österreichischer Hof, Schwarzstr. 5 (7 25 41). Elegant rooms (Roter Salon and Zirbenstube); Austrian and international cuisine. Different menus in Salzachgrill and Keller. Reserve. AE, DC, MC, V. Open late.

Paris Lodron, in Schloss Mönchstein, Mönchsberg 26 (84 85 55). One of the most stunning locations in Europe, and with food to match. Reservations and formal clothes essential. AE, DC, MC, V.

Moderate

Brandstätter, Liefering, Münch. Bundesstr. 69 (3 45 35). New, with lovely *Zirbenstube* (wood panelling). Renowned. Austrian specialties. Reserve. Closed 20 Dec. to 6 Jan. AE, DC, MC, V.

Brasserie "Zur Bastey", Kaigasse 7 (84 11 80). Good food, reader-recommended. Closed Sun. AE, DC, MC, V.

Flughafenrestaurant, at Airport, Innsbrucker Bundesstr. 95, Flughafen Maxglan (85 02 12). Plain decor but excellent food. AE, DC, MC, V.

Gablerbräu, Linzerg. 9 (7 34 41). Good Austrian food. Open daily. AE, DC, MC, V.

Hagenauer Stuben, Universitätsplatz 14 (84 26 57). In the house where Mozart was born. Small, with some tables outside next to a picturesque market. Good Austrian food and excellent wines. Exhibition of works by contemporary Salzburg painters on the upper floor. Closed Sat. afternoon and Sun. AE, DC, MC, V.

Maria Plain, Maria Plain Kasern (5 07 01). Old inn next to pilgrimage church. Good local food. Closed Wed. and 8 Jan. to 15 Feb.

Pitter (*Rainerstube*), Rainerstr. 6–8 (7 85 71). With coffeehouse and garden; vegetarian food available, along with local specialties. Excellent value. AE, DC, MC, V.

Purzelbaum im Schwarzwirt, Zugallistr. 7 (84 88 43). An attractive mixture of a pub and an old-fashioned Gasthaus. Attractively decorated in white and green. Fish specialties. Closed Sun. AE, DC, MC, V.

Zum Mohren, Judengasse 9 (84 23 87). Historic building with atmospheric vaults. Delicious Austrian and international food. Reserve. Closed Sun. and Nov.

Inexpensive

Be sure to have a beer and hearty Austrian meal in one of the Salzburg beergardens. They are as dear to the Salzburgers as the *Heurigen* are to the Viennese. Among the best are—

Augustinerbräu, Augustinerstrasse 4 (31 2 46). Where the Augustinian fathers have their beer on sale; in winter several large halls and in summer a shady garden.

Franziskischlössl, (7 41 39), on top of Kapuzinerberg. Good, simple fare. Closed Tues.

Krimpelstätter, Müllner Hauptstr. 31 (3 22 74). One of the oldest in Salzburg; hearty Austrian food; meeting place of locals. Reserve. Closed Mon.

Mundenhammer Bräu, Rainerstr. 2 (7 56 93). Reader-recommended for game.

Sternbräu, Getreidegasse 25, Griesgasse 34–6 (84 21 40). Self-service garden and semi-covered restaurant. Music on Fri. and Sun.; own butcher and sausage shops.

CAFES. Perhaps even more than in Vienna—for Salzburg is that much smaller—cafe life is a part of the city's traditions. Several cafes have a long history and have seen many famous people come and go. They are ideal as places to relax and keep an eye on the passing scene.

Bazar, Schwarzstrasse 3 (7 42 78). A Salzburg institution where locals go to see and be seen; lots of atmosphere. Closed Sun.

Ratzka, Imbergstrasse 45 (7 09 19). Pastries, *torten* and *petit fours* of unsurpassed quality. People from all over the country and the world come for Herrn Ratzka's *Zwetschkenfleck* or apple wine cake. Closed Mon. and Tues.

Schatz-Konditorei, Schatz-Durchhaus, Getreidegasse 3 (84 27 92). A tiny coffee house off an operetta stage. Delicious pastries, above all handmade *Mozart Kugeln,* which can be mailed. Closed Sun.

Tomaselli, Alter Markt 9 (84 44 88). Long tradition; usually crowded, but a must for every Salzburg visitor.

LAND SALZBURG

Sports and Spas in the High Alps

The shape of the Bundesland Salzburg (Federal State of Salzburg), or briefly, Land Salzburg, makes it look as if its boundaries had been drawn by drunken surveyors on the instructions of crazy mapmakers. But it was not the mapmakers who were mad; it was the country itself. The land had thrust itself upward into such weird and fantastic shapes that rivers, roads and boundaries were forced to follow them. The landscape is softer in the narrow neck of Land Salzburg, to the north and northeast of the city of Salzburg; here, blue lakes dream peacefully among the round-shouldered mountains covered by forests; here too is the beginning of the Salzkammergut region, most of which, however, lies across the state border in Upper Austria.

Exploring Land Salzburg

The narrow northern corridor which Land Salzburg thrusts upward between Bavaria and Upper Austria is the beginning of the Salzkammergut lake country. North of the city of Salzburg are the lakes of Wallersee, visited chiefly for scenic reasons, though there are a couple of interesting old churches on its shores, and a group of three connected lakes, with the principal town of Mattsee lying between two of them. The Gothic basilica of its 18th-century abbey was remodelled in a Baroque manner in 1766, but the notable 15th-century frescos and atmospheric cloisters have been preserved. The abbey museum contains splendid monstrances, and the library some very valuable early printed books. On a small hill close to Obertum called the Hausberg, is a huge beech tree, the "Kaiserbuche." This was planted by the Emperor Josef II in 1779 on the spot from which he first surveyed the lands of the Innviertel which had just been ceded to him from Bavaria by the Peace of Teschen, ending the War of Succession, or "Potato War".

To the east, the lake nearest to Salzburg, Fuschlsee, is close enough to the city (about 24 km., 15 miles) to be a weekend resort for Salzburgers, and the place where many festival visitors choose to stay in preference to the city itself. A few kilometers farther southeast is the romantic Wolfgangsee, most of whose shores are within the borders of Land Salzburg, but whose chief attraction, St. Wolfgang of White Horse Inn fame, is in Upper Austria.

At the western end of Wolfgangsee is St. Gilgen, which again is near enough to Salzburg so that it is possible to commute. This accounts for the fact that it possesses many modern villas belonging to members of the international set who are apt to be found in Salzburg at festival time. There is precious little local color left to St. Gilgen, since the foreign invasion has deprived it of the real thing, leaving it simply a pleasant resort on a beautiful lake, with a nice beach. Its chief claim to fame is that Mozart's mother was born here.

The main attraction of Strobl, at the eastern tip of Wolfgangsee, is its delightful setting. If you wish a quiet vacation, this is a place to go. North of Wolfgangsee, a very narrow strip of Land Salzburg reaches the southern bank of Mondsee, whose main localities, however, are all within the borders of Upper Austria.

The great bulk of shoe-shaped Land Salzburg lies to the south and southwest of its capital. This is mountain country, with much higher mountains than those of the lake region, the sort of towering rocky peaks that come to mind with the words "the Alps." The mightiest range stretches across the southern boundary of the state and continues eastward into Styria—a wall rearing from west to east right across the center of Austria.

However, the exploration of this country has been simplified by dynamite: the Pass Lueg and the tunnels of the Tauern Autobahn go straight through the mountains, while along the other three roads, snaking and climbing above them, the magnificent scenery compensates for the steep gradients.

The Tennengau

The territory south of Salzburg is blocked off before the higher mountains are reached by the Tennen range, from which the district gets its name of the Tennengau. If we start down into it on the left bank of the Salzach River, (motorway A10 or lesser road), we pass by Schloss Anif, a moated castle, which can also be visited conveniently as an excursion from Salzburg.

The first place of any size to which we come is Hallein, second largest town in Land Salzburg, a spa, with brine baths, now a winter sports center. It is an old town, with a history going back to Celtic and Roman times, and with some medieval structures still standing, like the town wall. The parish church is 15th century, and Franz Gruber, composer of "Silent Night, Holy Night" was buried here.

The most interesting sights of Hallein are not in the town proper, but in the mining settlement of Dürrnberg above it. Here you may visit, from

May 1 to Sept. 30, a salt mine—a weird trip to another world, a cleverly-lighted land of subterranean lakes and dark caves, not an excursion for the timid. An unusual underground museum not only shows you what salt mining was like in Celtic and Illyrian times, but displays prehistoric finds from the region as well. Above ground you can see the town's 16th–17th-century church, to which pilgrimages are made for its 17th-century statue of the Virgin. The church is all of marble, for this is marble country; Hallein possesses a flourishing marble industry today.

The main road south passes a little to the west of the small summer resort of Vigaun to Kuchl, an interesting old market town whose Gothic rock church, on the Georgenberg, occupies the site of the Roman temple of the fifth-century settlement of Cucullae. A curious feature of this church is its outside pulpit.

The World of the Ice Giants

The Tauern Autobahn (A10) by-passes Golling and as you plunge into the Pass Lueg Tunnel you leave Tennengau and emerge into the Pongau, whose first point of importance is Werfen. The approach is signaled some distance before you reach it by the Hohenwerfen Castle perched high above the town and consequently visible for miles. It was first built in 1077, but the present building, dating from the 16th century, replaced the original one, destroyed in the Peasants' Rebellion of 1525, and was itself restored in 1935 after a bad fire.

Werfen is visited in the summer by climbers and in the winter by skiers—it has a ski descent of nearly 2,400 m. (8,000 ft.), one of the longest single-slope drops in the eastern Alps—but its great attraction is ice. It is the starting point from which to visit the Eisriesenwelt (the Ice Giants' World), the largest known complex of ice caves, domes, galleries and halls in Europe. It extends for some 42 km. (25 miles) and contains fantastic frozen waterfalls, natural formations suggesting statues, and other wonders. It's about a 3½-hour climb to the Dr. Friedrich Öld-Haus, where the tours begin, but it is possible to drive to the resthouse a little more than halfway and thence to take the cable car to the cave entrance.

Radstadt

A town since the 13th century, Radstadt still possesses its old walls from that period, with the addition of towers built three centuries later at the corners. It has a fine Gothic parish church, two other interesting Baroque churches, law courts in neo-Classical style, two castles in Renaissance style and some fine old town walls. If it seems surprising to find so much architectural importance tucked away in a small mountain town the explanation is that Radstadt lies at the entrance to the Radstädter Tauern Pass, an important north–south way through the mountains which has been used since Roman times, lately of lesser significance because of the Tauern Autobahn, tunneling through the mountains slightly to the west.

Radstadt is itself a highly picturesque town and it is surrounded by some impressive scenery. The Radstädter Tauern Pass is very popular with Austrians as a high-altitude summer resort, a paradise of pure mountain air and of gentians and Alpine roses blooming beside minute lakes, and is even more popular in winter as a skiing resort.

After Untertauern, you are really climbing through magnificent scenery, and over a road whose original bed was laid down by the Romans.

At Obertauern you are at the mouth of the pass. At the summit of the pass itself, which is at an altitude of about 1,740 m. (5,900 ft.), is the Cemetery of the Unknown. It is the resting place of the bodies recovered here in the early days before the development of organized mountaineering.

Once across the pass, you are in the southernmost, and for that matter, the easternmost, part of Land Salzburg, the Lungau. The southward road passes through Tweng to Mauterndorf, a thousand-year-old market town. It has old buildings, old traditions (its Samson Procession), and a splendid castle-fortress watching over it, which is open to the public.

From Mauterndorf you can exercise one of the few choices which permit you, in these mountainous regions, to make a return trip by an alternative road instead of retracing your path. Take the eastern road (95) to Tamsweg, capital of the Lungau and an ancient Roman town of which some remnants still remain. A minor summer and winter resort near the Preber Lake, Tamsweg possesses a museum, the Baroque Künberg Castle and a 16th-century town hall, and the early 15th-century pilgrimage church of St. Leonhard is nearby, notable especially for its fine windows and Gothic carved confessional chairs and paintings.

Returning from Tamsweg, you start back by the same road, but just outside of town turn left, to the west, passing through Unternberg, and below the Schloss Moosham, a restored 13th-century castle which can be visited and is now a museum. Then comes St. Michael, wiped out by fire in the 17th century, but with a few surviving relics—the 13th- and 14th-century frescos in the Gothic parish church, and the nearby Agydius Church, outside of the fire area, which dates from 1278. From here the A10 continues down into Carinthia.

The Pongau

Back in the Pongau, Bischofshofen (with three fine churches) is important chiefly as a point of departure: as a rail and road junction and as the entrance to skiing country which has long been a traditional training ground of champions. The Hochkönig, which can be reached from this side as well as from Werfen, has a jump where leaps of more than 300 feet have often been made.

From Bischofshofen, the main route (311) passes through St. Johann im Pongau, a highly popular place in both summer and winter. In summer, visitors come for fresh air, folklore, and to take the bus excursion to the Lichtensteinklamm, the deepest, narrowest, most spectacular gorge in the eastern Alps, with a tremendous waterfall at one end. In winter, this spot is particularly favored by non-champion skiers, for its location, on the floor of a cup whose sides are formed by mountains all about it, provides an almost endless variety of good runs down into town.

At Schwarzach the routes divide, the rail line branching west and south, to Bad Hofgastein and Badgastein. The road, too, divides some kilometers from Schwarzach, 167 going to Badgastein, 311 continuing west.

The idiosyncracies of fashion have made Badgastein the main center, but smaller Bad Hofgastein is also attractive, though lower down the valley. It may appeal more to those who prefer relaxation among beautiful scenery to lively entertainment. As a spa, its advantages are the same, for the Badgastein waters are piped here, so that precisely the same cures are available. It is a minor resort only because it is so close to Badgastein; alone it would still draw many visitors, and it has plenty of facilities for them. There is a Gothic parish church with three old altars, a 16th-century castle, and a number of old houses with corner turrets dating from the valley's gold mining days.

Badgastein

In the Middle Ages, the riches of Badgastein came from the gold mines, long since worked out. But it has a new and more profitable gold mine in the tourist industry, which Frederick, Duke of Styria, must be credited with founding, in the 15th century. The story is that he was dying of a gangrenous wound, when he was told of a miraculous spring in the Gastein valley. He went to Badgastein, was cured, and royalty, nobility, the wealthy, and plain tourists have been flocking to it ever since.

The attractions of Badgastein are many. First, there are the springs, which have a temperature of nearly 120° Fahrenheit. But even without the springs, Badgastein would be attractive, for the mountain scenery here is exceptionally beautiful. As for the setting of the town itself, it is incomparable. It clings to the evergreen-wooded slopes on either side of a rushing mountain torrent, which pours down a spectacular waterfall in the very heart of the settlement, under its Steinbrücke. A third attraction is its importance as a winter sports center, which, with the newly developing Sport Gastein area above it (reached by cable car or toll road), makes it one of the best equipped in Europe.

The cheapest way of all to benefit by the Badgastein springs is to push on into the valley to the last station on the railroad before it leaves Land Salzburg, Böckstein. Here the hotels have no thermal baths of their own, but guests staying here may use the Badgastein Municipal Spa Establishment. Böckstein also has a very special sort of cure all its own.

The Pinzgau

Now resume your exploration of the main westward route, which we left to enter the Gastein valley. Beyond this point, you are in the largest district of Land Salzburg, the Pinzgau. The next north–south passage into the mountains is the Rauris valley, entered from Taxenbach if you're driving, or from Kitzlochklamm, which is where you get off if you come by train. The principal sight here is the 90-m. (300-ft.) Kitzloch waterfall and the gorges cut by the stream of which it is a part.

The Sonnblick peak at the end of this valley is the chief point of interest of those who enter it. There is a meteorological observatory on top of it, but its importance for visitors is its splendid ski runs. These are not for novices, however; this terrain is strictly for experts.

Resuming your westward journey, you reach Bruck, a summer resort with a famous view from nearby Fischorn Castle and a winter skiing center, but which is better known as the starting point for one of the most spectacular trips in Austria.

The Grossglockner Road

This is the excursion over the longest and most spectacular highway through the Alps, the Grossglockner High Alpine Highway (107), an engineering achievement of the first magnitude. You can do it by bus or by private car. This is a toll road and it is normally open from about mid-May until mid-November, but unusually heavy later spring or early fall snows may block it. Whatever the season, it is advisable to inquire about conditions ahead before starting out. Fog is often encountered and can be dangerous. It is unwise to attempt to drive through during the night.

There is a mystery about the Grossglockner road. Before it was built, there had been no passage anywhere between Brenner Pass and Radstädter Tauern Pass (more than 160 km. (100 miles) apart) leading over these high mountains, nor was it on record that there had ever before been a regularly used route across the barrier at this point. Yet when the engineers who built the High Alpine Highway were blasting for the Hochtor tunnel, through which it passes at one point, they found, deep in the bowels of the mountain, a Roman statuette of, appropriately, Hercules.

From Bruck you plunge into the Fuscher valley leading south, and immediately find yourself confronted by the finest mountain scenery imaginable. You pass first through Dorf Fusch, and then by the Embach Chapel. At Ferleiten, where the toll house stands, the grade becomes steeper. You are really going up now. You pass the Schleier waterfall, and notice that the trees have disappeared. You are above the timberline.

You may pause, or the bus carrying you may do so, at the Piffalpe parking place, to enjoy the view across to the Grosses Wiesbachhorn, and again, perhaps, at the Hochmais parking place. (Parking on the road except at the spots provided is forbidden.)

About now you will notice that the grass has disappeared too. The only vegetation that can exist at this altitude is moss, which you will see here and there, sparsely punctuating the otherwise unrelieved gray of the rocks. At nearly 2,140 m. (7,000 ft.) you pass a gully that presents an awesome aspect of desolation. It is strewn with great boulders among which wisps of fog wreathe eerily and bears an appropriate name—the Witches' Kitchen. In the neighborhood is an old inn which has been here for 500 years, centuries before the Grossglockner road, or any passage at all through these seemingly impenetrable mountains, was ever contemplated.

There are a number of parking places and rest houses on the ascent. At the Edelweisspitze, 2,577 m. (8,455 ft.) up, you can sit on a terrace, sip a beer, and gaze out over an incredible view, which includes 37 peaks higher than 3,000 m. (10,000 ft.) and 19 glaciers. Later, when you go through a pair of tunnels, the Mitteltörl and the Hochtor, you leave the second one to enter Carinthia. (The Grossglockner, like the Dachstein, is a great pivot from which three Austrian federal states radiate—in this case, Land Salzburg, Carinthia and Tirol, whose borders meet here.)

At Tauerneck, the road sweeps around a curve and suddenly the Grossglockner bursts on your vision for the first time. The impact of the sight of this glittering snow-covered 3,797-m. (12,457-ft.) peak silhouetted against the sky is breathtaking. The road now turns westward, heading straight for the majestic peak, and stops at the dead end of the Franz Josefs Höhe, where you can have lunch and gaze at the distant black dots moving painfully over the face of Europe's oldest, biggest glacier, the Pasterzen (they are really mountain climbers and those fine lines across the ice face on which they are clambering are actually a series of deep and dangerous ice crevasses).

The Upper Pinzgau

Returning to Bruck and exploring some more of Pinzgau, many tourists turn north on the third and last of the road and railroad paths that leave the main route, to Zell am See, the chief resort of the Pinzgau. We shall enter that region later, as we follow that track back to the city of Salzburg, so we look first at the rest of the westward trail, the part of this region known as the Ober Pinzgau.

We will simply name briefly the chief points on the route—

Kaprun: A little south of the main highway, in the next of those north–south valleys, the Kaprunertal (railways stop at Fürth, from which you can enter the valley, though most excursionists to this point come from Zell am See). The reason for making this trip is to go through the gorge, past the ruins of an old castle, to the Kessel waterfall, dramatically lighted at night. The Kaprun Dam, built with Marshall Plan money, is an interesting sight. Kaprun is also a summer resort and an increasingly important winter sports center. A three-section aerial cable car takes you up over the glaciers to an elevation of 9,935 feet, almost at the top of Kitzsteinhorn; up here, you can ski all year round.

Stuhlfelden: there is a 17th-century castle here, and from it is reached Heilbad Burgwies with radioactive sulphur and iron baths.

Mittersill: summer and winter resort, on the main line. Mittersill was a great hunters' rendezvous between the wars and has again resumed this role. South of the town a mountain toll road rises up through the Felber and Amer valleys, revealing breathtaking mountain vistas, and penetrates the Hohe Tauern Range through a tunnel which comes on the other side in East Tirol. It was in this little town that in 1945 composer Anton von Webern was accidentally shot dead while lighting a cigar in the night on the terrace of his home.

Neukirchen am Grossvenediger: a much-frequented main-line summer resort, with guides for climbing the nearby Grossvenediger and Wildkogel peaks, and a winter sports center as well.

Wald im Pinzgau: has a late Gothic churchyard, the gravestones are made of rare minerals. This is the point from which you go to Ronach, for Krimml: here is the last spectacle of Land Salzburg's Far West, the Krimml waterfall, the highest in Europe, dropping 380 m. (1,250 ft.) in three stages. If it's sunny, the falls are at their best at noon; take a raincoat. In summer the waterfall is floodlit every Wednesday night if the weather is good. This is the end of the line, for if you cross the Gerlos Pass, you find yourself in Tirol; so we will return to Bruck and turn northward.

The Middle Pinzgau

Just north of Bruck, on Zeller Lake, is the most important resort of the Pinzgau, Zell am See. Its main season is July and August. It is almost as frequented, however, in the winter season, chiefly by skiers, who find this an excellent terrain.

Bathing is pleasant in Central Europe's cleanest lake, whose water in summer maintains an average temperature of 73 degrees; a theater, tennis courts, attractive promenades, and good shops cater for the many tourists. The chief architectural features of the town are the Renaissance Rosenberg Castle; the 1250 tower, originally a granary; and the Romanesque parish church, built about 1230.

Among the wealth of local excursions are short daily Alpine and longer Panorama Flights from the local airport, motor boat trips around the lake, or across it to Thumersbach, a popular health resort on the far side of the lake from the road and railroad, so that it is much quieter, and the

cable-railway ascent of the Schmittenhöhe plateau. Both are remarkable
for the views they afford. From the lake, the outlook to the mountains
in which it is set is delightful; from the plateau (where in winter there are
ski courses) there is a sweep which will impress upon you the geology of
Austria as no written description could ever do; for with your own eyes
you see the great hard-rock ranges of the Alps to the south and the quite
different lower limestone ranges to the north.

There are a larger number of bus trips to points of great scenic beauty
from Zell am See, some of which we have described already from other
points, like the Grossglockner, Kapruner valley and Krimml falls excursions.

Proceeding north from Zell am See (Route 311), through the Mittelpin-
zgau, at Maishofen the Glemm valley opens to the west. Halfway up the
valley is the famous skiing village of Saalbach and, at the valley's head,
Hinterglemm. These two important winter sports centers have combined
with Kaprun and Zell to form the Europe-Sport-Region. They offer a large
range of sports in all seasons at an equally varied range of prices.

Farther up 311, Saalfelden is first and foremost a summer resort, from
which mountaineers like to take off, but all around it is excellent skiing
country, so that in winter it is a central point from which practitioners
of this sport branch out to the nearby slopes.

Interesting sights in Saalfelden include the parish church, with a late
Gothic winged altar; the 14th-century Farmach Castle; and the Christmas
Crib Museum, located in the Ritzen Castle near the town. Off at the edge
of the Steinernes Meer (Sea of Stone) is a late Gothic chapel in a cave,
containing a winged altarpiece, near the stone pulpit and hermit's cell.

Steinernes Meer is a climber's Mecca, but it should only be crossed by
mountaineers of some experience. This is even truer of the Hochkönig,
which can be approached from this side, as well as from the eastern and
southern slopes, which we passed at the start of our circuit. Mountain
guides are available in Saalfelden. This is also a point from which excursions are made to the Königsee in that part of Bavaria that thrusts its arrowhead into Land Salzburg.

St. Martin bei Lofer is a point from which you may visit the Lam-
prechtsofenlochhöhle caves, with their great domes and waterfalls, the
Vorderkaserklamm gorge, and the Hirschbichl Pass, a strategic route that
was the scene of several battles during the Napoleonic Wars.

Lofer is a starting point for a number of interesting excursions, among
them the ascent of the Loferer Alpe, which can be made on foot in about
2½ hours, and from which there is a remarkable view. A pilgrimage museum, featuring votive tablets from the 17th through the 19th centuries is
in Maria Kirchental near Lofer.

From Lofer, the road (now 312) continues through Reit and the summer
resort of Unken, to the Bavarian border, at the western end of the narrow
neck of the arrowhead of Bavarian territory which thrusts into Austria.
You cross the 9 km. (5½ miles) of Germany and come out through Bad
Reichenhall, on the border just within Bavarian territory, and on the direct
road to the city of Salzburg, a few miles away.

PRACTICAL INFORMATION FOR
LAND SALZBURG

TOURIST INFORMATION. The main Tourist Offices are, of course, in Salzburg itself. Elsewhere in Land Salzburg there are offices in most of the smaller towns. Among those which you may find useful are the following—with their postal codes and phone numbers.

Abtenau A-5441 (0 62 43–22 93); Badgastein A-5640 (0 64 34–2 53 10); Bad Hofgastein A-5630 (0 64 32–64 81 16); Bischofshofen A-5500 (0 64 62–24 71); Bruck A-5671 (0 65 45–295); Filzmoos A-5532 (0 64 53–235); Fuschl A-5330 (0 62 26–250); Hallein A-5400 (0 62 45–28 82); Kaprun A-5710 (0 65 47–86 43); Kuchl A-5431 (0 62 44–62 27); Lofer A-5090 (0 65 88–321, 322).

Mauterndorf A-5570 (0 64 72–72 79); Mittersill A-5730 (0 65 62–369); Neukirchen A-5741 (0 65 65–6256); Obertauern A-5562 (0 64 56–252); Radstadt A-5550 (0 64 52–305).

Saalbach A-5753 (0 65 41–72 72); Saalfelden A-5760 (0 65 82–25 13); St. Gilgen A-5340 (0 62 27–348); St. Johann im Pongau A-5600 (0 64 12–465); Strobl A-5350 (0 61 37–255); Stuhlfelden A-5724 (0 65 62–49 0 94).

Tamsweg A-5580 (0 64 74–416); Wagrain A-5602 (0 64 13–82 65); Wald A-5742 (0 65 65–82 43); Werfen A-54 50 (0 64 68–388); Zell am See A-5700 (0 65 42–26 00).

AREA CODES—MAIL AND PHONE. You will find the postal code (preceded by an "A") and the telephone code (in brackets) after the name of each town in the following *Hotel and Restaurant* list.

HOTELS AND RESTAURANTS. Land Salzburg offers all types of accommodations, from the tops in luxury at Badgastein to the most modest countryside Gasthof and mountain lodge. Except for Badgastein, Bad Hofgastein, Zell am See and a few castle hotels, the accommodations are mostly moderate and low-priced, and in the country spots you often get more for your money than you do in the large cities and more fashionable places.

Abtenau A-5441 (0 62 43). Reached by bus from Golling in Salzach valley; on main road and rail line from Salzburg. *Moisl* (E), (22 32–0). Founded in 1764 as *Lipplwirt;* pleasant old house with indoor pool, and sauna. Good restaurant and cafe. Closed mid-Oct. to mid-Dec. AE, DC, MC. *Post* (M), (22 09). Old house; big, comfortable rooms up to modern standards, all with bath or shower. Closed April and Nov. DC. *Roter Ochs* (M), Markt 32 (22 59). 38 rooms, all with bath or shower; spacious with rustic decor. Large children's room. AE, DC, MC, V.
Campsite (26 98).

Adnet A-5024 (0 62 45). *Hubertushof* (M), (21 72). 40 rooms, all with shower. Wonderful view; pool and lawn. Good restaurant. Closed Nov. AE, MC.

Altenmarkt A-5541 (0 64 52). On Zauchensee, near Radstadt rail and bus stop. *Markterwirt* (M), (420). 900-year-old house with antique furniture; very friendly and family-run. 70 beds, all with bath or shower. Good fishing in lake. Notable restaurant and cafe. Closed 1–26 Nov. AE, DC, MC, V.
Campsites (533, 78 21).

Anif A-5081 (0 62 46). 6.5 km. (4 miles) from the center of Salzburg. *Friesacher* (M), Anif 57 (20 75). All rooms with bath or shower, rustic furniture; some apartments. Good *heurigen*-style restaurant, popular with locals. AE, DC. *Romantik Hotel Schlosswirt* (E), (21 75). 32 rooms, all with bath or shower and antique furniture. Fine old building; notable restaurant. Closed Feb. AE, DC, MC, V.

Badgastein A-5640 (0 64 34). There are more than 100 hotels, inns and pensions of all categories, many with thermal baths and restaurant. *Elisabethpark* (L), (2 55 10). 180 beds, all rooms with bath and period style furniture. Very good restaurant. MC. *Grand Hotel de l'Europe* (L), (3 70 10). One of Europe's great hotels, offering old-style luxury. Large rooms and even two-floor penthouses. Therapy center, indoor pool with thermal water. Magnificent casino in house. *Kaiserhof* (L), (25 44). Schönbrunn Yellow building in beautiful private garden. 114 beds, all with bath; therapy center. Good restaurant. AE, DC, MC, V.
Bellevue Parkhotel (E), (25 7 10). Just above center of town. 200 beds, all rooms with bath; therapy center, period-style furniture. Restaurant. Closed 15 Oct. to 15 Dec. DC, MC. *Grüner Baum* (E), Romantik Hotel, Kötschachtal (2 51 60). 95 rooms, all with bath or shower. Aristocratic clientele, but rustic atmosphere. Very good restaurant serving local and international specialties in comfortable rooms. Closed mid-Oct. to mid-Dec. and after Easter. AE, DC, MC, V. *Savoy* (E), Waggerlstr. 165 (25 88). 59 rooms, all with bath. Traditional old place with friendly atmosphere. Notable restaurant in dining area resembling elegant living rooms. Closed mid-Oct. to mid-Dec. AE, DC, MC, V.
Gerke (I), (23 78). Pension, 19 beds, most with shower. Closed Dec. to April. *Steinbacher* (I), (24 28). Pension, 12 rooms, all with shower. Closed Nov. *Stelzhammer* (I), (23 12). Pension, 16 rooms, all with shower and thermal water; solarium. Closed Nov.
Restaurant. *Vinothek in Villa Solitude* (3 70 16 08). Owned and run by star chef Jörg Wörther. A must for gourmets. AE, DC, MC.
Youth Hostel (20 80).
Campsite (27 90).

Bad Hofgastein A-5630 (0 64 32). 15 minutes' bus ride from Badgastein, also a fast train stop.
Palace Gastein (L), Alexander Moserallee 13 (67 15). 196 rooms, all with bath; indoor pool, bar and good restaurant *Amadeus* (67 15–0). Closed Nov. AE, DC, MC, V.
Alpina (E) (62 08–0). 95 rooms, all with shower; indoor pool, sauna, solarium and restaurant. Facilities for the disabled. Closed Nov. *Carinthia* (E), Dr-Zimmermanstr. (83 7 40). 39 rooms, all with shower; indoor pool, sauna, solarium and tennis; restaurant. Closed April and Nov. AE, DC, MC, V. *Grand-Parkhotel* (E), Kurgartenstr. 26 (63 5 60). 86 rooms, all with bath. Central, with indoor pool, sauna, solarium and good restaurant. AE, DC.

Moser (E) (62 09). 53 rooms, all with bath or shower; restaurant. Closed April and Oct. to Nov. *Norica* (E), Rudolf Bachbauergasse (83 91). 80 rooms, all with bath or shower. Indoor pool and sauna. Closed Nov. AE, DC, MC, V.
Kärnten (M), (67 11–0). 100 beds, most with bath or shower. Indoor pool, sauna and tennis. Excellent restaurant. *Kärntnerstuben,* AE, DC, MC, V. *Volserhof* (M), (82 88). 26 rooms, all with shower. Bar and restaurant.
Alpen-Appartment-Hof (I), (82 34). 23 rooms, all with shower. Campsite (67 01). Closed Nov.

Bergheim A-5101 (0 62 22). *Gmachl* (M), Bergheim 12 (52 1 24). 40 rooms, all with bath or shower, rustic furniture. Indoor pool, sauna, lawn and table tennis, playground for children. Very good restaurant, popular for parties. AE, MC, V.

Filzmoos A-5532 (0 64 53). Reached by bus from the railway station at Eben im Pongau, 14 km. (9 miles) away.
Silencehotel Unterhof (E), (225). 37 rooms, all with bath or shower. Swimming pool, sauna, comfortable rooms and excellent food. Closed Nov. AE, DC, MC, V.
Sporthotel Filzmooserhof (E), Neuberg 85 (232). 25 rooms, all with bath or shower. Indoor pool, mini-golf course, tennis, skating in winter; chair lifts and T-bars close by. Very good restaurant with local specialties. Closed Nov. AE, DC, MC, V.
Hanneshof (M), Filzmoos 126 (276). 45 rooms, all with bath; apartments. Fitness room, riding. Good restaurant. Closed Nov. AE, DC, MC, V.
Alpenkrone (I), (280). 51 rooms, all with bath or shower; sauna, solarium and fitness room. Closed Nov. AE, DC, MC, V.

Flachau A-5542 (0 64 57). *Alpenhof* (E), (205). 28 rooms, all with bath or shower. Typical family hotel with pleasant party rooms and big indoor pool. Reputable restaurant. Closed Nov. AE. *Tauernhof* (E), (31 10). 66 rooms, all with bath, rustic decor; apartments. Pleasant restaurant and wine tavern. Closed Nov. AE, DC, MC, V.

Fuschl Am See A-5330 (0 62 26). *Parkhotel Waldhof* (E), (342). One of the Silencehotel group. 70 rooms, all with bath or shower. Pleasant, close to the lake with own beach. Good restaurant. Indoor pool. Closed 15 Feb. to 15 March. AE.
Restaurant. *Brunnwirt* (E), (236). One of the best in the Salzkammergut region. Lovely 15th-century building. Closed 1–25 Dec. AE, DC, MC, V.

Goldegg Am See A-5622 (0 64 15). *Post* (E), (81 03). 40 rooms, all with bath or shower; wooden ceilings and lobby with open fire-place. Notable restaurant with shady terrace and very attentive service. AE, DC, MC, V.
Bierführer (M), (81 02). 20 rooms; noted restaurant. Closed 15 Nov. to 10 Dec. DC, MC, V.

Hallein A-5400 (0 62 45). *Brückenwirt* (M), (20 94). 21 rooms, most with shower or bath; garage.
Restaurant. *Hohlwegwirt,* Salzburg Bundesstr. 62 (2415). On road between Anif and Hallein. Locally inspired cooking with imagination. Good salads and regional wines.

Hof Bei Salzburg A-53 22 (0 62 29). *Schloss Fuschl* (L), (2553-0). Former hunting castle of the Prince Bishops of Salzburg, set beside a romantic lake. Haunt of the jet-set in festival time. 84 rooms, all with bath, furnished with antique pieces. Beach, sauna, tennis, 9-hole golf course. Good food in elegant and atmospheric restaurant. AE, DC, MC, V.

Kaprun A-5710 (0 65 47). *Barbarahof* (M), (82 35). 29 rooms, all with shower; indoor pool, sauna, solarium; restaurant. *Sporthotel Kaprun* (M), (86 25). 59 rooms, all with bath or shower; sauna, solarium. AE, DC.
Pension Berg Heil (I), (83 39). 15 rooms, all with shower; sauna and solarium.
Youth Hostel (85 07).
Campsite (85 24).
Restaurant. *Zirbenstüberl* (85 04). In Hotel Hubertus. Ambitious treatment of local produce. Closed Mon. AE, DC, MC, V.

Kleinarl A-5602 (0 64 18). *Appartementhaus Alpina* (M), (272). 30 beds, all with shower; indoor pool, sauna, tennis; restaurant for guests only. Closed May, Oct. and Nov.
Restaurant. *Dorfkrug* (E), (374). Run with love and expertise. Try the locally-made goat's cheese. AE, DC, MC, V.

Leogang A-5771 (0 65 83). *Krallerhof* (M), (246). 40 rooms, all with bath. Attractive lounges, big indoor pool, outdoor pool, sauna; bar and good restaurant. Closed Nov. AE, DC.

Lofer A-5090 (0 65 88). Bus from Saalfelden (26 km., 16 miles) and Salzburg (51 km., 32 miles—via Bad Reichenhall in Germany). *Bräu* (E), Lofer 28 (20 70). 28 rooms, all with bath. Beautiful 16th-century building; cozy *stuben*-style restaurant with excellent regional cooking. AE, DC, MC, V. *Post* (M), Lofer 53 (30 30). 44 rooms, most with bath or shower. AE, DC, MC, V.

Maria Alm A-5761 (0 65 84). Bus from Saalfelden. *Norica* (E), Maria Alm 86 (74 91). 83 rooms, all with bath. Indoor pool, bowling, children's playroom. Restaurant. AE, DC, MC, V. *Wachtelhof* (E), Hinterthal (82 88). 50 beds; comfortable hotel with startlingly good restaurant. AE, DC, MC, V.
Café Pension Schafhuber (M), Hinterthal (81 47). Country-style, but modern; 25 beds, all rooms with shower, pleasant. Restaurant specializing in all kinds of delicious *strudels*.
Eder (M), (77 38). 63 beds, all with bath. New, Salzburg-style with big hall for *Bauerntheater* (peasant theater) which is quite funny even if you don't understand a word. Pleasant restaurant. Closed Nov.

Mauterndorf A-5570 (0 64 72). Bus from Radstadt or Unzmarkt in Styria. *Elisabeth* (E), (73 65). 43 rooms, all with shower. Indoor pool, sauna, solarium; restaurant.
Post (M), Mauterndorf 183 (73 16). 15 rooms, all with bath or shower. Courtyard garden. Closed Nov. MC, V.
Restaurant. *Mesnerhaus* (E), (7595). New gourmet restaurant for fine foods and some of the best wines in the region. Closed Mon. AE.
Campsite (74 26).

Mittersill A-5730 (0 65 62). *Sporthotel Kogler* (E), (46 1 50). 56 rooms, all with bath or shower. Indoor pool, sauna, solarium, playroom for children. MC.

Obertauern A-5562 (0 64 56). Bus service from Radstadt and Mauterndorf, both about 22 km. (14 miles) away. *Edelweiss* (E), Obertauern 124 (245). 72 rooms, all with bath or shower; modern, Alpine-style with indoor pool, sauna, solarium. Open Dec. to April. AE, DC, MC, V.
   Berghotel Pohl (M), (209). 17 rooms, all with bath or shower. Austrian specialties in restaurant. Closed May to June and Oct. to Nov. DC. *Kärntnerland* (M), (271). 15 rooms, all with bath or shower. Club atmosphere; library. Breakfast only. Closed May to June and Sept. to Oct. AE. *Kristall* (M), (323). 23 rooms, all with shower, some with four posters, balconies. Family-run. Closed May to June and Sept. to Nov.

Obertrum Am See A-5162 (0 62 19). *Bräugasthof Sigl* (I), Dorfplatz 1 (212). 25 rooms, all with bath or shower. Traditional atmosphere—run by one family since 1775. Rustic, antique furnishings. Well-known restaurant, famous local beer. DC, MC, V. *Neumayr* (I), Dorfplatz 8 (302). 30 rooms, some with bath. Restaurant known for local fish dishes, particularly trout, served in wood paneled *stuben*. AE, DC, MC, V. Closed Tues.
   Campsites (442; 263; 435).

Radstadt A-5550 (0 64 52). *Sporthotel Stegerbrau* (E), (590). 27 rooms, all with shower; elegant. Own fishing in lake and Enns River. Trophy-decorated restaurant serving delicious trout. Closed Oct. and after Easter. Campsite (78 61).

Rauris A-5661 (0 65 44). *Rauriserhof* (E), (213). 72 rooms, all with bath or shower, balconies. Pleasant and friendly atmosphere; tennis, pool. Good restaurant serving local and international dishes. Closed Nov.

Saalbach A-5753 (0 65 41). Bus service from Zell am See. *Alpenhotel Thomas* (E), (66 60). 180 beds, all with bath or shower. One of the biggest in the village; rooms spacious with alpine-style furniture; some apartments. Lots of entertainment and above par restaurant. *Kuhstall* (stable) bar. AE, DC, MC, V. *Glemmtalerhof* (E), Hinterglemm 150 (71 35). 150 beds, all with bath or shower, alpine-style, very comfortable and mostly with balcony. Large lobby and lounges; cafe, bar and night-club. AE, DC, MC, V. *Hinterhag* (E), (29 10). 50 beds, all with bath, beautifully furnished, many with four-posters. Paintings by the talented hostess; remarkable restaurant featuring hand-decorated plates and superb modern cooking. *Ingonda* (E), (26 20). 46 rooms, all with bath; sauna, solarium, tennis. Good restaurant. Closed Nov. AE, DC, MC, V. *Saalbacherhof* (E), (71 11). 170 beds, most with bath or shower. Sauna and tennis; restaurant. AE, DC.

Saalfelden A-5760 (0 65 82). Fast train stop on Salzburg to Innsbruck line. *Brandlhof* (E), Hohlwegen 4 (2 17 60). 150 rooms, all with shower or bath. Indoor and outdoor pool, tennis, riding hall, golf course, squash. Restaurant. AE, DC, MC, V.
   Campsite (26 60).
   Restaurant. *Schatzbichl* (E), Ramseiden 82 (32 81). Famous; specializing in unusual local dishes. Friendly. Rooms available. AE, DC, MC, V.

St. Gilgen Am Wolfgangsee A-5340 (0 62 27). Reached from Salzburg by bus or car, about 48 km. (30 miles); the road is kept in good condition in winter. *Billroth* (E), (217). Beautiful setting in huge park beside lake; elegant villa with sun terraces. 44 rooms, all with bath or shower. Restaurant. Closed Nov. to April. AE, V.
Post (M), (239). 90 beds, some with bath, some with shower. Dates back to 1415; very friendly. Good restaurant.
Youth Hostel (365).
Campsites (72 05; 72 28; 72 08; 0 61 38–25 95; 0 61 38–24 68).

St. Johann Im Pongau A-5600 (0 64 12). Fast train stop. *Sporthotel Alpenland* (E), (70 2 10). New hotel with every comfort and facility. Rustic restaurant. AE, DC, MC, V. *Prem* (M), (63 15–0). 18 beds, all with bath or shower; playroom for children; squash, indoor tennis. *Silbergasser* (I), (421). 22 rooms, all with bath or shower; sauna, solarium. Closed April and Nov.
Youth Hostel (62 22).
Campsites (60 12; 519).

Strobl A-5350 (0 61 37). *Kurhotel Schloss Strobl* (E), (310). 79 rooms, all with bath or shower; indoor pool, sauna, solarium, therapy center. Open March to Nov. AE. *Parkhotel Seethurn* (E), (202). 84 rooms, all with bath; indoor pool, sauna, solarium, tennis. Closed Nov. AE, DC.
Campsite (0 61 38–24 71).

Wagrain A-5602 (0 64 13). Bus service from St Johann im Pongau (13 km., 8 miles) and Radstadt (48 km., 30 miles). *Alpenhof Edelweiss* (M), (84 47). 15 rooms, all with bath or shower; indoor pool, sauna. Closed Oct. to Nov. *Alpina* (M), (83 37). 15 rooms, all with bath or shower; indoor pool, sauna; restaurant. Closed Nov. DC. *Enzian* (M) (85 02). 30 rooms, all with bath or shower; sauna. Restaurant. Closed Nov. AE, MC. *Grafenwirt* (M), (82 30). 17 rooms, all with bath or shower. Restaurant for huntsmen. Closed Oct. to Nov. AE, DC, MC, V.

Wald Im Pinzgau A-5742 (0 65 65). *Graf Recke* (E), (64 17). Romantik Hotel. Family run, very good food, personal attention. Sporting facilities. Closed Oct., Nov. and April. DC, V. *Kammerlander* (M), (62 31). 40 rooms, all with bath or shower. Closed Nov.

Werfen A-5450 (0 64 68). *Lebzelter* (M) (212). 5 rooms, outstanding restaurant (E)—one of the finest in the Salzburg area. Excellent wines. Closed Mon. Run by the Obauer family. AE.

Zell Am See A-5700 (0 65 42). *Grand* (L), (23 88–0). Large hotel newly built on lakeside. Swimming pool, rooftop bar, disco, terrace, every facility. 3 restaurants. Gourmet restaurant, *Hintertasche*. A superb addition to the resort. AE, DC, MC, V. *Salzburgerhof* (L), Aurspergstrasse 11 (28 28). 58 rooms, all with bath or shower. Indoor pool, sauna; quality food. Closed Dec. AE, DC, MC, V. *Erlhof* (E), Thumersbach (31 73). 20 rooms, all with bath. Typical old Salzburg estate with fine vaulted ceilings. Own beach, riding, tennis. Notable restaurant. Closed May and Nov. AE, DC, MC, V. *Katharina* (E), Kirchenweg 11 (73 10). 60 rooms, all with bath or shower; beautiful wooden ceilings and twin-bedded rooms which can be changed to living areas. Closed Nov. AE. *St Georg* (E), Schillerstrasse 10 (35 33). 37 rooms, all with bath. A bit above the lake, rustic decor; pool, sun terrace and bar; good restaurant. Closed May and Nov. AE, DC, MC, v. *Zum Hirschen* (E), (24 47). 45 rooms, all with bath. In center of town, but with sound proofed windows. Comfortable, with rustic furniture. Superb restaurant in beautifully paneled dining rooms. Closed Nov. DC.

Sporthotel Lebzelter (M), (24 11 0). 50 rooms, next to the old tower. Good food and local color in the *Felsenkeller.* DC.

Youth Hostel located on the lake.

Campsites (21 15; 62 28).

GETTING AROUND LAND SALZBURG. By Air. Salzburg airport is relatively small, but modern, and is open to international jet traffic, including regular flights (Austrian Airlines and British Airways) from London. Zell am See airport and a small airfield near Badgastein have been adapted for small aircraft traffic. Air taxis can be taken from Salzburg to these airports and round sightseeing flights can be made from all of them.

By Train. Land Salzburg is the meeting point of three main rail lines, all of them also international train routes. On the main line from Switzerland, Germany, and Innsbruck to Vienna, the fast train stops in this province are Zell am See, Schwarzach-St. Veit, Bischofshofen, and Salzburg; the medium fast trains stop also at Saalfelden, Bruck-Fusch, Taxenbach-Rauris, St. Johann im Pongau, Werfen (occasionally), Golling-Abtenau, and Hallein. A medium fast train takes about 2¼ hours from Salzburg to Saalfelden (several daily trains).

At Schwarzach-St. Veit the main line for Carinthia and Italy branches off with fast train stops at Bad Hofgastein and Badgastein. The fast train ride from Salzburg takes about 2 hours and several daily trains are available in both directions.

The third main line parts for Styria at Bischofshofen with the fast train stop at Radstadt and sometimes also in Eben in Pongau. A direct fast train covers the Salzburg-Radstadt section in about an hour (several daily services).

A local, narrow-gauge railroad connects Zell am See with the Upper Pinzgau as far as Krimml, making the trip in 2 to 2½ hours; six daily trains in both directions.

Steam locomotive fans can enjoy the summer schedules of the narrow-gauge lines running between Mauterndorf and Murau (Styria), and St. Georgen and Voecklamarkt north of Salzburg.

By Bus. In summer there is a direct bus Salzburg-Grossglockner. The Salzkammergut lake area is reached from Salzburg by postal buses or special excursion buses.

Tamsweg and the rest of the Lungau district, as well as Lofer on the other side of the province, can only be reached from Salzburg and Radstadt by road; a regular bus service covers these routes.

By Car. For the motorist, Land Salzburg offers many dramatic and dazzling roads, especially in the mountains, as well as many fast and modern autobahns. All the routes described below use Salzburg as their starting point.

To reach the Grossglockner and the southern areas of the province, there are two principal routes. The first is the more scenic and meandering, whilst the second is much more direct. Both, however, end in the magnificent climb up the Edelweisspitze. The first route leaves Salzburg heading southwest and cuts across the narrow strip of Germany at Bad Reichen-hall, re-entering Salzburg at Unken. From here it continues south through the whole of the province, via Saalfelden and Bruck and on to the Gross-glockner toll road. This then climbs to the Edelweisspitze and into Carin-thia through the Hochtor tunnel, which, at 2,505 m. (8,218 ft.) marks the highest point of the road and is on the Salzburg–Carinthia border. The second route takes the Tauern autobahn south from Salzburg and contin-ues past Bischofshofen and runs on to Bruck. From here the two routes merge.

To reach the eastern parts of the province, the most direct route is to drive to Bruck on the Tauern autobahn and then take the 311, from where this all-weather road continues east to Mittersill—where you can either turn north or south to reach the Tirol and the East Tirol respectively—and Neukirchen am Grossvenediger and finally to the Gerloss pass on the Salz-burg-Tirol border. The final part of this road is spectacular, reaching 1,630 m. (5,350 ft.).

The southeastern part of the province is reached again by the Tauern autobahn to Bischofshofen. Turning right here on 308, the road continues to Radstadt—and into Styria—and from there climbs dramatically up the Radstädter–Tauern pass to Tamsweg in the extreme southeast of Salzburg.

The Salzkammergut lake area, due east and north of the capital, is reached by the 24 km of the A1 autobahn. This then continues into Upper Austria.

PLACES OF INTEREST. Apart from its share of castles and monaste-ries, Land Salzburg has some exciting natural features to visit—especially spectacular waterfalls. All the places mentioned in the following list are given with route indications starting from Salzburg. Many of the museums have admission fees. Please ascertain the opening times locally—they are liable to sudden change.

Goldegg. A10 to Bischofshofen, 311 to Schwarzach, small local road to Goldegg. 16th-century **castle** with older sections, early Renaissance Knights' Hall. **Pongau Folklore Museum** in the castle. Tours May through Sept., every Thurs. and Sun. Also Tues. July and Aug. Oct. through April, Thurs.

Golling. 24 km. south of Salzburg on autobahn. Waterfall, restored har-bor on river; dramatic Lueg Pass.

Grossgmain. Salzburger Openair Museum. All sorts of buildings and houses from the 16th to the 19th centuries re-erected on this site. Open daily 9–5, except Mon.

Hallein. Route 341 to Anif, 159 to Hallein. **Celtic Museum** in old salt-mine offices. May through Oct. Look for grave of *Holy Night* composer in churchyard.

Bad Dürrnberg. Route 159 to Anif, 159 to Hallein. Pilgrimage church with magnificent 1750 altar. **Openair Celtic museum** (Keltendorf). Salt mines, tours May to Oct., 8–5. Entrance fee. Not possible for small chil-dren and disabled visitors.

Krimmler Wasserfälle (Krimml Waterfalls). A10 to Bischofshofen, 311 to Zell am See, 168 to Mittersill, then 165 to the falls. There's a bus service from Zell am Ziller. 900 ft. of falls in three tiers.

Lofer. Interesting trail along the banks of the Saalach. See the **Holztrift installations** which form part of a now extinct system for transporting felled timber. **Bauerntheater,** nightly performances of local farces by passionate amateur villagers. You won't understand, but the experience is unique.

Maria Kirchental (St. Martin near Lofer). A1 and E17 to Lofer, small toll road to Maria Kirchental. 1701 Baroque **Pilgrimage Church** with collection of votive tablets. Open all day.

Mattsee. North via Elixhausen. **Abbey Church** (Gothic, Baroqued) richly decorated, interesting tombstones in the cloisters. **Castle** has a museum with local displays, plus carriages. **Monastery museum,** religious and local material. June through Sept. 4–6 P.M.

Radstadt. A10 to Knoten Ennstal, then Route 146. **Castle Lerchen** has a **Folk Museum** with historical displays, sacred art and folklore.

Saalfelden. **Ritzen Castle** with **Pinzgau Museum;** Christmas cribs, local furniture and church art.

St. Johann Im Pongau. Liechtenstein Gorge. A10 to Bischofshofen, then 311. Rail, too, from Salzburg. Extremely popular gorge, 3 miles from St. Johann. Open May through Oct, tour takes about 45 minutes.

Tamsweg. A10 to Ennstal, 99 to Mauterndorf, 95 to Tamsweg. **St. Leonhard Pilgrimage Church,** magnificent Gothic glass; carvings and Baroquery. **Lungauer Folklore Museum** in the former Barbara Hospital; furniture, pictures, weapons. May through Oct.; closed Mon. Tours every hour.

Taxenbach. Kitzlochlamm (waterfalls in gorge). A10 to Bischofshofen, then 311. Also reachable by train from Salzburg. Tour visits (45 minutes) May through Oct. 10–12, 2–5 P.M.

Werfen. A10 south. **Hohenwerfen Castle,** 11th century. Open to vistors in the season. Nearby are the **Eisriesenwelt,** the Giant Ice Caves, the world's largest (just after the Lueg Pass). Open May to Oct.

CASINO. The Badgastein Casino is open daily from 5 P.M. in both the summer and winter seasons—that is from June to Sept., and from Christmas to the middle of March. Roulette, black jack and baccara available.

WINTER SPORTS. Almost all of Land Salzburg is excellent skiing country. The season usually begins in the second half of December or the first half of January and lasts until mid-March, in the high spots until May. On some very high elevations such as Kitzsteinhorn (above Kaprun and Weiss See), reached by cable cars and glacier lifts, and in the new Sport Gastein area above Badgastein (reached by toll road), there is skiing all

year round. Budget skiers should investigate the up-and-coming ski possibilities of Abtenau, Altenmarkt, Radstadt, Filzmoos, Flachau and Maria
Alm. Enquire, too, about the *Golden Ski Card* offering full use of 233 lifts
throughout the province at a special price.

Tennengau and Salzburg Salzkammergut. Attractive skiing area,
with easy intermediate slopes and a relaxed atmosphere. Alpine and Nordic skiing by the Wolfgansee, and on both the Zwölferhorn and the Pos-
talm.

Resorts: Abtenau (712 m., 2,336 ft.); Annaberg (777 m., 2,549 ft.); Bad
Durnberg (800 m., 2,625 ft.); Faistenau (786 m., 2,579 ft.); Hintersee (746
m., 2,448 ft.); Krispl-Gaissau (927 m., 3,041 ft.); Kuchl (469 m., 1,539
ft.); Lungötz (850 m., 2,789 ft.); Russbach (817 m., 2,680 ft.); St. Gilgen
(546 m., 1,791 ft.); St. Martin am Tennengebirge (1,000 m., 3,281 ft.);
Strobl (543 m., 1,782 ft.).

Facilities: The area has 15 indoor swimming pools, 2 cable cars, 5 chair
lifts, 62 T-bars and 206 km. (128 miles) of cross-country trails and floodlit
Bob-run.

From the Hochkönig to the Tennengebirge. A long series of skiing
villages which stretches all the way from the Mühlbach area near the
Höchkonig to the base of the Tennengebirge, close to the Tauern motorway, and so easily accessible. Not a smart skiing area, but friendly, with
plenty of variety for expert and tyro alike.

Resorts: Bischofshofen (547 m., 1,795 ft.); Dienten (1,071 m., 3,514 ft.);
Mühlbach am Hochkönig (853 m., 2,799 ft.); Pfarrwerfen (538 m., 1,761
ft.); Werfen (620 m., 1,934 ft.); Werfenweng (1,000 m., 3,281 ft.).

Facilities: the area has 9 indoor swimming pools, 5 chair lifts, 34 T-bars
and 72 km. (45 miles) of cross-crountry tracks.

Pinzgauer Saalachtal. A superb area for scenery, with high peaks,
lovely valleys and fine ski slopes. The Saalbach-Hinterglemm resort is one
of Austria's largest ski regions, with both excellent equipment and an elegant après-ski potential.

Resorts: Leogang (800 m., 2,622 ft.); Lofer (640 m., 2,200 ft.); Maishofen (765 m., 2,510 ft.); Maria Alm (802 m., 2,631 ft.); Saalbach-
Hinterglemm (1,003 m., 3,291 ft.); Saalfelden (744 m., 2,441 ft.); Unken
(564 m., 1,850 ft.); Viehofen (859 m., 2,818 ft.).

Facilities: the area has 22 indoor swimming pools, 1 cable car, 20 chair
lifts, 88 T-bars and 195 km. (121 miles) of cross-country trails.

Europa Sports Region, Upper Pinzgau. This is an up-and-coming
area with a lot of variety for choice of slope. There is a recent area, the
Weiss-See, with a fine Alpine Center at 2,130 m. (7,000 ft.). For the all-the-
year skiers, the Kitzsteinhorn is going in the summer.

Resorts: Bruck a. d. Grossglocknerstrasse (758 m., 2,487 ft.); Fusch a.
d. Grossglocknerstrasse (805 m., 2,641 ft.); Kaprun (800 m., 2,625 ft.);
Königsleiten (1,600 m., 5,250 ft.); Mittersill (789 m., 2,589 ft.); Neukirchen am Grossvenediger (856 m., 2,808 ft.); Uttendorf/Weiss-See (807 m.,
2,648 ft.); Wald in Pinzgau (884 m., 2,900 ft.); Zell am See (758 m., 2,487
ft.).

Facilities: the area has 20 indoor swimming pools, 10 cable cars, 15
chair lifts, 71 T-bars and 113 km. (70 miles) of cross country trails.

Grossarltal, Gasteinertal And Raurisertal. While the Grossarltal is better known as a spa region, it has the added attraction of being excellently placed between the other two areas which offer great skiing. The combination of sophisticated spa life and fine winter sports opportunities make this a region to look at.

Resorts: Badgastein (1,083 m., 3,553 ft.); Bad Hofgastein (870 m., 2,854 ft.); Dorfgastein (835 m., 2,740 ft.); Grossarl (920 m., 3,018 ft.); Hüttschlag (1,020 m., 3,347 ft.); Rauris (950 m., 3,117 ft.).

Facilities: the area has 28 indoor swimming pools (several of them thermal), 4 cable cars, 17 chair lifts, 53 T-bars and 136 km. (85 miles) of cross-country trails.

Radstädter Tauern Region. Obertauern, in the depths of the region, at 1,820 m. (6,000 ft.), is a famous skiing center. The whole area is about the tops for the province.

Resorts: Altenmarkt-Zauchensee (850 m., 2,789 ft.); Eben im Pomgau (855 m., 2,805 ft.); Filzmoos (1,057 m., 3,468 ft.); Flachau (925 m., 3,045 ft.); Goldegg (825 m., 2,707 ft.); Kleinarl (1,014 m., 3,327 ft.); Obertauern (1,740 m., 5,709 ft.); Radstadt (856 m., 2,808 ft.); St. Johann im Pongau (567 m., 1,857 ft.); Wagrain (900 m., 2,953 ft.).

Facilities: the area has 32 indoor swimming pools, 2 cable cars, 28 chair lifts (with 6 twin-sided lift systems for valley-to-valley connections), 110 T-bars and 195 km. (121 miles) of cross-country trails.

Lungau. Tucked into the join of Carinthia and Styria, this is an increasingly popular skiing region, with the attractions of Mautendorf-St. Michael's twin-sided lift system and several other opportunities for excellent slopes. All the resorts are well over 1,000 m. mark.

Resorts: Mariapfarr (1,120 m., 3,675 ft.); Mauterndorf (1,122 m., 3,681 ft.); Obertauern/Tweng (1,740 m., 5,709 ft.); St. Margarethen (1,064 m., 3,491 ft.); St. Michael (1,075 m., 3,527 ft.); Tamsweg (1,024 m., 3,360 ft.).

Facilities: the area has 18 swimming pools, 1 cable car, 7 chair lifts and 98 km. (61 miles) of cross country trails.

UPPER AUSTRIA

The Realm of Salt

The Federal State of Upper Austria (Bundesland Oberösterreich) lies in the north-central section of Austria. To the east, it borders on Lower Austria, its historic twin; to the south, there are two other Austrian federal states, Styria and Land Salzburg. Its western border with Bavaria is defined mostly by the river line Salzach–Inn–Danube and it is at the same time the frontier between Austria and Germany; to the north is Czechoslovakia.

The Danube flows through Upper Austria from the Bavarian city of Passau in the west, almost as far east as the Nibelungengau in Lower Austria, passing by Linz, the capital. Beyond the confluence of the Enns River with the Danube, however, the right bank of the Danube is already in Lower Austria while the left bank still remains in Upper Austria.

Mühlviertel is the hilly and forested country north of the Danube and it stretches as far as the Bohemian Forest (Böhmerwald), the range of wooded mountains at the triple border between Austria, Germany and Czechoslovakia. The rich, undulating agricultural land to the southwest of the Danube is called Innviertel because it slopes mostly towards the Inn Valley. But most of the scenic beauty in Upper Austria is displayed in its southern part—the Salzkammergut lake region and the adjoining, mountainous, Pyhrn District.

Vacationists flock to Salzkammergut because its lakes, streams, valleys, meadows and woods provide a perfect summer playground and the mountains attract skiiers in the winter. Not only is this an area of largely unspoiled landscapes, but it is also the realm of salt, of saltmines whose presence has shaped the country in many ways. Today, when this commodity is one of the commonest and cheapest that we buy, we are inclined to forget its importance in not-very-distant history. It was ordinarily a government monopoly, and the tax on salt was considered everywhere one of the most irksome of all, for it was applied to a basic necessity, almost as if air were taxed.

In Austria, too, salt was a government monopoly, and the Salzkammergut (Estate of the Salt Chamber) region was banned to visitors in order to prevent untaxed salt from being smuggled out. The peasants stayed locked in the valleys, citizens from other regions were, for the most part, locked out. This situation lasted until the early 19th century. The region was finally opened up because Emperor Franz Josef, in his youth, had discovered its attractions. He established his summer residence at Bad Ischl. The aristocracy flocked into the Salzkammergut and its salt-inspired isolation was ended.

Exploring Upper Austria

The Salzkammergut, which is the most frequented region of Upper Austria, lies northeast of Salzburg, and much closer to that city than to Linz. We shall therefore begin our round trip through Upper Austria by heading out from Salzburg on the autobahn, or by local bus, through pleasant rolling country to Mondsee, the largest town on the third largest of the Salzkammergut lakes. We are now in Upper Austria and enter the heart of the lake country, with the Zellersee, a small little-visited lake just to the north; the Wolfgangsee which we shall inspect on the return trip, to the south; the Attersee to the east; and the Mondsee—for the lake and the town bear the same name—confronting us.

Mondsee means Moon Lake. The name was given it by the Romans, who were impressed by the beauty of this eight-km. (five-mile) long, one-and-a-half-km. (one-mile) wide, body of water, reflecting in its placid depths the double-toothed mountain rising above it. The water is warmer than in any other of these high-lying lakes, making it a good place for swimming.

The town of Mondsee takes pride in pointing out that its parish church, built in 1470, is the largest in Upper Austria. The claim is a trifle spurious, since it was not originally constructed as a parish church, but for the more pretentious role of the abbey church of the Benedictine monastery established here in the eighth century and closed, like so many others, by the reforming zeal of Emperor Josef II. Another part of the abbey became the Schloss Mondsee, a castle that has come down in the world. Once owned by the German royal family, it became an American summer school, an epoch in its history that was ended by the war. It contains some exceptionally fine examples of Baroque art.

The Wolfgangsee, or Abersee, just south of the Mondsee, is visited most frequently from Salzburg; for the sake of following a consecutive route, we shall keep to the Linz road through the northern lakes and inspect this one as we swing back through the southern part of this region. If you approach this lake from Salzburg, therefore, simply follow in reverse the directions given at the end of this section.

With the next place of importance on the Linz road, Unterach, we come to the largest of the lakes, the Attersee, precisely twice the size of the Mondsee (16 km. kilometers by three, 10 miles by two). A boat trip is particularly interesting, for traffic on the Attersee is interesting—not only pleasure craft, but the working boats of the fishermen, the gravel boats carrying the product of the pits in the mountains, and the rafts peculiar to the lake, which may be loaded with almost anything.

Most settlements on Attersee are now summer residential areas; the railroad terminal is at Schörfling-Kammer at the north head of the lake, where trains connect with the boats making the lake circuit. The town of Attersee on the west shore is the seat of a sailing club, but the main attraction is the lake, favored especially by fishermen—the water is very clear and very cold, teeming with, besides *saibling* (char), lake trout and pickerel, and the neighboring streams with brook trout.

The Traunsee

The Höllengebirge is back at the southern end of the lake, where we started, but we had better return to that region in order to reach the Traunsee. If you actually follow this route on the ground, you can start at Weissenbach and take the good secondary road to Mitterweissenbach on the Traun River, the most important water course in the Salzkammergut. Turn left, follow along the stream, and you presently reach the Traunsee at Ebensee, where you can begin to ascend the Höllen range from its eastern end, as a cable railway starts here for the Feuerkogel, from which there is a magnificent view over the Totes Gebirge—the Dead Range (i.e. no vegetation)—to the nearly 10,000-foot-high Dachstein, at the point where the borders of Land Salzburg, Upper Austria, and Styria meet. Feuerkogel is mainly a winter sports center; although not so well known as many other skiing centers in Austria, it is well rated by the experts.

Traunsee is the second largest of the Salzkammergut lakes—about 11 km. long (7 miles) and one-and-a-half km. (one mile) wide—and it also has a steamer service during the summer. Moving up the lake, south to north, the following places are of interest: Traunkirchen (west shore); the famous Fishermen's Pulpit in the parish church; a pleasant walk to the old church on the top of a former small island off the shore, now joined by land. The view at sunset from the Kalvarienberg is worth the climb.

Altmünster (west shore) is the oldest settlement on the Traunsee, whose parish church dates from the 16th century. It seems to have had a particular attraction for musicians; many have lived here at one time or another, the most notable having been Brahms and Wagner—the latter composed *Tristan und Isolde* in Otto Wesendonk's villa here until his interest in Otto Wesendonk's wife deprived him of those lodgings.

Gmunden (north shore, foot of the lake) is the biggest place in the region, one much visited, and deserving of special attention. Gmunden is both an old town (important in Roman times because of the salt trade, and still the terminal port for the barges bringing salt from the mines of the Aussee, Bad Ischl, Hallstatt, and Ebensee down the Traun River and across the Traunsee) and a modern watering place. From its older days, it retains a few Gothic dwellings, a Gothic church, and several castles spread over the vicinity, of which the most famous is a double castle—a Landschloss on the shore, a Seeschloss connected to the other by a causeway on an island in the lake. The latter is the very picturesque Schloss Ort. The oldest paddle steamer in Austria, the *Gisela,* has been restored and now tours the lake under full steam.

As a resort center, its attractions are its location—the tree-shaded promenade along the lake shore is delightful—two theaters (one openair), a

Kurhaus, regular concerts, water sports, fishing and often, in the summer, sports festivals. It is a center from which a number of delightful excursions can be made—to a fine waterfall, the Traunfall; to the 1,690 m. (5,546 ft.) Traunstein; to the 1,006-m. (3,300-ft.) Grünberg; and to a number of other points. Finally, Gmunden will provide you with an excellent souvenir of your visit; it is famous for its ceramics and it is unlikely that you will want to depart without taking a sample with you.

Wels

North of Gmunden, the Traun River plunges through tremendous gorges, rushing turbulently to its approaching junction with the Danube. Following the valley toward Linz, you first come to Lambach, whose originally Romanesque monastery, later converted into Baroque style, has some of the earliest (1080) and best-preserved Romanesque frescos in Austria. Just 2 km. (1 mile) from Lambach is an architectural—and religious—curiosity, the Dreifaltigkeitskirche, (the Church of the Holy Trinity) at Stadl Paura. It is built as a physical expression of the concept to which it is dedicated, the whole place is in multiples of three. Triangles and pyramids are essential parts of the design and everything is triplicated. This can be very confusing when there are three altars equally demanding attention, but the idea was an interesting one.

Then on to Wels, which is a convenient center for trips into the Danubian hinterland to the northwest, or southward to the Almtal and the mountains beyond.

Although Wels is thus used chiefly as a point from which to visit other attractions, it is not without its own. The Baroque town hall, the parish church—originally Gothic, later renovated in Baroque style, and also boasting a Romanesque doorway—the Renaissance Pollheimer Schloss, the Lederer Tower and Gate, and several buildings with Renaissance and Baroque facades are its chief sights. You can also see the house in which legend has it that the shoemaker-poet Hans Sachs, the original of the character in Wagner's *Die Meistersinger von Nürnberg,* lived in 1513. On Mount Wels, overshadowing the city, stands the stronghold erected for Emperor Maximilian I in 1519, and in the town itself you can inspect the City Museum's prehistoric and Roman collections.

Linz

From Wels, we come to Linz on the Danube, the capital of Upper Austria. It was only after large steel works and chemical plants were erected here during the period of German rule in Austria, that the population number surpassed that of Innsbruck and Salzburg, Linz becoming the third largest city in Austria (after Vienna and Graz), Linz is also a center of river navigation (its river port has more cargo volume than any other port on the section of the Danube belonging to the West), an important junction on international railroad lines, and a key crossing point of a number of highways and main roads. In addition to being a busy industrial and trading city, it also harbors much of the charming old world in the town streets around the main square, in the shadows of the cathedral and under the castle hill. Since 1966 Linz has been a university town, too, though only teaching sociology and economy.

A large bridge across the Danube connects it with its left-bank suburb of Urfahr, which at one time was a market town in its own right.

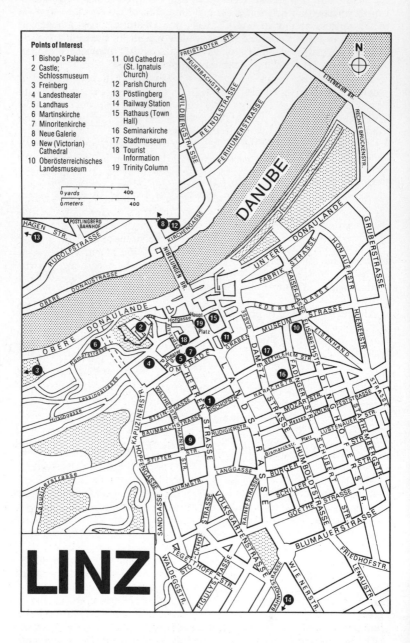

Points of Interest

1 Bishop's Palace
2 Castle;
   Schlossmuseum
3 Freinberg
4 Landestheater
5 Landhaus
6 Martinskirche
7 Minoritenkirche
8 Neue Galerie
9 New (Victorian)
   Cathedral
10 Oberösterreichisches
   Landesmuseum
11 Old Cathedral
   (St. Ignatuis
   Church)
12 Parish Church
13 Pöstlingberg
14 Railway Station
15 Rathaus (Town
   Hall)
16 Seminarkirche
17 Stadtmuseum
18 Tourist
   Information
19 Trinity Column

0 yards   400
0 meters   400

LINZ

The name of Linz comes from Lentia, a Roman settlement which existed here in the fifth century, and possibly earlier, since the word Lentia appears to be only a latinized form of an earlier Alpine Celtic name, as a salt trading post existed here already in prehistoric times. As early as the sixth century, there was a Bavarian settlement; in the ninth century, Linz became a market town and later on acquired full town rights. Emperor Friedrich III resided in Linz from 1489 to 1493.

Extensive redevelopment, restoration and the creation of traffic-free zones have transformed Linz, which is certainly a city of contrasts—with Austria's largest medieval square on the one hand, and the country's most modern multi-purpose hall which is used for concerts, conventions and all kinds of gatherings, the Brucknerhaus.

The center of the old town is the large, elongated Hauptplatz (Main Square) with the ubiquitous Baroque Trinity column in the middle; the square is lined by once patrician houses, among them the 17th-century Town Hall. Towering above one of the square corners are the two spires of the Baroque Old Cathedral (nowadays called also St. Ignatius Church or Jesuit Church), with splendid interiors, including a particularly beautiful Renaissance carved choir and the Krisman-made organ. Nearby is the city parish church, originally built in the 13th century and rebuilt in 1648 in Baroque style. The Victorian Cathedral is magnificent and worth a visit. Hofgasse, one of the narrow romantic streets which converge on the square from all directions, takes you to the castle, where Emperor Friedrich III lived.

Some of the gates, ramparts and walls of the original medieval schloss still exist, but the massive main building was reconstructed in 1599–1607 and later on served as military quarters for the imperial troops. Today the castle houses the most important collections of the Upper Austrian State Museum (Oberösterreichisches Landesmuseum), including prehistoric and Roman finds, historic Upper Austrian house interiors with rustic and other period furnishings, models of Upper Austrian farmhouses, rich samples of folk dress, old weapons including those of peasant rebellions, paintings, and a fine collection of carved church sculpture. The museum is splendidly arranged and is certainly worth a visit.

From the castle ramparts, now adapted as a park, there is a very good view of the Danube, of Pöstlingberg and other hills to the north. Beyond the castle park is Römerberg (Roman Hill), with the small Martinskirche, which is one of the oldest churches in Austria; it originates either from the late Roman or early Bavarian times and was rebuilt for the first time toward the end of the eighth century, reputedly by Charlemagne. Continuing on the Römerstrasse beyond Römerberg, one can get to the wooded hill of Freinberg, with fine vistas from the Höhenstrasse (high road) and good walks.

Retracing your steps on the Römerstrasse, you return to the center, passing by the theater building on a large, tree-lined street called Promenade. In front of you stands the Renaissance Landhaus (seat of the state government) built in the late 16th century, severely damaged during the great city fire of 1800. The original, beautiful arcaded courtyard with the fountain still remains. Next to the Landhaus is the Minoriten Church with late Baroque and Rococo interiors and some altar paintings by Kremser Schmidt.

Following Herrenstrasse from Promenade you come to the neo-Gothic New Cathedral, with a 444-foot tower. On the corner of Herrenstrasse and Bischofstrasse is the Bishop's Palace, built between 1721 and 1726 according to plans made by the Baroque master, Jakob Prandtauer. Continuing on Bischofstrasse you reach Landstrasse, the principal shopping precinct of Linz, which runs all the way from the vicinity of the main railroad station to the main square. Across Landstrasse in Harrachstrasse is another notable example of Baroque art—the Seminary Church, formerly of the Order of Teutonic Knights, completed in 1825 after the plans of Lukas von Hildebrandt, with portal sculptures by Rafael Donner and some paintings by Altomonte and Kremser Schmidt.

Across the Danube bridge from the main square is the suburb of Urfahr, which was administratively a separate town until 1919, when it was incorporated into the city of Linz. A "must" is the view from Pöstlingberg, the hill on the left bank of the Danube, clearly defined by a twin-spired church; the top can be reached by a special streetcar from Urfahr—the ride itself on the nostalgic tram, the steepest non-cog in the world, is well worth it—or by road if you are driving. On a clear day the view takes in a good deal of Upper Austria south of the Danube and a long chain of the Austrian Alps on the horizon.

The city's great industrial zone lies in the southeastern outskirts along the Danube. Closest to the city is the large freight harbor, with very modern installations and a free port section. Next are the chemical plants of Chemie Linz, founded by the Germans in 1938; they produce millions of tons of fertilizers, insecticides, pharmaceuticals and various other chemicals. Much larger are the steel works of VÖEST (Vereinigte Österreichische Eisen- und Stahlwerke), also built by the Germans in 1938 and subsequent years, presently one of the major steel-producing factories in Europe. VÖEST developed an entirely new method for steel-making and has since sold it to all the biggest steel producing countries.

Northern Upper Austria

Upstream from Linz comes the town of Wilhering, with its monastery and church, perhaps Austria's loveliest Rococo church. Farther along, a little back from the south bank of the Danube, is Eferding, with its 15th-century Gothic parish church and interesting castle with a museum. If you have always thought of the Nibelungs as a mythical race known only to old German legends and Wagner, this is the place to get that idea out of your head. The Nibelungs existed, though not quite as Wagner describes them, and Eferding was their stamping ground. The parish church has an unusual double-corkscrew staircase, some pretty Baroque altars and a cemetery with some interesting old graves. The Spitalkirche is also worth seeing.

The Danube now flows through a deeply-cut valley; after passing several castles, the boat traveler leaves it at Passau on the German side of the border, between the Danube and the Inn, which flows into it at this point. The Austrian town is Innstadt, on the east bank of the Inn—which may be followed south to Schärding—still possessing parts of its medieval walls as well as many old gabled buildings, a fine town hall, several old town gates, a Baroque parish church with a fine marble high altar and a painting by Rottmayr, and a museum housed in a Renaissance building. The Baroque houses in the main square are painted in a great array of colors and are a remarkable sight.

Continuing up the Inn, we come first to the Abbey of Reichersberg, founded in the 11th century and rebuilt in the 17th; the Abbey Church has some magnificent Rococo work and a lovely late-Baroque pulpit. Then on to Braunau, an old town which has retained its charming medieval character. Bürgerspitalkirche and the parish church are both 15th-century Gothic (the latter is overwhelmed by its 320-foot tower). The Glockengiesserhaus (bell foundry) is a good example of an artisan's workshop from the Gothic period. The Salzburg Tower Gate is the best preserved piece of the old walls, and there is an interesting city museum in the restored Herzogsburg, one of the oldest buildings in Braunau.

The more important centers on the way back toward Linz are:

Ried: home of the Schwanthaler family of Baroque architects and sculptors (at Schwanthalergasse 11) and the parish church with two altars by Thomas Schwanthaler; from here you can visit the village and the castle of Aurolzmünster, about 6 km. away;

Haag: an old town lying at the foot of the hill with Starhemberg Castle;

Gallspach: site of the renowned Zeileis Institute of Radiology;

Bad Schallerbach: a spa with hot sulphur springs, whose drinking and bathing cures are recommended for a large variety of ailments.

At this point, we are almost back to the Traun valley, and can return to Linz either via Eferding and along the Danube, or via Wels and along the Traun.

Linz is the most practical point of departure for visits to the Mühlviertel, the hilly region between the Danube and the border of Czechoslovakia. Two main roads roughly cover this area from Linz, with two local railroads following approximately the same direction.

On or near the road to the northwestern corner of Austria (Route 127) are several places of limited interest; among them are—Haslach, with a Baroque town hall, the remains of medieval fortifications, and the Lichtenau Castle on a hill not far away; and Aigen, at the end of the railroad line, with the Abbey of Schlägl, founded in the 13th century and later rebuilt several times. The Abbey Church has some rich Baroquery and paintings by Altomonte and others. This unspoilt part of the country was the spiritual home of the author Adalbert Stifter.

The other main road of Mühlviertel (E14) goes to Freistadt via Gallneukirchen in Gusen valley with the Castle of Riedegg. Freistadt is a charming town with old walls, towers, and gates (the Linzertor being particularly remarkable among the latter), a castle, a Baroque and a Gothic church. If you are interested in Gothic winged altars, you should not fail to visit the church in Waldburg, only a few miles from Freistadt, which has three.

The Southward Route—St. Florian and Steyr

Starting our backward trip from Linz, briefly east and then southwest, we pass first through a favorite excursion trip from Linz, St. Florian. The Augustinian Abbey (rebuilt between 1668 and 1751 by Antonio Carlone and Jakob Prandtauer and standing over the tomb of St. Florian, who was drowned in the Enns in 304 for refusing to sacrifice to the Roman gods), is considered among the finest Baroque buildings in Austria and among its most important art treasures is the *Sebastian Altar* painted by Albrecht Altdorfer, one of the most important painters of the so-called Danube School. A magnificent staircase rises to the marble hall, on the ceiling of which Altomonte depicted the Austrian victories over the Turks. The library contains 120,000 volumes and there are 14 sumptuously decorated

Kaiserzimmer (Imperial Apartments). In one stands Prince Eugene's superbly carved fourposter, in another the simple bed in which Anton Bruckner died in 1896. Under the church's white-and-gold organ, an 18th-century masterpiece with 7,000 pipes and 103 stops, is the grave of the great composer who was organist at the abbey and at the cathedral at Linz. During the summer, there is an organ concert daily at 4.30. Prandtauer also designed the abbey's hunting castle, Hohenbrunn, now a museum with a fine collection of porcelain. St. Florian has another claim to fame: there is a bell foundry here which cast the great bourdon bell for Vienna's Cathedral of St. Stephen, "Big Pummerin."

To the north, across the Autobahn, is Austria's oldest town, Enns, granted a charter in 1212. Finds from the original Roman town, Lauriacum, are in the Renaissance town hall and Ennsegg Castle. There is a fine view from the 200-foot Stadtturm (Town Tower), built in the 1560s, over the town's churches and old houses. When in this area note the magnificent, four-cornered farmhouses called "Vierkanter." Each generation is required to restore one of the four wings during its tenure, thus ensuring the entire structure is repaired every 100 years.

24 km. (15 miles) up the River Enns at its confluence with the River Steyr is Steyr, whose inhabitants are still working iron as they have done since Celtic times, though less lucratively since the break up of the Austrian Empire which cut the town off from its markets. Steyr has partly recovered from its depression by adding automobile manufacture to its activities. Fortunately, it has another string to its bow in addition to the industrial one. It is considered by some to be one of the best preserved old towns on German-speaking territory and gave its name to the neighboring province Styria.

It would be impossible to list here all the fine old buildings to be seen in Steyr. You should not miss the Hauptplatz—possibly the most beautiful in all Austria—the center of the old city, the Rococo town hall, the central parish church (one of the largest Gothic churches in the province, of which the earliest parts date from the 15th century), or, above all, the Bummerl-haus, built in 1497, which is considered the finest Gothic private dwelling in the city. There is also the Lamberg Castle; St. Michael's Jesuit church, with its fine organ; the Schnallen tower, built in 1613, the Bezirkshauptmannschaft (District Government building), in rustic Renaissance style; and the Baroque Dominican church built in 1550. Look for the Wehrgraben. This filled-in moat became the basis for several small industrial structures in the 18th century. Threatened with destruction, it has now been restored and bears witness to the start of the Industrial Revolution in Austria.

In Steyr you are still in Bruckner country. He composed his *Sixth Symphony* in the Parish House here, and there is a Bruckner room in the Mesnerhaus. Steyr is also a favorite center for boating enthusiasts, who make it their starting point for trips along either the Enns or the Steyr, which meet here.

West from Steyr is Bad Hall, a spa having the strongest bromine-iodine springs in Austria. Lying in lovely wooded surroundings, with all the amenities of a modern watering place, it caters to patients with a wide variety of maladies as well as to healthy visitors, who make this a starting point for excursions into the mountains to the south.

Kremsmünster Abbey

8 km. (5 miles) west of Bad Hall is Kremsmünster-Markt; its Benedictine abbey was founded in 777, but the present building dates from the much later Baroque period. Its great treasure is the *Tassilo Chalice* (named after Duke Tassilo of Bavaria, founder of this and many other abbeys), the oldest example of the goldsmith's art in either Bavaria or Austria (it is ascribed to the year 769), and the finest example of such work from early Christian times anywhere in the world, with the single exception of the Irish Cong Cross. In summer concerts are held both here and at St. Florian.

This monastery is the site of a famous school, which has numbered among its pupils many of Austria's greatest men. Its so-called Astronomic Tower, often called Europe's first skyscraper, contains a fine natural history collection, its art treasures include a 12th-century reliquary, and there are 100,000 volumes in its library, among them an illuminated Bible dating from the eighth century. Fish basins with arcaded passageways, built by Carlone and Prandtauer, and the Kaisersaal, with its paintings by Altomonte, are also not to be missed.

Southwest of Kremsmünster is Grünau (also reached from Traunsee) in the lovely Alm Valley. Southeast are the summer and winter resorts of Windischgarsten, with the nearby Gleinkersee, and Spital am Pyhrn, with a Baroque abbey church and the Vogelgesang gorge in the vicinity.

Hallstatt

From Spital am Pyhrn, Hallstättersee, the Salzkammergut lake located in the southernmost corner of Upper Austria and squeezed between Styria and Land Salzburg, can be reached in the easiest manner by traveling a short distance (about 53 km., 33 miles) through Styria. We proceed over the Pyhrn Pass (about 945 m., 3,100 ft.) and then through Mitterndorf and Bad Aussee, which once also belonged to the Salzkammergut salt estate, and afterwards cross back into Upper Austria on the beautiful mountain road over the Pötschenhöhe (about 975 m., 3,200 ft.). Immediately below this mountain pass are the shores of Hallstätter Lake. On its west bank is Hallstatt, believed to be the oldest community in Austria. More than a thousand graves of prehistoric men have been found here, and it has been such an important source of relics of the pre-Christian Celtic period that this age is known as the Hallstatt epoch. The prehistoric men built on piles in the lake, for safety's sake, and Hallstatt today is also on props, for it occupies a series of terraces on the side of the mountain to which it clings precariously.

For lack of space, the bones of the dead are dug up after 10 years and, with artistically painted skulls, placed in the much-visited charnel house, next to the 16th-century parish church, which contains a splendid winged altar with nine panels.

The museum (open May through October) has, of course, relics of the Hallstatt epoch and also, as already noted, recounts the history of salt; and you may likewise visit a salt mine here. There are guided tours from April through October. It would be difficult to imagine a more impressive spectacle than these caverns, of which the largest is more than 32 km. (20 miles) long. Taken together, they make up the largest underground complex in Europe. The antithesis to the descent into a mine is the trip by cable car from Obertraun up to the ice caves of the glacier of the Dachstein, that mighty mountain which is the anchor post of Upper Austria, Styria and Land Salzburg, for the borders of the three states meet here.

Bad Ischl

Continuing down the Traun valley, we come to one of the most important places in the Salzkammergut—Bad Ischl. This was the place, as we have already noted in the introduction to this chapter, where Franz Josef chose to establish his summer court, and the chief amusement of oldtimers still seems to be retailing the gossip of the vanished imperial society. One of the incidents connected with the emperor's sojourn at Ischl is that it was here, for the only time in his life, that he consented to ride in an automobile (he never used the telephone, either). This single break in the tradition was explained by the identity of the person with whom he shared the car—his fellow monarch, Edward VII of England, who was no mean force himself in establishing the social popularity of the spas of Europe.

It is an easy transition from Imperial Austria to Franz Lehar, the composer of so many operettas that glorified it, and sure enough, Lehar had a villa here, which today is a museum. You may also see the emperor's villa (Kaiservilla, now owned by his great-grandson, Markus von Habsburg), and its surrounding park. It is open from May to September. Bad Ischl today is a modern spa, one of the best equipped in Austria.

The Wolfgangsee

If we continued to follow the Traun from Bad Ischl, we should quickly come to Mitterweissenbach, where we joined it at the start of our circuit; instead we shall turn west to the Wolfgangsee, named after the most famous place on its shores.

St. Wolfgang is on the north shore of the lake, where you will find find yourself—literally—in the Austria of operetta. For you may stay if you like at the *White Horse Inn,* unfortunately recently given a facelift that has destroyed some of its oroginal charm, but you *are* at the White Horse Inn, the one which was the setting for the famous operetta. It is favored over other localities on the same lake because it is on the far side from the road and therefore off the beaten track.

The fame of the White Horse Inn has dwarfed that of St. Wolfgang's more serious drawing card, the winged altarpiece of Michael Pacher, made in 1481, which is one of the finest examples of Gothic wood carving in the world. The 16th-century parish church in which it is placed possesses two other notable altars, either of which would be the prize of any other church, but they sink into insignificance before this one. Its custodians treat it with great ceremony. The "wings" are kept closed on ordinary days. On Sundays they are half opened, on important religious festivals, like Christmas and Easter, they are opened wide, exposing the fine work within. If you pay it a visit, however, it will be opened for your inspection. St. Florian, that Austrian martyr whose acquaintance we have already made, the hermit St. Wolfgang, the local patron, and others are pictured in the scene of the crowning of the Virgin, with workmanship so minute that you can see even the stitches on the Virgin's clothing.

All other localities on Wolfgangsee are within the borders of Land Salzburg and we have described them in that chapter. Only a few kilometers northwest over the Schafberg Mountain (1,784 m., 5,850 ft.)—whose summit can be reached from St. Wolfgang by cogwheel railway—is Mondsee, where we started our round tour of Upper Austria. (However, there is no direct connection between St. Wolfgang and Mondsee.)

PRACTICAL INFORMATION FOR LINZ

TOURIST INFORMATION. Städt. Fremdenverkehrsbüro (City Tourist Office), Altstadt 17 (07 32–23 93–13 80). Open all year, Mon. to Fri. 8–6; June to Sept., also open Sat., Sun. and holidays 8–11.30 and 12.30–6. Also available here is information about short specialist tours out of Linz. There is also a bureau de change open Mon. to Fri. 8–12 and 1–7, Sat. 8–12 and 1–5, Sun. 8–12. Airport information, 0 72 21–72 70 00; train information, 17 17; bus information, 21 60.

AREA CODES. The postal code for Linz is A-4020, and 4040 north of the Danube, and the telephone area code 07 32.

HOTELS. Accommodations in Linz have developed at a great rate and are today comparable in price and quality with other provincial Austrian cities. The Tourist Accommodations Office is in the main railroad station (0 732–54 00 0). Open Oct. to May, Mon. to Sat. 9–12 and 1–6; June to Sept., Mon. to Sat. 9–12 and 1–7, Sun. 9–12 and 2–7.

Deluxe

Schillerpark, Rainerstrasse 2–4 (55 40 50). 111 rooms, all with bath. Brand new, in the center of town. Casino, underground garage, excellent staff; bar, Viennese coffee house, two restaurants. AE, DC, MC, V.

Expensive

City-Hotel, Schillerstr. 52 (52 6 22). 41 rooms, all with bath. Garage, parking lot. AE, DC, MC, V.

Domhotel, Baumbachstr. 17 (27 84 41). 50 rooms, all with bath or shower. Sauna, fitness room. Highly recommended after total facelift. AE, DC, MC, V.

Ebelsbergerhof, Wienerstr. 485 (42 1 25). In Ebelsberg suburb; cafe, wine tavern and restaurant serving Upper Austrian specialties. AE, DC, MC, V.

Novotel, Wankmüllerhofstr. 37 (47 28 10). 100 rooms, all with bath; modern, handy for autobahn. AE, DC, MC, V.

Spitzhotel, 4040, Karl-Fiedlerstr. 6 (23 64 41 0). Just over the Nibelungen bridge in new city complex. 56 rooms with every comfort. Conference rooms. Good restaurant *Paladino.* AE, DC, MC, V.

Tourotel, Untere Donaulände 9 (27 50 75). 180 rooms, all with bath; international standard, next to Bruckner Haus. Nightclub, sauna; good restaurant. AE, DC, MC, V.

Moderate

Drei Mohren, Promenade 17 (27 26 26). 22 rooms, all with bath. Across from Landhaus. Inn since 1595; well modernized. AE, DC, V.

Mühlviertlerhof, Graben 24–26 (27 22 68). 24 rooms, all with bath or shower. Newly renovated. Comfortable; excellent breakfast. Central location. AE, DC, MC, V.

Prielmayerhof, Weissenwolfstr. 33 (27 41 31). A bit out from the center, bus stop outside. Wine bar, restaurant. DC, MC, V.

Wolfinger, Hauptplatz 19 (27 32 91). On main square; entrance from historic courtyard lined with street lamps and crossed by open-terraced corridors. Restaurant on upper floor; period-style wine tavern approached from courtyard. Friendly and good. AE, DC, MC, V.

Inexpensive

Haselgrabenstuben, Ödmühlweg 6 (25 41 48). Across the river and a little out, but good value. 10 rooms. Restaurant and bar. Closed Sun.

Pöstlingberg, Pöstlingberg 14 (23 10 43). On hill, reached by car or streetcar. 6 rooms with bath. Cafe, cellar with wine tavern and excellent restaurant. AE, DC, MC, V.

Youth Hostels

Jugendgästehaus, Stanglhofweg 3 (66 44 34). Near the sports complex.

Jugendherberge, Blütenstr. 23 (23 70 78). Just across the Danube from the center of town.

Jugendherberge, Kapuzinerstr. 14 (28 27 70). Handy to center, close to Capucin cloister.

Camping

Campingplatz Linz, Wiener Bundesstr. 937 (Pichlinger See) (40 0 16).

RESTAURANTS. Linz lies in the middle of an intensive agricultural area with plenty of market gardens, so the produce that supplies its many restaurants is always fresh and tasty. Unfortunately, this is not a wine-producing part of Austria, so many of the wine taverns and other restaurants specialize in the wine of some other area of the country. The one local drink that is worth trying is cider, here called *Most.*

Expensive

Allegro, Schillerstr. 68 (66 98 00). Successfully established top restaurant, Austrian *nouvelle cuisine* at its best. Elegant setting. Closed Sat./Sun. and Aug. AE, DC, MC.

Antiquitätenstube, Alter Markt, Hofgasse 9 (27 54 65). Austrian and international specialties. Closed Sun. DC.

Kremsmunsterer Stube, Altstadt 10 (28 21 11). Regional cooking of high standard. Closed Sun. AE, DC, MC.

Le Bistro, Altstadt 8 (27 14 56). French specialties. Open from 6 P.M. to 2 A.M. daily. AE, DC, MC, V.

Theater Casino, Promenade 39 (27 76 61). Next to theater; formal. Closed Sun. eve. and Mon. Garden in summer.

Schloss Puchenau, Karl-Leitl-Str. 1, Puchenau 9 (22 15 15). In beautiful Renaissance palace on the Danube. A bit staid, but fine Austrian food. Closed Sun. Evenings only.

Moderate

Kaminloch, Baumbachstr. 18 (27 03 26). Unusual fireside restaurant. Exceptionally friendly; freshly-prepared dishes; wines direct from the grower. Popular with arts and theater people. Closed Sat.

Kaufmännisches Vereinshaus, Landstr. 49 (27 31 65). House of the Merchants' Association; large paneled hall, attractive courtyard-garden. Open 7 days a week.

Landhof, Pummererstr. 4A (27 98 32). Austrian cuisine, especially game, trout. Nice garden. Open Mon. to Fri. 11 to 2.30 and 6 to 11.

Zum Mühlviertler, Graben 24–26 (27 22 68). Good for game and fish; great variety of dumplings. AE, DC, MC, V.

Inexpensive

Klosterhof, Landstr. 30 (27 33 73). Formerly the library of the Kremsmünster Abbey—a vast establishment with a series of upstairs and downstairs rooms and halls with rustic hunting decor. Beer garden. Hearty Austrian dishes and good *Stiegelbräu* beer. Open 7 days a week.

Stiegl-Bierstuben, Volksgartenstr. 28 (51 6 97). Old-time interior, pleasant garden. Closed Sun.

The best bet for restaurants in this grade is to try the wine taverns or cafes—see below.

CAFES. Just to be even with Vienna, Linz boasts a cake of its own—*Linzer Torte*—which should not be missed. Pastry cooks send it all over the world to the considerable detriment of the world's waistline.

Cafe-Konditorei Tautermann, Klammstr. 14–16 (27 96 86). Winner of many international cake and pastry prizes. Open daily, except Tues.

Cafe Traxlmayr, Promenade 16 (27 33 53). Real Viennese coffee house. Nice terrace; popular meeting place of Linzers. Closed Sun.

Konditorei Wagner, Landstr. 15 (27 17 65). This and Tautermann specialize in *Linzer Torte.* From here they will mail it anywhere in the world. Closed Sat. eve. and Sun.

Konditorei Wrann, Landstr. 70 (27 32 88). Best pastries in Linz. Open daily. Also at Landstr. 70.

Schlosscafe, Tummerplatz 10 (27 34 16). Attached to Schlossmuseum (Castle Museum) with outdoor terrace on the ramparts; excellent view of the Danube, Urfahr and Pöstlingberg. Open April to Oct. Closed Mon.

WINE TAVERNS. Numerous wine taverns dot the old city section. They vary in quality of atmosphere and wine, but at their best they are excellent. In summer, try the outdoor wine gardens along the Obere Donaustr. on the Danube bank across the river.

Etagenbeisl, Domgasse 8 (27 13 46). Offers Schrammel music and Gemutlichkeit. Closed Sun.; open lunchtime and evenings till 2 A.M.

Wachauer Weinstube, Pfarrgasse 20 (27 46 18). Wachau wines—from the Danube valley (Melk-Krems). Closed Sun.

MUSEUMS AND GALLERIES. Neue Galerie (New Gallery), Blütenstr. 15 (23 93–36 00). Interesting exhibitions as well as German and Austrian paintings and sculpture of the 19th and 20th centuries, including Klimt, Schiele, Kokoschka. Mon., Tues., Wed., Fri. and Sat. 10–6, Thurs. 10–10, Sun. 10–1.

Museum Francisco Carolinum (Provincial Museum), Museumstr. 14 (27 44 82). The natural history collections of the Upper Austria Provincial Museum. Tues. to Fri. 9–6, Sat. and Sun. 10–6. Closed Mon.

Schlossmuseum (Provincial Museum), Castle Museum, Tummelpl. 10 (27 44 19). The historical, folklore, weapons and art collections of the Provincial Museum, housed in the 15th-century castle. Also has interesting reconstructions of Gothic and Renaissance interiors. Tues. to Fri. 9–5, Sat. and Sun. 10–4.

Stadtmuseum (City Museum), Bethlehemstr. 7 (23 93–19 00). City collections of art and archeology. Mon. to Fri. 9–6, Sat. and Sun. 3–5.

ENTERTAINMENT. Theater. The theater season lasts from Sept. to June. **Landestheater** (27 76 55) offers opera, operetta and drama performances; **Kammerspiele Theater** (27 78 55) produces drama and comedy—both at Promenade 39.

Music. A rich concert season is scheduled from fall to spring, with concerts in the **Bruckner-Haus,** Untere Donaulände (27 52 30), a beautiful piece of modern architecture on the banks of the Danube, voted one of the five best concert halls in the world by the London Symphony Orchestra. During July and August, weekly serenades are held in the Renaissance courtyard of the **Landhaus** at 8 P.M.

The top musical event is the Linzer Bruckner Festival, held in September.

A Modern Arts Festival including *Ars Electronica,* is held in the third week of June.

Nightlife. For dancing, try the **Bambi-Diele,** Landwiedstr. 140 (84 5 16); **City Club,** Bürgerstr. 3 (27 34 93), closed Tues.; **Grand Filou,** Blütenstr. 1 (23 70 21), closed Mon.; **Je t'aime,** Graben 27 (27 17 58), open daily; **Venturo,** Landstr. 13 (27 14 64), open daily.

For nightclubs— **Moulin-Rouge,** Wiener-Str. 217 (44 2 72), closed Sun; **Orient Bar,** Schillerstr. 49 (66 16 43), open every night.

The nicest chic cafe/bar is **Extrablatt,** Waltherstr. 15 (27 93 19).

There is a casino in the Hotel Schillerpark, open daily from 4 P.M.

SPORTS. Linz has several swimming establishments, among them— *Parkbad,* Untere Donaulände 11, with indoor pool open Oct. to April, outdoor swimming May to Sept.

Tennis courts—check with the Tennisverbrand (51 2 50) for available halls and courts.

Riding and instruction at *Linzer Reiterbund,* Roseggerstr. 51; *Union-Reitclub St. Georg,* in Ebelsberg Castle across the River Traun; *Reitklub Linz,* Museumstr. 31.

Golf. 18-hole course at St. Florian, Tillysburg (07 2 23–28 73) near the autobahn exit Asten-St. Florian.

Good **skiing** terrains are in the hilly area 8–16 km. north of the city, around the villages of Lichtenberg (ski tours), Kirchschlag (5 ski lifts, ski school, ski jump) and Hellmondsödt (3 ski lifts).

Ice skating at Untere Donaulände 11 (27 85 13), indoor and outdoor in season. Check for opening times.

SHOPPING. The main shopping area in Linz is along the Landstrasse, running its entire length from the vicinity of the main station to the Taubenmarkt, with some of the side streets such as Mozartstrasse, Bethlehemstrasse and Spittelwiese. Taubenmarkt marks the beginning of the old town, Graben, Promenade, Schmidtorstrasse and Hauptplatz (main square) being the main shopping lanes; and Herrenstrasse, which runs parallel to Landstrasse, is also important.

If you are looking for local handicrafts and souvenirs, you might try *O.Ö. Heimatwerk*, Upper Austrian folklore store, with shops at Landstr. 21, and Bürgerstr. 1, articles ranging from ceramics, glass, pewter and wooden objects, folk dress, folk furnishings to entire rustic room interiors.

PRACTICAL INFORMATION FOR
UPPER AUSTRIA

TOURIST INFORMATION. In its own way, Upper Austria is as relaxed and beautiful a vacationland as anywhere in central Europe. This is especially true of the part of the Salzkammergut that falls in the province, with its lake resorts, and of the Mühlviertel, forested and peaceful. The following list is of the local Tourist Offices you may want to consult, with their postal codes and phone numbers. There are twice as many scattered across the province, but these are the ones most likely to be needed. The main regional tourist office is at Schillerstr. 50, A-4010 Linz (0 732–66 30 21).

Aigen im Mühlkreis A-4160 (0 72 81–441); Altmünster/Traunsee A-4813 (0 76 12–86 11 40); Ampflwang A-4843 (0 76 75–27 49); Bad Goisern A-4822 (0 61 35–83 29); Bad Hall A-4540 (0 72 58–20 31); Bad Ischl A-4820 (0 61 32–35 20); Bad Leonfelden A-4190 (0 72 13–397); Bad Schallerbach A-4701 (0 72 49–20 71).

Eferding A-4070 (0 72 72–55 55 0); Freistadt A-4240 (0 79 42–29 74); Gmunden/Traunsee A-4810 (0 76 12–43 05); Gosau am Dachstein A-4824 (0 61 36–295); Grünau im Almtal A-4645 (0 76 16–82 68); Hallstatt am See A-4830 (0 61 34–255); Kremsmünster A-4550 (0 75 83–72 12).

Mondsee A-5310 (0 62 32–22 70); St. Wolfgang A-5360 (0 61 38–23 12); Spital am Pyhrn A-4582 (0 75 63–249); Steyr A-4400 (0 72 52–23 2 29); Wels A-4600 (0 72 42–34 95); Windischgarsten A-4580 (0 75 62–266).

AREA CODES—MAIL AND PHONE. You will find the postal code (preceeded by an "A") and the telephone code (in brackets) after the name of each town in the following *Hotel and Restaurant* list.

HOTELS AND RESTAURANTS. The Salzkammergut region is well equipped with hotels, with the emphasis on the moderate category. There are also a few luxurious converted castles and first-class lakefront establishments, as well as many low priced pensions, and Gasthof-type accommodations. Most lake hotels are open in summer only, usually May 1–Sept. 30 (sometimes up to a month earlier or later) with high-season prices during July and August. Many hotels and pensions offer reduced full-board rates if taken on a weekly or monthly basis.

Aigen A-4160 (0 72 81). *Wöber Hotel Waldhof* (E), (85 85). 54 rooms. Riding and conference facilities. Good food in Schloss-tavern. *Almesberger* (M), (87 13). 57 rooms, all with bath or shower; indoor and outdoor tennis courts, indoor pool, sauna; lawn. Good restaurant. AE, MC, V.

Youth Hostel (283).

Altenfelden A-4121 (0 72 82). *Kleebauer* (E), (55 88). Closed Feb. and Nov. Austria's finest riding hotel; indoor school, scenic location, woods and meadows; outdoor pool, tennis court. 40 rooms with bath. DC.

Ampflwang A-4843 (0 76 75). *Sporthotel Parcours* (E), (2421). All facilities in *the* riding village of Austria; tennis courts; 54 rooms, all with bath. AE, DC.

Attersee A-4864 (0 76 66). *Oberndorfer* (E), (364). 22 rooms, all with bath. On lake with own beach; excellent restaurant with game and fish dishes. AE, MC, V. Closed Jan. to Feb. and Dec.
Campsite (249).

Bad Goisern A-4822 (0 61 35). *Kurhotel* (E), (83 05). Outside village in park; cure facilities. 72 rooms, most with bath or shower. Closed Dec. to Jan. AE, DC, MC, V.
Campsite (81 36).

Bad Hall A-4540 (0 72 58). *Schlosshotel Feyregg* (E), (2591). 14 rooms, all with bath; small, exclusive castle pension with period-style furnishings. DC.

Bad Ischl A-4820 (0 61 32). *Kurhotel* (E), (42 71). 115 rooms, all with bath or shower; modern; cure facilities; restaurant. AE, DC, MC, V.
Zum Goldenen Schiff (M), (42 41). 56 rooms, most with bath or shower; pleasant apartments with balconies; fish a specialty. AE, DC, MC.
Restaurants. *Cafe Zauner,* Pfarrg. 7 (35 22). A *must* for all visitors to Bad Ischl. Long tradition and unsurpassed pastries. The famous specialty is *Zaunerstollen.* Closed in winter on Tues. AE.
Weinhaus Attwenger (E), Leharkai 12 (33 27). Pleasant *Stuben;* idyllic garden. Local specialties of very high standard, fish and game dishes. Reserve. AE, DC, MC. Closed Mon.
Youth Hostels (65; 34 83 8).

Bad Leonfelden A-4190 (0 72 13). *Böhmertor* (M), (231). 49 rooms, all with bath or shower. Indoor pool, sauna, solarium, cure facilities; restaurant.
Youth Hostel (383).

Bad Neydharting A-4654 (0 72 45). *Kurhotel Neydharting* (E), (89 16 0). 88 rooms, most with bath or shower. Indoor pool, cure facilities. Closed Jan.

Bad Schallerbach A-4701 (0 72 49). *Grünes Türl* (M), (81 63). 30 rooms, all with bath or shower; indoor pool, sauna, solarium, tennis, gymnasium, elegant restaurant. Closed Nov. AE, DC, MC, V.

Braunau A-5280 (0 77 22). *Post* (M), (34 92). 31 beds, all with bath. Pleasant *Stuben*-style restaurant. DC, MC.
Youth Hostel (23 21–281).
Campsite (73 57).

Eferding A-4070 (0 72 72). *Dannerbauer* (E), Brandstatt 5 (471). One of the many new-style, high-quality restaurants that have sprung up all over Austria in unlikely places. Closed Mon. and Tues. midday. DC, MC.

Enns A-4470 (0 72 23). *Lauriacum,* Wiener Str. 5–7 (23 15). 30 rooms, all with bath; traditional with modern conveniences. Garden; attractive beer restaurant. Closed in Dec. AE, DC, MC, V.

Freistadt A-4240 (0 79 42). *Deim Zum Gold. Hirschen* (M), Böhmerg 2 (22 58). 23 rooms, most with bath or shower. Ancient hostelry with modern comforts. Good food.
Youth Hostel (43 65).
Camping (26 24).

Gmunden A-4810 (0 76 12). *Parkhotel am See* (E), (42 30). 50 rooms, most with bath or shower; traditional with very attentive service. Restaurant. Closed Oct. to April. AE, DC, MC, V. *Schlosshotel Freisitz Reuth* (E), (49 05). Old castle with modern facilities. 26 rooms, all with bath or shower. Good restaurant. AE, DC, MC, V. *Goldener Brunnen* (M), (44 31). 32 rooms, all with bath and mini-bar, and overlooking the river. Old-fashioned, family-run hostelry; terrace. Marvelous home-cooking and good wines. Open all year. AE, DC, MC, V.
Campsite (30 60).

Grünau Im Almtal A-4645 (0 76 16). Can be reached from Wels by local railway. *Almtalhof* (E), (82 04–0). 21 rooms, all with bath or shower; *Romantik* hotel; beautiful old building; period furniture; good restaurant. Closed Nov. to April. DC, MC, V.

Hallstatt A-4830 (0 61 34). *Grüner Baum* (E), (263). 34 rooms, most with bath. On lakeshore, with lake-fish dishes in terrace restaurant. Open May to Oct. *Seewirt* (M), (246). 25 beds, all with shower; beach; good restaurant and wine tavern. MC, V.
Bergfried (I), (248). 83 beds, most with bath or shower. Restaurant.
Youth Hostel (279 or 681).
Campsite (329).

Hinterstoder A-4573 (0 75 64). By bus from the rail station of the same name on the Linz–Graz line. *Berghotel Hinterstoder* (E), (54.21). 40 rooms; indoor pool, sauna, solarium, tennis courts, cure facilities. First-rate restaurant and bar. Closed Oct. to Nov. and May.
Dietlgut (M), (52 48). 22 rooms, most with bath or shower; set in breathtaking mountain scenery. Heated pool, sauna, solarium. Restaurant. Closed in Nov.
Youth Hostel (52 27).

Mondsee A-5310 (0 62 32). *Eschlböck* (E), A-5310 Plomberg (2 91 20). 22 beds, all with shower; nicely furnished. Considered to be the best restaurant in Austria. Closed Mon. in winter. AE, DC, MC, V. *Motel Mondsee* (E), (21 54). Near autobahn exit; modern, 26 rooms, all with bath, refrigerator, balcony; restaurant. Closed Nov. to March. DC, V. *Weisses Kreuz* (E), (22 54). Comfortable rooms in which to sleep after enjoying a dinner in many ways equal to that of "Eschlböck." Closed Wed. except in Aug.

Restaurant. While *Eschlböck* gets highest marks, don't overlook *La Farandole* (E), (34 75). A top eating place in this small resort. Closed Mon. AE, DC, MC, V.

Youth Hostel (24 18).

Campsites (29 27; 26 00; 29 38; 29 02; 29 15; 25 36).

Obertraun A-4831 (0 61 31). *Berghotel Krippenstein* (M), (0 61 35–71 290). Located at an altitude of 2,000 m. (6,300 ft.), only accessible by cable car or on foot. 80 beds, most with bath or shower. Closed in Nov. DC, MC, V.

Youth Hostel (360).

Campsite (265).

St. Martin Im Innkreis A-4973 (0 77 51). On side road (near 143), about halfway between Braunau and Schärding. *Schlosspension St. Martin* (M), (61 02). 11th-century castle; swimming, tennis, riding, hunting and fishing in unspoilt country. DC.

St. Wolfgang A-5360 (0 61 38). *Romantik Hotel Weisses Rössl* (E), (23 06). 68 rooms, all rooms with bath or shower. Dine at the *White Horse Inn*. Terrace facing the lake; health program available; indoor pool; good service. AE, DC, MC, V. *Seehotel Cortisen* (E), (2367–0). 28 rooms, all with bath or shower; pool, beach. Restaurant. Open April to Oct. AE, DC, MC. *Strandhotel Margareta* (E), (23 79). 44 rooms, all with bath or shower; pool, beach. Restaurant and bar. Closed Nov. and April. AE, DC, MC, V. *Eden* (M), (23 26). 32 rooms, most with bath or shower; restaurant and bar. Closed Feb., March and Nov. AE, DC, MC, V.

Campsites (22 06; 25 43; 25 21).

Schärding A-4780 (0 77 12). *Forstinger* (M), (23 02). 18 rooms, all with bath; very good restaurant. AE, DC, MC, V. *Schärdingerhof* (M), (44 04 36). 30 comfortable rooms. Good cooking. Locally-brewed beer. DC, MC, V.

Seewalchen A-4863 (0 76 62). *Häupl* (E), (22 49). Silencehotel. 29 rooms, all with bath. Above the lake, with wonderful view. The seventh generation of the Häupl family run the hotel, creating a friendly atmosphere. The restaurant is famous for fish from the Attersee and other specialties, Austrian and international. Glorious terrace in summer. AE, DC, MC, V.

Spital Am Pyhrn A-4582 (0 75 63). On the railway line from Linz to Graz, under the Pyhrnpass in eastern Totes Gebirge. *Pension Göswiener* (I), (260). 22 rooms, some with shower. Good restaurant. MC.

Youth Hostel (214 or 213).

Steyr A-4400 (0 72 52). *Minichmayr* (E), (23410). 51 rooms, all with bath or shower. Finely-renovated old house. Good restaurant with terrace overlooking the confluence of Enns and Steyr rivers. AE, DC, V. *Hotel Mader* (M), Stadtplatz 36 (23 3 58). 53 rooms with bath. Comfortable. Good heurigen cellar. MC.

Campsite (61 12 03).

Restaurant. *Café Rahofer* (M), (24 606). On historic main square. Old restaurant with vaulted ceiling; excellent coffee and pastries. AE, MC, V.

Traunkirchen A-4801 (0 76 17). *Post* (M), (23 07). On main square; 60 rooms, all with bath or shower; sauna, solarium, gymnasium; restaurant and bar. AE, DC, MC.
Campsite (22 81).

Vöcklabruck A-4840 (0 76 72). *Auerhahn* (M), (34 56). 60 rooms, all with bath or shower; well furnished. Good restaurant. AE, DC, MC, V.

Weissenbach A-4854 (07663). *Post* (E), (240). 35 rooms, all with bath or shower. Recently renovated; comfortable rooms; restaurant. Closed Nov. to April.
Youth Hostel (220).
Campsites (220; 227).

Wels A-4600 (0 72 42). *Stadtkrug* (E), Kaiser-Josephs-Platz 21 (62 91 4). 92 rooms, all with bath or shower. Central. Good restaurant using produce from own farm and butcher's shop. AE, DC, MC, V. *Rosenbergerhotel Traunpark* (E), (62 2 36). 106 rooms, all with bath. Top-quality, modern-style hotel with every comfort and facility. Good (E) restaurant. AE, DC, MC, V.
Campsite (82 2 22).
Restaurant. *Wirt am Berg* (M), Berg 6 (44 3 81). On Route 1 to Lambach. Best restaurant in Wels with excellent cuisine. DC, MC. Closed Sun. eve. and Mon.

Windischgarsten A-4850 (0 75 62). *Sporthotel* (M), (82 82). 11 rooms, all with bath. AE, DC.
Restaurant. *Schwarzes Rössl* (M), (311). Local dishes, large helpings. AE, MC. Closed Mon.
Campsite (430).

GETTING AROUND UPPER AUSTRIA. By Train. Three main railway lines cross this region. Covering the Salzburg-Linz section of the main Austrian railroad line from Vienna to the west, a very fast train takes less than two hours and a slow train over three hours. Small local trains branch off at Steindorf for Braunau, at Vöcklamarkt for the town of Attersee, at Vöcklabruck for Kammer, at Lambach for Gmunden and Haag, and at Wels for Grünau; local trains of greater importance take off at Attnang-Puchheim for Braunau and Schärding to the northwest and for Gmunden, Ebensee, Bad Ischl, Hallstatt towards the southeast.

The second main line goes from Linz to Passau (Germany) via Bad Schallerbach and Schärding; about 1½ hours by fast direct train.

The third main line runs from Linz to Graz, passing through Rohr (local train to Bad Hall, about 5 km. away), Kremsmünster, Klaus, Hinterstoder (station only, bus to the village), Windischgarsten, Spital am Pyhrn (about two hours by fast train).

Freistadt and Aigen can be reached by the local trains from Linz. Enns is on the main line from Linz to Vienna; to get to Steyr by train, take the local train at St. Valentin a little beyond Enns.

By Bus. The local bus services cover the region very well, with the natural exception of the mountains to the south, though there are routes through to Almsee Hinterstoder and Rosenau.

Bus tours of the main places of interest originate in Salzburg, Linz, Bad Ischl, Gmunden and elsewhere. Inquire at the local Tourist Offices or travel agents.

By Boat. Between Linz and Passau fast steamer services on the Danube operate from early May to mid-September and from Linz the boats continue to Lower Austria and Vienna (07 32–27 00 11). In addition to the Danube shipping line, there are frequent lake ship services in summer on Traunsee, Attersee, Wolfgangsee, and Mondsee. The Hallstatt boat takes passengers to and from all the trains stopping at the Hallstatt railroad station, located across the lake from the town. Motorboat trips are also possible on all of these lakes.

By Car. Salzburg is the nearest large city to the lake region and most of the Salzkammergut area can be visited by making day trips out of Salzburg. By road it is about 43 km. (27 miles) to St. Wolfgang; 49 km. (30½ miles) to Bad Ischl, 75 km. (47 miles) to Hallstatt. Via the autobahn (A1, E14) it is about 25 km. (15½ miles) to Mondsee, 53 km. (33 miles) to Attersee, 74 km. (46 miles) to Gmunden on Traunsee, 130 km. (81 miles) to Linz.

From Linz to the Totes Gebige area on A1 southwest to Sattledt, then turning south on to 138, using local roads where necessary—the distance is about 90 km. (56 miles) to Almsee, 98 km. (61 miles) to Hinterstoder, 97 km. (60 miles) to Windischgarsten and 103 km. (64 miles) to Spital and Pyhrn. Route 138 continues 27 km. (17 miles) over the Pyhrnpass to Liezen in Styria.

From Linz it is 80 km. (50 miles) to Schärding (Route 129), 61 km. (38 miles) to Aigen (127), 42 km. (26 miles) to Freistadt (125, E14), 20 km. (12½ miles) to Enns (A1), and 40 km. (25 miles) to Steyr (A1 and 337).

PLACES OF INTEREST. Upper Austria may not be quite so rich in great abbeys and castles as Lower Austria, but it can certainly hold its own. The routes in the following list start in Linz, unless otherwise stated. Please ascertain opening times locally, as they are liable to sudden change and difficult to predict in advance.

Aigen Im Mühlkreis. In the very north of the province, on the Czech border; Route 127 all the way. The **Abbey of Schlägl.** Originally 13th-century. Gothic and Baroque paintings, portraits, special exhibitions. Usually open daily, mornings and afternoons; Sun. afternoons only.

Bad Ischl. A1 to Regau, then 145 (via Traunsee). The **Kaiservilla** (Emperor's Villa), with a superb garden, is in the north of the town. Guided tours May through Oct. Operettas in summer. **Lehar Villa** on river.

Braunau. A1 to Haid, A25 to Wels Nord, 137 then 137A and 309 the rest of the way. Picturesque old town on the German frontier. Birthplace of Hitler. Fine neo-Gothic **church** with early Gothic choir. **Bezirksmuseum** in the Herzogsburg—local history exhibits and church art.

Eferding. Route 129 due west. 15th-century **church;** 1416 **castle** (modernized around 1600). **Stadtmuseum,** Kirchenplatz 1, local history and material on the Starhembergs. May through Sept.

Enns. A1 east. Austria's oldest town. **Ennsegg Castle;** a Renaissance Townhall; **Museum der Stadt Enns,** prehistoric and Roman finds, town history, armory, church art, etc.

Freistadt. 125 (E14) north. Old walled town. **Local Museum** with town and district displays. Fine medieval/Baroque houses on main square.

Gmunden. A1 to Regau, then 145 for a few kilometers. An attractive old town. Double castle—one on land one on the lake, the latter **Schloss Orth. Museum der Stadt Gmunden** im Kammerhofgebäude, with Brahms room, Christmas cribs, local history and ceramics. Three weeks before Easter is **Liebstatt** Sunday. Since 1641 the citizens have put on their finery and walked in a magnificent procession through the town to the church. They carry *lebkucken* (gingerbread) hearts with loving messages on them in multicolored icing. The Renaissance town hall on the lakeside square has a ceramic glockenspiel. The *Gisela,* a paddlesteamer built in 1872 and traveled on by Franz Joseph, has been restored and now does tours round the lake, still using its original steam engines.

Haag. A1 to Haid, A25 to Wels Nord, then 137/137A, turn off at Rottenbach. **Schloss Starhemberg** above town.

Hallstatt. A1 to Regau, then 145 to Bad Goisern and continue down to foot of Hallstättersee. Prehistoric finds in the **Museum,** plus Roman provincial art. Local history and folklore in the **Heimatmuseum,** on the lakeshore. 16th-century **Parish Church;** charnel house (decorated skulls) in Gothic **St. Michael's Chapel.** There is a cable car up to a **salt mine,** one of the oldest in the world.

Kefermarkt. A few kilometers south of Freistadt (q.v.). Magnificent carved altarpiece in **Church of St. Wolfgang,** 40 ft. high, late 15th century.

Kremsmünster. 139 southwest. Great Benedictine **abbey.** Magnificent rooms (including the Kaisersaal, Emperors' Hall); fine Fischbehälter (Fish-pond) with 5 basins, arches and statues by Carlone and Prandtauer; other treasures include the *Tassilo Chalice,* late 8th century.

Lambach. A1 to Haid, A25 to Wels Ost, then 1 for 10 km. Important 11th-century Benedictine **abbey.** Restored Romanesque frescos, plenty of good Baroquery. Nearby, in **Stadl Paura** (2 km., 1 mile south), **Dreifaltigkeitskirche** (Holy Trinity) heavily symbolic church—all facets are multiples of 3—fine frescos by Altomonte etc.

Mondsee. A1 all the way, west. **Parish Church** is the former abbey church, Baroqued outside, Gothic in. Both the church and the **Heimatmuseum** have works by the local Baroque sculptor Meinrad Guggenbichler. **Mondseer Rauchhaus,** displays of local life, a smokehouse; on the outskirts of town, part of an open-air **musuem.** In summer there are open-air performances of the Mondsee *Everyman.*

Obertraun. A1 to Regau, then Route 145 to Bad Goisern; follow signs to Hallstatt. The take-off point for the cable car which goes up to the great

ice caves of the Dachstein (Dachsteineishöhle). Obertraun is across the Hallstättersee from Hallstatt.

Reichersberg Am Inn. A1 to Haid, A25 to Wels Nord, 137 then 137A/309 to Ried, north on 143 then left at Ort. 11th-century **abbey,** restructured in the 17th. Fine Baroque pulpit and Rococo decorations. Gothic panel paintings in the abbey museum.

Ried Im Innkreis. A1 to Haid, A25 to Wels Nord, 137 then 137A/309. Works of the Schwanthaler family of Baroque sculptors in the **Innviertler Volkskundehaus;** plus town history and regional folklore.

Rohrbach. 127 due northwest. Baroque **church;** the Pilgrimage Church of **Maria Trost** is nearby.

St. Florian. A1 to Asten turnoff, east of Linz. Great Augustinian **abbey.** Magnificent Baroque rebuilding from 1686 to 1750 under Carlone and Prandtauer. Collection of paintings, especially important for the works of Altdorfer; sculpture drawings, etc. Kaiserzimmer (Imperial Apartments), richly decorated; the great Marmorsaal (Marble Hall), with fine frescos; fine Baroque church with Bruckner's organ and tomb.

St. Wolfgang, Wolfgangsee. A1 to Mondsee, then 154 to the lake, round the lake to St. Wolfgang. Can be reached by boat from the foot of the lake. The **church** contains Michael Pacher's great carved altar (1481), one of the masterpieces of European Gothic.

Schärding. A1 to Haid, A25 to Wels Nord, then 137 northwest. Fine medieval remains, walls and parts of the old town, especially the main square. In the **Heimathaus,** Schlossgasse, there is a good collection of paintings, from Gothic to modern.

Steyr. A1 east to Enns, then 337 south. Picturesque old quarter, with the **Bummerlhaus** on the main square. **Dominikanerkirche** (Dominican Church) has heavily Baroqued interior. **Stadtpfarrkirche** (Parish Church), has Gothic elements. **Heimathaus,** museum with town history and Petermandl knife collection. The pilgrimage **church of Christkindl** (Christchild) is especially popular during Advent.

Tillysburg. Route 1 to east of Enns, then south; the road is not numbered. **Castle** built by nephew of the great Tilly in the first half of the 18th century. Evening candlelit chamber concerts during July.

Traunkirchen. A1 to Regau then south on 145 through Gmunden. Baroque **Fisherman's Pulpit** in the Parish Church—highly theatrical creation.

WINTER SPORTS. The main skiing areas of Upper Austria are the mountain groups of Dachstein and Totes Gebirge, the first partially and the latter mostly within Styria, and in the lower Höllengebirge, between Traun and Atter lakes. The skiing season in the high mountains lasts from December to May, in the Dachstein sometimes extending into June. In lower areas January to March are the most reliable months.

Experienced skiers can undertake exceptionally rewarding scenic tours across the high mountain plateaus dotted with lodges, while the less experienced will find enough challenge in lower localities, among them several spas which in winter become also centers of the white sport. The technical facilities in Upper Austria have increased greatly within the past years, matched by improved accommodations for guests.

This is economy country for skiers, with similar, albeit not so spectacular, facilities and terrain as in wider-known regions.

Salzkammergut. This is a classically beautiful landscape in summer and an up-to-date skiing area in winter. It is easily reached and well-supplied with accommodations.

Resorts: Altmünster (443 m., 1,453 ft.); Bad Goisern (500 m., 1,640 ft.); Bad Ischl (468 m., 1,531 ft.); Ebensee (429 m., 1,407 ft.); Gmunden (420 m., 1,378 ft.); Gosau (770 m., 2,526 ft.); Hallstatt (508 m., 1,667 ft.); Mondsee (481 m., 1,578 ft.); Obertraum (514 m., 1,686 ft.); Weyregg am Attersee (480 m., 1,575 ft.).

Facilities: the area has 12 indoor swimming pools, 9 cable cars, 1 chair lift, 56 T-bars and 140 km. (87 miles) of cross-country trails.

Pyhrn–Priel Region. For the ski buff this is a rather special area. It has high peaks and fine lift facilities. But the region is good for a quieter way of life, too, with plenty of local events to enjoy, and a marvelously relaxed atmosphere for just living the simple life.

Resorts: Hinterstoder (600 m., 1,969 ft.); Spital/Pyhrn (650 m., 2,133 ft.); Vorderstoder (808 m., 2,651 ft.); Windischgarsten (600 m., 1,969 ft.).

Facilities: the area has 10 indoor swimming pools, 1 cable car, 5 chair lifts, 30 T-bars and 105 km. (65 miles) of cross-country trails.

Other Areas. Among the other areas where winter sports are quieter and not quite so heavily accented are Innviertel–Hausruckwald, Linz–Danube region, Mühlviertel. They are all good for skating, minor skiing and, of course, can provide plenty of opportunities for superb winter wandering through attractive countryside. Mühlviertel is being developed as something of a ski center, though it does not have the spectacular locale of many others.

TIROL

Wonderland in Two Parts

Today, the Bundesland Tirol (Federal State of Tirol) has a population of some 541,000 and covers an area of nearly 13,000 square kilometers. Before World War I, the Tirol was much bigger; but the large, prosperous wine-growing area of South Tirol was ceded to Italy under the terms of the peace treaty, and the wealthiest part of the state was lost to Austria. As a result of this political surgical operation, the East Tirol has been entirely cut off from the main body of the state and can only be reached by passing through Italy or over the Alps through Salzburg. The Tirolese feel very deeply the loss of South Tirol, and have never given up agitating for the return of this rich fertile country, where they all have relatives, and many still own property. The red wine you will drink in the Tirol (called *Kalterer, Magdalener,* and other names) will come from South Tirol, and very good it is.

Italy, then, forms the long southern boundary of the state. To the north the Tirol has another international frontier with Bavaria. To the east lies Land Salzburg and—beyond East Tirol—Carinthia. Over to the west the great Arlberg massif marks the western limits of the Tirol, and once you are over the pass you are in Vorarlberg.

Early Tourists

Since the early 1930's the Tirol has been one of the most popular holiday centers for British visitors, though they have now been overtaken by the Germans as the backbone of the tourist trade, the youngest and most pros-

244

perous of Tirolean industries. It is said that the first missionaries to come to the Tirol were either Irish or English. From the beginning of the 18th century a procession of what might be called "pioneer tourists" from all parts of the British Isles came singly and in small parties to discover the Tirol as a country of great scenic beauty and as an ideal holiday center. Indeed, the Tirol can be said to owe a great deal to British pioneering. It was the British Kandahar Ski Club that played an important part in making the Tirol the world's most popular winter sports center: it was this club that encouraged and sponsored the late Hannes Schneider in teaching his revolutionary technique, which has made Austrian skiing world famous. During the late 19th century scores of adventurous and enterprising British businessmen came to the Tirol and built factories, and they too can claim to have had a major share in the credit for the rapid growth of its industry.

The Americans discovered this area as a holiday center only a few decades later. In 1906, the railroad millionaire Morgan spent a holiday in Innsbruck, and from then on the Tirol was much publicized and boosted as a holiday playground in the United States. Since the last war, Tirol has become very popular with American skiers who now come here in droves every winter, many returning every year. Tirol has also been selected by most U.S. downhill and slalom champions as the training ground for these Alpine skiing disciplines.

The history of the Tirol is full of romance. Up to the beginning of the 16th century it was a very powerful state, under a long line of counts and dukes of varying fortunes, as can be judged by some of their nicknames— "Friedl the Penniless," and his son, "Sigmund the Wealthy," for example.

Under Maximilian I the state reached the zenith of its power. But perhaps the best known historical figure is Andreas Hofer, the hero of the Tirol, who led the famed rebellion against the Napoleonic occupation, defeating the French troops at the Battle of Bergisel. Both the Golden Roof and the magnificent Maximilian's mausoleum are in Innsbruck, and the memorial to Andreas Hofer lies just outside the city.

Innsbruck, capital of the Tirol, is very conveniently situated for the tourist. Even if you have already settled on a resort for your holiday, you should certainly spend a day or two in the capital first; for Innsbruck is the treasure house of the whole Tirol, historically, esthetically and economically.

Exploring Innsbruck

The capital of the Tirol is one of the most beautiful towns of its size in the world. This 750-year-old town (it received its municipal charter in 1239) undoubtedly owes much of its fame and charm to its unique situation. To the north, the steep, sheer sides of the mighty Alps of the Northern Chain rise like a shimmering blue and white wall from the edge of the city; an impressive and awe-inspiring background to the mellowed green domes and red roofs of the picturesque baroque town. To the south, the mountains of the Tuxer range form a series of drop-curtains ranging from 2,100 to 3,000 m. (7,000 to 10,000 ft.) in height.

Innsbruck has great importance as a crossroads. The north/south axis carries traffic between Germany and Italy, while the east/west one connects Austria with Switzerland.

The charming old-world town, built largely in Baroque style, has remained virtually intact. The old part of the town, though the skyline has

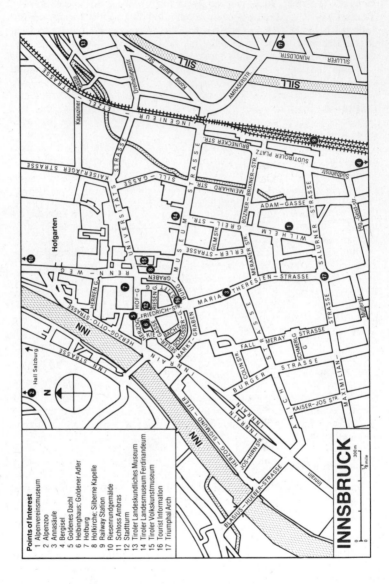

Points of Interest
1 Alpenvereinsmuseum
2 Alpenzoo
3 Annasäule
4 Bergisel
5 Goldenes Dachl
6 Helbinghaus; Goldener Adler
7 Hofburg
8 Hofkirche; Silberne Kapelle
9 Railway Station
10 Riesenrundgemälde
11 Schloss Ambras
12 Stadtturm
13 Tiroler Landeskundliches Museum
14 Tiroler Landesmuseum Ferdinandeum
15 Tiroler Volkskunstmuseum
16 Tourist Information
17 Triumphal Arch

INNSBRUCK

suffered from the encircling highrises, is built on the right bank of the swift-flowing Inn, which delimits its northern and western boundaries. The railway line and the smaller Sill River run around the old town to the south and east. Beyond the rivers and the railway line lie the newer, modern parts of Innsbruck for the most part either factory sections or attractive residential districts, with tree-lined avenues and large, spacious gardens. As the site of the Winter Olympics in 1964 and 1976, the city got a series of new sports facilities, among which were the Eisstadion (ice rink) and the beautiful ski jump on Bergisel, where many international competitions take place every year.

For the tourist bent on sightseeing, Innsbruck is not an exhausting city to explore. It is only a half-hour walk from one end of the old town to the other. You cannot stray far if you remember not to cross the railway or the rivers.

Innsbruck (Inn Bridge) is first mentioned in history books as a trading post in the 12th century. Owing to its commanding position on the most important trade route over the Alps into Italy and Central Europe's principal outlet to the south over the famous Brenner Pass, Innsbruck grew rapidly and towards the middle of the 13th century became a full-fledged town. In the early 15th century, Duke Friedrich (the one who was popularly known as Friedl the Penniless) transferred his official residence from Meran to Innsbruck, which thus became the capital of Tirol. Many of the beautiful buildings in Innsbruck were built by the powerful Emperor Maximilian, who loved the Tirol and its capital city; others by Austria's famous Empress Maria Theresa, who gave her name to the principal street of the town.

Any sightseeing in Innsbruck should begin at Maria-Theresien-Strasse, which runs through the heart of the city from north to south, and is the main shopping center. Within the pedestrian zone, you can see four of Innsbruck's best known sights in the space of an hour.

The first of these is the world famous view from the Maria-Theresien-Strasse toward the Nordkette range of mountains. Stand halfway down the street and face north. You will get the best uninterrupted view from the left-hand side of the road.

The second is the Roman-style Triumphal Arch, that spans the Maria-Theresien-Strasse at the southern end of the short street, and was built in 1767 by Maria Theresa. The sculptured reliefs on the southern face commemorate the marriage of her son Leopold, Archduke of Tuscany, who later became Emperor Leopold II, to the Spanish Princess Maria Ludovica in 1765, and those on the northern side are a memorial to the sudden and tragic death of Franz the First, husband of Maria Theresa, both events occurring at the same time in Innsbruck's Hofburg castle.

The third is another monument erected by the Tirol Diet, or council, in 1706 to commemorate the liberation of Tirol from the Bavarian army of invaders which occupied the greater part of the province during the Wars of the Spanish Succession. This is the Annasäule (St. Anne's Column), halfway down the Maria-Theresien-Strasse in the center of the road, so called because the Tirol was liberated on St. Anne's Day.

Next to the famous view of the Alps, Innsbruck is best remembered for that remarkable curiosity, the Goldenes Dachl (Golden Roof), which, together with the old town section surrounding it, is the fourth famous sight. To reach it, carry on past the Annasäule to the end of the Maria-Theresien-Strasse, and down the narrower Herzog-Friedrich-Strasse to the bottom, where this famous Innsbruck landmark faces you across the little square.

The shimmering golden roof covering the beautiful, ornate stone balcony is not of solid gold, but is a mass of heavily gilded copper tiles. The ancient mansion was originally built as a residence for Duke Friedrich onto the back of the old Hofburg castle, and it is said that the indignant Duke had the original roof covered with costly golden tiles to give the lie to the belief that he was poor. In later days the famous balcony was used by the Emperor Maximilian and his guests as a kind of "Royal Box" from which to watch the performances of strolling players in the square below. The original building was altered and added to at the beginning of the 18th century, and only certain parts, notably the balcony and alcove below it, with the magnificent, finely-wrought coats of arms of Austria, Hungary, Burgundy, Milan, the Holy Roman Empire, Styria, Tirol, and the Royal German emblem.

Opposite the Goldenes Dachl is the Helbinghaus, with its lovely 18th-century facade of bow windows in high Rococo style. A bit to the left lies the Goldener Adler, one of the oldest inns in Innsbruck (16th century). Over its long history of hospitality it has played host to many famous people, among them Goethe and the Tirol's great hero, Andreas Hofer, who fought the French and was executed by them in 1809.

The other sights you should not miss are the Hofburg palace, with the beautiful imperial park laid out in the English style, the Imperial (or Court) Church, with the tomb of the Emperor Maximilian, and the Silver Chapel adjoining it.

The Hofburg was originally built in the 15th century, but was later almost completely restyled and rebuilt by order of the Empress Maria Theresa in the latter half of the 18th century, and the original palace and the grounds were considerably enlarged. The banqueting rooms, especially the Giants' Hall, the paintings in the suite of reception rooms, and the elaborate furniture are of most interest.

The Hofkirche (Court Church) was built in 1553–63 solely as a great mausoleum for Emperor Maximilian I. At the beginning of the 18th century it was restyled in the Baroque idiom. The emperor's cenotaph of grained marble is the largest Imperial Germanic tomb ever known to have been built. But the church and the tomb are entirely dominated by the heroic-sized armor-clad statues of the emperor's ancestors and notable kings and emperors of history, who guard the kneeling figure of the Emperor Maximilian in bronze, a work of the Flemish master Alexander Colin of Mechlin. There are no less than 28 of them—14 to a side—some of them are ladies, all are in bronze except two, which are in copper. The legendary King Arthur of England is one of them, and another of the giants is Theoderich, the famous King of the Goths; both were sculptured by Albrecht Dürer. During those times Innsbruck was a great center of armor makers and this explains the elaborate armor suits of the statues. The remains of Emperor Maximilian, however, do not lie in the fabulous tomb. He is buried in the town of Wiener Neustadt, near Vienna. The Hofkirche does, however, house the body of Andreas Hofer.

The Silberne Kapelle (Silver Chapel), adjoining the Court Church, was built as a separate mausoleum in 1587 by Archduke Ferdinand (1529–95), the Regent of Tirol, so that he might be buried beside his wife Philippine Welser, a commoner, albeit the daughter of the rich and powerful merchant family of Welsers; her cenotaph and the statue of Ferdinand were sculptured by Colin of Mechlin. She was also a superb cook and left behind an excellent cookbook. She is commemorated in the excellent restaurant bearing her name at the Hotel Europa. The chapel owes its name to the silver altar figure of the Madonna.

The Tiroler Landesmuseum Ferdinandeum, in the Museum-Strasse, has a magnificent picture gallery specializing in Gothic and Baroque works by famous Tirolean, German, Dutch, and Italian masters. But the most interesting part of the museum is the comprehensive industrial art collection of bronze, glass, enamel and iron. There is also a large collection of old coins and medieval arms.

The Tiroler Volkskunstmuseum, next to the Imperial Chapel, has a complete collection of local folk costumes and antique rustic furniture, as well as of old farm and artisan tools and utensils. Anyone interested in the dirndl and its many variations, and in old house interiors, could spend a happy hour here. There are several other museums, all of great interest, in the city.

Short Excursions

To visit Schloss Ambras, a bus from the main Innsbruck station departs every half-hour for Ambras, a little village 30 minutes away. The magnificent castle, one of the finest and best preserved in Austria, was originally a Gothic castle built by the dukes of Andechs in the 11th century. It was rebuilt as a residence for the Archduke Ferdinand of Tirol in the German Renaissance style, between 1564 and 1582. Of particular interest is the Spanish Hall, the earliest known large Renaissance council chamber on German soil, which was built in the year 1570. Unfortunately, the greater part of the archduke's personal collection of fine arts was transferred long ago to the Kunsthistorisches Museum in Vienna, but there is still a very large collection of pictures, weapons, armor, *objets d'art,* furniture, various ingenious household gadgets, and other curiosities dating from medieval times to be seen. The castle grounds are very beautiful and extensive and contain the original tilting grounds and a little cemetery set deep in the woods, where heroes of the War of Liberation were laid to rest. Concerts are held in the castle hall during summer.

There are three other short excursions outside the town you must make. Two of them are trips by cable railway up to the Hungerburg (853 m., 2,800 ft.) and from there right up to the Hafelekar. You can do both trips in one, taking the cogwheel railway up to the Hungerburg from the valley station directly inside the town itself, and then transferring to the Hafelekar two-stage cable car, which starts from the Hungerburg and soars right up to the dizzy height of 2,286 m. (7,500 ft.), with the second stage (change of cars) beginning at the intermediate station of Seegrube (1,904 m., 6,248 ft.). At all three stops, Hungerburg, Seegrube, and the Hafelekar terminus, there are hotels and restaurants commanding a wonderful view over the Tirolean Alps with Innsbruck spread out at your feet.

If you are staying a few days in Innsbruck, you would enjoy the views better if you do not attempt more than one stage at a time. Start with the lower Hungerburg, and try a different altitude and perspective each day, enjoying a leisurely lunch at each halt. Don't miss the beautiful and interesting Alpine Zoo before going up.

The third excursion you should not miss is to Bergisel, just outside the southern limits of the town near the Sill gorge. The Isel Hill is a large beautifully laid out park, a Field of Remembrance to soldiers of the famous Tiroler Kaiserjäger Regiment and to the Tirolean fighters against the Napoleonic occupation and oppression. The hill became famous as the scene of several pitched battles fought during the war of Liberation in 1809, and there is a fine memorial to Andreas Hofer, leader and military commander during that war, and the national hero of Tirol, plus the Provincial Cenotaph, the Tomb of the Unknown Soldier and a little lookout tower. The great charm of the Bergiselgrounds is that the memorials and buildings are spaced widely apart amid beautiful woods and lawns, so that the place in no way resembles a cemetery.

An attraction in the vicinity of Innsbruck is the Ehnback–Klamm near Zirl (half-hour walk), where a romantic pathway was blasted through the rocks of a wild gorge.

Another excursion destination, particularly interesting for the unspoiled beauty of its mountain scenery, is Axamer Lizum which is 22 km. (13½ miles) away from the Olympic village in Innsbruck's Arzl-South district. Three chair lifts will take you to various elevations. Axamer Lizum came into the spotlight in 1964 as one of the sites of the IXth Winter Olympics and was again the site for all alpine events, except the men's downhill, in the XIIth Winter Olympics. In winter a free ski bus takes guests from the center to the skiing areas. Enquire at reception desk.

You will now have seen the most important landmarks and sights in Innsbruck, but the city is full of other historical buildings, and the museums are veritable treasure chests of the arts.

The Environs of Innsbruck

Only a few kilometers by road up the steep hill behind Bergisel is the village of Igls, perched a thousand feet above the city under the Patscherkofel mountain. Igls is well known as a winter sports center and many visitors to Innsbruck prefer to make their headquarters here rather than down in the valley below in the city itself. In winter there are the obvious advantages of the skiing facilities, but in summer, too, Igls is a pleasant place, and there are frequent buses to Innsbruck, as well as a country-style tram.

In the hot summer months there is a small bathing lake, the Lanser See, at the edge of the plateau and about a kilometer from Igls, which lies well back at the foot of the Alps. But the real lure at Igls is the famous Patscherkofel cable-car railway, which runs from the village to the top of Patscherkofel mountain (2,012 m., 6,600 ft.) in less than 20 minutes. The view over the whole valley and the town of Innsbruck is just as fine as that seen from the Hafelekar station on the other side of the Inn valley, and serves to round off the tourist's bird's-eye impression of the magnificent panorama of the Alps. Walkers will delight in the Zirbenweg, a long, well-marked trail following the ridge leading east away from the cable car station.

There is also an intermediary station called Heiligwasser (Holy Water), which used to be a popular place of pilgrimage, and the spring water was— and still is—said to be the panacea for all kinds of complaints.

The third lift out of Innsbruck is a chair lift from near Mutters to the Stubai valley and the Mutterer Alm. Here also there is a fine view, although not the equal of the other two.

To the South—Stubaital and Wipptal

The delightful little Stubaital (Stubai Valley), less than 40 km. (25 miles) in length, is noted for its beautiful and striking mountain scenery. No less than 80 glistening glaciers and more than 40 towering Alpine peaks have turned this valley into one of the showpieces of the Tirol. Only 16 km. (10 miles) from Innsbruck, the Stubai region is a popular summer center and offers splendid opportunities for mountain climbing and skiing on the glacier. In the winter, the valley is particularly favored by skiing parties wishing to make extensive tours along the glaciers and mountains of the Stubai Alps.

To see the whole of the Stubaital is a full day's excursion from Innsbruck. It is easily reached by car, bus, or on the narrow-gauge, single-line electric railway that serves the Stubai valley exclusively. Both the latter means of transport take different routes as far as Fulpmes, halfway up the valley and the terminus of the "Stubai valley railway," so it is a good plan to take the bus one way and return on the quaint little electric train, and you will see more of the beauties of the valley. Buses leave from the Mutterbergalm just outside Innsbruck at regular intervals for the valley.

At the little village of Schönberg (Lovely Hill) a road branches off from the Brenner road. This is the entrance to the Stubai Valley. Schönberg is perched on a hill, and from the village you can enjoy a fine all-round view over the surrounding Stubai and Tuxer Alps. From Schönberg the road dips down to tiny Mieders; it then passes through Telfes to Fulpmes.

After a longish stop at Fulpmes, the valley capital, the bus climbs up to Neustift, the old terminus. This is a good place to have lunch; the driver of the postal bus will be able to recommend the best place to patronize—he probably lunches there himself. From here the bus follows the narrow winding Alpine road into the Stubai Alps through gorgeous scenery laced with glaciers to the hamlet of Ranalt, under the great craggy peak of Zuckerhütl (Little Sugar Hat). This last part of the road is not asphalted.

Returning to Fulpmes, the Stubai train will take you back to Innsbruck, climbing up to the high plateau at the entrance to the valley through Telfes (the highest point reached by the train), then down to Mutters and Natters—where there is a little lake—and finally descending into the Inn valley at Innsbruck.

The valley of the Sill River is called Wipptal; it leads from Innsbruck to the Brenner Pass and over it into South Tirol (now in Italy). The autobahn crosses the valley near Innsbruck over the 600-foot high Bridge of Europe (Europabrücke) and continues along its western slopes to Brenner, while the international rail line runs through the valley. There is a good bus service up to the Brenner. Although Wipptal can hardly be classed as one of the most beautiful in the Tirol, the villages along its length are quite popular in summer, and in the wintertime cater for large numbers of winter sports enthusiasts.

Matrei is the first stop up the Wipptal. If you have a car, you can return to Innsbruck via Igls along the steep mountain backdoor road that gives you a marvelous view over the Tuxer Alps to the east, instead of by the rather dull road along the Sill.

You come next to Steinach at the foot of the Brenner Pass, a popular little resort in summer and winter, with an Alpine lake, swimming pool, and some excellent skiing slopes. The road for Gschnitztal, another small valley penetrating the Stubai range, branches off at Steinach.

After Steinach the road starts to climb steeply to Gries near the top of the pass, and parts company with the railway line that burrows into the Alps toward the Italian frontier. Gries is a small winter sports center frequented mainly by Austrian tourists. Near Gries there are some interesting Roman remains, for this was once the imperial military road from Rome to the North Sea. Shortly after passing the ruins you reach the top of the pass entering South Tirol across the Austrian–Italian frontier.

To the Northwest—Seefeld and Scharnitz

One of the most delightful excursions from Innsbruck is to travel along the length of the Karwendel railway. Starting at Innsbruck, the electric train leisurely winds across the Austro-Bavarian border roughly in the shape of a huge letter S to Reutte, tucked away in the northwestern corner of the Tirol. After leaving Innsbruck, the train first of all follows the Inn valley, then climbs steeply round the massive Solstein mountains, passing through several long tunnels until the line finally reaches the great Seefeld plateau on the edge of the Wetterstein range.

Seefeld, one of the Tirol's most fashionable winter sports centers, is only 26 km. (16 miles) from Innsbruck. Ranking with Kitzbühel and St. Anton as far as hostelry and atmosphere are concerned, it concentrates on cross-country skiing and was the site of the competitions in this sport during the Olympic Games.

In summer, too, Seefeld is a popular resort; it is a good base for exploring the countryside or visiting neighboring Bavaria, and is not far from Innsbruck. A remarkable feature of Seefeld is the little Wildmoos lake, which is apt to vanish suddenly, leaving a lush green meadow and a little bubbling spring to mark its location. At other times it is deep enough to swim in and, when available, is one of Seefeld's major summertime attractions. It is 4 km. (2.5 miles) outside Seefeld and buses there are few and far between.

Dipping down the receding high ground of the plateau we come to Scharnitz, a little town on the Austro-Bavarian border. There is not much left to see of the Porta Claudia fortress nowadays, but during the Napoleonic Wars the Austrian garrison—oddly enough commanded by an English colonel, an ancestor of the poet Swinburne—successfully defied a large French army under Marshal Ney. Scharnitz is a center for summer walking tours into the Karwendel mountains and along the Isar valley.

Detour Around the Zugspitze

The electric railway then leaves Austria, traveling in a large semicircle through Garmisch-Partenkirchen, and round the mighty Zugspitze back, at Ehrwald, to Austrian territory again. Ehrwald is a winter and summer resort at the foot of the Wetterstein Alps, and the great attraction here is, of course, the Zugspitze. An occasional bus from the center of town takes you to Obermoos with the valley station of the Austrian aerial cable car to Zugspitze which reaches to the very top of this great mountain (2,962 m., 9,716 ft.). From the summit there is a magnificent view over Austrian, Bavarian and part of the Swiss Alps. Zugspitze, which marks the Austrian-German border, is at the same time the highest mountain in Germany and its peak can also be reached by cable car from the German side, starting at the village of Eibsee.

Northwest of Ehrwald is Lermoos, in summer a health resort and in winter a popular winter sports center. Beyond, in the Lechtal Alps is Berwang, idyllic mountain village, winter and summer resort. Here you can be sure of fine powder snow from late autumn to late spring, and many skiing aces come here for serious training.

In the center of the district known as the Ausserfern lies Reutte, a pleasant and convenient spot for a summer holiday. There are some very colorful houses with richly painted facades, and a small, interesting museum. You may swim in the three lakes in the vicinity. The largest lake, the Plansee, connected to the Heiterwang lake by a short canal, is nearly 6 km. (3½ miles) long and is set in the heart of a beautiful forest. To the north of Reutte lies Vils, which has the distinction of being the Tirol's smallest township, and the German frontier. To the west, over the Gaicht Pass, there are two more delightful little mountain lakes within easy bus rides of Reutte.

To the southwest of Reutte, the long, straggling Lech valley follows the course of the mountain stream across the Lech Alps right up to the mighty Arlberg and the provincial frontier of Vorarlberg. In summer this rather out-of-the-way Alpine valley is a favorite base for mountaineering enthusiasts.

Exploring the Lower Inn Region

To the east of Innsbruck the Inn valley broadens out considerably, and courses right through the Tirol to Kufstein and the German border. Hall, a bare 8 km. (5 miles) from the Tirolean capital, is very ancient, and was founded by miners from the nearby salt mines, which have now fallen into disuse. The picturesque old part of the town is built on a steep slope in the form of an amphitheater with narrow cobbled streets running straight down the hill. From the main road you cannot get a proper perspective of the fine old buildings. The old Rathaus, or town hall, was built in the middle of the 15th century and is a fine example. The ornately-carved councillors' room should be seen, and also the beautifully-worked mosaics which cover the Rathaus walls. The Mint Tower, which you can hardly miss, and the monastery church, the oldest ecclesiastical building of the Renaissance period to be found in the Tirol, are all interesting examples of Tirolean craftsmanship.

Schwaz, on the right bank of the Inn, is even older than Hall and dates back to the 12th century. In the 15th century Schwaz was a rich and important mining center, whose chief sources of wealth were the silver mines burrowing deep under the towering Tuxer Alps. Many of the buildings built during those prosperous times still stand, and the market place has kept its atmosphere. The churches of Schwaz are full of interesting architectural detail and lovely works of art.

Jenbach, a main line station on the railway, is important to the tourist as the starting point for the Achen and Zillertal valleys, both very popular summer resorts.

A small railway takes passengers from the Jenbach railway station up the steep 1-in-4 gradient to Maurach near the head of the great Achensee lake. As the little train crawls jerkily up the Achen valley you get a magnificent view over the Alps to the right. Buses provide alternative means of transport from Jenbach, and travel all along the lake as far as the Achen Pass at the farther end of the valley, stopping at the three or four lakeside summer resorts on the way. From Maurach you can take a cable car to Erfurter Hütte, a mountain lodge about 1,820 m. (6,000 ft.) up in the Sonnwend mountain group.

The Achen Valley

Although you can have some excellent skiing in the Achen valley in the winter, the lake is the main attraction, and the whole valley is a very popular summer resort. The mountain lake is the largest and most beautiful in the Tirol. The great mountains of the Karwendel and Sonnwend ranges rise from its blue waters, nearly 137m. (450 ft.) deep in places. A small steamer plies between the different villages strung out along the lakeside, and is usually crowded with trippers at the height of the season. There is some excellent fishing in the lake and on the river, too, which flows out of the lake at the farther end and into Germany.

Pertisau, a small picturesque little village, the only one on the western shore of the lake, is the most popular place to go to, and less than a mile from the railway terminus at the level of the lake. Located nearly 900 m. (3,000 ft.) above sea level, Pertisau offers fair comfort, excellent bathing, sailing, tennis and fishing, and even boasts of a small nine hole golf course, all at budget prices.

On the eastern side of the lake, the road leads through Buchau to the northern end with various small settlements belonging to the commune of Achenkirch; Seehof is one of them and Scholastika another one. Although Pertisau and the western shore of the lake are more popular, the eastern side enjoys at least two hours of sunshine a day more, and the bathing is consequently warmer.

The drive, either by bus or in your own car, along the Achenbach to the Bavarian border is very lovely. It passes through the village of Achenwald and you reach the Austrian-German frontier on the Achen Pass.

Because it lies so conveniently close to Innsbruck, 48 km. (30 miles) away, the lake is always crowded with weekend holidaymakers from the city during the hot summer months. If you only plan to pay a fleeting visit to the valley, you would do well to choose a weekday.

The Ziller and Tuxer Valleys

On the other side of the Inn valley lies the Zillertal, biggest and most famous of the many beautiful valleys of Tirol. You may be a little disappointed traveling along the lower reaches of the Zillertal. As far as Zell am Ziller the valley is broad and shallow, and the scenery is certainly not very inspiring. It is only from Zell onwards that the valley really starts to live up to its name. On the way up the lower part of the valley you pass through the small pretty Alpine villages and then you come to Zell am Ziller, the first of the tourist centers.

The Gauder Festival, the traditional Ziller valley May fête, takes place on the first weekend in May. Thousands of tourists from far and wide pack the little market town to watch the events, which are very colorful and most amusing. These festivals have been held at Zell for over 400 years, and the different events are based on ancient customs. Here, too, you can hear some of the best Ziller valley singing, and listen to some expert harp and zither playing. For the Ziller valley folk are famous throughout Austria for their prowess on these ancient instruments.

At Zell am Ziller the valley divides. The main valley goes straight on up to Mayrhofen, the most important resort in the valley, and to the Tuxer valley, while an offshoot climbs to the Gerlos plateau, a favorite winter sports resort, and a center for mountain climbing. The Ziller valley railway doesn't run up this branch of the valley, but buses and sleighs take passengers from Zell up to the plateau. The dominating feature at Gerlos is the towering Kreuzjoch, 2,558 m. (8,392 ft.) high. Beyond Gerlos there is a scenic road leading over the Gerlos Pass to the village of Wald and Krimml waterfalls in the neighboring Land Salzburg.

The old Ziller steam railway makes daily scheduled runs between Jenbach and Mayrhofen, and can be rented—at a price—by steam-engine buffs. Mayrhofen is the main base for sightseeing tourists, and has been a favorite Tirolean summer resort of the British for many a year. At Mayrhofen the Ziller valley splits up into four. Three of these are called gründe (grounds): the Zillergrund, Stillupgrund, and Zemmgrund. Each of these narrow, pretty little valleys striking deep into the heart of the Ziller Alps is a perfect gem, a prime example of the picture-postcard Alpine valley, rising near the top to the glittering pale blue glaciers.

The fourth arm leads into the Tuxer valley, highest of the four, which ends at the foot of the massive Olperer and Rifflerspitz glaciers, nearly 3,350 m. (11,000 ft.) up. Frequent buses leave Mayrhofen for Lanersbach and Hintertux, the two villages in the valley. The view over the Tuxer Alps to the north is perhaps the finest of the whole.

Lanersbach is the first of these small mountain villages and at the top of the valley is Hintertux, right at the foot of the great glaciers that have made the Tuxer valley so famous a beauty spot and summer-skiing region. 1,493 m. (4,898 ft.) above sea level, Hintertux is also quite popular as a spa, and has a small thermal swimming pool. Apart from the magnificent landscape that surrounds the mountain village, Hintertux is also the center of an ancient wood-carving industry.

The Rattenberg District

Back in the main Inn valley, we come to Brixlegg, with its two famous castles, Schloss Kropfsberg, built to defend the approaches to the Ziller valley, and Schloss Matzen, a 12th-century castle on the mountainside. Brixlegg stands at the entrance to the short Alpbach valley, whose main attraction is the lovely small town of Alpbach, a winter sports center, but a delightful place at any time of the year. Alpbach is also the setting for the annual Europäisches Forum Alpbach (European Forum).

Two miles farther along the Inn valley from Brixlegg is Rattenberg, a quaint little medieval town, once a famous mining town like Hall and Schwaz, and now reduced to a small place with a tiny population. Rattenberg's prosperity came from silver mining and, when the mines were exhausted, the town lapsed into a trance of centuries. There are some very fine examples of Gothic architecture and the ruins of a powerful castle built by Emperor Maximilian I.

Rattenberg and Kramsach, across the Inn River, are known for fine glass workshops, owned by Sudeten German refugees from Czechoslovakia: in Kramsach there is also a school teaching the art of etching, engraving and painting on glassware—you can have your name or initials engraved on any glass within half an hour. Near Kramsach is the 17th-century Achenrain Castle with three small and charming lakes in the vicinity. Here is also the entrance to the short but lovely Brandenberg valley. About 8 km. (5 miles) up and high above the valley is the small village of Brandenberg, surrounded by beautiful woods.

We arrive next at Wörgl, a mainline junction, which is Austria's youngest township and a thriving market town. Here the main road and the railway divide. One route follows the Inn up to Kufstein and on to Bavaria, the other turns due east through Kaisergebirge and the Kitzbühel Alps to the famous skiing center of Kitzbühel. Just south of Wörgl is the Wildschönau district with the small skiing villages of Niederau, Oberau and Auffach, reached by a country road.

The Kufstein District

Like many other Austrian provincial towns Kufstein is dominated by a mighty castle. In this case it is the Geroldseck fortress, built by the Dukes of Bavaria in the 12th century on a spur of Kaisergebirge guarding the entrance to the Inn valley. It has withstood many sieges, and was later used as a political prison before becoming the town museum. Perhaps the most interesting feature of the fortress is the colossal Heroes' Organ built in one of the great towers. It is said that you can hear the organ quite clearly more than eight kilometers away on a windless day. On a clear day the view from the Wallachenbastion is magnificent.

Four chairlifts will take you up the nearby mountain, the Kaisergebirge, but the great attraction at Kufstein during the hot summer months is the large number of warm water lakes in the immediate neighborhood. There are no less than eight of these. Some of them, like the Pfrillsee and Längsee, are perched high up on the mountainside in the middle of dense forests. Others, like the Thiersee, are larger and in open country.

Thiersee is a picturesque mountain village on the lake of the same name, amidst magnificent Alpine scenery. The town is also known for its passion play, revived in 1955 and similar to that of Oberammergau in neighboring Bavaria. The passion play was started in the 17th century and still takes place from time to time in a special theater that seats 900. The play is acted by a village amateur group and non-villagers are not allowed to perform.

Up in the northwest corner, near the German border, is the village of Erl, whose ancient passion play was revived during the summer of 1959. One of the oldest of its kind in the Alpine regions, it traces its origins back to the religious plays first given there in the year 1613.

The Kitzbühel Alps

The main trunk road from Wörgl leads through the valley between the Kaiser and the Kitzbühel mountains via St. Johann in Tirol to Kitzbühel, one of the most famous winter sports centers in the world. St. Johann is also a place to choose for a summer vacation, as it has all kinds of activities on offer plus plenty of variety in walking paths, from gentle ones by the rivers to quite serious climbs. Another road, not quite as good a surface, but considerably shorter, goes right over the Kitzbühel Alps through Hopfgarten and Kirchberg—both winter sports centers. Wheel chains are essential if you take this route while it is snowing, but for most of the year it is easily usable, clear and much less busy than the main road round through St. Johann.

Long before Kitzbühel became a fashionable winter sports resort, the picturesque little old-world town, set in the heart of the magnificent Kaiser and Kitzbühel Alpine ranges, was popular as a summer resort. In those days the main attractions were the unrivaled scenery and the attractive warm water lake of Schwarzsee just outside the town. Nowadays, of course, the accent is wholly on skiing. The town's facilities are among the finest in the world. The famous Kitzbühel Ski Circus is a carefully planned, clever combination of lifts, cable railways, and runs, beginning at the foot of the Hahnenkamm (valley station of the main cable railway) by which you can ski downhill for over 80 km. (50 miles) without having to climb a single foot on your own power.

Many famous people have their own villas near Kitzbühel, and the place is teeming with celebrities during December and again in February. If you want a day off there are frequent bus services to Salzburg through Germany, and the trip takes an hour each way. But there is always plenty to do and see in Kitzbühel: ski races, festivals, fancy dress balls, and plenty of local color. Kitzbühel also has quite a name as a health resort.

A few miles north of Kitzbühel is the far less fashionable winter sports town of St. Johann in Tirol. Many sportsmen who cannot afford the luxury of actually living in Kitzbühel itself come here instead, enjoying the same skiing facilities as their better-off brothers.

High up in the Kitzbühel Alps, southeast of St. Johann, a 15-minute bus run from St Johann station is another smaller winter sports center— Fieberbrunn, one of the prettiest villages in this part of the Tirol, set amid beautiful scenery, with plenty of snow and first-class skiing. Another small winter and summer resort easily reached from St. Johann by bus is the village of Kössen near the German border. From Kössen you can take the bus also to Kufstein by the way of Walchsee, a beautiful lake among the mountains where all water sports are practised in the summer.

The Upper Inn Region

The Upper Inn valley from Innsbruck to the Swiss border is very beautiful, particularly the narrow mountain valleys which branch off to the south from the broad Inn up into the vast, glistening regions of the Stubai and Ötztal glaciers.

The first of these, and the shortest, the Sellrain, is only a few kilometers west of Innsbruck and is easily and rapidly reached by bus. At Zirl, the first town along the Upper Inn, the mountain road up to the high Seefeld plateau branches off over a steep mountain ridge to the north. Your Sellrain bus, though, crosses the Inn to Kematen, a small village at the entrance to the Sellrain valley, and then runs along the lovely Melach gorge to the villages of Sellrain and Gries in Sellrain. Both these places are popular skiing centers during the winter months, and are chiefly patronized by the city dwellers from nearby Innsbruck. In the summer the villages are starting points for extensive tours into the Stubai glaciers. At its end the valley climbs up to the mountain plateau at Kühtai with the renowned hunting castle of Emperor Maximilian I, converted into a hotel. Kühtai is a high summer and winter resort and at the same time a pass; the road continues from here down into the Ötz valley.

The 16-km. (10-mile) stretch of road from Zirl to Telfs is not very interesting to tourists. If you are traveling by car, you will find the old country road running along the southern bank of the Inn rather more diverting than the newer arterial highway which hugs the mountain cliffs all the way. Telfs, like Zirl, is another typical Inn valley market town. Traveling westwards from Telfs by car you have two choices. You can continue down the main road along the Inn or turn off towards the Mieminger plateau to Nassereith, then south to Imst where you rejoin the highway.

If you have the time to spare, the short extra trip is well worth while. From the top of the plateau, at Barwies, you have a magnificent view down over the Inn valley on your left, and to the right over the Wetterstein massif which you will miss by keeping to the Inn. If you are going to Reutte from Innsbruck by car and not via the Karwendel railway, this is the route to take. At Nassereith the road to Lermoos and Reutte branches off and climbs steeply out of the village and over the Fern Pass. The village of Nassereith is best known for its procession of grotesque masks which takes place every five years at Fasching.

Following the main road from Telfs you pass by the village of Stams with its 13th-century Cistercian abbey. If you are interested in architecture you will most certainly want to visit it. The monastery church, originally Romanesque, has been rebuilt several times and presently is one of the largest Baroque churches in Tirol; the interior is by various masters, including Feichtmayr and Vischer, and glories in a Rose Grille, a superb wrought-iron screen made in 1716, and a multitude of other beautiful sculptures and paintings. The abbey was closely associated with royal and aristocratic patrons for centuries, and boasts a whole complex of richly-decorated rooms, as well as lavish tombs.

The monastery building has also been rebuilt several times, the present Baroque structure dating from the early 18th century. It is now the Schigymnasium, a boarding school for would-be ski racers.

Imst, a thriving little market town, lying a kilometer or so back from the Inn River and the railway line, is an excellent center to choose for a summer holiday and base from which to visit the famous Pitz and Ötz valleys. Here is held the Schemenlaufen, another renowned masked Fasching procession. Many of the magnificently carved masks worn by the mummers—especially those of the fearsome witches—are very old and are works of art. Good specimens of these masks can be seen in the Imst museum. A great feature of these rustic carnivals is the ringing of cow bells of all shapes, sizes, and tones. If you have time, take a walk up the dramatic Rosengarten Gorge, which begins right in the heart of town. 40 minutes will take you through some breathtaking scenery, but wear strong shoes.

A bus from Imst will take you into the Pitz Valley, whose entrance is directly opposite Imst, across the Inn. The road rises steeply and abruptly to Arzl, a pleasant mountain village for a restful vacation.

The Ötz Valley

The Ötz Valley begins 11 km. (about 7 miles) east of Imst and rises in a series of great natural steps for nearly 42 km. (26 miles) from the Inn river to the glaciers around Obergurgl, nearly 1,951 m. (6,400 ft.) above sea level.

At the head of the first stop is Ötz, a typical Tirolean mountain village with an interesting old Gothic parish church. A kilometer farther on you pass through the tiny hamlet of Habichen; up another step to Umhausen, the oldest, and Längenfeld, the largest, village in the valley. Near Umhausen is the wild Stuiben waterfall.

We now come to Sölden, the first of the famous villages in the valley. Sölden (1,359 m., 4,460 ft.) is a winter sports center with an international reputation. The natural skiing facilities are extremely good, and by taking the chair lift up to Hochsölden (2,062 m., 6,800 ft.) you can be sure of excellent snow conditions for all the year. Hochsölden, by the way, is in no sense of the word a village, but merely the terminus of the chair lift graced by a collection of sports hotels. A modern cable car takes you from Sölden over the glaciers to an elevation of almost 3,050 m. (10,000 ft.) on Gaislachkogel, to the permanent snow area where skiing is done all year; this is the highest cable car in Austria.

Tiny Obergurgl is famous for three things: it is the highest village in Austria (1,926 m., 6,320 ft.), it is the place where Professor Piccard landed in his famous balloon, and it is a magnificent winter sports district. A vast expanse of snow and ice shimmers all around you during the winter, and all year round the great peaks and glaciers of the Ötztal Alps appear to be deceptively close at hand. A high Alpine road takes you from Obergurgl to the hotel settlement of Hochgurgl, an excellent skiing spot, and farther up to the Timmelsjoch pass (about 2,499 m., 8,200 ft.) through magnificent mountain scenery. From Hochgurgl, a three-stage chair lift takes you to an area where skiing is possible all year round.

The Venter Valley burrows even deeper into the Ötztal Alps, and finally ends at Vent, a small Alpine village, lying a mere hundred feet lower than Obergurgl. It, too, is a popular winter sports center. During the summer it becomes the base for serious mountain climbers, experienced in ice and rock climbing, who wish to attempt to scale—preferably with professional local guides—the formidable Wildspitze (3,795 m., 12,450 ft.) or other, even more difficult, neighboring peaks.

Landeck

24 km. (15 miles) farther west along the main Inn valley from Imst we come to Landeck, the largest and, perhaps, the least attractive town on the Upper Inn. Although the town has not the same charming atmosphere as Imst, it is a popular tourist center during the summer months, and is a convenient base from which to explore the nearby Paznaun Valley and the final stretch of the Inn Valley.

Landeck is famous for an ancient and awe-inspiring rite which takes place around Christmas time each year. At dawn the young men of Landeck set out to climb to the top of the great rocky crags that overshadow and hem in the old city on three sides. As dusk falls they light huge bonfires which can be seen for miles around, and then set fire to great discs of pinewood dipped in tar which they roll down to the valley below. The sight of scores of these enormous fiery wheels bounding down the steep slopes towards the town is a fearsome spectacle, and the more daring young bloods, clutching blazing torches and yelling at the top of their voices, race down the mountainsides on skis at breakneck speed in an attempt to beat the firebrands to the bottom of the valley.

At Landeck the river Inn turns southward along the edge of the Silvretta mountains toward Engadin in Switzerland and South Tirol in Italy. Ried is a small village where you turn off to the west up a small precipice to Ladis, and higher up Bad Obladis on the Samnaun range, with a wonderful view over the Inn valley and down to Landeck, with the Lech Alps in the far distance.

On the same side above the Inn valley, also perched up high on the plateau, is Serfaus (1,433 m., 4,700 ft.), an old village with interesting painted houses, a 14th-century and a Baroque church; it is also reached by a branch road from Ried. Serfaus is an important winter sports center with a good number of ski lifts and the Komperdell cable car will take you also in summer up to where you can take several interesting mountain tours or just enjoy the view.

At the head of the Inn valley, where the Austrian, Swiss and Italian frontiers meet, is Nauders, an unpretentious but delightful little winter sports center, dominated by the striking 14th-century Castle of Naudersberg. Due west of Nauders, up a steep pass to Martinsbruck, you reach the Swiss frontier post and the entrance to the Engadine. Carry straight on through Nauders for 5 km. (3 miles) and you are in South Tirol, in Italy. Nauders is a good place to stay overnight if you are driving to or from Italy.

The Paznaun Valley

Another interesting valley tour, easily undertaken from Landeck by bus, is up the enchanting Paznaun valley running southwest from the village of Pians, a kilometer to the west of Landeck. This valley follows the course of the Trisanna mountain river for 40 km. (25 miles) into the heart of the Blue Silvretta mountains, so called because of the shimmering ice-blue effect of great peaks and glaciers, dominated by the mighty Fluchthorn at the head of the valley at Galtür.

At Ischgl the biggest village of the Paznaun, lying just over halfway up the valley, you will find excellent skiing, particularly in the small Fimber valley, which branches off the Paznaun at this point. In summer Ischgl is a popular high altitude health resort. The almost 4-km.-long Silvretta cable car takes you even higher, to 2,317-m. (7,600-ft.) Idalpe.

Galtür, slightly higher, at the top of the valley road, a two-hour bus ride from Landeck, is the best-known resort in the Paznaun, equally popular as a winter sports center, summer resort, and as a base for mountain climbing. Although well known as a base for hardened, practised mountaineers, many of the climbs up the Blue Silvretta to the half dozen mountain rest huts belonging to the Alpenverein are very easy.

The Arlberg

Between the entrance to the computer-controlled Arlberg road tunnel, Europe's third-longest, and the railway, from which the *Arlberg Express* takes its name, at the foot of the great mountain pass, lies St. Anton am Arlberg, to use the town's proper title, one of the most famous winter sports centers in the world and the cradle of modern skiing.

It was to this small and—at that time—unpretentious little Alpine valley town that Hannes Schneider, an unknown young ski instructor with advanced ideas, came to teach his now world famous "Arlberg School" skiing technique at the invitation of the newly founded Arlberg Ski Club. Although there have been many important modifications—notably by other Austrian instructors—to the "Arlberg technique" as originally taught by Hannes Schneider just after the turn of the century, the basic features of all skiing courses the world over are based on the fundamentals laid down by him.

At the height of the season, the little town is seething with visitors. Many prominent people in public life, including royalty, come regularly every year to St. Anton for the winter sports.

The Skihaserl or ski bunny, as the beginner is referred to, will join the ski school. The nursery slopes are good at St. Anton and you will have plenty of company, often very distinguished company. Once you are past the Skihaserl stage—this may well take more than a season—you will want to get up into the Arlberg mountains and enjoy the superlative runs from the top of the Galzig and the Valluga above it. The summit of Valuga (2,809 m., 9,216 ft.) reached by aerial cable car, offers also in summer a splendid view over the Alps.

Two kilometers higher up is the hamlet of St. Christoph, where a hospice was founded as early as the 15th century to succour stranded and imperiled travelers caught by snowdrifts on the pass. St. Christoph is another important, but much smaller, winter sports center, and it is here that the Austrian government holds its exacting courses for would-be ski instructors.

While at St. Christoph there is not the same social round as at St. Anton, the skiing facilities are exactly the same, and are nearer to hand. In some respects, especially if you are determined to take your skiing seriously and willing to forego the distractions of high life (or cannot afford them), winter sports are more fun at St. Christoph.

East Tirol

The present-day Austrian Federal State of Tirol is roughly rectangular in shape, with East Tirol tacked on to the southeastern corner like an appendix. The state is one great mass of mountains, scarred by scores of Alpine valleys, some large, but mostly small and narrow, winding in and out of the great ranges of the Alps.

The isolated position of East Tirol is one of those strange historical accidents. In 1918, after World War I, South Tirol was ceded to Italy. This left East Tirol completely cut off from the rest of the Tirol by a narrow upthrust of Italy which joins the border of Land Salzburg. East Tirol, although separated, is an integral part, for administrative purposes, of Tirol proper.

Geographically, therefore, to the west and south of East Tirol runs the Italian frontier, while to the north stretches a massive, impassable barrier of the Alps, the Venediger and Glockner groups of Hohe Tauern. Except for the new Felbertauern Road and for the Drau Valley running to Carinthia, these mountains now separate it from the rest of Austria and, consequently, East Tirol has been neglected by the international tourist in spite of magnificent mountain scenery.

To reach East Tirol from inside Austria, there is a railway coming from Carinthia that enters East Tirol at Dölsach proceeding through Lienz and Sillian to South Tirol (now in Italy), and from there to Innsbruck. The so-called corridor trains (cars locked while in transit through Italian territory, but without passport and customs control) operate between Innsbruck and Lienz (about four hours by autorail; connections are often bad).

To enter by car you must either travel over the Felbertauern alpine road, the only link with North Tirol through Austrian territory, or from Carinthia. From Land Salzburg, you can take also the celebrated Grossglockner mountain road, whose Carinthian section will bring you to the Iselsberg

Pass. Each of these routes will bring you directly to Lienz, capital of East Tirol.

Lienz is a summer resort, a center for mountain climbers, and an up-and-coming winter sports headquarters. The 16th-century Liebburg castle-palace on the main square is now being restored to its former splendor. The most interesting sights in the 15th-century parish church include four late Gothic winged altars, frescos by Josef Adam Mölk, and late Gothic tombs. Near the church is the district war memorial with chapel frescos by the famous Tirolean painter Albin Egger-Lienz, who, as his name implies, was from Lienz, and who is also buried here. This is marvelous walking country. Take the Zettersfeld cable car to the top for easy, but rewarding, high-altitude walking. South of Lienz the walking is equally good in the Dolomites or on the Hochstein massif.

Just outside the market town there is a small bathing lake at Tristach with a little Lido. The old battlemented Castle of Schloss Bruck, at the entrance to the Isel valley, a kilometer-and-a-half outside the town, should not be missed. In the old days it used to be the seat of the Counts of Görz (now called Gorizia and located in Italy), and today it houses a very interesting museum with finds from the nearby Roman excavations, folklore collections, and paintings by Egger-Lienz and Franz Defregger, another Tirolean painter. The castle was first built in the 13th century and then rebuilt in the 16th century. It is remarkably well preserved and its most outstanding features are the tower and the Romanesque chapel with late 15th-century frescos. Another point of interest are the excavations of the Roman town of Aguntum, between Nussdorf and Dölsach, less than 5 km. (3 miles) from Lienz. Before the Roman times Aguntum was a Hallstatt-period market town.

Lienz owes its importance as a town to the fact that it stands at the junction of three valleys. The Isel valley to the northwest, the main Drau valley to the east, and Pustertal to the west. The East Tirolean section of Pustertal is also the valley of Drau River, but the long Puster valley crosses the Austro-Italian border and continuing through South Tirol (while retaining the name of Pustertal) becomes the valley of the River Rienz and ends near the town of Brixen in South Tirol. The Drau River crosses into Carinthia less than 16 km. (10 miles) below Lienz, but the Isel and its tributaries cover most of the East Tirol north of Drau.

The section of Pustertal to the Italian frontier at Toblach is not very exciting. To the south of the road you get a magnificent view over the Lienz Dolomites, and the road and railway finally reach the village of Sillian, the highest in this valley, and just before the frontier. Near Sillian is the 13th-century Heimfels Castle, also once owned by the Counts of Görz; although it is slowly decaying it is still a powerful sight, and if you are at all romantically inclined, very much worth roaming through its walls and courtyards. If you turn off north just before Sillian and travel 12 km. up the good road, you will come to the village of Innervillgraten. This remote valley head offers the perfect place for those who want to get away from it all. There is also excellent walking in the area.

From Sillian you'll have to turn back to Lienz unless you want to cross the frontier of Italy and visit South Tirol. North of Lienz, at the confluence of the Virgen and Tauern valleys, is Matrei, quite frequented as a summer resort. It has a late Baroque parish church built by Hagenauer; nearby is the old but remodeled Weissenstein Castle and the 13th-century Nikolauskirche (St. Nicholas Church) with Romanesque frescos from the early 13th century, among the oldest preserved in Austria. Matrei is a mountain climbing center. If you do not wish to engage in this somewhat strenuous activity you may take the bus to Matreier Tauernhaus, almost 1,525 m. (5,000 ft.) up in the Tauern valley, in order to enjoy the spectacular landscape of the Venediger range. If you drive, you can also reach this area by the new smooth and fast Felbertauern road amidst spectacular mountain scenery.

Retracing our steps back towards Lienz we come to a point where the Isel, Defereggen, and Kalser valleys meet. At the end of Kalser valley, deep under the pyramidal peak of Grossglockner, is the mountain village of Kals, one of the top mountain climbing centers in Austria. If you don't feel like climbing Grossglockner from this side, a walk into the nearby Lesach valley, up to the Lesacher Alpe, will reward you with beautiful mountain scenery and the absence of modern mechanical contraptions. Defereggen valley, a deep cut in the Defereggen Alps, is dotted with unspoiled villages, and St. Jakob in Defereggen, near its upper end, a small summer and winter resort, is one of the nicest mountain villages in East Tirol.

If you drive (or ride on a bus) from Lienz to the Grossglockner mountain road, you have to cross the Iselsberg pass on the border of East Tirol and Carinthia. From Iselsberg, a summer resort and winter sports center, there is a most magnificent view of the Lienz Dolomites.

There is a game reserve located between Oberassling and Bichl, high in the mountains, stocked with indigenous animals including chamois, wild boar and the golden eagle. Visitors are welcome and there is a car park and restaurant.

PRACTICAL INFORMATION FOR INNSBRUCK

TOURIST INFORMATION. Tiroler Fremdenverkehrswerbung (Tirol Tourist Office), Bozner Platz 6, (05 12–53 20 0); Städtisches Verkehrsbüro (Local Tourist Office), Burggraben 3 (05 12–53 56 0); Hotel Information at the Central Rail Station, (05 12–58 37 66); autobahn exit west (57 35 43); autobahn exit east (46 4 74); autobahn exit south (57 79 33); and Igls (77 1 01).

Post Offices. Hauptpostamt (Central Post Office), Maximilianstr. 2, open all week, round the clock. Brunecker Str. 1–3, Mon. to Sat., 6.30 A.M.–8 P.M.

Money. Banks are open Mon. to Fri. 7.45–12.30, 2.15–4. Bureaux de Change in the Tourist Office, Burggraben 3, daily 8–8. Another one in the Central Station is open daily 7.30 A.M. to 8.15 P.M. Others can be found in travel agencies and hotels. Compare rates.

AREA CODES—MAIL AND PHONES. The postal code for Innsbruck is A-6020. The telephone area code is 05 12.

HOTELS. The main station is centrally located, and most of the main hotels are within easy reach. You are advised to book your rooms well in advance for the high season (July to Aug. and in the winter). However, if you arrive without having booked, inquire at the rooms reservation office (Zimmernachweis) in the railway station: they will find you accommodation, either in a small hotel or a private house.

Innsbruck is a very visitor-conscious town, and offers all kinds of deals, especially in winter. These change from year to year but usually include advantageous hotel rates. There is also a Club Innsbruck guest card which gives reductions on cablecars and lifts, etc.

Deluxe

Europa, Südtirolerplatz 2 (59 31). 130 rooms with bath. In center of town, opposite railway station. Period furnished rooms, some modern; excellent *Philippine Welser* restaurant. AE, DC, MC, V.

Innsbruck, Innrain 3 (59 8 68). 70 rooms with bath. Modern, with good views of old town and Nordkette mountains. AE, DC, MC, V.

Scandic Crown, Salurner Str. 15 (59 3 50). International standard. 180 luxury rooms with bath. Indoor pool. Excellent panorama restaurant. Roof terrace. Piano bar. AE, DC, MC, V.

Expensive

Alpotel, Innrain 13 (57 79 31). Central, with 75 comfortable, quiet rooms, all with bath. Sauna. Outstanding restaurants. AE, DC, MC, V.

Central, Sparkassenplatz (59 20). 80 rooms with bath or shower; indoor pool. AE, DC, MC, V.

Clima, Zeughausgasse 7 (58 83 61). 51 rooms with bath; garage. DC, MC, V.

Goldener Adler, Herzog Friedrich Strasse 6 (58 63 34). 40 rooms with bath or shower. Founded in 1390 in the heart of the old town; hostelry for dukes and princes. AE, DC, MC, V.

Grauer Bär, Universitätstrasse 5 (59 2 40). 150 rooms with bath or shower. Well furnished rooms and spacious bathrooms. Rustic bar. AE, DC, MC, V.

Kapeller, Phil. Welserstrasse 96 (43 1 01). 35 rooms with bath or shower. Slightly out of town; cozy rooms, mostly with TV. Outstanding restaurant, closed Sun. AE, DC, MC.

Maria Theresia, Maria-Theresienstrasse 31 (59 33). 200 beds with bath. Friendly. Newly renovated. Right in the center of town. Underground garage. AE, DC, MC, V.

Roter Adler, Seilergasse 4–6 (59 4 47). 60 rooms with bath. AE, DC, MC, V.

Schwarzer Adler, Kaiserjägerstrasse 2 (58 71 09). Romantik Hotel. 50 beds with bath or shower. Excellent restaurant with Tirolean specialties. AE, DC, MC, V.

Villa Blanka, Weiherburggasse 8 (82 22 11). 36 rooms with bath or shower. Modern, above center of town; rooms with balconies. AE, DC, MC, V.

Moderate

Berg Isel, Bergisel (58 19 12). 21 rooms, 5 with bath. Bar and restaurant. Closed Nov.

Greif, Leopoldstr. 3 (58 74 01). 66 rooms. DC, MC.

Koreth, Hauptplatz 1 (67 5 67). 20 rooms, with bath or shower. Garage; bar and restaurant. Outside Innsbruck in the village of Mühlau.

Leipziger Hof, Defreggerstrasse 13 (43 5 25). 70 rooms, all with bath or shower. AE, DC, MC, V.

Mozart, Müllerstrasse 15 (59 5 38). 50 rooms, most with bath or shower. AE, DC, MC, V.

Neue Post, Maximilianstr. 15 (59 4 76). 60 comfortable rooms. Restaurant. AE, DC, MC, V.

Royal, Innrain 16 (58 63 85). 37 rooms, most with bath or shower. AE, DC, MC, V.

Weisses Kreuz, Herzog Friedrichstrasse 31 (59 47 90). 52 rooms, most with bath or shower. Central, next to Goldenes Dachl, in pedestrian-only street. AE.

Inexpensive

Internationales Studentenheim, Innrain 64 (59 4 71). Open July to end Sept.

Leopoldina, Bürgerstrasse 10 (58 90 27). Open July to end Sept.

Rapoldihaus, Hans-Untermüllerstrasse 6 (85 1 55). 90 rooms, most with shower; bar and restaurant. Open July to Sept. AE.

Student Hotel, Fischmalstr. 24 (83 3 61). Open July and Aug.

Weisses Lamm, Mariahilferstr. 12 (83 1 56). All rooms with shower.

Youth Hostels

Glockenhaus, Weiherburggasse 3 (85 5 03). Open all year.

Technikerhaus, Fischnalerstr. 26 (82 1 10). Open July and Aug.

Youth Hostel, Radetzkystr. 47 (49 17 42). Open all year.

Youth Hostel Reichenau, Reichenauer Strasse 147 (46 1 80). Open all year: except Dec. 24–26.

Youth Hostel Torsten-Arneus-Schwedenhaus, Rennweg 17b (25 8 14). Open July and Aug.

Youth Hostel St. Paulus, Reichenauer Strasse 72 (44 2 91). Open July and Aug.

Camping

Innsbruck has three camping sites at—

Reichenauer Strasse (46 2 52); **Innsbruck-West,** Kranebitter Allee 214 (84 1 80). Open Apr. to Oct.: **Seewirt,** Geyrstrasse 25 (46 1 53).

GETTING AROUND INNSBRUCK. By Tram and Bus.

Innsbruck is well served with internal transport, there are 3 tramlines and 25 bus lines. Tickets can be bought in books of 5, 10 and 25.

Post buses going all over the Tirol can be caught at the Central Bus Station (next to the Central Rail one).

Taxis. There are taxi stands all over town. For radio taxis call 53 11 or 45 5 00.

Car Hire. Avis, Salurnerstr. 15 (57 17 54) and at airport; Buchbinder, Burgenlandstr. 8 (48 5 65), very competitive prices; Denzel, Adamgasse 5 (58 20 60); Hertz, Südtirolerplatz 1 (58 09 01).

Horse Cabs. Horse-drawn cabs are still a feature of Innsbruck life. There is a cab stand in front of the Tiroler Landestheater on Rennweg.

Cable Cars. Three cable car systems will take you up the nearby mountains. The **Nordkettenbahn** is in three parts, bus line N to the Hungerburg funicular, Hungerburg to Seegrube, Seegrube to Hafelekar.

The **Patscherkofelbahn** goes by bus J, Igls to Heiligwasser, Heiligwasser to Patscherkofel house, Patscherkofel house to the Patscherkofel peak by chair lift.

The **Mutteralmbahn** goes from Mutters (Stubaitalbahn) to Nockhof, from there to Muttereralm, from there by chair lift to Pfriemesköpfl.

By Car. Parking in the town center means vouchers, bought from tobacconists, the Tourist Office (Burggraben 3) and machines. Or there are indoor parks at the Hotel Maria Theresia, Erlerstr.; Sparkassen Garage, Sparkassenplatz 1; Garage Tourist Center, Salurnerstr. 15; Markthallen Garage, Herzog-Sigmund-Ufer; Garage Tiroler Gebietskrankenstr., Klara-Pölt-Weg 2.

Sightseeing. Sightseeing tours of Innsbruck by bus, taking about an hour, leave from the Hofburg at 10.15, 12, 2 and 3.15. Longer tours lasting around 2 hours, leave Bozner Platz at 10.10, 12.10 and 2.10.

PLACES OF INTEREST. We give the admission times for those places of interest that can only be visited during certain hours. The Hofburg, Imperial Church and Silver Chapel are all close together, but to explore their treasures thoroughly you must allow half a day.

Alpenvereinsmuseum, Wilhelm-Greil-Str. 15. The history of the central Alps, with special emphasis on the story of skiing. June through Sept., Mon. to Fri. 9–12, 2–5; Oct. through May, Tues. to Thurs. 6–12, 2–5.

Alpenzoo, Weiherburg. A unique zoo, housing all species of Alpine vertebrate animals. Open all year, daily 9–6 (5 in winter).

Bergisel Museum, Bergisel. Panoramic view and museum to patriot Andreas Hofer and other Tirolean heroes. April through Sept., daily 8–5; Oct. through March, daily 10–3. Closed Mon.

Hofburg, Rennweg. The Imperial Palace, originally built by Maximilian and rebuilt magnificently by Maria Theresa (finished in 1777). Guided tours all year, open daily 9–4. Closed Sun.

Hofkirche und Silberne Kapelle (Court Church and Silver Chapel), Universitätsstr. 2. Maximilian I's monument with Dürer's statues; Andreas Hofer's tomb; the Silver Chapel (between the church and the palace) has silver altarpiece and more fine tombs. May to Sept., daily 9–5; Oct. to April, daily 9–12, 2–5, Sun. 9–12.

Olympiamuseum (Olympic Museum), Goldenes Dachl. Films and exhibits of the '64 and '76 Winter Olympics. Daily 9.30–12, 2–5.

Riesenrundgemälde, Rennweg 39, next to Hungerburg funicular station. Giant, circular painting of the battle of Bergisel, 1809. April to Oct., daily 9–4.45.

Schloss Ambras (Lower Castle). On outskirts, tram 3 toward Pradl, or line 6. Archduke Ferdinand II's art collection, plus fine apartments; lovely park. May through Sept., daily 10–4; closed Tues.

Stadtturm (The City Tower), Herzog-Friedrich-Str. 21. 15th-century tower with magnificent views. March through Oct., daily 10–5; July and Aug., daily 10–6.

Tiroler Landeskundliches Museum im Zeughaus Kaiser Maximilian I, (Tirolean Regional Museum), Zeughausgasse. In Maximilian's arsenal; exhibits of mineralogy, maps, mountain engineering, lumbering—a huge and interesting grab-bag of subjects. May through Sept., daily 10–5; Sun. and holidays 9–12.

Tiroler Landesmuseum Ferdinandeum, Museumstr. 15. Ancient and early history, especially strong on Gothic collection; Baroque gallery; German and Dutch art; modern art. Tues. to Sat. 10–12, 2–5; Sun. 9–12. Closed Mon.

Tiroler Volkskunstmuseum (Museum of Tirolean Folk Art), Univesitätsstr. 2. Tirolean farmhouse interiors from Gothic to Rococo, carved and painted peasant furniture, costumes and Christmas cribs. Daily 9–12, 2–5; Sun. and holidays 9–12.

ENTERTAINMENT. Theater. For an enjoyable evening out there is the **Tiroler Landestheater** and **Kammerspiele,** Rennweg, where you can see opera, operetta, drama and comedy. Advance booking office 52 0 74–30. Program information 52 0 74–01.

Music. Concerts are given in the modern Saal Tirol of the **Kongresshaus.** Performances usually start at 7.30 P.M. At Whitsun concerts are given by organists from all over the world during International Organ Week.

In summer, brass band concerts of folk music performed in the park or in one of the public squares are almost a daily event. In season you can hear the real Tirolean yodeling and zither music and see the authentic Tirolean dances as a part of the Tirolean folk shows, performed at **Stiftskeller** and in the **Hotel Europe.** Concerts are also held in **Ambras Castle** in July and August.

Nightlife. Innsbruck is not the place for nightclubs, but several bars have opened up recently and nightlife is slowly improving—as elsewhere in Austria. Try *Dorian Gray,* Valiergasse 10 (47 9 28) or *Pascha,* Anichstr. 7 (58 24 20).

Information. For up-to-date information about what to see and do, get *Innsbrucker Veranstaltungskalender* —or, more simply, *What's On in Innsbruck.* Also useful is the monthly booklet *Garçon!,* available in English.

SHOPPING. Shopping in Innsbruck means browsing leisurely through the historic streets of Maria-Theresienstrasse, Museumstrasse, Brixnerstrasse, Meranerstrasse and in and out among the arcades of Herzog-Friedrichstrasse. Everything can be found within a relatively small area. The best-known Tirolean specialties include: Tirolean hats, Loden cloth and handwoven materials, dirndls and lederhosen, leather clothing, wood carvings and wrought iron, glass and ceramics, mountain climbing and skiing equipment.

Normal business hours are Mon. to Fri. 8.30–12, 2–6; Sat. 8–12, except the first Saturday of the month, 8–12 and 2–5. Some shops stay open at lunchtime in the busier center area.

RESTAURANTS. All the hotels, of course, serve meals; the bigger hotels provide some of the best food in Innsbruck. But there are a number of excellent restaurants. As in most regions of Austria, local specialties are being rediscovered and are worth looking for.

Expensive

Altstadtstüberl, Riesengasse 13 (58 23 47). Tirolean specialties and wines. Closed Sun. Reserve. Open late. AE, DC, MC, V.

Belle Epoque, in Alpotel, Innrain 13 (57 79 31). Successfully relocated and remains one of the city's top restaurants. French cuisine and wines. Closed Sun. Reserve. AE, DC, MC, V.

Bistro, Pradlerstrasse 2 (46 3 19). Superb food, emphasis on fish and French style. AE, DC, MC, V. Open late.

Domstuben, Pfarrgasse 3 (57 33 53). Elegant front rooms, charming up-stairs, attentive service, creative cooking. AE, DC, MC, V.

Four Seasons, in Scandic Crown Hotel, Salurner Str. 15 (59 35 0). Su-perb modern cuisine in glass-roofed room with spectacular views. Fine selection of wines. AE, DC, MC, V.

Goldener Adler, Herzog Friedrichstrasse 6 (58 63 34). Upper floor most elegant. Tirolean and international food. Reserve. AE, DC, MC, V. Open late.

Kapeller, Philippine-Welser-Str. 96 (43 1 06). Ranked among Inns-bruck's top restaurants. Closed Sun. AE, DC, MC, V.

Philippine Welser, in Hotel Europa (59 31). Excellent modern cuisine with a regional touch. AE, DC, MC, V.

Picnic, Fallermayerstrasse 12 (58 38 59). Hearty Tirolean food on ground floor, more sophisticated on the upper floor. Very good choice of wines from France, Italy and Austria. AE, DC, MC, V. Open daily to 1 A.M.

Schwarzer Adler, Kaiserjägerstr. 2 (58 71 09). Elegant dining by candle-light. Local specialties, wide wine selection. Closed Tues. AE, DC, MC, V.

Moderate

Hirschstuben, Kiesbachstr. 5 (58 29 79). Atmospheric rooms, excellent Tirolean food with emphasis on game. Closed Sun. AE, DC, MC, V.

Löwenhaus, Rennweg 5 (58 54 79). Rustic, lovely garden. Tirolean and Bavarian food. Excellent pastries. Reserve. AE, DC, MC, V.

Rosengarten, Claudiastrasse 8 (58 33 62). Italian food. Closed Wed. AE, MC. Open late.

Weisses Rössl, Kiebachgasse 8 (58 30 57). Beautiful Tirolean *stube.* Local specialties. Closed Sun. and Nov.

Inexpensive

Gasthof Engl, Innstrasse 22 (83 1 12). Good local food. Closed Sat. and Sun.

Ottoburg, Herzog-Friedrich-Str. 1 (57 46 52). Excellent local dishes served in a warren of atmospheric upstairs rooms. Open daily. AE, DC, MC, V.

Stiegelbräu, Wilhelm-Greilstrasse 25 (58 43 38). Pleasant garden; lots of atmosphere; typical Tirolean dishes.

WINE TAVERNS. Under the ancient arcades along the narrow Herzog-Friedrichstr, which is a continuation of Maria-Theresienstr. and in many of the old side streets, you will find inviting taverns, some of them centuries old, and offering music.

The **Goethestube** of the Goldener Adler (58 63 34), where Goethe used to sip his *viertel* of the red South Tirolean during his stays here in 1786 and 1790, has the best music, wine and food. Open evenings only.

Happ, Herzog-Friedrich-Str. 14 (58 29 80), under the Arcades, a wine tavern with good Austrian specialties. Excellent value.

CAFES. Innsbruck has preserved the ancient Austrian tradition of the coffeehouse as well as, if not better than, most cities. Here you can relax and watch the world go by as you enjoy excellent coffee, pastries and other delicious tidbits.

Alte Teestube, Riesengasse 6, (58 23 09). On upper floor of Herzog Frie-drich restaurant. Cozy room; meeting place for tea lovers with a choice of 36 different varieties.

Central, Gilmstrasse 5, (59 20). In Central Hotel; large Viennese-style coffee house; many newspapers and magazines. AE, DC, MC, V.

Munding, Kiebachgasse 16, (58 41 18). In the old part of town; has been making pastries for over 100 years.

WINTER SPORTS. The Innsbruck area is one of great distinction. Twice selected for the Winter Olympics, this city and its environs has a magnificent range of skiing facilities. There is also the opportunity to combine days on the slopes with the advantages of a city renowned for its hotels, restaurants and cultural heritage. There is a daily ski bus from the city center to the ski slopes (58 31 76).

Nearby Resorts. Axams-Axamer Lizum (878 m., 2,881 ft.); Götzens (868 m., 2,848 ft.); Gries im Sellrain (1,240 m., 4,068 ft.); Igls (900 m., 2,953 ft.); Kühtai (2,020 m., 6,628 ft.); Mutters (830 m., 2,723 ft.); Patsch (1,002 m., 3,288 ft.); Praxmar (1,693 m., 5,550 ft.); St. Sigmund (1,516 m., 4,971 ft.); Sellrain (909 m., 2,982 ft.); Tulfes (922 m., 3,025 ft.).

Facilities: the area boasts 34 indoor swimming pools, 7 cable cars, 10 chair lifts, 35 T-bars and 115 km. (72 miles) of cross-country trails.

The best establishment for figure and speed skating is the new Olympic Ice Stadium in Innsbruck, skating in summer too; ice hockey as well; curling alleys, toboggan runs here and in Patsch; horse sleighs can be hired here and in Patsch.

OTHER SPORTS. Innsbruck is a first-class mountain climbing center and the locale of the Hochgebirgsschule Tirol, Kaiser Josefstr. 3 (58 59 86), which organizes rock and ice climbing courses. For further information contact Oesterreichischer Alpenverein (Austrian Mountaineering Club), Wilhelm-Greil-Str. 15 (59 5 47).

Hang-gliding. Nordkette Club, Felseckstr. 41 (36 06 03).

Horse Riding. You may have to join a club, but the fees are reasonable. Contact Campagnereiter-Gesellschaft Tirol, Langerweg 43 (47174).

Gliding. Information from the Airport (82 3 76, 83 1 57).

Golf. An 18-hole course is at Golfclub Innsbruck-Igls, Golfcourse Rinn (0 52 23–8177); 9 holes at Lans-Sperberegg (0 52 12–77 1 65).

Ice Skating. Year round in the Olympia center (59 8 38).

Squash and Tennis. Center Neu Rum in the Olympic Village (63 4 20). Parkclub Igls, Kurpark (77 2 07).

Swimming. Swimming pool Tivoli, Purtschellerstr. 1 (42 3 44) also has a sauna. Indoor pools at Amraser Str. 3 (42 5 85), and Olympisches Dorf, Kugelfangweg 46 (61 3 42); both of these have saunas, too. There are also several attractive lakes in the area for summer excursions and swimming.

Walking. For keen walkers the tourist office will arrange tours of any size from farmhouse to farmhouse.

PRACTICAL INFORMATION FOR THE TIROL

TOURIST INFORMATION. The main Tourist Offices are in Innsbruck, Bozener Platz 7 (05 12–53 20), (see the *Practical Information for Innsbruck*). Elsewhere in the Tirol there are offices in most of the smaller towns. Among the larger centers, with a greater selection of activities on offer are (with postal code and phone number)—

Achenkirch A-6215 (0 52 46–62 70); Alpbach A-6236 (0 53 36–52 11); Axams–Axamer Lizum A-6094 (0 52 34–81 78, 71 58); Fieberbrunn A-

6391 (0 53 54–63 05–0); Fulpmes A-6166 (0 52 25–22 35); Gerlos A-6281 (0 52 84–52 44); Ischgl A-6561 (0 54 44–53 18, 52 66); Kaltenbach A-6272 (0 52 83–22 18); Kirchdorf A-6382 (0 53 52–31 36); Kitzbühel A-6370 (0 53 56–21 55, 22 72–0); Kufstein A-6330 (0 53 72–22 07); Kühtai A-6183 (0 52 39–222).

Landeck A-6500 (0 54 42–23 44); Mayrhofen A-6290 (0 52 85–23 05, 26 35); Mutters A-6162 (0 52 22–57 37 44); Neustift A-6167 (0 52 26–22 28); Obergurgl–Hochgurgl A-6456 (0 52 56–258); Obernberg A-6156 (0 52 74–532); Pertisau A-6213 (0 52 43–52 60); Reutte A-6600 (0 56 72–23 36–0).

St. Anton am Arlberg A-6580 (0 54 46, 22 69–0); St. Johann in Tirol A-6380 (0 53 52–22 18); Scheffau A-6351 (0 53 58–81 37); Seefeld A-6100 (0 52 12–23 13, 23 16); Söll A-6306 (0 53 33–52 16); Steinach am Brenner A-6150 (0 52 72–62 70); Tux (Lanersbach) A-6293 (0 52 87–606); Walchsee A-6344 (0 53 74–52 23); Wildschönau A-6311 (0 53 39–82 55, 82 16, 89 80); Zell am Ziller A-6280 (0 52 82–22 81).

East Tirol: Lienz A-9900 (0 48 52–47 47); Matrei A-9971 (0 48 75–65 27, 67 09), 227 (65 27); St Jakob i. Def. A-9963 (0 48 73–54 84); Virgen A-9972 (0 48 74–52 10).

AREA CODES—MAIL AND PHONE. You will find the postal code (preceded by an "A") and the telephone code (in brackets) after the name of each town in the following *Hotel and Restaurant* list.

HOTELS AND RESTAURANTS. The warm-weather tourist traffic is at its peak in July and August, when to arrive at a summer resort without a reservation often means to be left without a room, or at least to have a very slim chance of getting the kind of room you want. Local tourist offices—which are very active and efficient in the Tirol—will often be able to help with accommodations, especially when it is a question of rooms in private houses or small pensions. Many hotels and restaurants close out of season without prior notice. Always check ahead.

Achenkirch A-6215 (0 52 46). *Zur Post* (E), (62 05). 107 rooms, all with bath or shower; indoor and outdoor pools, sauna, solarium, cure center, tennis; restaurant and bar. DC, MC, V.
Campsites (62 39; 6387; 65 68).

Alpbach A-6236 (0 53 36). *Böglerhof* (L), Romantik Hotel (52 27). 50 rooms, all with bath. Indoor and outdoor pools, sauna, tennis, superb restaurant. DC.
Alpbacher Hof (E), (52 37). Beautiful old Tirolean building. Indoor pool, sauna, fitness room. 110 beds, all with bath. Closed April to mid-May, Oct., Nov. Restaurant. *Alphof* One of the Silencehotel group. (E), (53 71). Just outside town. 78 beds, all with bath. Children's room, indoor pool, tennis, dancing. Closed Apr. to May, Oct to Nov. AE, DC, MC.

Arzl A-6471 (0 54 12). 10-minute bus ride from fast-train stop Imst–Pitztal. *Post* (M), (31 11). 120 beds, most with bath or shower. Outdoor swimming pool; restaurant and bar.

Axams A-6094 (0 52 34). *Neuwirt* (M), (81 41). 50 rooms, all with bath; restaurant and bar.

Berwang A-6622 (0 56 74). Bus service from Bichlbach on Innsbruck–Garmisch–Reutte rail line. *Kaiserhof* (E), (82 85). 140 beds, all with bath; apartments, sun-terrace, garden, disco, bowling and sauna. Cafe and cozy restaurant. DC, MC. *Berwangerhof* (E), (82 88). 260 beds, all with bath. In Tirolean style, elegant; beautiful lounges, apartments and rooms. Huge indoor pool.

Brixlegg A-6230 (0 53 37). *Brixleggerhof* (I), (26 30). 9 rooms, all with bath or shower. Restaurant and bar. Closed Oct.
Restaurant. *Tiroler Weinstuben* (M), Marktstr. 40 (23 58) Very good food and wines served in wood-paneled *stuben*. Try the *Schlitzkrapfen*, or the kid. Closed Mon., Tues. noon and June to mid-July. AE, MC.

Ehrwald A-6632 (0 56 73). On Innsbruck–Garmisch–Reutte railway. Cable car to Austrian side of Zugspitze 2,644 m. (8,676 ft.). *Alpenhof* (E), (23 45). 46 rooms, all with bath or shower. Spacious apartments or rooms, rustic lounges; modern gym, tennis, playroom for children. Bar. Closed April and Nov. AE, MC. *Sonnenspitze* (E), (22 08). 26 rooms, some with bath, most with shower. Closed Nov. AE, DC, MC, V. *Spielmann* (E), (22 25). 30 rooms, all with bath or shower. Beautiful location, fine Tirolean furniture and carpets. Good service and excellent restaurant.
Ehrwald–Obermoos winter caravan and campsites (26 66; 27 45).

Ellmau A-6352 (0 53 58). *Der Bär* (L), (23 95). 62 rooms, all with bath. Elegant furnishings in lounges, rooms and apartments; children's room, indoor and outdoor pools, sauna; superb restaurant (closed April) of great elegance.

Fieberbrunn A-6391 (0 53 54). *Schlosshotel Rosenegg* (E), (62 01). 85 rooms, all with bath or shower; children's room, nurse; restaurant and bar. Closed Nov.
Campsite (66 66).
Restaurant. *Herbert's Gourmet Stube* (E), Dorfstr. 9 (60 74). Small, personal, and exquisite. Closed Mon. *La Pampa* (M), Rosenegg 61 (64 42). Serves best steaks in Tirol, excellent desserts. Closed Wed. MC.

Fulpmes A-6166 (0 52 25). *Alte Post* (M), (23 58). 50 rooms with bath or shower; sauna, solarium; restaurant and bar. AE, DC. *Waldhof* (M), (21 75). 60 beds, all with bath or shower. Pension terms only. Sauna, solarium; restaurant and bar. DC.

Galtür A-6563 (0 54 43). Bus service from Landeck, fast train stop on Arlberg Express route. *Alpenrose* (E), (269). 42 rooms, all with bath. Good restaurant serving local specialties. Open only in season. MC. *Fluchthorn* (E), (202). 50 rooms, all with bath or shower. New and modern, but in Tirolean style. Sauna, solarium; restaurant and bar with dancing. DC.

Gerlos A-6281 (0 52 84). Bus service from Zell am Ziller. *Almhof* (M), (53 23). 45 rooms, all with bath. Sauna, solarium, tennis; restaurant and bar.

Going A-6353 (05358). *Stanglwirt* (E), (20 00). Holiday complex built around ancient coaching inn. 40 rooms, all with bath. Stables, tennis, swimming pools, sauna. Countless activities. Classic Tirolean and health cuisine. DC, MC.

Restaurant. *Rautnerwirt* (E), (27 84). Among the Tirol's top dozen restaurants. Closed Mon. to Tues. noon. DC, MC, V.

Gries Am Brenner A-6156 (0 52 74). **Restaurant.** *Alpenblick* (E), (257). Excellent cuisine using local ingredients. Closed on Tues., 5–15 Feb. and 15 Oct. to 20 Dec.

Hall A-6060 (0 52 23). *Maria Theresia* (M), (63 13). 25 rooms, most with bath or shower; attractive rooms; fire-side lounge. Excellent restaurant with attentive service. AE, DC, MC.
Campsite (73 45 28). May to Sept.

Heiterwang A-6611 (0 56 74). *Fischer am See* (E), (51 16). 19 rooms, all with bath or shower. Small, located on most beautiful lake in Tirol. Tirolean-style building and furniture. Fishing, swimming, boating. Closed 10 Jan. to 10 Feb. and 10 Oct. to 10 Dec. Remarkable restaurant serving local specialties.
Campsite (51 16).

Hintertux A-6294 (0 52 87). *Rindererhof* (E), (501). 39 rooms, all with shower. Sauna, solarium; restaurant and bar.

Hochsölden A-6452 (0 52 54). *Edelweiss* (L), (22 98). 30 rooms, all with bath. Indoor pool, sauna. Traditional atmosphere with modern comforts. Cocktail bar, disco; restaurant. AE, DC.
Enzian (E), (22 52). 49 rooms, all with bath or shower. Sauna, solarium, tennis; restaurant and bar. Closed April, May and Nov. DC, MC, V.

Hopfgarten A-9961 (0 48 72). *Waldpension* (I), (53 51). 25 rooms with shower. Simple comfort and friendly with good food; charming setting on edge of the woods.

Igls A-6080 (0 52 22). Can be reached from Innsbruck by frequent bus service (6 km.) or streetcar (8 km.), or private car; parking facilities available. *Parkhotel* (L), (77 3 05). 50 rooms, all with bath. Villa in park; big pool on roof; sauna, massage. Special packages for golfers and tennis players. Good restaurant serving local food. Closed 1 Nov. to 15 Dec. AE, DC, MC, V. *Schlosshotel Igls* (L), (77 2 17). 19 rooms, all with bath; apartments and rooms are attractively furnished. Indoor and outdoor pools; restaurant. AE, DC, V. *Sporthotel* (L), (7 72 41). 90 rooms, all with bath. Indoor pool, sauna. Quality restaurant. Closed 10 Oct. to 15 Dec. AE, DC, MC, V.
Astoria (E), (77 48 10). 32 rooms, all with bath. Tirolean house in quiet location. AE, DC, MC, V.

Imst A-6460 (0 54 12). *Linser* (E), Teilwiesen 10 (24 05). 30 rooms, all with bath or shower. Indoor pool, sauna. Good restaurant. AE, MC, V.
Post (E), (25 54). 77 beds, some with bath or shower. A Romantik Hotel in former castle. Big garden. Restaurant. DC, V. *Stern* (E), (33 42). 25 rooms, all with bath or shower. Indoor and outdoor tennis. Well above par restaurant serving first-class Tirolean food. AE, DC, MC, V.
Campsites (28 66 and 2293).

Innervillgraten A-9932 (04843). *Gannerhof* (I), (52 40). 13 rooms in peaceful country Gasthof. Every comfort, lovely restaurant, good food and wines. Originally a farmhouse built in 1719.

Ischgl A-6561 (0 54 44). Bus service from Landeck. *Madlein* (E), (52 91). 130 beds, all with bath. Indoor pool, sauna, solarium. Bar and restaurant. Closed in May and Nov.

Jungholz A-6691 (0 56 76). *Kur-und Sporthotel Tirol* (E), (81 62). Silencehotel. 97 rooms, all with bath or shower. Can only be reached via Deutsche Alpenstrasse. Elegant lobby, comfortable rooms and apartments; indoor pool, cure facilities. Notable restaurant. Closed 2 Nov. to 14 Dec.
Campsite (81 82).

Kirchberg A-6365 (0 53 57). *Parkhotel* (E) (2 38 30). 42 rooms, all with bath or shower. Modern, with elegant period furnished rooms; playroom for children. Restaurant. AE, DC, MC. *Sonne* (E), (24 02). 49 rooms, all with bath. Sunny location, friendly rooms with balconies. Tennis court. Restaurant.

Kitzbühel A-6370 (0 53 56). About 1½ hours by fast train from Innsbruck. *Goldener Greif* (L), (43 11). 55 rooms, all with bath. 700 years old but with modern facilities; casino, indoor pool, magnificent lobby with vaulted ceiling and fireplace. Bar, dancing, casino and good restaurant. AE, V. *Maria Theresia* (L), (47 11). 108 rooms, all with bath or shower. New and elegant. AE, DC, V. *Schloss Lebenberg* (L), (43 01). 100 rooms, all with bath; apartments, indoor pool, cure facilities, tennis, playroom for children. Good restaurant. AE, DC, MC, V.
Schloss Münichau (L), A-6370 Reith (29 62). 58 rooms, all with bath. Former hunting lodge (14th-century) with fine Tirolean-style rooms; hunting, fishing in nearby Schwarzsee. Restaurant. AE, DC, V. *Tennerhof* (L), (31 81). 42 rooms, all with bath. Romantik Hotel. Old mansion in big garden. Tirolean furniture; indoor pool; near new golf course. Closed April, May, 4 Oct. to 17 Dec. AE, DC, MC, V.
Sporthotel Reisch (E), (33 6 60). Central, set in large garden. Every comfort, spacious rooms, excellent restaurant. *Tenne* (E), (44 44). 92 beds, all with bath. "Society" meeting place; nightclub; restaurant. AE, DC, MC, V. Open all year. *Weisses Rössl* (E), (25 41). 70 rooms, most with bath or shower. Friendly but elegant. Nightclub and restaurant. AE, DC, MC, V.
Campsite on Schwarzsee nearby (28 06).
Restaurants. *Unterberger Stuben* (E), (21 01). Considered the Tirol's top restaurant. International specialties. Reserve. Closed Tues. and Wed. midday, June. DC.
Cafe Praxmair (M), (26 46). Cafe and *après-ski* place. Always crowded; very good cakes and pastries. A *must*. Open until 8 P.M. MC, V. *Schwedenkapelle* (M), Klausenbach (58 70). On road to Kirchberg. Well-prepared international dishes; very good Austrian, Italian and French wines. DC, MC, V.

Kössen A-6345 (0 53 75). *Peternhof* (E), (62 85). 76 rooms, all with bath. Indoor pool, sauna, solarium; restaurant and bar.

Restaurant. *Zum Postillon* (E), (62 04). First-rate Tirolean specialties; in modern style. Excellent red wine and good, strong coffee. Closed Mon. DC, MC, V.

Kühtai A-6183 (0 52 39). Bus service from Innsbruck and Kematen; when road conditions between Gries in Sellrain and Kuhtai are very bad, a caterpillar vehicle is used. *Alpenrose* (E), (205). 36 beds, all with bath. Apartments. Beautiful location, wonderful sun terrace. Lounge and rooms tastefully furnished.

Jagdschloss (E), (201). 90 beds, all with bath. Former hunting lodge of Emperor Maximilian. Aristocratic atmosphere; wooden ceilings and antique furniture. Restaurant serving Tirolean and international specialties. Closed May to Nov. DC, MC.

Kufstein A-6330 (0 53 72). *Alpenrose* (E), (21 22). 19 rooms. Pleasant hotel outside town. Excellent, with outstanding restaurant, among the top dozen in the Tirol.

Landeck A-6500 (0 54 42). Fast train stop on rail line from Innsbruck to Vorarlberg and Switzerland. *Schrofenstein* (E), Malserstr. 31 (23 95). Good restaurant, comfortable rooms. AE, DC, V. *Tourotel (Post),* (E), (23 83). 97 rooms, all with bath. Completely renovated old building; modern functional rooms; attractive apartments on top floor. Restaurant. AE, DC, MC, V.

Schwarzer Adler (M), (23 16). 70 beds, some with bath or shower. Good restaurant with Tirolean food. AE.

Campsites (46 36; 39 4 05).

Lanersbach A-6293 (0 52 87). *Forelle* (M), (214). 68 beds, some with bath or shower. Indoor pool, sauna. Good restaurant. V. *Tuxerhof* (M), (211). 35 rooms, all with bath or shower. Fireside lounge. Cocktail bar and restaurant. AE, DC, MC, V.

Lans A-6072 (05 12). **Restaurant.** *Wilder Mann* (E), (7 73 87). Long-established spot, popular locally. Excellent value. AE, DC, MC, V.

Lermoos A-6631 (0 56 73). On same railway as Ehrwald. *Drei Mohren* (M), (23 62). 100 beds, most with bath, some with shower. Ideal for active stay. Lifts and cross-country skiing trail behind the hotel. Fishing in brook and lake; hunting. Guest kindergarten. Good restaurant serving local food—large helpings. Closed 20 March to 30 April and 20 Oct. to 20 Dec. AE, DC. *Post* (M), (22 81). 125 rooms, most with bath. Indoor pool, sauna.

Campsites (29 80, 21 97).

Leutasch A-6105 (0 52 14). *Aparthotel Xander* (E), (65 81). 56 apartments with all modern facilities; indoor pool, sauna, solarium, massage, gym, bowling. Restaurant. DC.

Campsite (65 70).

Lienz A-9900 (0 48 52). Reached by railway on the Salzburg–Mallnitz–Lienz line from Carinthia, and by car on the Felbertauern road. *Sonne* (E), (63 3 11). 57 rooms, all with bath or shower, all with modern facilities. Playroom for children. Restaurant. AE, DC, MC, V. *Traube*

(E), (64 4 44). Romantik Hotel. 52 comfortable rooms. Central location. Beautifully appointed. Swimming pool on top floor with breathtaking view of Lienzer Dolomites. Elegant vaulted restaurant. Excellent food and wines. Less expensive Italian restaurant in cellar. Own fishing rights; terrace café. *Tristachersee* (67 66 60). A mile or two out of town on a hidden, elevated lake. Magical setting. Totally renovated, and run with care and concern. Good food and wines. Lovely lakeside terrace.

Gribelehof (I), just outside town on Schlossberg (62 1 91). Magnificent views. Beautifully-cooked, local farm produce. 30 pleasant rooms, some with showers.

Youth hostel, by river (63 3 10).

Campsites (65 4 63; 64 0 22).

Matrei In Osttirol A-9971 (0 48 75). On the Felbertauern road; bus from Lienz. *Rauter* (E), (66 11). 120 beds, all with bath or shower. In modern alpine-style. Indoor pool, tennis, riding hall. Famous restaurant serving local specialties. Closed mid-Nov. to mid-Dec. AE, DC, MC, V. *Tauernhaus* (I), (88 11). Located some way out of town in a valley at base of Felbertauern pass. Old rest house founded in 1207 by the Archbishops of Salzburg. Now a simple, comfortable Gasthaus. Excellent home cooking. Good for walking and skiing.

Campsite (66 79).

Mayrhofen A-6290 (0 52 85). *Elisabeth* (E), Einfahrtmitte 432 (29 29). 70 beds, all with bath. New, in Tirolean-style, nice rooms, indoor pool. Restaurant. AE, DC, MC, V. *Kramerwirt* (M), (26 15). 151 beds, all with bath or shower; *stuben* with wood paneling. Fitness center on top floor. Restaurant with friendly staff. *The* center of activity.

Neue Post (M), (21 31). 155 beds, most with bath. Parking. Restaurant. Garage. AE, DC, MC, V.

Campsite (25 80).

Restaurant. *Wirtshaus Zum Griena* (M), (27 78), in 400-year-old building, with wood paneling. Lots of atmosphere and first-rate local dishes. Red wines from south Tirol, white wines from Austria.

Mieming A-6414 (0 52 64). *Römisch Deutscher Kaiser* (E), (56 68). 51 rooms, all with bath. In quiet location on sun plateau of Mieming. Two tennis courts, heated pool. Restaurant. Closed 1 Nov. to 15 Dec. AE, DC, MC, V.

Mutters A-6162 (0 52 22). *Muttererhof* (M), (27 4 91). 24 rooms, most with bath. Indoor pool, sauna, solarium; magnificent view of surrounding mountains. Good restaurant. Closed April, Nov. and Dec. AE, V.

Nassereith A-6465 (0 52 65). *Post* (M), (52 01). 36 rooms, all with bath or shower. Pool; restaurant. AE, DC, MC, V.

Campsite (52 10).

Nauders A-6543 (0 54 73). *Almhof* (L), (313). 53 rooms, all with bath. Evening entertainments. Good restaurant. Closed Nov. *Astoria* (E), (310). 49 rooms, all with bath. Indoor pool, sauna. Closed 20 April to 15 May and 10 Oct. to 17 Dec. AE. *Margarete Maultasch* (E), (236). 120 beds all with bath. Indoor and outdoor pools, sauna. Restaurant. AE, DC, MC, V.

Obergurgl A-6456 (0 52 56). Bus service from Otztal (Arlberg Express stop). *Bellevue* (M), (228). 57 beds, all with bath. Skiing right in front of building. Restaurant. *Edelweiss* (E), (223). 170 beds, most with bath, some with shower. Lots of tradition, family-run. Restaurant. AE, DC, MC, V. *Hochfirst* (E), (231). 82 rooms with bath or shower. Indoor pool, sauna. Restaurant. Closed 1 May to 9 June, 2 Oct. to 12 Nov. DC, MC, V.

Laurin (M), A-6456 Hochgurgl (227). 30 rooms, all with bath or shower. Good restaurant and bar. MC.

Ötz A-6433 (0 52 52). *Alpenhotel* (M), Bielefeld Str. 133, (62 32). 45 rooms, all with shower. In center of village. Good value. Restaurant. *Drei Mohren* (M), (63 01). 24 rooms, some with bath or shower, and all comfortable. Tennis; restaurant. MC, V.

Posthotel (M), (63 03). 100 beds, some with bath or shower. Nostalgic, old house, very pleasant rooms; apartments for families. Simple furnishings. Restaurant. AE, DC, MC, V.

Campsite (64 85).

Pertisau A-6213 (0 52 43). *Fürstenhaus* (E), (54 42–0). 64 rooms with every comfort. Fine setting on lake, built in 1469 as palace for Duke Sigismund. Sigmund Freud stayed here in 1900. Own boats, pool, sauna, restaurant. *Kristall* (E), (54 90). 81 beds, some with bath and some with shower. Pool, sauna, solarium, fitness room; restaurant and bar.

Restaurant. *Rieser* (M), (52 51). With garden; excellent salads.

Pettneu Am Arlberg A-6574 (0 54 48). *Gridlon* (E), (208). 38 rooms, all with bath or shower. Indoor and outdoor pools, tennis, riding, evening entertainment including dancing, barbecues and competitions. Restaurant. Closed 29 April to 9 June, 29 Sept. to 15 Dec.

Reutte A-6600 (0 56 72). Same line as Ehrwald and Lermoos. *Ammerwald* (M), Grenzstrasse, (81 31). 103 rooms, most with bath. Quiet location; ideal for hiking, cross-country skiing; sauna, bowling and curling. Restaurant and bar. AE, DC, MC.

Youth Hostels (30 39; 26 44).

Campsites (28 09; 20 58; 20 71).

St. Anton Am Arlberg A-6580 (0 54 46). Fast train stop on Arlberg Express route. *Schwarzer Adler* (L), (22 44). 112 rooms, all with bath. 400-year-old stone building that pre-dates the castle. Pleasant rooms, Tirolean-style lounges. Disco and cafe. *Sporthotel* (L), (3111). 57 rooms, all with bath; indoor pool with waterfall; nightclub, bar and restaurant. Closed Oct. to Nov. AE, DC, MC, V.

Arlberg (E), (22 44). 59 rooms, all with bath. Modern, standard rooms, tennis court, dancing. Known restaurant. AE, DC, MC, V. *Karl Schranz* (E), (25 55). 23 rooms, all with bath. Spacious house, lobby with open fire and trophies won by the owner. *Mooserkreuz* (E), (22 30). 39 rooms, all with bath. Indoor pool and sauna. Above town, in old house. AE, DC, MC, V.

Restaurant. *Berghaus Maria* (M), (20 05). International specialties; delicious fresh salads. Genial atmosphere. AE, DC, MC, V.

St. Christoph Am Arlberg A-6580 (0 54 46). On mountain pass, above St. Anton and reached from there by bus. *Hospiz* (L), (2 61 10). 102 rooms, all with bath. Fully modernized 600-year old building; refuge for travelers crossing through the Arlberg pass. Indoor pool; bar and superlative restaurant famed both for its food and its wines. Closed out of season. AE, DC, MC, V.

St. Jakob i. Def A-9963 (0 48 73). *Alpenhof* (E), (53 51). 87 rooms, all with bath. Superb setting, with skiing and walking galore; swimming pool and good restaurant.

St. Johann A-6380 (0 53 52). *Europa* (E), (22 85–0). 50 beds, all with bath. Next to recreation center; indoor and outdoor pools, tennis lawn. Attractive restaurant, for residents only; brunch served until noon. AE, DC, MC, V.

Campsite (25 84).

Seefeld A-6100 (0 52 12). About 30 minutes from Innsbruck by fast train; also by bus (24 km.); parking facilities. *Astoria* (L), (22 72). 46 rooms, all with bath and balconies. Indoor and outdoor pools, sauna. A little above village, chalet-style. *Klosterbräu* (L), (26 21–0). 108 rooms, all with bath; apartments. 450-year-old former monastery with columns and cross-vaulting. Central location; very good restaurant. AE, DC, MC, V. *Tümmlerhof* (L), (25 71–0). 66 rooms, all with bath. All modern conveniences; indoor and outdoor pools; elegant rooms and lounges; bar and outstanding restaurant. Closed April to May, Oct. to mid-Dec.

Dreitorspitze (E), (29 51–0). 80 rooms, most with bath or shower. Indoor pool, sauna. Restaurant. AE, DC, MC, V. *Karwendelhof* (E), (26 55). 90 beds. At station, chalet-style, 18th-century cellar tavern; excellent dining; casino. AE, DC, MC, V. *Wildsee Schlössl* (E), (23 90). 19 rooms in idyllic forest setting. Superb restaurant. Closed Nov. AE, DC, MC, V.

Post (M), (22 01). 86 rooms, most with bath or shower. Tennis; good restaurant. AE, DC, MC, V.

Restaurants. Birklstüberl (E), (23 22). Stüberl specialties. *Sir Richard* (E), (20 93). One of the best in Tirol; fine local cuisine, very personal atmosphere. Closed Mon. in summer; Nov. AE, DC, MC, V.

Casino in town.

Serfaus A-6534 (0 54 76). Bus service from Landeck on Arlberg Express route. *Cervosa* (E), (62 12). 130 beds, most with bath, some with shower; apartments available. Indoor pool; massage parlor. Good restaurant with excellent winelist. AE, DC, V. *Maximilian* (E), Silencehotel (65 20). 80 beds. Cosy blend of ancient and modern. Superb food and wine. MC.

Sölden Im Ötztal A-6450 (0 52 54). Bus service from Ötztal on Arlberg Express route.

Alpina (E), (25 59). 20 rooms, all with bath. AE, DC. *Central* (E), (22 60). 70 rooms, all with bath; indoor pool; tennis. Antique furniture in lobby and lounges. Restaurant.

Sonne (M), (22 03). 110 beds. DC.

Campsite (26 27). Jan. to Apr., June to Sept.

Telfs A-6410 (0 52 62). *Interalpen* (L), (42 42). Huge, 313-room resort hotel, brand new, all facilities. Surprisingly good restaurant. AE, DC, MC, V.

Campsites (28 49 or 33 3 13; 31 2 23).

Walchsee A-6344 (0 53 74). Bus service from Kufstein and St. Johann. *Bellevue am See* (E), (57 31). 400 beds, most with bath or shower. Indoor pool; solarium. Restaurant. Closed April, Nov. DC, V.
Campsites (53 39; 53 59).

Wildschönau–Oberau A-6311 (0 53 39). *Angerhof* (E), (84 02). 30 rooms, all with bath or shower. Indoor and outdoor pools; sauna; solarium. Restaurant and bar. Closed May.
Kellerwirt (M), (81 16). 70 beds, most with bath. Richly atmospheric.

Wörgl A-6300 (05332). *Parkrestaurant Golf* (37 60). Good local and health food.

Zell Am Ziller A-6280 (0 52 82). *Zellerhof* (M) (26 12). 32 rooms. Restaurant.
Bräu (M), (23 13). 39 rooms, all with bath. 16th-century building in center of village. Hunting and fishing. First-rate restaurant.
Campsite (22 48). Open all year.

Zirl A-6170 (05238). *Goldener Löwe* (E), (23 29). Comfortable but modest hotel with outstanding restaurant serving local and health specialties.

GETTING AROUND THE TIROL. By Train. The main railway line of the Tirol, coming from Vorarlberg to St. Anton am Arlberg, crossing the main part of North Tirol, and leaving it shortly after St. Johann for Land Salzburg, is also the route of the Arlberg-Orient Express. The latter, however, makes stops only at St. Anton, Landeck, Ötztal, Innsbruck, Jenbach, and Kitzbühel. Other fast trains on this line stop also at Imst, Telfs (some), Wörgl, and St. Johann.

The second most important railway line enters Tirol from Germany at Kufstein and proceeds to Wörgl, Innsbruck, Brenner, and from there to Italy. Fast-train stops are at Kufstein, Wörgl, Jenbach, Schwaz (occasionally), Innsbruck, Matrei am Brenner, Steinach, and Brenner.

A local railway line connects Innsbruck with Seefeld, Scharnitz, and continues through a short stretch of German territory at Garmisch with Ehrwald, Lermoos and Reutte. Narrow-gauge local railways connect Jenbach with Mayrhofen in the Ziller valley and with Achensee, and Innsbruck with Fulpmes.

By Bus. The state and private bus service net is well organized; in a few mountain sections caterpillar vehicles and motor sleighs have to be used sometimes in bad weather to make the last stretch.

Bus sightseeing tours, often covering also the sights of South Tirol, originate in many localities (mostly only in summer), in addition to Innsbruck; among them Igls, St. Anton am Arlberg, Landeck, Reutte, Kitzbühel, St. Johann in Tirol, Brixen im Thale.

By Boat. In summer motorboat roundtrips take place on Walchsee and there is frequent lake boat service between the localities on Achensee.

By Car. The best way of seeing Tirol is, of course, by car. In the official travel offices in Tirol you can obtain an attractive booklet containing suggestions for some 45 automobile roundtrips in Tirol, including a description of the roads and traffic rules. Driving is recommended, however, only in the snow-free months unless you are an expert in high-mountain snow driving. From Innsbruck you can cover all of North Tirol in day trips. The west Autobahn (A12) enters Austria from Germany at Kufstein and runs southwest past Innsbruck to Telfs. From there the 171/A12 continues comfortably west to the Arlberg. From Innsbruck the Brenner Autobahn (182/A13), an outstanding example of Alpine road construction, runs south to the Brenner to connect with the Italian Autostrada to Bolzano. Among its engineering achievements is the Bridge of Europe (Europabrücke), almost 600 feet high above the Sill Valley near Innsbruck, and the 6,000-foot-long Lueg Bridge shortly before the Brenner Pass; the Europabrücke is so called because it is the key passageway between the fast highway systems of northern, central and southern Europe.

Another supermodern mountain road is the Felbertauernstrasse (108) between East Tirol and Mittersill in Land Salzburg, whose most outstanding feature is the 5-km. (3 mile) tunnel cutting through the main range of the Hohe Tauern at an elevation of 1,590 m. (5,250 ft.) while the gradient is never higher than 7 percent; this road is now the fastest link between Bavaria, northeastern Tirol and Salzburg on one side and East Tirol, Carinthia and northeastern Italy (Trieste, Venice) on the other side.

Among other roads offering exceptional vistas are: the Timmelsjoch road from Untergurgl in Upper Ötz Valley to the Timmelsjoch mountain pass (about 2,500 m., 8,200 ft., 14 percent gradient) through magnificent mountain scenery; the scenic road along Achen Lake which leads to Germany and has shortened the driving time between Innsbruck and Munich to 1¼ hours; the Gerlos Pass road from the Ziller Valley to the Krimml Waterfalls and Mittersill in Salzburg province, also in beautiful mountain landscape (highest point about 1,630 m., 5,350 ft., maximum gradient only 9 percent); Burgital Panorama Road from Nassereith north of Imst to Holzleitensattel in Mieminger Range.

PLACES OF INTEREST. The Tirol is essentially a mountain province, and its churches, abbeys and castles seem to grow out of the wild and rocky landscape. Some of the most impressive works of art of the region are created from wood—especially the superb statuary without which no self-respecting Tirolean church is complete. Given the remoteness of most of the Tirolean villages, it is not surprising that Gothic is a style that hung on long after it had been transmuted elsewhere. Please check locally what the latest situation is regarding days and times of opening, before setting off to explore; they change with very little warning, quite apart from being irregularly seasonal. The routes we suggest in the following list all begin from Innsbruck.

Alpbach. A12 east to Rattenberg, 171 to Brixlegg, local road from there. Annual locale for the European Forum. Picturesque chalets all over the area. **St. Oswald,** late Gothic, frescos by Mayr, plus fine 1770 carvings. **Folk Museum** at Inneralpbach.

Axams. 7 km. (4 ½ miles) from Innsbruck on local road. Site of 1964 Winter Olympics. **Parish Church of St. John the Baptist.** Gothic, converted to Baroque (1732). Wall frescos and subterranean chapel of bearded female saint (St. Wilgefortis).

Ehrwald. A12 west to Telfs, 189 to Nassereith, then 314 north. The 1920s cablecar was extended to the **Zugspitz** summit (2,962 m., 9,716 ft.)

in 1962. An awe-inspiring trip. Take your passport with you and cross the border on the summit.

Fieberbrunn. A12 east to Wörgl, then 312. St. **Johannes Nepomuk Chapel,** with frescos by Matthäus Günther (1762) and Rococo stuccowork. Also massive **Presbytery** (1771).

Imst. A12 west to Telfs, then 171. **Parish Church** (1492) with outside frescos; **Calvary Church,** with Gothic frescos; **Capuchin Monastery** (1680). **Museum.** Site of the first SOS Children's Village.

Kitzbühel. A12 east to Wörgl, then 170 via Brixen. Fine example of Tirolean town architecture. Half-a-dozen interesting churches, especially the **Parish Church of St. Andrew,** with its lavishly Rococo Rosakapelle, and the **Church of St. Catherine** (Gothic winged altar of around 1520). Museum in the old courthouse—mining history and reconstructed 16th-century farmhouse.

Kufstein. A12 all the way northeast to near the Bavarian border. **Festung** (The Fortress), built 1200 then restored and enlarged early 1500s, a huge structure, romantically sited. Houses the **Local Museum** and the **Heldenorgel** (Heroes' Organ) which plays daily. The town also has some attractive Art Nouveau architecture. Every six years at nearby Erl the oldest *Passion Play* in Austria is performed.

Landeck. A12 west to Zams, then 171. 13th-century **castle** on the southeast mountainside, containing a museum with excellent Baroque sculpture. **Parish Church of the Assumption of the Virgin** in Angedair, with Gothic altar and paintings. **Plague Church,** with interesting paneled ceiling and 16th-century altars. The town has several historical houses.

Lienz. East Tirol. To get to East Tirol from Innsbruck you can either go down through the Brenner Pass into Italy, then east via Bruneck (on Route 49); or on the A12 east to Jenbach, 169 to Zell am Ziller, 165 via the Gerlos Pass (toll road) and the Krimml waterfalls to Mittersill, then 161 through the Felber Tauern tunnel and 108 to Lienz. **Schloss Bruck,** well-kept castle, housing the **Osttiroler Heimatmuseum** (East Tirol Museum), with local folk material and Roman discoveries, 19th and 20th century art, especially the works of Albin Egger. **St. Andrew's Church,** rediscovered frescos plus fine 16th-century tombstones. 5 km. out of (Route 107) is **Aguntum** and **Lavant,** Roman sites.

Matrei in East Tirol. 28 km. (17 ½ miles) before Lienz on Route 108, after the Felber Tauern tunnel. Two interesting churches (**St. Alban** and **St. Nicholas**) both with paintings and Gothic statues. St. Nicholas is a fine medieval building (13th century) with Romanesque frescos.

Oetz. A12 west to Öztal, 171, 186 to the south. Decorated Gothic houses (Stern Inn). **Parish Church,** with Gothic elements and fine Baroque sculptures. Bone house and splendid Gothic altar. This is the beginning of the Ötz Valley, with the splendid **Stuiben Falls.**

Rattenberg. A12 east along the Inn Valley. Ancient municipality (1393). Picturesque medieval mining center with two richly endowed churches (**St. Vigil** and the **Servite Church**). Imposing castle ruins.

Reutte. A12 west to Telfs, 189 to Nassereith, then 314 north for 43 km. (27 miles). Township since 1441. Finely decorated houses with wrought-iron signs and window grilles. **Monastery Church** and **Local Museum**, with regional Baroque painters' work.

St. Anton Am Arlberg. A12 west, then 171 and 316/S16. Famous skiing center with appropriate **Local Museum** which covers the history of skiing. Notable wood carving on the pulpit in the **Parish Church** (The Fall of Satan).

St. Johann. A12 east to Wörgl, then 312. Magnificently decorated Baroque **Parish Church**. Gothic **Spitalskirche** with fine late-medieval stained glass. Many interesting houses.

Schwaz. A12 east. Once a rich silver and copper mining town. Wealthy 15th- and 16th-century houses, especially of the Fugger family. **Parish Church**, Gothic with Baroque embellishments. **Franziskanerkirche** (Franciscan Church) has statuary and choir stalls worth noting, plus a foremost example of Gothic in the cloister, with frescos and local armorial paintings. The **Schloss Freundsberg** is a medieval castle housing the **Stadtmuseum** (local history and mining).

Seefeld. A12 west to Zirl, then north on 177 (very steep). Elegant skiing center, home of Olympic cross-country competitions. **Parish Church**, built during the first three-quarters of the 15th century. Interesting Gothic statues and frescos. Marble stairs lead to the 1574 Chapel of the Holy Blood, Baroque frescos and stucco-work. Baroque **Seekirchl**, small chapel by the lake (west of the village).

Stams. A12 and 171 west. Great Cistercian **Abbey**, founded 1273. The Baroque Abbey Church is full of magnificent works of art; the wrought-iron Rose Grill (1716); the Tree of Life altarpiece with its 84 carved saints (1613); the Tirolean Princes' Vault with late-1600s carvings; the Chapel of the Holy Blood (1717); and a whole complex of other elaborately-decorated chapels, rooms and halls. If you can only make one trip out of Innsbruck, and a short one, this should be it. The **Parish Church** is Gothic (1318), with Baroque and Rococo changes. Near Stams is the last oak forest in the Tirol.

Volders. Just east of Innsbruck on 171. **Servitenkirche** (Church of the Servites), a delightful mid-1600s Baroque building, packed full with paintings and carvings of the Baroque and Rococo periods. Attached to a Servite seminary, and so of limited access. A nearby castle, **Friedberg**, is a massive Gothic structure with interesting frescos in its Knights' Hall.

CASINOS. The casino at **Kitzbühel,** in the Hotel Greif, is open year-round, daily from 7 in the evening; roulette, baccara and black jack.

The one in **Seefeld** is open daily from 7 in the evening in summer, from 5 in winter; also roulette, baccara and black jack.

WINTER SPORTS. Tirol is the best winter sports area in Austria and very probably the best skiing center in the world. Here can be found some fine skiing schools and many brilliant skiing techniques originated here. They are constantly being improved, and are taught by the old masters and by the new ones who are growing up on every hill. Tirol is the home country of such skiing masters of the past as Hannes Schneider and Toni Seelos, of such record holders of yesterday as Toni Sailer, Josl Rieder and Andreas Molterer, and of dozens of present-day champions. Scores of international and national competitions take place here throughout every winter season. More hotel comforts and more *après-ski* entertainment may be provided for the skiing tourist in other countries, but none equals Tirol when it comes to real skiing.

Equipment can be rented in most places. The best time for skiing in the lower areas is from early January until mid-March, but you can usually ski from mid-December until the end of March. In the higher areas skiing goes on from early December until the end of April. The best time for the high mountain skiing tours is early spring, and for glacier tours May and June. Above Hochgurgl, on Rettenbachferner above Sölden, and on Stubai and Tuxer glaciers, there is year-round skiing.

Arlberg. For information on the Arlberg ski area (Tirol/Vorarlberg) see the *Practical Information* for the Vorarlberg chapter.

Paznautal. Backed by the severe bulk of the Silvretta massif, this mountain valley is an impressive place to ski. The Silvretta skiing region is within easy reach, and this is an ideal district for those who favor ski-touring.

Resorts: Galtür (1,584 m., 5,197 ft.); Ischgl (1,377 m., 4,518 ft.); Kappl (1,258 m., 4,128 ft.); See (1,058 m., 1,468 ft.).

Facilities: the area has 5 indoor swimming pools, 4 cable cars, 6 chair lifts, 35 T-bars and 48 km. (30 miles) of cross-country trails.

Upper Inntal. The perfect combination of high plateaux and delightfully-picturesque Tirolean architecture makes this a winter sports region with great character. There are modern facilities, ski tours going above 2,750 m., (9,000 ft.), and skating on a natural rink under floodlighting.

Resorts. Fiss (1,436 m., 4,711 ft.);Ladis (1,200 m., 3,937 ft.); Landeck (816 m., 2,673 ft.); Nauders (1,365 m., 4,479 ft.); Pfunds (971 m., 3,186 ft.); Prutz (866 m., 2,838 ft.); Ried (879 m., 2,884 ft.); Serfaus (1,427 m., 4,682 ft.). Has first underground railway connecting town center with the ski slopes.

Facilities: the area has 13 indoor swimming pools, 5 cable cars, 7 chair lifts, 31 T-bars and 167 km. (104 miles) of cross-country trails.

Pitztal. A region of high peaks surrounding an unspoilt valley. The combination of great views and excellent skiing is hard to beat.

Resorts: Jerzens (1,100 m., 3,609 ft.); Mandarfen (1,682 m., 5,519 ft.); Plangeross (1,616 m., 5,302 ft.); St. Leonhard (1,200 m., 3,937 ft.); Wenns/Piller (979 m., 3,212 ft.).

Facilities: the valley has 2 indoor swimming pools, 3 chair lifts, 10 T-bars, 29 km. (18 miles) of cross-country trails.

Ötztal This one is the highest on every count! The Wildspitze is the Tirol's highest peak, and it carries the highest cable-car service and Austria's highest winter-sports resort, Hochgurgl. Many of the hotels match the surroundings for height of luxury and cost.

Resorts: Gries (1,573 m., 5,161 ft.); Hochgurgl (1,685 m., 5,513 ft.); Hochsölden (2,070 m., 6,789 ft.); Längenfeld (1,180 m., 3,872 ft.); Niederthei (1,537 m., 5,040 ft.); Obergurgl (1,927 m., 6,318 ft.); Oetz (820 m., 2,690 ft.); Sölden (1,377 m., 4,518 ft.); Umhausen (1,036 m., 3,399 ft.); Vent (1,893 m., 6,207 ft.).

Facilities: indoor swimming pools in the area number a distinguished 16, there are 3 cable cars, 18 chair lifts, 38 T-bars and 108 km. (67 miles) of cross-country trails.

The Ausserfern Region. An internationally popular area south of the Zugspitze. Plenty of variety in the orientation of the ski runs.

Resorts: Berwang (1,336 m., 4,383 ft.); Biberwier (995 m., 3,264 ft.); Bichlbach (1,075 m., 3,527 ft.); Breitenwang (849 m., 2,785 ft.); Ehrwald (1,000 m., 3,281 ft.); Grän-Haldensee (1,124 m., 3,688 ft.); Holzgau (1,103 m., 3,612 ft.); Jungholz (1,100 m., 3,609 ft.); Lermoos (1,004 m., 3,294 ft.); Nesselwängle (1,147 m., 3,763 ft.); Reutte (854 m., 2,802 ft.); Tannheim (1,097 m., 3,599 ft.); Weissenbach am Lech (887 m., 2,920 ft.).

Facilities: the area has 13 indoor swimming pools, 5 cable cars, 13 chair lifts, 57 T-bars and a stimulating 226 km. (140 miles) of cross-country trails. Holzgau and Reutte have floodlighting on their slopes.

Mieming and the Seefeld Plateau. Lying high and with well-varied terrain, these areas are very popular with all brands of ski enthusiast. There are Olympic tracks at Seefeld, which was the venue for the Winter Olympics in '64 and '76. Après ski is also a big feature of the region—with everything from intimate taverns to a casino.

Resorts: Leutasch (1,130 m., 3,708 ft.); Mieming (800 m., 2,622 ft.); Mösern (1,235 m., 4,047 ft.); Obsteig (1,000 m., 3,281 ft.); Reith (545 m., 1,785 ft.); Seefeld (1,181 m., 3,870 ft.); Scharnitz (964 m., 3,163 ft.); Seefeld (1,200 m., 3,937 ft.).

Facilities: the area has 34 indoor swimming pools, 3 cable cars, 7 chair lifts, 43 T-bars and an exciting 285 km. (177 miles) of cross-country trails. Reith has floodlighting on its slopes.

Stubai, Wipptal and the Side Valleys. The Brenner motorway gives easy access to this area and ensures its popularity. Once in the region, the attractive old villages provide the needed touch of authenticity to ski life. The glacier gives year-round sport and the variety of slopes make certain that even the tyro can get in a satisfying day's skiing.

Resorts: Fulpmes (960 m., 3,150 ft.); Gries/Brenner (1,200 m., 3,937 ft.); Gschnitz (1,242 m., 4,075 ft.); Mieders (982 m., 3,222 ft.); Navis (1,343 m., 4,406 ft.); Neustift (1,000 m., 3,281 ft.); Obernberg am Brenner (1,400 m., 4,593 ft.); Steinach am Brenner (1,050 m., 3,445 ft.); Trins (1,214 m., 3,983 ft.).

Facilities: the area has 17 indoor swimming pools, 2 cable cars, 9 chair lifts, 37 T-bars and 228 km. (142 miles) of cross-country trails. Neustift has floodlighting on its slopes.

Zillertal. This is an area which goes way back in skiing history. It was one of the early regions to become popular, but it has managed to modernize with the best. The glacier, well-served by lifts, provides all-the-year skiing.

Resorts: Finkenberg (839 m., 2,753 ft.); Fügen, Fügenberg (550 m., 1,805 ft.); Gerlos (1,246 m., 4,088 ft.); Hintertux (1,500 m., 4,921 ft.); Hippach (589 m., 1,932 ft.); Lanersbach (1,300 m.,4,265 ft.);Mayrhofen (630 m., 2,067 ft.); Zell am Ziller (580 m., 1,903 ft.).

Facilities: the region has 23 indoor pools, 8 cable cars, 16 chairlifts, 63 T-bars, and 104 km. (65 miles) of cross country-trails. Gerlos has floodlit slopes.

Wildschönau and Alpbachtal. An area where a certain international element adds to the glamor of Alpbach, while the traditional Tirolean rusticity reigns elsewhere.

Resorts: Alpbach (973 m., 3,189 ft.); Auffach (900 m., 2,952 ft.); Niederau (823 m., 2,698 ft.); Oberau (936 m., 3,069 ft.); Reith im Alpbachtal (640 m., 2,100 ft.); Thierbach (1,175 m., 3,849 ft.).

Facilities: the district has 14 indoor swimming pools, 7 chair lifts, 58 T-bars and 57 km. (35 miles) of cross-country trails. The Wildschönau slopes are floodlit.

Achental. A lovely district, even for the Tirol. It is popular not just for skiing, but also for curling—on the frozen Achensee. Cross-country skiing is also magnificently served around the lake.

Resorts: Achenkirch (923 m., 3,024 ft.); Maurach (957 m., 3,435 ft.); Pertisau (930 m., 3,051 ft.).

Facilities: the valley has 10 indoor swimming pools, 1 cable car, 6 chair lifts, 19 T-bars, and 107 km. (67 miles) of cross-country trails. Achenkirch has floodlit skiing.

Kaiserwinkel. A small region, up by the Bavarian border. Popular for its easily accessible slopes—free bus services to the lifts—and plenty of variety of activities, tobogganing, skating, riding, as well as the mandatory skiing.

Resorts: Kössen (588 m., 1,929 ft.); Schwendt (697 m., 2,287 ft.); Walchsee (668 m., 2,192 ft.).

Facilities: 3 indoor swimming pools, 4 chair lifts, 16 T-bars and 161 km. (100 miles) of cross-country trails. Schwendt has floodlit ski slopes.

The Kitzbühel Area. Now, this is one of the high spots for fashionable life on the slopes. Whatever you want is here—and plenty of it. The skiing is superb (as long as the snow obliges), there is a magnificent supply of cross-country trails all blazed and ready, riding, skating, swimming . . . you name it and Kitzbühel can provide it.

Resorts: Aurach (790 m., 2,589 ft.); Brixen im Thale (800 m., 2,625 ft.); Ellmau (812 m., 2,664 ft.); Erpfendorf (630 m., 2,067 ft.); Fieberbrunn (788 m., 2,585 ft.); Going (798 m., 2,618 ft.); Hopfgarten im Brixental (622 m., 2,041 ft.); Jochberg (924 m., 3,032 ft.); Kirchberg in Tirol (856 m., 2,808 ft.); Kirchdorf in Tirol (643 m., 2,110 ft.); Kitzbühel (760 m., 2,493 ft.); Oberndorf in Tirol (700 m., 2,297 ft.); Reith bei Kitzbühel (800 m., 2,625 ft.); St. Johann in Tirol (663 m., 2,175 ft.); Scheffau am Wilden Kaiser (752 m., 2,467 ft.); Söll (703 m., 2,306 ft.); Waidring (781 m., 2,562 ft.); Westendorf (800 m., 2,625 ft.).

Facilities: the statistics show how effectively serviced for the winter-sports enthusiast the Kitzbühel region is. There are 32 indoor swimming pools, 8 cable cars, 41 chair lifts, 111 T-bars and a stimulating 503 km. (313 miles) of cross-country trails. Oberndorf has 500m. of floodlit slope, open to 10 at night.

East Tirol. An area which veers to the simple side, though with superb sun-drenched landscape. Lienz leads the pack for its lift-system and Zettersfeld is a mecca for sun-worshippers. Brand new cable car cuts waiting to a minimum. The villages mostly can provide stunning views of surrounding mountains, as well as good basic winter-sports terrain.

Resorts: Hopfgarten (1,104 m., 3,622 ft.); Kals (1,325 m., 4,347 ft.); Lienz (673 m., 2,208 ft.); Matrei (1,000 m., 3,281 ft.); Obertilliach (1,450 m.,4,757 ft.); Prägraten (1,312 m., 4,305 ft.); St. Jakob im Defreggen (1,389 m., 4,557 ft.); Sillian (1,097 m., 3,599 ft.); Virgen (1,194 m., 3,918 ft.).

Facilities: 7 indoor swimming pools, 1 cable car, 10 chair lifts, 38 T-bars and a fine 269 km. (167 miles) of cross-country trails.

OTHER SPORTS. Tirol is a sports mecca in summer as well as in winter. In most resorts, large and small, there are healthy activities going on all over the place, usually extremely strenuous. Apart from the slightly esoteric sports such as archery, the more widely-popular ones that don't need a great deal of expertise are easily practiced.

Fishing. Fishing is possible all over the Tirol in lakes and mountain streams, and good fishing, too. The local tourist offices will have details of where to go and how to get the necessary permit.

Golf. Apart from the two courses outside Innsbruck, there are another two at Kitzbühel, the Golf-Club Kitzbühel, A-6370 Kitzbühel (0 53 56–30 07), season April through Nov., 9 holes, and the Red-Bull-Club, A-6370 Kitzbühel (0 53 56–52 61).

At Seefeld there is an 18-hole course, Golf-Club Seefeld-Wildmoos, A6100 Seefeld (0 52 12–30 03), season May through Oct.; Pertisau boasts a 9-hole course, Golf-Club Achensee, A-6213 Pertisau (0 52 43–53 77). A new course is under construction at Kitzbühel-Schwarzsee.

Horseback Riding. Naturally, the Tirol countryside is marvellous for riding and there are 75 riding centers to provide the wherewithal. The local tourist offices have all the details and prices of hire etc.

Mountaineering. For details of this essentially Tirolean sport contact the Oesterreichischer Alpenverein (The Austrian Mountaineering Club), Wilhelm-Greil Str. 17 (59 5 47) in Innsbruck. There are somewhere around 22 mountaineering schools, all with fully trained guides to help novices up the sheerest face. Most of the schools are in areas that are world-famous for the difficulty and challenge of their mountains. If you are interested in courses, contact Bergsteigerschule, Wilhelm-Greil-Str. 17, A-6020 Innsbruck (59 5 47–34).

Swimming and Sailing. Many of the Tirolean lakes are ideal for water sports. On Achensee and Plansee you can either sail or swim. Swimming is excellent in the cool waters of Haldensee, Hechtsee, Heiterwanger See, Piburger See, Reintaler See, Schwarzsee, Thiursee, Tristachersee and Walchsee. Sailing on Durlassboden as well.

VORARLBERG

Rural, Remote—and Relaxed

Tiny Vorarlberg covers an area of slightly more than 2,600 square kilometers, and is (with the exception of Vienna) the smallest of Austria's federal states. As its name implies, the state lies "before the Arlberg," that massive range of Alps, the watershed of Europe, and forms the western tip of Austria. To the north lies Bavaria, and to the west and south Vorarlberg is bounded by the Swiss frontier.

The history of Vorarlberg goes much further back than the times of the Alemannic tribes, for remains from the Stone Age and prehistoric times have been found in all parts of the state. The Vorarlbergers claim, according to legend, that when Noah landed from the ark after the flood he found himself in Vorarlberg. Timbers from the ark are said to have been found on the top of the Widderstein Mountain.

The countryside has much in common with neighboring Switzerland, and the inhabitants of the state have close affinities with the Swiss. Both peoples are descended from the same ancient German Alemannic tribes that flourished in the 3rd century B.C. and both have the same characteristics of thrift, hard work, and a deeprooted instinct for democracy and independence. Indeed, after the collapse of the Habsburg monarchy, Vorarlberg nearly became a part of Switzerland. In May 1919 about 80 percent of the inhabitants voted for starting negotiations with Switzerland for an eventual union with that country, but the Peace Conference at St. Germain decreed otherwise, and Vorarlberg became a part of the newly created Austrian Republic.

Today, Vorarlberg is the center of Austria's important textile industry, playing a vital role in the country's export trade and bid for self-sufficiency.

While the seat of the Vorarlberg state government is in Bregenz, the official capital of the state, the highest court, the chamber of commerce, and the financial administration have their headquarters in Feldkirch, and the state institute for economic promotion selected Dornbirn for the seat of its office.

Exploring Vorarlberg—Bregenz

Bregenz is a picturesque little town, lying at the eastern extremity of Bodensee (Lake Constance), that vast sheet of water 64 km. (40 miles) long and nearly 13 km. (8 miles) across at the widest point. The town is built on the slopes of the wooded foothills that rise gently from the shores of the lake. The old part of the town is built on higher ground and overlooks the new, modern part of Bregenz, which is spread out along the lakeside, where a long promenade follows the shoreline. More than any other town in Austria the face of Bregenz has changed. With the opening of the new rail freight yards outside the town, acres of lakeside land have been redeveloped as a recreation area.

The time to visit Bregenz is during the four weeks of the Music Festival (July to August). This is a spectacle you shouldn't miss if you have any time to spare, since the Bregenz Festival takes place on the lake itself and offers a unique and memorable evening you are sure to enjoy. A vast floating stage is the setting for one of the world's most beautiful water-borne musical festivals. The orchestra pit is built into the lower part of the stage, and the whole is linked to the shore by a long jetty.

You can take in most of the important sights of Bregenz during a short walk. There is the Vorarlberger Landesmuseum, exhibiting the history and art of Vorarlberg (including works by Angelica Kaufmann, 1741–1807), on Kornmarkt square, which also contains an attractive theater. Just round the corner to the left is Rathausstrasse, with the 17th-century Town Hall and the Seekapelle (dedicated to St. George in 1668) attached to it. Following the Maurachstrasse will bring you to Oberstadt, the upper town; here, on the site of a former Celtic settlement and a Roman camp, called Brigantium, is the mighty Martinsturm—a relic of the medieval fortifications. The tower houses a museum of local art and folklore, plus the Martinskapelle, with remarkable frescos from the 1360s. Close by is the Altes Rathaus, the Old Town Hall, while on a rise is the Gothic parish church of St. Gall, built in the 14th century and Baroqued in the 17th. The lovely choirstalls came originally from the Abbey of Mehrerau.

Another must in Bregenz is a trip to the top of the Pfänder Mountain above the town. A funicular from the heart of the town will take you up in a matter of 6 minutes. From this vantage point you get one of the finest panoramic views to be found on the Continent. On a fine, sunny day the breathtaking scene takes in the entire length of the lake. At your feet lie the compact group of houses of the Old Town, and lower down, the bustling New Town of Bregenz. To the right a few miles away, lies the German frontier, with the Bavarian town of Lindau clearly seen in the foreground, and the large city of Friedrichshafen in the middle distance. To the left, you can catch a glimpse of the Rhine, 16 km. (10 miles) away, and beyond it lies Switzerland.

The Bregenz Forest

Directly behind Bregenz lies the Bregenzerwald (Bregenz Forest). This is the name given to a wide area of densely wooded highlands, charming valleys, and lovely alpine meadows dotted with thick clusters of red, white, blue and yellow alpine flowers, all set against a fabulous backdrop of majestic Alps.

Should you be searching for the ideal place for the family summer holiday, particularly if some of the family are very young, then you couldn't do better than to choose the Bregenz Forest. Even if you are just passing through, a day's tour of the Bregenz Forest is most rewarding. Here you will see the Vorarlbergers as they really are. In the picturesque little villages the women still wear the handsome, stiffly starched folk dress of their ancestors, as it has been the usage for the past five or six hundred years. The women take a great pride in their national dress, and with great justification. On festive occasions the girls carry a golden headdress shaped like a small crown, and the married women a pointed cap. Old men's folk dress is still worn by the members of local brass bands, and it differs from place to place according to the shape of the cap and the color of various parts of clothing. In the Bregenz Forest white is the color of mourning, while in other districts the more usual black is worn at funerals and on Sundays.

At Egg—an easy name to remember—the valley branches into two. The left-hand fork leads down a country road to the villages of the lower part of Bregenzerwald, all with an old-world charm of their own: among them Langenegg, Lingenau, Krumbach, Hittisau, Riefensberg, and Sibratsgfäll.

The right-hand fork, continuing the main road through the Bregenz Forest, takes you through Andelsbuch, where the main valley of the area starts to spread out. On the other side above the valley is Schwarzenberg, which can be reached also from Dornbirn by the road over Bödele. Then, round a bend, Bezau, the best known of the Bregenzerwald villages, comes into view. All these villages lie at about 600 m. (2,000 ft.) above sea level, but now the winding country road climbs steeply round the spurs of the Alps to another string of villages, Mellau, Schnepfau and Au. From Au—which really is pronounced "ow"!—a side road leads to Damüls, the highest village of Bregenzerwald.

Dornbirn and Feldkirch

Dornbirn is important because it is the center of Vorarlberg's main industry—textiles. Every year an important international trade fair, with textiles a specialty, is held that coincides in time with the Bregenz Music Festival. A cable car joins the town with the Karren heights, with a very fine view.

From Dornbirn, still traveling up the Rhine valley you pass through Hohenems, with its outstanding Renaissance Palace and the remains of the once very powerful Alt-Ems fortress. The town is the location for an international music festival, the Schubertiade, now considered one of the finest musical events anywhere in Europe. Further up the valley is Götzis, a small town with interesting churches and castle ruins, and known for its textile industry.

Still farther is Feldkirch, Vorarlberg's oldest town. This is the first stop on the main railway line after crossing into Austria from Switzerland.

Parts of Feldkirch date from the Middle Ages and it is still a town with great character. Picturesque arcades line the busy, narrow main street, and the ancient town hall and city gates are splendid examples of 13th- and 15th-century craftmanship. The great castle of Schattenburg, the 12th-century former seat of the powerful valley barons, is open to the public (museum and restaurant).

At Feldkirch both road and railway turn into the Ill valley toward Bludenz, the fourth of Vorarlberg's democratic little towns. Bludenz, a main-line station, is the starting point for three of Vorarlberg's loveliest valleys, which all emerge into the deep Ill valley in this area.

The Great Walser Valley (Grosswalser Tal)

To the north lies the Grosswalser Tal (Great Walser Valley), first colonized by Walliser highland clans from the Valais area in Switzerland (of Burgundian origin). At the entrance to the valley, which is easily accessible from the Bludenz railway station by bus, lies Thüringen, a charming little summer resort with a small lake, waterfall, and splendid view down over the Ill valley with the Rhätikon mountains in the distance.

From Thüringen, the bus climps steeply up the gradient into the Walsertal, to Sonntag, or "Sunday village," in the heart of the valley. Be sure to get a seat on the right-hand side of the bus, or you will not be able to enjoy the magnificent panorama of Alps—the back door to the Bregenz Forest—as you go along. Beyond lies Buchboden, a tiny hamlet high up in the outer range of the Arlberg. This hamlet, Sonntag, and Fontanella, another mountain village at the foot of a spur three kilometers to the north of Sonntag, are well known bases for mountain climbers in the summer, and in winter for proficient skiers.

The Brandner Valley (Brandner Tal)

Turning southwest across the Ill river from the railway station at Bludenz, you reach Bürs, a pleasant village at the foot of the Brandner valley, which straggles steeply on through the narrow, sheer mountain gorge, and after about half-an-hour's drive from here we arrive in Brand, a mountain village at the foot of Scesaplana in the Rätikon range.

Brand (975 m., 3,200 ft.) is becoming increasingly popular among foreign tourists as a health resort and winter sports center. If you are fond of walking, you can climb by easy stages along the forest paths without much exertion to the beautiful Lüner glacier lake (about a 3-hour climb). You can shorten your walk by half if you take the cable car which brings you from Schattenlagant, farther up the valley from Brand, to Lünersee in five minutes. This cable car operates only in summer, but the chair lift to Niggenkopf (1,615 m., 5,300 ft.) runs in summer and winter.

Anyone interested in geology should pay a visit to the tiny village chapel, which is built of a local rock called "trowel stone." This stone may be cut into shape quite easily with an ordinary saw; when exposed to the air, the masonry then shrinks slightly, hardens and becomes rather brittle.

The Montafon Valley

The third valley leading from Bludenz is the lovely Montafon, famous for its brown castle, the most attractive of Vorarlberg's many tourist-frequented valleys.

Tschagguns and Schruns, about halfway up the valley, both lie within a mile of each other, both equally well known as summer and winter sports resorts. Neither place is of the fashionable variety, but the picture postcard views over the Ferwall Alps to the east and the mighty Rätikon on the western side of the valley are unsurpassed anywhere in Austria, while in wintertime the skiing is as good here as in any of the more internationally famous centers.

Shortly before St. Gallenkirch the valley divides. To the southwest, a narrow offshoot from the main valley leads up to Gargellen (1,423 m., 4,667 ft.), a tiny Alpine village sandwiched in between the massive Rätikon and the towering Silvretta mountains. In the summer Gargellen is famous as a base for mountaineers intent upon getting to grips with the challenging Alpine peaks. Those less athletically inclined may enjoy really excellent trout fishing in the fast mountain streams. In the winter there is some very fine skiing, but to make the most of the facilities, you should have considerable ability.

Continuing on, Gaschurn is still another popular little place for winter sports enthusiasts. This is the touring region par excellence. Local guides will take skiing parties on 2- or 3-day tours across the peaks and glaciers of the Silvretta and the Ferwall, sleeping in the snug, well-appointed rest huts at night. But it is not necessary to be a skiing expert to enjoy winter sports at Gaschurn, and there are plenty of facilities for beginners.

The Bielerhöhe

Less than 5 km. (3 miles) from Gaschurn, along the main road, is Partenen, another pleasant village, particularly for skiers. One of the huge Vermunt power plants is at Partenen, with two others in the region. The plants were opened before World War II, but enlarged after the war when the dams for the artificial lakes on Silvretta were built.

Just beyond Partenen is the beginning of the Silvretta Hochalpen-Strasse, a private toll road owned by the Vorarlberger Illwerke power company, leading through 24 km. (15 miles) of curves and bends over the Bielerhöhe Pass (2,036 m., 6,680 ft.) and the Vorarlberg-Tirol border to Galtür in the Paznaun valley of Tirol. Built in connection with the giant Vermunt electricity works that collect water from the Silvretta glaciers in two artificial lakes, it is a masterpiece of high Alpine road engineering. Many curves and a narrow width make it difficult to drive; it is normally open early June to mid-October. At the top enjoy magnificent views of the Piz Buin (3,312 m., 10,866 ft.) to the south which was first climbed in 1865.

The Other Arlberg

Bludenz is the departure point for the Arlberg massif, that Mecca of winter sports. Passing through the narrow Klostertal valley and the small hamlet of Dalaas, the road begins the steep ascent up the Arlberg, while the railway started its slower climb to Langen am Arlberg right after leaving Bludenz. Langen is the main-line-stop for the internationally known winter sports centers on the Vorarlberg side of the Arlberg. If the Arlberg pass is closed temporarily to motorists during the winter due to a sudden avalanche, then the Arlberg tunnel with its fast approach road will soon see you into Tirol.

Stuben (1,407 m., 4,615 ft.), at the beginning of the climb, is famous as the birthplace of Hannes Schneider, Austria's most distinguished ski pioneer. Like every village on the Arlberg, it offers magnificent skiing from December until the end of April. Although not as fashionable as the resorts farther up, beyond the Flexen Pass, it is very popular, particularly with tourists who take their skiing seriously.

Just past Stuben the famous Flexen road over the pass begins. This is a triumph of bold engineering. From Stuben the Alpine road looks like some gigantic caterpillar crawling along the face of the steep mountain cliffs. For much of its length the Flexen road is completely covered over by short tunnels of reinforced concrete, or complicated structures of massive wooden beams. For the short stretches where the road emerges into the sunlight, the mountain side is shored up with formidable concrete barriers, while higher up immense barricades guard against the danger of avalanches.

In summer the treeless slopes are covered with Alpine flora, and in wintertime, with eight to fifteen feet of snow on the ground, they become a winter sports paradise. Zürs itself is nothing more than a collection of large hotels. Various ski lifts and chair lifts will take you up to heights of over 2,400 m. (8,000 ft.) to the start of some of the finest downhill runs in Europe.

From Zürs the valley dips down a shallow slope for a few kilometers to Lech, the second of the two international winter sports resorts on top of the Arlberg. Although some people maintain that Lech is not quite as fashionable as Zürs, the fact is that there are more hotels, better technical facilities, bigger ski schools, more life, and prices almost as high as in Zürs. But there is really not much to choose between them. Zürs has the advantage of being a little higher up, but Lech is a genuine and very pretty village.

From Lech, the road takes you to Warth am Arlberg, another small village in beautiful mountain scenery, the point of departure for many walks and climbing tours, and an up-and-coming winter sports resort. At Warth, the road splits: one route runs into Tirol down the wild Lech Valley, eventually reaching Reutte, while the other crosses the high plateau of Hochtannberg, over the pass of the same name (1,676 m., 5,500 ft.), to the high resort, and winter sports center of Schröcken.

This old village, framed by towering mountains, was originally settled by Walliser, as were the Grosses Walsertal to the southwest and the Kleines Walsertal to the northeast. Kleines Walsertal or Kleinwalsertal (Small Walser Valley), with its tiny villages of Riezlern, Hirschegg, Mittelberg, and Baad—all renowned summer and winter resorts—represents a sort of geographic anomaly because, thrusting itself into Bavaria from the other side of the high Alpine range above Schröcken, it can be reached from the Austrian side only by a few high mountain paths, whereas its only road communication is with Oberstdorf in Germany. For this reason, the Kleinwalsertal has an economic union with Bavaria, and the currency here is the German Mark.

From Schröcken, the Hochtannberg road descends along the swift flowing Bregenzer Ache to Au, and then on to Bezau and Egg in Bregenzerwald.

PRACTICAL INFORMATION FOR VORARLBERG

TOURIST INFORMATION. Vorarlberg has just over 100 local tourist offices, mostly in very small places. Many of them have accommodation advice facilities as well as plenty of help to give to visitors to their district. Among the larger ones are the following (with their postal codes and phone numbers):

Bezau A-6870 (0 55 14–22 95); Bludenz A-6700 (0 55 52–62170); Bregenz A-6900 (0 55 74–23 3 91); Dornbirn A-6850 (0 55 72–62 1 88); Egg A-6863 (0 55 12–24 26); Feldkirch A-6800 (0 55 22–23 4 67).

Gargellen A-6787 (0 55 57–63 03); Gaschurn A-6793 (0 55 58–82 01); Hohenems A-6845 (0 55 76–46 47); Langen A-6932 (0 55 82–75 44 15); Lech A-6764 (0 55 83–21 6 10); Lochau A-6911 (0 55 74–25 3 04); Partenen A-6794 (0 55 58–83 15); Riezlern A-6991 (0 55 17–51 1 40).

Schröcken A-6888 (0 55 19–267); Schruns A-6780 (0 55 56–21 66); Stuben A-6762 (0 55 82–761); Tschagguns A-6774 (0 55 56–24 57); Warth A-6767 (0 55 83–35 15); Zürs A-6763 (0 55 83–22 45).

Bregenz Information: Ship information, Harbor (22 8 68); Pfänder Cablecar, Steinbruchg. 4 (22 1 60); Bus excursions, Weiss, Bahnhofstr. 27 (23 2 00); Bregenz Festival (22 8 11); Bicycle hire, Jahnstr. 11 (22 3 19) and Rheinstr. 64 (36 3 36); Car rental, Avis, Am Brand 2 (26 8 89) and Buchbinder, Rheinstr. 4 (23 7 60).

AREA CODES—MAIL AND PHONE. You will find the postal code (preceded by an "A") and the telephone code (in brackets) after the name of each town in the following *Hotel and Restaurant* list.

HOTELS AND RESTAURANTS. Vorarlberg is well provided with accommodations ranging from the international first class to the low-priced regional Gasthof-types. In smaller and less-known resorts you will often find that the bottom prices do not always represent the lowest quality when compared to the other areas inside, as well as outside Austria. The highest prices are charged during the peak winter season in such renowned skiing centers as Zürs and Lech, and here, together with extras, your daily expenses may run as high as in any other top-priced locality in the country.

When staying in summer or winter resorts you will find that the best arrangement is to take *en pension* terms. When traveling through the countryside or visiting a town, the exploration of local-style taverns and non-hotel restaurants will be more interesting.

There are accommodation bureaux in many of the local tourist offices to help you find a room if you are in difficulties.

Bezau A-6870 (0 55 14). *Bad Reuthe* (E), A-6870 Reuthe (22 65). 127 rooms, all with bath; apartments, with all conveniences. Spa treatments with medical supervision. *Gams* (E), (22 20). 40 rooms, all with bath or shower. Traditional atmosphere; outdoor pool, tennis courts, elegant lounge; good restaurant. *Kur-Sporthotel Post* (E), (22 07). 42 rooms, all with bath or shower. Indoor pool, sauna, spa facilities. Quality restaurant, game in season. Closed Nov. to mid-Dec. MC.

Restaurant. *Engel* (E), (22 03). Charming, friendly restaurant with fine regional cooking and good wines. Closed Tues.
Campsite (23 82; 29 64).

Bludenz A-6700 (0 55 52). On the main rail line, about 1 hour from Bregenz. *Schlosshotel* (M), (63 0 16). 36 rooms, all with bath or shower. Located above center of town with wonderful view of Ratikon mountains. Minigolf, billiards, bowling; average restaurant. AE, DC, MC, V.
Campsite (62 5 12).

Brand A-6708 (0 55 59). Bus from Bludenz. *Scesaplana* (E), (221). 63 rooms, all with bath. One of the best hotels of Vorarlberg. Geared to meet international standards; indoor and outdoor pools, indoor tennis courts; restaurant. Closed Nov. AE, DC, MC, V. *Walliserhof* (E), (24 10). 44 rooms, most with bath or shower. Indoor and outdoor pools, sauna, tennis. Closed Nov.
Lagant (M), (285). 35 rooms, all with bath. Friendly chalet-style; indoor pool, lawn, sun terrace; restaurant, also serving health food. AE, DC, MC, V.

Bregenz A-6900 (0 55 74). *Schwärzler* (E), Landstrasse 9 (2 24 22). 75 rooms, all with bath. Quiet site, a bit out of town; international standards. Good restaurant. AE, DC, MC, V. *Mercure* (E) (26 1 00). 94 rooms. Modern, purpose-built hotel close to Festspielhaus. Every comfort and facility. Recommended restaurant, casino. AE, DC, MC, V. *Messmer* (E), Kornmarktstrasse 16 (22 3 56). 45 rooms, all with bath or shower; sauna, solarium; bar and excellent restaurant. DC, MC, V.
Weisses Kreuz (E), Romerstrasse 5 (22 4 88). 44 rooms, all with bath or shower, color TV and minibar. Family-run, particularly friendly. AE, DC, MC, V.
Berghof Fluh (M), Fluherstrasse 7 (24 2 13). 12 rooms, all with bath. Restaurant, bar. AE, DC, MC, V. *Bodensee* (M), Kornmarktstrasse 22 (22 3 00). 28 rooms, all with bath or shower. DC, MC, V. *Central* (M), Kaiserstr. 26 (22 9 47). 41 rooms, in traffic-free zone. Modern, friendly, and convenient. *Germania* (M), Am Steinebach (22 7 66). 17 rooms, most with shower. Excellent value, good cooking, nice atmosphere. Restaurant. Closed Sun. MC.
Camping at *Seecamping* (31 8 95), mid-May–mid Sept; *Camping Weiss,* Brachensweg 4 (35 7 71), June–Sept.; *Camping Mehrerau,* (31 7 01)), on the lake 3 km. in the direction of Switzerland, April–Oct; and *Camping Mexico,* Hechtweg 4 (33 2 60), June–Sept.
Restaurants. *Ilge Weinstube* (E), Maurachg. 6 (23 6 09). Cozy, intimate, excellent food and stunning wines; also food to take out. Closed Thurs., and Sun. eves. V. *Zoll* (E), Arlbergstr. 118 (31 7 05). Considered by many to be Austria's finest restaurant. Small, on Lake Constance, with fish from the lake; traditional Austrian cuisine imaginatively prepared in a completely new way. Closed Thurs. AE.
Goldener Hirsch (I), (22 8 15), Kirchstr. 8. Oldest tavern in Bregenz. Noisy and cheerful, good food and drink at low prices. Closed Tues.
Youth Hostel, (22 8 76). Open April to Sept.

Damüls A-6884 (0 55 10). *Damülserhof* (E), (210). 84 beds, all with bath or shower. All modern conveniences; indoor pool, sauna, tennis; restaurant. DC.

Dornbirn A-6850 (0 55 72). 15 minutes by fast train from Bregenz. *Parkhotel* (E), (6 26 91). 62 beds, all with bath or shower. Meeting place for businessmen, especially during the Dornbirn trade fair. Outside town; near a great variety of sports facilities. Good restaurant *Jägerstüble*. AE, DC, MC, V. *Rickatschwende* (E), (6 53 50). 44 rooms, all with bath. At 823 m. (2,700 ft) with wonderful view. Indoor pool, tennis; good restaurant. DC, MC.

Campsite (69 1 19).

Restaurants. *Gasthof Hirschen* (M), (6 63 63). Prime food and garden. Closed Mon. AE, MC, V. *Krone* (M), (62 7 20). Good use of fresh local ingredients. Closed Wed. and Sat. midday. *Rotes Haus* (M), (6 23 06). In center of town; lovely old building with *stuben*-like living rooms; good food with large helpings. DC, MC.

Egg A-6863 (0 55 12). *Post* (M), (22 30). 25 rooms, all with bath or shower. Restaurant. Closed Nov. MC.

Restaurant. *Löwen* (M), (22 01–12). The place to go if you like cheese. Rustic atmosphere in old barn, with Bregenz Forest specialties. AE, MC, V.

Feldkirch A-6800 (0 55 22). About 35 minutes from Bregenz by fast train. *Bären* (E), (2 20 50). 26 rooms, all with bath. Fine building in center of town, with soundproof windows. First-rate restaurant serving local and international specialties. AE, DC, MC. *Illpark* (E), Leonhardsplatz 2 (24 6 00). 92 rooms, all with bath. Large, modern hotel with every comfort. Centrally located, conference facilities. Restaurant. AE, DC, MC, V.

Alpenrose (M), (2 21 75–0). 21 rooms, all with bath or shower. In center of medieval town, run by Gutwinsky family and giving personal service. AE, DC, MC, V.

Youth Hostel (23 1 81).

Campsite (24 3 08).

Gargellen A-6787 (0 55 57). Bus from Schruns. *Alpenhotel Heimspitze* (E), Romantikhotel, (63 19). 19 rooms, all with bath or shower. Montafon-style, tastefully furnished. Excellent food and good wines served in pleasant *stuben*. Closed May, Oct. and Nov. MC. *Feriengut Gargellenhof* (E), (62 74). 23 rooms, all with bath or shower. On hill; horseback riding. Restaurant. DC, MC.

Gaschurn A-6793 (0 55 58). Bus from Schruns or Bludenz. *Epple* (E), (82 51). 63 rooms, all with bath or shower. Indoor pool, tennis; restaurant. Closed May to June and Oct. to Nov.

Campsite (85 48).

Restaurant. *Alt Montafon* (E), (82 32). Exceptional cozy restaurant with a lot of wood paneling, serving mainly local food imaginatively prepared. Excellent wines. Closed Mon. AE.

Hard A-6971 (0 55 74). *Angelika* (M), (33 3 43). 44 beds, all with bath or shower. Popular with businessmen, and performers during the Festival. Spacious rooms with balconies. Above par restaurant; good soups and wonderful ice cream. Closed Dec. MC.

Youth Hostel (33 92 03 or 35 01 82).

Kleinwalsertal A-6992 Hirschegg (0 55 17). *Ifenhotel* (L), (50 71). 72 rooms, all with bath or shower. Beauty farm. Pleasant rooms, all modern conveniences and sports facilities; best restaurant in town. Closed Nov. AE, DC, MC.

Almhof Rupp (E), A-6991 Riezlern (50 04). 25 rooms, all with bath or shower. Reasonable for pleasant rooms, delicious buffet breakfast. Superb restaurant. Closed Nov. *Walserhof* (E), A-6992 Hirschegg (56 84). 34 rooms, all with bath, many with balcony. Indoor pool, tennis court; restaurant. Closed Nov. to 20 Dec.

Stern (M), A-6991 Riezlern (52 08). 50 beds, all with bath. Modern, in center of village. Free fishing for guests. Closed May and Oct. to 15 Dec. AE, DC, MC, V.

Campsites (57 92; 57 27; 61 38; 56 96).

Lech Am Arlberg A-6764 (0 55 83). Bus from Langen or St. Anton (Tirol), both on main rail line. *Gasthof Post* (L), (2 20 60), 41 rooms, all with bath. Really romantic; painted facade, antique rustic furniture, wooden ceilings, lots of atmosphere. Haunt of aristocrats and royalty. Excellent restaurant serving international specialties. Best restaurant in town. Closed May to June and Oct. to Nov. v. *Almhof Schneider* (L), (35 00). 70 rooms, all with bath. Elegant rooms and lounges of international standard—heated chest for ski boots! Outstanding restaurant serving local produce. AE, MC, V.

Angela (E), (24 07). Silencehotel, (24 07). 25 rooms, all with bath. Homey atmosphere; gym. Closed May to July and Sept. to end Nov. *Arlberg* (E), (21 34). 78 beds, all with bath. Indoor and outdoor pools, sauna; tennis. Restaurant. AE, MC, V. *Brunnenhof* (E), (23 49). 32 rooms, rustic comfort. Excellent restaurant; sauna. Closed May to Nov. DC, *Kristiania* (E), (2 56 10). Indoor pool, sauna. Owned by Olympic ski champion Othmar Schneider. 32 rooms, all with bath or shower. Good restaurant. Closed May to Nov. AE, DC, MC. *Krone* (E), (25 51). 54 rooms, all with bath. Sauna, solarium and massage parlor. Excellent restaurant. Closed May and Oct. to Nov. *Montana* (E), A-6764 Oberlech (2 46 00). 40 rooms, all with bath. On sunny slopes of Oberlech. Indoor pool, open fireplace, balconies; remarkable restaurant whose owner comes from Alsace.Closed May to Nov.

Solaria (M), (2214). 24 rooms, most with bath. Restaurant; pension only in winter.

Restaurant. *Alpenblick* (M), (27 55). Discovered by cross-country skiers; small and unspoilt. Little choice, but well-prepared local dishes. Good value. AE.

Lochau A-6911 (0 55 74). **Restaurants.** *Mangold* (E), Pfänderstr. 3 (2 24 31). Cozy rooms; regional specialties and good pastries. Closed Mon., 9 Jan. to 2 Feb. MC, V. *Messmer* (E), (2 41 51). Highly recommended, serving local as well as Italian cuisine. Closed Thurs. and mid-Nov. to 2 Dec. *Klause* (M), Bregenzerstr. 7 (2 33 90). Beside lake, sun terrace; fish from Lake Constance, good pastries. Closed Tues. and 15 Oct. to 15 Nov. DC, MC.

Mellau A-6881 (0 55 18). *Kreuz* (M), (22 08). 53 rooms, all with bath; apartments. Indoor pool, sauna, solarium, children's rooms; fine restaurant. Closed Nov.

Röthis A-6832 (0 55 22). **Restaurant.** *Torggel* (E), (4 40 52). Attractive place on two floors; lovely garden; select international cuisine. Closed Tues. and Jan. AE, DC, MC, V.

St. Gerold A-6700 (0 55 50). *Kloster St. Gerold* (E), (21 21). 25 rooms, some with bath or shower. Romantic location in Grosswalsertal 11th-century abbey. All modern facilities; excellent restaurant in Klosterkeller. Cultural events during summer months; remarkable library. Closed Tues. DC, MC, V.

Schruns A-6780 (0 55 56). Local rail and bus from Bludenz. *Montafon Kurhotel* (L), (27 91). 93 beds, all with bath. Swimming pool, sauna, solarium, cure center. Restaurant and bar. Silencehotel. Closed Nov. DC. *Alpenhof Messmer* (E), (26 64). 39 rooms, all with bath or shower. Indoor pool, sauna, solarium. Restaurant and bar. Silence Hotel. *Löwen* (E), (31 41). 85 rooms, all with bath. Comfortable, mansion-style; big indoor pool, tennis, disco. Fine *Restaurant Français* serves light regional specialties as well as French fare. AE, DC, MC, V.
    Campsite (26 74).
    Cafe. *Feuerstein* (M) (21 29), in small side street; antique furniture, especially in upstairs rooms; delicious pastries and *petit fours*.

Stuben Am Arlberg A-6762 (0 55 82). Bus from Langen on the main rail line. *Albona* (E), (712). 22 rooms, all with bath or shower. Sauna, solarium; restaurant and bar. Closed Nov. *Mondschein* (M), (721). 30 rooms, all with bath or shower. Old house full of atmosphere. Indoor pool. Restaurant. Closed Nov.

Zürs Am Arlberg A-6763 (0 55 83). Bus from Langen and St. Anton am Arlberg, both on main railway line. *Alpenhof Sporthotel* (L), (21 91). 41 rooms, all with bath. Indoor pool, sauna. Good restaurant. Closed May to Nov. *Lorünser* (L), (22 5 40). 76 rooms, all with bath; comfortable and elegant. Open fire in lobby; restaurant for residents only.Closed May to Nov. *Zürserhof* (L), (25 13). 107 rooms, all with bath; beautiful apartments. Indoor tennis, bowling, golfomat, billiards, table-tennis, sauna; disco in basement. Excellent restaurant. Closed May to Oct. MC.
    Alpenrose-Post (E), (22 71). 87 rooms, most with bath, some with balconies. Attractive lounges; indoor pool. Restaurant. Closed May to Nov. MC, V. *Edelweiss* (E), (26 62). 74 rooms, all with bath. Sauna, bar and disco. Closed May to Nov. *Flexen* (E), (22 43). 60 beds, all with bath; fancy new apartments. Traditional atmosphere. Closed May to Nov.

GETTING AROUND VORARLBERG. By Train. The main railway line from Vienna and Innsbruck enters Vorarlberg at Langen after coming out of the Arlberg tunnel. This is the route of both the *Arlberg* and *Orient Express* trains. It proceeds through Bludenz to Feldkirch, where it splits into two lines, the Arlberg Express route going through tiny Liechtenstein to Switzerland and Vorarlberg Express route through Dornbirn to Bregenz, continuing from there to Lindau in Germany. The shortest connection between Bregenz and Switzerland is via St. Margrethen (in Swiss territory).
    A fast train takes about 1½ hours from Bregenz to Langen and about 3½ hours from Bregenz to Innsbruck. Small local railroads connect Bre-

genz with Bezau in lower Bregenzerwald, and Bludenz with Schruns in Montafon valley.(Steam locomotives ply this route in July and August.) Narrow-gauge steam locomotives with old cars take passengers through the Bregenzerwald on the museum railroad between Bezau and Schwarzenberg. For information, call 0 55 14–22 95.

By Bus. State and private bus services connect all the towns and villages not served by the railroad. Half-track vehicles and sleighs are used in winter in the higher places when necessary. Some of the highest roads become impassable for motor vehicles in heavy snow and then you have to hire horse sleighs. Sightseeing bus tours originate in Bregenz.

By Car. If you are driving, the A14 Autobahn leads south from Bregenz to Dornbirn (11 km., 7 miles), Feldkirch (35 km., 22 miles), and Bludenz (53 km., 33 miles); Route S16/E17 continues west to the entrance of the Arlberg tunnel at Langen (80 km., 50 miles) and winds up to Stuben and the Arlberg Pass (92 km., 57 miles).

From Feldkirch it is 15 km. (9 miles) to Vaduz in Liechtenstein.

From Bludenz, very narrow roads lead south to the Brenner Tal and Route 193 north into the Grosswalser Tal. Route 188 leads southeast up the Montafon valley to the Silvretta Pass (43 km., 27 miles). The Silvretta high mountain toll road begins at Partenen and climbs up at a maximum of 12% in many sharp curves to a height of 2,042 m. (6,700 ft.). If the weather conditions are normal it is open for traffic from early June until late October.

Shortly above Stuben (by the Arlberg tunnel) the Flexen Pass (1,784 m., 5,853 ft.) Route 198 branches off for Zürs and Lech (kept open in winter months as far as Lech) and continues to Warth (18 km., 11 miles), where it meets Route 200 coming from Bregenz through Bregenzerwald. The latter is a beautiful drive through the lower and upper sections of the Bregenzerwald mountains (77 km., 48 miles, from Bregenz to Warth), although the entire road is not in tip-top condition and the last section near Warth quite narrow.

PLACES OF INTEREST. The routes for the items on the following list are given with the starting point from Bregenz. Please check for opening days and times locally, as they are difficult to establish in advance, and change without warning.

Bezau. Route 200. **Heimatmuseum,** Ellenbogen 181. Local history museum, 17th-century sacred art, portraits. Closed in winter. Narrow-gauge steam trains on what remains of the Bregenzerwaldbahn.

Bludenz. Good as a center for trips into the surrounding countryside. **Heimatmuseum,** im Oberen Tor. Regional history, sacred art (especially the Muttersberg Altar). Closed winter.

Bregenz. Vorarlberger Landesmuseum (The Vorarlberg Provincial Museum), Kornmarkt. Prehistory and Roman exhibits, with the history of the province up to date. Art exhibits include Angelica Kauffman's work. **Martinsturm** (St. Martin's Tower), 13th century tower with exhibits (including frescos) and views. **Parish Church,** (22 7 97). 15th century, interesting furnishings (especially the carved choir stalls). Closed Mon.

Dornbirn. A14 south. **Vorarlberger Naturschau** (Vorarlberg Natural History Museum), Marktstr. Modern techniques in displays of the Province's natural history. Some attractive local architecture (e.g. **Rotes Haus,** the Red House).

Feldkirch. A14 south. The old town has a lot of Gothic buildings of interest—**Katzenturm** (the Cats' Tower), **Churetor** (Chur Gate) and the arcaded Market Place. **Schattenburg** castle, a massive medieval fortress has a handy cafe and the **Heimatmuseum** with local history displays, armor, frescos and crafts. Good overviews of Feldkirch. 15th-century **Parish Church.** Two fine town squares, one with vaulted sidewalk arcades.

Götzis. A14 south. **Castle** ruins. **Parish Church** with 16th-century frescos and Baroque high altar.

Hohenems. A14 south. **Castle,** Renaissance palace, with displays of weapons, paintings etc. Summer concerts during Schubert Festival, and plays. **Parish Church** has 18th-century carved altar. Nearby castles at **Alt-Ems** (ruins), and **Schloss Glopper.**

WINTER SPORTS. Similar to the neighboring Tirol, Vorarlberg is an excellent area for skiing, including high mountain ski tours. Several top winter sports centers, such as Zürs, Lech-Oberlech, Bielerhöhe, and Hochkrumbach are located quite high and skiing is possible here from early December until the end of April and even later, particularly on Bielerhöhe. On some of the glaciers you can ski in August. The best time for skiing in lower areas is usually between early January and mid-March. International and national competitions take place throughout the winter. Skiing equipment can be rented in most places. In several places ski lifts are lit for night-time skiing. Snowmobiles are banned altogether, but there is some magnificent tobogganing to be had in the area. During summer months, many resorts—Mellau and Brand for two—offer tennis, hiking and fitness packages.

Tobogganing is widely practiced in the region and several competitions take place every year. Ice skating competitions and ice hockey games can frequently be seen on the most important skating rinks. Horse sleighs are often a necessity in higher areas and are therefore easy to find.

Arlberg. Straddling the border between Vorarlberg and the Tirol, this area is one of the classic ski regions. It lies fairly high, as Austrian ski areas go, and is rightly famous for its magnificent slopes and snowfields. As it has been so long in the running, the Arlberg can provide plenty of off-the-slopes things to do, as well . . . skating, horse-riding and many of the other enjoyable things that a glorious winter landscape inspires.

Resorts: Lech (1,444 m., 4,738 ft.); Zürs (1,717 m., 5,633 ft.); Pettneu (1,228 m., 4,029 ft.); St. Anton (1,304 m., 4,278 ft.); St. Christoph (1,802 m., 5,912 ft.).

Facilities: the Arlberg has 22 indoor swimming pools, 9 cable cars, 15 chair lifts, 37 T-bars and 75 km. (47 miles) of cross-country trails.

St. Anton has the largest ski school in the world, where 300 instructors teach under the championship guidance of Karl Schranz. The après-ski life of St. Anton, with its discos, restaurants and general go-go-go atmosphere will ensure that you reach the morning sessions on the slopes in the right frame of mind.

Grosswalsertal. Lying between Lake Constance and the classic Arlberg ski area, this is a beautiful valley, typical of the best Alpine scenery. Well-supplied with cable cars and accommodations, it is one of the quieter spots for winter sports, and none the worse for that.

Resorts: Blons (902 m., 2,959 ft.); Faschina (1,500 m., 4,921 ft.); Fontanella (1,200 m., 3,937 ft.); Raggal (1,016 m., 3,334 ft.); Sonntag (890 m., 2,919 ft.); Thüringerberg (878 m., 2,881 ft.).

Facilities: the valley has 3 indoor swimming pools, 3 cable cars, 2 chair lifts, 12 T-bars and just 18 km. (11 miles) of cross-country trails.

Brandnertal–Walgau. Rising up from Bludenz to the Brandner glacier this is an easily accessible skiing valley, with good clear slopes. There are also fine walking paths with superb views at 1,500 m., (5,000ft).

Resorts: Bludenz (588 m., 1,929 ft.); Brand (1,037 m., 3,402 ft.); Bürserberg (900 m., 2,952 ft.).

Facilities: 8 indoor swimming pools, 1 cable car, 4 chair lifts, 8 T-bars and 28 km. (17 miles) of cross-country trails.

Montafon. A big, busy area for winter sports, rapidly reaching an international clientele. With excellent equipment for moving skiers around the district and a good selection of terrain—from easy beginners' slopes to the really tough ones. The surrounding high peaks make both for wonderful panoramas and good snowfalls.

Resorts: Bartholomäberg (1,087 m., 3,561 ft.); Gargellen (1,423 m., 4,667 ft.); Gaschurn (1,000 m., 3,281 ft.); Partenen (1,051 m., 3,448 ft.); St. Gallenkirch (878 m., 2,881 ft.); Schruns (700 m., 2,295 ft.); Silbertal (889 m., 2,917 ft.); Tschagguns (700 m., 2,295 ft.); Vandans (649 m., 2,129 ft.).

Facilities: 22 indoor swimming pools, 6 cable cars, 12 chair lifts, 38 T-bars, and 68 km. (42 miles) of cross-country trails. There is a 2-mile toboggan run requiring skill.

Klostertal. This long valley runs all the way up from the Walgau and Bludenz to the Arlberg Tunnel and beyond. As the motorway runs the entire length of the valley, all the side shoots are easily reached.

Resorts: Dalaas/Wald (836 m., 2,743 ft.); Klösterle (1,073 m., 3,521 ft.); Stuben am Arlberg (1,407 m., 4,616 ft.).

Facilities: 2 indoor swimming pools, 4 chair lifts, 8 T-bars, 33 km. (21 miles) of cross-country trails.

Bregenzerwald. This is a favorite region for family skiing as the facilities range from good nursery slopes right up to those which challenge the experienced skier. Also, this is an area of magnificently varied alpine scenery—as beautiful in summer as it is under its winter cloak.

Resorts: Alberschwende (721 m., 2,366 ft.); Andelsbuch (613 m., 2,011 ft.); Au (800 m., 2,625 ft.); Bezau (649 m., 2,129 ft.); Bizau (681 m., 2,234 ft.); Damüls (1,430 m., 4,692 ft.); Egg (600 m., 1,969 ft.); Hittisau (791 m., 2,595 ft.); Mellau (688 m., 2,257 ft.); Schoppernau (852 m., 2,795 ft.); Schröcken (1,269 m., 4,164 ft.); Schwarzenberg (696 m., 2,284 ft.); Sibratsgfäll (927 m., 3,041 ft.); Warth (1,459 m., 4,787 ft.).

Facilities: 14 indoor swimming pools, 3 cable cars, 14 chair lifts, 61 T-bars, 183 km. (114 miles) of cross-country trails.

Kleinwalsertal. This is a high-lying area with good skiing on treeless slopes carrying lots of snow. One of the joys of this area is that it is fairly remote, indeed it can only be got at from Germany, as the circle of high peaks cut it off from the rest of Austria. It is a cognoscenti's hunting ground.

Resorts: Hirschegg (1,113 m., 3,649 ft.); Mittelberg (1,218 m., 3,996 ft.); Riezlern (1,084 m., 3,557 ft.).

Facilities: 21 indoor swimming pools, 2 cable cars, 6 chair lifts, 26 T-bars and 35 km. (22 miles) of cross-country trails.

CARINTHIA

Blue Lakes—Ancient Forests

Few regions of Europe are such well-defined geographical units as Carinthia (Kärnten). High mountains frame it on all sides, with only a few very narrow valleys cutting through this frame. The northern ranges lower slowly—the southern abruptly—into the center, which is composed of the Klagenfurt plain and its extensions, the principal lakes, and the undulating hills between.

If you observe the Carinthian landscape from the top of Pyramidenkogel above Wörther Lake or from Kanzelhöhe above Ossiacher Lake, both of which offer excellent views over most of the state, Carinthia will appear before your eyes as a huge arena. The Drau River winds its way through, passing by Gothic and Baroque steeples of village churches, and together with the lower Gurk and Glan valleys forms its floor. Blue-green lakes rest comfortably between the shoulders of low forested hills and reflect the golden white light of rocky faces of the Karawanken and Carnic Alps, the highest southern steps of the arena. To the northeast the lower, balding Koralpe and Saualpe, and to the north the heavily wooded Gurktaler Alps, close off the region toward Styria; and to the northwest the snowy peaks of the Hohe Tauern soar to the mighty Pasterzen glacier of the Grossglockner, king of Austrian Alps (3,797 m., 12,457 ft.).

Because of this geographic compactness, it is no wonder that Carinthia became a political unit very early in history. Many Bronze Age graves have yielded rich prehistoric finds. Various Illyrian tribes lived here during the Hallstatt period. The first known state organization, however, was the kingdom of the Alpine Celts, set up a few centuries B.C., with the capital in Noreia, the site of which is still unknown and disputed by historians. It lasted until the Romans conquered the area in the late 1st century B.C., setting up the Roman province of Noricum. The Romans left around A.D. 600. The ancestors of the Slovenes, then called Carinthians or Carantanians, established a state organization in this region, with its probable center in the Zollfeld area; it was ruled by independent dukes and was, according to medieval chronicles, called Carantania.

In the mid-eighth century the Slovenes asked the neighboring Bavarian dukes for assistance in staving off Avar invasions from the east, and an alliance was born which later resulted in Bavarian lordship over Carantania. During the time of Charlemagne, Carantania, together with Bavaria, became his vassal state; thus Carinthia became a part of the Holy Roman Empire of the German Nation at its very birth and remained with it until its end. In the early ninth century, after an unsuccessful rebellion, the Slovenian rulers were replaced by Franks and in 976 Carinthia became the first imperial duchy in the present Austrian territory. In 1335 the Habsburgs added Carinthia to their possessions, ruling benevolently till 1918. Since the disintegration of the Austrian Empire in 1918, Carinthia has been a federal state of the Austrian Republic.

After the Slovenian settlement many parts of the country remained only thinly inhabited, but through the following centuries many new settlers arrived, mostly from Bavaria and also from other German areas, and the German language gradually prevailed. Numerous old Slovenian customs and also old pagan Celtic beliefs, however, have still been preserved together with a Slovenian minority in South Carinthia which in a plebiscite in 1920 voted to remain with Austria.

Exploring Carinthia

Traveling by the main road or railroad from Vienna, and after crossing Styria, your first town in Carinthia will be Friesach, in the narrow Metnitz valley. Here begins an area, extending to the Wörthersee and Villach, that can be called the heart of the state and the hub of Carinthian history. The most important historic finds have been made in this area; here the main Roman settlements existed, the first churches were founded, the oldest castles and towns built.

Romantic Friesach, which is still surrounded by double ramparts and a moat, was first mentioned in the 9th century, and the market town has existed at least since the 11th century. For a long period it belonged to the prince-bishops of Salzburg and was the seat of the administrator of their estates in Carinthia. Gallant medieval tournaments used to take place here and 600 knights participated in the famous one of May 1224 and broke 1,000 lances; the Styrian Minnesinger Ulrich von Liechtenstein, who appeared dressed and equipped all in green, calling himself the "May Knight," alone broke 53 lances on his adversaries.

The town is huddled underneath the hill of Petersberg, where the once-powerful bishop's castle is mostly in ruins but still well worth visiting, particularly the donjon or watchtower with the Rupertus Chapel and 12th- and 13th-century frescos, among which the one of Bishop Romanus from around 1130 is supposed to be the oldest in Austria; and in summer for the openair classical plays, performed by the local amateur company in the upper courtyard. Next to the castle ruins stands the ninth-century Peterskirche, a small pre-Romanesque church facing Geiersberg Castle on another hill. Carinthia's two largest churches are the 12th-century, twin-spired, Romanesque parish church with Gothic interior additions, somewhat spoiled by 19th-century restoration, but with exquisite stained-glass windows; and the 13th-century Gothic church of the Dominicans' first monastery on German soil, with a 14th-century stone statue of the Madonna and other remarkable sculptures. Also of great interest in this romantic medieval town are the two winged altarpieces and the 12th-century frescos in the church of the Teutonic Knights; the Renaissance fountain on the main square with reliefs representing scenes from Greek mythology.

If you believe that Tannhäuser was a creation of Wagner's imagination, you will be surprised to learn that descendants of his family were Salzburg administrators in Friesach and a Tannhäuser Chapel was erected in 1509 in the Dominican Church, with a red marble tomb of Deputy Dean Balthasar Tannhäuser added after his death in 1516.

A few kilometers south of Friesach, on the main road to Klagenfurt, is the village of Hirt, where beer has been brewed since 1270, and, in its vicinity, the climatic health resort of Agathenhof, supposed to be the largest of its kind in Europe. A little beyond Hirt lies Zwischenwässern, where the Metnitz River flows into Gurk and a local road branches off for the upper Gurk valley. The neo-classic Schloss Böckstein, looking rather like a country palace, is located at this crossroad. It was built for the bishops of Gurk by Hagenauer, the 18th-century Salzburg architect.

The Cathedral of Gurk

The upper Gurk valley road, and the small narrow-gauge railroad running alongside, first reach the small town of Strassburg with the majestic castle dominating the valley from the hill above it. Until the late 18th century, when they moved to Klagenfurt, the prince-bishops of Gurk had their secular residence in this castle which is now partially in ruins.

Farther up the narrow valley is Gurk, an old village first mentioned in medieval manuscripts in the ninth century. Its interest lies in the twin-spired cathedral church, once the religious seat of the Gurk bishops, and one of the greatest architectural treasures in Austria. The first church was built at this site by Countess Hemma of Friesach-Zeltschach, a legendary figure from early Carinthian history, who after the death of her husband and son in battle, devoted her life and money to religion, built some ten churchs, died in the convent founded by her at Gurk in 1045, and was proclaimed a saint in 1938.

The construction of the present prevailingly Romanesque basilica was started around 1140 by Bishop Romanus, whose fresco-portrait is in the Petersberg Castle in Friesach. It took more than half-a-century to erect this impressive structure of three naves, separated by pillars and ending in three apses. Beneath the cathedral a crypt of 100 gracefully slender marble pillars was built to entomb the body of Countess Hemma.

Around 1200, when the construction was completed, the church was decorated with several works of art, among them the beautifully simple main portal and the more ornate Samson tympanum relief. Through the ensuing centuries it was further embellished with many additions in various period styles. Among the most valuable ones are: the 13th-century frescos, among the most important of the Romanesque period, ascribed to Master Heinrich, precise in design although biblically complicated, located in the so-called Bishop's Chapel; the Gothic *Poor Man's Bible* (frescos depicting scenes from the New and Old Testaments) and painted glass windows in the 14th-century vestibule enclosing the main portal; other Gothic frescos and a Romanesque wall painting of St. Christopher (around 1250) near the main altar; the largest and oldest Carinthian *Fastentuch* (Lent Curtain, a linen cloth still used to cover the altar during Lent), with biblical scenes painted in 1458; six lively woodcarved reliefs (around 1500) representing scenes from the life of St. Hemma; a small Renaissance winged altarpiece; the richly elaborate main altar, the chief Baroque creation of Michael Hönel; the lovely lead 18th-century *Pietà* by Raphael Donner; and the Rococo pulpit (1740).

Weitensfeld is known for the oldest preserved painted glass window in Austria, originating from 1170. Today only its copy can be seen in the small St. Magdalen Church, while the highly valued original is in the safety of the Diocesan Museum in Klagenfurt.

Not far is Klein Glödnitz, a crossroad where one road continues to Feldkirchen and the Ossiacher Lake. Another road rises to Flattnitzer Höhe, bypassing Flattnitz, three kilometers away, and then drops steeply into the Metnitz valley to Metnitz, from where it proceeds via Grades to Friesach. Flattnitz (1,396 m., 4,580 ft.) is an unpretentious resort in an idyllic location in the middle of Gurktaler Alps, with a small lake nearby, frequented in summer by vacationists in search of mountain quiet and in winter by skiers. Metnitz has an interesting parish church and is particularly known for its octangular Gothic charnel house with outside *Totentanz* (Dance of Death) frescos. A finely woodcarved Gothic winged altarpiece can be seen in St. Wolfgang Church in Grades, and another castle of the Gurk bishops on the other side of the river. If you do not wish to make the full circle of upper Gurk and Metnitz valleys (about 88 km., 55 miles, altogether), you have to turn back to Klein Glödnitz or Weitensfeld, returning through Gurk to Böckstein Castle crossroad.

Medieval Strongholds

The next larger town is St. Veit an der Glan, which from the 13th to the early 16th century was the capital of the Duchy of Carinthia. Architectural evidence of its medieval origin is still visible in spite of the conflagration of the early 1800's which destroyed many old buildings. The most outstanding structure on the picturesque main square is the Rathaus, with a richly ornamented facade and a Rococo stuccoed ceiling in the grand hall. Only the main tower has remained of what was once a mightly ducal castle: it is located in the northeastern section of the town, housing the local museum.

More than a dozen castles are located in the surroundings of St. Veit. Some of them are ruins, others have been preserved in their original form or were renovated during a later period. They usually can be reached by narrow roads, but occasionally you will just have to walk. Just north of St. Veit are the two Kraig Castle ruins, the 11th-century Hochkraig and the 14th-century Niederkraig, both with mighty towers. In their vicinity is the lovely and romantic six-towered Frauenstein, built in the early 16th century and completely preserved. A few miles toward the southwest are the 12th-century Hardegg ruins and the old and the "new" Karlsberg castles; two Romanesque towers are the best parts of the old one still standing, whereas the "new" (17th-century) castle is preserved. Near St. Veit, in an easterly direction, are the ruins of the once-powerful Taggenburg, nowadays attracting visitors also for the view from the hill on which it is located and for a tavern which has been set up inside.

A little farther east is the famed Hochosterwitz, literally crowning the steep, isolated hill on which it is built. This is probably the most beautiful of all the castles in Austria. When you observe it from afar it does not look real but rather like a picture from a fairy tale, and one almost expects a dragon to appear in a puff of smoke or to hear troubadours sing. By branching off the main road to St. Donat, you may drive up (there is also bus service from Klagenfurt) as far as the first gate. From the parking lot the fortified castle lane winds up around the rocky hill through 14 tower-gates before reaching the main entrance. They all date from the 16th century, when the 13th-century castle was converted into the present stronghold by Freiherr Georg Khevenhüller, whose descendants still own it. Conducted tours through the armory and portrait gallery of ancestors; there is a restaurant. The view of the surrounding area is magnificent. If you are in a hurry and wish to return to your car in a few minutes, take the *Narrensteig* (Fool's Ascent), a precipitous footpath that begins at the castle church beside the eighth gate.

Magdalensberg and the Four-Hills Pilgrimage

A couple of miles from St. Donat, back on the main road, is the hamlet of Willersdorf; from here a road takes you up Magdalensberg, well known for the excavations of a Celtic-Roman town. As early as 1502 a farmer, while plowing, found here the statue of the *Youth from Magdalensberg*, today one of the prized possessions of the Kunsthistorisches Museum in Vienna (copies of it were made for the Klagenfurt and Magdalensberg museums). The *Youth*, probably a Roman copy of a fifth-century-B.C. Polycleites original, was sent by the Roman merchants of Aquileia on the Adriatic as a gift to the flourishing Celtic town on Magdalensberg, where it was installed in the temple as the image of Latobius, the local god of war. After this discovery a few other objects were found, but digging started only in the second half of the 19th century, whereas systematic excavating began only after World War II. Parts of a Celtic and Roman town have been uncovered so far, and a particularly interesting feature is what appears to be a government building with an assembly hall for representatives of various tribes and a section for archives and records. The Alpine Celts used to build their towns on hills, and the settlement on Magdalensberg appears to have been one of the most important of their federal state organizations.

Magdalensberg is also known as the starting point for the age-old Vierberglauf (Four-Hills-Pilgrimage), which takes place every year on the second Friday after Easter. The participants gather on Magdalensberg on the eve of that Friday and light campfires around the 13th-century church and the Gothic chapel on the top of the hill. A midnight Mass is read and then everyone hurries downhill, burning torches in hand. The simple procession, with only a small cross leading it, and rather resembling a group of hikers, now proceeds across the Zollfeld on Ulrichsberg (1,021 m., 3,350 ft.), the second hill, from here down into the Glan valley and up again on the third hill, the Veitsberg (1,193 m., 3,870 ft.) and then through the village of Sörg on the Lorenziberg (984 m., 3,200 ft.), which is the fourth and the last hill and close to St. Veit. Masses and other religious services are performed on the top of the hills and in some churches on the way. The pilgrimage has to be completed within 24 hours, hardly a generous concession in view of the considerable amount of walking involved (about 40 km., 25 miles, half of it uphill). This ancient and mysterious observance apparently originates from a number of pagan rites connected with sun worship. The direction taken and the time limit point to the movement of the sun: Magdalensberg is in the east, Ulrichsberg in the south, Veitsberg in the west, and Lorenziberg, reached after nightfall, in the north.

The Zollfeld

The small plain of the Zollfeld is actually a wider section of the Glan River valley, beginning shortly after St. Veit and reaching almost to Klagenfurt. Magdalensberg on the eastern side and Ulrichsberg to the west watch over this north–south passage. The Roman legionary, marching north, did so and founded the city of Virunum, which was the capital of the Roman province of Noricum and was located approximately in the middle of the Zollfeld: its sophisticated life is still reflected in the Dionysiac mosaic floor found here and today preserved in the Landesmuseum in Klagenfurt, and in the post horses depicted in a Roman relief, now immured in the south wall of the church in Maria Saal. The tribes migrating south smashed to bits Virunum's way of life and its splendid buildings. But those who decided to tarry longer on Zollfeld picked up the pieces and constructed forts, churches, farmhouses, and a new period of history.

A large number of Roman stones can still be seen in the buildings in the Zollfeld area, particularly in the walls of the churches of Karnburg and Maria Saal. St. Peter-and-Paul at Karnburg dates from Carolingian times, but the place is better known, from ancient documents as well as through some excavating, as the site of a castle-fortress which was the seat of the earliest rulers of Carantania and referred to in those times as *Curtis Carantana* (Carantanian Court). Across the valley, on another elevation, was Sancta Maria in Solio, the earliest version of the present Maria Saal Church, founded in the mid-eighth century by Bishop Modestus, sent by the Bishop of Salzburg upon the request of Cheitmar, a Slovenian Carantanian duke, himself already a Christian and wishing to introduce Christianity among his people. St. Modestus is supposed to be entombed in a Roman sarcophagus below a ninth-century altar. The present Church of Maria Saal, built in the 15th century, is one of the best examples of Gothic architecture in Carinthia though the twin towers end in Baroque helmets. Of special interest is Christ's genealogical tree on the ceiling of the central nave.

Not far from Maria Saal, in the middle of the Zollfeld and shaded by a group of trees, lies the Herzogstuhl (Duke's Chair), a double-seated throne made with stones from the ruins of Virunum. Another stone chair, the Fürstenstein (Prince's Stone), made from the base of a Roman column, and also originating from the remnants of Virunum, used to stand in the open field near Karnburg (it is now in the Landesmuseum in Klagenfurt). The remarkable ceremony of the investiture of Carinthian rulers, one of the earliest examples of constitutional law, took place on these two chairs in medieval times.

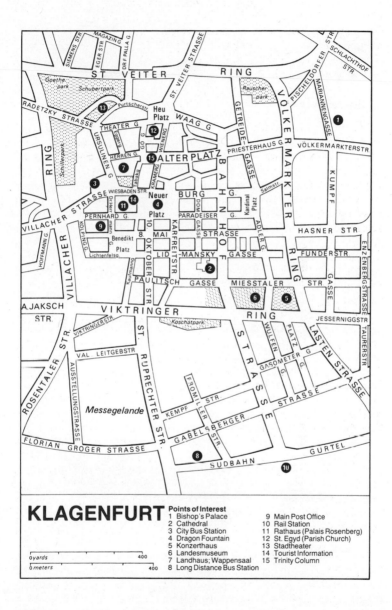

KLAGENFURT

Points of Interest

1 Bishop's Palace
2 Cathedral
3 City Bus Station
4 Dragon Fountain
5 Konzerthaus
6 Landesmuseum
7 Landhaus; Wappensaal
8 Long Distance Bus Station
9 Main Post Office
10 Rail Station
11 Rathaus (Palais Rosenberg)
12 St. Egyd (Parish Church)
13 Stadtheater
14 Tourist Information
15 Trinity Column

0 yards 400
0 meters 400

Klagenfurt

Only about 8 km. (5 miles) south of Maria Saal and the Herzogstuhl is Klagenfurt, founded in the 12th century and the capital of Carinthia since 1518. The center of the city has a quadrangular form, designed by an Italian architect, and defined by four "Rings," streets running along the sides of the no-longer-existing walls. Exactly in the center of this quadrangle is the Neuer Platz with the city's emblem, the dragon fountain carved from a schistblock in the 16th century. The usual dragon tale was given a realistic undertone when the fossilized cranium of a prehistoric rhinoceros (now in the Landesmuseum) was found near Klagenfurt. On the same square is a statue of Empress Maria Theresa. Behind the statue is the former Palais Rosenberg (1650), Klagenfurt's current town hall.

A block north of the dragon square is the longish Alter Platz, which is not only an old square as its name implies, but the oldest part of the city. It acquired the present form, however, only after the great fire of 1514. Near the west end of the Alter Platz are the Landhaus and Baroque parish church. The arcaded twin-towered Landhaus (seat of the provincial Diet)—the front facade of which is far less impressive than its courtyard side—was built towards the end of the 16th century; in the Hall of Arms (Wappensaal), ornamented with 665 coats of arms of Carinthian estates—spanning the period of 1590 to 1848—you can also see the Fürstenstein investiture ceremony portrayed by Josef Ferdinand Fromiller, the most important Carinthian painter of the Baroque period. Also on the Alter Platz are the Altes Rathaus (Old Town Hall), with a picturesque 3-floor arcaded courtyard, the 1650 Haus zur Goldenen Gans (House of the Golden Goose), and a Trinity Column.

Other important sights in the city include the 16th-century cathedral, which was originally built as a Protestant church, but which became the cathedral when the bishopric was moved from the now remote basilica at Gurk; the Diocesan Museum in Lidmanskygasse next to the cathedral, with a good collection of medieval church art; and particularly the Landesmuseum with the Fürstenstein, objects from Magdalensberg, the mosaic floor and other finds from Virunum, prehistoric collections, paintings and *objets d'art,* natural history collections, Carinthian folk dress, rustic house furnishings and decorations.

About 5 km. (3 miles) south of Klagenfurt is the village of Viktring with a moated 12th-century Romanesque church, which has suffered from rebuilding; the three 14th-century stained-glass windows, however, have retained their unspoiled beauty; worth seeing also are the two huge arcaded courtyards of the former Cistercian monastery, today housing a school.

Wörthersee

The blue waters of Wörther Lake are beautifully framed by its wooded sloping shores and by the jagged chain of Karawanken mountains in the background. The Wörthersee is the warmest of the larger lakes in Carinthia, perhaps owing to the existence of subterranean thermal springs. During the summer months its banks swarm with holiday-makers actually enjoying a pleasurable swim. A beautiful way to see the Wörthersee is by one of the small steam boats that ply from one end to the other. The *S.S. Thalia,* built in 1908, has been lovingly restored and now offers trips on the lake. In winter there is skating on the partially or totally frozen lake. Fog is a frequent visitor during fall and spring in the entire Carinthian lake area.

Proceeding from Klagenfurt-See to the north shore we come first to Krumpendorf, at the end of the Klagenfurt city bus line. The center of the village is located on the main road, while the majority of small hotels, pensions, and private villas are scattered along the lake about a mile away. Krumpendorf is an unpretentious and primarily family-type resort.

Midway on the north shore is Pörtschach, one of the two top vacation spots on the Wörthersee. Here, as well as in other places on the lake, the water is often warm enough for swimming as early as May, which is very early indeed for an Alpine region. Pörtschach is mainly a settlement of hotels and summer villas, parts of it built on a narrow peninsula with pleasant walks.

Velden, at the western end of the Wörthersee, is the most fashionable resort in the entire province, with a more international atmosphere, and livelier and longer night hours in the Casino, than Pörtschach. Many visitors, however, may find this almost Mediterranean exuberance too much to take, particularly on a Saturday night in summer.

The south shore is quieter, more modest, and more genuinely Carinthian. The road on this side is narrower. Less than 8 km. (5 miles) from Velden is Dellach with an attractively situated golf course, the only one in the area. A little farther, on a small peninsula, almost completely surrounded by water, is picturesque and ancient Maria Wörth, the most outstanding landmark on the Wörthersee. Although it is an unpretentious lake resort, it boasts two attractive old churches. A church existed here at least as early as the ninth century, if not earlier, but the present two date from the 12th century. The small one, called the Winter, or Rosary, Church, is basically Romanesque with later Gothic additions: the interior has a Romanesque choir with fragments of 12th-century frescos of the Apostles, a Madonna stained-glass window from 1420, and Gothic wood-carved figures. The larger parish church has a Romanesque portal, but its architecture is mainly Gothic and its interior décor mostly in Baroque style. Skulls and bones can still be seen in the round Romanesque charnel house in the cemetery.

Only a little over two kilometers (a mile) from Maria Wörth is Reifnitz, a lesser lake resort, from where you can take a short side road to the small, emerald green Keutschacher Lake, with the Romanesque church of St. George, a Baroque castle and an 800-year-old linden tree. A winding 5-km. (3-mile) road ascends to the observation tower on the top of the 850-m. (2,789-ft.) Pyramidenkogel. From its platform, on a fine day, there is a view over half of Carinthia.

Ossiach and Villach

Leaving Klagenfurt by Route 95 in a northwesterly direction, the first small town you meet is Moosburg, with the ruins of a Carolingian castle where Arnulf, the late-ninth-century German emperor, was born. Continuing through this area of rolling hills you leave on the left side the round-towered Renaissance Castle of Gradisch near the village of Glan and reach Feldkirchen, an ancient town that for several centuries belonged to the bishops of Bamberg. The parish church, a defense tower, and Biedermeier-style houses are the main sights. Feldkirchen is also an important crossroad. One road, mentioned earlier, goes to Klein Glödnitz and Gurk. Northward, Route 95 climbs, at a gradient of 23 percent, 37 km. (23 miles) through the mountainous Nockgebiet up to the Turracher Höhe, a high pass between Carinthia and Styria, a mountain summer resort and fine skiing center, on a lovely small lake.

Only 20 km. (12½ miles) west of Velden are the Ossiachersee and the city of Villach. Ossiacher Lake, is the third largest in Carinthia (after the Wörthersee and the Millstättersee), and it still retains some of that peaceful atmosphere Boleslaw II, King of Poland, came here to find in the 11th century. According to the story he stayed in the Benedictine Abbey at Ossiach for eight years as a simple brother, without revealing his identity and pretending to be mute, all in self-imposed penance for his murder of the Bishop of Cracow, and only on his deathbed confessed the truth. Though historians claim that Boleslaw's sojourn in Ossiach is only a legend, the king is commemorated by a tombstone and a fresco on the church wall facing the cemetery where many old wrought-iron crosses can be seen. Only the crypt—closed by a huge concrete slab—remains of the Romanesque abbey church, whose Gothic successor was remodeled into baroque in 1720. Fromiller is the painter of the frescos, as well as those in the Baroque Hall of the secularized monastery, where some of the Carinthian Summer Festival events take place. Other events of this annual festival are held in Ossiach and attract large audience, who flock to hear the international artists.

The other lake villages, however, have remained quiet summer resorts. Near the other end of the lake is Annenheim, from where a cable car takes you to the Kanzelhöhe (1,509 m., 4,950 ft.) and with a bit of walking and by combining two chair lifts from here on, you easily reach the top of Gerlitzen (1,920 m., 6,300 ft.). The view is magnificent from both elevations and includes a large chunk of Carinthia, as well as the Slovenian Alps across the border. Back in Annenheim we proceed around the bottom of the lake to St. Andrä, and then by a good side road up to the castle-fortress Landskron (Crown of the Land), today only partially preserved but with still-visible traces of past might. From the castle café terrace there is a fine view of distant Villach framed by Dobratsch Mountain and the Karawanken.

The small city of Villach is the second largest in Carinthia and an important railroad junction. Its history goes back to the times of the Romans, who used to take the waters in an early version of the present spa establishment at Warmbad Villach, just outside the city; parts of a Roman road can still be seen, but the Roman bridge and the fortress of Bilachium have disappeared. Medieval Uillah eventually became Villach, whose old section lies on the right bank of the Drau River, which makes a semi-circle around it. Stately Renaissance houses with arcaded courtyards surround the main square (with a Baroque Trinity column), and also frame the narrow, picturesque streets around it, including the house where, in the 16th century, Theophrastus Paracelsus of medical fame lived as a youth with his father, who was the town physician. The churches to visit are the prevailingly Gothic parish church with a 313-foot steeple and the pinkish Baroque Heiligenkreuzkirche on the edge of the city, with two towers and a cupola. Other interesting sights include the 16th-century Rathaus, the Heimatmuseum with prehistoric, folklore, and other collections, and a huge relief of Carinthia (65 × 31 feet) displayed in a building in the Schiller Park. Villach, together with the Dobratsch plateau above it and nearby

Gerlitzen, is also a leading winter sports center. Take the *M.S. Villach* on a fine summer's evening and watch the sun set over the mountains while you dine (28071).

Millstättersee

Spittal an der Drau, in the Drau Valley, about 40 km. (25 miles) northwest of Villach, is the main town of Upper Carinthia and is particularly known for its architecturally superb Schloss Porcia, built in the 16th century for the Count of Salamanca, the Imperial Treasurer. This castle-palace, located in the center of town next to a lovely park, is one of the most beautiful Renaissance buildings in Austria, especially in its gracefully arcaded court stairways and open corridors, which provide a dream-like setting for performances of classical plays in the summer.

From Spittal there are only a few kilometers to the blue waters of Millstättersee. Millstatt, about halfway on the north shore, is the main town on the lake to which it gave its name—or perhaps it was the other way around. The season of this lively resort culminates in the International Organ Music week held in August. The imposing abbey with its mighty towers, many courtyards and centuries-old linden trees, was founded in the 11th century but secularized in the 18th. The twin-towered Romanesque church, originating from the same period, has become the parish church. During later periods the church was partially rebuilt in Gothic style and also received some distinguished Baroque additions, but its 12th-century Romanesque portal has remained the most exquisite feature of its architectural décor. From the same period, and highly interesting for its complicated pillar ornaments, is the Kreuzgang, the arcaded court connecting the church and the monastery.

Seeboden, at the western end of the lake, is growing in importance as a water sports center. A little beyond Seeboden, the lake road joins the main road connecting Carinthia with Salzburg and Rennweg, where you have the choice of the Autobahn tunnel (Route A10) or the steep climb over the Katschberg Pass via Route 99. Less than halfway up the valley is the colorful town of Gmünd, with its medieval wall, gates and town square, and where the Malta mountain stream rushes into the Lieser. The Malta Hochalm toll road follows the waterfalls and artificial lakes, formed by the torrent, up to Austria's largest dam, where the glaciers of the High Tauern are mirrored in the glassy waters of a lake.

The small village of St. Peter in Holz, about 5 km. (3 miles) from Spittal, lies on the site of the ancient town of Teurnia, which was already Christian in Roman times. Only a little excavating has been done here, but the small museum contains a well-preserved mosaic floor and some other remains of a building supposed to have been an early Christian church.

A few kilometers farther up the Drau valley the Möll River flows into the Drau. If you proceed up the larger Drau valley, cut between the Kreuzeck and Gailtaler mountain ranges, the two largest localities before reaching East Tirol will be Greifenburg and Oberdrauburg. From Greifenburg, a steep 11-km. (7-mile) ascent leads in a southeasterly direction to Weissensee, the fourth largest lake in Carinthia and considered by some to be the most beautiful. On its shores are only a few small villages, which in summer are becoming more and more lively resorts, with hotel accommodations increasing every season. Techendorf is the principal locality and here the lake, narrowing to about 350 feet, can be crossed by a wooden bridge. Neusach is at the end of the road, and to reach the other end of the lake, you walk or take a motorboat.

Both the Drau and Möll valleys are dotted with medieval castles. The well-preserved 13th-century Groppenstein near Obervellach in the Möll valley is particularly worth a visit. The parish church at Obervellach has a three-section altar painting from 1520 by Jan van Scorel, a Dutch disciple of Dürer. From Obervellach a steep road branches north (right) to Mallnitz, a mountain village and a winter sports center of increasing importance. Mallnitz is at the Carinthian end of the Tauern railroad tunnel, and here you load your car on the train if you wish to drive straight into Land Salzburg, because no road crosses the high mountain chain.

Proceeding farther up the Möll valley, Route 106 rises steadily into the realm of the Hohe Tauern, turning sharp north at the village of Winklern where it is joined by the road coming from Lienz, capital of East Tirol. The ascent of the Grossglockner via Route 107 begins after the unpretentious summer and winter resort of Döllach; bypassing a splendid waterfall, the road climbs to Heiligenblut, a winter sports center (1,288 m., 4,226 ft.), and the seat of the famed mountain climbing school. The sharply pointed spire of the Gothic church appears almost a duplicate of the conic peak of the Grossglockner in the background. The greatest treasure inside the church is the winged and richly woodcarved main altarpiece (1520).

At the upper end of Heiligenblut is the toll gate of the Grossglockner road, which from here on curves up to Franz-Josefs-Höhe after joining its counterpart coming from Land Salzburg over Hochtor. Franz-Josefs-Höhe (almost 2,440 m., 8,000 ft.) is so called because Emperor Franz Josef got this far in his exploration of the Grossglockner area (no roads, of course, existed in those times).

South Carinthia

The swift Gail flows along the southwest edge of Carinthia through small scattered villages with ancient churches and aged, often wooden, farm homes. The narrow valley is peacefully soft, with many old linden trees, but its fir-treed slopes rise steeply, particularly on the south side, and craggy peaks peer from behind them. The main town in the Gail valley is Hermagor, situated approximately in its center, and together with the nearby Pressegger Lake, comprises an invitingly modest vacation spot.

Further down, where the valley becomes wider, lies the village of Nötsch below the wild rocky face of the Dobratsch Mountain, which has a lovely alpine garden surrounding the towering peak, (also called Villacher Alpe), and a little further the village of Feistritz with a 1,000-year-old linden tree and an old Gothic church on a steep hill. A few kilometers east of Feistritz we reach the main road from Villach to Italy. The Austro-Italian border, only about 3 km. distant, is near the village of Thörl, where some very fine 15th-century Gothic frescos can be seen in the parish church, representing one of the chief works of Thomas von Villach, a famed Carinthian painter of that period.

The Gail flows into the Drau near Villach. In the vicinity is the round blue-green Faaker Lake with a tiny island in the middle, a few small but rapidly growing resorts, and the mighty pyramid of Mittagskogel watching over it from the Karawanken range. The best view of the lake and the surrounding area is from the nearby hill of Tabor (about 730 m., 2,400 ft.) which can be reached by a good road.

Proceeding along the Drau valley, called here Rosental, we come eventually to Ferlach, the centuries-old town of gunmakers. In modern times these individualistic and independent craftsmen, who pass the secrets of their skill from generation to generation, have been producing handmade hunting weapons, chiefly the excellent combination guns, adorned with artistic engravings. There is an interesting gun museum.

North of Ferlach, across the Drau, are the Baroque pilgrimage church of Maria Rain and the Castle of Hollenburg with 14th-century chapel frescos and wall paintings on the gate tower and in the arcaded court. South of Ferlach on the steep Loibl Pass road, crossing the Karawanken into Slovenia (the northwestern Yugoslav republic), offers grandiose scenery which you miss if you take the tunnel; from the Small Loibl Pass, halfway up, a narrow road leads into the Bodental, perhaps the range's most beautiful high valley.

The parish church in the village of Abtei, on the Drau some 16 km. (10 miles) east of Ferlach, contains the *Lamentation over Christ* by Thomas von Villach, considered to be the best Gothic painting in Carinthia. To the southeast is the Seeberg Pass, over which Route 82 climbs into Slovenia through spectacular Alpine landscape, which begins after the small spa of Eisenkappel, which has a Gothic church and the Renaissance Hagenegg castle. A steep, narrow side road leads from Eisenkappel through a wild waterfall-filled gorge to tiny Trögern.

North of Eisenkappel lies Klopeiner Lake, among the warmest lakes in Carinthia, where you can usually swim from early May until the end of September. It is crowded in summer.

Völkermarkt, across the Drau to the north, acquired town rights in the 13th century, when the Gothic church was erected; the rich frescos and tombs in the three naves all belong to the Middle Ages. The town hall is part of the 14th-century ducal castle, whose gate opens on the square with houses belonging to the Baroque and Biedermeier periods. The tower of St. Ruprecht's church below Kolhof Castle is the oldest and loveliest in Austria. The River Drau, which has recently been dammed in this section, forms a large artificial lake, called Volkermarkt reservoir and now one of the largest lakes in Carinthia, crossed by a gracious bridge on Route 82 to Eisenkappel and Seeberg Pass. To the east is Bleiburg, a 750-years-old town, dominated by a 16th-century castle and the high Petzen mountain on the border of Slovenia.

The Lavant Valley—Klagenfurt to Graz

The main road (Route 70) from Klagenfurt to Graz goes through Völkermarkt and the Lavant valley, which separates the almost twin-like Saualpe and Koralpe mountain plateaus. Of exceptional interest in this valley is the 11th-century Benedictine Abbey at St. Paul, with its basically Romanesque basilica, a small museum of paintings, drawings, engravings, and a valuable library containing manuscripts and a Gutenberg Bible. The Gutenberg Bible used at the swearing in of the U.S. Presidents originally came from St. Paul.

The Lavant flows into the Drau at the small town of Lavamünd with the nearby castles of Kollegg and Thürn. Higher up the Lavant valley, St. Andrä possesses two churches of note; the former Jesuit monastery has been converted into a comfortable senior citizens' home. At Wolfsberg the Romanesque parish church contains a Baroque altar with a painting by Kremser-Schmidt.

In the upper Lavant valley are the spa of St. Leonhard with sulphuric springs and a very impressive Gothic church, and Preblau, known for its mineral table water. From the Twimberg Castle ruins, and passing Waldenstein Castle, the main road curves up over the Pack Sattel into Styria.

PRACTICAL INFORMATION FOR CARINTHIA

TOURIST INFORMATION. With its lakes surrounded by a backdrop of magnificent mountains, Carinthia is ideal vacation territory. There are Tourist Offices in almost every town and village, many of them equipped to help with accommodation problems, should they arise. The following list is of the offices in the larger centers, all with their area code and phone number.

Bad Bleiberg ob Villach A-9530 (0 42 44–28 93). Bad Kleinkirchheim A-9546 (042 40–82 12); Döllach im Mölltal A-9843 (0 48 25–52 1 21); Eisenkappel-Vellach A-9135 (0 42 38–245); Faaker See–Finkenstein A-9583 (0 42 54–21 10); Feld am See A-9544 (0 42 46–22 80–74); Friesach A-9360 (0 42 68–23 16).

Gmünd A-9853 (0 47 32/21 97); Gurk A-9342 (0 42 66–81 25); Heiligenblut A-9844 (0 4824–2101–22); Klagenfurt A-9020 (0 4 63–53 72 23 or 20 01–21) Kötschach-Mauthen A-9640 (0 47 15–85 16); Krumpendorf A-9201 (0 42 29–23 13).

Mallnitz A-9822 (0 47 84–290); Malta A-9854 (0 47 33–240); Maria Saal A-9063 (0 42 23–22 14); Maria Wörth A-9082 (0 42 73–22 40); Metnitz A-9363 (0 42 67–220–11); Millstatt A-9872 (0 47 66–20 22–32); Moosburg A-9062 (0 42 72–83 4 00–22); Ossiach A-9570 (0 42 43–497); Pörtschach am Wörther See A-9210 (0 42 72–23 54).

St. Veit an der Glan A-9300 (0 42 12–55 55 13); Seeboden A-9871 (0 47 62–81 2 10); Spittal an der Drau A-9800 (0 47 62–34 20); Techendorf A-9762 (0 47 13–22 20 13); Velden am Wörther See A-9220 (0 42 74–21 03); Villach A-9500 (0 42 42–24 4 44–0); Völkermarkt A-9100 (0 42 32–25 71 47); Warmbad Villach A-9504 (0 42 42–27 2 44).

AREA CODES—MAIL AND PHONE. You will find the postal code (preceded by an "A") and the telephone code (in brackets) after the name of each town in the following Hotel and Restaurant list.

HOTELS AND RESTAURANTS. The principal lake resorts are well provided with hotels of all categories, some of them luxurious. Hotels elsewhere are usually of the modest and provincial type, although you will find some exceptions in such large localities as Klagenfurt and Villach and in some mountain resorts. In the mountain areas in general, however, the picturesque Alpine-style hostelries will often give you more in return than you expect. Prices on the whole are a little lower than in such tourist-conscious provinces as Salzburg and Tirol; during the peak summer season first class accommodations in the top lake resorts of Velden or Pörtschach, may run into about the same amount of money as in most other fashionable Austrian vacation spots. During the high season you will find it advantageous to take room-and-board terms in resort areas.

Bad Kleinkirchheim A-9546 (0 42 40). *Das Ronacher* (L), (282). 160 beds, all with bath; thermal pool, cure center. Good restaurant. Closed 1 Nov. to 20 Dec. AE, DC, MC
Alte Post (E), (212). 120 beds, most with bath. Pool, sauna, tennis. Restaurant. AE, DC, MC, *Kristall* (E), (82 92). 70 beds, all with bath. Modern, comfortable rooms. Restaurant. DC, MC. *Pulverer* (E), (244). 150 beds, all with bath. Indoor and outdoor pools and spa bath. Restaurant. Closed Nov. *Römerbad* (E), (82 34). 68 beds, all with bath. Beautiful view of mountains from balconies; spacious lounges, rustic furnishings. Outstanding restaurant with local specialties, wide choice of wines. Closed mid-April to mid-May and Nov. AE, DC, MC, V. *St. Oswald* (E), (591). 90 beds, 43 with bath. Indoor pool, sauna and tennis. Restaurant.
Kolmhof (M), (216). 90 beds, all with bath or shower. Thermal pool. AE, DC, V. *Trattlerhof* (M), (81 72). 100 beds, all with bath or shower. Tennis, riding, indoor pool, cure center. Restaurant. Closed Nov. to 15 Dec.
Cafe. *Hutter* (454). Where everybody goes in the afternoon for delicious cakes and great variety of coffee.

Bleiberg Ob Villach A-9530 (0 42 44). *Bleibergerhof* (E), (22 05). 104 beds, all with bath and all modern conveniences, including thermal water supply to baths. Restaurant *Dobratschstüberl,* considered among the finest restaurants in Austria and worth a special visit. 1986 cook of the year award. AE, DC, MC, V.

Döbriach A-9873 (0 42 46). *Zanker* (M), (77 80). 98 rooms, all with bath or shower. Indoor and outdoor pools, sauna, solarium; pension terms only. Restaurant and bar. Closed Oct. to March. MC.
Campsites (77 74 or 77 21; 71 89 or 73 86; 7187 or 72 06; 77 14 or 78 93; 73 15; 77 35 or 72 13; 77 15 or 71 94).

Döllach Im Mölltal A-9843 Grosskirchheim (0 48 25). *Schlosswirt* (E), (211). 60 beds, all with bath, some with four posters. Tennis, riding, outdoor pool, rifle range, fishing, small game reserve. One of Carinthia's top restaurants, serving genuine local food. AE, DC, MC, V.
Campsite (415).

Faakersee A-9583 (0 42 54). *Inselhotel* (E), (21 45). 80 beds, all with bath. Romantic, quiet location on island. All kinds of activities possible; tennis, table tennis, swimming, fishing and walking in the lovely grounds. Restaurant. *Karnerhof* (E), (21 88). 210 beds, most with bath or shower. Silence Hotel. Situated between Drobollach and Egg, in an isolated position overlooking the lake; country-style main building with highly-rated restaurant, two modern annexes. Indoor and outdoor pools, sauna and tennis, thermal pool. Closed mid-Oct. to end April.
Finkensteinerhof (M), (21 76). 80 beds, all with bath or shower. Close to mountains and lake; outdoor pool, sauna, Average restaurant, friendly service. Closed Nov. and 15 Jan. to 15 March. *Strandhotel Fürst* (M), Faak (21 15). 65 beds, most with shower. Lawn leading down to lake and private beach. Restaurant. *Tschebull* (M), (21 91). 24 beds, all with shower. Pool. Excellent restaurant with imaginative regional cooking, some unusual wines. AE, V.
Campsites (28 88; 27 3 92; 22 61; 21 37; 22 97 or 22 98; 26 70; 27 18).

Restaurant. *Da Luciano* (E), Oberferlach 74 (31 22). Happy union of Carinthian with Italian cuisine. Closed Oct., Nov., March and Mon.

Feld Am See A-9544 (0 42 46). *Lindenhof* (E), (22 74). 50 beds, all with bath or shower. Quiet location, lawn, beach, tennis courts, bar and outstanding restaurant serving fine local cuisine. Homey atmosphere, ideal for families. DC, MC.

Gmünd A-9853 (0 47 32). *Kohlmayr* (M), (21 49). 24 rooms, all with bath or shower. Friendly family atmosphere. Good restaurant.
Restaurant. *Stadtschänke Zu den Grafen Lodron* (M), (22 18). Remarkably good food, in choice of elegant upstairs rooms or picturesque *Keller*. MC, V.

Heiligenblut A-9844 (0 48 24). *Glocknerhof* (E), (22 44). 120 beds, all with bath or shower. Rustic building in romantic village; all modern amenities, indoor pool and restaurant. MC, V. *Kärntner Hof* (E), (20 04). 70 beds, most with shower. Indoor and outdoor pools, sauna, solarium, fitness room; restaurant and bar. Closed May and Nov. AE, MC, V.
Senger (M), (22 15). 45 beds, most with shower. Old farmhouse, carefully expanded without ruining genuine atmosphere; restaurant. Closed 20 April to 20 May and 1 Oct. to 15 Dec. AE.
Youth Hostel (22 59).
Campsite (20 48).

Kanzelhöhe A-9520 (0 42 48). On the Gerlitzen Plateau, reached by cable car from Annenheim. *Sonnenhotel Zaubek* (E), (27 13). 58 beds, all with bath. Indoor pool, sauna, solarium, fitness room; restaurant and bar. Closed April and May. AE.

Keutschachersee A-9074 (0 42 73). *Brückler* (I), Keutschachersee 5 (23 84). 40 rooms, most with shower. In lovely countryside, with grill-restaurant and wine tavern in converted barn; beside the lake. *Gabriel* (I), Plescherken 15 (24 41). 27 rooms, some with bath or shower. Some apartments. Near lake, own beach, rowing boat; restaurant. *Höhenwirt* (I), (23 28). 70 beds, all with bath or shower; bar and restaurant.
Cafe. On the top of Pyramidenkogel at 855 m. (2,800 ft.), reached by 5 km. of mountain road.
Campsites (23 84; 25 17; 27 73 or 22 92; 23 75; 23 57 or 29 64).

Klagenfurt A-9020 (0 46 3). *Dermuth* (E), Kohldorferstr. 52 (21 2 47). 85 beds, all with bath, some rather small and noisy—try to get one facing the wood. A bit outside town; indoor pool, sauna, solarium. Closed 22 Dec. to 10 Jan. DC. *Kurhotel Carinthia* (E), 8-Mai Str. 41 (51 16 45). 45 beds, all with bath and well-furnished with radio, TV and refrigerator. Cure facilities. AE, DC, MC, V. *Moser Verdino* (E), Domgasse 2 (5 78 78). 138 beds, all with bath. Central, recently renovated; cafe. AE, DC, MC, V. *Musil* (E), 10-Oktober Str. 14 (51 16 60). 28 beds, all with bath and period-style furnishings. *Romantik* hotel. Breakfast until noon. AE, DC, MC, V. *Porcia* (E), Neuer Platz 13 (51 15 90). 80 beds, all with bath or shower. Central; underground garage. AE, DC, MC, V. *Wörthersee* (E), Villacherstr. 338 (21 15 80). Most rooms with bath and balcony, well renovated. Good restaurant. AE, DC, MC, V.

Sandwirt (M), Kolpinggasse (5 62 09). 80 beds, most with bath, some with shower. Fine old house in center. Restaurant. AE, DC, V.
Youth Hostels (51 31 72; 56 9 65).
Campsite (28 17 79 or 2 11 69).
Restaurants. *Lido am See* (E), (26 17 23). Restaurant on lake, excellent food, elegant terrace. AE, DC, MC, V. *Wörthersee* (E), Villacherstr. 338 (2 11 58). Elegant restaurant in hotel of same name. Highly rated for international and local specialties. Closed Mon. and Jan. AE, DC, MC, V.
Berghof (M), A-9073 Viktring, Jugenddorfstr. 4 (24 18 90). Local specialties and fish dishes. AE, DC, MC, V. *Knödelstube* (M), Villacher Str. 11 (51 17 74). Casual *Heuriger/*town inn atmosphere. Good wine, fresh salads, many kinds of dumplings. Closed Sun. *Weinstube* (M), Kardinalplatz 2 (51 22 33). In friendly courtyard; simple, but very well-prepared local food.
Cafe. *Musil,* 10 October Str. 14 (51 16 60). Real Viennese-style coffee house, especially good on Sunday mornings. Lots of newspapers and magazines, excellent pastries. MC.

Kolbnitz A-9815 (0 47 83). *Marhof* (M), (22 43). 50 beds, all with bath or shower. 16th-century farm, transformed with all modern conveniences; vaulted dining room and bar. Outdoor pool; hunting. Choice cuisine, interesting wines. Closed Nov. to 14 Dec. AE, DC, V.

Kötschach-Mauthen A-9640 (0 47 15). *Kürschner* (M), (259). 95 beds, all with bath or shower, pension terms only. Outdoor pool, sauna, solarium, tennis, cure center; restaurant and bar. Closed Nov. AE, DC, MC, V. *Post* (M), (221). 60 beds, most with bath or shower. In center of village. Nice restaurant and bar. Closed March and Nov. MC, V.
Campsite (429).
Restaurant. *Kellerwand* (E), Mauthen 24 (269). Inconspicuous building, elegantly refurbished. Carinthian cooking with a modern, imaginative touch. It is worth a detour to eat in this remarkable restaurant, rated as Carinthia's best. Closed Dec. and Tues. in winter.

Krumpendorf A-9201 (0 42 29). *Habich* (M), (29 52). 80 beds, all with shower. Attractive hotel in large garden, with terrace; playground for children, table tennis and beach. Indoor pool, sauna and tennis. *Schloss Hallegg* (M), (0 46 3–4 93 11). 30 beds, all with bath. 13th-century castle with arcaded courtyard; fishing ponds in grounds, tennis, riding, swimming. Closed 1 Oct. to 15 May. *Seehotel Koch* (M), (22 26). 84 beds, all with bath. Atmospheric house in own garden beside lake. Restaurant. AE, DC, MC, V.
Restaurant. *Ganymed* (E), Hallegerstr. 1 (29 31). Pleasant setting and food. Closed Wed. and Feb. AE, DC, MC, V.

Mallnitz A-9822 (0 47 84). *Alpenhof Alber* (M), (525). 105 beds, most with bath. Lawn, terrace; good restaurant with local specialties. Closed 10 Oct. to 12 Dec. MC, V.
Gasthof Egger (I), (214). 39 beds, all with bath or shower. Quiet; restaurant serving simple but good local food. Closed Nov.

Malta A-9854 (0 47 33). *Burgrestaurant-Hotel* (M), (28 51). 60 beds, all with shower. Located in an unusual round building. Bar. Closed Oct. to April. AE.

Campsite (21 92). Open April–Oct.

Maria Wörth A-9082 (0 42 73). *Linde* (E), (22 78). Attractive rooms and lounges; lawn leading down to the shore. Above-par restaurant. *Wörth* (E), (22 76). 65 beds, all with bath; outdoor pool. Good restaurant and bar. Closed from Oct. to April. DC. *Astoria* (M), (22 79). 80 beds, all with bath. Quiet, with own beach, indoor pool, indoor tennis, play room for children. Good restaurant. Closed Oct. to April. AE, DC.

Millstatt Am See A-9872 (0 47 66). *Alpenrose* (E), Obermillstatt (25 00). 46 beds, all with bath or shower. First "Bio-Hotel" in Austria— attractively built in magnificent location. Organically grown vegetables used in healthy but tasty cuisine. *Die Forelle* (E), (20 50). 100 beds, all with bath. Elegant hotel with guests to match. Attractive beach and restaurant. AE, DC, MC. *Postillon am See* (E), (25 52). 49 beds, all with bath; indoor pool, lawn. Closed 25 Oct. to 24 April.
Post (M), (21 08). 80 beds, all with bath or shower. Traditional, newly renovated. Children welcome. Restaurant, fish specialties in atmospheric *Wappenstuberl. Strandhotel Marchetti* (M), (20 75). 92 beds, all with bath. Pleasant; directly on lake. Restaurant.
Campsites (25 30, 26 65).

Nassfeld A-9620 (0 42 85). *Gartnerkofel* (E), (81 75). 90 beds, all rooms with bath, apartments. Sauna, solarium, tennis. Very pleasant. Closed May, Oct., Nov. *Wulfenia* (E), (81 11). 120 beds, all with bath, apartments. Indoor pool, tennis, sauna. First-rate restaurant, bar. The friendly hosts will take guests mountain climbing. Closed May, Nov.

Ossiachersee A-9570 (0 42 43). *Marienheim* (I), Annenheim (0 42 48–27 56). 26 beds, most with shower. Closed Nov. to April. *Strandpension* (I), Ossiach (432). 64 beds, most with shower; outdoor pool, restaurant.
Campsites (436, 379, or 529, 456; 82 23 or 446; 421; 318; 83 14; 304; 0 42 42–41 1 33; 0 42 42–41 8 86).

Pörtschach A-9210 (0 42 72). *Parkhotel* (L), (26 21–0). 313 beds, all with bath and every comfort. Scenic location on lake; restaurant. Closed Oct. to April. AE, DC. *Schloss Seefels* (L), Toschling 1 (23 77). 70 rooms, all with bath; elegant meeting place of chic clientele. Indoor and outdoor pools, tennis. Restaurant, nightclub. Closed mid-Oct. to mid-Dec. and March to mid-April. AE, DC, MC, V.
Österreichischer Hof (E), (23 91). 92 beds, all with bath or shower. In center of resort with indoor pool, sauna; beach with barbecue area; restaurant. DC, MC. *Rainer* (E), (23 00). 60 beds, all with bath. Three excellently furnished villas in garden on lake; 150 yds from beach; tennis, waterskiing, board-sailing (instruction available), riding, cycling. *Schloss Leonstain* (E), (28 16–0). 38 rooms, all with bath. Finely-furnished small castle; close to road and railway. Good restaurant in beautiful setting. Closed Oct. to mid-May. AE, DC, V. *Werzer Astoria* (E), (22 31). Resort hotel in its own park on the lake. Private beach. Every comfort and facility. Spacious and well-run. AE, DC, V.
Dermuth (M), (22 40). 100 beds, all with bath or shower. Old house by lake, new one by road. Both comfortable, with friendly service. Restaurant. Closed Oct. to April. DC.

Campsites (31 33; 23 16).
Restaurants. *Schiffwirt* (E), Bundesstr. (22 71). Good fish. Reserve. *Hubertus* (E), (20 75). Hearty Carinthian fare; excellent wines; view.

St. Kanzian A-9122 (0 42 39). *Promenaden Strandhotel Marolt* (M), (23 36 or 23 21). 300 beds, all with bath or shower; sauna, solarium, tennis; restaurant and bar. Closed Nov. to April. *Krainz* (I), (22 08). 98 beds, most with shower; outdoor pool; restaurant and bar. Closed Nov. to April. Campsite (22 24–32).

St. Veit/Glan A-9300 (04212). **Restaurant.** *La Colonne* (E), (53 93). A place that has fast become one of Carinthia's best restaurants. A jewel, and amazing value. Closed Mon. DC, MC. *Pukelsheim* (E), (24 73). Surprising to find a second gourmet restaurant in so small a town. Regional food and good wines. Closed Tues.

Seeboden A-9871 (0 47 62). *Bellevue* (E), am Waldrand 24 (81 3 46). 90 beds, all with bath or shower; indoor pool, sauna, solarium; bar. Closed March, April and Nov. DC, MC. *Sporthotel Royal* (E), (81 7 14). 80 beds, all with bath; indoor and outdoor pools, sauna, solarium, tennis, cure center; bar and restaurant. Closed Nov. to April.
Campsites (81 1 91, 81 2 67, or 81 9 35; 27 23; 81 9 27).

Spittal An Der Drau A-9800 (0 47 62). *Alte Post* (M), Hauptplatz 13 (22 17). 82 beds, all with bath or shower. Carinthian-style restaurant specializing in fish and game. *Ertl* (M), Bahnhofstrasse 26 (20 48). 85 beds, all with bath or shower; close to station, with own garden; indoor pool. Restaurant. AE.
Youth Hostel (32 52).
Campsite (24 66).

Techendorf A-9762 (0 47 13). *Alte Post* (M), (22 28). 26 rooms, all with bath. Own beach and balcony. Cafe and small restaurant. Closed Nov. DC, MC, V. *Strandhotel Weissensee* (M), (22 19). 70 rooms, most with bath or shower. Ideal for families; terrace, lawn, beach, tennis, sauna, sailing and windsurfing instruction. Closed 10 Oct. to 10 May.
Forelle (I), (23 56). 25 beds, all with bath or shower. Pool; restaurant and bar.
Campsites (22 34, 22 82).
Restaurant. *Kellerstuben Müller* (M), (22 71). In center of village, pleasant *stuben* with terrace; homemade cakes. Closed Nov. and April, Mon. out of season. DC, MC, V.

Turracher Höhe A-9565 (0 42 75). Bus from the rail stations of Feldkirchen in Carinthia and Turrach in Styria. *Hochschober* (E), (82 13). 120 beds, all with bath. Ideal for families, on lake in mountain scenery; indoor pool, tennis, lawn. Fine restaurant with Austrian fare.
Jägerwirt (M), (82 57). Indoor pool. Good restaurant.

Velden A-9220 (0 42 74). *Parkhotel* (L), (22 98–0). 180 beds, all with bath; garden with old trees. Superb restaurant, parks. Closed Oct. to April. AE, DC, MC, V. *Seehotel Engstler* (E), (26 44). 76 beds, all with bath; renovated, quiet garden. Closed 15 Oct. to 30 April. AE, DC, MC, V. *Schloss Velden* (E),

(26 5 50). 94 rooms, all with bath. Converted Baroque 15th-century castle with antique decor in public rooms. Tennis, private beach; restaurant, rustic tavern and lakeside bar. Open April to Oct. AE. *Hubertushof* (E), Europaplatz 1 (26 76). 90 beds, all with bath; old and elegant, in magnificent setting; own beach, indoor pool. Restaurant. Closed 20 Oct. to Easter. MC. *Veldenerhof-Mösslacher* (M), (20 18). 180 beds, all with bath or shower, many with balcony. Tennis and watersports, with instruction. Large restaurant by lake and garden. AE.

Casino in town.

Campsite (45 69).

Villach A-9500 (0 42 42). *Parkhotel* (E), Moritschgasse 2 (2 33 00). 250 beds, all with bath. In spacious park; traditional atmosphere, cure center and cafe. AE, DC, MC, V. *Post* (E), Hauptplatz 26 (2 61 01). 130 beds, all with bath. A Romantik Hotel. Beautifully-adapted Renaissance palace on main square. Personal and friendly. Fine vaulted ceiling in restaurant which serves prime Austrian fare. In summer dine by candlelight in the courtyard "Orangerie" among cascades of plants and fountains. Sauna. AE, DC, MC, V.

Youth Hostel (28 8 62).

Campsites (27 4 02 or 27 8 33).

Warmbad Villach A-9504 (0 42 42). *Warmbaderhof* (L), (2 55 01). 205 beds, all with bath; considered a deluxe hotel; indoor and outdoor pools with thermal water, therapy center, tennis. Excellent *Kleines Restaurant* and cafe in quiet part of Kurpark. AE, DC, V. *Karawankenhof* (E), (2 55 03). Newly rebuilt, every comfort. 95 beds, all with bath or shower; indoor and outdoor pools, tennis, therapy center in huge Kurpark. Restaurant. AE, DC, MC, V.

Josefinerhof (M), (2 55 31). 110 beds, most with bath or shower. Indoor and outdoor pools, sauna, tennis, riding. Restaurant. AE, MC, V.

PLACES OF INTEREST. All routes outlined below start from Klagenfurt. Please ascertain opening days and times locally. They change irregularly and are difficult to predict in advance.

Ferlach. Route 91 south. **Büchsenmachermuseum** (Gunsmiths' Museum), Rathaus. Exhibitions of the local gunsmiths' craft.

Frauenstein. Route 83 to St. Veit, then local road. Possible on foot from St. Veit (via Obermühlbach), about 3 miles. **Castle,** 16th-century and attractive.

Friesach. Route 83 north; also on main rail line. Medieval town with lots to see. **Fortifications,** with gates, towers and moats; **Parish Church,** poorly restored but with some good glass; early-Gothic **Dominican Church; Deutschenordenskirche** (Teutonic Order) has remnants of frescos, Gothic carvings. Open-air performances of plays in the courtyard of Schloss Petersberg in summer.

Gurk. Route 83 north to Pöckstein, then 93 west to Gurk. Romanesque **Cathedral** (around 1200) with interesting architectural elements; tomb of St. Emma; *Pietà* by Georg Raphael Donner.

Heiligenblut. Autobahn A2 to Villach, E14 to Möllbrücke, 106 to Winklern, then 107 to Heiligenblut. Romantic mountain resort beside the Grossglockner with wonderful views. **Parish Church,** Gothic of 1491. Outside fresco, winged altarpeice.

Hochosterwitz. Route 83 north to St. Donat, then local road. One of Austria's most beautiful castles, pure fairytale, crowning a hill; 14 gateway towers; collection of weapons and armor; cafe/restaurant; bronze 1580 altar in the church.

Hollenburg. South on 91. Massive 16th-century fortress; fresco in castle chapel (around 1380). Fine views; arcaded courtyard. Strategically placed to guard the Rosental. Close to Maria Saal. **Chapel** with 14th-century frescos.

Magdalensberg. Route 83 north to Willersdorf, then small local road. **Roman/Celtic Excavations,** guided tours available. Magnificent views to the north. **Pilgrimage Church,** with fine carvings.

Maria Saal. Route 83 just north of Klagenfurt. **Pilgrimage Church** with frescos, carvings and fine interior (Gothic). Tomb of St. Modestus; Plague Chapel, with frescos. **Openair Museum** with old farmhouses (on the Zollfeld).

Maria Wörth. On Wörthersee, due west of Klagenfurt. **Winterkirche** (Winter Church), one of two pilgrimage churches, side by side, with frescos in Romanesque choir, Gothic carvings and stained glass. **Charnel House** (see page 321).

Millstatt. A2 to Villach, Route E14/100 to Spittal, 99 to Seeboden, 98 to Millstatt. **Abbey.** Magnificent Romanesque doorway and cloisters in abbey remains. The foundation went through three main periods, and has architectural and decorative treasures from all three. Small but interesting **Museum.** Organ weeks are held here in summer.

Obervellach. A2 west to Villach, Route E14/100 to Möllbrücke, then 106. **Parish Church** (Gothic) with fine Dutch altarpiece (1520), carvings and fresco (1509); Garden of Olives carving in the chancel. East of Obervellach is **Oberfalkenstein** castle, now ruined. Niederfalkenstein was renovated in 1906.

Ossiach. A2 to Villach turnoff, 94 to Ossiach. Former **Abbey Church** with colored stucco decorations; Gothic chapel with valuable altarpiece (early 1500s); once very wealthy, has other well-furnished rooms. Setting of Carinthian Summer Music festival.

St. Veit An Der Glan. Route 83 due north. Interesting old town with 18th-century architecture. **Parish Church** mainly Gothic as is the **Rathaus** (Town Hall)—guided tours.

Spittal. A2 to Villach, then Route E14/100. **Schloss Porcia.** 1597, one of Austria's great buildings, a Renaissance palace/castle, arcaded courtyard, used for summer performances. **Bezirkheimatmuseum** (Regional Museum), local history displays, housed in Schloss Porcia.

Strassburg. Route 83 north to Pöckstein, then 93 west. **Bischofsburg** sizeable castle; **Parish Church** and **Spitalskirche** (Gothic circular building with frescos); **Local** and **Church Museum.**

Villach. Due west on A2. Interesting houses on the main square (**Paracelsushof, Hirschegger Hof**). **Parish Church,** Gothic with Baroque additions; 1480 stuccowork; stone carvings, etc. **Stadtmuseum** (Town Museum), Widmangasse 38, with Roman and other early finds, late-Gothic collection; material on Paracelsus; paintings. In the Schiller-Park is a huge **Relief Map of Carinthia.**

WINTER SPORTS. Here, as in the rest of Austria, skiing is the principal winter sport. The skiing season in the mountain areas lasts from December to March, high up in Hohe Tauern it extends into late spring with the international Grossglockner glacier ski racing, usually in early June.

Carinthia has slopes of all degrees of difficulty, from the gentler ones for novices to real challenges for the experienced Alpine skier, with accommodations at considerably lower prices than in many other areas. Particular bargains are Katschberg and Turracher Höhe. There is winter camping for skiers at Döbriach on Millstättersee.

Heiligenblut and the Upper Mölltal. This area is backed by Austria's mightiest mountain, the Grossglockner, which joins with other lesser peaks to provide some spectacular views from the ski slopes.
Resorts: Döllach (1,024 m., 3,360 ft.); Heiligenblut (1,301 m., 4,269 ft.); Winklern (967 m., 3,176 ft.).
Facilities: the area has 4 indoor swimming pools, 1 cable car, 3 chair lifts, 11 T-bars and 25 km. (16 miles) of cross-country trails.

Mallnitz And The Drautal Region. This region can provide some magnificent downhill runs, one of them has a vertical drop of over 4,000 ft. Most of the slopes are treeless, while the surrounding scenery is an added incentive for the skier.
Resorts: Berg/Drautal–Embergeralm (630 m., 2,064 ft.); Kolbnitz–Reissbeck (700 m., 2,295 ft.); Mallnitz (1,200 m., 3,937 ft.); Obervellach (680 m., 2,231 ft.); Spittal an der Drau (556 m., 1,824 ft.).
Facilities: 7 indoor swimming pools, 7 cable cars, 2 chair lifts, 16 T-bars, and 136 km. (85 miles) of cross-country trails

Sonnenalpe and Nassfeld–Weissensee. A variety of heights in a good-sized area down by the Italian border. Attractive for the hiker, too, as the marked paths through the woodlands and along the banks of the lake are especially scenic.
Resorts: Hermagor (603 m., 1,977 ft.); Kötschach–Mauthen (710 m., 2,329 ft.); Nassfeld (1,500 m., 4,921 ft.); Weissbriach (818 m., 2,684 ft.); Techendorf (980 m., 3,213 ft.); Weissensee (930 m., 3,051 ft.).
Facilities: 7 indoor swimming pools, 5 chair lifts, 16 T-bars and 154 km. (96 miles) of cross-country trails. There are also opportunities for ski-bobbing.

Nockberge Around Bad Kleinkircheim. Another ski area which is centered on a good spa town, giving the winter-sports enthusiast the best of both worlds. There is a massive 2½ mile downhill run for the courageous.

Resorts: Bad Kleinkirchheim (1,100 m., 3,609 ft.); Ebene Reichenau–Falkert (1,097 m., 3,594 ft.); Feld am See (743 m., 2,438 ft.); Turracherhöhe (1,763 m., 5,784 ft.).

Facilities: the area has 16 indoor swimming pools, 1 cable car, 6 chair lifts, 20 T-bars, and 91 km. (57 miles) of cross-country trails.

The Environs of Villach. While not among the very high ski regions, this one has a lot to recommend it to the skier and non-skier alike. The slopes of the Kanzelhöhe are attractive in themselves and give marvelous views of the Karawanken range. For those who like variety, Villach offers both its old-world atmosphere and some good spa facilities.

Resorts: Arnoldstein (597 m., 1,956 ft.); Finkenstein–Faak am See (560 m., 1,837 ft.); Annenheim–Gerlitzen (500 m., 1,640 ft.); Verditz bei Treffen (600 m., 1,969 ft.); Villach (501 m., 1,644 ft.); Warmbad Villach (503 m., 1,650 ft.).

Facilities: 12 indoor swimming pools, 1 cable car, 8 chair lifts, 22 T-bars and 123 km. (76 miles) of cross-country trails.

OTHER SPORTS.

Golf. Golfers have four courses at their disposal: an 18-hole course at Golf-Club Bad Kleinkircheim, A-9546 Bad Kleinkircheim (0 42 75–594); at Golfanlagen Velden-Köstenberg, A-9220 Velden (0 42 74–45 82); near Klagenfurt at Kärntner Golf Club, A-9082 Dellach/Maria Wörth (0 42 73–25 15); and 9 holes at Golfanlage Pörtschach-Moosburg, A-9210 Pörtschach (0 42 72–83 4 86). New courses are under construction at Pörtschach and Velden.

Hiking. Most resorts have marked hiking trails, many allowing a climb in one direction, with return either via an alternate route or with a bus.

Swimming and Sailing. Carinthia's lakes are known for their pure waters. Windsurfing is excellent as the lakes are long and narrow. Power boating and water skiing are limited to certain lakes and areas.

STYRIA

White Horses and Hills of Iron

Styria (Steiermark) is a romantic country, a country of virgin mountains and Austria's largest and densest forests, rife with game. It is a country of old folk traditions and a long historic record. Her rich deposits of iron attracted both the Celts and the Romans who left many traces of their presence behind. Later on Styrian iron provided the armor for the Christian armies fighting the Turks. Styria became the "Western Wall" against the Turkish invasions and in the 15th century when Emperor Friedrich III resided there, as well as thereafter, Graz was the strongest fortress of Christianity and the Turks never succeeded in taking it. The silent witness of those glorious days are the 27,000 pieces of armor and weapons preserved in Graz Armory, the largest remaining collection of its kind in the world. But the "Styrian green," more than anything else, symbolizes to the Styrian his love for nature, his old traditions, and his home.

Exploring Styria

The geography of Styria is largely dominated by the Mur River which collects its waters from most of the Styrian valleys. Its source, however, is in the Lungau region of Salzburg province, from where it enters Styria at Predlitz following its long northeastern course as far as Bruck, where, joined by Mürz—the "Little Mur"—it suddenly turns southeast and runs through Graz.

The fastest way from Vienna to Graz is by the A2 through east Styria. Both this and the alternative route via Semmering and the Mürz-Mur valley are scenically rewarding. The train journey over the Semmering from Vienna to Graz is memorable. To savor this triumph of 19th-century railway engineering to the full, with its bold viaducts and tunnels, try to get a window seat facing the engine on the left of the train—but do it soon: plans are afoot to re-route the line via a new tunnel *under* the Semmering.

Mariazell

Mariazell began in 1157 as a cabin housing five monks, who built a church and set up in it a statue of the Virgin carved from limewood. As time went on, curious stories began to emanate from Mariazell: the statue was performing miracles! Its reputation grew and by the end of the 14th century Mariazell was drawing pilgrims from all parts of Europe, particularly from Slavic and Hungarian lands. Today it is the country's foremost pilgrimage church and contains Austria's national shrine, the Chapel of Grace. The miracle-working statue is still to be seen in Mariazell, surrounded by a splendor unknown to it in the 12th century. It stands on a silver altar designed by the great Austrian architect Fischer von Erlach (who also created the Baroque high altar) in the parish and pilgrimage church, a 14th-century basilica rebuilt in the 17th century by Sciassia. Its fine treasury with, among other beautiful items, the Virgin's rich wardrobe, is open, summer mornings.

A cable car takes you from Mariazell to the Bürgeralpe, over 1,250 m. (4,100 ft.) high. On the main road south of Mariazell (20) is the Seeberg Pass with a fine view of the surrounding mountain ranges of Hochschwab and Veitschalpe. The road proceeds farther south through the quiet summer and winter resort of Aflenz and by the Schachenstein Castle ruins and the 14th-century fortress at Thörl to Kapfenberg in the Mürz Valley.

From Semmering through the Mürz Valley

Taking the train from Vienna you literally penetrate Styria through a tunnel over half-a-mile long underneath the Semmering Pass, while the excellent road crosses over the Pass. The first communities on the Styrian side of Semmering are Steinhaus and Spital, unpretentious summer resorts, sharing in winter a first-class skiing area. The Semmering Railway is one of the great Victorian railway achievements in the world. It has tunnels, elegant viaducts and breathtaking views.

At Mürzzuschlag we reach the Mürz River. Here is the heart of Austrian skiing, and, in a sense, of the Winter Olympics, since the first Nordic Games were held here in 1904. The main current has moved to Innsbruck, but there is still a winter sports museum here in honor of past glories. The old parish church was rebuilt in Baroque style and partially redecorated in Rococo, and there are also several interesting old houses; see the Gutschelhoferhaus, distinguished by the fact that Czar Alexander I of Russia and Emperor Franz I of Austria slept here.

Further up the Mürz Valley are Neuberg with a 14th-century Cistercian monastery reputed to possess the most beautiful cloisters in Styria, and Mürzsteg with a hunting castle that belonged to Emperor Franz Josef, currently the summer residence of the presidents of Austria.

Down the valley from Mürzzuschlag is Krieglach, known chiefly for the fact that Peter Rosegger, the famed Styrian folk poet, spent part of his life here. He was born in the nearby Alpl (about 8 km., 5 miles), in the beautiful wooded mountain area that is called his Waldheimat (forest homeland) and which inspired many of his poems. His birth house as well as the Waldschule (school in the forest), founded by him, have been preserved. His grave is in the Krieglach cemetery. The road, river and railway continue through Kindberg to Kapfenberg, with its Oberkapfenberg Castle.

Bruck an der Mur

Bruck an der Mur lies at the confluence of Mur and Mürz and is a good center for one of the best walking areas of Austria. Most people who arrive here are too busy changing trains to notice that Bruck has marked merits of its own. Its most notable structure is the fine Kornmesserhaus, built between 1499 and 1505 in late Gothic style, and well restored. The original owner was called Pankraz Kornmess, hence the name. The wrought-iron Renaissance fountain on the main square is the most beautiful of its kind in Styria. Another wrought-iron masterpiece is the late Gothic sacristy door of the 14th-century parish church, itself well worth an inspection. Maria im Walde is an interesting church, with one of the best Austrian 14th-century frescos. Another old fresco, depicting the Last Judgement and originating from around 1420, can be seen in the Church of St. Ruprecht.

A treasure of Gothic art is contained in the 14th-century St. Ulrich Church in Utsch near Bruck: a crucifixion fresco from 1390 and sculptures and glass window paintings from 1430.

Following the Mur River to Graz we pass through Mixnitz, the starting point for a highly interesting trip that takes you first to the savage Bärenschützklamm gorge, which you have to negotiate on steps and ladders, but whose raging waterfalls are worth all the trouble; then across mountain meadows that seem incongruously peaceful in the midst of such tormented scenery; and finally to the 1,722 m. (5,650 ft.) Hochlantsch.

Farther south is Frohnleiten, an old town with rich Rococo interiors in its parish church. On an abrupt rock about 3 km. southwest of town is Rabenstein Castle, a medieval structure built on the ruins of a Roman fort and subsequently redone in Baroque style. A couple of other castles are nearby, the 18th-century Neupfannberg in a pleasant park, and the ruins of Pfannberg.

Near Peggau, only about 20 km. (12½ miles) from Graz, is the largest stalactite and stalagmite cave in Austria, the Lurgrotte with a small underground lake, artificial pathways, electric lighting, and conducted tours of varying length.

Through East Styria to Graz

Proceeding from Vienna on the eastern route, we enter Styria just beyond Mönichkirchen, crossing the Wechsel mountain range. There are two roads here, either the fast A2, or the more leisurely 54, which is the one we follow. The first Styrian communities are the twin towns of Pinggau and Friedberg, the first sitting modestly in the narrow valley and the second towering above it on a steep hill. Friedberg was once a fortress town, founded in the 12th century, allegedly with part of the ransom paid by Richard the Lionheart. At Rohrbach we reach the Lafnitz river and the secondary road leading west to Vorau where there is a renowned Baroque abbey with many visitable treasures. A few kilometers north of Vorau is Festenburg Castle, now partially converted into a church and belonging to the Vorau Abbey, but once a meeting place of Minnesingers.

Lafnitz river branches off from the main road at the town of Lafnitz and from here on forms the border between Styria and Burgenland. A secondary road approximately parallels it through the towns of Neudau with a castle, and Burgau, where the 13th-century fort provides a spectacular backdrop for the huge swimming pool.

But Europe's largest pool is in East Styria's main town, Fürstenfeld, founded in the 12th century as a fortress-town in the chain of the Empire's eastern defenses, later a district seat of the Knights of Malta. The architectural evidence of this period can still be seen, including fine old town houses and churches, remains of fortifications, and several castles in the vicinity. To the southwest of Fürstenfeld is Riegersburg Castle-Fortress, the most powerful Styrian castle, dominating the town of the same name below it from the top of a basalt pile of rocks. First record of its existence goes back to 1100, it was last rebuilt in the 17th century: it has seven gates, arcaded courtyards, decorated halls, a collection of armor and weapons, and a fine view over East and South Styria. It was savagely fought over in World War II.

If instead of following the course of Lafnitz river we continue from the town of the same name along Route 54 to Graz (the railroad line goes via Fürstenfeld) we first come to Hartberg, another old town with a castle and a Baroque church but with a Romanesque charnel house and murals from the same period. West of Hartberg is Pöllau with the former abbey church, the best example in Styria of High Baroque, and with a 16th-century Rathaus with a whipping post. Nearby is the Pöllauberg pilgrimage church, one of Austria's loveliest.

Three kilometers or so upstream from where the main road crosses the Feistritz river is the 13th-century Schloss Herberstein, owned by the famous South Styrian aristocratic family of the same name, one of the most magnificent Styrian castles, last rebuilt in the 17th century, with rich internal and external decorations, a family and castle museum, and a game preserve. Nearby is Austria's largest artificial lake—Stubenbergsee. Farther up the Feistritz valley are several small summer resorts, the best known among which is Birkfeld.

Back on the main road we continue to Gleisdorf, a marketing center for the fruit grown in this fertile region and, after crossing the low hills between Raab and Mur valleys in a westerly direction, we come to Graz. North of this section are Weiz with a 17th-century church built as a fort for defense against the Turks and the vividly decorated Weizberg pilgrimage church; and Passail, an unpretentious summer resort with the picturesque gorges of Raabklamm and Weizklamm and several underground caves in the vicinity.

Graz, Styria's Capital

Napoleon's play on words, *"Ville de grace aux rives de l'amour,"* aptly describes this elegant Baroque center, framed by parks and gardens, on the banks of La Mur. There was probably a Celtic settlement on the spot, and almost certainly a fortress in the 9th century. However, documentary evidence only begins early in the 12th century, and it was one century later that it acquired officially the status of a town, and enclosed itself in the

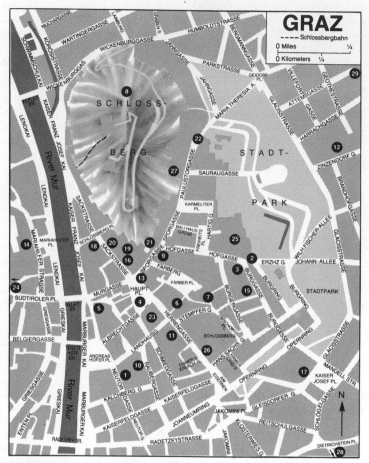

Points of Interest

1	Alte Galerie	12	Leech Church	23	Rathaus
2	Burgtor	13	Luegg House	24	Schloss Eggenberg;
3	Cathedral	14	Mariahilf Church		Rail Station
4	Erzherzog Johann Fountain	15	Mausoleum of Ferdinand II	25	Stadtburg
5	Franciscan Church	16	Neue Galerie	26	Stadtpfarrkirche
6	Gemaltes Haus	17	Opera House	27	Styrian Folklore Museum
7	Glockenspiel	18	Palais Attems	28	Technical University
8	Glockenturm	19	Palais Herberstein	29	University
9	House of the Teutonic Knights	20	Palais Khuenburg Stadtmuseum		
10	Joanneum	21	Palais Saurau Goess		
11	Landeszeughaus; Landhaus	22	Paulustor		

walls that helped it later on to escape capture by the Turks. It was the capital, not only of Styria, but of all Inner Austria—Carinthia, Carniola, Görz, Istria, and Trieste as well—from the late 14th to the early 17th century. Today, it is a prosperous city, spread out over both banks of the Mur. The left bank, on which the Old Town is located, is the richer in relics of the past, although there are also some interesting old buildings on the right bank, the Lend and Gries sections. These two areas are fast turning into a Grazer "Quartier Latin."

The easiest way to get an overall view of Graz is to take the cable-railway, the Schlossbergbahn, from the Kaiser-Franz-Josef-Kai up to Schlossberg, the steep wooded rock that dominates the town, crowned, till the Napoleonic Wars, by a large castle-fortress. From it you will be able to see all of Graz and a good part of East, South and Central Styria as well. Orientation tables, located at various points offering the best views, will help you to identify what you see. Near the top is also an openair theater where opera and drama performances are staged in summer, particularly during the Graz Festival. Only the Bell Tower or Glockenturm, remains of the old fortifications. It was saved during the Napoleonic Wars when the townspeople paid the French 3,000 guilders not to destroy it. Thus Styria's largest bell, the Liesl, weighing more than four tons, is still pealing forth the musical tone for which it has been famous since 1588. The *big* hands on the gigantic dials show the hours and the *small* hands the minutes, an endless source of confusion to unsuspecting visitors.

The castle hill is included in the vast park area of the City Park (Stadtpark) which forms a crescent around the eastern part of the old town. From the Bell Tower you can take a pleasant pathway to the city gate called Paulustor and to the Styrian Folklore Museum, housed in an old monastery, and then proceed through Sporgasse, lined with interesting old buildings, such as the House of the Teutonic Knights and Palais Saurau-Goess, to the main square. If you decide to return from the Schlossberg by the railway then you reach the main square walking through Sackstrasse, which also has several old palaces, among them Palais Herberstein with an outstanding stairway and ceiling frescos; Palais Khuenburg, where Archduke Franz Ferdindand was born in 1863 and which now houses the Stadtmuseum; and particularly the Baroque Palais Attems with stucco decorations and frescos, very valuable furnishings, rare 18th-century tapestries and the largest private art collection in Styria.

On the main square (Hauptplatz) stands the Erzherzog Johann Fountain with the statue of the Styrian Governor and the four female figures representing the four principal rivers of Styria. The Rathaus, a structure from the end of the last century, is of less interest; remarkable however is the richly ornamented Luegg House with arcaded passageway on the corner of Hauptplatz and Sporgasse. Artistically superior is the row of facades in Herrengasse, which begins at the other end of the square, among them particularly the 15th-century Herzogshof or Gemaltes Haus (Painted House) at No. 3. In the same street is the Landhaus, the seat of the Styrian state parliament and government, whose main wing was built by Domenico dell'Allio, a native of Lugano, in Italian Renaissance style. Its arcaded courtyard is magnificently proportioned and the star exhibits among the interiors are the Knights' Hall and the Council Chamber. The 16th-century courtyard fountain is an unusually fine example of the old Styrian wrought-iron art. Historic coats of arms of Styrian cities figure over one of the doorways on the Herrengasse façade. Adjoining the Landhaus is the Landeszeughaus, the original Armory built in 1642 and still arranged in the same manner. It contains about 27,000 pieces of armor, weapons, and other military equipment, mostly from the 16th and 17th centuries comprising the actual weapons of the Styrian soldiers, last used at the end of the 17th century, and never out of the armory since: probably the only one of its kind.

Farther down on the other side of the street is the twin-naved Gothic parish church, the Stadtpfarrkirche, built early in the 16th century, to which have been added a Baroque facade and spire, both 18th century. Tintoretto's *Assumption of the Virgin* decorates the altar. Across the street from the parish church begins a short narrow street, called after the great architect Johann Bernhard Fischer von Erlach because he was born in one of the houses there. From the parish church you can wander through the heart of the old town toward the cathedral. If it happens to be 11 A.M. or 6 P.M., you might stop and watch the Glockenspiel on the square to which it has given its name.

The cathedral is 15th-century Gothic, and its most notable exterior decoration is a fresco painted in 1485 depicting the *Divine Torments*—which turn out to be (a) plague, (b) locusts, and (c) war. Inside are a number of details you should not miss—the high altar, the beautiful choir stalls, Raphael Donner's tomb of Count Cobenzl, and Konrad Laib's *Crucifixion.* Fine concerts are held in the summer months. The Diocesan Museum and cathedral treasure are also worth seeing. The treasure includes two magnificent ivory reliquaries, which were originally the hope chests of Paola Gonzaga, daughter of Ludwig II of Mantua.

Adjoining the cathedral is the Baroque mausoleum in which Emperor Ferdinand II is buried. The interior, designed by Fischer von Erlach, is particularly attractive. Across the square from the cathedral and the mausoleum is the Stadtburg, begun by Friedrich III in 1438 but including sections from every succeeding century. Its most notable detail is the double spiral Gothic staircase, added in 1499—unless you call the medieval Burgtor Gate attached to it a detail.

Through the Burgtor you again find yourself in the City Park. If you cross it approximately to the left you eventually come to the Teutonic Knights' twin-spired early Gothic Leech Church with a 13th-century stone relief of Madonna with Child, and beyond it to the University, noted for its creation of eminent jurists, philologists and physicians. Near the southeastern end of the City Park is the superbly restored and enlarged Opera House and beyond it in the same general direction, the Technical University, founded by Erzherzog Johann. Some 150 years ago Erzherzog Johann also founded the Joanneum, the Styrian Provincial Museum with the main building in Neutorgasse, three blocks from the Landhaus. Rather like a smaller version of the Victoria and Albert in London, this museum was designed to foster the progress of industry and the arts. This, one of oldest museums in Europe, is really a group of museums. The old buildings contain the natural history museum and a coin collection.

The new buildings, in the other half of the same block, contain the picture galleries and the applied art museum. The first shows works from medieval to modern times. Among famous artists represented are Hans von Aachen, Lukas Cranach, Jan Breughel, Pieter Breughel. The *Admont Madonna,* carved in wood in 1315, is Styria's most admired Gothic work of this kind. The other chief treasures are the 14th-century Mühlau crucifix, a 15th-century Madonna from the St. Lambrecht Monastery and the

St. Peter by the unknown master from Grosslobming, of the same period. In the applied arts museum is the Augsburg Chalice, 16th century, the largest Renaissance chalice in Austria. The wrought-iron work here is particularly admirable.

After crossing Andreas Hofer Platz, the terminal for out-of-town buses, Neutorgasse takes you to the Franciscan Church which provides an appropriate backdrop for an ancient, tiny square, and to the main bridge connecting the Old Town on the left bank with its right bank sections. Several old town houses are to be seen here, especially on Mariahilferstrasse and Griesgasse, and among the churches the twin-spired Mariahilf Church is particularly appealing. Annenstrasse, the principal business artery of the right bank becomes increasingly modern as it approaches the railway station.

Excursions around Graz

There are many pleasant spots for short trips from Graz. Among them is Maria Trost, where there is a fine Baroque church with two towers and famous paintings, and an attached convent. It is beautifully located on high land. (Tram No. 1.)

Eggenberg Castle (3½ km., 2 miles to the west) about 20 minutes with streetcar 1 (get off at Schloss strasse and walk to the end of the road) is a magnificent 17th-century residence, with no less than 26 large rooms for receptions, in addition to normal living quarters. It is grandly decorated and furnished, and the Baroque stucco work and mural and ceiling paintings are remarkable. It also houses the small Graz City Museum and an interesting Jagdmuseum (Museum of Hunting). Mouflons, deer, and peacocks roam in freedom in the large park around the castle. Entrance at end of Eggenberger Allee. Beautiful chamber concerts are held in the big gallery in summer.

Plabutsch—an elevation west from the city—has lovely walks and a fine view of the western Styrian mountains.

St. Radegund-Schöckel is a health resort, wonderful for walkers—there are 42 km. (26 miles) of walking paths here. There is also a swimming pool. Take the funicular, one of Europe's most modern, up the Schöckel (1,445 m., 4,741 ft.) for a view extending from the Alps to the Hungarian plain.

Stift Rein, near Gratwein, reached by bus, is also a popular excursion spot with Graz citizens. The monastery church, originally Romanesque, was rebuilt in the 18th century; one of its main attractions is the altar painting by Kremser Schmidt, but practically every part of it is magnificent. Only a few km. away is the Gothic Maria Strassengel, the "daughter church" of the Rein monastery with the main altar by Fischer von Erlach and some paintings by Kremser Schmidt.

Just 15 km. (9½ miles) from Graz, at Stübing, is the Austrian Openair Museum, where some 70 rural buildings from all over Austria have been reconstructed. Spaced out through the Mur valley the grouped houses, mills and barns are all in working order. On Sundays in summer a bus leaves Andreas Hoferpl. in Graz at 2 P.M. for a tour of the Wine Road.

South Styria

South Styria is mostly a region of undulating hills, carpeted with vineyards in its middle section, becoming higher and more forested toward the west, and slowly disappearing into the plain in the east. Only a fraction of South or Lower Styria (Untersteiermark) was left to Austria after World War I; the bulk of it had had to be ceded to the newly created Yugoslav State.

The largest community in the present Austrian South Styria is Leibnitz, dominated by Seggau Castle which since the ninth century had been a stronghold of Salzburg Prince-Bishops and later went into the hands of the Styrian Bishops of Seckau. The castle houses a collection of Roman stone reliefs, for Leibnitz stands on the site of the Roman town Flavia Solva, founded by Emperor Vespasian in the first century. More remains from Roman times can be seen at Frauenberg near Seggau, where a Roman temple once stood and a pilgrimage church stands today. Leibnitz itself has an interesting parish church, originally Gothic with an impressive 18th-century main altar.

East of Leibnitz, on the Mur river which forms here the frontier between Styria and Slovenia, is the small, picturesque town of Mureck, and farther down the river the larger Radkersburg. Its Gothic parish church contains a famous *Black Madonna,* while the 165-foot clock tower on the Rathaus rises above fine patrician houses. Both towns have old castles which are on the hills across the river and therefore across the border. North of Radkersburg in quiet green surroundings lies Bad Gleichenberg, the most important Styrian spa.

At Ehrenhausen, south of Leibnitz, begins the Styrian Wine Road, leading across undulating hills through the wine villages Platsch, Gamlitz and Leutschach. The Austrian-Yugoslav border runs down the middle of the wine road for several miles—there is different paving on each side! The scenery is spectacular; the steep slopes of the hills are ornamented with vineyards and little wine press houses.

West of the wine region, the wooded slopes of Koralpe rise to a considerable height along the border of Carinthia. Deutschlandsberg, a summer resort at the foot of Koralpe and an old town with a medieval castle, is the main center. North of Deutschlandsberg are the towns of Voitsberg and Köflach, both defined by long history, medieval castles and coal mining, and actually already in central Styria.

If you are fond of horses, you will probably want to visit the Lippizaner stud farm at Piber, in the vicinity of Köflach. These snow-white horses trace their lineage back to 1580 when Archduke Karl of Styria established a stud farm at Lippiza near Trieste, using stallions imported from Arabia and mares from Spain. Born black, the steeds gradually turn white between the ages of two and seven. After World War I, when Austria lost Lippiza, the farm was transferred to Piber. Of course, the farm provides the horses for the famous Spanish Riding School in Vienna. Every Monday in summer a bus leaves Andreas Hoferpl. in Graz at 8 A.M. for a guided tour of the stud farm, returning at noon.

Iron Alps and Upper Mur

Leoben, a few kilometers upstream from Bruck in the Mur Valley, is the largest town in central Styria and the center of this important mining and heavy industry region. It is an old town and the heritage of its past includes the 17th-century parish church; the Baroque column commemorating the passage of the plague, which stands on the handsome main square lined with fine old buildings, including the Rathaus and the 17th-century Hacklhaus. Maria Waasen Church with brilliant 12th-century Gothic windows is worth visiting. There are many interesting old houses as well as the Massenburg Castle ruins. One unique feature is the Schwammerl ("little mushroom"), a name irreverently bestowed on the former Customs Tower (Mautturm), the town symbol, because of its shape.

In the southern suburb of Göss is the oldest monastery in Styria, founded around 1000; its most outstanding features include the Gothic church and Bishop's Chapel with frescos from 1285, and a Romanesque crypt. The monastery has long been secularized and presently houses the renowned Göss Brewery.

To the north is the Donawitz basin, an important factor in European steel production. Donawitz itself is the northern suburb of Leoben and the Alpin Montan Gesellschaft operates several blast furnaces and a modern rolling mill here. This whole area is seeking a new identity and new industry (not least tourism) as it suffers the fate of all steel centers in Western Europe.

The atmosphere changes abruptly from industrial to touristic at Trofaiach, where interest centers about summer holidays and two old Gothic churches with 14th- and 15th-century statuary. Both elements, however, are combined again at Vordernberg, the oldest center of the Styrian iron industry, where the Romans worked the metal from the surrounding mines of what are accurately called the Iron Alps. There are a couple of interesting churches and some 17th-century guild houses that are worth looking at.

We now come to the most amazing place in this entire region, Eisenerz. What is unique at Eisenerz is Erzberg, the mountain that towers above it. Erzberg is literally a mountain of iron. The ore is 34 percent pure iron. It does not have to be mined; it is quarried. For centuries, men have been chipping off pieces of the mountain. In modern times, the stuff of which the mountain is made has been pulled away in strips, so that now it rises in terrace after terrace, some forty of them. 1,520 m. (5,000 ft.) high, it is rated as the largest ore field in Europe capable of open-face mining. Guided visits of the mine can be made. Production will soon be discontinued and the region, together with its mountain, will be turning more and more to tourism in the future.

In Eisenerz itself there are several things of interest. The St. Oswald Church, built in 1509, is the biggest fortified church in Styria, built to resist the onslaughts of the Turks. The Schichtturm, or Shift Tower, used to tell when it was time to change the shifts at the mine.

Near Erzberg, in the northerly direction, is the lovely Leopoldsteiner See, hidden among the mountains, while to the south, on the main road between Eisenerz and Vordernberg is Präbichl, near the pass of the same name, a point of departure for climbing and skiing tours.

Back at Leoben, we continue upwards through the Upper Mur Valley. At St. Michael the main road leading to the Enns Valley and farther to Salzkammergut and Salzburg branches off. Knittelfeld is a small industrial town with the dreamy Ingering Lake nearby, framed by forests. About 16 km. (10 miles) north is the 12th-century Seckau Abbey, another famed Styrian monastery, with the original Romanesque style of its church still visible despite later additions, containing many outstanding features of all periods, such as the Renaissance-style Mausoleum of Archduke Karl II as well as the modern apocalyptic frescos in the Angel's Chapel by Herbert Boeckl, one of the most prominent 20th-century Austrian painters. For five-and-a-half centuries Seckau was the episcopal center for Styria, and the whole complex of buildings bears rich testimony to the wealth that was lavished on it. The stained-glass, wrought iron, paintings and carvings are well worth spending time to visit.

Farther up the valley is Judenburg; as its name implies it was a Jewish town several centuries ago. An old building still displays a 500-year-old sculptured head of a Jew. Judenburg has several interesting churches (especially the Parish church with a Rococo pulpit and some interesting sculptures), private dwellings, remains of the city wall, the ruins of the old Liechtenstein Castle nearby with the 17th-century new Liechtenstein Castle below it. At St. Georgen the road crossing the range of Niedere Tauern takes off, reaching after less than 16 km. (10 miles) the old silver mining town of Oberzeiring where a former silver mine can be visited.

Back in the Mur Valley we come to Unzmarkt with the ruins of the still impressive Frauenburg Castle on an elevation across the river. Among his castles this was the one that the famous Styrian Minnesinger Ulrich von Liechtenstein liked most, and here he died in 1275. At Scheifling the main road for Carinthia leads south, but the valley itself continues toward the west.

At Niederwölz a short side road takes you to the 800-year-old Oberwölz with medieval walls, three gates, old churches and the Rothenfels Castle perched on a red cliff. You can still see here how a medieval town was laid out.

At Teufenbach, with an old and a new castle, another side road takes you to St. Lambrecht, another famed abbey, founded in the 11th century. This, like Seckau, is a richly endowed abbey, full of items to interest anyone who likes church art and architecutre. There are fine medieval wood carvings, Rococo altars and splendid vestments.

Murau, founded in the 13th century, with remains of the 14th-century walls, several Gothic churches, the Rathaus that was once part of the fortifications, many old dwellings in the narrow streets, and crowned by Schwarzenberg Castle, is a historic jewel. But the main attraction of this area is, perhaps, the old steam-engine narrow-gauge Murtal railway, which puffs and whistles through the lovely Mur Valley between Murau and Tamsweg (in Land Salzburg). It runs only on certain days in summer, and is accompanied by bright red and green cars (one of them a bar), and often also by the Murau brass band.

At Predlitz, the last village in Styria, with a remarkable wood-paneled ceiling in its church, a rough side road takes you up to Turrach, where the first blast furnaces and Bessemer converters on the Continent were put to use, and farther up to Turracher Höhe, a mountain resort with a small lake and famed for its Alpine flowers and skiing.

The Enns Upstream to Dachstein

The most spectacular entrance into the Enns Valley, which dominates northwestern Styria, is near its lower or eastern end, reached either from Eisenerz (Route 115) or via Altenmarkt if coming from Upper Austria (also 115). Immediately upstream from Hieflau, where the two mentioned routes join, begins the spectacular gorge of Gesäuse. The rocky faces of craggy peaks soar up on all sides, almost straight from the river bed, and the Enns cuts its way through them in a rushing, foaming, wild stream, white and green. This is one of the most splendid examples of natural mountain architecture anywhere in the Alps (Route 112).

Once out of Gesäuse the Enns Valley widens and it is here that the famous Abbey of Admont is located in the town of the same name. The
abbey is particularly renowned for its library with ceiling frescos by Altomonte and Rococo bookshelves. The rocky Ennstaler Alps provide a magnificent frame for the town. On a hill near Admont is the twin-spired pilgrimage church of Frauenberg.

At Liezen the Enns Valley road is joined by the road coming from St.
Michael near Leoben over the Schober Pass and through Rottenmann,
one of the oldest towns in Styria, and Selztal. Stainach, located under the
mighty Grimming mountain group, is famous for its Glöcklerlauf (masked
procession) on Twelfth Night. In the vicinity are several castles, the lovely
Putterersee, and the medieval fortress settlement of Pürgg with the Gothic
parish church and 12th-century frescos in the Romanesque Johannes
Chapel.

Near Stainach, the main road forks into two directions. One road (145)
climbs to Klachauer Höhe, and from there passes into Ausseer Land,
which is the Styrian section of Salzkammergut. The other road (146) continues up the Enns valley along the base of the powerful Grimming to
Gröbming, a very pleasant climatic resort and one of the centers of Styrian
horsebreeding.

At Schladming, a picturesque old town that was the site of the Alpine
Skiing World Championship in 1982, the Enns Valley narrows between
the Dachstein mountain range and Schladminger Tauern. Schladming, a
renowned summer and winter resort, has remains of old walls, the town
hall, which was formerly a hunting castle, and a Gothic church. The nearby mountain resort of Ramsau is the principal climbing base for the majestic Dachstein (2,995 m., 9,826 ft.), covered by glaciers on its north side,
vertically cut on its south side, the highest peak of Styria, reached by a
super-modern cable car.

Ausseer Land

In the high valley beyond the Klachauer Höhe are the summer resorts
and first-class skiing centers of Tauplitz, with Tauplitzalm (1,965 m.,
6,447 ft.) and Mitterndorf, and the giant ski jump of Kulm nearby.

The heart of this region is Bad Aussee, with Altaussee on the lake to
which it gives its name, as a secondary center. The former is a big spa,
especially beneficial for respiratory troubles because of its altitude and its
location, which protect it from wind and fog, so that sun baths as well
as brine and mud baths can be a dependable part of the cure here. You
can choose between a swimming pool and lake bathing, climb mountains
on foot or take a chair lift, inspect the 5,000 different Alpine flowers in
the Alpine garden or the costumes in the museum, go to the Kurhaus theater or the cinema, look at the 15th-century parish church with its statue
of the Virgin or the 14th-century Hospital Church, with its Gothic statues
and frescos, or simply watch the pageantry of everyday life in a town
where folk costumes survive in full ceremony. Bad Aussee is the center
for such Trachten for both sexes. Special folk festivals are held during the
year and this is the best spot for buying any Trachten articles you might
fancy. It is also a good place for hunting, fishing, tennis or, in winter, skiing.

Altaussee is by comparison a quieter, more reposeful place than its cousin, dominated by the endless spectacle of the Dachstein glacier, always

the same and always changing with each minute variation in the light. It adds to the baths of the larger center a variant of its own—the pineneedle bath.

Grundlsee on the lake of the same name is also a quieter resort, and Gössl at the end of the lake is recommended for those who want complete peace and do not mind simple accommodations. From Gössl there is a 20-minute walk to the beginning of Toplitzsee, which you can cross by a motor raft; from the other end it is five minutes to the rustic Kammersee and the Traun waterfall pouring down a rocky cliff.

With various new ski lifts and more under construction, the district around Bad Aussee, Altaussee and Grundlsee is a winter sports center of major importance.

PRACTICAL INFORMATION FOR GRAZ

USEFUL ADDRESSES. Tourist information, Herrengasse 16 (in Landhaus). 83 52 41 (for Graz); and 7031–22 87 (for Styria). Also at the railway station (91 68 37); open daily 9 A.M. to 9 P.M.
Money. Apart from all the normal banks, there is a bureau de change at the main rail station. Exchange offices are open on Sundays at the main Post Office on Neutorgasse and in the Post Office next to the main station.

AREA CODES—MAIL AND PHONES. The postal code for Graz is A-8010 for the Old Town side of the River Mur and A-8020 for the railway side.The telephone area code is 0 31 6.

HOTELS. There is a wide selection of good hotels, most of which have been extensively refurbished in the last few years. Ask your hotel receptionist for a "Visitor's Pass," which will provide you with reductions for many facilities.

Deluxe

Alba Wiesler, Grieskai 98 (91 32 41). 98 superbly appointed rooms. Turn-of-century hotel with magnificent mosaic by a pupil of Klimt. Overlooking the river. Has been rebuilt inside and is now unquestionably Graz's top hotel. Stylish café, bars, bistro and gourmet restaurant. AE, DC, MC, V.

Expensive

Daniel, Europaplatz 1 (91 10 80). 96 rooms, all with bath or shower; close to station and main traffic route, but windows soundproofed; restaurant. Closed 22 Dec. to 7 Jan. AE, DC, MC, V.
Erzherzog Johann, Sackstrasse 3–5 (81 16 16). 70 rooms, all with bath or shower. Dating back to 16th-century, beautiful lobby. Small rooms in old part - ask for a new room, more comfortable and quieter. Good restaurant and cafe. AE, DC, MC, V.
Europa, Bahnhofgürtel 89 (91 66 01). 120 rooms with every comfort. Conference facilities, bar, sauna, cafe, *Four Seasons* restaurant.
Gollner, Schlögelgasse 14–16 (85 25 21). 40 rooms, most with bath or shower; in center of Graz but windows are soundproofed; sauna, solarium; very friendly; comfortable rooms. AE, DC, MC, V.

Parkhotel, Leonhardstrasse 8 (33 5 11). 65 rooms, all with bath. Central, close to City Park, University and Opera. Functional rooms, nice garden in courtyard. AE, DC, MC, V.

Schlossberghotel, Kaiser Franz Joseph Kai 30 (80 7 00). 43 rooms, all with bath. Totally renovated, beautifully furnished, full of antiques. AE, DC, MC, V.

Weitzer/Goldener Ochs, Griesgasse 15 (91 38 01). 205 rooms, all with bath or shower. Run by Weitzer family for many generations. Traditional atmosphere with modern amenities; nice view of river, old town and Schlossberg. Soundproofed windows. Good restaurant. AE, DC, MC, V.

Moderate

Academia, Schönbrunng 7–11 (33 5 58). Open July to Sept.

Drei Raben, Annenstrasse 43 (91 26 85). 50 rooms, 37 with bath or shower. DC, MC, V.

Mariahilf, Mariahilfstr. 9 (91 31 63). 44 rooms, 38 with bath or shower. DC, V.

Rosenhotel Steiermark, Liebiggasse 4 (34 0 41). 112 rooms, all with shower. Open July to Sept.

Zum Kreuz, Kärntnerstr. 451 (28 34 36). 12 rooms, all with bath. On the outskirts; in the same family for over 100 years. Small but with good restaurant. MC.

Inexpensive

Engel, Lendplatz 1 (91 37 57) 18 rooms, 10 with bath or shower; reasonable and just across the river from the center.

Strasser, Eggenbergergürtel 11 (91 39 77). 30 rooms. MC.

Youth Hostel

Jugendgästehaus in Idlhofgasse 74 (91 48 76). Open all year.

Camping

Camping Central, Strassgang, Martinhofgasse 3 (28 18 31).
Camping Nord, Grabenstr. 146 (62 76 22).
Camping Graz-West, Reininghausstr. 1 (52 78 03).
Camping Graz-Ost, Neue Welthöhe 71 (45 1 96).
Camping Graz-Mantscha Riederhof-Mantscha 1 (28 43 80).

GETTING AROUND GRAZ. By Bus and Tramcar. The nexus of the bus/tram network in Graz is Jakomini Square, from which you can reach most of the city. There are 7 streetcar lines and many bus routes. For the edges of town you can take a streetcar and then transfer to bus. For information about City Transport there is a 24-hour phone service on 78 9 31.

Guided Tours. Bus tours, which will help you get an overall view of the city, operate daily June through to the beginning of Sept., except Sat. and Sun. Buses leave the Grazer Congress at 3. Tour lasts about 2¼ hours.

There are also guided tours through the Old Quarter, tours of the Citadel, of the Eggenberg Palace State Rooms and of the Armory. Check with the Tourist Office for the latest arrangements.

By Taxi. Call 28 01 or 983.

RESTAURANTS. The food in Graz is traditional and, by and large, excellently prepared. Naturally there are plenty of international dishes available, but the main emphasis for the visitor should be on the typical

Styrian specialties—*Wurzelfleisch,* a sort of stew; variations on the theme of *Sterz,* a dish made from buckwheat; any of the seemingly innumerable sausages; or *Hendl,* chicken done in local ways. Try pumpkin-seed oil (Kernöl) on your salad. Don't be put off by the green/black color; its nutty flavor is delicious. Wine restaurants are every bit as good here as they are elsewhere in Austria.

Expensive

Hofkeller, Hofgasse 8 (83 24 39). Old beer and wine cellar, transformed into a most elegant restaurant. Food beautifully prepared and served; Austrian and international specialties; very good choice of Austrian wines. Closed on Sun. AE, DC, MC, V.

Pichlmaier, Petersbergerstrasse 9 (41 5 97). Gourmet meeting place of Graz, some way out. Regional specialties; good Austrian wines. Closed Sun. AE, DC, MC.

Plabutscher Schlössl, Gostingerstr. 149 (57 10 55). Delightful small Schloss. Wine and dine well by candlelight. Closed Sun. DC.

Weincomptoir Stündl, Heinrichstr. 55 (33 4 13). Excellent cooking with Italian influence. Superb wine list. AE, DC, MC, V.

Moderate

Brandhof, Gleisdorfergasse 1a (82 42 55), just behind the Opera House. Excellent game, family-run, the best Schilcher Rosé in town available by the glass. Closed Sun., open late.

Goldene Pastete, Sporgasse 28 (82 34 16). In Renaissance building at the center of Graz; very pleasant rooms, friendly host; mostly Styrian cuisine. Closed 15–31 Aug. and Sat./Sun. Open late.

Milchmariandl, Richard Wagner Strasse 31 (34 4 00). One of the most popular in Graz. Nice rooms, quiet garden. Fresh salads; Styrian specialties. Closed Sun. AE, DC, MC, V.

Stainzerbauer, Bürgergasse 4 (82 11 06). In the center of the Old Town, very popular. Styrian specialties. Reserve. DC, MC.

Inexpensive

Gambrinuskeller, Färbergasse 6–8 (81 01 81). In the heart of the old town. Large garden in summer. Delicious salads and charcoal-grilled specialties at amazing prices. Styrian wines and good beer. Closed Sat./Sun.

Puntigamer Brauhausrestauration (29 12 25). In the southern suburbs at the terminus of tram 5, by the Puntigam rail station, with a large garden and several halls; located in the brewery of the same name, with its own excellent beer.

Schuberthof, Zinzendorfgasse 17 (31 3 36), near city park, is known for its hearty food. Closed Sat./Sun. MC.

Weisses Rössl, Lendplatz 37 (91 43 71), with garden and good Styrian food.

Zum Kreuz, (see *Hotels*), Kärntnerstr. 451, in Strassgang south suburb, (28 34 36), good Styrian wines and food, especially the home-made sausages.

WINE TAVERNS. The locals enjoy a glass of wine and like to be able to listen to a song at the same time, often to join in. The best places for this are the evening wine taverns (Weinstuben), all of them also serving food. Most of these stay open into the small hours.

Herzl-Weinstube, Prokopigasse 12 (79 8 49), typically Styrian.

Keplerkeller, Stempfergasse 6 (82 24 49). Home of astronomer Johannes Kepler from 1597 to 1600. Lovely wine lodge; music, outside tables in beautiful Renaissance courtyard. Open evenings only; closed Sun. AE, DC, MC, V.

Landhauskeller, Schmiedgasse 9 (83 02 76). Food and drink in the originally-decorated Stuben, such as the Ritterstube (Knights' Room) and the Jägerstube (Hunters' Room). Closed Sun. DC, V.

Stadtheuriger, Hans Sachs Gasse 8 (83 24 82). *Heurigen* in 400-year-old house in the Old Town. Well assorted buffet; good Austrian wines. Closed Sun.

CAFES. As with so many of the old regional towns in Austria, the cafes are a focal point of local social life. Graz is no exception to the rule, and many of the city's cafes are full of atmosphere. In the summer there is a whole different breed of cafe enjoying the openair life. Among the hotel cafes those of the Erzherzog Johann and the Parkhotel are notable.

Cafe am Tummelplatz, Hans Sachs Gasse 8 (83 24 82). Same set-up as Stadtheuriger. Meeting place of the elegant young; not just Grazers. Vaults, period furniture. Closed Sun.

Glockenspiel, Glockenspielplatz 4 (83 02 91). New, meeting place of local trendies. Excellent coffee; good sandwiches and pastries. Closed Sun.

Leinich, Kaiser Joseph Platz 4 (83 05 86). Situated on picturesque market square, so it's especially interesting on Saturday morning—market day. Delicious *torten;* home-made preserves make an unusual present.

All of these are closed on Sundays. But all over town are "Sorger" cafes, which *are* open on Sundays and serve excellent coffee and pastries.

PLACES OF INTEREST. While Graz has several interesting galleries, the town itself will amply reward time spent in wandering, especially the Old Quarter, which is full of architectural fascination. The city has put up green information plaques to help with the identification of the highlights. These are keyed to a map that can be obtained from the Tourist Office.

Landeszeughaus (State Armory), Herrengasse 16 (877–36 39). A pure survival; built in 1642 and still full of contemporary weapons—though restored and properly displayed. Tues. to Fri. 9–4; Sat., Sun. and holidays 9–12. Closed in winter.

Mausoleum of Ferdinand II. Next to the cathedral. Mon. to Sat. 11–12. Entrance only possible at 11.

Schloss Eggenberg, Eggenberg Allee 90. A bit out of town to the west. In a large game park. A Baroque masterpiece, it is visitable with guided tours (check with 53 2 64).

Stadtmuseum (Graz City Museum), Sackstr. 18 (82 25 80). In the former Khuenburg Palace. Changing exhibitions. Mon. to Fri. 10–6, also Tues. 10–9, Sat. 9–1. In the same building is a **Pharmaceutical Museum** and the **Robert Stolz Museum.** Mon. to Fri. 10–1, closed Sat. Closed holidays.

Steiermärkisches Landesmuseum Joanneum (The Joanneum). This complex of museums is housed in several places. The "old" nucleus of the set-up is in the Joanneum building on Raubergasse 10 (mainly Natural History), (87 70). Then the main galleries are the **Alte Galerie** (The Old Gallery), Neutorgasse 45 (877–24 57) and the **Neue Galerie** (New Gallery), Sackstr. 16 (82 91 55). The **Styrian Museum of Folklore** is at Paulu-storgasse 13, (83 04 16). Open Easter–Nov., Mon.–Fri. 9–4, Sat./Sun. 9–1. **Prehistory and Early History,** with Roman material, is in an openair pavilion at **Schloss Eggenberg** (53 2 64). The Armory is also part of this conglomeration of museums. Opening times may differ between the various departments, but the average times are Tues. to Fri. 9–4, Sat., Sun. and holidays 9–12. Best check first.

PRACTICAL INFORMATION FOR STYRIA

TOURIST INFORMATION. With Graz as its central point, Styria is a province rich in vacation possibilities, from the spas and lakes of the Salzkammergut, through the mountainous scenery of the Dachstein-Tauern area to the gentle, remote villages of the Upper Mur valley. Almost every small town and village has its own Tourist Office, but the following are the ones the visitor is most likely to want to consult. Each is given with its postal code and phone number. Provincial Tourist Office, Herrengasse 16, Landhaus, Postfach 800 (8010, 0316/7031–2287).

Admont A-8911 (0 36 13–21 64); Altausee A-8992 (0 61 52–71 6 43); Bad Aussee A-8990 (0 6152–23 23); Bad Gleichenberg A-8344 (0 31 59–22 03); Bad Mitterndorf A-8983 (0 61 53–24 44); Bad Radkersburg A-8490 (0 34 76–25 45); Bruck an der Mur A-8600 (0 38 62–51 8 11); Eisenerz A-8790 (038 48–37 00); Fladnitz-Teichalm A-8163 (031 79–23 238).

Gröbming A-8962 (0 36 85–21 31); Grundlsee A-8993 (0 61 52–86 66); Irdning A-8952 (0 36 82–32 43); Kapfenberg A-8605 (0 38 62–22 5 01); Leibnitz A-8430 (0 34 52–26 20); Leoben A-8700 (0 38 42–44 0 18); Mariazell A-8630 (0 38 82–23 66); Murau A-8850 (0 35 32–27 20); Mürzzuschlag A-8680 (0 38 52–24 60).

Neuberg an der Mürz A-8692 (0 38 57–83 21); Obdach A-8742 (0 35 78–203); Oberzeiring A-8762 (0 35 71–387); Pichl-Mandling A-8973 (0 64 54–342); Predlitz-Turracher Höhe A-8863 (0 35 34–82 62); Ramsau am Dachstein A-8972 (036 87–81 9 25); Schladming A-8970 (0 36 87–22 2 68); Stubenberg A-8223 (0 31 76–282); Tauplitz-Tauplitzalm A-8982 (0 36 88–24 46).

AREA CODES—MAIL AND PHONE. You will find the postal code (preceded by an "A") and the telephone code (in brackets) after the name of each town in the following Hotel and Restaurant list.

HOTELS AND RESTAURANTS. Styria has a very large number of low-priced but delightful and unspoiled little countryside hotels and inns of the Gasthof variety. The capital of Graz, the Styrian lakes of Salzkammergut and certain other localities also offer first-class accommodations, but in the countryside as a whole the stress is on the unpretentious and inexpensive type of hotel.

You will find that the prices in Styria are lower than anywhere else in Austria, with the possible exception of Burgenland. But for these prices, you will often receive a higher quality accommodation.

Aflenz A-8623 (0 38 61). About 20 minutes from Kapfenberg by local bus. *Aflenzer Hof* (I), (22 45). 65 beds, most with bath or shower. 15th-century building with new wing and comfortable rooms. AE, DC, V. *Hubertushof* (I), (3 13 10). 19 rooms, most with bath or shower. Rustic furniture in lobby and rooms. DC, MC, V.

Alpl-Waldheimat A-8671 (0 38 55). *Waldheimathof* (M), (82 52). 110 beds, all with bath or shower. In green countryside; rustic interior; quiet and relaxing atmosphere. Cozy restaurant, with good food and wines. DC.

Altaussee A-8992 (0 61 52). *Seevilla* (E), Fischerndorf 60 (7 13 02). 30 rooms, all with bath or shower. Indoor and outdoor pools, sauna, solarium; restaurant. AE, DC. *Zum Loser* (M), (7 13 73). 15 beds, most with bath or shower; nice and simple. Pleasant restaurant serving excellent food. AE, DC, MC, V.

Bad Aussee A-8990 (0 61 52). *Alpenhof* (E), (27 77). 10 rooms, all with bath. In lovely garden. MC. *Erzherzog Johann* (E), Kurhausplatz 62 (25 07). 62 rooms, all with bath. In center of town, excellently run, all modern amenities; cure center, indoor pool. Good restaurant serving national and international specialties. Attractive coffee house. AE, DC, MC, V. *Kristina* (M), Altausseer Strasse 54 (20 17). 12 rooms, all with bath; hunting-lodge style; in big garden with old trees. Elegant lobby and rooms. DC, MC, V. *Paradies* (M), Marktleite 211 (25 71). 39 beds all with bath. A bit outside town. Restaurant for residents only. MC, V. *Wasnerin* (M), (21 08). 30 rooms, 22 with bath or shower. Styrian chalet type, above town; magnificent views of the Dachstein.
Campsite (24 27).

Bad Gleichenberg A-8344 (0 31 59). *Austria am Kurpark* (M), Brunnenstrasse 124 (22 05). 31 rooms, all with bath or shower; restaurant and bar. Closed Dec. to March. AE. *Grandhotel Stenitzer* (M), (22 50). 30 rooms, all with bath or shower. Restaurant and bar. Closed Dec. to March. AE, V. *Hindenburghof* (M), (23 22). 40 beds, all with bath or shower. Pool, sauna, solarium. Closed Nov. to Feb.

Bad Mitterndorf A-8983 (0 61 53). About 4 hours by fast train from Graz and about 3 hours from Salzburg (via Bischofshofen), changing trains at Stainach–Irdning. *Kurhotel Heilquelle Heilbrunn* (E), Neuhofen 108 (24 86). 104 rooms, all with bath. Indoor and outdoor pools, sauna, solarium, cure center; restaurant and bar. AE, DC, MC.
Hubertushof (M), (25 95). 27 rooms, all with bath or shower. On plateau above the village, country-house style, in garden. Restaurant. Closed April and Oct. to Nov. *Lord* (M), (25 53). 19 rooms, all with bath. Indoor pool, sauna. Restaurant. Closed Nov. to Jan.
Kochalm campsite (23 94).
Restaurant. *Grimmingwurzen* (E), (31 32). Styrian cuisine refined into something very special; worth a detour. Closed Tues. AE, DC.

Bad Radkersburg A-8490 (0 34 76). *Kur-und-Sporthotel* (E), (25 71). 88 rooms, all with bath. Cure center, indoor and outdoor pools. AE, DC, MC, V.
Österreich (I), (21 27). 65 beds, most with shower. Restaurant. AE, DC. Closed Dec.
Campsite (24 11).

Bruck An Der Mur A-8600 (0 38 62). *Bahnhof* (M), (51 2 20). 92 beds, most with shower. Sauna, solarium; restaurant. MC. *Bauer* (M), Minoritenplatz (51 3 31). Newly rebuilt, and likely to be best in town when complete. AE, MC. *Bayer* (M), Hauptplatz 24 (51 2 18). 60 beds, some with bath or shower. Sauna, solarium; restaurant. AE, DC, MC, V.
Youth Hostel (53 4 65).

Fladnitz A-8163 (0 31 79). *Kraltaverne* (I), (27 41 11). 11 rooms, all with shower. Sauna, tennis; bar and restaurant. Closed Nov. MC.

Frohnleiten A-8130 (03127). *Murhof* (E), (21 01 or 22 28). 40 beds, all with bath; indoor and outdoor pools, sauna, tennis; bar and restaurant. Associated with 18-hole golf course. Closed from Nov. to April.
Restaurant. *Weissenbacher* (M), (23 34). An institution for decades with locals and visitors. The big rooms and the garden by the river are usually crowded. Good food in large helpings.

Fürstenfeld A-8280 (0 33 82). *Hitzl* (M), Bahnhofstrasse 13 (21 44). 32 rooms, all with bath; indoor and outdoor tennis, horseback riding, lawn, children's room. Good restaurant. Closed Mon. DC, MC, V.

Gröbming A-8962 (0 36 85). *Landhaus St. Georg* (E), (27 40). One of the Silencehotel group. 24 rooms, all with bath; indoor pool, sauna, solarium, cure center; restaurant. Closed Nov. DC.

Hartberg A-8230 (0 33 32). *Ring* (E), (25 45). 103 rooms, all with bath. Deluxe amenities; indoor pool, sauna, solarium, tennis, cure center. Bar and restaurant. DC, MC, V.
Campsite (22 50).

Haus Im Ennstal A-8967 (0 36 86). 15 minutes by train from Gröbming. *Hauser-Kaibling* (M), Hauptstrasse 26 (25 78). 32 rooms, all with bath. Modern, in center of village; indoor pool. AE, DC.

Irdning A-8952 (0 36 82). *Schloss Pichlarn* (L), (28 41). 76 rooms, all with bath. In the lovely Enns-valley, huge park; indoor and outdoor pools, tennis, horseback riding, 18-hole golf course. Restaurant. Closed Nov. AE, DC, V.

Judenburg A-8750 (0 35 72). *Grünhübl* (M), (24 37). 14 rooms, all with shower; tennis. Bar and restaurant.
Restaurant. *Lindenwirt* (M), Wöllmersdorf 12 (23 06). Pleasant atmosphere; well-prepared international specialties. Famous, with excellent wine list. Closed Mon. AE, DC, MC, V.

Kapfenstein A-8353 (0 31 57). *Schlosswirt* (M), (22 02). 16 beds, all with bath. Romantic old castle with all modern amenities. Famous restaurant with attractive rooms and a panoramic terrace. Styrian food plus a good wine list.

Kitzeck A-8442 (03456). *Weinhof Kappel* (M), (23 47). Ambitious regional cooking and local wines (a unique dry Muskateller). Startling view of the vineyards.

Köflach A-8580 (0 31 44). *Zum Kleinhapl* (M), (34 94). This gasthaus has been transformed into a place of pilgrimage for those in search of new-style Styrian cuisine. Regarded as one of Austria's finest restaurants, it has retained its character and simplicity, as well as its low prices. Closed Sun., Mon. AE, DC, MC, V.

Leoben A-8700 (0 38 42). Less than 1½ hours by autorail from Graz. *Brücklwirt* (E), (8 17 27). Outside town in Niklasdorf on old main road. 70 rooms, all with bath. Comfortable; sound-proofed windows. Indoor pool, sauna. Well-known restaurant. AE, DC, MC, V.

Leutschach A-8463 (0 34 54). *Eichberghof* (I), (226). 16 beds, all with bath, and balcony; horseback riding. Restaurant using local ingredients for local specialties. Pretty rooms and superb local wines. Closed Dec. to March.

Mariazell A-8630 (0 38 82). 3 hours by narrow gauge local train from St. Pölten on Vienna–Linz railway line; 2½ hours by bus from Bruck an der Mur; 4 hours from Graz; about 4½ hours from Vienna. *Feichtegger* (M), Wienerstr. 6 (24 16). 55 rooms, all with bath or shower; next to basilica. Closed in April and Nov. AE, DC, MC, V. *Mariazellerhof* (M), Grazerstr. 10 (21 79). 14 rooms, all with bath and well furnished. Noted for traditional home-made gingerbread. Closed March. AE, DC.
Rohrbacherhof (I), (23 20). 57 beds, some with bath, some with shower. Closed April and Nov.
Youth Hostel (26 69).
Campsite (21 48) at nearby St. Sebastian.

Murau A-8850 (0 35 32). 1 hour by bus or small train from Unzmarkt. *Lercher* (M), (24 31). 26 rooms, all with bath or shower. Attractive dining-room, new pension annex, sauna, sun terrace; good food, good wine, family atmosphere. AE, DC, MC, V.

Obdach A-8742 (0 35 78). *Groggerhof* (M), (22 01). 16 rooms, all with bath or shower. Perhaps the most perfect *gusthof* in Austria—family-run, Styrian wines, beautifully cooked local dishes, homemade cakes. Closed Tues., and during part of Nov.

Pichl-Mandling A-8973 (0 64 54). Train stop on the Salzburg–Graz line. *Pichlmayrgut* (M), (305). 96 rooms, all with bath or shower and handsomely furnished, some with four-posters. Tasty local cuisine. Closed Nov. AE, V.

Präbichl A-8794 (0 38 49). 1 hour from Leoben by bus; also local railway, but slower. *Hubertushof* (M), (214). 55 beds, all with bath or shower; sauna; disco, cellar bar and good restaurant.

Ramsau Am Dachstein A-8972 (0 36 87). *Edelweiss* (E), (81 9 88). 50 rooms, all with bath or shower; sauna, solarium, tennis; restaurant and bar. *Sporthotel Matschner* (E), Ort 61 (81 7 21). 60 rooms, all with bath or shower and balconies. Indoor pool, sauna, solarium, tennis; bar and restaurant. DC, MC, V.

Almfrieden (M) (81 0 21). 42 rooms, all with bath or shower. Well-located; attractive *stuben*-style restaurant. Closed May and Nov. MC.

Alpengasthof Peter Rosseger (M), (8 12 23). 13 rooms, all with bath and rustic furniture; best restaurant in town. Closed Nov.

Campsite (81 2 80).

Riegersburg A-8333 (0 31 53). *Zur Riegersburg* (I), Riegersburg 29 (216). 33 rooms, all with bath, balconies, quiet location. Very good value. AE, DC, MC, V.

Youth Hostel (217).

Schladming A-8970 (0 36 87). Can be reached by autorail from Salzburg in under 2 hours, and from Graz in under 4 hours. Bus service between Schladming and Ramsau.

Sporthotel Royer (L), Europlatz 583 (2 32 40). 130 rooms, all with bath (but ask for a quiet one as main traffic routes are close). Modern; indoor and outdoor pools, tennis, horseback riding; restaurant. AE, DC, MC, V.

Alte Post (E), Hauptplatz 89 (2 25 71). 74 beds, all with bath or shower. Romantik Hotel. On main square; delightful restaurant serving beautiful food. Closed Nov. AE, DC, MC, V.

Youth Hostel (24 5 31).

Campsite (23 1 95).

Restaurant. *Tritscher* (M), (2 24 35). Central, beer garden; local and international cuisine. Closed Tues. V.

Söding A-8661 (0 31 37). Motorway exit A2 Mooskirchen. *Gasthaus Hochstrasser* (I) (23 38). Good country food and fine genuine Schilcher wine; magnificent home-made schnapps. Cheap to take away too. Try their clear apricot schnapps or the unique blueberry schnapps. Also pear and cherry.

Stainz A-8510 (0 34 63). *Wolfbauer* (M), (22 91). 10 rooms, all with shower; bar and restaurant. Closed Wed.

Restaurant. *Engelweingarten* (M), (23 81). One of the nicest restaurants of Styria, high above the vineyards. Cozy *stuben* with tiled stove, fine view; excellent Styrian specialties. Closed Mon. MC. Just outside village in Sommereben, *Jagawirt* (I), (0 31 43–81 05). Excellent Schilcher in pretty Stuben. Closed Wed.

Stubenberg Am See A-8223 (0 31 76). *Alphotel* (E), Zeil 136 (33 10). 87 rooms, all with bath and balconies. Indoor pool, horseback riding, tennis; terrace restaurant and bar. Bus to lake. AE, DC, MC, V.

Campsite (390).

Restaurant. *Buschenschank Herberstein* (M), (278). A *Heuriger* with character. Closed Nov.–March.

Tauplitz A-8982 (0 36 88). Some 6 km. (4 miles) from Bad Mitterndorf—10 minutes by train. Chair lifts connect Tauplitz and the Tauplitzalm Plateau (4 km. long), and Tauplitzalm with Lawinenstein. *Berghotel Tauplitzalm* (M), (23 25). 85 beds, all with bath or shower; sauna. Restaurant and bar. Closed May, Oct. and Nov. *Sporthotel Tauplitzalm* (M) (23 06). 34 rooms, all with bath or shower. Indoor pool, sauna, solarium; restaurant and bar. Closed May and Oct.

Haus Rosskogel (I), (22 37). 9 rooms, most with shower.

Weiz A-8160 (0 31 72). *Modersnhof* (E), Büchl 32 (37 47). 21 beds, all with bath. A Romantik Hotel; quietly sited in the middle of orchards. Restaurant with excellent cuisine. Closed Mon. AE, DC, MC, V.

GETTING AROUND STYRIA. By Train. Graz is connected with Vienna and Salzburg by inter-city trains, sleek, fast and very comfortable. The Vienna–Bruck–Graz–Leibnitz route is served by the *Laibach Express* and *Balkan Express;* and several other intercontinental express trains traverse Styria. The line from Graz to Bruck, Leoben, St. Michael, Trieben, Selztal, Steinach, Schladming, and on to Salzburg and Germany, follows the *Steiermark Express* route, and from Selztal you may also proceed directly to Upper Austria and Linz. Train information Graz (17 17).

Secondary train routes link Graz with Vienna via Feldbach, Fürstenfeld, Hartberg and Burgenland; Leoben with Präbichl, Eisenerz, Hieflau, Gstatterboden, Admont and Selztal; Steinach with Tauplitz, Bad Mitterndorf, and Bad Aussee.

Among the small local lines—several of these are narrow gauge—are: Feldbach–Bad Gleichenberg, Spielfeld–Radkersburg, Graz–Köflach, Kapfenberg–Aflenz–Seewiesen, Unzmarkt–Murau–Predlitz.

By Bus. Styria, like all Austria, is well-connected by bus. The main centers from which the bus routes radiate are Graz, Leibnitz, Feldbach, Gleisdorf, Weiz, Hartberg, Bruck an der Mur, Judenberg and, in the west of the state, Liezen, Steinach and Gröbming. Far and away the greatest concentration of bus routes is in the southeast area, as one would expect from the land formation. However, the valleys, to quite a height, are served by the postal buses and private routes right up to tiny spots.

For information on cross-country buses, call Graz 0 31 6–81 18 18.

By Car. The short route from Vienna to Graz is by the road through East Styria, scenically very rewarding and a bit shorter than via Bruck (185 km., 115 miles, Vienna—Graz): at Wiener Neustadt branch off for Aspang, then proceed via Mönichkirchen (maximum gradient 12 percent), Hartberg and Gleisdorf to Graz, all this on Route 54; the alternative autobahn, A2, follows roughly the same route, avoiding the towns, and is of course faster, though less attractive.

From Leoben Route 115 leads to: Trofaiach (10 km., 6 miles), Präbichl (about 24 km., 15 miles, maximum gradient 9½%), Eisenerz (28 km., 17 miles), Gstatterboden (about 57 km., 35½ miles), Admont (69 km., 43 miles), and continues to Liezen.

The A9 autobahn is only finished from Graz to St. Michael, whence it is 75 km. (47 miles) on Route 113 over the Schober Pass (maximum gradient 18%) to Liezen. From there 308 follows the Enns southwest to Schladming and Radstadt in Salzburg, while 145 branches northwest at Stainach to Bad Mittendorf and Bad Aussee.

Among the most scenic high Alpine roads are the short road from Bad Mitterndorf to the Tauplitz plateau (about 990 m., 5,250 ft.), open and plowed in winter, the much longer road over the Sölker Tauern (1,800 m., 5,900 ft.) connecting Gröbming in the Enns Valley with Murau in the Mur Valley, and the road to Planneralm from Wald near Steinach.

PLACES OF INTEREST. The routes suggested in the following list start from Graz. Please check locally for opening times and days, as these are very difficult to forecast accurately in advance.

Admont. A9 northeast (through the Gleinalmtunnel), 115 through Trieben an Rottenmann, rejoin A9 then double back eastwards on 112. Great Benedictine **Abbey,** reconstructed after serious fire in mid-1800s which missed the magnificent Rococo library. Manuscripts on display. **Natural History Museum.**

Arnfels. South on A9, 69 west just above Yugoslav border. **Domineum Arnfels,** musical collection, clocks and folk art.

Brandhof. North on A9 and S35 to Bruck, then Route 20 through Au. **Jagdschloss,** 1820s Hunting Lodge; living quarters of Archduke Johann. Summer guided tours only.

Herberstein. A2 east to Gleisdorf, then 54 left just after Hirnsdorf. **Schloss.** Dominating castle, built over five centuries; collection of armor, historic kitchens etc.

Kainach. West on A2, then 70 to Voitsberg, north on local road through Afling. **Schloss Alt-Kainach.** Renaissance castle (1526–33). Castle Museum (i.e. a museum that deals with castles, models, plans and so on); weapon collection. Summer only.

Krieglach. A9 and S35 to Bruck, northwest on S6 and 116. **Roseggermuseum,** the house of the poet Peter Rosegger. **Heimatmuseum,** Museum of local history and customs.

Leoben. A9 to St. Michael, then right onto S6. **Stadtmuseum** (Town Museum), Kirchengasse 6. Art and local history, especially of mining. **Maria-Waasen-Kirche,** 14th century church with stained glass. Interesting Renaissance patrician houses.

Mariazell. Due north on A9, S35 at Friesach, then Route 20 from Bruck. **Gnadenbasilika,** Pilgrimage Church. Various periods, but unified in Baroque. Treasury and fine decorations, especially high altar of J.B. Fischer von Erlach. Gnadenkapelle (Chapel of Miracles) ornate in the extreme. Take the cablecar up to the **Bürgeralpe** for magnificent views.

Murau. A2 southwest, 70 from Liebach, 77 to Judenburg, then 96. **Burg,** mid-1600s castle on medieval base. Museum of weapons and poaching. **Parish Church,** early-Gothic; 1350 frescos; attractive high altar. Two other early churches. Narrow-gauge railroad with some steam power.

Oberzeiring. A2, then 70 and 77 east to Judenburg, 114 to Unterzeiring and take a local road to the left. **Schaubergwerk und Heimatmuseum,** former silver mine with mining museum. **Cemetery Church** (1378) with early frescos and interesting interior.

Piber. A2 west to Mooskirchen. Route 70 west to Voitsberg. After town, follow signs right to Barnbach and Piber. Stud farm of the famous white **Lippizaner Horses.** Open Apr. to Nov., 9–11 and 2–4. Information (0 31 44–32 23).

Riegersburg. East on A2, at Ilz take Route 66 south. **Burg,** huge 13th-century castle on dominating site. Fine rooms—Knights' Hall, state rooms, Roman and Turkish—plus arms and armor collection. Magnificent views.

St. Lambrecht. A2 then 70 east to Köfflach, 77 to Judenburg, 96 to Teufenbach, then local road. **Abbey** with high Gothic nave; collections of religious art, painting and sculpture; folklore; interesting apartments. Gothic **Peterskirche,** fine carved altar pieces.

Stainz. A2 south of Liebach, then 76. **Schloss,** with collection of antique household and working utensils. Former **Abbey Church,** part-Gothic, part-Baroque with fine interior.

Stübing/Gratwein. North on A9. **Österreichisches Freilichtmuseum** (Austrian Openair Museum). A collection of rural buildings from all over Austria.

Trautenfels. The route to Rottenmann (as for Admont), then 113 and 308 west. **Schloss,** 13th-century castle (rebuilt in the 1600s). Interesting stuccowork and frescos. **Local Museum** is a branch of the Graz Joanneum.

Vorau. Northeast on 72 to Birkfeld, then a local road east to Vorau. 1662 **Abbey Church** with magnificent interior. Interesting abbey buildings with library (Kaiserchronik). Nearby is **Festenburg,** a medieval church fortified by the Abbots of Vorau, especially against the Turks. Frescos and a museum.

WINTER SPORTS. Styria's excellent skiing terrains became much better known following the Alpine World Skiing Championships which were held in Schladming in 1982. However, the area suffers from a lack of top-quality hotels though its technical facilities are first class—there are over 500 ski lifts, chair lifts and cable cars as well as more than 60 ski schools. If nice bars and fancy après ski activities do not figure as musts in your winter sports program, you may find that the skiing in Styria is just your cup of tea, certainly the ski lodge Gemütlichkeit is real and sincere. But there are a few places, such as Mariazell, where all the fashionable amenities of winter resort life are available, and at even lower prices than elsewhere in Austria. Styria also has the longest chair lift in the world at Tauplitz (4 km.) and one of the biggest ski jumps in the world near Bad Mitterndorf. The skiing season lasts from December to March, in the higher areas several weeks longer, and many races as well as jumping events take place during this time. All-year skiing is now possible on the Dachstein Glacier, and there are outstanding high-mountain ski tours.

Tobogganing is extremely popular and there are frequent competitions. Many curling matches are featured. Ice hockey is played at Graz, Bruck an der Mur, Leoben, Mariazell, and Mürzzuschlag. Skijoring is practiced both with horses and motorcycles, and in several localities horse sleigh rides can be taken.

Western Styria. Relaxed slopes on the eastern side of the Koralpe. Plenty of virgin snow and some excellent high ski touring to be had.
Resorts: Glashütten (1,274 m., 4,170 ft.); Gaberl–Salla (1,551 m., 5,089 ft.); Hirschegg (896 m., 2,940 ft.); Modriach (1,009 m., 3,311 ft.); Pack (1,125 m., 3,691 ft.); Trahütten (1,000 m., 3,281 ft.).

Facilities: not a great area for the mechanics—42 T-bars and 25 km. (16 miles) of cross-country trails.

Upper Mürztal. Families on vacation from Graz favor this area, which is specially geared to catering for the family trade. The region stretches from the Semmering to the Mürztal, well-sprinkled with good, if fairly simple, resorts.

Resorts: Alpl (1,100 m., 3,609 ft.); Altenberg am der Rax (782 m., 2,565 ft.); Fischbach (1,000 m., 3,279 ft.); Kapellen (703 m., 2,306 ft.); Kindberg (567 m., 1,860 ft.); Krieglach (610 m., 2,001 ft.); Langenwang (638 m., 2,093 ft.); Mürzsteg (783 m., 2,569 ft.); Mürzzuschlag (667 m., 2,184 ft.); Neuberg an der Mürz (730 m., 2,394 ft.); St. Kathrein am Hauenstein (822 m., 2,697 ft.); Spittal am Semmering (778 m., 2,550 ft.); Steinhaus am Semmering (830 m., 2,721 ft.); Veitsch (664 m., 2,179 ft.)

Facilities: 3 indoor swimming pools, 3 chair lifts, 65 T-bars, and 91 km. (57 miles) of cross-country trails.

Hochschwab Alpine Region. Here the simplicity of Styria comes into its own. This is a true country district, with small resorts grouped round the bulk of the Hochschwab. For the skier with a yen for history, Mariazell will satisfy his thirst and provide good après ski, too.

Resorts: Aflenz Kurort (765 m., 2,510 ft.); Breitenau bei Mixnitz (658 m., 2,159 ft.); Eisenerz (736 m., 2,412 ft.); Etmissl (712 m., 2,336 ft.); Mariazell (870 m., 2,854 ft.); Seewiesen (974 m., 3,192 ft.); Turnau (755 m., 2,475 ft.); Vordernberg–Präbichl (820 m., 2,690 ft.).

Facilities: 2 indoor swimming pools, 1 cable car, 2 chair lifts, 49 T-bars and 70 km. (44 miles) of cross-country trails.

The Upper Murtal and its Side Valleys. A mixture of attractive old villages and more modern winter-sports centers. Great scenery and plenty to occupy those on and off the slopes.

Resorts: Hohentauern (1,274 m., 4,176 ft.); Judenburg (737 m., 2,418 ft.); Lachtal–Schönberg (812 m., 2,664 ft.); Murau (832 m., 2,730 ft.); Neumarkt in der Steiermark (842 m., 2,763 ft.); Obdach (874 m., 2,868 ft.); St. Georgen–St. Lorenzen ob Murau (860 m., 2,822 ft.); St. Johann am Tauern (1,053 m., 3,455 ft.); St. Lambrecht (1,028 m., 3,369 ft.); Turrach–Turracherhöhe (1,763 m., 5,784 ft.).

Facilities: 4 indoor swimming pools, 3 chair lifts, 51 T-bars, and 97 km. (60 miles) of cross-country trails.

Dachstein–Tauern Region. The area around the Dachstein glacier provides both all-year skiing and a good choice of trails. Highspot of the region is, of course, Schladming with its incredibly fast downhill run. But there are plenty of less hair-raising things to do in a varied landscape.

Resorts: Donnersbachwald (960 m., 3,147 ft.); Gröbming (776 m., 2,546 ft.); Haus im Ennstal (772 m., 2,532 ft.); Kleinsölk (979 m., 3,207 ft.); Pichl–Mandling (800 m., 2,625 ft.); Pruggern (681 m., 2,232 ft.); Ramsau (1,200 m., 3,933 ft.); Rohrmoos–Unterthal (900 m., 2,952 ft.); St. Nikolai–Sölktal (1,023 m., 3,351 ft.); Schladming (745 m., 2,444 ft.).

Facilities: the area has 14 indoor swimming pools, 4 cable cars, 6 chair lifts, 77 T-bars and 164 km. (101 miles) of cross-country trails.

Styrian Salzkammergut. Yet another spa/winter-sports area, where the combination of the two acts as a draw to a great variety of vacationers.

Having this good mix also makes for more interesting après ski activities. Being a lake area, the summer and winter attractions are very much a continuous process.

Resorts: Altaussee (720 m., 2,362 ft.); Bad Aussee (650 m., 2,133 ft.); Bad Mitterndorf (812 m., 2,664 ft.); Grundlsee (711 m., 2,333 ft.); Kainisch (850 m., 2,787 ft.); Tauplitz (896 m., 2,937 ft.).

Facilities: 6 indoor swimming pools, 3 chair lifts, 37 T-bars, and 72 km. (45 miles) of cross-country trails.

Other Areas. Apart from the regions with a high-profile winter-sport content, Styria has several areas that are able to provide a slightly gentler winter vacation. Among them are—Southern Styria, the Environs of Graz, Upper Styria and the Gesäuse, Palten and Liesingtal district. All these have less high-powered skiing, but attractive scenery for hikes and lots of other winter sports such as skating and curling.

OTHER SPORTS. Golf. Golf courses can be found at Bad Gleichenberg (0 31 59–37 17); Murhof (0 31 27–21 01, 22 28); Irdning, Schloss Pichlarn (0 36 82–43 93, 28 41); and at Weissenbach-Liezen (no telephone).

Index

The letters H and R indicate Hotel and Restaurant listings.

(See also "Practical Information" sections at the end of each chapter for Sports, Special Events and other useful information.)

Fodor's Travel Guides

U.S. Guides

Alaska
Arizona
Atlantic City & the
  New Jersey Shore
Boston
California
Cape Cod
Carolinas & the
  Georgia Coast
The Chesapeake Region
Chicago
Colorado
Dallas & Fort
  Worth

Disney World & the
  Orlando Area
Florida
Hawaii
Houston &
  Galveston
Las Vegas
Los Angeles, Orange
  County, Palm Springs
Maui
Miami, Fort Lauderdale,
  Palm Beach
Michigan, Wisconsin,
  Minnesota

New England
New Mexico
New Orleans
New Orleans (Pocket
  Guide)
New York City
New York City (Pocket
  Guide)
New York State
Pacific North Coast
Philadelphia
The Rockies
San Diego
San Francisco

San Francisco (Pocket
  Guide)
The South
Texas
USA
Virgin Islands
Virginia
Waikiki
Washington, DC
Williamsburg

Foreign Guides

Acapulco
Amsterdam
Australia, New Zealand,
  The South Pacific
Austria
Bahamas
Bahamas (Pocket
  Guide)
Baja & the Pacific
  Coast Resorts
Barbados
Beijing, Guangzhou &
  Shanghai
Belgium &
  Luxembourg
Bermuda
Brazil
Britain (Great Travel
  Values)
Budget Europe
Canada
Canada (Great Travel
  Values)
Canada's Atlantic
  Provinces
Cancun, Cozumel,
  Yucatan Peninsula

Caribbean
Caribbean (Great
  Travel Values)
Central America
Eastern Europe
Egypt
Europe
Europe's Great
  Cities
Florence & Venice
France
France (Great Travel
  Values)
Germany
Germany (Great Travel
  Values)
Great Britain
Greece
The Himalayan
  Countries
Holland
Hong Kong
Hungary
India, including Nepal
Ireland
Israel
Italy

Italy (Great Travel
  Values)
Jamaica
Japan
Japan (Great Travel
  Values)
Jordan & the
  Holy Land
Kenya, Tanzania,
  the Seychelles
Korea
Lisbon
Loire Valley
London
London (Great
  Travel Values)
London (Pocket Guide)
Madrid & Barcelona
Mexico
Mexico City
Montreal &
  Quebec City
Munich
New Zealand
North Africa
Paris
Paris (Pocket Guide)

People's Republic of
  China
Portugal
Rio de Janeiro
The Riviera (Fun on)
Rome
Saint Martin &
  Sint Maarten
Scandinavia
Scandinavian Cities
Scotland
Singapore
South America
South Pacific
Southeast Asia
Soviet Union
Spain
Spain (Great Travel
  Values)
Sweden
Switzerland
Sydney
Tokyo
Toronto
Turkey
Vienna
Yugoslavia

Special-Interest Guides

Health & Fitness
  Vacations
Royalty Watching

Selected Hotels of
  Europe

Selected Resorts and
  Hotels of the U.S.
Shopping in Europe

Skiing in North America
Sunday in New York